The Pastry Chef's Companion

A Comprehensive Resource Guide for
the Baking and Pastry Professional

Glenn Rinsky
Laura Halpin Rinsky

WILEY

JOHN WILEY & SONS, INC.

This book is printed on acid-free paper. ∞

Copyright © 2009 by Glenn Rinsky and Laura Halpin Rinsky. All rights reserved.

Published by John Wiley & Sons, Inc., Hoboken, New Jersey.

Published simultaneously in Canada.

For general information on our other products and services, or technical support, please contact our Customer Care Department within the United States at 800-762-2974, outside the United States at 317-572-3993 or fax 317-572-4002.

Wiley also publishes its books in a variety of electronic formats. Some content that appears in print may not be available in electronic books.

For more information about Wiley products, visit our Web site at http://www.wiley.com.

Library of Congress Cataloging-in-Publication Data

Rinsky, Glenn.
    The Pastry chef's companion: a comprehensive resource guide for the baking and pastry professional/Glenn Rinsky, Laura Halpin Rinsky.
       p. cm
    Includes bibliographical references.
    ISBN 978-0-470-00955-0 (pbk.)
       1. Cookery—Encyclopedias.   2. Pastry—Encyclopedias.   3. Baking—Encyclopedias.
I. Rinsky, Laura Halpin.   II. Title.
    TX349.R484   2008
    641.3'003—dc22

                                             2007038112

Printed in the United States of America
10   9   8   7   6   5   4   3   2   1

Contents

This book is dedicated to our son, Elliott—
the best bun that ever came out of the oven.

How It All Began

We wanted to preface *The Pastry Chef's Companion* with a poignant and clever quote from a well-respected culinarian, but after exhaustive research we came back to something one of our less than enthusiastic pastry students once said at the culinary school where we met as instructors in 2001. He had what we refer to as "pastry phobia." He detested the balance beam scale and cringed at the sight of a cake recipe. During midterm review he was asked how he liked the pastry class, and without skipping a beat he replied, "You see, I'm a devout southern Baptist, and all of my life I've been taught that hell is fire and brimstone and eternal damnation, but now I know that hell is really sugar and flour and yeast and butter and eggs!" We are sure that at one time or another every culinarian has shared this spiritual assessment, but the passion for our craft always prevails. Like the bits of shaved chocolate that lodge under your fingernails, it is part of you; once ingrained, there is no escaping its sweet and satisfying grip.

The Pastry Chef's Companion was conceived one night over dinner as we were talking about how great it would be to have a reference book that included all sorts of information about pastries, breads, desserts, and confections. As we stared across the table from each other, a collective light went on and this book was born. We naively thought, "How hard can it be? Just gather up some words, define them, alphabetize them, and voilà!—we have a book." Despite our working full time, having a child, and going to school, two years seemed like a reasonable time to accomplish it all. Needless to say, we were in for the biggest shock of our lives. But 4,800 definitions, 10 appendices, 2 master's degrees, and 3,600 diapers later, we made it.

This book is designed to offer a comprehensive assortment of well-defined pastry, baking, and confectionery arts terms and products, including interesting information about the origin, history, and folklore of the items. *The Pastry Chef's Companion* is part dictionary, part encyclopedia.

The vast amount of information contained in this book provides readers with a thorough reference to the components that make up the baking, pastry, and confectionery arts. Whether you are a chef, pastry chef, culinary student, or devoted foodie, this book will broaden your knowledge and enhance your gastronomic library. In addition, we have included pronunciations for as many terms as possible; for ease of use, the pronunciations are given in simple syllable sounds rather than phonetic symbols.

In an effort to reconcile the conflicting demands of teaching, researching a book, raising a child, and earning our master's degrees, we brainstormed new and innovative ways of educating our students that also yielded some of the results you read in this book. The lecture portions of our classes were four hours long, and no matter how entertaining a teacher is, there is only so much you can say about making a pie. To make the lessons more interesting and interactive, we began assigning research homework. Each student was given a specific dessert or pastry to research and asked to prepare a presentation for the class. Though it was a challenge for the students to uncover quality facts, many came through with fascinating, educational reports that we were able to include here. Although there are many books on the subjects of baking, pastry, and the confectionery arts, there has been no single, comprehensive resource devoted to the topic. It is our hope that *The Pastry Chef's Companion* will be that resource.

We trust chefs, pastry chefs, bakers, confectionery artists, and pastry enthusiasts will relish the wealth of information here, and that it will satisfy their sweet tooth for knowledge.

From us to you—read, learn, and enjoy.

The Rinskys

Acknowledgments

The inspiration for this book came from our shared love and passion for the baking, pastry, and confectionery arts.

We would like to thank our editors, Julie Kerr, Rachel Livsey, Jackie Beach, copyeditor Carole Berglie, and the entire Wiley team for their constant support and expertise in giving our work aesthetic substance and life. We would also like to thank Susan Ginsburg, our book agent from Writers House, LLC for her generous counsel throughout this process. We owe a special debt of gratitude to our last-minute linguists, Stephen Sansom and Mona Hammoud; thank you!

We greatly appreciate the guidance and knowledge of those who reviewed this book: John Bandman, The Art Institute of New York City; Martha Crawford, Johnson & Wales University; Catherine Hallman, Walters State Community College, Tennessee; Richard Kennedy, The Art Institute of New York City; and Chris Thielman, College of DuPage, Illinois. Their contributions have increased the overall quality of this endeavor.

The love and encouragement from our friends and family were a great comfort to us during the lengthy process of bringing "the book" to fruition, and for that we are eternally grateful.

Finally, we would like to thank our mentors, colleagues, and students for giving us the opportunity to learn from them and for their unwavering dedication to the betterment of our craft.

About the Authors

Glenn Rinsky A native of Cincinnati, Ohio, he is a graduate of The Culinary Institute of America. He holds a B.S. in Business Administration from Virginia College and a M.Ed. in Leadership and Higher Education from Capella University. He has worked as a chef for Cummins Diesel, Marriott and Kroger Corporations and owned and operated a specialty wedding cake business for 12 years. He is a contributing writer for *Pastry Arts and Design* magazine and is certified by The American Culinary Federation as an Executive Chef, Executive Pastry Chef and Culinary Educator. He is currently a Senior Chef Instructor at Jefferson State Community College in Birmingham, Alabama.

Laura Halpin Rinsky A native New Yorker, she is a graduate of The Culinary Institute of America. She holds a B.A. in Communications from Rutgers University and a M.Ed. in Adult Education and Training from Colorado State University. She has worked in some of the finest hotels and restaurants around the country including The Russian Tea Room in New York; Mr. B's in New Orleans; The Anatole Hotel in Dallas; Bread Alone in Woodstock; The Palace Hotel in San Francisco; Bacara Resort and Spa in Santa Barbara and The Monte-Carlo Hotel in Europe. She is a contributing writer for *Pastry Arts and Design* magazine and is certified by The American Culinary Federation as an Executive Pastry Chef and Culinary Educator. She was the Program Coordinator for Baking, Pastry, and Confectionery Arts at Culinard, The Culinary Institute of Virginia College in Birmingham, Alabama and is currently designing and implementing a Hospitality and Culinary Arts Academy for Hewitt-Trussville High School in Trussville, Alabama.

Glenn and Laura married in 2003 and currently live in Birmingham, Alabama with their son Elliott and crazy dog, Mrs. Rosen.

Your feedback about the book would be warmly received. Please contact us at eatcake101@hotmail.com.

Aa

abaissage (ah-bay-'zahjh) A French term that denotes the rolling out of pastry dough.

abaisse (ah-'bays) A French term that describes a rolled-out piece of pastry, specifically *puff pastry*, into thin sheets. It may also refer to a thin slice of *sponge cake*.

Abernathy biscuit A firm cracker flavored with caraway seeds. Created in the 1800s by a Scottish physician named Dr. John Abernathy as a digestive cure.

aboukir (ah-boo-'kir) 1. A Swiss dessert made with sponge cake and pastry cream flavored with chestnut alcohol. The round cake is finished with coffee-flavored fondant and garnished with chopped pistachios. 2. A *bombe* consisting of almond/ praline ice, praline-flavored *pâte à bombe*, and garnished with toasted almonds and marzipan.

aboukir almonds (ah-boo-'kir) A petit four of green-colored marzipan studded with two roasted blanched almonds, dipped into a sugar syrup and cooled, forming a hard crust.

abricot (ah-bree-'coe) The French word for *apricot*.

absinthe ('ab-sinth) A sweet and highly flavored emerald green spirit distilled from the leaves of the wormwood plant, flavored with herbs such as fennel, Chinese anise, hyssop, and veronica. It was first produced by Henri Louis Pernod but is banned by most countries because it is believed to be dangerous to one's health. In recipes, Pernod is often cited as a substitute.

absorbition The ability of a bread flour to absorb water.

acaçá (ah-'ka-sah) A Brazilian porridge of coconut milk and rice flour that is steamed, usually in banana leaves.

acacia (ah-'kay-sha) A food additive derived from the acacia tree. It is used as an emulsifier, thickener, or flavoring agent in processed foods such as chewing gum, confections, and snack foods. Also known as *gum arabic*.

acacia honey See *honey*.

acerola (as-uh-'roh-luh) A small tree grown in the West Indies and adjacent regions, as well as the small cherry-type fruit that it produces. The fruit is also known as *Barbados cherry*, *Puerto Rican cherry*, and *West Indies cherry*; it has a tangy, sweet flavor and is an excellent source of vitamin C. Used in desserts and preserves.

Acesulfame-K (ay-see-'suhl-faym-K) A noncaloric artificial sweetener, commercially sold as Sunette and Sweet One. It was discovered in 1967 by the German life-sciences company Hoechst AG and was approved by the FDA in 1988. It is 200 times sweeter than sucrose, and retains its sweetness when heated, unlike other artificial sweeteners. Used in many foods, including puddings, gelatin desserts, candies, and yogurt.

acetate ('ah-sa-tate) A clear, flexible plastic, which can be purchased as sheets, rolls, or strips in various thicknesses, often used in chocolate work and cake making.

acetic acid (ah-'see-tic) 1. A colorless pungent liquid that is the essential ingredient in vinegar—it makes it sour. 2. An acid in sourdough culture and sourdough bread. Along with lactic acid, it provides the sour flavor in sourdough bread. The acid develops best in bread doughs that are cool and stiff. It is formed when wild yeast bacteria interact with alcohol present in fermented solutions such as wine and beer.

Acetobacillus (ah-'see-toe-'bah-sill-us) Bacteria that create *lactic acid* and *acetic acid* by eating sugars present in bread dough. This creates a distinct sour flavor in the bread.

aceto dolce (ah-'see-toh 'dohl-chee) Literally, "sweet vinegar" in Italian. Refers to a fruit spread made by preserving fruit in vinegar and then cooking it with honey and grape juice. The spread is served like jam for breakfast or as an afternoon snack.

acetome ('ah-sah-tome) A syrup made from honey and vinegar, once used as a preservative for fruits in many parts of Europe, but rarely used today.

achiote (ah-chee-'oh-tay) The red, inedible seed of the *annatto*, a small shrub native to tropical America and also cultivated in Southeast Asia and other tropical climates. The seeds contain a natural coloring pigment called annatto.

acid From the Latin acidus, which means "sour." Acids are found in vinegar (acetic acid), wine (tartaric acid), lemon juice (citric acid), sour milk (lactic acid), and apples (malic acid). They may be used as tenderizers because they break down connective tissue, and also to prevent fruit from oxidizing. Acids are also used in making meringue because they help strengthen the cell wall of egg white protein.

acidic (ah-'sihd-ihk) A culinary term that describes an item with a tart or sour flavor.

acidophilus milk (ass-ah-'doph-a-lus) Whole, low-fat, or nonfat sweet milk to which *Lactobacillus acidophilus* bacteria have been added, as a way of restoring the bacteria present in raw milk but destroyed in the pasteurization process. The addition of the bacteria converts the lactose milk to lactic acid, which is linked to health benefits, including improved digestion.

acidulant, acidulated water (ah-'sihd-yoo-lay-ted) Water to which a small amount of an acid has been added, used to prevent discoloration of some fruits and vegetables, such as peaches and artichokes. The acids used may include vinegar, lemon juice, lime juice, and ascorbic acid.

acitróne (ah-sih-'troh-nay) Candied *nopale*.

ackee (ah-'kee) A bright red tropical fruit that, when ripe, bursts opens to reveal a soft yellow flesh and black seeds. Some parts of the fruit are toxic when under-ripe, and therefore ackee may be subject to import restrictions. The fruit was brought from the West Africa to Jamaica in the late 1700s by Captain Bligh. It is served with salt fish at breakfast in Jamaica.

Aclame See *alitame*.

acorn Nut produced by the oak tree. Of the many varieties of oak trees, the acorns of the white oak and live oak are the most commonly used for food. The nuts may be eaten raw or roasted. Ground acorns may also been used as a coffee substitute.

acqua ('ahk-wah) The Italian word for water.

active dry yeast See *yeast*.

additive A natural or synthetic ingredient added to food products to enhance flavor and/or appearance, prolong shelf life, and/or improve nutritional value.

ade A cold drink that combines sugar, water, and citrus fruit juice.

adobe oven See *oven*.

advocaat ('ad-voh-kaht) A Dutch drink of brandy, sugar, and egg yolks, similar to eggnog. A favorite in Amsterdam. Also called *advocaatenborrel*.

adrak ('ahd-rack) The Indian word for fresh *ginger* root.

adzuki bean (ah-'zoo-kee) A russet-colored dried bean with a distinctive white streak and a sweet flavor; used extensively in Japanese and Chinese puddings and confections, such as Yokan. Adzuki beans can be found in Asian markets; may also be spelled *azuki*.

aeblepidsvin A Danish dessert of apples, lemon juice, and toasted almonds.

aebleskiver ('eh-bleh-skee-vor) Literally "apple slice," this is a small Danish doughnut made with a beer batter flavored with spices and citrus zest. The doughnuts are baked stovetop in a special pan called an aebleskivepandle, which has deep half-sphere indentions to form the pastry as it cooks. A slice of apple or small amount of jam may be inserted into the centers after baking or they may be dusted with confectioners' sugar; served warm.

aenjera See *injera*.

aerate ('ay-uh-rayt) To fill with air; to lighten, so as to create volume in pastry products. Aeration may be accomplished by physically or mechanically whisking, creaming or laminating, or by adding a leavening agent such as yeast or baking powder.

aerometer (air-'oh-mee-tehr) See *Baumé*.

African Red tea See *rooibos*.

afternoon tea A traditional English light meal served in the afternoon and consisting of finger sandwiches, petit fours and scones, crumpets, and/or muffins served with clotted cream and jam. It is traditionally accompanied with tea and sometimes Madeira, Port, or Sherry. See also *high tea*.

agar-agar ('ah-gahr) A dried, tasteless seaweed used by commercial processors because of its strong setting properties to thicken soups, sauces, ice creams, and jellies. May be used as a gelatin substitute. Agar-agar is unique in that it will set at room temperature, unlike gelatin, which needs refrigeration to set. Can be found in many Asian markets.

aging The maturing of foods under controlled conditions, for the purpose of obtaining a particular flavor or texture.

agitate To move with rapid, irregular motion. In pastry, agitation is often done to induce crystallization of fats and sugars, as with agitating chocolate during the tempering process.

agiter (ah-ghe-'tay) The French verb meaning to stir or shake.

agraz A North African sorbet made from *verjuice*, sugar, ground almonds, and often sprinkled with Kirsch.

agrio (ah-'gree-yoh) The Spanish word to describe something as sour.

agrumes (ah-grue-'may) The French word for citrus fruit.

aguardiente (ah-gwar-dee-'en-tee) A strong Spanish liqueur similar to *grappa* or *marc*.

aigre (ay-gruh) The French word that describes something as tart, sour, or bitter.

aigre-doux (ay-gruh-'doo) The French term to describe something as bittersweet.

A
a

airbrush A small, air-operated tool that sprays edible color for the purpose of decorating cakes, confections, and showpieces.

air pump A tool used in the production of *blown sugar*. It consists of a long tapered nozzle with a hose that connects to a bulbous hand pump. A ball of cooked sugar is placed over the nozzle and air is blown into the sugar by hand-squeezing the pump, while at the same time the sugar is formed into the desired shape.

Airelle (ah-'rehl) A cranberry-flavored *eau-de-vie.*

airelle rouge (ah-'rehl 'roo-zha) The French word for *cranberry.*

aiysh (eye-'yesh) Egyptian flatbread.

ajouter (ah-zhu-'tay) The French verb meaning to join, or add ingredients.

ajowan ('ahj-wah-ahn) A light brown to purplish seed used as a spice in Indian breads and chutneys. It has the flavor of thyme and is the size and shape of a celery seed. Also called *ajwain* or *carom.*

ajwain See *ajowan.*

akala (ah-'kah-lah) A Hawaiian berry similar to a raspberry, eaten raw or used in jams and pies. The color may vary from red to purple.

akee See *ackee.*

akwadu A Ghanan dessert of bananas or other fruits combined with shredded coconut, citrus juice, and sugar and baked until the coconut is golden brown. Usually served hot or cold after a spicy meal.

à la carte (ah lah carht) A menu term used to indicate that each item is priced separately.

à la minute (ah lah mee-'noot) The French term for "of the minute," referring to dishes that are prepared at the last moment or are made to order.

à la mode (ah lah 'mohd) The French term for "in the style of" or "in the manner of." During the last century, it has come to mean American pie with a scoop of ice cream on top.

Albariño (ahl-bah-'ree-n'yoh) A white grape varietal grown in California as well as parts of Portugal and Spain. It produces a crisp, light-bodied wine.

Albert Uster Imports See *Specialty Vendors* appendix.

albumen (al-'byoo-mehn) From the Latin word *albus,* which means "white," this is the protein of the egg white, which makes up approximately 70% of the edible portion of the egg.

alcazar (al-kah-'zahr) See *alkazar.*

alchermes (al-'kehr-mess) A bright-red spicy Italian liqueur. The color is from a naturally occurring dye called *cochineal,* which is a substance extracted from insects such as ladybugs. The liqueur is used to flavor and/or color desserts and confections.

alcohol A tasteless, odorless, highly flammable liquid that is the intoxicating agent in liquors and fuels. Alcohol suitable for human consumption is known as ethyl alcohol, or ethanol. These spirits are made by fermenting the juices and concentrations of grains or fruits and then distilling the liquids to produce alcohol. Water is usually added to bring the solution to a rating of 80 proof, or 40% alcohol by volume. Unlike water, which boils at 212°F (100°C), alcohol boils at 173°F (78°C), and not all of the alcohol may be cooked or burned off, as has been proved by a USDA study. Also, alcohol will not freeze completely, and therefore is used in many frozen desserts, when a complete hard freeze is undesirable.

alcohol burner A small tool with a flame, used extensively in the production of *pulled sugar* and *blown sugar*. The glass or metal burner has a cloth wick that is soaked in denatured alcohol. When the wick is lit, the burner is used to heat or melt pieces of sugar so they can be connected. Also known as a spirit lamp.

A
a

aldehyde An organic compound that contributes flavor and aroma to bread.

aleurone layer The outermost layer of the wheat endosperm, which is typically removed with the bran prior to milling.

alfajore (al-fah-'hoar-ray) A South American pastry popular in Peru and Ecuador, consisting of short dough rounds baked and sandwiched together with cinnamon-flavored custard or cooked milk pudding.

algin (al-jihn) A thickening agent derived from seaweed and similar to gelatin. It is used as a stabilizer in commercial puddings, ice creams, pie fillings, and other foods. Also known as *alginic acid*.

alginic acid See *algin*.

alitame (al-ih-taym) An artificial sweetener that is 2,000 times the sweetness of sugar. It is not yet approved by the FDA. It is currently marketed in some countries under the brand name Aclame.

alkali ('al-kah-lie) A substance with a pH of 7 or above. Alkalis are used to neutralize acids. The most common alkali in baking is baking soda, which is also known as bicarbonate of soda. See *baking soda* and *pH*.

alkanet ('al-kuh-neht) A Eurasian plant that is a member of the borage family. Its roots produce a bright red color that is used as a food dye, particularly in margarine.

alkazar (al-kah-'zahr) An Austrian cake that is made with a base of shortdough pastry that is covered with a layer of apricot marmalade and topped with a Kirsch-flavored almond meringue. After the cake is baked, it is garnished with more marmalade and a latticework of marzipan, and then returned to the oven to brown the marzipan. Also spelled *alcazar*.

Allegrini An Italian, red semisweet wine named for the late Giovanni Allegrini, who founded the Allegrini wine estate in the 1950s. It has intense blackberry fruit flavors with a hint of licorice and eucalyptus, and it pairs well with ripe, creamy cheeses and cheesecake.

alleluia (ah-lay-'loo-yah) A citrus-flavored French confection made during Easter time. It is believed that the cake is named after Pope Pius VII. Legend has it that a dying soldier found the recipe during battle and gave it to a pastry chef; upon hearing the story, the Pope baptized the cake and named it Alleluia, which is French for "hallelujah."

alligator pear See *avocado*.

all-purpose flour See *flour*.

all-purpose shortening See *shortening*.

allspice The dried brown berry of the *Pimenta dioica* tree, found in Central and South America and the West Indies. The flavor is similar to that of cinnamon, nutmeg, and cloves. Sold both whole and ground, allspice is used in a variety of baked goods including pumpkin pie. Also known as *Jamaica pepper*.

allumette (ah-loo-'meht) The French word for "matchstick," which refers to thin strips of puff pastry that are baked and then topped with a sweet filling or royal icing; in the savory kitchen, the strips are topped with savory fillings.

almendras garrapinadas (al-'mahn-drahz gah-rah-pihn-'yah-dahz) Toasted almonds cooked in caramelized honey syrup. The almonds are cooled on a marble slab and broken into bite-size pieces. These candied almonds are popular in Spain and usually made for celebrations.

almond The nut of the almond tree, grown in California, South Africa, Australia, and the Mediterranean. Almonds are either sweet or bitter. Sweet almonds are most common in the United States; bitter almonds are illegal here because the prussic acid in the raw bitter almond is poisonous. The toxins can be destroyed by heating, however, and processed bitter almonds are used in liqueurs, extracts, and *orgeat syrup*. Sweet almonds are available blanched or unblanched; whole, sliced, slivered, or chopped; smoked; and in paste form.

almond cream A thick pastry cream enriched with ground almonds and almond-flavored liqueur.

almond extract A flavoring agent made from sweet or bitter almond oil and alcohol, used in many pastries, cakes, icings, and confections. This is a concentrated flavoring ingredient and so is used in small quantities.

almond flour Finely ground blanched almonds. Also called *almond meal*. See *meal*, no. 2.

almond meal See *almond flour.*

almond milk A mixture of milk or water and marzipan, heated until the mixture is smooth. It is used in custards, cakes, and sauces.

almond oil The oil extracted from sweet almonds. Used in the preparation of desserts and salad dressings.

almond paste 1. A soft paste made from ground blanched almonds, sugar, and glycerin. It is used in a variety of confections including frangipane, macaroons, and *Hippenmasse*. Marzipan is made from almond paste. 2. The British term for *marzipan.*

alpine strawberry Another name for *fraise des bois.*

alum ('al-uhm) 1. A crystalline salt used to retain the crispness of fruits and vegetables. 2. An ingredient in baking powder.

aluminum cookware A type of cook or bake ware made from aluminum. It is popular because of its high conductivity and low cost, but is limited to stovetop cooking because of its tendency to discolor foods, particularly acidic foods. It is recommended to use a heavy-gauge pan lined with parchment paper or a *Silpat* to obtain a better baked product. See also *anodized aluminum.*

aluminum foil A thin flexible sheet of aluminum used for baking and storing food products. The foil comes in two weights, regular and heavy-duty, and may also be used to wrap foods for the freezer to protect them from freezer burn.

alveograph A European testing instrument used to measure the strength and baking ability of flour.

am (ahm) The Indian word for *mango.*

amai (ah-mah-ee) The Japanese word to describe something as sweet.

amande ('ah-mahn) The French word for *almond.*

amandine ('ah-mahn-deen) A French term that refers to a food preparation garnished with almonds.

amaranth A native American herbaceous plant whose nutritive seeds have a unique, slightly spicy flavor. They can be used whole, cooked, or ground into flour. Amaranth contains no gluten, so it should be used in combination with wheat flour if making breads or cakes.

amardine A dried-apricot paste that has been processed into a sheet, produced in the Middle East.

amaree cookie A thin spice-flavored cookie with a base of dark chocolate and topped with roasted sesame seeds, created in 1990 by Australian pastry chef Aaron Maree.

amaretti (am-ah-'reht-tee) An Italian *macaroon* made from bitter almond paste or apricot kernel paste. The most popular brand is Lazarroni di Saronno.

amarattini (am-ah-reht-'teen-ee) A miniature version of *amaretti* cookies.

amarena cherry Moist, fleshy ripe wild cherries preserved in syrup or brandy, an Italian specialty. The Fabbri brand is the most well known.

amaretto (am-ah-'reht-toe) An almond-flavored liqueur originally produced in northern Italy. It is a combination of sweet and bitter almonds, and may also contain the flavor of apricot kernels. The word *amaro* means "bitter" in Italian.

amarula (ah-mah-'rue-lah) A cream liqueur from South Africa, made from the fruit of the African marula tree; it has a fruity caramel flavor.

ambasha An Ethiopian spice bread made with wheat flour, yeast, fenugreek, cardamom, salt, and coriander.

ambassador cake A French gâteau consisting of a sponge cake flavored with Grand Marnier, filled with pastry cream and candied fruit, then covered with a thin sheet of marzipan.

ambrosia (am-'bro-zha) 1. An American fruit dessert of bananas, oranges, and toasted coconut. Marshmallows and whipped cream may also be found in this southern favorite, served as a dessert or salad. *Ambrosia* means "immortality" and has its roots in Greek mythology, where it was considered the food of the gods. 2. A cocktail of *Champagne, Calvados, Grand Marnier,* and lemon juice.

American Culinary Federation See *Professional Development Resources* appendix.

amigdalozoúmi (a-meeg-dah-loots-'oom-ee) A Greek almond milk drunk during Lent and at funerals.

ammonium bicarbonate A leavening agent popular before the utilization of baking soda and baking powder, with certain unique features well suited to making small, dry baked goods such as cookies and crackers. It is not recommended for use in large or moist products because the ammonia gas will not bake out and the product will have a strong ammonia taste. Also known as *hartshorn salt* because it was originally produced from a hart's (male deer) horns and hooves.

Amontillado (ah-mohn-tee-'yah-doh) See *sherry.*

amylase ('ah-mah-laze) An important enzyme in yeast-risen baked goods. It is present in ingredients such as malted barley flour and breaks down starches into sugars, which softens the bread and helps prevent it from staling. Also known as *diastase.*

amylopectin A component of starch characterized by a branch molecular structure. See *starch.*

amylose ('ah-mah-lohs) 1. A category of sugar that includes maltose, sucrose, glucose, fructose, and dextrose. 2. A component of starch that has a straight chain of glucose molecules. See *starch.*

amylose starch The network of glucose molecules found in wheat and most other bread grains. These starches play an important role in the gelatinization process of bread baking. See *starch.*

an (ahn) A Japanese sweet bean paste.

anadama bread (anna-'dahm-mah) An earthy yeast bread containing molasses and cornmeal, from New England. Legend has it that this bread came about from a farmer's frustration at his wife serving him cornmeal and molasses gruel on a daily basis. One day he was so fed up that he added yeast and flour to the mush while yelling, "Anna, damn her!"

ananas ('ah-nah-nahs) The French word for *pineapple*.

anesone (ah-neh-'soh-nay) A clear, anise-flavored liqueur with a distinct licorice flavor.

angel food cake A light and airy cake made from beaten egg whites, sugar, flour, and flavorings and baked in a tube pan. Thought to have originated in Pennsylvania in the early 1800s, it has become an American favorite.

angel food cake pan A tall, round baking tube pan that has a removable bottom. It is specifically designed for making angel food cakes.

angel hair See *spun sugar*.

angelica (an-'jehl-la-kah) An aromatic herb native to northern Europe and Scandinavia. Its bright green stems are candied and used for flavoring and decoration. The fresh stems and leaves can also be used to flavor custards and jams. Owing to its expense, it is not widely available in the United States.

anethol The oil in *anise seed, fennel,* and *star anise* that give them their licorice flavor.

anice ('ah-nee-cheh) The Italian word for *anise*.

animal fat The fat that comes from an animal, including butter, suet, and lard. Animal fats are saturated, and so are commonly replaced by vegetable shortenings in pastry preparations.

anise, anise seed ('an-ihss) A herbaceous member of the parsley family, *Pimpinella anisum,* whose greenish-brown oval seeds have a sweet licorice flavor and are used in confections. The seeds also flavor several liqueurs, including ouzo and Pernod. They are also chewed as a digestive aid and to freshen one's breath.

anisette ('an-ih-seht) A clear, sweet, licorice-flavored liqueur.

anisyl butyrate A food additive used to enhance the flavor of candy, baked goods, and the vanilla flavor in ice cream.

anisyl formate A food additive used to add berry flavor to candies and baked goods.

anisyl propionate A food additive used to enhance the flavor of vanilla and various fruits, including plums and quince.

Anjou pear ('ahn-zhoo) See *pear*.

ankerstock ('ahn-ker-stahk) A sweet, rectangular rye bread flavored with spices and currants. It is believed to have originated in Scotland in the early 1800s, and is similar to gingerbread.

annatto (uh-'nah-toh) Yellow-red food coloring derived from soaking *achiote* seeds in water or cooking them in oil. Available in seed or liquid extract. Popular in Latin American and Indian cooking, primarily to color food and pastries; also used to color butter and cheese. Lends a slight astringent, earthy flavor.

anodized aluminum A hard, durable aluminum that is not reactive with food. Though it does not conduct heat as well as traditional aluminum, its dark color allows some heat to be transferred through radiation and its heavy gauge promotes more even baking.

antioxidant A substance in food that prevents oxidation. Found naturally in citrus fruits, broccoli, and Brussels sprouts, antioxdants aid in preventing the discoloration of fruits and some vegetables. Ascorbic acid and vitamin E are popular antioxidants. It is believed that they may also help reduce the risk of some cancers and heart disease.

anzac ('an-zic) A hard, sweet biscuit popular with the Australian and New Zealand army corps. They are known for there "resilience" and soldiers joke that these tile-shaped cookies are more suitable for armor protection than consumption.

apee ('ay-pee) A sugar cookie with a sour cream base. Invented in the 1800s by a Philadelphia cook named Ann Page, the name of the cookie comes from her initials.

aperitif (ah-pehr-uh-'teef) A light alcoholic beverage typically served before lunch or dinner.

Apfel ('ahp-phul) The German word for *apple*.

Apfelstreudel (ahp-phul-'strew-dull) A thin pastry roll filled with apples, spices, and raisins. Popular in Germany and Austria.

aphrodisiac (ahf-roh-'de-ze-ahk) Food or drink believed to give people a heightened sense of desire and sexual arousal. It is named after Aphrodite, the Greek goddess of love. The most well-known pastry aphrodisiac is chocolate.

appareil (ahp-pah-'ray) The French word denoting a mixture of ingredients used in a preparation.

apple The primarily round fruit of a tree in the *Roseacea* family. The apple is grown in many temperate regions around the world and thousands of varieties exist, offering flavors from tart to sweet. The fruit has firm flesh surrounded by a thin skin, which can range in color from yellow to red to strips of orange and gold. There are small seeds in the center of the fruit. Apples are popular raw, cooked, or pulped for their juice. Though some varieties are seasonal, others are available year-round. The most common varieties are:

> **Baldwin** A small, red apple with yellow streaks and a mild, sweet-tart flavor and crisp texture. Good for baking and eating. Available late fall.

> **Braeburn** A red apple with yellow streaked skin and a crisp, sweet-tart flavor. Available October to April.

> **Caville Blanc d'Hiver** A popular French dessert apple not commercially grown. Available mid-fall through spring.

> **Chenango** A medium American apple with a pale yellow skin that is striped with red. It has white flesh with pinkish-red marbling and is good for eating or cooking. Available mid-to late fall.

> **Cortland** A large apple with smooth, shiny, dark red skin with yellow patches and a juicy, sweet-tart flavor. Good resistance to browning when cut. Available late fall.

> **Crabapple** A wild or cultivated variety with small, pinkish-red fruit marked by hard, tart flesh. Its sour flavor makes it undesirable fresh but is popular for jams and jellies. Available September to November.

> **Criterion** A bright red apple with light green streaks and a slightly tart, juicy flesh. Available year-round with peak season in the fall.

> **Empire** Developed in New York state, a cross between a McIntosh and a red delicious, this apple has dark red skin and sweet-tart flavor. Available year-round.

> **Fuji** An attractive, aromatic, medium apple with a greenish-yellow skin heavily blushed with red. It has a sweet, crisp, juicy flesh and is good for baking and poaching. Available year-round.

Gala Originally from New Zealand, the apple's pale yellow skin is generously spotted with reddish streaks and it has a crisp, juicy flesh. Good for eating but not baking. Available year-round.

Golden Delicious Originally from West Virginia, this apple has a pale, greenish-yellow skin and a sweet, crisp, juicy flesh. It has good resistance to browning when cut and is excellent for baking because it retains its shape when cooked. Available year-round but at its peak in early fall.

Granny Smith Originally from Australia, the apple is named after the grandmother who developed it. With a golden-green skin and a slightly juicy, tart flavor, it is popular for baking or eating raw. Available year-round.

Gravenstein A round, crisp apple with a distinct acidic flavor. It is good both raw and cooked. Available early summer through early fall.

Ida Red A cross between a Jonathan and a Wagener. It is red with a hint of yellow and excellent for baking owing to its firm texture and medium acidity. Available fall through spring.

Jonagold A cross between a golden delicious and a Jonathan. It has a reddish-yellow skin and a juicy, sweet-tart flavor. Good raw or for cooking and baking. Available early fall through late winter.

Jonathan A crisp, bright red apple with a juicy, sweet-tart flavor. Only available October through November.

Lady A small, bright red apple that is a cultivated crab apple. It has a sweet, white flesh and is popular as a decorative item or fresh on desserts. Available fall to early winter.

Macoun A large red American apple that is derived from crossbreeding with a McIntosh apple. It has a crisp texture and juicy sweet-tart flavor that is good eaten raw or for baking. It has a short season that begins in late fall and ends in January.

McIntosh Named for its discoverer, John McIntosh, it is originally from Canada and was developed in the early 1800s. It is medium and has a red color with greenish-yellow streaks. Its sweet-tart flavor and crisp, juicy texture make it excellent for eating but it is not recommended for baking. Available year-round.

Newton Pippin A common American variety of the Pippin apple that originated in France. It has a greenish-yellow skin and a crisp, juicy, slightly tart flavor. Available fall to early spring.

Northern Spy A large apple native to North America, with a reddish-yellow striped skin and a sweet-tart flavor. A good all-purpose apple. Available fall to late winter.

Pink Lady A small, crisp apple with a pinkish-red skin and sweet-tart flesh that has a hint of raspberry and kiwi flavor. Available mid-winter.

Pink Pearl A medium American apple with a light green skin and unique pink flesh. It ranges in flavor from tart to sweet. Available fall to late winter.

Red Delicious A crisp, juicy, slightly elongated apple with a bright, deep-red color and slightly sweet flavor. Good for eating but turns mushy when baked. Available year-round.

Rhode Island Greening A popular commercial apple for applesauce and pie fillings, it has a green skin and sweet-tart flavor. Available mid-fall through spring.

Rome Beauty A large, red American apple discovered in the 1800s in Rome, Ohio. Good for baking owing to its ability to retain its shape when cooked. Available mid-fall through spring.

Stayman Winesap A cross between the red delicious and the Winesap, it has a red skin with greenish-yellow stripes and a crisp, juicy, tart flesh. Good all-purpose apple. Available late fall through late winter.

Winesap A dark red American apple with a crisp, juicy, tart flesh. Good for cooking. Available late fall through late winter.

York Imperial An American apple with a yellow streaked red skin and crisp, tart flesh. Good for cooking. Available mid-fall to April.

apple brandy Brandy that has been distilled from apples. See *applejack* and *Calvados*.

apple brown betty An American dessert of sliced apples baked with spices and sugar and topped with a crumb topping. It originated in colonial America.

apple butter A thick, sweet puree of apples with sugar, spices, and sometimes cider. Used as a fruit preserve.

apple charlotte A buttered bread shell filled with spiced, sautéed apples. Unlike other charlottes, this is baked and served warm. See also *charlotte*.

apple Connaught (kah-'nowt) A British custard named in honor of the Duke of Connaught. It is topped with the syrup from glazed apples.

apple corer A small, sharp edged, cylindrical hand tool that is used to remove the core from an apple.

apple dumpling An apple dessert consisting of a whole apple that has been peeled, cored, and filled with sugar, nuts, spices, and butter, then encased in a square of short dough or puff pastry, egg washed, and baked. See also *dumpling*.

applejack A strong American apple brandy distilled from apple cider. It ranges from 80 to 100 proof and is aged in wooden casks for a minimum of two years before being bottled. See also *Calvados*.

apple juice The natural juice of apples, usually pasteurized and filtered. Sugar may or may not be added.

apple pandowdy A rustic baked American dessert of buttered bread sprinkled with sugar and topped with apples, molasses, brown sugar, cinnamon, nutmeg, cloves, lemon juice, and butter, then another layer of buttered bread with the sugared side up. The crisp top and soft, moist interior are an interesting texture contrast. It is typically served warm, with whipped cream.

apple pear See *Asian pear*.

apple pie A two-crust pie with spiced apple filling. Originally from England, this popular dessert was brought to America by early European settlers. The apple filling is flavored with sugar, butter, and spices, and always topped with pie crust. Often served with ice cream; also served with Cheddar cheese in some regions of the country. See also *French apple pie*.

applesauce A puree of cooked apples, often flavored with sugar and sometimes spices such as cinnamon. Applesauce can be made by passing the cooked fruit through a food mill for a smooth puree or by crushing the apples manually, which results in a chunky version.

apple schnitz (shnihts) Dried apple slices, used in many Pennsylvania Dutch recipes.

apple snow A cold dessert of applesauce, spices, lemon juice, and whipped egg whites. Sometimes gelatin is added to increase the body of this soft mousse-like dessert. It is often served in individual glasses or dishes, and garnished with whipped cream.

apple strudel ('shtroo-duhl) A long pastry roll filled with apples, nuts, sugar, spices, and bread or cake crumbs. See also *strudel*.

apple sugar A sweet confection of apple juice, sugar, glucose, and an acid. The mixture is cooked to the hard crack stage and then poured onto marble, cut into sticks, and coated in fine sugar crystals. Originally from Rouen, France; the rice papers used to wrap the candies are stamped with a picture of the famous Rouen landmark, its clock tower. These candies are also shaped into small drops and slabs.

apple turnover A small individual pastry filled with apples, sugar, and spices enveloped in short dough or puff pastry. The traditional shape is a half-moon, formed by cutting circular shapes from the dough. The filling is placed on half of the circle, and the remaining half is turned over to enclose the filling. The pastry is egg washed and baked. Turnovers may also be filled with savory items or other fruits.

appliqué (ahp-lah-'kay) A method of cake decoration made by rolling out natural or colored fondant or marzipan and cutting designs of various shapes and sizes, such as flowers, leaves, and blossoms. The pieces are then placed on the surface of the cake, starting with the largest cutouts. Smaller cutouts are added on top of the larger pieces to create a three-dimensional effect, with the overall goal of adding depth and color to the finished product.

apprentice/apprenticeship A person learning a craft by working with experts in the field for a set period of time. An apprentice does an apprenticeship. Some apprenticeship programs are sanctioned by educational institutions and professional organizations, and they may offer certification or credits toward a diploma or degree.

apricot The small, oval fruit of the tree *Prunus armeniaca*. Apricots have thin, velvety skin that ranges in color from pale yellow to deep burnt orange. The fruit is fleshy cream to bright orange color and similar in texture to a peach. In the center of the fruit is a small almond-shaped stone, which detaches easily from the fruit when the apricot is cut in half. The American crop is grown primarily in California, and used in pastry in a variety of forms, including fresh, dried, and jam or glaze. The kernels in the stones are also roasted and used to flavor liqueurs or ground into a slightly bitter paste and used to flavor confections. The most common varieties are:

> **Early Gold** Originally from Oregon, this round, medium fruit has a bright golden skin that encases a rich, juicy flesh. It is best eaten raw or used for canning. Available early summer.

> **Golden Amber** Originally from California, this large, uniform fruit has a golden, yellow skin that encases a firm, slightly acidic, yellow flesh. Available late summer.

> **Moorpark** Originally from England, this large, oval fruit has a red-dotted orange skin that encases a fragrant orange flesh. Available mid-summer.

> **Perfection** Originally from Washington, this large, oval fruit has a pale orange skin with a tasty, bright orange flesh. Available early summer.

> **Royal** Originally from France, this large fruit has a yellowish-orange skin that encases a juicy flesh. There is a similar variety called Royal Blenheim that is originally from England. Available mid-summer.

> **Tilton** Originally from California, it is similar to the Royal but has an inferior flavor. Available mid-summer.

apricot brandy Any form of brandy distilled from *apricots*.

apricot glaze A clear, apricot-colored glaze made from apricot jam and water. It is most commonly brushed on desserts and pastries to provide shine and to protect fruit toppings from the air so they will have a longer shelf life. The glaze may be made fresh or purchased in bulk from specialty vendors. Also known as *nappage*.

aprium ('ap-ree-uhm) A hybrid fruit that combines plum (25%) and apricot (75%). It has the taste and appearance of apricots but a slightly sweeter flavor. Available May to June.

apry ('ap-ree) An alternative name for *apricot brandy*.

aqua vitae ('ahk-wah 'vee-tee) Literally, "water of life" in Latin. A clear distilled brandy, served as a cold shot in the Scandinavian countries.

Arabian coffee Coffee that has been ground to a fine powder and flavored with cardamom, cloves, and saffron. It is served black with no sugar, and its preparation signifies an offer of hospitality.

Arabica coffee bean (ah-rah-bih-kah) See *coffee*.

arachide (ah-rah-'sheed) The French word for *peanut*.

arak ('ahh-rrak) 1. In Asia and the Middle East, this is a fiery liquor whose ingredients vary from country to country but may include rice, sundry-palm sap, and dates. 2. A strong-scented, light-bodied rum from Java. Also spelled *arrack*.

arancia (ah-'rahn-chah) The Italian word for *orange*.

arborio rice See *rice*.

Arctic cloudberry See *berry*.

arepasau (aah-ruh-'pahs-oo) A Latin American cornbread, especially popular in Venezuela and Colombia. They are made from *masa* and are first grilled and then fried, which gives them a crisp exterior and soft, chewy interior. Arepas de chocolo are made with fresh corn kernels that have been roasted, ground, and kneaded. A simple version may be made by mixing equal amounts of boiling water and cooked white cornmeal with a bit of butter and salt; shaping the dough into tortillas and baking on a griddle.

Armagnac ('ahr-mahn-yak) One of the world's great brandies, it is produced in the French region of Gascony under strict controls. It is a single distilled full-flavored brandy made from white grapes, with a dry, smooth flavor, a strong bouquet, and an amber color owing to its oak cask aging. The aging may take up to 40 years. The age of the brandy is classified as follows: XXX is three years, VO is five to 10 years, VSOP, is up to 15 years, and Hors d' Age is at least 25 years.

Armenian cracker bread See *lavash*.

aroma Synonymous with smell, an important component of flavor because it enables tasters to separate and describe different products.

aromatic A word to describe an aroma that is imparted from spices, plants, or herbs that enhances the fragrance and/or flavor of food or drink.

arrack See *arak*, no. 2.

arrowroot A white, starchy thickening agent derived from a tropical tuber of the same name. It has a thickening power that is twice as strong as wheat flour; it is used to thicken sauces, puddings, and other foods. Arrowroot is tasteless and becomes transparent when cooked. When dissolved in water, it is known as a slurry, and is added cool to a hot liquid.

arroz con leche ('ah-rohs kon 'leh-cheh) A Spanish rice pudding flavored with vanilla, lemon, and cinnamon.

artificial coloring A synthetically or inorganically produced color used in many sweets, such as candies, decorations, and commercial pastries. Artificial colorings must meet FDA safety regulations for human consumption.

artificial flavor A chemically manufactured flavor as defined by the FDA. It is used as a food additive in commercial cakes, candies, frozen desserts, and pastries to mimic a natural flavor.

artificial sweetener A nonnutritive, synthetically produced sugar substitute. Artificial sweeteners include *aspartame, Acesulfame-K,* and *saccharin.* These sweeteners are 150 to 200 times sweeter than sugar. New sweeteners are becoming available that are chemical derivatives of sucrose, including *Splenda.*

artisan bread A high-quality bread that contains no artificial ingredients or preservatives and is made with only flour, water, yeast, and salt and sometimes grains and/or seeds. Artisan breads are created by artisan bakers who are trained in the skill and science of mixing, fermenting, shaping, and baking a hand-crafted product. They are typically made with a *pre-ferment* and baked directly on the oven deck.

artois, gâteau d' A pastry that combines a filling of apricot jam and almond cream sandwiched between two puff pastry strips. The top of the pastry is then egg washed and decorated with a diamond pattern, marked with a knife. It is baked and finished with additional apricot jam brushed over the surface, then decorated with *crystal sugar* on the sides.

artos (ahr-tahs) The general name for Greek celebration breads. There are many varieties and they differ in size, shape, color, and taste, depending on the festivity. Each is unique, with a history and involving family traditions. Many home bakers bring their breads to a priest for blessing before donating the loaves to the less fortunate.

ascorbic acid (as-'kohr-bihk) A water-soluble vitamin found in citrus fruit and the scientific name for vitamin C. It is used to prevent browning of fruits and vegetables, and also as an oxidizing agent in doughs to improve gluten quality.

ash The mineral content of a flour. Ash is measured in flours and grains by burning a sample at very high temperatures and weighing the remains. The ash content is important to bread baking because it helps determine what portion of the grain has been milled, as well as the mineral content; minerals increase yeast fermentation by providing food for the yeast.

asfor A Middle Eastern ingredient made from the stamens of the safflower. It has a golden, pale-orange color and is used to tint and flavor foods and desserts.

Asian pear A variety of juicy pear with a sweet aroma. They were first brought to America by Chinese miners during the gold rush of the 1800s. Also known as an apple pear owing to its similar shape. The most common varieties are:

> **Hosui** Medium pear with a crisp, apple flavor. It has a golden reddish-brown skin. Available early August.
>
> **New Century** See Shinseiki, below.
>
> **Nijisseiki** The most common type of Asian pear, it has a soft, smooth, yellowish-green skin that encases a slightly tart white flesh. Also known as Twentieth Century. Available early September.
>
> **Shinseiki** A flat, round pear with a tough, yellow skin that encases a white flesh with a sweet, crisp taste. Also known as New Century. Available mid-August.
>
> **Twentieth Century** See Nijisseiki, above.
>
> **Yali** A hardy variety with a pale yellow skin that encases a lightly sweet flesh. Available early October.

aspartame ('ah-spahr-taym) A synthetic artificial sweetener, 180 to 200 times sweeter than sugar. It has approximately 4 calories per gram and is a good choice for sweetening cold dishes. If heated, it breaks down and looses it sweetness, but a new form is being created for use in baking.

aspic ('as-pihk) A clear gelatin preparation. In the savory kitchen, aspic is made from broth to which gelatin been added and is used to coat cold dishes such fish and poultry in order to produce a shiny glaze. In the pastry kitchen, aspic is made with fruit juices, and although limited in use, may be a mold lining for *riz à l'impératrice* or other molded desserts.

assam tea ('as-sahm) A black tea with a reddish tinge that is full-bodied. Found in India's Assam district.

Asti Spumante ('ah-stee spoo-'mahn-tee) A sweet, sparkling dessert wine made from the Muscat grape. It is produced in the Asti area of the Piedmont in northern Italy. It may be used as an *aperitif* and also pairs well with fresh fruit and cheese.

asure (ah-'shoo-ray) A pudding of hulled wheat, chickpeas, nuts, and dried fruit. Originally from Turkey, it is also known as *Noah's pudding* and has religious significance to Muslims because it is believed that this was the last meal served on Noah's ark.

ataïf (ah-'ttah-yif) A fried half-moon pancake filled with nuts and syrup or cheese. Also known as Arab pancake.

ate (aah-tee) A sweetened, slightly grainy fruit paste typically made from guava or quince. It can be used as a dessert component or cake frosting or filling, and also pairs well with cheese. Ate keeps a long time and is popular in Mexico, Cuba, and the Middle East.

atemoya (ah-teh-'moh-ee-yah) A fruit native to South America and the West Indies, a cross between a *cherimoya* and a *sugar apple*. It has creamy custard-like center that contains dark flat seeds and has a tough, leathery green skin. The flavor is similar to a mango but with a hint of vanilla. Atemoyas are in season from late summer through the end of fall and contain high amounts of potassium and vitamins C and K.

athole brose (ah-thohl broz) A Scottish drink of oats, heather, whisky, and cream or eggs. This is typical of Brose dishes and was created during the Highland Rebellion in 1476.

atole (ah-'to-lay) A thick Mexican drink of corn masa, milk, crushed fruit, and sugar or honey. It dates back to pre-Columbian times and is served hot or at room temperature.

atr ('ah-ter) The Arabic word for a sugar syrup often flavored with citrus or rosewater.

atta flour ('at-taa) See *flour*.

au lait (oh lay) The French term that signifies an item is made "with milk," as in *café au lait*.

Auflauf ('uhf-luhf) The German word for a *soufflé*.

Auslese (ouse-lay-zuh) The German word for "selected harvest," which refers to a rich, sweet wine made from very ripe grapes that have been harvested in selected bunches.

autolyse (aw-toh-leeze) A resting period in the production of *artisan breads*. After the flour and water are mixed, this blend is allowed to rest for approximately 20 minutes so that the protein molecules may completely hydrate and bond to each other. The method was created by the famed baker Professor Raymond Calvel as a way to increase the volume and extensibility of the dough, as well as to reduce the oxidation that causes natural bleaching of the flour.

auvergnat (o-fehr-n'yah) A French bread shape, a ball of dough (*boule*) with a second piece of dough rolled out into a disk and attached to the top of the round dough. After baking, it appears as though the round dough is wearing a flat cap.

A
a

aveline (ah-veh-'leen) The French word for *hazelnut* or filbert.

avocado A tropical fruit of a tropical tree in the laurel family. Prized for its creamy, buttery flesh rich in oils, vitamins, and protein. The pale yellow-green flesh and large stone are enclosed in a skin that ranges in color from green to greenish-black. Depending on the variety, an avocado can weigh anywhere between 3 ounces (85 grams) to 3 pounds (1 kg 365 grams) and can vary from round to pear shape. The most well-known varieties are the black Hass and the green Fuerte. In Asia, the fruit is pureed and sweetened with condensed milk. It also makes an interesting ice cream.

awwam ('aah-'wwahm) A Lebanese yeast-raised ball of pastry dough that is fried and then dipped in a honey, lemon, and rosewater syrup.

azodicarbonamide A chemical sometimes added to flour during the milling process. It artificially oxidizes the flour and increases loaf volume.

azúcar (ah-'thoo-kahr) The Spanish word for *sugar*.

azuki bean (ah-'zoo-kee) See *adzuki bean*.

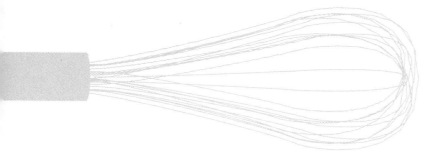

Bb

B & B A mixture of the liqueur *Benedictine* and *brandy*. It is bottled in Fecamp, the Normandy region of France. 2. The abbreviation for a bed and breakfast-type inn.

baba See *baba au rhum*.

baba au rhum ('bah-bah oh rhum) A rich yeast cake studded with raisins or currants and soaked in a syrup flavored with rum or Kirsch. Also known as a *baba*, this cake was developed in the late 1600s, when the king of Poland, Stanislas Leczyinski, dipped his dry Gugelhupf in rum and named it after the storybook hero Ali Baba. A classic baba au rhum is baked in a tall cylindrical mold, but it may also be baked in individual forms. If the cake is baked in a ring mold, it is known as *savarin*.

babáco (buh-bah-koh) Native to Ecuador, this tropical fruit is a relative of the papaya. It has a distinct shape with five sides that form a star when the fruit is cut. A pale flesh-colored interior is surrounded by a green skin that turns yellow when ripe. The flavor has overtones of strawberry, pineapple, and papaya and the smooth, thin skin is also edible. It is best eaten raw and is popular for both its creamy flesh and fragrant juice. Also called *chamburo*.

Babcock peach See *peach*.

babka ('bahb-kah) A rich, buttery rum-scented yeast bread studded with almonds, raisins, and orange rind or chocolate or cinnamon. Its origin is highly debated but Poles lay claim to its creation and traditionally serve it on Easter Sunday. The Eastern European Jews also claim they invented it and introduced it to America when they immigrated.

babovka (bah-'bove-kah) Traditional Czech tall, round cake with alternating layers of chocolate and vanilla sponge. The cake is flavored with rum and nuts.

Baby banana See *banana, finger*.

Baby Hawaiian See *pineapple*.

Baby kiwifruit See *kiwifruit*.

Baby Ruth A candy bar made with chocolate-covered peanuts and nougat. Invented by the Curtiss Candy Company in 1920, it was originally named after President Grover Cleveland's daughter, Ruth, but became popular because it was identified with the famous baseball player Babe Ruth.

Bacchus The Greek god of wine.

baci ('bah-chee) The Italian word for "kiss." It also refers to the small, round chocolate-covered hazelnut candies produced by the Perugina company in Italy.

backen ('bah-ken) The German verb meaning "to bake."

Bäckerei ('bay-kah-rye) The German word for a bakery.

Backobst ('bahk-obst) The German word for dried fruit.

Backofen ('bahk-ofen) The German word for oven.

back of the house A slang term that refers to the kitchen area of a restaurant or other commercial food-service establishment.

bagatelle (bahg-ah-'thel) A French dessert of *génoise* layers with *crème diplomat* and fresh strawberries. The strawberries are hulled and sliced lengthwise, then decoratively arranged vertically around the outside of the cake, creating an artistic band of berries. The cake is topped with a thin layer of pale green marzipan and served chilled. Also known as *fraisier*.

bagel A yeast bread shaped like a doughnut, with a dense chewy texture and shiny crust. A unique double-cooking technique is employed by first boiling the dough circles and then baking them. This popular Jewish bread was introduced to America in the late 19th century by Eastern European immigrants. Bagels are traditionally served with cream cheese and cured salmon (lox).

bag-out A term used in the pastry shop that refers to pressing a mixture out of a pastry bag onto a sheet pan in a particular pattern to form a decoration.

baguette (bah-'geht) The traditional long, thin French bread known for its crisp crust and light, chewy interior. *Baguette* is the French word for "stick." Classically, it weighs 8 ounces (240 ml) and is 30 inches (75 cm) long. Since the end of World War II, the French government has regulated the size and price of baguette loaves made and sold in France. A 1912 law states that the baguette must contain nothing but flour, water, yeast, and salt.

baguette pan A long metal pan that consists of two half-cylinders joined together lengthwise. It may be used to shape and bake French bread loaves and is sometimes perforated.

Baileys Irish Cream An Irish liqueur consisting of Irish whisky, cream, and cocoa.

bainiku (bah-nee-koh) See *umeboshi*.

bain-marie (bane-mah-'rhee) 1. French name for a double boiler used to promote slow, even, indirect heat to prevent overcooking. 2. A metal container that holds food over hot water for the purpose of keeping it hot. See also *water bath*.

baiser (beh-zay) The French verb for "to kiss." In pastry, it is a traditional petit four of two meringue kisses dipped in chocolate and sandwiched with a sweetened filling, such as pastry cream, whipped cream, or buttercream.

bake 1. To use an oven or other dry-heat chamber to cook a food item. Baking may be accomplished with the item covered or uncovered, but most pastry products are baked uncovered. 2. A Caribbean bread-like biscuit made with coconut milk and fried like a pancake on a griddle or in a pan.

bake-apple berry See *cloudberry*.

Baked Alaska A classic bombe with a sponge-cake base, topped with ice cream, and covered in meringue, which is browned with a torch or salamander just before serving. The dessert was created by a Parisian chef in 1860 and originally called *Omelette Norvégienne*, or Norwegian omelette; it is believed it was so named because the meringue resembled snow and the French consider Norway the land of snow. Americans adopted the dessert and renamed it Baked Alaska, after the dome igloos found there. It is traditionally served flaming, table side, to guests.

baked custard See *custard*.

baker A person who makes baked goods.

baker's cheese A pasteurized cheese produced from skimmed cow's milk. It is similar to cream cheese but contains virtually no fat. Although it is less rich, it is used in many pastry products because it is also less expensive.

baker's chocolate See *chocolate*.

Baker's German sweet chocolate A baking chocolate that was invented in 1852 by Sam German for the Baker's Chocolate brand. See also *chocolate, Baker's*.

baker's dozen One dozen (12) plus one (13).

baker's flour See *flour*.

baker's joy A pan-release spray used to coat baking pans so that goods are easy to remove. It is a combination of vegetable oil and flour, packaged in an aerosol spray can.

baker's knife See *cake slicer*.

baker's linen See *couche*.

baker's math See *baker's percent*.

baker's peel See *peel*.

baker's percent A system that bakers use to calculate formulas for baking. Flour is always 100% and all of the other ingredients in the dough are expressed as a percentage of the flour weight. This system allows recipes to be increased or decreased without compromising the quality of the product. Also known as *baker's math*.

baker's rack A portable rack that holds full and half sheet pans. Its mobility allows a large quantity of baked goods to be stored or moved through the work area.

baker's scale See *scale, balance*.

bakeware A term used to describe the tools used to produce items in a bakeshop including bread pans, sheet pans, cake pans and molds, cake rings, tart pans and rings, ramekins, pie pans, muffin pans, and others.

bakery A place where baked goods are made and sold.

Bakewell tart An English tart with a puff pastry crust brushed with jam and filled with eggs, sugar, and butter. After the tart is baked, it is dusted with confectioners' sugar or glazed with a simple icing or fondant. The tart was created by accident by a female cook working in the Rutland Arms Hotel in Bakewell, England.

baking ammonia See *ammonium bicarbonate*.

baking chocolate A chocolate made of pure chocolate liquor, without cocoa butter or sugars. It is also known as bitter or unsweetened chocolate. See *chocolate*.

baking cup A fluted paper or foil cup used to line muffin tins for baking muffins, cupcakes, and other small items. The cup holds the liquid batter and then becomes a wrapper after the item is baked. Baking cups come in standard 2 inch (5 cm) wide by 1¼ inch (3.1 cm) deep size but other sizes are available as well.

baking pan See *bakeware*.

baking powder A leavening agent for baked goods that consists of baking soda, cream of tartar or other acid, and a moisture absorber such as cornstarch. Baking powder is produced in both single-action and double-action forms. Single-action does not require heat and the baking soda reacts once it has dissolved in the liquid; it is no longer sold because it releases carbon dioxide too quickly and results in a low-quality product. Double-action baking powder reacts twice, once when dissolved and again when exposed to heat.

baking powder biscuit A small, round, American quickbread that is leavened with baking powder.

B
b

baking sheet A metal sheet used for baking. Most baking sheets are aluminum and are rigid and flat. Shiny heavy-gauge aluminum sheet pans are good conductors of heat and brown the food evenly. Dark metal sheet pans absorb heat, causing the bottoms of baked goods to darken and have a crisper crust.

baking soda An alkali leavener for making baked goods. When baking soda is combined with an acid and moisture, it produces carbon dioxide, which causes batters to rise. Baking soda reacts immediately when it comes in contact with a moist substance, so it should be mixed with dry ingredients before adding any liquid. If too much baking soda is used it may produce a yellowish-green discoloration and a strong chemical flavor. Also known as *bicarbonate of soda*.

baking stone A heavy, thick brown stone used in standard ovens to duplicate the constant heat attained from the brick floors of traditional bread and pizza ovens. Baking stones may be found in many shapes and sizes; however, round and rectangular shapes are most common. Items to be baked on the stones are slid directly onto the heated stone with the aid of a baker's peel. As an alternative, baking pans may be placed on the stones to extract some of the beneficial heat.

baklava (bahk-'lah-vah) A popular Greek and Turkish confection of multiple layers of phyllo dough brushed with butter and liberally sprinkled with spices and chopped nuts, usually almonds, walnuts, and/or pistachios. The pastry is scored into traditional triangle or diamond shapes, baked, and then soaked in honey syrup. Some regional variations flavor baklava with rosewater or orange flower water.

baladi (bell-a-dee) A 100% whole wheat Egyptian flatbread. The quality and price of the bread is strictly controlled by the government.

balance beam scale See *scale, balance*.

balance scale See *scale, balance*.

Baldwin apple See *apple*.

balka ('bahl-kah) A Polish yeast cake similar to brioche served at Polish Easter.

ballooning A cake-decorating technique whereby the decorator pipes a series of shells for a border but does not allow a tail to form. The shells are piped one after the other, with no spaces in between, with the result looking similar to a herringbone. This technique may be accomplished with a star or a round decorating tube.

balloon whisk See *whisk*.

balouza (bah-'loo-zha) A Middle Eastern pudding of cornstarch and nuts, flavored with orange flower water or rosewater.

balsamic vinegar See *vinegar*.

balsam pear See *muskmelon, bitter*.

balushahi (bah-'loo-shahi) An Indian dessert of sweet pastry dough deep-fried in clarified butter and dipped into sugar syrup.

banana A long, soft fruit of a perennial herb in the Musaceae family, cultivated in tropical climates around the world. Bananas are picked green and best ripened off the tree. They should be stored in a cool place and may be refrigerated; though the skin will turn black, the flesh will remain unchanged. Once peeled, banana flesh will begin to oxidize and turn brown unless kept in acidulated water. There are hundreds of varieties, with the most popular being:

> **Baby** Another name for Finger bananas.

> **Blue Java** With a splotchy grayish-blue skin and an ice cream-like flavor.

Burro A chunky, square-shaped banana that is 6 to 7 inches (15 to 17.5 cm) long. It has a deep yellow peel with black streaks and a soft, pale yellow flesh that tastes like sweet lemon.

Cavendish The most common yellow banana. It is typically 6 to 8 inches (15 to 20 cm) long with a golden yellow peel and creamy white, sweet flesh.

Finger A highly prized tropical banana that is only 3 to 4 inches (7.5 to 10 cm) long. It has a thin yellow skin and soft, creamy white to dark yellow flesh with a sweet tropical flavor. Also known as Baby banana.

Manzano Only 4 to 5 inches (10 to 12.5 cm) in length, with a thin yellow skin and firm, creamy white flesh that has an apple-like flavor with hints of strawberry.

Plantain A large, firm, flattish banana used extensively in Latin American and African cooking. About 12 inches (30 cm) in length and can weigh up to 1 pound (454 grams). The thick skin turns from green to black as it ripens and should be cut off with a knife. The flesh ranges from creamy white to pale pinkish orange. It is typically cooked green and used much like a potato, or when ripened, has a squash-like sweet flavor sweet and soft, spongy texture.

Red About 6 inches (15 cm) long, it turns from greenish-maroon to blackish-bronze as it ripens. The sweet, firm flesh ranges from pinkish-ivory to reddish-pink.

banana cream pie An American dessert of a baked pie shell lined with fresh bananas and filled with custard. It is typically topped with sweetened whipped cream or a meringue that is browned.

banana flour A flour made from dried bananas.

banana leaf A large, flat green leaf from the banana plant, used extensively in Southeast Asian and Central and South American cooking to wrap foods for baking.

banana liqueur See *crème de banane.*

banana passion fruit See *passion fruit.*

bananas Foster Famous New Orleans dessert of sliced bananas sautéed in butter, brown sugar, and banana liqueur, then flambéed with rum and served over vanilla ice cream. Named for a popular customer, Richard Foster, this table-side dessert was created in the 1950s at Brennan's restaurant.

banana split An ice cream dessert that consists of a banana split in half and topped with scoops of vanilla, chocolate, and strawberry ice cream, then covered with chocolate, fruit, or butterscotch sauce and finished with whipped cream and a *maraschino cherry.*

Banbury cake A sweet oblong English cake made with an outer crust of flaky puff pastry, filled with mincemeat. This was a popular 17th-century wedding cake, named after the Oxfordshire town of Banbury, where it was first baked; one the oldest forms of English cakes. Also known as *Banbury tart.*

Banbury tart See *Banbury cake.*

banh troi (behn-troy) Literally "floating cakes." A sweet Vietnamese rice dumpling. The *mung beans* are of soaked, steamed, and pureed, then mixed with sugar and chilled; then combined with sesame paste and formed into balls. The balls are encased in a *glutinous rice flour* pastry round and then boiled and simmered in a sugar syrup flavored with ginger. The finished dumplings are cooled, garnished with toasted sesame seeds, and served with a sauce.

banneton ('bahn-than) A French cloth-lined woven round or oval basket in which bread is allowed to rise before it is baked. Bannetons are used extensively in French bakeshops, as well as in the United States for making *artisan breads.*

B
b

bannock ('bahn-nuhk) A Scottish griddle cake made from barley meal and oatmeal, sometimes flavored with orange or almond, and sometimes containing currants, raisins, or other dried fruits. The cake is leavened with yeast or baking powder, and is the precursor of the scone.

bap A Scottish breakfast yeast roll with a floury taste.

Baptist cake A deep-fried doughnut-type cake popular in New England during the 1930s.

bara brith (baa-rah breeth) A Welsh fruitcake that is lightly spiced and packed with dried fruits. *Bara* means "speckled or spotted crust" and refers to the cake's exterior appearance.

barack ('bah-rahk) A Hungarian *eau-de-vie* made from apricots.

Barbados cherry See *acerola*.

Barbados gooseberry A small West Indian cactus fruit with yellow to red color and a tart flavor.

Barbados sugar See *sugar*.

barbagliata (bahr-bah-l'yah-tah) An Italian beverage made with espresso and cocoa that may be served warm or cold.

barbari (barr-bah-ree) An Iranian flatbread, similar to *lavash*.

barberry See *berry*.

bar cookie See *cookie*.

barfi ('bar-fee) A fudge-like candy from eastern India, consisting of milk cooked slowly until it has the consistency of cream. The mixture is then sweetened with sugar, colored with rosewater, and flavored with pistachios or almonds. Once cooled, it is cut into squares or diamonds, and often decorated with *vark*, an edible silver leaf. Also spelled *burfi*.

barista (bah-rhee-stah) A coffee professional highly knowledgeable about and trained in the preparation of coffee and espresso drinks.

bark 1. A flat chocolate candy of nondescript shape, studded with toasted nuts and dried fruit. The candy is made in large quantities and broken into chunky pieces. 2. Generic name for a chocolate coating of cocoa solids and vegetable oil, used as a nontempered form of coating chocolate.

Bar-le-duc A currant preserve made from both white and red currants and other berries. Developed in the French town of Bar-le-Duc, in Lorraine, this preserve was once made from white currants whose seeds were removed by hand.

barley The oldest known cereal grain, dating back to the Stone Age, now used in cereals, breads, soups, and many other dishes. Much of the barley grown is used for either animal feed or the production of beer and whisky, if it is malted first. The hulled barley is the most nutritious form of the grain, with only the husk removed. Scotch and barley grits are husked barley that has been ground. Pearl barley has the bran removed and has been precooked and polished. Barley flour and barley meal is pearl barley that has been ground. Lacking *gluten*, barley must be combined with wheat flour for bread making. Bread made with barley is dark, with a dense texture.

barley sugar A candy made from sugar cooked to the light yellow color of barley. It is then cut into strips and twisted.

barley syrup See *malt syrup*.

barm (bahrm) 1. The English term for a sourdough starter; see *sourdough culture/starter*. 2. The yeast that is drawn off of fermented malt.

barmbrack ('bahrm-brak) An Irish bread made from yeast or other leavening agents, studded with raisins, currants, and candied fruit peel, and usually spread generously with butter. It is often served with tea in Ireland.

barquette ('bahr-keht) A boat-shaped pastry shell filled with either a savory or a sweet filling.

barquette mold A metal boat-shaped tin used in the production of a barquette. The mold may have straight sides or be fluted, and is generally 3 to 4 inches (7.5 to 10 cm) long; 1¾ inches (4.5 cm) at the widest point; and ½ inches (1.2 cm) deep.

barriga de freira (bah-'ree-gah day free-'air-rah) A Portuguese sweet made by cooking sugar and water to a thick syrup and adding bread crumbs, butter, and beaten eggs. After cooling, it is poured into a serving dish and decorated with dried fruits and nuts. The name translates to "nun's belly" and is believed to be called this because in the 17th century nuns made and sold many such delicious sweets to raise money for their convents.

Bartlett pear See *pear*.

basboosa (baz-boo-zah) A Middle Eastern cake made with a thick batter of semolina flour and yogurt. Before baking, the top is scored in a diamond pattern and a whole blanched almond is put into each diamond. After baking, the cake is moistened with syrup of sweet rosewater and lemon.

Baseler leckerli See *leckerli; leckerlie*.

basil ('bay-zihl) An annual herb from the mint family, with an aromatic flavor of licorice and cloves. The name comes from the Greek *basileus,* which means "king" and so it is often referred to as the royal herb. Although native to India, basil can be found growing all over the world; it varies in size, flavor, and color with each region. An important herb in cooking, the most popular varieties include sweet basil, holy basil, opal basil, hairy basil, purple basil, and lemon basil.

basket weave A cake-decorating technique resembling a basket weave, often used for bridal cakes. A vertical line of buttercream is piped on the sides of the cake from the bottom to the top. A series of horizontal lines are then piped across this vertical line, leaving space between each one.

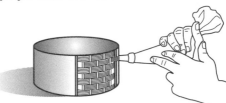

A second vertical line is piped over top of the edge of the horizontal lines, and then additional horizontal lines are piped, starting from the spaces found on the previous series of horizontal lines and over the new vertical line. Most basket weaves are piped using the #47 or #48 decorating tip; however, other tips may be used.

Baskin Robbins An ice cream store started by brothers-in-law Burton Baskin and Irvine Robbins in 1945 known for its "31 flavors" one for every day of the month. The company has grown into one of the world's largest franchises, with over 4,500 stores around the country.

basmati rice See *rice*.

bastard saffron See *safflower oil*.

baste To spoon onto or brush foods with a fat or other liquid as they cook.

B b

bastila (best-ee-lah) See *brik*.

ba-ta-clan (bah-tah-clahn) A French almond-flavored cake baked in a brioche pan and covered with vanilla fondant. It was invented in the 19th century by pastry chef Pierre Lacam.

bâtard (bah-'tahrd) Similar to the baguette, but smaller, this French bread traditionally weighs 8 ounces (240 ml) and is 24 inches (60 cm) long, not 30 (75 cm). The literal translation is "bastard," which refers to the loaf's not being the standard size.

batch The quantity of a product made at one given time.

Bath biscuit A derivative of English Bath buns (see *Bath bun*), a quickbread studded with currants and baked into small round biscuits. The biscuits were created by Dr. Oliver in Bath, England, and are also known as *Oliver biscuits* and *Bath Olivers*.

Bath bun A sweet yeast bun studded with golden raisins and candied peel. Before baking a generous amount of crystal sugar and currants are strewn about the top. The bun was created in the city of Bath, during the 18th century.

Bath Oliver See *Bath biscuit*.

batia roti See *roti*.

batido (bah-'tee-doh) A Latin American drink of water, fresh fruit pulp, and a small amount of milk, ice, and sugar.

bâtonnet (bah-tohn-nay) A classic French knife cut that resembles a stick. The dimensions are ¼ (6 mm) by ¼ (6 mm) by 2 inches (5 cm).

Battenberg A German checkerboard cake of pink and yellow cake squares held together with apricot jam and wrapped in marzipan. Originally named for German royalty, the cake was renamed tennis cake after World War I because it resembled the design of a tennis court and was often served at matches. It is an English favorite and is generally known by its original name.

batter A semi-liquid mixture that forms the basis for cakes, pancakes, waffles, muffins, and other pastries. It may be thick or thin before cooking or baking, and is generally made from flour, liquid, and eggs; it is poured or spooned into the baking pan.

batter bread A yeast bread with a thin batter-like consistency. The gluten is formed by vigorous stirring. See *Sally Lunn*.

batterie de cuisine ('bah-tree duh kwiz-'zeen) The French term that indicates the area in the kitchen that houses the equipment used in the production of food and pastries.

batter whisk See *whisk*.

Baumé See *Baumé scale*.

Baumé scale (bo-'may) A hydrometer scale of measurement used to determine the sugar concentration in a liquid by measuring its density; the sugar reading is expressed in degrees. The scale is named after its inventor, the French chemist Antoine Baumé. The baumé scale has been replaced by the *Brix scale*, which measures the density of sugar syrup in decimals.

Baumé thermometer See *thermometer, saccharometer*.

Baumkuchen ('bowm-koo-chen) A traditional German Christmas Cake, made only by specialty bakeries. The cake is made by brushing a thin layer of batter over a

Baumkuchen

turning rod placed over a hot grill. When the layer is set, another layer is applied over it, forming many thin layers of concentric rings. This layering forms what resembles the rings of a tree trunk. When the cake has a large number of rings, a long wooden comb is pressed into the sides, which gives the cake its characteristic screw-like indentations. The warm cake is then glazed with apricot, and then with either chocolate or a transparent sugar icing.

bavarese (bah-vah-reh-zeh) The Italian word for *Bavarian cream*.

Bavarian cream A classic French chilled custard dessert of *crème anglaise*, flavoring, whipped cream, and gelatin. This creamy mixture is set in a mold or used as a filling for cakes such as charlottes. Also known by its French name, *crème bavarois*.

bavarois (bah-vah-rwah) The French word for *Bavarian cream*.

beach plum See *plum*.

bead tea See *gunpowder tea*.

beat To rapidly combine ingredients in a circular motion to alter their consistency. Beating may be accomplished with a *whisk, paddle*, or spoon.

beaten biscuit A hard and crisp Southern biscuit. It dates to the 1800s, and its unique texture comes from how the dough is made. It is beaten with a rolling pin or mallet for an extended time, until it becomes blistered, elastic, and smooth. The dough is then stamped out into rounds, pricked with the tines of a fork, and baked. A beaten biscuit machine may be used, resembling an old-fashioned clothes wringer; it takes no less time, yet helps prevent tired bakers' arms.

beaumes de venise (bohm deh veh-'nez) A sweet Muscat wine from a village in the Vaucluse of the southern Rhône valley of France. It is known for its taste of honeyed apricots and is a popular dessert wine.

Beauty plum See *plum*.

bebida (beh-'bee-dah) The Spanish word for drink.

bee balm A member of the mint family, this herb is used to make tea and to flavor savory items.

Beerenauslese (bayr-nouse-lay-zuh) The German term for a "berry selected harvest," which refers to a rare and costly wine sweet wine made from grapes that are selected by hand, then exposed to *Botrytris cinerea*, which gives them an intense honeyed richness.

bee sting A sweet yeast pastry filled with custard and topped with a Florentine mixture. This is an English version of the German *Bienenstich* pastry. The name comes from the baker who was stung by a bee attracted to the honey topping he was preparing for the cake.

beet sugar A root vegetable from which sugar is produced. Indeed, one of the greatest sugar resources in the world; the European Union, United States, and Russia make up the three largest sugar beet processors. Beet sugar accounts for over 30 percent of all sugar production.

beggar's purse A crepe filled with caviar and crème fraiche, gathered together and tied to resemble a sack. This popular appetizer was created at the now-defunct Quilted Giraffe restaurant in New York City. More recently, the phrase refers to the sacklike shape and may be made with various products, including phyllo dough and sweet fillings.

beignet ('ben-yay) The French word for fritter. Refers to a doughnut-type yeast pastry popularized in New Orleans. The pastry is deep-fried and heavily dusted with confectioners' sugar. Beignets may also be savory and are best served warm.

beijo de anjo ('bay-ho-day 'an-yo) A small Brazilian sweet of rich, eggy little cakes coated in syrup and served in a bowl with additional syrup. The name means "angel kisses" in Portuguese.

bejinho de coco (bay-'hin-yoh day 'coe-coe) A Brazilian sweet and spicy candy. Sweetened condensed milk and butter are cooked until thick, coconut is added, and the candy is kneaded on an oiled surface, shaped into individual balls, coated in confectioners' sugar, and decorated with a whole clove.

Belgian waffle See *waffle*.

Bellini (beh-'lee-nee) A refreshing Italian summertime cocktail that consists of cold *Proseco* and fresh white peach juice. It was invented in the 1930s at Harry's Bar in Venice. Modern versions may use any variety of sparkling wine and frozen white peach juice.

bel paese (bell pay-'ay-zay) Literally, "beautiful country" in Italian, this refers to a semi-soft cheese with a mild buttery flavor, served as a dessert. It was originally produced in Bel Paese, a town outside of Milan.

belle Hélène (bell ha-'leen) A classic French ice cream dessert of a poached pear served on a scoop of vanilla ice cream and drizzled with warm chocolate sauce. It was created by the great Chef Auguste Escoffier in honor of an 1864 operetta of the same name. Also known as *pear belle Hélène* and *poire Hélène*.

bench 1. A table, traditionally of wood, in a pastry kitchen or bakery used for making breads and doughs. 2. See *12 Steps of Baking* appendix.

bench brush A horizontal brush with flat, vertical, thick bristles attached to a short handle, used to brush or sweep off excess flour or confectioners' sugar from a sheet of dough and/or from the table as the dough is being rolled out. May be plastic or wood.

benching See *12 Steps of Baking* appendix.

bench scraper A hand-held rectangular tool used for cleaning and scraping the work surface for baking. It is also a popular tool for tabling chocolate. The stainless steel blade is approximately 6 inches (15 cm) long and 3 inches (7.5 cm) wide, and is attached to a wooden or plastic handle of the same length.

Benedictine A liqueur flavored with herbs, honey, and dried fruit, named after a Benedictine monk of the Abbey of Fecamp, Normandy, France. This sweet Cognac-based liqueur was first produced in 1510. The letters D.O.M. on each bottle stand for *Deo Optimo Maximo,* meaning "To God Most Good, Most Great."

benne seed ('behn-ee) The African slave word for *sesame seed*.

benne wafer A traditional Southern cookie made with sesame seeds, pecans, and brown sugar. The cookies are thin and crisp, and were made in the slave kitchens of Southern plantations.

benzoyl peroxide A bleaching agent added to flour during the milling process to oxidize and whiten it.

bergamot orange ('ber-gah-mot) See *orange*.

Berliner doughnut See *Bismarck*.

berlingot (bayr-lin-gaht) A pyramid-shaped, striped, hard sugar candy. Although the origin is unknown, it is thought to derive from the Italian cake called berlingozzo which is traditionally flavored with peppermint. Today, many are made with a fruit flavoring, while a true berlingot is made by wrapping two colors together. In England and other countries they are also known as humbugs and boiled lollies.

Bernachon A world-renowned chocolate shop located in Lyon, France. Started by master chocolatier Maurice Bernachon, the shop sells his hand-crafted chocolates made with chocolate that is made in-house.

berry Any of a variety of small fruits that contain seeds but not pits. The most common varieties of berries are:

Barberry A bright red berry found throughout Europe and New England. This highly acidic berry is used in pies, preserves, and syrups. The unripened berries are sometimes pickled, but most people do not consume the tart fruit raw. Available June to August.

Bilberry A dark blue-purple berry that grows wild in Great Britain and other parts of Europe. A smaller, more tart version of the blueberry, it is used in the preparation of jams, syrups, and tarts. It is in season from July to September and is also known as *whortleberry*.

Blackberry A large, wild, elongated berry with a purplish-black, shiny skin and juicy, sweet-tart flavor. They are cultivated in North America and Europe and pair well with apples. They are popular as garnishes, sauces, jams, and fruit fillings. They may be purchased fresh or frozen year-round, but peak season is during the summer months. They are highly perishable and should be stored in the refrigerator in a single layer to prevent molding.

Blueberry A small, round, sweet, juicy berry with a smooth, purplish-blue skin. They grow wild in Maine; these are not readily available outside the state. They are cultivated throughout the rest of the United States and are popular as garnishes, sauce, jams, fruit fillings, and in muffins. They may be purchased fresh or frozen year-round, but peak season is during the summer months. They are highly perishable and should be stored in the refrigerator in a single layer to prevent molding.

Boysenberry A cross of a blackberry, raspberry, and a loganberry. Named after its creator, Rudolph Boysen, they are grown mainly in California and have a mildly sweet flavor. They are reddish-black and have a large, elongated shape. Available mid-summer.

Cape Gooseberry A bittersweet, juicy berry that is cultivated in tropical climates around the world. They resemble a small, golden-amber cherry tomato and have a thin, papery husk that must be removed before use. They are good for pies, jams, jellies, and for eating them fresh. Also known as *physalis*, *poha*, and *ground cherry*. Available March to July.

Cranberry A small, round, bright red berry with a very tart flavor. The wild cranberry is native to North America, but cultivated primarily in Massachusetts, Michigan, and Canada. They are popular in combination with apples for cobblers, pies, and other desserts and are available fresh, frozen, dried, canned, and sometimes sweetened. Available mid-October to late December.

Cowberry A tart, red berry that is a member of the cranberry family. It grows wild in Maine, Canada, and northern Europe and is used to make jams and sauces. Also known as *mountain cranberry*. Available October to December.

Currant See main entry for *currant*.

Dewberry Closely related to the blackberry. It is similar to the raspberry but is purplish-black instead of red. The berries are sweet and may be eaten raw or used to make jam or cobbler. Available June to August.

B
b

Elderberry The fruit of the elder tree. The very tart fruit with skin that is purple-black is used for jams and jellies, and of course the famous elderberry wine. The berry is poisonous when eaten raw owing to an alkaloid poison that is destroyed during the cooking process. Available June to early September.

Gooseberry A large, tart berry native to northern Europe. The skins may be smooth or fuzzy, and there are white, red, green, and yellow varieties. They are popular for jams, jellies, fruit fillings, and desserts. Available canned year-round or fresh during the summer.

Huckleberry A wild berry that resembles a blackberry but with a thicker skin and more acidic flavor. They have small, hard seeds in the center and are not commercially cultivated. They may be eaten as is or used in baked goods such as pies and muffins. Available June through August.

Juniper Berry An astringent, blue-black berry that is native to America and Europe. They are too bitter to eat raw and are generally sold dried and crushed before use to release their pungent flavor. They are the major flavoring ingredient in gin. Available August to September.

Lawtonberry This sweet fruit is a cross between the blackberry and the loganberry.

Laxtonberry A berry hybrid similar to the raspberry.

Lingonberry Known as "the red gold of the forest" in their native Sweden, these tiny cowberries are grown wild and look and taste like a small cranberry. They contain a natural preservative called benzoic acid, so little to no sugar is required and they do not need to be refrigerated. They ripen in September and are available only in the regions where they grow, such as Scandinavia, Russia, Canada, and Maine. They are very popular as a preserve and are also used as to make dessert toppings, parfaits, mousses, and sauces.

Loganberry A hybrid of the raspberry and blackberry. It is high in vitamin C and resembles a large oblong raspberry. It has a reddish-purple color and a sweet-tart flavor. They are good both fresh and cooked and are popular for jams, preserves, sorbets, tarts, pies, and coulis. Available July to early September.

Mountain Cranberry Another name for *cowberry*.

Mulberry There are three varieties: red, white, and black. The red are found mainly in the eastern United States while the white is of Asian origin and the black grows wild in Europe. They resemble blackberries and have a sweet-sour flavor, and are typically used to make jams, sorbet, ice cream, and mulberry wine.

Olallieberry A cross between a loganberry and a youngberry. They are grown mainly in California are available midsummer. They resemble a large elongated blackberry and the dark shiny skin encases a sweet juicy flesh; excellent as jams, jellies, and may also be used cooked or fresh in other desserts, pastries, and confections.

Raspberry A delicate, petite, sweet-tart berry that is used extensively in the pastry shop for garnishes, sauces, and jams. Red is the most common variety, but black and golden are also available. They may be purchased fresh or frozen year-round, but peak season is during the summer. They are highly perishable and should be stored in the refrigerator in a single layer to prevent molding.

Strawberry A hardy, sweet, red berry that is used extensively in the pastry shop for toppings, fillings, sauces, and jams. They are commercially cross-bred and vary in size, but generally the smaller varieties are more flavorful owing to a lower water content. They are available fresh or frozen year-round, but peak season is during the summer months. See also *fraise des bois.*

Thimbleberry Any of the thimble-shaped raspberry varieties, particularly the black ones.

Whortleberry See *bilberry.*

Wineberry Native to Japan, they resemble raspberries in size and color, but have a juicy, grapelike flavor.

Youngberry A large, shiny blackberry hybrid that has a reddish wine color and sweet, juicy flesh. It is native to Louisiana, but is now cultivated in southern California.

besan See *flour.*

besan roti See *roti.*

beta carotene ('bay-tuh 'khar-rah-teen) A nutritional supplement naturally occurring in fresh vegetables such as carrots, broccoli, squash, spinach, and sweet potatoes. It is believed to be an *antioxidant,* capable of helping reduce the risk of cancer and heart disease. Beta carotene is also used as a *food additive* because its characteristic orange-yellow pigments can color butter and margarine. It may also be used in foods such as flour and shortenings as a nutritional supplement.

beta crystal A component of cocoa butter, these crystals play a major role in the proper tempering of chocolate. A large number of stable beta crystals must be formed to gain the most appealing appearance, texture, and flavor of tempered chocolate. See also *cocoa butter.*

beta prime crystal See *cocoa butter.*

betise (beh-'tee-say) A small mint-flavored confection made by boiling sugar syrup. As the candy cools, air is injected into the mixture, producing tiny air bubbles that result in an airy texture. Betise is believed to have been invented in France in 1850, when a confectionery apprentice made a mistake, pouring the sugar syrup onto the marble slab incorrectly and inadvertently creating the microscopic bubbles that are characteristic of this candy.

bettleman A pudding similar to bread and butter pudding, made by soaking stale bread crumbs in boiled milk and then sweetening the mixture with sugar, spices, candied peel, eggs, cherries, and a stiffly beaten meringue. The mixture is then baked in individual dishes or a large baking dish with additional bread crumbs strewn about the top. *Bettleman* translates to "beggar's pudding," reflecting the times of hardship when people use whatever scraps are about the house.

betty A baked pudding of alternating layers of sweetened spiced fruits and buttered bread crumbs. Betties originated in colonial America and are also known as brown betty. Apple brown betty is the most well known, made with apples and brown sugar.

beugnon (bojhn) A traditional French fritter. This less sweet version of the American doughnut is made with a yeast dough formed into a ring and fried in hot oil. Although it was created after the *savarin,* they are similar in that they both may be soaked in a sweet syrup after cooking.

beurre (burr) The French word for *butter.*

beurre noir (burr nwar) The French term for "blackened butter," referring to whole butter that is melted and heated until it turns a deep brown.

B b

beurre noisette (burr nwah-'zeht) The French term for "brown butter," referring to whole butter that is melted and heated until it turns a hazelnut (noisette) color and aroma.

beveling The act of cutting off the edge of an un-iced cake so as to soften and round the edge. Beveling is done when rolled fondant is placed over the cake, so the edges will not tear. It also increases the area of the cake for decorating purposes.

bhakri (bahk-ree) A round, flat unleavened bread made from sorghum. A food staple of India.

bharaat ('bhhu-rrat) A sweet spice mixture from the Middle East, consisting of cinnamon, allspice, nutmeg, and cloves.

bialy (bee-'ah-lee) A large, round, flat and chewy yeast roll with a depression in the center. Often topped with chopped onions before baking, this Jewish-American bread was named after the Polish city of Bialystok.

bianco (bee-'ahn-koh) The Italian word for white.

Biber ('bi-bear) A Swiss honey cake made of rich gingerbread filled with a spiced mixture and glazed with a potato glaze while hot to give the cake its characteristic shine. Legend has it that a honey cake was fed to a helpful bear by Saint Gall, and so the cake is decorated with the picture of a standing bear.

bicarbonate of soda See *baking soda*.

Bienenstich ('bee-nen-steekh) The German version of a *bee sting*, differing from the English version in that the cake is topped with a generous amount of honey, butter, and almonds rather than a Florentine mixture.

biga ('bee-gah) An Italian-style pre-ferment used in the production of artisan bread. It consists of flour, water, and a very small quantity of yeast (.08 to 1%). The amount of water used determines whether it is loose (90 to 100% hydration) or firm (50 to 60% hydration). It does not contain any salt and therefore the yeast has no inhibitor and can digest all of the natural sugar during fermentation. This process assists in giving the final bread a stronger, more pronounced flavor.

bigarade (bee-gah-rahd) The French word for a bitter orange.

bilberry See *berry*.

Billings camambola A variety of *carambola*, used to make preserves.

bind To cause ingredients to come together by using butter, flour, eggs, cornstarch, cream, or other thickening agents. This culinary technique is used to hold ingredients together.

Bing cherry See *cherry*.

Bircher muesli A cereal mixture of oats, milk fresh cream, and fruits invented by Dr. Bircher Benner as a healthful, complete breakfast. This mixture may be made daily or stored for two to three days, allowing the oats to soak in the milk and become thicker and more flavorful.

birch sugar See *xylitol*.

Bireweck ('bee-a-re-veck) An Alsatian sweet of ball-shaped fruit dough flavored with Kirsch and fresh and candied fruits.

birmuelo (beer-'mway-low) A deep-fried cake of matzo meal, shaped like a doughnut and made during Passover. The may also be made with potatoes for a savory dish or with honey for a sweet confection. Of Sephardic origin.

Birne ('beer-ner) The German word for *pear*.

birthday cake A celebration cake given to someone to mark the anniversary of his or her birth. It is usually made of a sponge or shortening-based cake and iced with buttercream. It may vary in shape, flavor, style, and size. Traditionally, lit candles are placed on top of the cake and the person is supposed to make a wish before blowing them out.

Bischofsbrot ('bee-showfs-braut) An Austrian cake containing dried fruit and chocolate pieces.

biscotin A small, thin, crisp biscuit usually served with ice cream or other frozen desserts. It may also be served as a petit four with coffee and tea.

biscotte The French word for *rusk*.

biscotti (biss-'coe-tee) A dry, crunchy Italian cookie whose name means "twice baked." It is baked first as a loaf and then the loaf is cut into slices and baked again. It may be flavored with a variety of nuts, spices, or dried fruits and is traditionally dipped in espresso or dessert wine.

biscuit ('biss-kwee/'biss-kiht) 1. A French term that refers to various types of sponge cake. 2. A round, flakey quickbread made without sugar and with baking powder. 3. A thin British cookie or cracker.

biscuit à la cuiller A finger-shaped biscuit made from a sponge batter and piped out with a pastry bag, then baked. The finger biscuit was created when Charles Maurice de Talleyrand suggested to Antoine Carême that biscuits should be shaped differently so that they were easier to dip into a glass of Madeira. Carême formed the biscuit batter by pouring it through a funnel to create the now classic shape. See also *ladyfinger*.

biscuit base 1. A cake base made from short dough that is baked into a disk; used underneath cakes to make cutting and serving easier. 2. A mixture of cookie or graham cracker crumbs and melted butter, used as a base for cheesecakes or mousses.

biscuit cutter A round, square, oval, alphabet letter, or other shaped metal cutter used to obtain pastry shapes. Made from thin metal and with a sharp edge for accurate cuts; nesting sets of cutters are sold in several diameters.

biscuit de savoie ('biss-kwee duh-sa-'vwah) A very light French sponge cake. First made in the 14th century for Amadeus of Savoy; can be made into a single cake or into individual biscuits that are usually served with *afternoon tea*. The sponge is also used in the production of cakes, petit fours, and gâteaux. Also known as *savoy sponge*.

biscuit glacé ('bisskwee glah-'say) A molded frozen dessert consisting of egg yolks and sugar (prepared like a *gênoise*) whipped cream, and sometimes *Italian meringue*. It may be flavored with liqueurs, chocolate, or other flavorings and is usually served with an egg custard. It is also known as biscuit Tortoni, after its Italian inventor.

biscuit method See *mixing methods*.

biscuit press A cylinder-shaped extruder used to form biscuits and cookies. The dough is loaded into a metal chamber that is fitted at one end with a plunger-type press and the other end is fitted with a metal dye of varying shapes or images. The dough is forced through the dye to "extrude" the shape of the biscuit or cookie on the baking sheet.

bishop's bread An American quickbread from the 19th century. This sweet loaf is studded with dried fruit and traditionally served to visiting clergy.

Bismarck An elongated jelly-filled doughnut that is either baked or fried and is coated with either sugar or frosting. Also known as a *long john* or *Berliner doughnut*.

B
b

bistro ('bees-troh) 1. The French word for pub. 2. A small informal restaurant serving local fare, or classic French fare, that often has outdoor seating.

bitter melon See *muskmelon.*

bitter orange See *orange.*

Bitters A bitter flavored liquid made with herbs, spices, bark, roots, plants, and other aromatics that have been infused, distilled, and blended with a liquor, usually rum. Used most commonly in the mixing of particular alcoholic beverages, they may also be utilized as an *aperitif* and a *digestif* and in the preparation of some foods. They can be purchased in a variety of flavors including orange, and peach.

bittersweet chocolate Chocolate that is processed with only a small amount of sugar to produce a sharp-sweet flavor that is desirable in many pastries. See *chocolate, dark.*

bizcochito (bizz-coe-'hee-toe) A Mexican cookie flavored with anise and sprinkled with cinnamon and sugar.

bizcocho boracho (bizz-'coe-cho buh-'rotch-o) A small Spanish cake similar to a cupcake but flavored with cinnamon and soaked in wine. It is sometimes referred to as a tipsy cake because it may make the person tipsy.

biznaga (bizz-'nah-gah) A candied cactus pod, used as both a sweet and a savory ingredient in Mexican cooking.

blaanda bread (blahn-dah) A flat bread made with whole meal and oatmeal, and baked over an open fire on a griddle or rock. It first appeared in England around 1500 b.c., and is similar to *barmbrack,* with a distinct heavy, dense texture.

blackberry See *berry.*

black bottom pie A custard pie that is a layer of rich dark chocolate custard in a short crust or graham-cracker crust, topped with a layer of rum-flavored custard. The pie is finished with whipped cream and garnished with chocolate shavings.

black bread A dense, chewy European peasant bread made with dark rye flour, cocoa, molasses, and coffee. It gets its name from the very dark color created by these ingredients and may be slightly sweet.

black bun A Scottish mince pie with a pastry crust and filled with spiced nuts and candied and dried fruits. This traditional dessert is served on New Year's day and is known as *hogmanay* in Scotland.

black cow 1. A slang term for a root beer float. 2. A slang term for chocolate milk.

black currant See *currant.*

Black Forest torte A traditional cake from the Black Forest of Germany. It consists of Kirsch-soaked cherries and sweetened whipped cream, between layers of rich chocolate sponge. It is covered in whipped cream and garnished with shaved chocolate and cherries. Known in Germany as *Schwarzwälder Kirschtorte.*

black Hass See *avocado.*

black jack A bitter, burnt-sugar mixture used as a coloring agent in gingerbread, fruit cakes, pastillage pieces, and other items where a dark color is desired. It is made by cooking sugar past the caramel stage until a distinct black color is achieved, and then adding water to make a thick black syrup.

black onion seeds See *nigella.*

black pepper(corn) See *peppercorn.*

black Spanish fig See *fig.*

Black Tartarian cherry See *cherry.*

black tea See *tea.*

black treacle See *treacle.*

black walnut See *walnut.*

blackstrap molasses See *molasses.*

blade mace See *mace.*

blanc (blahn) The French word for white.

blanc de blanc (blahn duh blahn) The French term for "white of white," referring to Champagne that has been made with 100% Chardonnay grapes. It is typically light bodied, with a delicate flavor.

blanc de noir (blahn duh nwahr) The French term for "white of black," referring to a sparkling wine that is made with red grapes only. It typically has a full body and flavor.

blanch To parcook food by submerging it in boiling water for a brief period. In pastry, blanching is a way to remove the skins from peaches or nuts.

blancmange (blahng-mahnzh) A milk pudding or custard made with cornstarch, sugar, and vanilla. It is cooked on the stovetop and typically served chilled with fresh fruit or a sweetened sauce in individual dishes.

bleached flour See *flour.*

blend To combine ingredients or flavors to form a homogenous mixture.

blender An electric appliance used to chop, blend, puree, or liquefy ingredients.

blind-bake To prebake a pie or tart shell before filling it. First the dough is docked to prevent blistering and then lined with parchment paper before filling it with weights, beans, or other heat-resistant items. The weights help the dough keep its shape while baking. Halfway through the baking, the beans and paper are removed to allow the crust to brown. This technique is used for pies and tarts that have a precooked filling, such as custard, or a filling that does not require additional baking, such as Key lime pie.

blini ('blee-nee) A small yeast-raised Russian pancake traditionally made with buckwheat flour. This griddle cake is usually served with sour cream and caviar.

blister The uneven bumps that form in a dough during baking because of pockets of steam. Blistering can be prevented by docking the dough, or weighting it down before baking, so that the steam can escape.

blintz (blihnts) A crepe-like pancake filled with a sweet or savory filling. These pancakes are rolled up and sautéed to a golden brown, then traditionally served with sour cream, often in connection with a religious rite or festival in Eastern European and Jewish cultures.

Blitzen Kuchen ('blit-sen 'coo-ken) Literally, "lightning cake," referring to the quick rise of the cake because of its baking soda. It is flavored with orange and is a traditional German favorite.

Blitz puff pastry *Blitz* is the German word for lightning and refers to the quick preparation of this dough. The dough is prepared by the biscuit method and then rolled and folded like puff pastry. Although it is faster and easier to make than classic puff dough, there are not as many layers, it does not rise as high, and the texture is not as fine. It is often used for napoleons and other desserts that are layered with cream filling because it is crisp and flakey after baking.

block method See *tempering.*

blondie A bar cookie similar to a brownie, but flavored with butterscotch and vanilla rather than chocolate.

B
b

blood orange See *orange*.

bloom 1. The grayish-white coating that forms on chocolate as a result of improper tempering. It develops when the cocoa butter separates if the chocolate is overheated and the fat rises to the top. Although bloom is undesirable, it does not affect the taste and the chocolate may be retempered. Also known as *chocolate bloom*. 2. The process of softening gelatin in cool water it for use.

Bloom gellometer A professional tool used to measure the strength or firmness of set gelatin, invented by a French scientist named Bloom. The calibrated rod is marked in increments of 50 to 300 Bloom; most gelatin sets between 225 to 250 Bloom.

blown sugar Pulled sugar that is blown into thin, decorative objects with the use of an *air pump*. The technique is used to form animals, figures, and other garnishes or showpieces.

blowtorch A large propane-powered industrial torch or a small butane-powered hand-held torch, used to caramelize sugar on crème brûlée, brown meringue and marzipan, loosen chilled molded desserts, and warm mixing bowls of cold buttercream or frostings to make them smooth. Although the small, squat version is easier to handle and less likely to tip over than the tall, narrow, large cylinder version, the gas runs out more quickly and is not recommended for mass production.

blueberry See *berry*.

Blue Java See *banana*.

blush wine See *rosé wine*.

boil A moist-heat method of cooking that involves applying heat to liquid and raising the temperature to 212°F (100°C). The highly agitated water cooks food rapidly.

boiled custard 1. A mixture of eggs, milk, and sugar cooked on the stovetop. 2. An eggnog-like beverage from the American South, made from an egg custard.

boiled icing A cooked icing made by combining sugar syrup with egg whites and whipping the mixture until it is fluffy, with a glossy shine. The icing should be used immediately, as it does not keep well. See also *Swiss meringue* and *Italian meringue*.

boiled lollie See *Berlingot*.

boiled peanuts See *peanut*.

boiled sweet A candy made with a boiled-sugar mixture, flavored usually with peppermint, and poured onto a marble slab, then cut into pieces.

boil-point method See *thermometer*.

boisson ('bwah-sone) The French word for drink or beverage.

bola ('bow-lah) The Portuguese word for dough or pie.

bolzanese (bol-tahn-'eez-ee) Fat Italian sweet buns packed with fruits and nuts and covered in whole almonds. They are typically eaten for breakfast or as a snack with coffee, espresso, or tea.

bombe (bahm) A molded, dome-shaped frozen dessert with an outer crust of ice cream and filled with a flavored *pâte à bombe* mixture. Also known as *bombe glacée*. Some chefs prefer to use the term dome rather than bombe, owing to the negative connotations of the word. A dessert bombe is also sometimes referred to as a *pâte à bombe*.

bombe glacée (bohm glah-'say) Another term for *bombe*.

bon appétit The French term for "good appetite," often associated with the cookbook author Julia Child because she always closed her TV cooking programs with this phrase.

bonbon (bahn-bahn) The French word for a variety of small confections, including pralinés, fondant-centered chocolates, pastilles, and candied fruits.

boniatillo (boh-nyah-'teel-yo) A rich dessert made from the boniato root. The yam-like *boniato* is pureed, sweetened, and dusted with cinnamon.

boniato (boh-'nyah-toh) A white-fleshed tuber with reddish-brown skin, a member of the sweet potato family. The yam may reach up to 12 inches (30 cm) in length. It is used extensively in Caribbean cooking.

book fold A method of folding laminated dough. The rectangular piece of dough is smeared with butter and then the ends of the dough are folded into the center and then folded in half. Also known as *four fold*.

borage A coarse, hairy herb in the Boraginaceae family, with bright blue star-shaped edible flowers; used in salads.

border The decorative edging of a cake, made with a variety of products, such as buttercream, royal icing, or piped ganache. The size and shape of the border is determined by the tip used and by the chef's creativity. A border may be simple, as in a shell border, or elaborate, such as an overpiped border.

bordure ('bohr-durh) A border of pastry or bread, used as both a decorative accent and a dam to hold the contents inside a baking dish.

börek ('boor-ehk) A thin packet of pastry, usually *phyllo*, stuffed with a sweet or savory filling. When savory fillings are used, this pastry may be known as *bourekia*. They are popular in Turkey and other Middle Eastern countries. Also spelled *burek*.

Bosc pear See *pear*.

Boston brown bread A steamed quickbread made with rye, wheat flour, cornmeal, molasses, and sometimes raisins or other dried fruits. It is traditionally served with Boston baked beans.

Boston cream pie A traditional American cake of vanilla sponge cake split and filled with custard, and topped with a chocolate glaze. The French chef Sanzian, of the Parker House hotel, is credited with its invention in the mid-1800s; it is now the official state dessert of Massachusetts.

Botrytis cinerea (boh-'tri-this sihn-'her-ee-uh) A mold that develops on grape skins under certain environmental conditions. It dehydrates the grapes and increases the sugar concentration and flavor without minimizing its acidity. It is an important fungus in the production of sweet wines. Also known as *noble rot*.

bouchée (boo-'shay) The French term for "mouthful," referring to a small, round puff pastry filled with a sweet or savory mixture. *Bouchée à la reine* translates to "of the Queen," referring to its being inspired by King Louis XIV's wife, Marie Thérèse. See also *vol au vent*.

boulage (boo-'lahje) The French word that describes the round shape of bread dough before baking.

boulanger (boo-lohn-'jehr) The French word for baker. See *brigade*.

boulangerie (boo-lohn-jehr-ree) The French word for bakery.

boule (buhl) The French word for "ball," referring to a round loaf of bread.

boule de neige (bohl duh nezh) Literally, "ball of snow" in French, referring to either 1. A petit four of two small white meringues sandwiched together with chocolate buttercream and iced with vanilla buttercream before being rolled in grated chocolate; or 2. A large cake with layers of génoise and vanilla buttercream that, once firm, is cut to resemble a ball and then enrobed in vanilla buttercream and rolled in shredded coconut.

bounceberry An alternative name for *cranberry*.

Bourbon See *whisky*.

bourdaloue tarte A classic French tart of a short crust topped with pear halves, covered with frangipane and baked. The tart was developed in 1850 at a patisserie next to Notre-Dame de Lorette, the famous Parisian cathedral; it is traditionally served warm with a dusting of confectioners' sugar.

bourdelot (bohr-duh-loh) A baked apple encased in a square of puff pastry, with the four corners folded in to meet at the center. The apple is usually cored and filled with raisins, spices, and sugar before being wrapped. The pastry is then baked until the apple is tender and the pastry golden brown. This dessert comes from the French town of the same name in Normandy.

bourekia See *börek*.

bowl scraper A thin, flexible plastic tool used to scrape the sides of a bowl or rolling pin to remove batter or dough. Also known in the industry as a *pastry scraper*.

bowl truck See *mixer attachment*.

box grater See *grater*.

Boysenberry See *berry*.

braeberry See *bilberry*.

Braeburn apple See *apple*.

braewat (bray-what) A small, baked pastry triangle filled with a sweet or savory item. This popular Moroccan pastry is served warm.

braided loaf A bread design made by braiding two to six ropes of dough and baked. The most common braided loaf is *challah*.

bran See *wheat kernel*.

brandy A spirit distilled from grape wine or other fermented fruit, with a minimum proof of 60. It is usually aged in oak casks; the color, flavor, and aroma depend on the fruit used and the length of aging. Often served as an after dinner drink.

brandy butter A traditional English hard sauce of butter, sugar, and brandy, often served with steamed puddings and always served with Christmas pudding.

brandy snap A thin, crisp, cookie flavored with molasses, brandy, and spices. It is a derivative of the French *gaufre*, and was introduced to America by the first colonists.

brasserie ('brah-sayr-ee) A casual French restaurant that serves beer, wine, and hearty fare.

Brazil nut The seed of a large Brazilian tree, sometimes used in pastry. The seeds grow in clusters and resemble coconuts; within each seed are 20 to 30 hard, dark brown, triangular nuts with creamy white flesh that is high in fat and rich in flavor. Also known as *creamnut*, *para*, and *savory nut*.

bread A leavened and baked made from flour or meal. Bread is an ancient food staple that dates back to the Egyptians, who cooked flat cakes made of millet and barley on heated stones and who are credited with baking the first leavened bread. About 3000 B.C., they started fermenting a flour-and-water mixture by using wild yeasts present in the air. Since wheat is the only grain with sufficient gluten to make a raised or leavened loaf, wheat quickly became favored over other grains grown at the time, such as oats, millet, rice, and barley. The Egyptians also developed ovens in which several loaves of bread could be baked at the same time. Bread for the rich was made from wheat flour; bread for many others was made from barley; and bread for the poor was made from sorghum. Bread was put in the tombs of ancient Egyptians to provide nourishment for their travels to the nether world.

Many hieroglyphics depict Pharaohs surveying bountiful wheat fields or overseeing the production of bread in what would be the first bakeries. Although exact dates for the first baked bread and its use as a common staple are not known, the Bible has many references to both leavened and unleavened breads and "manna." The Greeks gained their bread knowledge from the Egyptians, and the Romans learned the art from the Greeks.

In the great Roman cities, bread was thought to be of greater importance than meat. The first bread bakers guild was formed in Rome around 168 B.C., and began the distinction of classifying the art of baking bread as a separate trade. During the Middle Ages, the bakery trade began to develop, and it was during this time that many varieties of bread emerged. In 1202, England adopted laws to regulate the price of bread and limit bakers' profits. Many bakers were prosecuted for selling loaves that did not conform to the weights required by local laws. As a result of the "bread trials" in England in 1266, bakers were ordered to mark each loaf of their bread so that if a nonconforming loaf turned up, the baker could be found. Thus, bakers' marks were among the first trademarks.

The production of bread was revolutionized with the advent of the steam engine, which mechanically ground the grain into flour and replaced the slower water mills. In addition, commercially prepared yeast was developed in the 1800s, which enabled bread to be produced for the masses. By the mid-1850s there were over 2017 bakeries in the United States, employing over 6700 workers. Bread continues to be an important food staple around the world and has many religious, cultural, and political meanings in different countries. The term *bread* encompasses a vast variety of products that are made with flour, water, salt, and yeast. The yeast may be wild or commercially produced and sometimes the bread is leavened chemically with baking powder or by steam. Milk or other liquids may be used in place of or in addition to water; and grains, seeds, nuts, and dried fruits may also be added depending on the flavor and texture of bread desired. Breads may be baked in a variety of ovens, on a griddle, steamed, or fried. There are hundreds of varieties of breads around the world, with each being distinct in flavor, shape, size, and texture. See *anadama, artisan, artos, barmbrack, Boston brown bread, brioche, challah, chapatti, ciabatta, cornbread, flatbread, focaccia, foo-foo, French bread, lavash, limpa, matzo, miche, naan, pain à l'ancienne, pain de campagne, pain d'epeautre, pain d'épice, pain de mie, panettone, panmarino, peasant bread, pueblo bread, pugliese, quickbread, roti, rye bread, sourdough bread, steamed bread, Stollen,* and *12 Steps of Baking* appendix.

bread and butter pudding An English dessert made by pouring a spiced custard base over buttered bread cubes, flavoring it with vanilla and raisins, and baking to a golden brown. It is traditionally dusted with confectioners' sugar and served warm.

bread crumbs Powdered or ground bits of fresh or dry bread, used for stuffings or for coating foods before frying. In pastry, bread crumbs are often used to soak up juices of fruits in pies and strudels.

bread dough See *lean dough* and *enriched dough.*

bread flour See *flour.*

breadfruit A large, round fruit found in the South Pacific, India, and the West Indies. It is related to the fig and has a bumpy green skin, with a cream-colored flesh.

Although picked green, it must ripen to develop its mild sweet and light yellow color. In Asia, breadfruit is treated as a vegetable, typically cooked in coconut milk to make a curry or fried in thin strips and sprinkled with salt, chili powder, or sugar syrup. The seeds may also be boiled in salted water and served as a snack.

bread machine A self-contained computer-programmed machine that prepares bread from start to finish. Most machines are geared toward the home baker and can prepare 1- to 2-pound (455 to 910 g) loaves within 3 to 4 hours. The bread machine may also be used to mix, knead, and proof yeast products that are then finished by hand.

bread pudding The American version of *bread and butter pudding* without the butter. It may also include various flavorings, nuts, or dried fruits.

breadstick A long stick of yeast bread, either very crisp or soft. They are often flavored or garnished with herbs and/or seeds.

breakfast Traditionally, the first meal of the day. Breakfast foods include breads, English muffins, fruit, muffins, danish, doughnuts, coffee cakes, croissants, or other baked goods. Other items served at breakfast include eggs prepared in a number of ways, breakfast meats, and batter cakes such as pancakes and waffles. These items are served with fruit juices and hot drinks such as coffee, tea, and hot chocolate.

breakfast bun See *danish pastry.*

breakfast tea See *English breakfast tea.*

brestois (breh-'stwah) A French cake that is a génoise sponge flavored with almonds and citrus peel, baked in a brioche mold and then split and filled with apricot jam. It is then garnished by rolling it in toasted almond pieces. The cake derives its name from the French town of Brest.

breton ('breh-tohn) Table decoration of small almond-flavored cookies iced in different flavors and stacked in either a pyramid or tower shape. Created by pastry chef Dubuse in 1850, this popular table decoration is presented with coffee.

breton crêpes Crêpes made with buckwheat flour; from northern France.

breton gâteau A dense sponge cake of French origin, traditionally decorated by brushing on a thick egg yolk glaze just after baking and scoring the top in a diagonal design with the point of a knife.

brevé ('brev-ay) Any coffee drink made with half-and-half instead of milk.

brewer's yeast See *yeast.*

bridge Australian style of cake decoration consisting of a swag of royal icing in a scallop shape piped on the side of the cake. A second piping of icing, usually positioned at the bottom of a cake layer, forms a second bridge. These then become a support structure for string work that is attached to both the top and bottom of the bridge work. Royal icing is piped through a #0 tube to the swags and is connected to the bottom bridge. This creates an extremely delicate design that stands out from the cake and somewhat resembles the suspensions on a bridge. The technique is also known as *extension work.*

brie (bree) From France, one of the world's great cheeses, characterized by a buttery, soft center and a powdery white rind; pairs well with fruit and nuts.

brigade The hierarchy system that the French use to organize the kitchen staff, instituted by Auguste Escoffier. Each position has a specific station and well-defined responsibilities. In pastry, the positions are:

> **Boulanger** The person responsible for all bread products.
>
> **Chef de pâtisserie** The executive pastry chef who is responsible for all of the products and cooks in his or her department.

Chocolatier The person responsible for all chocolate products including truffles, bonbons, and pralines.

Commis The pastry apprentice.

Confiseur The person responsible for confectionery items including fondants, sugar mixtures, syrups, decorative marzipan, and centerpieces made from chocolate, sugar, and pastillage. This position is often replaced by the chocolatier and chef de patisserie.

Glacier The person responsible for all frozen desserts including sorbets, ice creams, bombes, and parfaits; also often produces ice carvings and ice displays.

Pâtissier A pastry cook.

Sous chef Second in command, who takes over the executive pastry chef's responsibilities in his or her absence.

Tourier The person responsible for all dough production in the kitchen; may also bake the dough.

brik (breek) A triangular Tunisian pastry of *malsouqua* filled with sweet or savory items and then baked or fried. Also known as *bastila* in Morocco.

brine A solution that is used for the pickling of fruits and vegetables that consists of water and salt and may be sweetened with honey, sugar or molasses. It is also used to preserve and flavor food.

brioche ('bree-ohshh) A light, tender, classic French yeast bread enriched with eggs and butter, traditionally baked in a brioche mold with a large ball of dough on the bottom and a smaller one on top; this is classically called *brioche à tête*. Tête is the French word for "head" and suggests the top looks like a person's head. Brioche can also be molded into hexagon shapes with marked-out sections (*brioche Nanterre*) or shaped into a ring and used as a *Twelfth Night cake*. In many regions, brioche is stuffed with nuts, raisins, dried fruits, or cheeses and eaten for breakfast or afternoon tea. *Brioche mousseline* is a delicate tall and cylindrical version that has additional butter. This versatile bread has many sweet and savory uses.

brioche à tête See *brioche*.

brioche mold A round, fluted metal baking pan that flares out toward the top. This is the traditional shape for making the classic brioche.

brioche mousseline See *brioche*.

brioche Nanterre A variation of the traditional brioche, with hexagon shape made of four sections and cut on top with a scissors.

briouat (bree-o-ooh-'aht) Fried pastry triangles made of phyllo dough, filled with a sweet almond filling flavored with cinnamon and orange flower water. These popular Moroccan pastries are immersed in honey before serving.

brischtner nytlae (breesht'-nur neet-ll) A Canadian dessert of dried pears poached in spiced wine. It is often served warm as a topping for vanilla ice cream.

brittle Candy made of caramelized sugar and nuts that has been poured onto a flat surface, such as marble, to cool. Once hardened, it is broken into irregular pieces. Peanut brittle is the most common; however, other nuts may be substituted. Brittle is highly susceptible to moisture and humidity, and will become sticky and crumbly when not properly protected.

Brix hydrometer See *thermometer, sugar density refractometer.*

Brix scale A scale used to measure the sugar content in a liquid. Invented by German scientist Adolph Brix, it is based on the decimal system and the density is measured with a *hydrometer.* Commonly used to measure the sugar density in sorbet syrup and by the wine industry to measure the sugar content in grapes. See also *Baumé scale.*

broa ('bro-ah) The Spanish word for cornbread, a yeasted Portuguese bread made with olive oil and ground cornmeal.

bromate A chemical additive for bread that artificially matures white flour and increases loaf volume.

bronze stamp A specialty chocolate and sugar decorating tool from France. Sold in sets, they are quite expensive because they are molded in bronze to be different sizes of flowers, leaves, or star designs. The stamp is chilled and then quickly dipped into the melted chocolate or boiled sugar, which immediately hardens and creates a thin shell of the chocolate or sugar in the shape of the stamp's design.

Brot (braht) The German word for *bread.*

brown betty See *betty.*

brown butter See *beurre noisette.*

brownie A classic American bar cookie, of flour, eggs, sugar, butter, cocoa powder or chocolate, and a possible leavening agent such as baking soda or baking powder. Brownies are always chocolate in flavor and, depending on the proportion of ingredients, can have a cakelike or fudgelike texture. They usually have nuts, but may also have other ingredients such as chocolate chips.

brown rice See *rice.*

brown sugar See *sugar.*

Brown Turkey fig See *fig.*

broyage (broy-'ahjh) The Swiss term for a meringue-nut disk, such as *dacquoise.*

brûlé (broo-'lay) The French word for "burned." See also *crème brûlée.*

brunch A meal served between 10:00 AM and 2:00 PM, eaten in lieu of breakfast and lunch. It takes its name from a combination of both words. Menus generally offer both breakfast and lunch items. Sunday brunch is very popular at many hotels and restaurants.

brune kager ('broo-neh-'kah-gur) The Dutch term for "little cakes," referring to Danish spice cookies traditionally served during Christmas season. They are flavored with light or dark corn syrup, brown sugar, lemon zest, cloves, cardamom, cinnamon, and ginger, and are typically cut into 2-inch (5 cm) rounds and decorated with blanched almonds.

brush To apply a liquid, glaze, or coating to a dough or baked good.

brush embroidery A technique used by cake decorators and sugar artists that involves using *royal icing* to outline a design such as a flower onto the rolled fondant that covers a cake, either by freehand or tracing it. Each petal is piped separately and then the edges of the petal are brushed inward toward the center using a paintbrush lightly moistened with water. This creates an embroidered look that may be enhanced with additional piping. The technique became very popular in the 1990s.

bruttle A peanutty confection made by pulling a mixture of peanut butter, sugar, vanilla, baking soda, and salt until it resembles a soft peanut brittle. It is then cut into bite-size squares and dipped half-way in dark chocolate. The candy was created in 1951 by Sophia Gerkensymeyer of Spokane, Washington, then the recipe was passed to Carol Measel, who in 1988 began manufacturing it from her Spokane-based Bruttles Candy Company. The name is a combination of *brittle* and *butter*.

Bual See *Madeira*.

bubble sugar A decorative sugar technique made by poring a prepared sugar syrup across the top of parchment paper that has been lightly covered with spirit alcohol. As the paper is lifted, the sugar runs down the paper and reacts with the alcohol to create an array of bubbles throughout the sugar. This may also be accomplished by spreading a thin layer of *isomalt* between 2 *Silpats* and baking it until the sugar melts and forms the desired bubble appearance.

bublanina (boob-lah-'nee-nah) A Czech cake of sponge batter baked with fresh cherries or plums and sprinkled with vanilla sugar while still warm.

buccellato (booh-chuh-lah-to) A Sicilian dried fruit and spice cake shaped like a ring. It is traditionally served at Christmas, but may also be found year-round. In Tuscany, sometimes it is flavored with anise and given to children on their confirmation day.

bûche de Noël (boosh duh noh-'ehl) A traditional French Christmas cake in the shape of a log. The cake is a flavored génoise filled with rich French buttercream. It is designed to resemble a yule log and is  traditionally decorated with meringue mushrooms, and marzipan holly and berries. Also known as *yule log* and *Christmas yule log*.

buchteln ('book-teln) An Austrian sweet bun filled with jam.

buckeye A ball of creamy peanut butter dipped ¾ of the way in chocolate. It is a favorite in Ohio because it is meant to resemble the nut of the state's native buckeye tree.

buckle A deep-dish fruit dessert created in colonial America.

buckwheat The fruit of an herbaceous plant native to Russia, whose seeds are crushed to make buckwheat flour.

buckwheat flour See *flour*.

buckwheat groat Buckwheat kernels that are stripped of their inedible outer coating and crushed into smaller pieces. They are popular in Eastern Europe, where they toast them in oil to make breakfast cereals and side dishes.

Buddha's hand A subtropical finger-shaped citron fruit. It is prized for its thick, flavorful peel, which may be candied or made into *citron oil*.

budin (boo-deen) The Spanish word for *pudding*.

budino (boo-'dee-noh) The Italian word for *pudding*.

budino di riso (boo-'dee-noh dee 'rhee-soh) Italian *rice pudding*, baked in a sweet pastry crust rather than a baking dish.

buffet A meal where a central table is set with a variety of hot and cold items, including desserts, and guests are invited to serve themselves.

bugishu (boo-'gee-shoo) A Ugandan coffee made from a robusta bean of the same name.

bugne ('booh-yn) A large French fritter served with *crème anglaise* or *treacle*. It is traditionally served on Shrove Tuesday.

bülbül yuvasi (buhl-buhl yoo-vah-seu) The Turkish word for "bird's nest," referring to a pastry of phyllo dough filled with pistachios and rolled up to resemble a nest before baking. It is traditionally served in a syrup flavored with rosewater or orange flower water.

bulgar See *bulgur wheat.*

bulghur wheat See *bulgur wheat.*

bulgur wheat A wheat berry with the bran removed. It is steamed and dried before being ground into various degrees of coarseness. This Middle Eastern wheat staple may be used for the production of breads and is also spelled *bulgar* and *bulghur.*

bulkie A nickname for a Kaiser roll.

bulking agent A food additive used to add body or to thicken a particular food. It is typically used in commercial food production to "bulk up" the product and make production more economical.

bull's eye A large, round English peppermint.

bull's eye loaf A dark rye bread dough encased in a light rye dough and baked. When the bread is sliced, a "bull's eye" is formed.

bun A small round yeast roll, either sweet or savory.

bundi ('boon-dee) An Indian sweet of a chickpea batter poured through a sieve into hot fat. The resulting fritters are served with hot syrup. Bundi may also be made by preparing a thicker batter that is formed into balls and then fried. See also *besan.*

Bundt pan A tube pan with curved, fluted sides. Typically it measures 10 inches (25 cm) in diameter and 3½ inches (8.7 cm) in height, and is used to bake cakes and quickbreads.

buñuelo (boohn-'yhel-loh) A deep-fried Mexican pastry that is sprinkled with cinnamon sugar.

buon appetito (bwon ah-peh-'tee-toh) The Italian term for "Good Appetite."

buranelli (boo-rah-'nehl-le) An Italian-inspired knot-shaped deep-fried pastry, flavored with cinnamon sugar.

burek (bou-reck) See *börek.*

burfi See *barfi.*

burnt cream The British version of *crème brûlée.*

burro ('boo-roh) The Italian word for *butter.*

Burro banana See *banana.*

butter Pasteurized cream churned until it forms a solid mass. Butter is used extensively in the production of laminated doughs, cakes, pies, creams, and other products. In baked goods it provides moistness, tenderness, flakiness, volume, flavor, and mouthfeel. The two types of butter are sweet cream and cultured butter. Sweet cream has a mild flavor and is so called because it is made with cream that has not been soured. Cultured butter is made from sour cream and has a distinct sour flavor. Both types are available salted and unsalted. In the United States and Canada, the minimum amount of *butterfat* required in butter is 80%. European-style butters, such as *Plugra*, have a butterfat content of 82% or higher. A higher percentage of butterfat typically means the butter is smoother, with a creamier mouthfeel. The remaining ingredients in butter are water, usually 16%, and milk solids, which are the proteins, lactose, and minerals that contribute to the *Maillard browning* in baked goods. The water and small amount of air in butter assists in leavening. Other ingredients that may be added to butter are salt, natural butter flavor, and/or *annatto*, a natural coloring. Butter is graded in the United States based on flavor, texture, and color. The three grades are:

AA Made from the freshest cream, it has a fresh, mild butter flavor, smooth, creamy consistency, and uniform color.

A Stronger, slightly sour butter that is a good product but not as high in quality as AA grade.

B Has a distinct sour flavor.

In Canada, there is one grade for butter called Canada 1; it may be sweet or sour depending on whether it is made from sweet or sour cream.

Unsalted butter is recommended for pastries and baked goods because the amount of salt added to butter can vary from 1.5 to 2.5%. In addition, flavor can be controlled more easily with unsalted butter. It is important to properly store butter because it absorbs the odors of the products around it; it is best wrapped airtight and kept in the refrigerator or freezer. Other butter products include whipped butter, which has air incorporated into it; this increases the volume and gives it a softer, more spreadable consistency. Light or reduced-calorie butter has half the fat of regular butter owing to the addition of water, skim milk, and gelatin. It cannot be substituted for regular butter in recipes without significantly altering the texture and flavor of the product.

buttercream A type of icing or filling made from butter, sugar, eggs, and flavoring. There are several types, including:

Decorator's Another name for *buttercream.*

French or Common A rich buttercream made by whipping softened butter into a *pâte à bombe* mixture.

German A rich buttercream with a pastry cream base that is whipped with softened butter.

Italian A light, sweet buttercream made by whipping softened butter into Italian meringue.

Simple A quick version made by whipping the fat with confectioners' sugar. It is typically used to decorate with; also known as *decorator's buttercream.*

Swiss A stable buttercream made by whipping softened butter into Swiss meringue.

butterfat The saturated fat found in butter. See *butter.*

butterfly cake An English tea cake filled with cream and made to resemble a butterfly.

buttermilk Originally the milk left after butter had been churned, now made by adding *Streptococcus lactis* bacteria to nonfat or low-fat milk, which gives the milk a heavier texture and a sweet/tangy flavor.

buttermilk pie A Southern custard pie made with buttermilk, butter, eggs, sugar, and flour, with additional flavorings such as vanilla, lemon, or nutmeg.

butternut The seed of an American tree in the walnut family. The nut has a rich oily meat and is used in the production of candies and confections. The butternut tree is native to New England and is also known as a *white walnut.*

butterscotch A flavor derived by cooking brown sugar and butter; it is used in a variety of confections and bakery items. Butterscotch is also a type of hard candy.

butter tart A Canadian tart of sweet pastry dough filled with raisins and a buttery-rich cream sweetened with brown sugar and flavored with vanilla. This is Canada's national dessert.

Butterteig ('boo-ter-tike) The German word for *puff pastry.*

butyric acid (byoo-tihr-ihk) A food additive that comes from butter.

Cc

C The abbreviated form of *Celsius*.

cabinet pudding A baked or steamed English pudding with a custard base that is mixed with dried fruits and bread or cake crumbs. Thought to have originated in the 18th century. This rich dessert may be served warm or chilled.

cacao (kah-'koh) 1. The tropical tree from whose seeds (cacao beans) *chocolate* products are made. 2. Another name for *cocoa*.

cacao bean See *chocolate*.

cachaça ('cah-shah-sah) A Brazilian distilled liquor similar to rum, made from sugarcane that has been briefly fermented and then aged in wooden barrels for a minimum of one year. See also *Caipirinha*.

cachous A small scented tablet used to freshen the breath, popular in England during the 1800s.

cactus pear Another name for *prickly pear*.

cafe (ka-'fay) A small, casual restaurant.

café (ka-'fay) The French word for *coffee*.

café au lait ('kay-fay oh lay) The French term for "coffee with milk," generally with equal parts strong coffee and scalded milk.

café brûlot (ka-'fay broo-'low) A tableside preparation of coffee that has been steeped with sugar, cloves, cinnamon, and lemon zest, served in New Orleans. A thin long spiral of orange peel is placed above the coffee mixture; the waiter ignites a mixture of brandy and alcohol and pours the flaming mixture down the spiral of the orange peel. The term brûlot means "burnt brandy," "highly seasoned," or "incendiary."

café complet ('ka-fay com-'play) The name for the traditional French breakfast of coffee or café au lait, croissant, butter, and jam.

café con leche ('ka-fay kohn 'lay-chay) The Spanish name for coffee with hot milk.

café continental Hot coffee mixed with coriander, sugar, and warmed sweet red wine, traditionally served in a mug and garnished with an orange slice.

café crème ('ka-fay crehm) The French name for a small cup of coffee with cream or milk.

café en grains ('ka-fah ehn grahn) The French word for *coffee beans*.

café filtré ('ka-fay 'feel-tray) The French name for coffee that is made by pouring hot water through a filter holding ground coffee. It is traditionally served black, in demitasse cups.

café glacé ('ka-fay 'glah-say) The French word for iced coffee, made by pouring black coffee over ice cubes in a glass; usually served with cream and sugar.

café liégeois ('ka-fay lehz-whah) A Belgian dessert made with coffee ice cream topped with strong coffee and crème chantilly, and garnished with chopped toasted nuts. Originally called *café viennoise* because it originated in Vienna, but the name was changed during World War II because it sounded German.

café mocha ('ka-fay 'moh-kah) A coffee drink of espresso, chocolate syrup, steamed milk, and a thin layer of milk foam; typically served topped with whipped cream.

cafetière (kaf-tee-ay) Another name for *French press.*

café viennoise ('ka-fay veen-'nwahz) See *café liégeois.*

caffè (ka-'fay) The Italian word for *coffee.*

caffè Americano (kay-'fay ah-mer-ih-'kah-noh) The Italian term to describe a coffee drink with one or two shots of espresso, diluted with 6 ounces (180 ml) water. It was so named because it closely resembles American coffee, which is weaker than espresso.

caffè con latte (ka-'fay kohn 'lah-tay) The Italian term for coffee with milk, a combination of espresso and steamed milk topped with a thin layer of soft milk foam; commonly referred to as just *latte.*

caffè corretto (ka-'fay kohr-'eht-toh) An Italian coffee drink of a single or double espresso mixed with a small amount of brandy or liqueur.

caffeine (ka-'feen) A natural compound found in foods such as coffee, tea, and chocolate, believed to stimulate the nervous system and known for keeping some people awake.

caffè latte (ka-fay 'lah-tay) See *caffè con latte.*

caffè lungo ('ka-fay 'loon-goh) Literally, "long coffee," the Italian term for a long pour of espresso.

caffé macchiato See *macchiato.*

caffé mocha The Italian term for *café mocha.*

caffé nero ('ka-fay 'nay-roa) The Italian term for black coffee.

caffeol ('ka-fay-ohl) A fragrant oil produced from roasting coffee beans, which gives coffee its distinct flavor and aroma.

caffè ristretto ('ka-fay ree-'streht-toh) Literally, "restricted coffee," the Italian term for a strong espresso drink made by prematurely stopping the brewing and thus concentrating the flavor.

Caipirinha (ki-pee-'reenyah) A Brazilian cocktail of *cachaça*, sugar, and lime; thought of as the national cocktail.

cajasse (kah-'jhahs) A dessert of rum-flavored crêpes mixed with fruit and eaten cold. A specialty of the town of Sarlat, in the Périgord region of France.

cajeta (kah-'hay-tah) A sweet Mexican topping or sauce for ice creams and desserts. It consists of caramelized sugar and goat's milk, and is thick and creamy There are some Latin American variations made with caramel and fruit.

Cajun syrup cake See *gâteau de sirop.*

cake A general term that refers to a vast array of baked goods, ranging in texture from light and airy to rich and dense, and made in a variety of sizes and shapes. They may be single or multilayered, with almost endless flavor combinations. *Pound cakes* and *angel food cake* are served as is, while others may be filled and iced with *buttercream,* fruit, *crème chantilly, ganache,* and jam.

The two major categories of cakes are high-fat and low-fat, or egg-foam cakes. High-fat cakes tend to have a richer, moister, and more tender crumb, as well as a longer shelf life because of their high fat content. The three basic methods to prepare high-fat cakes are (1) creaming, (2) one-stage method, and (3) two-stage method (see *mixing methods* for individual descriptions). Low-fat or egg-foam cakes, such as *sponge cakes* and *angel food cakes*, rely on sugar for tenderizing and air whipped into the eggs for leavening. The three basic methods used to prepare these cakes are (1) angel food method, (2) chiffon method, and (3) sponge or egg-foam method (see *mixing methods* for individual descriptions).

The main ingredients in cakes are flour, liquid, and fat. Each of these plays an important role in the final texture of the cake. In order to get the desired result, it is important to understand the purposes of each, and although some ingredients play a dual role, in general tougheners should balance tenderizers and driers should balance moisturizers. The classifications are as follows:

Tougheners (eggs and flour) provide structure.

Tenderizers (fat, sugar, and chemical leaveners) provide tenderness owing to the softening and shortening of protein fibers and gluten development.

Driers (flour, starch, cocoa powder, milk solids) absorb moisture.

Moisteners (milk, water, syrups, honey, eggs) provide moisture.

European-style cakes are referred to as *tortes* and *gâteau*. See also *What Went Wrong and Why* appendix.

cake board A thin board of corrugated cardboard placed underneath sheet cakes to provide support, stability, and ease of mobility. Typically it is natural color on the bottom and coated with a white synthetic layer on top. Boards come in full and half sheetpan sizes.

cake circle A thin circle of corrugated cardboard that is placed underneath round cakes to provide support, stability, and ease of mobility. Typically it is natural color on the bottom and coated with a white synthetic layer on the top; circles come in sizes that range from 6 to 16 inches (15 to 40 cm) in diameter.

cake comb A small, flat, triangular hand-held tool with different sizes of serrated teeth on each of the edges. It is made of stainless steel and is used to create decorative curvy or straight lines on cakes. Also known as *icing comb* and *pastry comb*.

cake flour See *flour*.

cake knife See *cake slicer*.

cake marker A round metal or plastic tool used to score the top of round cakes into equal wedges. Markers are often double-sided and have a different number of slice markers on either side. They are available as 10, 12, 14, and 16 slices.

cake pan A metal or silicone (*fleximold*) baking pan designed specifically for baking cakes. Pans may be made from aluminum, tin, coated steel, or stainless steel, although the most popular are aluminum and heavy-gauge steel because they are the best conductors of heat. Cake pans come in a variety of sizes and shapes, with the most common being a round, straight-sided pan, which can range from 1 to 4 inches (2.5 to 10 cm) deep and in diameter from 3 to 24 inches (7.5 to 60 cm). Other shapes include square, rectangular, spherical, heart, teardrop, hexagonal, and triangular. See also *angel food cake pan, Bundt pan, Kugelhopf mold,* and *springform pan.*

cake ring A stainless steel, bottomless ring used to bake and mold cakes and desserts. The ring ranges in diameter from 3 to 14 inches (7.5 cm to 35.6 cm), 1 to 4 inches (2.5 cm to 10 cm) inches high. The ring is placed on a sheet pan lined with parchment and then the batter or filling is poured into the ring.

Cake rings are also used as molds when assembling cakes or desserts that have multiple layers or fillings; it enables the cakes to be built in sections and leaves the finished products with smooth, even sides. Some rings have adjustable sides to the diameter can be changed. Also known as an *entremet ring.*

cake slicer A serrated knife used to slice cakes horizontally into thin layers. They range from 12 to 14 inches long (30 to 35 cm) and 1⅜ inches (3.4 cm) wide with a rounded tip. Also known as a *cake knife* or a *baker's knife.*

cake smoother A small, hand-held tool used to smooth out rolled fondant on cakes. It is made from plastic and looks like a thin rectangle with rounded edges, a flat bottom, and a center handle.

cake tester A long, thin metal wire with a finger handle at one end, used to test the doneness of cakes. It is inserted into the center of a baked cake; if the tester does not display any batter residue when removed from the cake, the cake is completely baked.

cala ('kah-lah) The African word for rice, referring to a deep-fried pastry made with rice, sugar, yeast, and spices. The pastries resemble small, round doughnuts without the hole and are traditionally dusted with confectioners' sugar and served warm.

calcium phosphate A food additive used to increase the leavening power of baking powder in doughs or batters that contain a large amount of acidic ingredients, such as buttermilk.

calibrate See *thermometer.*

Calimyrna fig See *fig.*

calisson (kahl-ee-'sohn) A centuries-old diamond-shaped confection from Aix-en-Provence, in the South of France. The candies have a soft, smooth mixture of 40% almond paste and 60% candied fruit flavored with orange flower water, and are coated with royal icing. They should be stored in an airtight container because they dry out quickly. In the 17th century, they were given to the congregation during religious ceremonies in memory of the plague of 1630, but have since become a traditional Easter treat.

calorie ('kal-uh-ree) A unit measure of the energy value of foods, measured by determining the amount of heat needed to raise the temperature of 1 gram of water by 1°C. The four sources of calories are carbohydrates, proteins, fats, and alcohol. Each has a different ratio of calories per gram, as follows: alcohol, 7 calories per gram; carbohydrates and proteins, 4 calories per gram; and fat, 9 calories per gram.

Calvados ('kal-vah-dohs) A high-quality dry apple brandy that is twice distilled from cider. It is made in the town of Calvados, in Normandy, France, and is aged in small oak casks for a minimum of 1 year. It is categorized as follows:

> **Trois étoiles or Trois pommes** Aged for two years.
>
> **Vieux or Réserve** Aged for three years.
>
> **V.O. (Very Old) or Vieille Réserve** Aged for four years.
>
> **V.S.O.P.** Aged for five years.
>
> **Extra or Napoléon or Hors d'Age** Aged for six or more years.

Calvados is used to flavor desserts, pastries, and confections and it pairs exceptionally well with apples.

cambric tea ('kaym-brihk) An American drink of milk, hot water, and sugar. It is named after a fabric called cambric because it is similarly white and thin. The tea was popular in the late 19th century.

Camembert ('kam-uhm-behr) A soft cow's milk cheese with a powdery white rind and smooth, creamy interior. It pairs well with fruit and nuts.

C
c

camomile ('kam-uh-meel) An aromatic flower that is dried and steeped in hot water to make a mild tea.

Campari (kahm-'pah-ree) A bright red, bitter Italian aperitif that is most commonly served mixed with soda water.

Canadian butter tart A tart of buttery pastry filled with a sweet custard flavored with raisins and walnuts.

Canadian whisky See *whisky*.

canapé ('kan-uh-pay) A small, hand-held item that consists of a base of toasted or untoasted bread or a cracker or pastry shell that is topped with a spread of butter or soft cheese and garnished with a savory item. They may be hot or cold and are typically served with cocktails.

canary melon See *muskmelon*.

candied flowers See *crystallized flowers*.

candied fruit See *glacé fruit*.

candlenut A hard-shelled nut that is chopped and eaten as a snack or ground into a smooth paste and used as a seasoning, particularly in Indonesian cooking. They are approximately 2 inches (5 cm) in diameter. They are toxic when raw and must be roasted whole, then cracked open; the kernels are then cooked again to make them edible. Afterwards, they are chopped and eaten as a snack or ground into a smooth paste and used as a seasoning. The name is derived from their use in Indonesia and Malaysia to make candles. The high fat content makes them highly susceptible to rancidity and so they should be stored in a cool, dry place.

candy 1. A general term for small sweets or confections, such as gumdrops, candy bars, and licorice. 2. To cook fruit or other item in a sugar syrup until crystallized or candied.

candy apple An apple, usually granny smith, that has been dipped in a hard, red sugar coating and placed on a wooden stick for eating. The contrast of sweet coating and tart apple makes an interesting flavor profile. Candy apples are sometimes also flavored with cinnamon.

candy bar A general term for a block, rectangle, or elongated piece of chocolate. Many times the bar will contain other ingredients, such as marshmallow, nougat, caramel, nuts, raisins, or other fruit. They come in variety of sizes that range from bite size to giant, and are one of the most popular snacks in the world.

candy coffee bean 1. A candy shaped like a coffee bean and tasting like coffee. 2. A chocolate-dipped espresso bean. Both are used to decorate cakes, pastries, and confections.

candy floss The British term for *cotton candy*.

candy thermometer See *thermometer*.

canella (kahn-'nehl-lah) The Italian word for *cinnamon*.

canelle knife A small, hand-held tool that is a V-shaped piece of metal attached to a handle, used to make a decorative fluting on the sides of sliced fruits and vegetables. Also known as a *channel knife*.

cane syrup A very sweet, thick syrup made from sugarcane and used in Caribbean and Creole cuisine.

canna A tropical plant with a thick underground stem that is dried and ground to be used as a starch. In Australia, it is known as *Queensland arrowroot*.

canneler (kahn-neh-'lar) To make small, V-shaped grooves over the surface of fruits or vegetables, using a *canelle* knife; when the fruit or vegetable is sliced, it has a decorative, fluted border.

cannelle (kah-'nehl) The French word for *cinnamon*.

cannelon (kahn-'nehl-ah) A French pastry of thin strips of puff pastry wrapped around a long, narrow cylindrical mold and baked to a golden brown. The hollow center is then filled with *crème chantilly* or *mousse* and dusted with confectioners' sugar.

cannoli (kah-'noh-lee) A Sicilian Italian pastry of a thin, oval piece of dough wrapped around a *cannoli form* and deep-fried, then filled with a sweet mixture of whipped ricotta cheese, rum, candied citron, and chocolate chips. Traditionally, the ends are dipped in dark chocolate and rolled in toasted chopped pistachios.

cannoli form A tinned steel or aluminum specifically designed for making cannolis. They come in a variety of sizes ranging in diameter from ½ to 1 inch (1.2 to 2.5 cm) and from 4 to 6 inches (8 to12.5 cm) long.

canola oil (kah-'noh-lah) A flavorless oil extracted from the seeds of the rape plant. It is a popular oil because, among all other oils, it is the lowest in saturated fat and, with the exception of olive oil, it has the most cholesterol-balancing *monounsaturated fat* and highest proportion of Omega-3 fatty acids, which are believed to lower cholesterol and triglycerides. Its high *smoke point* also makes it ideal for frying. Known as *lear oil* in Canada, and also known as *rapeseed oil.*

cantaloupe See *muskmelon.*

cape gooseberry See *berry.*

cappuccino (kah-puh-'chee-noh) An Italian coffee drink that consists of ⅓ espresso, ⅓ steamed milk, and ⅓ milk foam. It is often served with a light dusting of cinnamon.

Cara Cara orange *See orange.*

carafe (kuh-'raf) A decorative glass container used to serve beverages at the table. It typically holds 16 to 32 ounces (½ L to 1 L) and has a narrow neck that is topped with a stopper, which controls the flow of the liquid. House wines are typically offered as half carafe (16 ounces/.5 L) or full carafe (32 ounces/1 L).

carambola (kah-rohm-'boh-lah) A tropical fruit native to Malaysia that is easily distinguished by its five prominent ridges that run the length of the fruit. It has a thin, glossy, golden-yellow skin and juicy, golden-yellow flesh that ranges in flavor from sweet to tart depending on the variety. It ranges in size from 3 to 5 inches (7.5 to 12.5 cm) long. When sliced crosswise, it resembles a 5-pointed star, and so it makes an interesting garnish for pastries and desserts, and also an interesting addition to fruit salads. Grown in Florida, Hawaii, the Caribbean, and Central and South America, it is available from early fall to winter. Also known as *star fruit.*

caramel ('kahr-ah-mel) 1. A stage of cooked sugar that ranges in color from golden brown (320°F/160°C) to deep brown (350°F/175°C) as the temperature increases. Caramel can be made using the wet or dry method. The wet method mixes water with the sugar and sometimes an acid such as lemon juice or cream of tartar to prevent crystallization; the sides of the pan should also be brushed with water to prevent *crystallization.* The dry method uses no water and cooks the sugar directly in the pan (this saves time because there is no water to boil off, but is easier to burn); as the liquid caramel cools it takes on a hard, glass-like consistency and cracks easily. Caramel is used extensively in the pastry shop for coating pastries, making brittles and pralines, as a flavoring for creams and confections, and as a base for caramel sauce. It is also used to make decorative sugar pieces such as *spun sugar* and *caramel cages.* 2. A soft or hard caramel-flavored confection; the texture of the caramel is determined by how long the sugar is cooked.

caramel apple An apple dipped in a semi-firm caramel coating, then often rolled in chopped, roasted peanuts and placed on a wooden stick for portable eating.

C
c

The contrast of the sweet caramel and tart apple makes an interesting flavor profile.

caramel bar Another name for a *caramel ruler.*

caramel cage An impressive sugar garnish made by drizzling thin strands of semi-cooled caramel over the back of a lightly oiled ladle or bowl in a criss-cross motion. Once cooled, it is gently removed and can be placed over a dessert for a stunning presentation. The thinness of the cage and its susceptibility to moisture will cause it to break down somewhat quickly; this may be slowed by making the cage from *isomalt* and storing it in an airtight container with a *dessicant.*

caramel corn A snack of popcorn coated in a caramel mixture of butter, brown sugar, and corn syrup. The coated popcorn may be gathered while the caramel is still warm and made into larger balls or eaten as small, individual pieces. See also *Crackerjacks.*

caramelization The process that sugars undergo when heated to high temperatures. In short, a series of chemical reactions occur that break down the sugars and create flavors and colors in caramel and in baked goods. In bread making, caramelization contributes to the browning of the crust and occurs at surface temperatures between 300° and 400°F (149°/400°C). See also *Maillard reaction.*

caramelize 1. To brown the sugar on a product such as *crème brûlée.* This may be accomplished with a *blowtorch* or *salamander* and contributes to the flavor and texture of the product. 2. To heat sugar until it liquefies and becomes a clear syrup. The color and flavor of the resulting sugar is determined by the temperature; sugar begins to caramelize at 320°F (160°C) and will begin to burn at around 365°F (185°C).

caramel ruler A stainless steel or chrome metal rectangular bar used to contain hot caramel, chocolate, fruit jellies, or fondant mixtures while they cool. They range in height from ¼ to 1 inch (6 mm to 3.7 cm) and 20 to 30 inches (50 to 75 cm) in length. The bars are generally oiled and placed on an oiled marble surface in a square or rectangle so that the caramel or other liquid mixture may be poured into the dammed area without seepage. Once the liquid has  hardened, the rulers are removed and the resulting square or rectangle is sliced as needed. Also known as *caramel bar, chocolate bar,* and *chocolate ruler.*

caramel sauce A sweet dessert sauce that consists of a sugar syrup that is cooked to a caramel color (320°F/160°C) and thinned with water, milk, or cream. Its flavor, richness, body, and color varies depending on whether cream, milk, or water is added. It may be served warm or at room temperature and pairs particularly well with apple and chocolate desserts.

caraque (kah-rahk) The French word for long, fine curls of chocolate. The 3- to 4-inch (8 to 10 cm) curls are made by gently scraping tempered chocolate just before it sets.

caraway ('kahr-uh-way) The tiny, grayish-black seeds of an herb that is a member of the parsley family. The seeds have a strong, aniselike flavor and are used extensively in German, Austrian, and Hungarian cuisine. They are particularly popular as a topping and ingredient in breads such as rye bread and also as a flavoring for cakes, cheeses, and a liqueur called *Kümmel.*

carbonate of ammonia See *ammonium bicarbonate.*

carbon dioxide A gas that is used as a leavening agent, formed from either fermentation or the use of chemical leaveners such as baking powder or baking soda. It plays a crucial role in making baked goods.

carbonation The process that results from combining a liquid and carbon dioxide in order to create a sparkling or effervescent effect.

cardamom ('cahr-duh-muhm) The aromatic seed of a plant in the ginger family. It is native to India, but is also cultivated in other tropical areas in Asia, South America, and the South Pacific Islands. The tiny seeds are clustered in a small pod the size of a large blueberry; there are approximately 20 seeds in each pod. Cardamom has a pungent aroma and a sweet-spicy flavor. It can be purchased either in the pod or ground, but the ground form begins quickly to lose the essential oils, which reduces the flavor. The seeds are removed from the pod and ground, or the entire pod may be ground. Cardamom is used extensively in Scandinavian and Indian cuisine to flavor breads, cakes, and confections.

carmine A food coloring derived from the dried bodies of female cochineal insects. It is used to give a deep red hue to jams, jellies, sauces, and candies.

carob ('kahr-uhb) The sweet, edible pulp in the long, leathery pods of the carob tree, an evergreen of the Mediterranean. It is used as a stabilizer in commercial foods and also as a flavoring agent in baked goods and candies. The pulp may be eaten fresh or dried, roasted, and ground to a powder. The flavor is similar to chocolate and so it is often used as a chocolate substitute in health food products because it is lower in calories, fat, and caffeine. Carob is also known as *Saint John's bread* and *locust bean* because the pods are said to resemble the locust insect, and a bible story describes how John the Baptist survived in the desert by eating locusts and honey.

Carolina rice See *rice*.

carom ('kah-raum) See *ajowan*.

carotene ('kahr-uh-teen) A yellow to orange fat-soluble pigment found in many fruits and vegetables, such as carrots. Also known as carotenoid. See also *beta carotene*.

carotenoid See *carotene*.

carrot A root vegetable that is a member of the parsley family. Owing to its high sugar content, carrots were used in the Middle Ages to sweeten cakes and desserts; and as early as the 1700s, Britain was using it as a sweetener for puddings. Today, carrot cake is one of the most popular American desserts. See *carrot cake*.

carrot cake An American cake made with flour, sugar, butter, grated raw carrots, walnuts, raisins, and cinnamon. It is traditionally iced with *cream cheese frosting*.

casaba melon See *muskmelon*.

Casatiello (ka-'sah-tee'ehl-loh) A spicy Italian cheese bread flavored with freshly ground pepper and chunks of salami. It was originally made for Easter in the countryside around Naples, but is now eaten year-round. Traditionally the bread is made in the shape of a doughnut, with hard-boiled eggs in the shell held in place on top by two bands of dough. Today, variations include shelled eggs on top, which sink into the dough as it is baked, and a brioche-like sweet version filled with candied fruits.

casein ('kay-see-ihn) The main protein in milk, and the basis for cheese, yogurt, sour cream, and other cultured dairy products. The casein proteins coagulate in the presence of acids or enzymes and thicken.

cashew A kidney-shaped kernel of the fruit of the tropical cashew tree. The kernel, which grows out from the bottom of the *cashew apple,* is protected by a double shell that is filled with a toxic oily brown liquid, so the nuts must be heated before shelling to destroy the toxicity. They have a sweet, buttery flavor and pair well with fresh fruits such as mangos, peaches, and nectarines. As with all other nuts, roasting them brings out the nutty flavor. Their high fat content (50%) makes them highly perishable, so they should be stored in a cool, dry place.

cashew apple The pear-shaped fruit of the cashew tree, native to Brazil, India, and the West Indies. It has a yellow-orange skin and a crisp, sweet, juicy peach-like flavor. If unripe it may be tart and astringent flavor. See also *cashew.*

cassadeille (cahs-sah-'dayl) A French turnover made from puff pastry and filled with a walnut mixture flavored with anise. They are traditionally served warm during the winter.

cassareep ('kas-sah-reep) A bittersweet Caribbean condiment made by boiling *cassava* juice with brown sugar and spices until it thickens to a syrup.

cassata (kah-'sah-tah) Literally, "little case" in Italian, referring to the rectangular shape of two different classic desserts. 1. A brick-shaped cake from Sicily traditionally served for Easter, Christmas, and weddings, which is a rectangular mold lined with *pan di spagna* cake brushed with rum syrup and filled with ricotta, candied fruit, and grated chocolate. After it is unmolded, it is covered in a thick layer of chocolate. Some variations are made in round or domed shapes and may be layered and/or covered in pale green marzipan. 2. A frozen dessert from Naples, consisting of either different flavors of ice cream shaped like a brick and filled with *crème chantilly* or a rectangular mold (see *cassata mold*) lined with fruit-flavored ice cream and filled with a *pâte à bombe* mixture flavored with candied fruit.

cassata mold A long, rectangular, stainless steel mold that is open on top and has a round base. It is designed specifically for making frozen *cassatas* and typically has a scraper with the same rounded shape as the base of the mold. The molds come in graduated sizes that are ½ inch (1.2 cm) apart so that each layer of ice cream can be smoothed into an even layer before the next layer is added. Once frozen, the mold is turned over and the product released. The result is a multilayered dessert with smooth, even layers and a rounded top. See also *cassata napoletana.*

cassata napolatena A frozen *cassata* made with multiple layers of ice cream, typically made in a *cassata mold.*

cassava (kah-'sah-vah) See *yuca.*

cassava flour The flour made from *tapioca.*

Casselman plum See *plum.*

casse museau (kahs mew-'zoh) The French word for "jaw breaker," referring to a very hard, dry cookie. It is made with a mixture of ground almonds and curd cheese that is rolled into a small cylinder and baked. Once cooled, it is sliced and baked again until it is dry and crisp. The name is derived from a festival tradition of people's throwing cookies at each other while trying to get them in each other's mouths. Unfortunately the ones that miss are said to "break the person's jaw."

cassia ('kah-see-uh) See *cinnamon.*

cassis (kah-'sees) The French word for black currant, referring to the European currant used to make *crème de cassis* liqueur, flavored syrup, and puree.

castagnaccio (kah-'stah-n'yah-chee-oh) A thin, round rustic Italian cake made with chestnut flour and flavored with pine nuts, fresh rosemary, and golden raisins. A specialty of Florence.

caster sugar See *sugar, castor.*

cast iron cookware Thick, heavy black cookware that is a good conductor of heat. It is not often used in the bakeshop, except sometimes to bake cornbread.

Before use, cast iron pans should be seasoned to prevent the food from sticking; a thin layer of oil is rubbed on the bottom and heated to approximately 300°F (149°C) for about 1 hour. The pans are best cleaned with a dry paper towel and should not be immersed in water if they are to remain well seasoned.

castle pudding A steamed or baked pudding that is made with a light, buttery sponge mixture that is poured into a small, cylindrical mold with a small amount of raspberry jam on the bottom. After cooking, the mold is inverted and the jam sauce runs over the pudding.

castor sugar See *sugar*.

cast sugar See *poured sugar*.

Catawba grape See *grape*.

cat's eye See *dragon's eye*.

cat's tongue A crisp, dry, sweet cookie with an elongated, slightly rounded shape that resembles a cat's tongue. The cookies may be flavored with citrus as well as chocolate or spices, and are traditionally sandwiched together with jam or a cream filling. Many times the batter is piped out using a pastry bag; however, special molds may also be used. Also known by the French name *langue-de-chat*. See also *cat's tongue mold*.

cat's tongue mold A flat, rectangular metal pan with 10 shallow indentions each approximately 3 inches (7.5 cm) long, designed for making the cat's tongue cookies but may also be used to make *éclairs* and *ladyfingers*. Also known by the French name *langue-de-chat* pan.

caudle (kaw-dl) A Scottish and English hot drink of gruel, eggs, sugar, spices, and wine or ale. An old-fashioned drink, it was believed to have restorative powers for the sick.

cava (cah-vah) A sparkling wine from Spain made in the *méthode champenoise* style (see *Champagne*). Its flavor ranges from dry to sweet.

Cavendish banana See *banana*.

Cayenne pineapple See *pineapple*.

CCE Acronym for Certified Culinary Educator, a teaching certification awarded by the *American Culinary Federation*.

cell pad A rectangular foam pad used in the production of gum paste flowers. It measures approximately 4 by 6 inches (10 by 15 cm). Cut-out flowers are placed on the pad and thinned out, shaped, or veined with *gum paste tools*. The softness of the foam helps in creating a realistic flower. The pads are generally constructed so that one side is firmer than the other, and which side is used depends on how much pressure needs to be applied to the gum paste to achieve the desired results.

Celsius (sehl-see-uhs) The metric measurement of temperature created by Swedish astronomer Anders Celsius. In Celsius, 0°C (32°F) is the freezing point and 100°C (212°F) is the boiling point. See also *Important Temperatures Every Pastry Chef and Baker Should Know* appendix.

cenci (sehn-'cee) An Italian pastry of thin strips of sweet dough that are tied into a knot and deep-fried, then dusted with confectioners' sugar. Traditionally served during carnival celebrations.

centigrade Another name for *Celsius*.

centiliter See *Liter*.

centimeter A metric measurement of length that is the equivalent of .39 inches. See also *meter*.

CEPC Acronym for Certified Executive Pastry Chef, which is the second-highest pastry certification awarded by the *American Culinary Federation*.

cereal Processed breakfast food made from cereal grains. There is an extensive variety to choose from; C. W. Post and W. H. Kellogg were among the first to mass-produce these foods.

cereal grain Any plant from the grass family that yields edible grains, such as barley, millet, rice, rye, quinoa, wheat, and sorghum. They are high in protein and carbohydrates, and are a food staple around the world. The word is derived from the name of the goddess of agriculture, Ceres.

Ceylon cinnamon See *cinnamon*.

Ceylon tea A popular black pekoe *tea* from Ceylon (Sri Lanka). It has a distinct flavor and aroma, with a hint of citrus.

cha (chah) The Japanese word for *tea*.

chafing dish A round or rectangular metal dish used to keep foods warm. A heat source is placed beneath another dish containing water, and the chafing dish is placed on top of that. The water helps keep the heat evenly distributed and prevents the food from burning.

chai (chy) An aromatic, spiced *tea* from India. It is typically made with black tea, milk, and spices such as cinnamon, cloves, ginger, nutmeg, pepper, and cardamom.

chalazae (kuh-'lay-zee) The thick, white, cord-like strands of egg white that are attached to the sides of the yolk, which keep it centered in the shell. If the chalazae are prominent, it means the egg is very fresh. They do not affect the quality of the product, but if a very smooth consistency is desired, such as in custards, they may be strained out.

challah ('hah-lah) An enriched yeasted bread with a soft, golden-brown crust and yellowish, light, tender interior. Challah is a traditional Jewish ceremonial bread that is symbolic of God's goodness and bounty, and it is served on the Sabbath, holidays, and other special occasions such as weddings. It is traditionally braided into 12 distinct sections to represent the 12 tribes of Israel. The high proportion of eggs to flour gives it its rich flavor and color; it is sometimes topped with poppy seeds.

chamanju (cha-mahn-joo) A Japanese steamed dumpling formed from a sweet paste of *adzuki beans*, sugar, and arrowroot. This mixture is cooked over low heat to form a stiff paste and then additional ingredients, such as sugar, flour, and baking soda, are added and worked into the stiff paste. Once cooled, it is rolled out into a cylinder and cut into small circles. Bean paste is placed in the centers of the circles and the dough is brought together and pinched to form dumplings, which are then steamed. They are typically served as dessert, after a Japanese meal or with afternoon tea.

Chambord ('sham-bord) A rich, natural raspberry liqueur from France, made from raspberries, blackberries, Madagascar vanilla, Moroccan citrus peel, honey, and Cognac. It is a popular flavoring in creams, sauces, and confections.

chamburo See *babáco*.

Champagne (sham-'payn) A sparkling wine which must come from the Champagne region of France in order to be labeled champagne. The high cost of this luxury item is due to the labor-intensive process it takes to create it. This process is called *méthode champenoise* and each step in the process will affect the quality and flavor profile of the finished product. The three major grapes used are Chardonnay (white); Pinot Noir (red), and Pinot Meunier. Once the grapes are harvested, usually by hand, they are pressed and traditionally fermented in seasoned wood casks but more commonly in stainless steel vats. The wine is then blended by a skilled wine master and a small amount of yeast and a *liqueur de triage*, which is a combination of sugar and wine, is added. The wine is bottled and capped, and aged in cellars for a minimum of one year. During this time the yeast eats the sugar (second fermentation) and creates alcohol and carbon dioxide, which enhance the complexity of the wine and create its distinct bubbles. The bottles are placed in wooden A-shaped frames called *pupitres* and "riddled," which requires each bottle to be turned slightly every day and the bottle to be slightly angled so that it ultimately ends up with the top of the bottle facing down. Traditionally this was done by a skilled worker called a *rémueur* who could riddle 30,000 to 40,000 bottles a day. Although about 25% of Champagne is still hand-riddled, the majority are riddled by large machines called *gyropalettes*. Slowly, as the bottles are riddled, the yeast cells move down the sides of the bottle until they collect in the neck of the bottle. The next step of the process is called *dégorgement*, which removes the collected yeast cells from the bottle, by placing the neck of the bottle in a brine solution that freezes its contents. When the bottle is turned right side up, the cap is removed and frozen yeast plugs removed. At this point the wine is bone-dry and has a small space where the yeast was. This space is filled with a combination of wine and sugar; the amount of sugar added determines the sweetness of the wine. The wine is now ready for corking and shipping. Champagnes are categorized by their levels of sweetness and are labeled as follows:

Extra brut Very, very dry with 0 to 0.6% sugar.

Brut Very dry with less than 1.5% sugar.

Extra dry Dry with 1.5% to 3% sugar.

Sec Lightly sweet with 2% to 3.5% sugar.

Demi-sec Sweet with 3.5% to 5% sugar.

Doux Very sweet with more than 5% sugar.

Unlike méthode champenoise, which must be fermented in the bottle it was made in, there are two other, less expensive methods for producing sparkling wine of the Champagne style. Both processes eliminate the time-consuming and labor-intensive process of riddling and dégorgement. The first one is called the transfer method, and although the second fermentation takes place in a bottle, after the bottles have aged they are emptied or transferred to a large tank, where they are filtered and treated with a dosage before being rebottled. The second method is called the charmat, or tank method. This process is the least labor intensive because the second fermentation takes place in a large tank and then the wine is filtered and bottled.

Champagne is an excellent accompaniment with desserts and pairs exceptionally well with strawberries, chocolate, and raspberries. See also *blanc de blanc, blanc de noir,* and *rosé.*

Champagne grape See *grape.*

chapata (cha-'pah-tah) See *zapatilla.*

champigny (shahm-'peen) A rectangular French puff pastry tart filled with apricot jam.

channel knife Another name for *canelle knife.*

chantilly cream See *crème chantilly.*

chantrenne pastry (shahn-'trehn pastry) A quick, easy, light pastry dough made via the biscuit method, consisting of flour, butter, eggs, salt, cold water, and lemon juice. The lemon adds flavor and also relaxes the gluten in the dough so as to reduce shrinkage while baking. It is used to make tarts, pies, and cookies.

chapatti (chah-'pah-tee) A soft Indian flatbread. It is traditionally baked on a *tava*, which is a cast iron plate, but a cast iron griddle or skillet can also be used. The soft dough is made from a mixture of water, *atta flour*, or whole-wheat flour and a little salt. The dough is shaped into balls and rolled into 8-inch (20 cm) rounds before being baked to a golden brown.

chapeau rolls (shah-'poe) Literally, French for "hat," referring to rolls that are topped with a thin piece of dough that resembles a hat. It is important to dust the "hat" dough with rye or rice flour so that the flour will not absorb moisture and can remain attached to the roll during baking.

charbat (sharr-bat) A thick Middle Eastern drink that is flavored with fruit juice and/or flower petals.

Chardonnay ('shar-doh-nay) A variety of white grape used to make a broad spectrum of wines, such as chardonnay and Champagne.

Charentais melon (shah-rehn-'tay melon) See *muskmelon.*

Charleston Chew A candy bar of chocolate-covered marshmallow-like nougat flavored with vanilla, chocolate, or strawberry. It was created in 1922 and named after the Charleston, a popular dance at that time.

Charleston Gray watermelon See *watermelon.*

charlotte ('shahr-lette) Originally a warm dessert made by baking a fruit-filled mixture in a mold lined with buttered bread, named in honor of Queen Charlotte, the wife of George III of England. *Apple charlotte* is the most well known of the hot charlottes; this popular 18th-century dessert inspired the famed pastry chef Antoine Câreme to create a cold charlotte named *charlotte Russe* in the

charlotte mold

19th century. It is a mold lined with ladyfingers and filled with vanilla Bavarian cream, then topped with another layer of ladyfingers; it is then chilled and inverted. (It is originally called *charlotte à la Parisienne* but was later changed to charlotte Russe ("Russian") when it was fashionable in France to serve food in the Russian style or with a Russian name. The name charlotte is believed to be derived from the old English word charlyt, which means "dish of custard filling."

Although any mold may be used to make a charlotte, they were originally baked in a *charlotte mold*, which is a pail-shaped mold with tapered sides and heart-shaped handles on either end. Other variations of cold charlottes are made in molds lined with cake, cookies, or macaroons and are filled with Bavarian cream, mousse, or other creams. The charlotte is then topped with a layer of cake, chilled, and then inverted. See also *charlotte pompadour* and *charlotte royale.*

charlotte à la Parisienne ('shar-leht ah lah pah-'ree-zhe-ehn) See *charlotte*.

charlotte mold See *charlotte*.

charlotte pompadour (shar-leht pohm-pah-'doo) An elaborate charlotte made by lining a mold with éclairs that have been filled with chocolate and coffee pastry cream. The different- flavored éclairs are alternated around the mold and filled with a coffee and/or chocolate-flavored *bavarois*. Once set, it is unmolded and decorated with alternating *cream puffs* that are flavored with either chocolate- or coffee-flavored pastry cream and glazed with coffee and chocolate *fondant*.

charlotte royale ('shar-leht roy-'ehl) A cold charlotte made by lining a domed mold with small slices of jelly roll, packed tightly, then filled with a flavored *Bavarian cream* and topped with a round of sponge cake. Once chilled and set, the mold is inverted and glazed with apricot jam. This charlotte was invented by Antoine Câreme. See also *charlotte*.

charlotte Russe ('shar-leht roose) See *charlotte*.

charmat method (shahr-'maht method) See *Champagne*.

Chartreuse (shar-'trooz) An ancient French herb liqueur originally made by the Carthusian monks in La Grande Chartreuse monastery. There are green and yellow varieties; the green version is pale yellow-green derived from chlorophyll, and has an intense aroma and minty, spicy flavor; the yellow gets its color from saffron and is lighter in body, lower in alcohol, and sweeter than the green.

chausson aux pommes ('sha-sewn oh pohm) A French apple turnover made with puff pastry.

che chuoi (cheh 'choy) A Vietnamese sweet pudding made from a cooked mixture of coconut milk, sugar, water, and sliced bananas, and thickened with tapioca, then garnished with toasted sesame seeds. It is traditionally served as an afternoon snack and/or with tea.

checkerberry Another name for *wintergreen*.

checkerboard cookie Dutch cookies named because of their resemblance to a checkerboard. They are made with two doughs, one vanilla typically flavored with cinnamon and the other chocolate. The cookie doughs are alternately stacked and shaped into a roll, then sliced and baked.

Cheddar cheese A firm cow's milk cheese. It ranges in flavor from mild to sharp. The natural color of this cheese is white, but it is often dyed orange with a natural ingredient called *annatto*. The name derives from the English town of Cheddar, where it originated. As well as an eating cheese, it is popular in America as an accompaniment to apple pie.

cheese A major food product produced all over the world, from cow, buffalo, goat, sheep, or other mammal's milk. The milk is treated with rennet or a bacterial culture that causes the milk to curdle and separate into liquids (whey) and curds, which are formed when the milk proteins coagulate. There are thousands of varieties of cheese, and the unique characteristics of each depends on the type of milk used, the length and method of aging, the region where it is made, and the individual cheesemaker's style. The main categories of cheeses are:

Blue-veined An aged cheese such as Roquefort that is distinguished by the blue or green mold that runs through the cheese.

Fresh Uncooked and unripened cheese that may or may not have the curds drained off. The cheese may be shaped into a form, as with cream cheese and baker's cheese or placed in a container to scoop as needed, as with cottage cheese and ricotta cheese.

Natural rind An aged cheese such as Stilton that is not treated with mold and forms its rind naturally. These are typically aged for a longer time than most other cheeses.

Pressed Either hard, as with Parmesan, or semi-firm, as with Cheddar, the cheese has a texture determined by whether or not the curds are heated before pressing (hard) and how long the cheese is aged.

Soft ripened A shaped cheese with a thin, white crust, such as Brie and Camembert. The surface of the cheese is treated with a mold, which causes it to ripen from the outside in.

Washed rind A ripened cheese such as Pont l'Evêque and Talleggio, that has been washed or treated with brine or an alcohol solution during the ripening process in order to create a mold on the outside of the cheese. These cheeses typically have a tan to pale-orange rind.

In baking, cheese is used as a filling and flavor agent. Cheese is also a major component of *cheesecakes* and cheese-based tarts. Cheese is also often an accompaniment to fruits and nuts, and may be served between courses or as a savory alternative to sweet desserts. See also *baker's cheese, Brie, Camembert, Cheddar, Chenna, chèvre, cottage cheese, cream cheese, Crema Dania, double cream cheese, Edelpilzkäse, faiscre grotha, farmers cheese, mascarpone, Neufchâtel, panir, Parmesan, Petit Suisse, Pont l'Evêque, Port-Salut, pot cheese, pyramide cheese, quark, ricotta, Roquefort, Stilton, Talleggio,* and *triple cream cheese.*

cheesecake A creamy cake made typically with cream cheese but other cheeses such as cottage cheese, ricotta, or mascarpone can be used. It is usually baked in a *springform pan.* The bottom crust may be crushed cookies, usually graham crackers, or finely ground nuts. The filling is a mixture of cheese, eggs, sugar, and flavorings, poured over the crust and baked until set. The cake must be thoroughly chilled before unmolding or it may not retain its shape. The texture ranges from light and airy to rich and dense, depending on the ingredients and baking method. Some cheesecakes are baked in a *water bath* while others are baked directly in the oven. A rich, dense, popular version is New York–style cheesecake, which is made with both cream cheese and sour cream. Many cheesecakes are topped with a sweetened sour cream mixture, but other toppings include confectioners' sugar, fresh or cooked fruit, and chocolate glaze. Savory cheesecakes may also be made and served as appetizers or entrées.

cheesecloth A lightweight, inexpensive white cotton cloth available in weaves that range from coarse to fine. It is used to strain liquids and as a holder for infusions. Cheesecloth retains its shape when wet and does not impart any flavor to food.

cheese straw A long, thin strip of puff pastry flavored with cheese and sometimes herbs, and baked to a golden brown. They are often twisted into a corkscrew shape before baking.

chef (shef) 1. In bread baking, a piece of ripe *sourdough starter* set aside to be used as a starter for the next batch of bread. 2. A person skilled in the culinary arts. Depending on the establishment and position in the kitchen, the person may also be responsible for employee management, cost control, and overall production.

chef de patisserie See *brigade*.

chef's knife See *French knife*.

Chelsea bun An English yeast bun filled with dried fruit and spices, glazed with jelly and served warm with butter or jam. A specialty of the town of Chelsea, they were created at the end of the 17th century. The dough is rolled as one piece, then cut into small buns and baked together in a round cake tin.

chemical leavener An ingredient that is added to a product for the purpose of leavening. See *baking powder, baking soda,* and *ammonium bicarbonate*.

chemiser To coat or line the bottom or sides of a mold. This is done either to prevent the food from sticking and allow for ease of unmolding or to be an integral part of the dessert, such as in lining a flan mold with caramel for *crème caramel*.

chenna ('chehn-nah) A fresh, unripened Indian cheese made from cow or buffalo milk. It is moist and crumbly with a soft, smooth texture, and particularly popular in Bengal and Orissa. It is used extensively in the production of desserts such as *rasgulla*.

cherimoya (chehr-uh-'moy-ah) The large tropical fruit of the annona tree, native to Ecuador and Peru but now cultivated in other temperate climates such as California and Florida. It has a leathery green skin that looks like a cross between a pineapple and an artichoke. The creamy, ivory flesh is dotted with inedible black seeds; the flesh has a custardy texture and unique pineapple-banana-mango flavor. They may be eaten fresh or used to make ice creams and sorbets. Available November to May. Also known as *custard apple*.

Chéri-Suisse (shay-hree swees) A Swiss liqueur flavored with chocolate and cherries.

cherries jubilee A flambéed cherry dessert of pitted cherries soaked in a sugar syrup, lightly thickened with arrowroot, and then flambéed with Kirsch and served over vanilla ice cream.

cherry The fruit of the cherry tree, any of several varieties cultivated in cool temperate parts of the world. These stone fruits are categorized as either sweet or sour, and the main varieties are as follows:

>**Bing** A popular, large sweet cherry with a deep red-purple to almost black skin and deep-red, juicy, sweet flesh. Available May to July.

>**Black Tartarian** Another name for Tartarian cherry, below. Available May to July.

>**Duke** A hybrid of sweet and sour cherry varieties that is primarily used for cooking and preserving. Available May to August.

>**Guinette** A small, semi-sour cherry with red skin and flesh and very long stem. They are popular for macerating in Kirsch. Available June to July.

>**Lambert** A sweet cherry that is large, round, and has a deep ruby-red color. The flesh is sweet, firm, and meaty and it is used both fresh and cooked. Available May to August.

>**Maraschino** Not a variety, but rather a sweet cherry typically made from Royal Ann (see next page) cherries. They are pitted and macerated in sugar syrup or, less often due to expense, maraschino liqueur. They are dyed red or green and are used as a garnish for desserts and cocktails. They may be purchased with or without stems, and come packaged in the syrup. Available year-round.

C
c

Mazzard From the wild mazzard tree, native to Europe and Asia. It has a rich flavor and is used as a flavoring agent for liqueurs. Available May to August.

Meteor A sour cherry with a bright red skin and slightly tart flavor. Available June to July.

Montmorency A well-known sour cherry developed in France. The bright to medium-red skin encases a juicy, firm, creamy-yellow flesh that has a semi-tart flavor. Available June to July.

Morello A large sour cherry that is primarily used in processed foods. The blackish-red skin encases a juicy flesh that is slightly tart; its deep red juice is used in liqueurs and brandies. Available canned in syrup, dried, or as preserves. Available June to July.

Napoleon Another name for Royal Ann cherry; see previous page.

Ranier A sweet, golden cherry with golden-yellow flesh blushed with red. The fruit is sweet and juicy. Available May to August.

Royal Ann A large, heart-shaped sweet cherry with golden-pink skin and flesh. It is firm and juicy, and is primarily used for commercial canning and to make maraschino cherries. Also known as Napoleon cherry. Available May to August.

Tartarian A large, heart-shaped, sweet cherry with purplish-black skin and juicy flesh. Also known as Black Tartarian. Available May to August.

cherry cordial A fondant-coated cherry encased in dark chocolate. Over time, the sugar in the fondant breaks down from the moisture in the cherry and creates a sweet liquid center around the cherry.

Cherry Heering See *Peter Heering*.

cherry liqueur See *Chambord, Framboise*, and *maraschino*.

cherry pitter A small hand-held tool used to remove the pits of cherries. It resembles a large pair of pliers, with a plunger on one end and a small cup, which holds the cherry, on the other. When the handles are squeezed together, the plunger pushes into the cherry and forces out the pit. There is also a version in which the cherries sit in a funnel container above the plunger mechanism, and when the plunger is raised, a cherry slides into position and the plunger pushes out the pit into a bottom container and the pitted cherry into another container.

cherry plum See *mirabelle plum*.

chess pie A specialty pie of the American South, with a single bottom crust filled with a rich, satiny mixture of sugar, butter, eggs, and a little flour. There are many variations, which include being flavored with lemon and replacing granulated sugar with brown sugar.

chestnut The sweet nut of the chestnut tree, native to Europe and America. The small golden nuts are surrounded by a bitter, reddish-brown papery skin and a hard, smooth dark brown shell. They may be purchased roasted, candied, preserved, canned in brine, frozen, ground into flour, or as a sweetened or unsweetened puree. They are used during the winter months in sweet and savory preparations, particularly in Europe, where they flavor creams, ice creams, and confections or serve as an ingredient or garnish for cakes. Available fresh from September to February. See also *marron glacé*.

chestnut cream A sweetened cream made from cooked chestnuts that have been pounded into a puree and mixed with *buttercream*. It is used to flavor pastries and confections.

chestnut puree A canned product made from pureed cooked chestnuts. It is used as a filling and/or flavoring in pastries, desserts and confections.

chèvre ('shehv-ruh) Literally, French for "goat," referring to goat's milk cheese that ranges in texture from moist and creamy to dry and semi-firm. The cheeses are made in a variety of shapes, including rounds, cylinders, cones, and pyramids and are sometimes coated with herbs or cracked peppercorns. It pairs well with nuts and sweet fruit.

Chiboust cream (chee-'boost) A rich custard cream lightened with meringue and set with gelatin. It was invented in 1846 by the French pâtissier Chiboust for the preparation of *gâteau Saint-Honoré*. Also known as *crème Chiboust*.

chichifrégi (shee-shee-'frayg) A small fluted fritter made from yeast dough, deep-fried and rolled in granulated sugar; a popular French street snack.

chickpea flour See *flour*.

chicory (chihk-uh-ree) A perennial herb in the endive family, whose roots can be roasted and ground, and used as a coffee substitute. Chicory may also be blended with coffee to add body and aroma. See also *chicory coffee*.

chicory coffee A Louisiana coffee drink made by infusing chicory root in coffee. It has a strong, bitter flavor and is a popular accompaniment to *beignets*.

chiffonade (schif-oh-'nahd) To finely cut slices and/or shred leafy ingredients such as mint or basil leaves.

chiffon cake (sha-'fohn) A sponge cake leavened with a whipped egg whites and baking powder and made with the chiffon method (see *mixing methods*). It is made with vegetable oil instead of solid shortening, which gives it extra moistness and a soft, delicate texture. The cake may be flavored with extracts, chocolate, cocoa powder, citrus, spices, and fruit or nuts. It was created by an insurance salesman named Henry Baker, who invented it in 1927 as a variation of *angel food cake* and sold it to the famed Brown Derby restaurant, for over two decades keeping the secret of the recipe well guarded. He sold the recipe to General Mills in 1947, who in turn printed "the first really new cake in 100 years" in the May 1948 edition of *Better Homes and Gardens*. The cake was commercially packaged with this slogan and became an immediate success.

chiffon pie See *pie*.

chile The fruit of the herbaceous *Capsicum* plant, noted for its pungency. There are over 200 varieties of chiles, with over 100 indigenous to Mexico. They vary in size, shape, color, and flavor, ranging from mild to intensely hot. Chiles are generally considered a savory item but some contemporary recipes use them in ice creams, sauces, sorbets, and creams to create a hot-sweet contrast. Also called *chili pepper*.

chili pepper See *chile*.

chimney A small opening made in a top pastry crust before the pie or other item is baked. Generally the hole is made with a small tube that allows the steam to escape during baking or to allow a filling or sauce to be poured into the pastry before serving.

china cap A perforated, stainless steel, cone-shaped strainer with a handle at the top. The holes may be small, medium, or large depending on the desired consistency of the food being strained.

China Martini ('kee-nahr mahr-'tee-nee) A bittersweet Italian liqueur with a syrupy consistency and strong herbal-quinine flavor.

chinchin (kihn-kihn) A Nigerian dessert of dough flavored with orange zest, deep-fried, and rolled in sugar and nutmeg before serving.

Chinese date See *jujube,* no. 2.

Chinese five-spice powder A combination of ground Chinese spices that features cinnamon, cloves, fennel seed, star anise, and Szechwan peppercorns.

C
c

Chinese gooseberry Another name for *kiwifruit.*

Chinese grapefruit Another name for *pomelo.*

Chinese pine nut See *pinenut.*

Chinese red date See *jujube,* no. 2.

chinois (shihn-'wah) A metal sieve shaped like a cone, used to strain custards and sauces and for making purees by forcing the soft fruit through the mesh. It has a reinforced metal band to prevent the very fine flexible metal mesh from becoming misshapen.

chinois confit (shihn-'wah kohn-'fee) The French name for a small, bitter orange that is native to China but grows wild in Sicily, used to flavor desserts, pastries, and confections. It is macerated in a strong sugar syrup, then dried and crystallized.

chiqueter (shee-keh-'tay) To flute the edge or rim of pastry dough for both decorative effect and to help it swell during baking.

chiu hwa (tchee-yo 'ha-'wah) The Chinese word for *chrysanthemum tea.*

chlorinated cake flour See *chlorine.*

chlorine A gas added during the milling process to artificially whiten flour, particularly cake flour. See *flour, bleached.*

chocart (show-'cahr) A large puff pastry turnover filled with thick apple puree and flavored with cinnamon and lemon zest. It is baked to golden brown and served warm.

chocolate The processed bean of the Theobroma *cacao* tree, native of the West Indies and South America and the source of chocolate, cocoa, and cocoa butter. The word *chocolate* is derived from the Aztec word *xocolatl,* which means "bitter water" and refers to a drink made by grinding cacao beans into a paste and adding, water, honey, and chiles. The history of chocolate dates back to 400 B.C. The Mayans established the earliest known cacao plantations, and the cacao beans were so highly prized that they were used as currency and also to make xocolatl, which they believed gave them wisdom and power. This tradition was passed on to the Aztecs, and when Christopher Columbus was introduced to this New World discovery in 1502, he was not impressed by the drink and returned to Spain with the "coins," or cacao beans, as a trinket of his exploration. In 1519, the Spanish explorer Hernandez Cortés realized the benefit of the magical elixir and established a cacao plantation in the name of Spain. He returned to his country with the beans and hid the secret recipe, which now included sugar, for almost 100 years. By 1606 Europe had become enthralled with this elite beverage and chocolate houses were opened all over Europe. In 1753, Swiss botanist Carolus Linneaus named the cacao tree *Theobroma cacao,* which means "food of the Gods." In 1828, Dutch chemist Van Houten invented a hydraulic press and alkalinizing process for the cacao bean, which made large-scale manufacture of cheap chocolate possible. In 1875, Daniel Peter of Switzerland put the first milk chocolate on the market. In 1895, Milton S. Hershey, of Pennsylvania, created the first chocolate bar. The tree thrives in hot, rainy climates and can be found today in South America, West Africa, Southeast Asia, Mexico, Venezuela, and Ecuador. The Ivory Coast and Brazil are the largest producers of cacao beans and the three main varieties are:

> **Crillo** Considered the highest-quality bean, it makes up only about 10% of world production. It is grown in Ecuador, Venezuela, and some parts of

Indonesia. It is expensive because the trees are not hardy and harvesting of the beans is labor-intensive. The trees produce soft, red pods that contain 20 to 30 white or purple beans. The bean has a mild aroma and is used for blending and the production of high-quality chocolate.

Forastero A hardy and easily cultivated tree that produces a good-quality, somewhat bitter, strong-flavored bean. It makes up about 85% of world production. It is grown mainly in West Africa and Brazil and is used for blending and making medium to fine-quality chocolate. The tree produces smooth yellow pods that contain 30 or more pale to deep purple beans.

Tintario A hybrid of the Crillo and Forastero beans, this makes up about 5% of the world's production. It is grown mainly in the Caribbean and Papua New Guinea. The bean has a higher yield and hardiness than Çrillo but is less bitter than Forastero. The tree produces hard pods that vary in color and contain 30 or more beans.

The labor-intensive production of chocolate involves many steps, and the factors involved in each affect the quality of the final product. A brief description follows:

Harvesting The beans are generally harvested at either the beginning or the end of the rainy season. The pods are removed from the trees by hand and broken open by skilled pod breakers, who can open up to 500 pods per hour. Depending on the type of cacao pod, 20 to 50 beans are harvested from a single pod; it takes approximately 400 beans to produce 1 pound (455 g) of chocolate.

Fermentation The beans are placed in heaps and fermented in the sun for 2 to 10 days. They must be turned consistently to ensure even fermentation. This stage diminishes the beans' bitterness and develops the chocolate flavor and aroma.

Drying The beans are spread out and sun-dried to enhance the chocolate aroma and evaporate the water content so they do not mold during shipping.

Shipping Once the beans are dried, they are packed and shipped to chocolate manufacturers worldwide.

The manufacturing process continues and the following steps vary among chocolatiers, depending on the quality and type of finished product desired.

Blending the beans The beans are weighed and blended according to unique recipes developed by the chocolate factory. This is an important step in influencing the final flavor of the chocolate. Like fine wine, it takes a skilled blender to produce a complex but balanced flavor.

Roasting The beans are roasted to develop the flavor and aroma. The amount of time and temperature at which they are roasted will impact their final flavor. Slow-roasted beans are generally less bitter and therefore require less sugar to balance the flavor. The higher quality the roast, the more intense flavor and aroma of the bean. This stage also serves to loosen the husk from the bean and prepare it for winnowing.

Winnowing The beans are cracked and the husks removed to expose the inner nib. The nib is the "meat" of the bean and is what is used to produce chocolate.

Grinding The nibs are heated and ground to a fine paste called *chocolate liquor*. The name is deceiving because it does not contain any liquor. This process also causes the fat or cocoa butter in the beans to separate; it is at this point that *cocoa powder* can be made by pressing the cocoa butter out of the chocolate liquor and processing it. See also *Dutch-process cocoa*.

Conching The word is derived from the Spanish word *concha*, which means "shell," because it was the shape of the first machine. This process kneads and stirs the chocolate liquor between large heavy rollers in order to produce a smooth, velvety texture by breaking down the sugar particles and blending in the *cocoa butter*. It aerates the chocolate and reduces any remaining bitter acids so that the fine chocolate flavor and aroma are enhanced. This may be done from a few hours to several days, depending on the quality of the chocolate being made. The longer the conch, the smoother and creamier the chocolate will be.

Tempering This involves heating and then cooling the chocolate in order to align the cocoa butter crystals and allow the chocolate to harden in a hard, shiny form. See *tempering*.

Molding The tempered chocolate is poured into various molds depending on the desired size and shape of the desired product. Once cool, it hardens into that form and is ready to be packaged and shipped.

The type of chocolate produced is determined by the type and proportion of ingredients added during the manufacturing process. The types include:

Baker's Pure chocolate liquor that contains between 50 and 58% cocoa butter. Depending on the brand, vanilla and/or salt may also be added. The lack of sugar renders it unpalatable for eating out of hand, but it is typically used as an ingredient in brownies, mousses, creams, and other desserts, pastries, and confections. Also known as *unsweetened chocolate*.

Dark A category of chocolate that is made with chocolate liquor, cocoa butter, sugar, *lecithin*, and vanilla. The proportion of these ingredients determines whether it is bittersweet, semisweet, or sweet. *Bittersweet chocolate* contains approximately 70% chocolate liquor and 30% sugar. *Semisweet chocolate* contains approximately 60% chocolate liquor and 40% sugar. *Sweet chocolate* contains approximately 50% chocolate liquor and 50% sugar. Varying amounts of cocoa butter are also included in those percentages.

Milk The sweetest of all the chocolates, it is made with chocolate liquor, cocoa butter, sugar, milk solids, lecithin, and vanilla. It should contain a minimum of 12% milk solids and 10% chocolate liquor.

White Although it is not considered a real chocolate because it does not contain any chocolate liquor, *white chocolate* is made with cocoa butter, sugar, milk solids, lecithin, and vanilla.

When judging the quality of chocolate the following criteria should be taken into consideration:

Appearance It should be rich in color, with a smooth, glossy surface. Cracked or dull-colored chocolate is an indication of poor quality.

Aroma It should have a strong chocolaty aroma that is pleasant to the nose.

Snap High-quality chocolate should have a crisp "snap" when it is broken.

Taste It should be well-balanced, not too bitter or sweet.

Color It should be even throughout, with no gray streaking.

Texture/mouthfeel It should taste creamy and smooth not gritty, waxy, or greasy.

Aftertaste The taste should linger pleasantly.

See also *coating chocolate, couverture*.

chocolate bar 1. Another name for *caramel ruler*. 2. Another name for *candy bar*.

C
c

chocolate bloom See *bloom,* no. 1.

chocolate chip A small drop of dark chocolate, made using vegetable fats and stabilizers to help it retain its shape while baking. Chocolate chips may not be used interchangeably with regular chocolate because of this difference in fat; the lack of cocoa butter prevents chips from being tempered and the stabilizers cause mousses, puddings, and other chocolate products to set firmer. Also called *chocolate morsel.*

chocolate chip cookie See *Toll House cookie* and *cookie, drop.*

chocolate cigarette A thin, cigarette-shaped chocolate garnish made by spreading a thin layer of tempered chocolate on a marble or other cold, hard surface and quickly scraping, in a forward motion, with a metal scraper so that the chocolate rolls up into a thin cylinder. It is very important that the chocolate be at the correct temperature and consistency or it will be too soft and will misshape the chocolate or be too hard and crack. These may be made with dark, milk, or white chocolate or, although more difficult, used in combination to create a striped pattern.

chocolate curl A decorative chocolate garnish made in a variety of ways, including scraping a knife or vegetable peeler on the surface of a block of chocolate or spreading a thin sheet of tempered chocolate on a marble or other hard surface and then scraping it up with a metal scraper. These can be made with dark, milk, or white chocolate and used to decorate the sides of cakes or as a garnish on cakes, pastries, or confections.

chocolate glaze A shiny and glossy coating for cakes, pastries, and confections. Made with melted dark, milk, or white chocolate combined with cream and/or butter, vegetable oil, or corn syrup. The mixture may be thick or thin depending on the amounts and types of ingredients used. See also *pâte à glacer.*

chocolate liqueur See *crème de cacao.*

chocolate liquor Also known as *cocoa mass,* the thick, liquidy paste made from finely ground cocoa nibs. It contains only the cocoa solids and cocoa butter that is inherent in the beans, and is the foundation from which chocolate is made. See also *chocolate.*

chocolate mold A heavy plastic mold for shaping chocolate confections and showpieces. The first type of mold is hollow, used for making three-dimensional chocolate figures; they are two pieces that can be clamped together with a small hole in the bottom for draining the excess chocolate. These come in a variety of sizes and shapes, including Easter bunnies and eggs, animals, and Santa Claus. They can also be used to mold various shapes that can be fitted together with chocolate to form interesting showpieces. The second type of mold is a flat tray with shallow indentions in a variety of designs such as stars, hexagons, pyramids, rounds, ovals, hearts, and squares. They are used to mold solid chocolates or chocolates with a soft center.

chocolate morsel A small, kiss-shaped drop of chocolate that is used primarily in chocolate chip cookies.

chocolate mousse A rich, creamy dessert that is made with eggs and white, milk, or dark chocolate that is lightened with whipped cream and/or meringue. It is also used as a filling in cakes, pastries, and confections.

chocolate ruler Another name for a *caramel ruler.*

chocolate sauce A pastry sauce used to enhance the flavor and appearance of desserts, ice creams, and pastries. There are many formulas for making the sauce, and the consistency and richness depend on the amounts and types of ingredients used. Rich, chocolatey sauces are typically made with melted chocolate, butter, and cream. Other variations use water and/or cocoa powder. Dark, milk, or white chocolate can be used, and the sauce may also be flavored with extracts or liqueurs.

chocolate syrup A topping for ice cream desserts made from cocoa powder, sugar, high fructose corn syrup, and other ingredients blended to a smooth, pourable liquid. It is also used to flavor beverages and ice cream sodas. Hershey and Bosco chocolate syrups are two of the most well-known brands.

chocolate thermometer See *thermometer*.

chocolate truffle A chocolate confection made from chocolate *ganache* and formed into small, bite-size balls that are then dipped in tempered chocolate or rolled in cocoa powder. The ganache may be flavored with liqueurs, extracts, or fruit purees. Its name derives from its resemblance to a truffle, which is a highly esteemed fungus that grows at the base of oak trees.

chocolatier See *brigade*.

chokecherry Any of several varieties of small, wild cherries native to North America. They are astringent and turn from red to almost black when ripe. They are not recommended for eating fresh, but make excellent jams and jellies.

chop To cut food into smaller pieces, either by hand or with a blender or food processor.

Chouquette (shoo-'keht) A small, round pastry made from *choux paste* and sprinkled with granulated sugar before.

choux gland (shoo-glahn) A pastry made from *choux paste* that is piped into the shape of a large acorn and baked. It is then filled with rum-flavored *crème chantilly* and glazed with green *fondant*, then topped with chocolate sprinkles on one half only.

choux paste (shoo paste) Another name for *pâte à choux*.

choux Salambô (shoo sah-lahm-'bo) A small, oval pastry made from *choux paste* and baked, then filled with a Kirsch- or rum-flavored pastry cream and glazed with a light brown caramel. The pastries are garnished with almonds and typically served as afternoon tea cakes. They were created by a Parisian pâtissier in honor of the 1890 opera *Salambô*.

chrabeli ('krah-behl-ee) A small, sweet, pear-shaped biscuit made from meringue and flour. It is formed, dried at room temperature for 8 to 10 hours, and then baked in a low oven until the outside is crisp while the inside is soft and bread-like. They are typically served as a petit four or snack with coffee or tea.

Christmas cake A traditional British holiday cake, a large, round, flat-topped fruit cake made with dried fruits, almonds, spices, and brandy, and iced with apricot jam and enrobed in marzipan. The cake is finished with a decorative piping of royal icing and garnished with candied cherries and marzipan holly leaves.

Christmas ice pudding A frozen dessert of ice cream packed with brandied fruits and flavored with chocolate or chestnut puree. It was popular in hot-climate European countries during the 19th century because the traditional hot Christmas pudding was not desirable.

Christmas melon Another name for *Santa Claus melon*. See *muskmelon*.

Christmas pudding Another name for *plum pudding*.

Christmas yule log Another name for *bûche de Noël*.

christopsomo (kris-'tohp-soh-moh) A traditional Greek Christmas bread that is decorated with a cross of nuts on top.

chrysanthemum tea (crih-san-the-muhm) A Chinese tea made from a blend of small dried chrysanthemum blossoms and black or green tea. It is sweetened with rock candy and typically served with a pastry after a meal. Also known as *chiu hwa.*

chufa ('choo-fuh) Another name for *earthnut.*

chuoi chien (choy chehn) A warm Vietnamese dessert of bananas stuffed with a sweet filling of nut paste such as pistachios or hazelnuts. They are dipped in a mixture of flour, sugar, cornstarch, and salt and are deep-fried and dusted with confectioners' sugar.

churn 1. To agitate cream quickly in order to separate the fat from the liquid and form a solid butter. 2. An old-fashioned, hand-cranked machine for churning butter; it consists of a container with wooden blades.

churro ('choor-roh) A sweet pastry from Spain and Mexico made from yeast dough and shaped into a long, thin spiral, then deep-fried and rolled in cinnamon sugar.

chutney ('chuht-nee) An East Indian condiment of fruit, vinegar, sugar, and spices. It ranges in texture from chunky to smooth and may be mild, spicy, or hot. Sweet chutneys are used as a spread for bread and also pair well with cheese.

ciabatta (chyah-'bah-tah) The Italian word for "slipper," referring to a slipper-shaped rustic bread made from a very wet dough, with large amounts of either *poolish* or *biga.* It has a golden brown, crisp and thin crust with a soft interior that has big holes.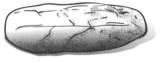

ciambella (chee-ahm-'behl-lah) Italian for "ring-shaped," refers to a rich, buttery lemon pound cake that is baked in a tube pan. Depending on the region, cornmeal and/or raisins soaked in brandy or rum may be added.

cicely (chee-'chel-ee) A fragrant herb member of the parsley family, with anise-flavored leaves and seeds.

cider A drink made from fruit juice, usually apple. If it not fermented, it is referred to as *sweet cider* and if it is fermented, it is referred to as *hard cider.* It is sometimes diluted with water and may be served warm or chilled. It is also used to make *vinegar* and *brandy.*

cider vinegar See *vinegar.*

cilantro (see-'lahn-troh) The pungent, green leaves and stems of the *coriander* plant. It is widely used in Latin American, Asian, and Caribbean cooking.

cilindrati (chee-leen-'drah-tee) The Italian word for "rolled," referring to crescent rolls made from a very thin bread dough that has been rolled out repeatedly before being rolled up.

cinnamon ('sih-nuh-mihn) A spice derived from the bark of an evergreen laurel tree that is native to Ceylon (Sri Lanka) and China. It is made by cutting off the thin shoots or young branches of the tree when the bark is easily separated from the tree. The pieces are cut into 4-inch (10 cm) sticks and fermented for several hours. The thin outer skin is then scraped off to reveal the inner bark. As the pieces dry, they tighten into hard sticks, which are known as *cinnamon sticks.* The sticks keep indefinitely in a cool, dry place. *Ground cinnamon* is made by grinding the sticks into a powder. Cinnamon is used to flavor custards, cookies, cakes, confections, and other pastry items. The two types of cinnamon are Ceylon (*Cinnamomum zeylanicum*) and cassia (*Cinnamomum cassia*). *Ceylon cinnamon* is lighter in color and mildly sweet. *Cassia cinnamon* is a dark, reddish brown and has a stronger, slightly bittersweet flavor. Cassia is the most common form of cinnamon sold in the United States.

cinnamon bun An American breakfast bun made from a yeast-risen sweet dough rolled into a rectangle and filled with cinnamon sugar and sometimes raisins, then rolled into a cylinder and sliced into individual rounds. The buns are usually drizzled with *flat icing.*

cinnamon stick See *cinnamon.*

cinnamon sugar A mixture of granulated sugar and ground cinnamon, used as a topping and flavoring for pastries.

cioccolata (chee-koh-'lah-tah) The Italian word for chocolate.

ciseler ('see-zeh-leh) The French verb "to chisel," referring to a small hole or slash cut into the top crust of breads or pastries to prevent the top from splitting open because of the rising steam within.

citral ('sih-trehl) An essential oil found on the outer layer of *lemongrass* and gives it its distinct lemony flavor and aroma.

citric acid ('sih-trihk) A water-soluble acid extracted from the juice of citrus fruits. It can also be produced from fermented glucose, and is available in both liquid and powdered form. It has a strong, tart taste, and is added to sugar syrups to prevent crystallization and also as a flavoring agent for food and beverages.

citron ('sih-trohn/'see-trawn) 1. A subtropical citrus fruit that resembles a lumpy, yellowish-green lemon. It is prized for its thick rind that has a strong lemon flavor and aroma. It is candied and typically sold in strips or chopped. The peel is also processed in brine and pressed to extract *citron oil,* which is used as a flavoring agent. 2. The French word for lemon.

citronella (sih-truh-'nehl-uh) Another name for *lemongrass.*

citron oil See *citron.*

citron vert (see-'trawn vehr) The French word for lime, literally "green lemon."

citrus fruit A large family of fruits from trees in the Citrus genus, native to Asia but now cultivated in temperate climates all over the world, particularly Central and South America, Florida, Texas, and Arizona. See *citron, clementine, grapefruit, lemon, lime, mandarin orange, pomelo, tangelo, tangerine,* and *ugli fruit.*

citrus reamer A wood or plastic hand-held tool that resembles a rigid, ribbed cone. The pointed end is pressed into a citrus fruit half and twisted to extract the juice.

citrus stripper A small, hand-held tool used to cut long, thin strips of citrus zest. The notched stainless steel edge allows the zest to be uniformly stripped.

citrus zester Another name for *zester.*

cl The abbreviation for *centiliter.* See *Liter.*

clabbered cream Unpasteurized milk that has soured and thickened naturally. An old-fashioned product of the American South typically served very cold as a beverage or topping for fruit, and sometimes sweetened or topped with black pepper and cream.

clafoutis (clah-'foo-tee) A rustic French fruit tart made by placing a layer of black cherries in a fluted tart pan or dish and covering them with a thick, pancake-like batter. The batter puffs slightly when baked and produces a golden brown crust in between the tops of the cherries. The dessert originated in the Limousin region; the name is derived from the local dialect word *clafir,* which means "to fill." Classically the cherries are unpitted because the pits add flavor, but many variations pit them and also use other fruits. The top is dusted with confectioners' sugar and it is served warm.

clarified butter ('klahr-ih-fyed) Unsalted butter that has been slowly melted to separate the milk solids from the fat and to evaporate most of the water. The solids sink to the bottom and the remaining golden liquid is the clear (clarified) butter. The top is skimmed for any residue, and the butter is strained before use. Owing to the removal of milk solids, which can burn at high temperatures and turn rancid more quickly, the butter now has a higher *smoke point* and keeps longer. The flavor, however, is less rich and buttery.

clarify ('klahr-ih-fye) To clear a cloudy liquid by removing the sediment. This is most commonly accomplished with the use of egg whites because the whites attract any particles in the food and draw them to the surface. The bits are then skimmed off and the resulting liquid is clear. See also *clarified butter.*

clear flour See *flour.*

clementine ('klehm-ihn-tine) A seedless citrus fruit that is a cross between a tangerine and a Seville orange, cultivated in North Africa and Spain. It has a thin, deep-orange skin and juicy, red-orange flesh with a tangy-sweet flavor. It is named after its inventor, Father Clément, who cross-bred the fruit in 1902. Available November to April. See also *mandarin orange.*

clingstone A stone fruit whose flesh "clings" to the pit, such as some peach varieties. See also *freestone.*

cloche (klohsh) The French word for "bell" or "dish cover," referring to a bell-shaped, unglazed, stoneware cover used in bread baking. The cover is first soaked in water and then placed over the bread prior to baking. The heat from the oven reacts with the water-soaked clay and produces steam, which coats the dough and creates a crisp crust.

clotted cream A thick, spreadable cream made by heating a rich, unpasteurized cream to approximately 180°F (82°C) until it thickens and forms a semi-solid layer of cream on top; after it is cooled, the thickened cream is removed and served. This is a specialty of Devonshire, England, and is made with a minimum fat content of 55%. It is traditionally served with jam and scones. Also known as *Devon cream* and *Devonshire cream.*

cloudberry A tart, amber colored version of a raspberry, to which it is related. They are primarily used for making jam and found wild in Scandanavia, New England, and Canada.

clove 1. The reddish-brown, dried, unopened bud of a tropical evergreen tree native to the Maluku Islands. Their tiny round tops sit on a short, thin spike; the name is derived from the Latin word *clavus*, which means "nail." They are available whole or ground and have a strong spicy flavor that is mildly sweet. They are a popular pastry spice, particularly in combination with other spices such as cinnamon, for flavoring gingerbread, cakes, cookies, pastries, and confections. 2. A single segment of a garlic bulb.

cloverleaf roll A soft roll with a top that resembles a three-leaf clover. They are typically made from enriched dough and baked in a muffin pan. The shape is achieved by placing three small balls in the pan so that when the roll rises, the top forms the cloverleaf.

club soda See *seltzer water.*

cm The abbreviation for *centimeter.*

CMB The acronym for Certified Master-Baker, which is the Retailer's Bakery Association's highest professional designation for a baker.

C
c

CMPC The acronym for Certified Master Pastry Chef, which is the highest pastry certification awarded by the American Culinary Federation.

coarse salt A term used to describe salt that has large granules.

coat In culinary terms, to cover the outside of a product, either by dipping it in a wet or dry mixture or by brushing or glazing a liquid onto it, such as in coating fruit with apricot jam. See also *nappé*.

coating chocolate A type of chocolate that replaces the cocoa butter with another fat such as vegetable oil, so that the chocolate hardens without being tempered. It is easy to use but does not retain the same crisp snap, shine, or true chocolate flavor of tempered *couverture*. It may be purchased as dark, milk, or white chocolate from specialty vendors and is used extensively to coat, dip, and decorate products. See *chocolate*.

coat the back of a spoon See *nappé*.

cobbler 1. An American baked dessert of a thick fruit mixture topped with a biscuit-like dough. It typically is served warm, with vanilla ice cream or sweetened whipped cream. 2. A punch drink of fruit juice, sugar, and brandy, rum, or wine, served over crushed ice and garnished with mint and citrus slices.

cobnut Another name for *hazelnut*.

cocada (koh-'kah-dah) A sweet Spanish coconut custard.

cocada amarela (koh-'kah-dah ah-mah-'reelyah) A yellow coconut pudding from Mozambique, made by cooking sugar, water, and cloves to a thick syrup and then adding freshly grated coconut and egg yolks. The mixture is cooked until thick and then chilled until set. It is traditionally served in small shallow bowls and sprinkled with cinnamon.

cochineal ('cosh-ee-nehl) See *carmine*.

cocktail grapefruit A sweet, juicy citrus hybrid that is a cross between a pomelo and a mandarin orange. It has an orange-yellow skin and flesh, and is available January through March.

cocoa ('koe-koe) 1. Another name for *cacao*. 2. The shortened name for a cup of *hot cocoa*. See *chocolate*.

cocoa bean Another name for *cacao bean*. See *chocolate*.

cocoa butter The natural fat present in the cacao bean. It is sold in pale-yellow bars or compressed cakes, and has been extracted from the beans during the chocolate manufacturing process. It may be used to thin melted chocolate or mixed with coloring to paint on decorations. It is very hard and brittle at room temperature because it is so high in saturated fatty acids but has a low melting point that gives it its "melt in your mouth" quality. An understanding of its unique composition is critical for properly tempering of chocolate because its different cocoa butter crystals melt at different temperatures:

> **Alpha crystals** melt between 70° and 75°F (21° to 24°C).
>
> **Beta crystals** melt at 95°F (35°C).
>
> **Beta prime crystals** melt between 81° and 84°F (26° to 29°C).
>
> **Gamma crystals** melt at 63°F (17°C).

cocoa mass Another term for *chocolate liquor*.

cocoa nib The inner portion of the *cocoa bean* that is heated and processed to make *chocolate*. Nibs may be purchased in small, dried bits and used as an ingredient in ice creams, fillings, and creams; they contain no sugar and have a strong bitter chocolate taste.

Coco Lopez See *coconut cream.*

coconut The fruit of the coconut palm tree, which grows in tropical climates around the world, including Malaysia, Hawaii, South America, and India. The hard, dark-brown hairy husk has three small indentions on the bottom that resemble eyes. Under the shell is a thin, smooth, brown skin that covers the creamy white coconut flesh and the thin, opaque coconut water. The palm tree produces approximately 20 coconuts each year, which take about a year to ripen. Since the tree has a long lifespan and bears fruit continuously through the year, coconuts are harvested year-round. The entire coconut is used in many ways, making it a very valuable commodity. The fibers around the shell are used to make ropes and fishing nets; the leaves are made into mats, baskets, and thatching material; the shell is broken in half and used as bowls; the shoots of the palm are eaten as a vegetable; the trunk is used for building materials; the nutritious flesh is used as food and to make coconut oil; and the juice is used as a beverage and to make coconut milk. See also *coconut cream, coconut milk, coconut oil,* and *desiccated coconut.*

coconut cream 1. A highly sweetened liquid made from coconut, sugar, and various thickeners, used in mixed drinks and desserts. Originally from Puerto Rico, it is primarily sold under the brand name Coco Lopez, which was named after its creator, Don Ramon Lopez-Irizarry. 2. The thick top layer of canned coconut milk. Owing to the milk's high fat content, the cream rises to the top.

coconut cream pie An American dessert of baked bottom pie crust filled with coconut-flavored pastry cream and topped with *crème chantilly* and toasted coconut.

coconut haystack An American coconut confection made by heating egg whites and sugar, and then adding dried coconut until the mixture is moist but firm. Small portions of the mixture are piled onto a baking sheet so that they resemble small haystacks, then baked and the bottoms dipped in tempered chocolate. They may be eaten as a snack or used as a petit four or item on a cookie tray.

coconut ice A rich, sweet confection of two layers of gelled coconut milk, one pink and the other white. Once set firm, they are rolled in granulated sugar and served in small pieces.

coconut macaroon A coconut-flavored macaroon. See *macaroon.*

coconut milk A milky liquid made by grating fresh coconut meat and steeping it in warm water, then straining the mixture. It is available unsweetened, in cans exported mainly from Thailand.

coconut oil The oil extracted from dried coconut after it has been sweetened and shredded. It is one of the few nonanimal saturated fats and is used widely in the commercial manufacturing of candies, cookies, and baked goods.

cocoa powder A powder made from the cocoa that remains when *cocoa butter* is extracted from *chocolate liquor.* It is dried and forms a cake that is then ground to a fine powder. It is a naturally acidic product that ranges in color from pale brown to a rich, reddish brown depending on the type of bean used and the roasting process. Cocoa does not contain any sugar or cocoa butter, so it is significantly less expensive than chocolate. It acts as a drier (it absorbs moisture) in baked goods and should always be sifted before use. The cocoa powder used to make *hot cocoa* is generally mixed with sugar and other flavorings. See also *Dutch-process cocoa.*

coconut sugar See *sugar, palm.*

coddle To simmer something just beneath the boiling point for a short period of time.

C
c

coeur à la crème ('core ah lah 'krehm)
Literally, French for "heart of cheese,"
referring to a cheese dessert made with
a mixture of cream cheese, sweetened
whipped cream, and sour cream. It is
molded in either a heart-shaped porcelain
coeur à la crème mold, which has drain
holes on the bottom, or a heart-shaped
wicker basket lined with cheesecloth.
Both molds allow the whey to drain off
and the cheese obtains a firmer texture.
Once chilled and set, it is unmolded and

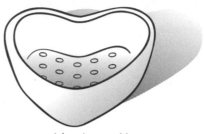

coeur à la crème mold

served with fresh berries or a berry sauce. The molds are approximately 1 inch
(2.5 cm) high and range in size from 3 to 7 inches (7.5 to 17.5 cm) in length and
diameter, which allows the dessert to be made individually or as one large dessert.

coeur à la crème mold See *coeur à la crème*.

coffee A beverage made from the seeds of the tropical coffee plant. The fruits of
the tree are called the *coffee cherry* and beans are actually the seeds of this fruit.
Although there are hundreds of different coffee species, the two most commercially produced are:

> **Arabica** A coffee plant that grows at higher altitudes. It is indigenous
> to Ethiopia and is named for the Arabs, who were the first to cultivate it
> commercially. It produces a coffee that has a more full-bodied, complex
> flavor than Robusta and accounts for 70% of the world's coffee.

> **Robusta** A coffee plant that grows at lower altitudes. It produces a less
> rich coffee than Arabica but is popular for commercial production because
> the beans are less expensive to harvest and the trees are heartier and more
> fertile.

Coffee plantations can be found in tropical climates all over the world, including
Hawaii, Indonesia, Africa, and Cuba, but Brazil and Colombia are the two largest
coffee producers today. The labor-intensive process begins with hand-harvesting
the multilayered coffee cherry. It has an outer skin that encases the white pulp of
the fruit, which holds the seeds or beans. Each bean is surrounded by a
parchment-like skin, and the fruit goes through a series of processes designed to
remove one of the layers. The beans are then cleaned, dried, and hand-inspected
for color and quality. At this stage the beans are referred to as green, and are
exported. The color, flavor, body, and quality of the coffee are determined not
only by the beans but also by how the coffee manufacturer roasts and blends the
beans. The stronger the roast, the more color, flavor, and body the coffee will
have. The most common roasts are:

> **American** The beans are medium-roasted and produce a coffee with mod-
> erate color and flavor.

> **European** A blend of ⅔ heavy-roasted beans and ⅓ medium-roasted
> beans.

> **French** The beans are heavy-roasted, which gives the coffee a strong flavor
> and dark color.

> **Italian** A very strong roast that is used to make espresso.

> **Viennese** A blend of ⅔ medium-roasted beans and ⅓ heavy-roasted beans.

Once ground, the beans begin to lose their flavor quickly, so it is recommended
to purchase them whole and grind them on an as-needed basis. The beans and/or
ground coffee may be kept in the freezer for prolonged freshness and shelf life.

There are many by-products made from coffee, with the most popular being:

Decaffeinated Coffee that has had the *caffeine* removed. This is done before the beans are roasted in one of two methods. The first chemically extracts the caffeine with the use of a solvent, which is washed out before the beans are dried. The second, which is known as the Swiss water method, steams the beans and then scrapes away the caffeinated outer layer with a high-pressure water process.

Freeze-dried A granular form of brewed coffee that has been frozen. It is added to hot water and is slightly more expensive and flavorful than instant coffee.

Instant A powdered coffee made by drying freshly brewed coffee. It is added to hot water but does not possess the same richness and flavor as freshly brewed coffee.

Coffee is an important flavoring component in pastry and confectionery making. It is used to soak *ladyfingers* in the production of *tiramisu* and as a flavoring agent in syrups, fillings, creams, and sauces (see *coffee extract*). It is also an integral component of warm and cold coffee-based beverages (see *café* and *caffè*).

coffee bean The seed of the *coffee cherry*. See *coffee*.

coffee cake A breakfast or brunch pastry served with coffee or tea. There are many possibilities, made with a yeast-risen dough or leavened with baking powder and/or baking soda. It typically contains fruit and/or nuts, and may or may not be iced or topped with *streusel*.

coffee cherry See *coffee*.

coffee cream See *cream*.

coffee extract A concentrated coffee product used to flavor creams, sauces, confections, and other pastry products. It is sold in liquid form by specialty baking-supply vendors.

coffee paste A concentrated coffee product used to flavor creams, sauces, confections, and other pastry products. It is sold in paste form by specialty baking supply vendors.

coffee plunger Another name for *French press*.

coffin The colonial American term for a pie crust. See *pie*.

coffyn The Old English term for a pie crust. See *pie*.

Cognac (kon-yak) A fine French brandy distilled from white grapes grown in the town of Cognac, France. The famous brandy should be complex, balanced, and smooth, with long-lasting aromas and flavors that have a hint of citrus, honey, vanilla, flowers, smoke, and earth. It is made by heating the white wine derived from the Cognac grapes and then aging the resulting liquid in oak barrels, where it obtains its unique flavor. The brandy is aged for a minimum of three years and the bottle is labeled with stars to designate the number of years it was aged: 1 star = 3 years; 2 stars = 4 years; 3 stars = 5 years. Older cognacs are labeled as follows: V.S. (very superior); V.S.O.P. (very superior old pale); V.V.S.O.P (very, very, superior old pale). The labels X.O., Extra, and Reserve indicate that it is the oldest Cognac a producer distributes. The highest-quality cognacs are labeled "Fine Champagne," which indicates that at least 60% of the grapes used in the production of the brandy came from the superior grape-growing region of Cognac called Grande Champagne. It is traditionally served in a snifter as an after-dinner drink, and is also used by pastry chefs to flavor desserts, pastries, and confections.

Cointreau ('kwahn-troh) A French orange-flavored liqueur made from the peel of sweet and sour oranges, with an intense orange flavor that is slightly bitter. It has been made by the Cointreau family since the mid 19th century, and is used to flavor desserts, pastries, and confections. Although more expensive, *Grand Marnier* is a good substitute.

cola ('koh-lah) A sweet carbonated beverage made from *cola nut* extract.

cola nut The nut of the cola tree, cultivated in South America, Africa, and the West Indies. In these countries it is eaten raw as a snack and is believed to relieve fatigue and have aphrodisiac powers. Cola nuts contain caffeine and theobromine, and are used in the manufacturing of some soft drinks, particular *cola*.

colander ('kahl-uhn-dehr) A plastic, ceramic, or metal bowl with perforated holes and used to drain the liquid from solids.

cold pressing See *olive oil.*

colette (koh-'leht) A petit four with a chocolate base, an almond cream filling, and a chocolate disc for a lid. It is chilled until firm and then dipped in chocolate.

Colheita (kohl-hee-'tah) See *Port.*

college pudding An English steamed pudding made by placing jam at the bottom of a *dariole mold* and then filling it with a pudding mixture. After it is baked, the mold is inverted and the pudding is coated with a rich jam sauce. Its name derives from its popularity with British college students.

colomba (kah-'lohm-bah) Italian for "dove," it refers to a traditional Easter cake shaped like a dove. The cake is made from a rich yeast-risen dough packed with candied fruit and flavored with spices and citrus zest. It is topped with crystallized sugar and toasted almonds.

coloring A food additive used to color food, pastries, confections, cakes, creams, and beverages. It may be natural or synthetic, and comes in many forms, including water- and oil-based liquids, pastes, and powders. Depending on the type, it may be added directly to the product, applied with a brush, or sprayed on with an airbrush. Coloring is used extensively in chocolate and sugar work for centerpieces and garnishes.

column See *pillar.*

combi oven See *oven.*

Comice pear See *pear.*

commis (koh-mee) See *brigade.*

common fennel See *fennel.*

common meringue See *meringue.*

common millet See *millet.*

common pineapple See *pineapple, gold.*

compote ('kohm-poht) A mixture of fresh or dried fruit that has been slowly cooked in sugar syrup and often flavored with liqueur, citrus zest, and/or spices. The slow cooking allows the fruit to retain its shape. It is often served with desserts, as a topping for ice cream, or as a filling for turnovers and tarts.

compound butter A flavored sweet or savory butter spread made by blending softened butter with ingredients such as maple syrup, brandy, citrus zest, spices, or chopped fruit or nuts. The sweet varieties are often served with pancakes, scones, muffins, or tea cakes.

compressed fresh yeast See *yeast.*

concentrate A food item that has had most of the water evaporated out of it, which makes the flavor more intense. In pastry, concentrated oils and extracts are used to flavor pastries, sauces, creams, and confections.

conching See *chocolate.*

concord cake A French cake of chocolate meringue layers sandwiched together with chocolate mousse, and garnished with small strips of chocolate meringue on the sides and dusted with confectioners' sugar. It was created by French pastry chef Gaston Lenôtre.

Concord grape See *grape.*

Condé (kohn-'day) The name given to a variety of desserts created in honor of the great French general Condé. They are all based on rice cooked in milk and a fruit sauce. The original cold dessert consists of apricots poached in a sugar syrup and arranged in a crown around a ring of rice that has been cooked in milk. The rice ring is coated with apricot and Kirsch sauce, and decorated with cherries and candied fruit.

condensed milk See *sweetened condensed milk.*

confection (kuhn-'fehk-shuhn) A general term used to describe a bite-size candy or sweet.

confectioners' sugar See *sugar.*

confectionery 1. A shop where confections are made. 2. A broad term to describe sweet items based on sugar, such as caramels, candy, and marzipan.

confiseur (kohn-feez-yuh) See *brigade.*

confisserie (kohn-'fihs-sihr-ree) The French name for confections or a confectionery shop.

confit (kohn-'fee) The French word for a method of preserving foods; in the pastry shop, it typically refers to partially candied citrus peels.

confiture (kohn-fee-'tyoor) The French word for *preserves* or *jam.*

Conjolais (kohn-joh-'lay) A small confection made with Italian meringue and grated coconut. It is dried in a low oven and served as a petit four or snack with coffee or tea.

congress tart A small, sweet puff pastry made by spreading the bottom of a pastry shell with jam and then filling it with *frangipane.* Thin slices of pastry dough are laid diagonally across the top of each tart, they are baked, and then brushed with apricot jam and glazed with *fondant* that has been thinned with *Kirsch.*

conserve ('kohn-surv) A thick, sweet spread made from cooked fruit, nuts, and sugar, often served with biscuits and scones.

continental breakfast A light breakfast that typically consists of coffee or tea, served with toast, *croissants,* or pastries and jam and butter.

convection oven See *oven.*

cookie A vast variety of small cakes characterized by how the dough is made and shaped for baking. The mixing methods are similar to cake mixing methods, but in general less liquid is used, so the flour develops less gluten and the batter is smoother. The three basic cookie methods include one-stage, creaming, and sponge (see *mixing methods*). Cookies are made in a wide array of flavors, textures, shapes, and sizes, as follows:

> **Bar** 1. A firm cookie dough shaped into long, flat rectangular bars. The bars are baked, cooled, and then sliced, and baked again until dry and crisp. *Biscotti* are the most well known bar cookie. 2. The term used by home

cooks to describe sheet cookies (see below) because the baked cookies are cut into bars.

Drop A soft, moist dough that is dropped onto a baking sheet with a small spoon or ice cream scoop. It is important to leave adequate space between the cookies because they have a tendency to spread during baking. Popular examples include *chocolate chip cookies, peanut butter cookies,* and *oatmeal cookies.*

Molded A semi-firm to firm dough that is either shaped by hand or in a *cookie mold.* Hand-molded cookies are formed by rolling the dough into balls that may or may not be flattened before baking. Sometimes, as with *peanut butter cookies,* additional impressions are made on the cookie with a fork or other tool to create a decorative design.

Piped A soft dough that is either piped with a piping bag or a *cookie press.* The design of the cookie is made with a decorative tip, which can produce a variety of shapes and sizes. *Spritz cookies* are a popular example.

Refrigerator or ice box A stiff dough is rolled into logs and stored in the refrigerator or freezer until firm, then sliced and baked. The benefit of this type is that the dough can be made ahead of time and the cookies sliced and baked as needed. *Checkerboard cookies* are a popular example.

Rolled A stiff dough that is rolled and cut with shaped *cookie cutters.* The dough must be chilled to harden the fat; owing to the labor involved, these are typically made during holidays or for special occasions because they are usually also hand-decorated after baking. Popular examples include *gingerbread* men and *sugar cookies.*

Sheet A thin or thick batter is poured or spread into a rectangular baking pan. Sometimes a base of short dough or cookie dough lines the bottom of the pan. After baking, the cake is cut into bars, squares, triangles, or diamonds. This category includes a wide variety of products, but *brownies* and *lemon bars* are popular examples.

Stencil A somewhat thin batter, also known as a *stencil paste,* is spread over a stencil cutout and baked. The stencils come in a variety of designs or can be hand-made using a thin piece of cardboard or plastic. The cookies are thin and crisp and many times are formed into shapes while still warm. Popular examples include *tuile* and *Hippenmasse.*

Since certain characteristics are desirable in cookies, it is important to understand what causes them and how to manipulate the ingredients to produce these specific traits:

Softness Achieved by using a high proportion of liquid and low proportion of sugar and fat; also, using *hygroscopic* ingredients such as honey and molasses to absorb moisture from the air. A low-protein flour absorbs less moisture. Large or thick cookies will likewise retain more moisture. Under-baking and adding a small amount of acid, such as sour cream or yogurt, will reduce spreading and browning. Storing the cookies in an airtight container keeps them softer.

Crispness Achieved by using a low proportion of liquid and a high proportion of fat and sugar; by using butter instead of shortening to increase spread; also, by using a high-protein flour, which absorbs more moisture. Adding baking soda will weaken the gluten strands and also increase spread. Slicing or spreading the cookie dough very thin and baking until most of the moisture is evaporated likewise produces crispness. Storing the cookies in an airtight container with a *dessicant* to absorb the moisture will keep them crisp.

Chewiness Achieved with a high proportion of liquid, eggs, and sugar and low proportion of fat. Also, using a high-protein flour will help develop gluten and cause chewiness.

Increased spread Achieved with a high proportion of liquid, granulated sugar, and baking soda. Baking soda weakens the gluten strands and neutralizes acidity, which increase spread. Using a low-protein flour to absorb less moisture and a fat with a low melting point such as butter also increases spread. When using the creaming method, beat the mixture until light and fluffy; the incorporation of air increases spread. Grease the cookie sheet and bake at a low temperature.

Decreased spread Achieved with a high-protein flour to develop gluten and absorb more moisture; using confectioners' sugar instead of granulated sugar because confectioners' contains cornstarch, which absorbs moisture and creates a stiffer, drier dough; using baking powder because it leavens without decreasing acidity, which sets the dough quicker; using a fat with a higher melting point, such as shortening. When using the creaming method, cream the fat and sugar only until combined; less air will decrease spread. Chill the dough before baking, and bake at a higher temperature on an ungreased cookie sheet.

See also *What Went Wrong and Why* appendix.

cookie cutter A sharp-edged metal or plastic cutter for cutting rolled cookie dough into various shapes and sizes. The cutters may be dipped in sugar or flour prior to cutting to prevent their sticking to the dough; they are sold individually or in sets.

cookie cutter sheet A professional pastry tool that allows cookies to be cut in one full sheet. The rolled dough is placed on a lined sheet pan and the cutting sheet is pressed into the dough by a rolling pin being rolled over the top. The sheet is removed, and once the scraps are removed, the cookies are lined up on the pan, ready for baking. The sheets are made of heavy plastic and come in a variety of shapes that can cut anywhere from 20 to 100 cookies at a time.

cookie dough The mixture that results form combining specific ingredients used in the preparation of cookies. The consistency ranges from wet to dry depending on the type of cookie being made. See also *cookie*.

cookie gun Another name for *cookie press.*

cookie mold A decorative mold used to imprint a design onto cookie dough before it is baked. The design is imprinted by pressing the cookie dough into the mold and leveling it off with a knife. The mold is then inverted to release the cookie which is now ready to be baked. The molds are available in a variety of designs, shapes, and sizes and may be made from wood, plastic, ceramic, or glass. They are popular in the production of *Springerele* cookies and *Scottish shortbread.*

cookie press A tool used to make decorative cookies, consisting of a long, hollow cylinder affixed with a plunger at the top and a decorative nozzle at the bottom. The cookie dough, which needs to be soft and pliable, is placed in the tube, and as the plunger is pushed down, it forces the dough out of the decorative nozzle directly onto the baking sheet. Design plates create a range of designs, and some models can be fitted with specialty plates for piping out buttercream and other frostings. Although most professional chefs  use a *piping bag,* this is a popular tool for the home baker, particularly for making *spritz cookies* and other traditional holiday designs. Also known as a *cookie gun.*

cookie stamp A flat disc with a decorative design carved or imprinted on one side and a short knobbed handle on the other, used to imprint the design onto cookies to be baked. Stamps can be made from wood, plastic, glass, or ceramic and are available in a variety of designs, both individually and in a set. It is important to use the stamp on firm doughs, otherwise the design will not hold its shape.

cooling The process whereby a food item releases the heat that has been produced by cooking or baking. Depending on the food, this can be accomplished in a variety of ways. Baked goods are typically removed from the oven and allowed to stand at room temperature to cool. Stovetop items such as *crème anglaise* and *caramel* must be cooled quickly, so the pan is put directly into an *ice bath* and stirred until it has cooled. Other items, such as *pastry cream,* can also be cooled down quickly by spreading it out on a thin sheet and placing the sheet, covered, in the refrigerator. Breads should be cooled on racks that allow the air to circulate around them so they retain their crunchy exterior and do not become soggy. See also *12 Steps of Baking* appendix.

cooling rack A metal rack with closely spaced rows of metal that sit on short legs (½ inch/1.2 cm). This allows air to circulate completely around a baked good while it cools; otherwise, steam may build up around the product and make it soggy. Racks are available in different shapes and sizes, including circles, squares, and rectangles. They are also used for icing and 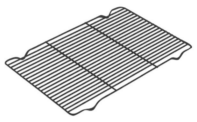 glazing cakes, petit fours, and cookies with fondant and chocolate. It is recommended to place a pan lined with parchment paper under the cooling rack to catch excess drippings; this allows some of the coating to be reused and also makes for ease of clean up.

Copha The brand name of a coconut butterfat extracted from pressed coconut flesh. It is clear and transparent when warm and solidifies into an opaque white when chilled.

copper cookware Heavy-duty cookware used primarily in the pastry kitchen for cooking sugar and whipping egg whites. It has high heat conductivity and can reach high temperatures in a relatively short period of time. The heaviness of copper pans allows for even heat distribution and reduces chances of crystallization during sugar cooking. When egg whites are whipped in a copper bowl, it strengthens the proteins and makes them more stable and resistant to overwhipping; volume will also be greater than if whipped in a stainless steel bowl.

coque (kohk) A crown-shaped cake made from brioche-like dough and, depending on the region, flavored with candied fruit, citron, orange flower water, and/or rum. Traditionally made for Easter in the south of France.

coque à petit four (kohk ah 'peh-tee fohr) Small, shell-shaped petit four made with mixture of ground almonds and meringue, baked until dry and crisp, then then sandwiched together with jam, *ganache,* or *buttercream* and glazed with *fondant icing.*

coquito nut (koh-'kee-toh) A nut of a tree native to South America. They resemble tiny coconuts, with a brown exterior and a hollow white interior that has a crunchy, sweet, coconut-like flavor.

cordial 1. A confectionery term that refers to chocolates with a liquid center, such as a *cherry cordial.* 2. Another term for *liqueur.*

core 1. The center of a fruit such as a pineapple, apple, or pear, typically removed because it is tough and/or woody. 2. To remove the core from a fruit.

corer A hand-held utensil for removing the core and seeds from fruits such as apples and pears. There are several variations depending on the fruit to be cored.

coriander (kor-ee-'an-der) An herb and spice member of the parsley family, native to the Mediterranean and Middle East. the plant is cultivated for its seeds, which are used dried, and for its dark green, lacy leaves, which are used fresh and are known as *cilantro*. The tiny, yellowish-tan seeds are used whole or ground as an aromatic spice to flavor desserts and baked goods, particularly in Scandinavia. Their flavor is a combination of lemon, sage, and caraway with a hint of sweet orange.

cordial Another name for *liqueur*.

cornbread An American quickbread that substitutes most or all of the flour with cornmeal and ranges in texture from light and airy to rich and dense. It may be sweet or flavored with savory items such as cheese, scallions, or bacon. Some versions are baked stovetop in a cast iron skillet with lard or another fat while others are baked in a pan in the oven. It is particularly popular in the southern United States. See also *cornstick pan*.

Cornell bread A nutritious formula to enrich bread, developed at Cornell University in the 1930s. It consists of 1 tablespoon each soy flour and nonfat milk powder plus 1 teaspoon wheat germ for each cup of flour used in the bread recipe.

cornelli lace A decorating technique used on cakes to create a lace pattern. The technique involves piping random curves all over the cake with a #2 or #3 decorating tip. The curvy lines never touch each other.

cornet (kohr-'neht) 1. The French word for "cone," referring to cone-shaped products that may be made from *puff pastry,* as in *cream horns,* or wafer batter, such as *tuile* or ice cream cones. They are typically filled with ingredients such as *crème chantilly,* ice cream, and *pastry cream.* 2. A cone-shaped piece of *parchment paper* that is filled with an ingredient such as *chocolate, buttercream,* or *royal icing* and used to write on and decorate cakes, pastries, and confections.

cornelli lace

cornetti (kohr-'neh-tee) The Italian name for a croissant, referring to a traditional *croissant* enriched with eggs. They are served hot in Milan and Rome, and may be plain or filled with apricot jam, pastry cream, or almond paste.

cornflake Toasted flakes made from the coarse meal of hulled corn for use as a breakfast cereal.

cornflour 1. The European term for *cornstarch.* 2. See *flour.*

cornmeal Dried yellow, blue, or white corn kernels that have been ground to a fine, medium, or coarse texture. Yellow cornmeal is the most popular, used on the bottom and/or top of English muffins, breadsticks, and breads to add crunchy texture and prevent the dough from sticking to the pan. It is also an important ingredient in the production of *cornbread* and *corn muffins.*

cornmeal flatbread Any of several round, flat breads made with cornmeal and sometimes flour. They may be cooked over the ashes of a campfire, on hot stones, on a griddle, in a cast iron pan, or in the oven. The name, exact type of batter, and cooking method varies. See also *johnnycake* and *hoe cake.*

corn muffin An American muffin made from a quick bread batter containing flour and cornmeal, typically in equal ratios, eggs, milk, and leavening. Sugar is an optional ingredient depending on the region of the country and local preferences.

corn oil An odorless, flavorless, pale yellow oil produced from dried, crushed corn kernels. It is low in saturated fats; polyunsaturated corn oil is cholesterol free and a major ingredient in *margarine*. Its high *smoke point* makes it a good choice for frying; also, it is used in many pastries, confections, and desserts. Other vegetable oils, such as *peanut oil, canola oil,* and *soybean oil,* can be substituted.

corn pone An eggless cornbread that is shaped into small ovals and fried or baked. It is popular in the southern United States.

cornstarch A powdered starch derived from finely ground cornmeal, used extensively in the bakeshop to thicken stirred custards and pie fillings because the product will remain translucent. It is typically mixed with a small portion of liquid before being added to a mixture in order to prevent it from lumping up. It also needs to be fully cooked or it will leave an unpleasant starchy taste. It is also an ingredient in *confectioners' sugar* because it absorbs moisture and helps prevent the product from lumping up. Known as *cornflour* in Europe.

cornstick pan A cast iron pan used to bake individual portions of cornbread batter. It has shallow indentions that are shaped like an ear of corn.

corn sugar Another name for *dextrose.*

corn syrup A clear syrup produced from the breakdown of starch, particularly cornstarch. It contains a certain amount of sugar, particularly glucose and maltose, which sweetens, moistens, browns, and tenderizes products. Whatever is not converted to sugar is called saccharides, which thicken, add body, and enhance pliability of foods. The corn syrups are classified by the amount of conversion to sugar that the starch has undergone and are referred to as high-conversion, medium-conversion (also known as regular glucose corn syrup), and low-conversion syrups. High-conversion syrups are high in sugar and low in saccharides. Low-conversion syrups are low in sugar and high in saccharides. Medium-conversion syrups are a balance between the two. Most bakeshops use a medium-conversion corn syrup in candies, confections, and pie fillings such as pecan pie. The most common brand is Karo light corn syrup and Karo dark corn syrup. The light version also contains fructose, salt, and vanilla while the dark version is regular light corn syrup with molasses, caramel coloring, salt, and added flavor. Dark corn syrup may be used as a less expensive substitute for molasses but it has a milder flavor. Low-conversion syrups are very thick, mildly sweet, and less likely to crystallize or brown; for this reason they are the recommended choice for icings, confections, pulled and blown sugar, and frozen desserts. Glucose crystal is an expensive, low-conversion glucose corn syrup from France. It is highly refined and has a crystal-clear appearance. High-fructose corn syrup, known as glucose-fructose in Canada, is equal parts fructose and glucose. It is used by food processors to increase the sweetness of items without adding additional sucrose. It was formulated in the 1970s by Japanese researchers, and is primarily used in the commercial production of confections, candies, and soft drinks.

Cortland apple See *apple.*

cotignac (koh-tee-'nyak) A French confection made from sweetened quince paste that is cut into rounds, which are then packaged in small round wooden boxes and air-dried. It is a specialty of the city of Orléans. It is believed to have been made during the time of Joan of Arc, so her image decorates the wooden boxes they are packaged in. She is also embossed on the larger version of cotignac by pressing the paste into molds.

Cotswold cake An Irish butter cake of butter, mashed potatoes, sugar, vanilla, flour, and baking powder. Its name derives from its popularity in the Cotswold district of England.

cottage cheese A moist fresh cheese made from whole or partly skimmed pasteurized cow's milk, originally produced as a homemade farm cheese in cottage kitchens and now made commercially. The soft, white, lumpy cheese is available as small curd, medium curd, or large curd. Creamed cottage cheese is enriched with 4 to 8% cream. Low-fat cottage cheese has 1 to 2% fat, and non-fat has zero. It is available plain or flavored. It is used as a low-fat alternative to cream cheese and as an ingredient in cheesecakes and fillings. It is also a popular low-fat dessert when topped with fresh fruit.

cottage pudding A simple dessert of a rich, plain cake that has been soaked in a sweet lemon or chocolate sauce.

cotton candy A snack of long, thin strands of aerated sugar spun around a cardboard cone. This is a popular circus and fairground confection that dates back to 1904, when William Morrison and John C. Wharton introduced it at the World's Fair. The sweet, fluffy mass is highly susceptible to moisture and melts in the mouth upon contact. It is typically colored pink, but purple and blue are also popular. Also known as *candy floss* in Britain and *fairy floss* in Australia.

cottonseed oil A refined oil extracted from the cotton plant. It is light and flavorless, and is typically blended with other vegetable oils to make vegetable oil products. It is also used as an ingredient in margarine, salad dressings, and commercially fried products.

couche ('coo-shh) 1. A canvas cloth made from untreated natural fiber, used to proof (ferment) dough. The rough surface absorbs the extra moisture in the dough, giving the bread a thick, crisp crust, which is characteristic of French bread. It is also sturdy enough to hold a round shape to create a dividing wall between the loaves so that they don't stick to each other. They are reusable if the excess flour is shaken off and are stored in a cool, dry place. 2. An old-time Cajun breakfast of fried cornmeal mush, a mixture of oil, yellow cornmeal, milk, water, salt, and baking powder made into a batter and fried. It is served like a hot cereal, with milk and sugar.

coucoulelli (koh-koh-'lehl-lee) A moist diamond-shaped cake from Corsica, made with flour, spices, wine, and olive oil.

coulis ('koo-lee) A thick puree of fresh or cooked fruit, used as a sauce or accompaniment to desserts, ice creams, and other pastry products. The name derives from the French *coulis*, which means "strained juice from meat" because this was the original application.

counterweight See *scale, balance*.

coupe (koop) A frozen dessert made from virtually any combination of ice cream, fruit, and sauce flavored with liqueur, and topped with whipped cream and/or nuts, chocolate, candied fruit, or meringue pieces. Also refers to the stemmed, wide, deep bowl in which it is served.

coupler A two-piece plastic device used to attach a *pastry tip* to a *pastry bag*. It allows the tips to be changed without having to change the pastry bag. The cone-shaped piece is placed in the bottom of the pastry bag until the top of it protrudes from the bag. The desired tip is fitted onto the threaded edges of the cone-shaped piece, and a plastic ring is screwed over the top of the tip onto the cone-shaped piece to keep the tip in place. When a different tip is desired, the plastic ring is unscrewed and the new tip is put in place. Once the ring is screwed back on, the product may be piped with a

different design. It is an important pastry tool, particularly when using various tips to decorate wedding cakes and other celebration cakes, because it saves time and product. They are available in large and small sizes to accommodate different tip sizes, and may be purchased separately or as part of a pastry tip set.

couque (kook) A Flemish pastry of brioche dough filled with golden raisins, currants, and candied fruit. Its name derives from the Dutch word *koekje*, which means "cake." They are typically made in individual portions and served warm with butter.

couronne (koo-'ruhn) The French word for "crown," referring to crown-shaped breads and pastries.

couscous ('koos-koos) Granulated semolina, a food staple of North African cuisine. For breakfast, it is cooked in milk and served as a porridge. For dessert, it is sweetened and mixed with fruit. It is also a popular savory accompaniment that is flavored with spices and served with vegetables and/or meat.

coush-coush ('koosh-koosh) A thick, cereal-like Cajun breakfast specialty made by adding boiled water to yellow cornmeal, salt, pepper, and baking soda, and frying it in a skillet with bacon fat or lard. As it cooks, a toasty brown crust forms that is crumbled into the cereal before serving. It is topped with butter, milk, or cream and sweetened with sugar or cane syrup.

couque de Dinant (kook duh day-'nah) A dry, hard cookie from the small town of Dinant in the Belgian province of Namur.

couverture ('coo-vehr-churr) The term for a high-quality *chocolate* with a minimum of 32% *cocoa butter*. It is the only type of chocolate that can be tempered, and is also used in high-quality confections and desserts. It may be dark, milk, or white.

Coventry puffs A triangular puff pastry turnover filled with rich mincemeat. They originated in the British city of Coventry during the 1500s and were traditionally given at Easter as a present from godparents to their godchildren. The three corners of the turnover are meant to represent the three spires of the Coventry cathedral.

cowberry See *berry*.

Crabapple See *apple*.

cracked stage, sugar See *Sugar Cooking Stages* appendix.

cracked wheat Whole, unprocessed wheat kernels that have been broken or cracked into coarse, medium, or fine pieces. Used to add texture and flavor to bread.

Crackerjacks A snack mixture of caramel-coated popcorn and roasted peanuts. It was introduced at the 1893 Chicago World's fair by its inventors, Frederick William Rueckheim and his brother, Louis. The original version was a combination of popcorn and peanuts that were coated in molasses, but it was not popular because it was sticky and messy. After experimenting with the recipe, they developed a dry caramel coating that did not stick to the hands. This version became well known after being included in the 1908 song "Take Me Out to the Ball Game." In 1912 they added a small trinket or toy surprise in the box, which turned it into a childrens' favorite. See also *caramel corn*.

cramique (krah-meek) A currant and raisin-filled brioche bread from Belgium and northern France. It is served warm with butter for breakfast or as a snack with coffee and tea.

cranachan A traditional Scottish dessert made with beaten double cream, toasted oatmeal, sugar or honey, and seasonal fruits. It is typically served in individual portions with shortbread cookies. Also known as *cream crowdie*.

cranberry See *berry*.

cream 1. To beat fat and sugar together until the mixture is smooth and creamy. See *creaming method*. 2. The fat contained in whole milk. When unhomogenized milk stands at room temperature for several hours, it naturally separates into the milk-fat rich cream on top and fat-free milk on the bottom. In commercial production the top layer, or cream, is skimmed off using centrifugal force and pasteurized. Cream is categorized based on its fat content and is labeled as follows:

> **Coffee** Another name for light cream.
>
> **Light** Contains between 18 and 30% fat. Also known as coffee cream.
>
> **Light whipping** Contains 30 to 36% fat and sometimes emulsifiers and stabilizers.
>
> **Heavy** Contains a minimum fat content of 36%. It doubles in volume when whipped. Also known as heavy whipping cream.
>
> **Heavy whipping** Another name for heavy cream.
>
> **Manufacturing** Contains 40% fat and no stabilizers. The lack of a stabilizer allows it to be added to a slightly warm mixture such as melted chocolate without it separating. The extra fat content also produces a very rich whipped cream.
>
> **Ultra-pasteurized** Cream that has been heated to 300°F (149°C) in order to kill bacteria that causes milk products to sour. It has a longer shelf life than regular cream but does not whip as well or have the same rich flavor.

See also *clabbered cream, clotted cream, crème fraîche, half-and-half, sour cream,* and *whipped cream.*

cream bun A round bun made from sweetened dough with fruit mixed in. After baking, the buns are split open and filled with jam and whipped cream and dusted with confectioners' sugar.

cream cheese A smooth, creamy cheese made from cow's milk that is cultured with bacteria and sometimes a stabilizer such as *gum arabic* to increase shelf life and firmness. It has a slightly tangy flavor, and is available in a variety of styles, including light or low-fat, nonfat, and whipped. It contains a minimum of 33% milkfat and a maximum of 55% moisture. Light or low-fat cream cheese has half the calories as regular cream cheese; nonfat cream cheese has zero fat grams; and whipped cream cheese is easily spread because it has air whipped into it until it is soft and fluffy. Commercial cream cheese is typically packaged in 3-pound (1 kg 365 g) units and is used extensively in the bakeshop in the production of cheesecakes, pastry doughs, cookies, and tarts.

cream cheese dough A short dough that uses cream cheese to replace all or part of the fat. The cream cheese is cut into the flour of the recipe as in the preparation of pie pastry. Cream cheese dough is used as the dough for the Jewish crescent-shaped cookie *rugalach.*

cream cheese frosting A sweet, creamy icing made of softened cream cheese, vanilla, and confectioners' sugar, traditionally used to fill and ice *carrot cake.*

cream crowdie Another name for *cranachan.*

cream horn A puff pastry cone filled with *crème chantilly*. It is made by wrapping a thin strip of puff pastry around a cone-shaped metal form, brushing it with egg wash, and sprinkling it with sugar, then baking to a golden brown. It is filled after it has cooled.

creaming method See *mixing methods*.

creamnut Another name for *Brazil nut*.

cream of coconut A thick, very sweet mixture of coconut paste, water, and sugar, used to flavor pastries and drinks such as piña colada.

cream of tartar An acid salt with several different functions in the bakeshop. 1. When dissolved in a dough or batter, tartaric acid is released, which reacts with the baking soda and produces carbon dioxide for leavening. It is a common ingredient in fast-acting baking powder because it releases over 70% of its carbon dioxide during mixing. This lowers the *pH* of some baked goods, such as *baking powder biscuits*, which weakens the *gluten* strands, resulting in a more tender pastry with a whiter, finer crumb. It also has a clean flavor with minimal aftertaste. 2. In sugar syrups, cream of tartar helps prevent crystallization and browning. This provides confections with a smooth texture and shiny appearance, which means they are less likely to dry and crack. 3. Cream of tartar is the most common acid used to stabilize meringues and it also enhances the whiteness of the beaten whites. 4. In fudge recipes, a small amount of cream of tartar helps break down some of the *sucrose* into *invert sugar*, which helps yield a smoother, creamier fudge.

cream puff A puffy, round pastry made with *choux paste*, often filled after baking. The baked puffs are either filled from a small hole made in the bottom or split open and filled with ice cream, pastry cream, or crème chantilly. They may be topped with confectioners' sugar, fondant, caramel, or chocolate glaze. Cream puffs are used in the production of *croquembouche, profiteroles*, and *gâteau Saint-Honoré*. They are also popular as a petit four or individual dessert.

cream sherry See *sherry*.

cream yeast See *yeast*.

crema ('krehm-uh) 1. The Italian word for cream, often used as part of the name for a custard or cream such as *crema pasiticceria*. 2. The creamy, beige froth on the top of an espresso.

crema caramella The Italian name for *crème caramel*.

crema dania ('krehm-uh 'dahn-yuh) A rich Dutch double cream cheese with a white powdery rind and soft ivory-colored interior. It is 72% milkfat and pairs well with Port, fruit, and nuts.

crema inglese ('krehm-uh een-'gleh-she) The Italian name for *crème anglaise*.

crema pasticceria ('krehm-ah pah-stee-cheh-'ree-ah) The Italian name for *pastry cream*.

crème (krehm) 1. The French word for cream. 2. A descriptive word used for sweet liqueurs such as *crème de menthe* and also custards such as *crème brûlée*.

crème anglaise (krehm ahn-'glayz) A classic French custard sauce flavored with vanilla but sometimes also with chocolate, coffee, liqueurs, and spices. It can be served warm or chilled, and makes an excellent topping for fruit or pastry. It is also used as a base for making ice cream and *Bavarian cream*. Also known as vanilla sauce.

crème au beurre (krehm oh behr) The French word for *buttercream*.

crème au beurre au lait (krehm oh buhr oh lay) French for cream with butter and milk, referring to a French buttercream to which pastry cream been added. This produces a very flavorful buttercream; however, it is softer and less stable than classic buttercream and is often used as filling for pastries and cakes.

crème bavarois (krehm bah-vuh-'rwaz) The French name for *Bavarian cream*.

crème bourdaloue (krehm boor-dah-'lou) A classic French cream made with a cooked mixture of eggs, yolks, sugar, and cornstarch. It is flavored with Kirsch and lightened with meringue, and used as a filling in tarts and pastries.

crème brûlée (krehm broo-'lay) French for "burnt cream," referring to a creamy custard dessert with a caramelized top. It is traditionally baked in a shallow ramekin. The custard flavor can range from light to very rich depending on whether it is made with milk, half-and-half, or cream. It is usually flavored with a whole vanilla bean but other ingredients such as chocolate, coffee, fruit, liqueurs, or spices may be used. Before serving, it is sprinkled with a thin layer of sugar that is then caramelized with a *blowtorch* or under a *salamander*. Superfine sugar is recommended because it is least likely to clump up, but brown sugar or granulated sugar may be used as well. It is important to make sure the sugar is properly caramelized or it will be gritty. The crisp sheet of caramel contrasts nicely with the creamy custard.

crème caramel (krehm kehr-ah-'mehl) A French custard dessert made by baking the custard in a mold with a small amount of *caramel* in the bottom. The custard is baked until set and then chilled. Before serving, the mold is inverted to release the custard and the caramel, which has been softened during the baking process and now glazes the top of the custard; and the excess caramel provides a sauce. The dessert is also known as *crème renversée* in France; *renversée* means "upside down." It is known as *flan* in Spain and Mexico and as *crema caramella* in Italy.

crème chantilly (krehm shanh-'tee-yee) Whipped cream that is sweetened with confectioners' sugar and flavored with vanilla. It is a popular topping or garnish for desserts, cream pies, and cakes. It was created in 1660 by a French man named Vatel, who worked as a head waiter at the Château de Chantilly for the Prince of Condé.

crème Chiboust (krehm chee-'boost) See *chiboust cream*.

crème d'abricots (krehm 'dah-bree-koh) A sweet apricot liqueur. *Abricot* is the French word for *apricot*.

crème d'amande (krehn dah-'mahnd) 1. The French word for *almond cream*. 2. A pink almond-flavored liqueur. *Amande* is the French word for almond.

crème d'ananas (krehm 'dah-nah-nahs) A pineapple-flavored liqueur. *Ananas* is the French word for pineapple.

crème de banane (krehm deuh bah-'nahn) A sweet banana liqueur. *Banane* is the French word for banana.

crème de cacao (krehm deuh kah-'kah-oh) A dark chocolate-flavored and colored liqueur with a hint of vanilla.

crème de cassis (krehm deuh kah-'sees) A black currant-flavored liqueur. *Cassis* is the French word for black currant.

crème de cerise (krehm deuh 'sehr-eez) A cherry-flavored liqueur. *Cerise* is the French word for cherry.

crème de menthe (krehm deuh menth) A refreshing mint-flavored liqueur. It is available green or clear. *Menthe* is the French word for mint.

crème diplomat A French cream that is equal parts pastry cream and whipped cream, sweetened and flavored with vanilla. It is used as a filling for cakes and pastries, and is often stabilized with *gelatin* if it is being used in a pastry that requires it to be firm. Also known as *diplomat cream*.

crème fraîche (krehm 'fresh) French for "fresh cream," referring to a semi-thick, rich cream with a tangy flavor and soft, creamy texture. It is made from pasteurized cow's milk to which a lactic bacteria culture has been added to thicken it and give it its distinct sharp flavor without souring the cream. It may be purchased fresh, but an inexpensive version can be made by adding 2 tablespoons (30 ml) of buttermilk or sour cream to 8 ounces (160 ml) cream. The mixture will thicken if left at room temperature (70°F/21°C) for 12 to 24 hours. Once thickened, it should be mixed well, and can be kept covered in the refrigerator for up to 10 days. It makes an excellent topping for fruit and desserts, and can also be used as a filling in cakes, pastries, and confections.

crème de noyaux (krehm deuh 'nwah-yoh) A sweet, pink liqueur flavored with the pits of fruit such as apricots and/or cherries; it tastes like almonds. *Noyau* is the French word for a seed kernel.

crème pâtissière (krehm pah-tee-see'her) The French name for *pastry cream.*

crème praliné (krehm 'prah-lee-nay) French for "praline cream," referring to a praline-flavored cream made by adding a caramelized paste of almonds or hazelnuts to buttercream. It is used as a filling for cakes and pastries.

crème de rose (krehm deuh rose) A rose-flavored liqueur that is made with rose petals, vanilla, and spices.

crème de violette (krehm deuh 'vyoh-leht) A violet-flavored and colored Dutch liqueur. *Violette* is the French word for violet.

crème renversée (krehm reh-vehr-'say) Another name for *crème caramel.*

Crenshaw melon See *muskmelon.*

Creole cream cheese A thick, tart sour cream, eaten for breakfast with sugar and fruit. It is a specialty of New Orleans.

crêpe (krayp) The French word for *pancake*, referring to a paper-thin, unleavened pancake used to make sweet and savory dishes. A thin, pourable batter is used and lightly cooked in butter or oil. Depending on the region, the batter may be made with buckwheat flour or wheat flour, water or milk, and varying amounts of eggs and sugar. Dessert crepes are filled with crème chantilly, fruit, chocolate, jam, nuts, ice cream, and/or topped with butter, sugar, spices, or flavored sauces or liqueurs. The name derives from the Latin *crispus*, meaning "curly" or "wavy" and refers to the wavy edges of the crêpe after it is cooked. See also *crêpe normande* and *crêpe suzette.*

crêpe normande A warm crêpe filled with sautéed apples, butter, sugar, and cinnamon, then rolled into a cylinder and dusted with confectioners' sugar.

crêpe pan A round, carbon steel pan for making *crêpe*s. It has a flat bottom and shallow, sloping sides, with a flat, wide handle that makes it easy to hold when spreading the thin batter around the pan and flipping the crêpes. The pans are available in a variety of sizes that range in diameter from 5 to 10 inches (12.5 to 25 cm).

crêperie ('kray-pehr-ee) A restaurant or shop that serves sweet and savory crêpes. They originated in Brittany, France, but are now found throughout Europe.

crêpe suzette (krayp soo-'zeht) A crêpe heated in a sauce of sugar, butter, orange and lemon juices, orange zest, rum or brandy, and orange liqueur such as Grand Marnier. The dessert is classically prepared tableside and flamed just before serving. Traditionally, the crêpes are folded into triangles. The recipe was created in 1901 by a chef working at the Café de Paris in Monaco; he named them in honor of a beautiful young woman named Suzette who accompanied Edward, the Prince of Wales, to dinner.

crescia al formaggio ('creh-see-ah ahl fohr-'mah-gee-oh) A rustic Italian Easter bread from Umbria. Eggs and cheese such as *Parmesan* and pecorino romano are added to a rich, brioche-like dough and baked in a seasoned flowerpot. The name is from *crescia*, which means "grow" and refers to the dramatic doming of the bread over the top of the flowerpot.

crespelle (krehs-'pehl-leh) Thin Italian pancakes that are either filled and rolled into cylinders or stacked with different fillings between the layers.

crillo ('kreehl-oo) See *chocolate*.

crimp 1. To press or pinch two pieces of dough edges together to seal it and form a decorative edge. This may also be done on a single piece of pie dough to form a decorative pattern and create a dam for the filling so it does not spill out during baking. 2. A method of cake decorating for rolled *fondant*-covered cakes, whereby a *crimper* is used to imprint a decorative pattern around a cake edge or top.

C
c

crimper A flat metal hand-held tool that resembles a pair of tweezers but with much wider sides. The grooves make a decorative pattern on the dough's edges and seal it. Mini crimpers are also available for extra-fine decorative work on *marzipan*, *gum paste*, and *rolled fondant*.

Crisco A popular shortening first produced by Procter & Gamble in 1911, most often today used by home bakers today for making pie dough and quickbreads. It was the first shortening to be made of 100% vegetable oil.

crisp 1. An American dessert of a thick fruit mixture topped with *streusel* and baked. Typically served warm with vanilla ice cream or sweetened whipped cream. 2. A culinary term used to describe a food item that has a firm but easily breakable texture.

Criterion apple See *apple*.

croissant (kruh-'sahnt) A rich, buttery pastry shaped like a crescent, with a crisp, flaky golden brown crust and soft, semi-hollow interior. They originated in Austria in 1686, during the war between Austria and Turkey. A group of bakers were in their bakery during the night and heard the Turkish troops tunneling under them; they sounded a warning, which aided in the Turkish defeat. The bakers were honored with the task of creating a pastry shaped like the crescent on the Turkish flag. They are a classic breakfast pastry in France, typically served with butter and/or jam.

croissant cutter A hand-held pastry tool for cutting uniform triangles of dough to be rolled into croissants. The cutter consists of four sharp, slanted, stainless steel blades that rotate around an axle attached to wooden or metal handles. They are available in sizes to produce mini, regular, or large croissants, and there is also a large model that cuts three rows of triangles simultaneously.

croquant (kroh-'kahnt) Another name for *krokant*.

croquembouche ('kroh-kuhm-boosh) French for "crisp in the mouth," referring to a pyramid-shaped dessert composed of cream puffs that have been filled with rich cream and dipped in caramel. The pyramid is embellished with an assortment of decorations that include *spun sugar*, candied fruits, *nougatine*, *sugar flowers*, *royal icing*, and *marzipan* sweets. It is traditionally served at weddings, buffets, and First Communion celebrations.

croquembouche mold A tall, stainless steel cone-shaped mold for making *croquembouche*. It is available in heights that range from 10 to 24 inches (25 to 60 cm).

croquet (kroh-'kay) A petit four shaped like a stick and made from a mixture of almonds, sugar, and egg whites that are dried in a low oven until crisp.

croquignole (kroh-kwee-'nohl) A small, light, crisp cake made with sugar, flour, and egg whites, baked and covered with vanilla icing. It dates to the 16th century.

crostata/crostate (kruhs-'tah-tah/kruhs-'tah-tay) A rustic Italian tart made only with *pasta frolla* and named after the fruit or jam that fills the tart. It is topped with a lattice of dough before being baked.

crostini (kruhs-'tee-nee) Italian for "little toasts," referring to small, thin slices of toasted bread that are brushed with olive oil and served as *canapé* bases or as a garnish for soups and salads.

croustade (kruhs-'tahd) A hollowed-out case of baked puff pastry that is filled with sweet or savory fillings such as *crème chantilly* and fresh fruit. It may be large or small; the sweet versions are typically served with a dessert sauce such as *crème anglaise* or fruit *coulis*.

croûte (kroot) A baked pastry case or hollowed-out piece of bread used to hold sweet or savory fillings. When served as a dessert, it is typically made from dried *savarin* or *brioche* that is moistened with a flavored syrup and spread with jam and/or poached or candied fruit.

cruchade (krew-'shahd) 1. In Saintonge, France, a thin, round cake made from a corn batter that is fried and served with jam. 2. In the Landes region, a sweet or savory biscuit that is fried.

cruller ('kruhl-uhr) A deep-fried doughnut made from dough that is either yeast-raised or leavened with baking powder, cut into a long thin strip, and twisted before being deep-fried. It is sprinkled with granulated sugar and brushed with a sweet glaze. *French crullers* are made with *choux paste*. The name derives from the Dutch word *krulle*, which means "twisted cake."

crumb 1. A term that describes the interior of cakes and breads. 2. The action of removing crumbs a diner's table between courses; the table is "crumbed" with a small tool called a crumber that is run across the surface to gather the crumbs and present a clean setting for the next course.

crumb coating A technique for icing cakes whereby a thin layer of icing is spread across the sides and top of a cake layer in order to trap the crumbs in the icing. These trapped crumbs are less likely to resurface when the cake has the final icing coat applied. Some pastry chefs chill the cake between the crumb coating and final coating to further ensure that no crumbs will be exposed.

crumble 1. A British dessert of fresh fruit topped with a crumbly pastry mixture and baked. 2. To break food into small pieces.

crumpet ('kruhm-piht) A small, round, flat, straight-sided yeast-raised bread made from a batter that is cooked in a *crumpet ring* on the griddle. They are a specialty of the British Isles. They are toasted whole and served at afternoon tea with *clotted cream* and jam.

crumpet ring A bottomless metal ring approximately 3 inches (7.5 cm) in diameter, used to shape crumpet batter as it is baked on the griddle. Once the bottom is browned, the crumpet is flipped over and the ring removed. The rings are also used to shape *English muffins* while baking.

crush To reduce a food item to fine particles, often with a *rolling pin* or *mortar and pestle*.

crust 1. The outer layer of bread, pies, pastries, and other baked items. 2. The bottom lining of a pie; see *pie crust*. 3. The sediment that forms in bottle-aged red wines and Ports.

crystal sugar See *sugar*.

crystallization The process of sugar particles clumping or clinging together, often as a result of not being properly melted during cooking. Crystallization can occur when granulated particles of sugar come in contact with melted particles, or when the melted sugar is agitated too much during cooking. The latter often occurs because the mixture was stirred while still hot, allowing large sugar crystals to disperse themselves through the mixture. Crystallization may be prevented by brushing down the sides of the pan with water during the cooking process. There are times, however, when crystallization is desired. When making fudge, controlled sugar crystallization is needed for obtaining the correct texture, and is completed by stirring the fudge mixture after it has cooled, forming small sugar crystals that give a creamy texture. *Fondant* and *taffy* are other products where small crystallization has occurred in order to achieve the desired texture. Some ingredients, such as lemon juice, cream of tartar, corn syrup, or citric acid, are added to sugar mixtures to prevent crystallization; the acid creates *invert sugar*, which is resistant to crystallization.

crystallized flowers Flowers such as violets and rose petals that have been dipped in a thick sugar syrup and then drained and dried to form small sugar crystals on the petals. The flowers are then dusted with granulated sugar to enhance the crystallized appearance. These are primarily used as garnishes on desserts and for decorative purposes. Also known as *candied flowers*.

crystallized fruit Another name for candied fruit; see *glacé fruit*.

cuba libre ('koo-buh 'lee-bruh) An iced cocktail made with rum, lime juice, and cola.

cube sugar See *sugar*.

Cucumber melon Another name for *Kiwano melon*.

cuka See *vinegar*.

cumin ('kyoo-mihn) An aromatic seed of a plant in the parsley family. It resembles a caraway seed but has a warm, nutty flavor. The seeds come in three colors: amber (the most widely available) and the more peppery and complex flavored white and black varieties, which may be found in Asian markets. Cumin is available in whole or ground form, and should be stored in airtight containers in a cool, dark place. It is a popular spice in Middle Eastern and Mediterranean cuisine, and is also used in Europe, particularly in Scandinavia and Germany, to flavor breads and liqueurs.

cupcake An individual cake typically baked in a muffin pan with a paper or foil baking cup. It may be made in a variety of flavors and is usually frosted and/or decorated with colored icing and sometimes sprinkles.

cupuacu (koo-'pah-choo) The fruit of the cupuachu tree, native to Brazil, whose seeds are dried and processed like *cacao beans* to produce a light brown "chocolate" with a mild, bittersweet flavor and a hint of fruit. The pod resembles a fuzzy football and contains moist pulp with seeds. It is available in ground or bar form, and is used in the same way as *cocoa powder* and *chocolate*.

Curaçao ('kyoor-uh-soh) An orange-flavored liqueur made from the dried peel of the bitter and sour oranges found on the Caribbean island of Curaçao. Although the original liqueur is clear, it is also available in red, blue, orange, and green. There are also several flavor blends, including coffee, chocolate, and rum raisin. It is used to flavor desserts, pastries, confections, and beverages.

curd 1. A rich, creamy pastry filling made from a mixture of citrus juice, sugar, butter, and egg yolks. It thickens as it cooks and sets when cool. The satiny curd is used as a filling for tarts, pies, pastries, and cakes. 2. The semi-solid portion of milk after it coagulates and separates. It is used to make cheese.

curdle A term that describes the separation of a product owing to souring, temperature differences, or too much acid.

currant ('kuhr-uhnt) 1. A seedless Zante grape that when dried resembles a tiny, dark raisin. Currants are a popular ingredient to add sweetness and texture to breads, pastries, and desserts. 2. A tiny berry produced on currant bushes and is related to the gooseberry. Fresh currants are available from June to August, and the three varieties are:

> **Black** Found in Scandanavia, France, and Germany these small, dark, bitter berries are used primarily for preserves, liqueurs, and syrups.

> **Red** Native to Europe and very popular in Scandinavia, these small, tart red berries grow in clusters. They are rich in citric acid, pectin, and vitamins and are used mostly to make jams and jellies or as a decorative garnish.

> **White** Although more difficult to find, these are similar to red currants but with a white skin. They are good for eating out of hand and also to make jams and sauces.

cuscus dolce (kuss-kuss 'dohl-chay) Italian for "sweet couscous," referring to a specialty dessert from the Santo Spirito Monastary in Agrigento, Sicily. It consists of a pistachio nut paste flavored with almonds and cinnamon and kneaded into a cooked couscous mixture. It is then combined with a sugar syrup and served in mounds topped with grated chocolate.

cush (koosh) 1. A cornmeal pancake from the American South. 2. A sweet, mushy cornmeal mixture that is fried in lard and eaten as a cereal with cream or *clabbered cream* and sugar or cane syrup.

cushion lattice A decorating technique of piping a large puff of *royal icing* and allowing it to dry, then piping a *lattice* design over the puff and letting it dry. This process is repeated until the desired height and fullness is achieved. The trick of this technique is making perfectly piped, multiple criss-crossing lines.

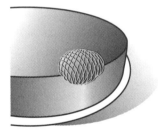

cushion lattice

custard Any of a variety of pastry products made with a liquid that is thickened by the coagulation of egg protein. The two types of custards are *stirred custards* and *baked custards*. Stirred custards, such as *pastry cream* and *crème anglaise*, are made on the stovetop and stirred as they cook. Sometimes, as with pastry cream, they contain a starch such as cornstarch to thicken and stabilize them. Baked custards, such as *crème brûlée* and *crème caramel* are baked in the oven until set and then chilled. They should be baked in a *water bath* to ensure even distribution of heat and protect from overcooking. With the exception of pastry cream and other custards that contain starch (because the product should be boiled to cook out the starch), both types of custard should not reach an internal temperature that exceeds 185°F (85°C) because the eggs will start to coagulate and curdle. If overheated, custard will become watery because the moisture separates from the toughened protein. See also *What Went Wrong and Why* appendix.

custard apple Another name for *cherimoya*.

custard pie See *pie*.

custard powder A powdered thickening agent used in lieu of flour. It is made up of cornstarch or arrowroot, vanilla, colorings, and sometimes sweetener. It typically needs to be added to liquids such as milk, cream, or water and cooked to remove the starchy flavor. It was invented by a chemist named Alfred Bird, who made it as a substitute for egg custard because his wife was allergic to eggs.

cut in To gently blend small pieces of fat into a flour mixture, as with the *biscuit method*. It is important to keep the fat cold in order for it to retain its shape and prevent it from melting into the flour. Cutting in may be done by hand or with a pastry blender.

Cynar ('chee-nahr) A dark brown, bitter Italian liqueur made from artichokes and herbs. It can be served as an *apéritif* over ice, either plain or with soda water, or as a cocktail mixed with cola or tonic water.

C
c

Dd

dacquoise (dahk-koo-'wahz) 1. A *meringue disc* that includes ground almonds folded in before baking; used in the preparation of confections, cakes, and petit fours. 2. A French cake of three hazelnut or almond meringue discs sandwiched together with sweetened whipped cream or flavored *buttercream*.

dadar (dah-'dahr) An Indonesian specialty of stuffed and rolled crêpes, served with coffee or tea. The crêpes are made with a batter of coconut milk, salt, and rice flour or cornstarch, and filled with freshly grated toasted coconut, brown sugar, vanilla, cinnamon, and salt.

Dairy Queen A chain of roadside stands featuring soft ice cream, founded by a father and son team. Their first sale of this soft frozen dairy product was in 1938, at a friend's ice cream store. The treat was so successful that they opened their first store in 1940, in Joliet, Illinois. By 1960, there were 3,000 Dairy Queens in 12 countries. Although other items have been added to the menu, such as hotdogs and hamburgers, ice cream is still its main feature.

Dalloyau ('dahl-why-oh) A well-known Parisian gourmet shop, known for its macaroons, chocolates, cakes, and pastries.

damming The technique of applying a thin or thick border of icing around the outside edge of a cake layer, so that the filling between each layer does not seep out.

Damson plum See *plum.*

Dancy orange See *orange.*

danish pastry A popular breakfast pastry made in a variety of sizes and styles and filled with fruit, cheese, jams, or nuts, and often brushed with apricot jam. The pastry originated in Denmark, but the Danes call their version *wienerbrod,* or *Viennese bread,* because in the late 1800s the bakers of Copenhagen went on strike and were replaced by Viennese bakers, who produced this crisp, layered pastry. The yeast dough is laminated with butter and enriched with eggs. Over 100 shapes can be made, ranging from snails to pinwheels.

dan ta an (dahn 'tah ahn) A small pastry tart from Singapore, filled with a golden-yellow egg custard.

Danziger Goldwasser ('dahn-tsig-uhr 'golt-waz-zer) See *Goldwasser.*

Dapple Dandy See *pluot.*

darazsfeszek ('dah-rahz-sfehs-zehk) A yeast-raised Hungarian coffee cake made by filling individual pieces of pinwheel-shaped dough with a rich mixture of butter, milk, sugar, walnuts, and raisins. The pinwheels are baked in a large pan and pulled apart after baking to a golden brown.

dariole (dah-ree-'ohl) A French term to describe both a small cylindrical mold and the dessert baked in it. Traditionally the dessert is made by lining the mold with *puff pastry* and filling it with *frangipane.* It may also be savory.

dariole mold See *dariole.*

Darjeeling tea (dahr-'jee-ling) One of the finest varieties of black tea. It is grown at a high altitude, up to 7,000 feet in the Darjeeling area of northern India; the cooler air enables it to grow more slowly and produce leaves that give it a medium-body, floral aroma and slightly astringent taste.

dark brown sugar See *sugar, brown*.

dark chocolate See *chocolate*.

dark corn syrup See *corn syrup*.

dark raisins See *raisins*.

dartois (dahr-'twah) A French pastry made by filling two strips of *puff pastry* with a sweet or savory filling. Sweet fillings include *frangipane*, jam, or *pastry cream* sometimes flavored with candied fruit. The pastry is believed to be named after a 19th-century vaudeville artist named François Victor Dartois.

dash A measuring term that is synonymous with "a pinch." The actual weight is approximately ¹⁄₁₆ teaspoon.

dasher See *ice cream machine*.

date The fruit of the date palm. It is picked green and ripens to a yellow, reddish brown, golden brown, or black, color, depending on the variety. The cylindrical fruit ranges from 1 to 2 inches (2.5 to 5 cm) long. The paper-thin skin surrounds a fleshy mass with a single elongated seed. With a sugar content over 50%, dates are very sweet. They may be found fresh, dried, whole, and chopped. Dates can be traced back to 6000 BC and are believed to have originated in the Persian Gulf region.

DATEM The acronym for diacetyl tartaric acid esters of mono and diglycerides. It is an emulsifier used in dough conditioners to increase water absorption and strengthen gluten.

DDT See *desired dough temperature*.

DE The acronym for dextrose equivalence. It is a specification used for glucose syrup to determine how much the starch molecule has been broken down into simpler sugars. It affects the flavor, viscosity, and browning ability of glucose syrup.

dead dough An unleavened dough used in the production of bread sculptures and display products. The absence of leavening allows the decorative shape, such as a cornucopia or bread basket, to retain its form during baking. After baking they are typically coated with food lacquer and may be stored in the freezer for future use. Also known as *salt dough*.

decaffeinated coffee See *coffee*.

deciliter A metric measurement of volume that is equivalent to ½ cup.

deck oven See *oven*.

decorative cutter A metal or plastic tool used for making decorative cut-outs of gumpaste, marzipan, cookie dough, and other pastry products. It is available in a wide variety of shapes, sizes and designs and may be purchased individually or as a set.

decorator's buttercream See *buttercream*.

decorator's icing See *royal icing*.

decorating sugar See *sugar*.

deep-dish 1. Refers to a deep pie pan with straight sides that is used to make a pie containing either a sweet or savory filling. 2. A shallow casserole made with only a top crust.

deep-dish pizza A pizza is known for its thick, chewy crust, developed in Chicago.

deep-fry To cook foods using a high *smoke point* fat. The food is often breaded before being dropped into hot fat; the temperature of the fat varies according to the food but is typically 375°F (190°C). The food may be fried in a wire basket or directly in the oil and the desired result is a crisp exterior with a juicy interior.

deep-frying thermometer See *thermometer*.

deglaze To add a liquid, usually stock or wine, to a pan so as to capture the flavor bits that remain sticking to the pan after cooking a food item. This liquid then becomes the base for a sauce.

degrease To remove fat from the surface of a hot liquid. This is typically done with a skimmer or spoon.

dehumidifying agent See *dessicant*.

dehydrate, dehydration To remove moisture from a food product. This is done with a low, dry heat and acts a preservative. The thinly sliced food items are placed on a perforated tray in a low-temperature oven or in a special piece of equipment called an electric dehydrator.

dehydrated beets A food additive made from beets that imparts a deep red color to baked goods, jams, and jellies.

dejeuner (day-zhoo-'nay) The French term for lunch.

Delaware grape See *grape*.

del giorno (dehl 'jhorn-oh) Italian for "of the day," equivalent to the French *du jour*. A culinary term that refers to a menu item that is made especially for that day.

Delicious apple See *apple*.

Demerara rum A dark, rich rum produced from sugarcane grown along the Demerara River in Guyana, South America.

demerara sugar See *sugar*.

demi-feuilletage (deh-mee fo-'ee-tahjh) French for "half puff pastry," referring to leftover scraps of *puff pastry* dough that are rerolled and used.

demitasse ('dehm-ee-tahs) 1. The French name for a small (2 oz./55 g) coffee cup used to serve very strong coffee such as *espresso*. 2. The French word for "half cup."

denature To breakdown protein molecules as a result of heat, acid, or mechanical agitation.

denatured alcohol An ethanol treated with an additive such as methanol, isopropanol, methyl ethyl ketone, methyl isobutyl ketone, or denatonium that renders it unfit for consumption. It is used by pastry chefs in the production of *pulled sugar* and *blown sugar* to fuel the *alcohol lamp* that provides the flame for heating and melting the sugar. Also known as *methylated spirit*.

dendê (dha-n-'dha) An oil obtained from palm fruit, used in Brazilian cooking for its flavor, texture, and bright orange color.

densimeter An instrument used to measure the density of a sugar syrup by floating the device in the syrup. See *hydrometer* and *saccharometer*.

depression cake A cake made from shortening instead of butter and brown sugar and water instead of milk and eggs. It was popular during the Great Depression and World War II.

Derby pie A pie with a chocolate and pecan filling flavored with Bourbon. It is often associated with the Kentucky Derby, and because it is a registered trademark, it may be served only by Kern's Kitchen, where it was created by George Kern in 1968.

desdemona A pastry of *ladyfingers* sandwiched together with *crème chantilly*, then brushed with apricot jam and covered in a Kirsch-flavored *fondant*. The pastry is named after the Shakespearean character Desdemona, the love of Othello.

desem ('dehs-sehm) 1. A firm sourdough starter of fresh organic wheat flour, developed in the Netherlands. It is regenerated by removing a small piece of dough from the day's production and storing it in flour so that it may develop additional natural yeasts. This fermented ball is then used as the starter for a fresh batch of sourdough bread. 2. A Flemish style of naturally leavened bread that uses whole wheat flour.

desicate To preserve food by cutting into small pieces or shredding it and drying it completely.

desiccant A product that absorbs moisture in the air. It is used to help protect items such as *tuile* and sugar showpieces when placed in an air tight container with the product. The most common dessicants are *silica gel* and *limestone*. Also known as a *dehumidifying agent*.

desiccated coconut Dried shredded coconut, made from the white portion of the coconut kernel after the brown skin has been removed. Depending on the dryness of the coconut and how finely it was shredded, the product will absorb different amounts of moisture and the recipe should be adjusted accordingly.

desired dough temperature The ideal temperature of a dough while you are working with it. For lean doughs, the ideal temperature is typically 75° to 80°F (24° to 27°C), while enriched doughs are slightly higher. Use the following formula to calculate the temperature of the water needed to achieve the ideal dough temperature:

$$\text{Flour temperature} + \text{room temperature} + \text{friction factor} = x;$$

$$x - \text{desired dough temperature} = \text{water temperature}.$$

See also *12 Steps of Baking* appendix.

dessert The final course of a meal, consisting of a sweet preparation or an assortment of cheeses. The word derives from *desservir,* the French term for "to clear the table."

dessert wine A sweet wine served as is or with dessert. Some of the more popular sweet wines include *sparkling wines*, *Sauternes*, and *fortified wines* such as *Port* and *Sherry*. See also *Allegrini, Asti Spumante, Auslese, Beerenauslese, Champagne, ice wine, maculan, Prosecco, sherry, Spätlese, Tokay wine*, and *Trokenbeerenauslese*.

détendre (deh-tahn-drah) A French term that refers to the softening of a mixture, usually a dough, with the addition of milk, eggs, or stock.

détrempe (day-'trohmp) A French term referring to a mixture of flour, water, and salt that is used as a foundation for *laminated doughs*.

devil's food cake An American cake of moist, rich chocolate layers iced with a fudgey chocolate icing. Its name is related to the reddish brown color that is a result of the baking soda used as a leavening, which neutralizes the acid of the chocolate. It is often considered the counterpart of *angel food cake* and was created in 1905.

Devon cream Another name for *clotted cream*.

Devonshire cream Another name for *clotted cream*.

dewberry See *berry*.

dextrin A starch fragment produced when high heat breaks down a starch. The fragments absorb water and thicken products, just like starch does.

D
d

dextrose ('dehk-strohs) A naturally occurring form of glucose found in grapes and corn. It is produced by dehydrating *high-conversion glucose corn syrup*. It is less sweet than *sucrose*, browns at a lower temperature, crystallizes more slowly, and is less soluble in water. Also known as *corn sugar* and *grape sugar*.

dextrose equivalence See *DE*.

dhom palm (dahm) See *doum palm*.

diastase See *amylase*.

diastic malt Malt that has amylase enzymes in it.

dice To cut into small, symmetrical cubes, generally ranging from ¼ to ⅛ inch (3 to 6 mm) in size.

dietary fiber A component of plants, fruits, and vegetables that cannot be digested by the human body, therefore passing through the digestive system and acting as a cleansing agent. This is more commonly known as *roughage*.

digestif (dye-jest-'teefe) An alcoholic beverage consumed at the end of a meal. It is believed to aid in the digestion of food and is typically served in a small amount in a *snifter*.

digestive biscuit A semi-sweet British cookie made from whole wheat flour and sometimes dipped in chocolate.

digestive enzyme A natural food enzyme that helps the body digest foods and reduces the gases that may be experienced from particular foods, such as grains, cabbage, broccoli, and onions. These foods along with others contain complex sugars that collect in the digestive system, causing excess gas from fermentation. Digestive enzymes are found in drugstores in tablet form and may be taken after eating the troublesome foods.

digital thermometer See *thermometer*.

dilute To reduce the concentration of a liquid by adding additional liquid, usually water.

Dinkel See *spelt*.

dioul (dee-O-'oohl) See *malsouqua*.

diple ('deep-lee) A deep-fried Greek pastry shaped like a bow or circle. It is typically topped with cinnamon honey syrup and walnuts.

diplomat cream See *crème diplomat*.

diplomat pudding A chilled, molded dessert of rum- or *Kirsch*-soaked *ladyfingers* layered with *Bavarian cream*, apricot jam, and crystallized fruit.

dipping fork A small handheld pastry tool to dip confections into chocolate or fondant. It resembles a football goal post, with three spaced wire prongs in the center. The fork is attached to a short metal or wooden handle.

direct dough A yeast bread dough produced via the *straight dough method*. See *mixing methods*.

disaccharide A compound of two simple sugars, or sacharides linked together, as in *maltose*, *lactose*, and *sucrose*.

dissolve To break down a dry ingredient by incorporating it into a liquid.

dipping fork

distillation The process of separating alcohol from a liquid through the heating of the liquid and capturing the resulting steam, which contains the alcohol vapors. This vapor is than condensed into a separate container to derive the desired alcohol.

distilled water Water that has had all the minerals and other impurities removed by the process of *distillation*.

divinity An American confection made by beating a cooked sugar syrup into egg whites. It may be flavored spices, nuts, citrus, or chocolate. Once the mixture is cool, it is formed into small mounds and has a fluffy, creamy texture that resembles fudge. If brown sugar is used it is known as *seafoam*.

Dixi-red peach See *peach*.

dl The abbreviation for *deciliter*.

Dobos torte ('doh-bohs) A Hungarian cake with five to nine ultra-thin layers of *sponge cake* sandwiched with a rich coffee or chocolate *buttercream* and topped with a crisp caramel glaze. The cake was created in the late 19th century by Josef Dobos.

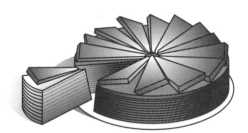

dochinhos de amendoim (do-'kee-nos dee ahmehndo-eem) A bite-size square of sweet peanut cake made by slowly cooking sugar, eggs, roasted peanuts, and freshly grated coconut until thick. Once cooled, it is cut into squares, rolled in confectioners' sugar, and garnished with roasted peanuts.

docker A spiked roller used to pierce holes in rolled dough before baking in order to eliminate air bubbles and allow steam to escape.

dodol (doh-'dohl) 1. A Southeast Asian sweetmeat made from overripe *durian*. 2. A Malaysian pudding made from sticky rice, coconut milk, palm sugar, and brown and granulated sugars. It is cooked in a deep skillet for several hours and stirred continuously until a sticky, brown, shiny, taffy-like mass. Once cooled, it is poured into containers that are made from *pandanus leaves*. This, rich, sweet dessert is served as a snack or spread on toast; it may also be purchased in individual foil or plastic containers.

dolce ('dohl-chay) Italian for "sweet," referring to sweets and including desserts, candies, cakes, and pastries. Also known as *dolci*.

dolce Milanese ('dohl-chay mihl-'ah-neys) A rich, buttery sweet bread from Milan that is packed with raisins and flavored with rum and orange.

dolci ('dohl-chee) See *dolce*.

dollop A small drop of food, usually whipped cream, that is often used as a garnish.

donut Alternate spelling for *doughnut*.

double-acting baking powder See *baking powder*.

double boiler A cooking implement that consists of a bottom pan, usually a saucepan, that holds water and has a second pan that sits above the water so that a gentle steam-induced cooking results. This is used to prepare delicate sauces such as *vanilla sauce*, which would break or cook too quickly when placed over direct heat. Also popular for melting *chocolate*.

double cream A thick, rich cream with over 48% milk fat.

double-cream cheese A variety of naturally sweet cow's milk cheese that is enriched with cream. It contains a minimum of 60% milk fat and has a soft, creamy texture and mild, sweet flavor. These cheeses make an excellent dessert course when served with fruit.

D
d

double magnum See *magnum*.

dough A combination of flour and liquid, usually water or milk, that is mixed together to form a mass that ranges from soft to firm. Other ingredients may also be added depending on the desired dough type. It may be leavened or unleavened and sweet or savory. The texture and consistency will vary as well as the color and flavor. See also *bread dough, pastry dough, pie dough.*

dough conditioner A granular product added to yeast-raised baked goods to ensure good gluten development and a fine crumb. They are used mostly by high-production facilities to compensate for poor flour quality and/or strengthen dough that undergoes rough handling in the automated equipment. They also reduce mixing and fermentation time, but if overused, will result in poor volume and texture. Also referred to as *dough improver.*

dough cutter An expandable, accordion-like metal frame with straight-edged pastry wheels on one side and fluted pastry wheels on the other. The pastry tool is used to cut several pieces of dough at one time, and the width may be adjusted to make the strips thick or thin.

dough hook See *mixer attachments.*

dough improver See *dough conditioner.*

doughnut A deep-fried, individual round of sweet dough that may or may not have a hole in the center. The dough

dough cutter

is leavened by either yeast or baking powder, and can be flavored with nuts, spices, and other ingredients. Typically, the ring-shaped doughnuts with the hole in the center are covered with a flavored glaze or granulated or confectioners' sugar. Doughnuts without the hole are typically filled with jam, cream, or custard. See also *doughnut hole.*

doughnut cutter An aluminum or stainless steel tool used to cut doughnut dough into rings with a hole in the center. It is recommended to dip the cutter in flour as needed to prevent sticking.

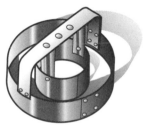

doughnut hole The center of a doughnut dough that remains after the dough has been cut into rings. Typically this dough is also fried and flavored, and sold separately. There is much folklore surrounding the origin of the doughnut hole, but a popular story claims that in 1847, a New England sea captain named Hanson Gregory punched holes in the dough because his mother's doughnuts were not cooked in the center.

dough reaction rate A measurement of how quickly baking powder releases carbon dioxide at room temperature and how much is released with heat. Also referred to as *DRR.*

dough sheeter See *sheeter.*

doum palm (doo-uhm) A palm tree native to the Nile region in Africa, whose edible fruit tastes like gingerbread.

doux (do) The French word for sweet.

dowel A thin, cylindrical piece of plastic or wood that varies from 12 in. to 24 in. (30 cm to 60 cm) in length and ¼ in. to 1 in. (6 mm to 2.5 cm) in diameter. It is primarily used to support cakes that are stacked or tiered.

dowel rod A straight rod, usually wood or plastic, inserted into cake layers to support the weight of tiers. They may be cut to size and are often used in wedding cakes.

dragée (drah-'zhay) 1. A French confection of an almond or other flavored center surrounded by a hard, shiny sugar coating. 2. Tiny, glossy gold or silver sugar balls used to decorate pastries and confections.

dragon's eye A cherry-size, round fruit indigenous to Southeast Asia. The thin, light brown exterior contains a grapelike white flesh that surrounds a single shiny brown inedible seed, giving the appearance of an eye. The fruit has a delicate, mildly sweet flavor and a slightly woody aroma. They may be cooked, but are most often eaten raw. If dried, the fruit has a smoky flavor and is used to make fruit tea. Available October to May. Also referred to as *longan* and *cat's eyes*.

drain To draw off the liquid from a product, usually with a *colander*.

Drambuie (drahm-'boo-ee) A golden Scotch whisky made from spices and herbs, and sweetened with heather honey. Its name derives from a Gaelic expression that translates into "the liquor that satisfies." It is used as a flavoring in desserts and confections.

drapery A swaglike decoration made from *icing, rolled fondant, gum paste, chocolate,* or other pliable pastry product. It is a common design on celebration cakes, particularly wedding cakes. Also known as *garland.*

dredge To coat a product in flour, cornmeal, or finely ground crumbs before frying or sautéing, in order to improve browning of the product. Products may also be dredged in a liquid such as an egg mixture.

dredger A plastic or metal container with a perforated lid, used to sprinkle sugar, cocoa powder, spices, or other ingredients over a product.

dresil (dra-scal) A Tibetan dessert of white rice flavored with butter, brown sugar, nuts, and raisins.

dried fruit Fruit that has been *dehydrated* to remove the moisture. This process concentrates the natural sugars and intensifies the flavor. It also acts as a preservative and increases shelf life. The fruit may be sun-dried or dehydrated mechanically, and used dried or reconstituted in liquid. A large variety of fruits, such as cherries and apricots, can be dried; they are a popular ingredient in desserts, pastries, and confections.

dried milk See *dry milk.*

dried plum or prune paste A paste of dried fruit, frequently used as a fat replacer in baked goods. It is best used in dark products and is effective as a moistener and tenderizer, but does not have the same leavening power as traditional fats. It may be purchased as a paste or made by blending 12 ounces (360 ml) of water for every pound (455 g) of dried plums or prunes.

drier An ingredient that absorbs moisture in products, such as flour, cocoa powder, or starch.

drizzle To lightly pour a liquid, such as chocolate or icing, in a thin steady stream over a product.

drop cookie See *cookie.*

DRR See *dough reaction rate.*

drum sieve See *tamis*.

drupe fruit (droop) Any thin-skinned fruit, such as apricots, plums, cherries, or peaches, that contain one hard central seed surrounded by soft flesh. They are classified as either *freestone* or *clingstone*. Also known as *stonefruit*.

dry ice A crystallized form of carbon dioxide that assumes temperatures of 0°F (−18°C) or below, used for storage and preservation of foods, especially in transport, as it will keep frozen items frozen. When the vapors interact with the air, it gives off its characteristic white smoke. Caution must be taken when working with dry ice because it will burn skin on contact.

dry milk Common name for dried milk. It is made by removing 96% of the water from fat-free (nonfat dry milk) or whole milk (dry whole milk). This process is called spray-dried, and is done by spraying partially evaporated milk into a heat source so that it dries instantly and becomes powder. It is not recommended for use in custards or creams because it does not have the fresh dairy flavor of milk, but may be used in yeast-raised baked goods and cookies. Also known as *dried milk* and *powdered milk*. Also referred to as *dry milk solids* (*DMS*).

dry milk solids See *dry milk*.

ducat ('doo-kaht) A small, delicate Austrian yeast-risen cake dusted with cinnamon sugar and served with warm custard.

duff A Scottish pudding made with dried fruit and spices and steamed or boiled.

du jour (doo'zheur) French for "of the day," referring to a menu item made that day.

duku ('doo-koo) A Malaysian fruit that is a member of the langsat family. It is the size of a large golf ball, with a tough, golden-brown skin that surrounds a sweet, juicy flesh with hints of grapefruit. The small seeds are bitter and not eaten, but the flesh is eaten fresh as a snack or for dessert.

dulce ('dool-say) The Spanish word for sweet.

dumpling A sweet or savory food item that may be poached, steamed, fried, or baked. Sweet dumplings are commonly made of sweet pastry dough that is filled with a fruit mixture and baked or poached in a flavored syrup.

Dundee cake A light-textured fruit cake packed with currants, almonds, spices, candied fruit, and citrus zest and topped with whole blanched almonds. It was created in the 1800s when a cook used the leftover citrus peelings from a marmalade factory and created this cake; named after the Scottish town of Dundee.

Dunkin' Donuts The largest coffee and baked goods chain in the world, with 52 varieties of doughnuts. Founded in 1950 by Bill Rosenberg in Quincy, Massachusetts.

durian ('duhr-ree-en) A fruit of the durian tree, native to Southeast Asia, that resembles a yellowish-green football with spikes. It is highly prized for its intense fragrance, but known for its equally intense odor, which is so strong that the fruit is banned in many hotels in Southeast Asia. Inside its tough exterior are five white segments that surround a few portions of tender, pale-yellow flesh wrapped 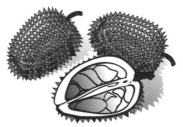 around a large, single, light-brown seed. Both the flesh and the seeds are edible, typically eaten fresh within hours of being split open because the flesh deteriorates quickly once it is exposed to air. Overripe durian is used to make *dodol*, or jam.

durum flour See *flour*.

durum wheat See *wheat*.

dust To sprinkle a powdery substance, such as cocoa powder or confectioners' sugar, over a product.

Dutch-process cocoa A process for treating *cocoa powder* with an alkali, usually potassium carbonate, to neutralize the natural acidity of the cocoa and raise the *pH* level to 7 or above. This results in a richer, darker color and a smoother, less astringent flavor. It also helps the cocoa powder dissolve more easily in water. It is called Dutch process after Dutchman Conrad Van Houten, who invented the machine that extracts the cocoa butter from the cocoa mass.

D
d

Ee

Earl Grey tea A black tea named after the British Prime Minister Earl Charles Grey in the 1830s. Earl Grey is infused with *bergamot orange oil*. This fragrant citrus fruit gives the tea its distinct, refreshing flavor.

earth almond See *earthnut*.

earthenware Porous cooking vessels made of kiln-fired clay. They are glazed on the interior and must be soaked in water before being heated.

earthnut The small, wrinkled tuberous root of an African plant. It has a bumpy brown skin and white flesh that has a sweet nutty flavor similar to almonds. It can be dried and candied or eaten as a snack. It can also be ground into flour or roasted as the base for a coffee drink. The nuts are gluten, cholesterol, and sodium free. In Spain and Mexico, they are used as a base for a popular drink called *horchata*. Also known as *chufa*, *earth almond*, and *tiger nut*.

eau-de-vie (oh-deuh-'vee) French for "water of life," referring to any distilled spirit made from grape wine or fermented fruits.

eau parfumée (oh par-foo-'may) A Moroccan beverage of orange-flavored water scented with burnt *gum arabic*.

Ebbelwoi ('ehb-behl-y) A German apple wine from the town of Sachsenhausen, near Frankfurt, traditionally served in ribbed glasses with wooden lids. It is a dry wine with slight acidity and an alcohol content of 6%.

Eccles cake An oval puff pastry filled with a rich currant mixture and topped with sugar. Originally from the town of Eccles in Lancashire, England, these are typically made individually and served with tea.

éclair (ay-'klehr) An elongated pastry made by piping *pâte à choux* paste into a cylinder and filling it with vanilla *crème pâtisserie* and glazing with *fondant*. They vary from 2 to 6 inches (5 to 15 cm) in length. One of the most popular choux pastries in the world, it may also be made with other flavored fillings.

éclair paste See *pâte à choux*.

Edelpilzkäse ('eh-dehl-piltz-kahs) A firm German dessert cheese made from cow's milk. It has a crumbly, white interior streaked with blue veins and has a strong fruity flavor.

egg The unfertilized ovum produced by a female chicken. It has a hard, porous shell that can absorb odors and flavors; the color is determined by the breed of hen. The two main parts of an egg are the white and the yolk. The white, also known as *albumen,* is protein (10%) and water (90%) The yolk consists of lipoproteins, fats, and emulsifiers such as *lecithin.* The color of the yolk is due to yellow-orange *carotenoids* and is also affected by the hen's feed. All parts of the egg are edible,

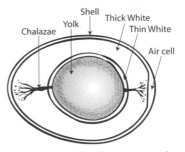

although most people discard the shell. Eggs are classified by a grading system of AA (the highest quality), A, and B. They are sorted and sold in various sizes from jumbo to peewee; however, for commercial purposes, the large egg is preferred. The average egg weighs 2 ounces (55 grams), which is broken down as 1 ounce (30 g) for the white, ⅔ ounce (20g) for the yolk, and ⅙ ounce (5 g) for the shell.

egg cream A New York beverage of milk, *chocolate syrup,* and *seltzer water.* This popular drink contains no egg, but derives its name from the frothy top that resembles beaten egg whites. New Yorkers have been enjoying this soda fountain specialty since the 1930s.

egg-foam method See *mixing methods.*

egg jam A Southeast Asian condiment that is a jam-like custard made from sugar, eggs, and coconut milk and flavored with pandanus leaves or vanilla. It is traditionally spread on toast and eaten for breakfast, with strong coffee that is flavored with sugar and condensed milk.

eggnog A beverage of eggs, cream or milk, sugar, and spices such as cinnamon, nutmeg, and allspice, traditionally served during the Christmas holidays. The mixture is cooked until thick and finished with rum, brandy, or whisky. It may be served warm or chilled.

egg piercer A tool to make a tiny hole in the large end of an egg, which prevents it from cracking during cooking. The egg piercer has a sharp steel pin that is usually spring-loaded.

egg ring A stainless steel ring without a bottom, used to hold an egg while it is being poached or fried.

egg roll wrappers A very thin square of dough traditionally used to wrap egg rolls and spring rolls, but can also be filled with sweet items. The dough is made of flour, water, and salt.

egg separator A tool used to separate eggs into whites and yolks by allowing the egg white to flow through the saucer-like piece while the yolk is held in the cup.

egg substitute A mixture of egg whites, corn oil, a food starch, and artificial coloring, used as a healthy alternative to eggs because it contains no cholesterol. The substitute may be used for making muffins and pancakes, but is not recommended for products that require air being whipped into them, because the gums and other additives prevent it from foaming.

egg timer An hourglass with enough sand to drain from one side to the other in 3 minutes, which is the recommended time to prepare a soft-boiled egg.

egg wash An egg mixture that is brushed onto goods before they are baked; it gives enriched browning, shine, and/or acts as a moisture barrier for the finished item. The wash may be made from whole eggs, yolks only, or whites only, and may or may not include water or milk.

E
e

egg whisk See *whisk*.

egusi (eh-'goo-see) The small, flat, pale seeds of an African watermelon, eaten as a snack or ground and used as a thickener.

eighty-six (86) A kitchen term that refers to running out of an item: when it is no longer available, it is "86ed."

einkorn ('eye'n-korhn) A variety of coarse-grained wheat believed to be the ancestor of modern wheat varieties. It is traced back to southeastern Turkey some 10,000 years ago, when agriculture first began.

Eisenlebkuchen ('eye'z-en-layb-koo-ken) A German spiced cookie covered with chocolate. It is a specialty of Nuremberg.

Eiswein ('eye'z-vine) See *ice wine*.

elasticity A baker's term that refers to a dough's springiness. It significantly contributes to loaf volume and structure. See also *gluten*.

election cake A dried-fruit laden cake flavored with sherry and spices, from New England. It was created in the 18th century and is made to celebrate Election Day.

Electra See *Quady*.

elephant ear See *palmier*.

elephant skin An undesirable crust that forms on the surface of bread doughs when they are *overoxidized* or not properly covered during the *benching* process. The name derives from the appearance of the crust—it resembles wrinkly elephant skin.

Elisen ('eh-liz-en) A German gingerbread leavened with egg whites.

Elsay ('ehl-say) A French custard powder. See *custard powder*.

Elysium (ee-lihs-'see-uhm) See *Quady*.

embroidery piping A style of cake decorating used to create fine-detailed designs that resemble embroidery. This can be done freehand or a pattern can be traced onto the rolled *fondant* covering the cake. To achieve quality embroidery piping, use a very fine round tube, either #00 or #000, with a slightly thinned *royal icing*. See also *brush embroidery* and *eyelet embroidery*.

Emerald Baut See *pluot*.

Emmental cheese ('em-mehn-tahl) Named for Switzerland's Emmental valley, this creamy cheese has a nutty, buttery flavor and pale yellow rind and interior. It is made from partially skimmed unpasteurized cow's milk and pairs well with fruit and dessert wines.

emmer wheat A form of wheat that dates back to Babylonia, where it was first cultivated. Regarded as a cereal grain, it is found in Switzerland and southern Germany. Also called *two-grained spelt* or *starch wheat*.

empañada (ehm-pah-'nah-dah) A deep-fried turnover that may be filled with meat, vegetables, or something sweet, popular in Central and South America.

Emperor grape See *grape*.

emulsified shortening See *shortening, high-ratio*.

emulsifier A chemical additive used to achieve a permanent uniform suspension of two liquids.

emulsion A uniform mixture of two unmixable liquids. Emulsions may be divided into two categories: temporary and permanent. A *temporary emulsion* will stay suspended for a limited period of time; a *permanent emulsion* uses an *emulsifier* such as egg yolk to form a permanent suspension.

enamelware Cookware or bakeware made of cast iron or steel that has been enameled to prevent rusting.

encapsulated flavoring A dry flavoring or spice that has been coated to protect the flavor from heat, light, and moisture. It has a longer shelf life and can also withstand the heat of the oven better than other flavorings.

en croûte (ahn 'kroot) The French term for a food wrapped in pastry dough and baked.

endosperm See *wheat kernel.*

Engadine ('ehn-gah-din-uh) A Swiss covered tart of short dough filled with a rich mixture of walnuts caramelized in sugar, cream, and honey. From the Graubünden canton of Switzerland, it is also known as *Engadiner Nusstorte.*

Engadiner Nusstorte ('ehn-gah-din-uh 'nuhs-stuhrt-uh) See *Engadine.*

English breakfast tea A robust blend of black teas from several areas, including India, Sri Lanka, Kenya, and China. The tea was created in Edinburgh, Scotland. Tea houses in London began adding the name "English" to the tea in the 19th century, and it is still a favorite there today.

English Morello cherry See *cherry.*

English muffin A small, round yeast pastry formed in an *English muffin ring* and baked on a griddle. It is recommended to split open the muffin with a fork in order to reveal the nooks and crevices that are characteristic of this product. The muffin is usually toasted before serving.

English muffin ring A bottomless ring used to shape *English muffins* and *crumpets.* See also *crumpet ring.*

English Swiss roll The English version of the American jelly roll, with a thicker layer of sponge cake so it is not rolled as tightly. See *jelly roll.*

English walnut See *walnut.*

enology (ee-'noh-loh-jhee) See *viniculture.*

en papillote (ehn-pah-pee-'yoht) A cooking technique by which food is placed in a piece of *parchment paper* that is folded to seal. As the food bakes, it lets off steam, which puffs the parchment paper into a dome and cooks the food.

enriched dough A bread dough that contains some fat, dairy, eggs, or sugar. Products made from enriched doughs are generally richer and tenderer than those from lean yeast doughs, because the fat shortens the gluten strands and prevents them from forming too strong a structure. Common examples of enriched breads are *brioche* and *challah.*

enriched flour Flour from which the bran and germ have been removed from the endosperm during milling. The milling also removes many vitamins, minerals, and fiber. Enrichment replaces certain vitamins and minerals, such as niacin, riboflavin, and thiamin. Flour enrichment began in the United States in the 1940s to help prevent diseases caused by vitamin and mineral deficiencies, and the process is subject to U.S. Food and Drug Administration regulations.

enrobe To coat a candy or pastry with chocolate, sugar, or fondant. Enrobing is usually done by pouring rather than dipping, and may be done with a machine called an *enrober.*

enrober A machine that coats chocolates and other confections with chocolate.

entremet (ehn-trah-'may) 1. French for "between courses," referring to desserts served after the cheese course. 2. A composed dessert, which means it has several components, that may be hot, cold, or frozen.

entremet ring See *cake ring.*

E
e

enzyme A protein that acts as a catalyst to increase the speed of chemical reactions that would otherwise occur slowly.

épi ('eh-pee) The French word for wheat, referring to a bread shape that resembles a sheaf of wheat. It is traditionally made from French bread dough and cut with scissors.

epicure ('ehp-ih-kyoor) A person with a fascination and deep interest in all things related to the culinary and gastronomic arts.

Epiphany cake See *Twelfth Night cake.*

ergosterol, irradiated A vitamin D food additive used to fortify milk.

Eskimo Pie A square of vanilla ice cream surrounded by a hard chocolate shell. It was invented in 1920 by Christian Nelson in Onawa, Ohio, and was originally called the I-Scream-Bar.

épi

espresso A very strong Italian coffee made by forcing hot water through finely ground coffee beans by means of high pressure. The resulting beverage is thicker and blacker than drip coffee, and is distinguished by reddish-brown foam, called *crema,* which floats on the surface. Espresso is traditionally served in a 1.5 ounce (45 ml) cup, or may be used as a base for a variety of coffee drinks. A single shot of espresso is made with ¼ ounce (7 to 8 g) of coffee and a double shot of espresso is made with ½ ounce (14 to 15 g) of coffee.

espresso con panna An *espresso* coffee served with a dollop of whipped cream.

espresso cup The 1.5-ounce (45 ml) cup that *espresso* is traditionally served in.

espresso lungo (ehs- preh-z 'loon-goh) *Espresso* made with twice the amount of water as a regular espresso.

espresso machiatto (ehs-'prehs-oh mah-kee-'aht-toh) An *espresso* with a dollop of steamed milk.

espresso powder Finely ground powder made from roasted espresso beans that dissolves instantly in water. It is often used to infuse a strong coffee flavor into desserts and pastries.

essence A concentrated liquid flavoring derived from natural sources such as herbs, spices, or flowers.

Essencia (eh-'sehn-see-ah) See *Quady.*

essential oil See *volatile oil.*

ethylene gas A natural gas produced by ripening fruits and vegetables that promotes further ripening.

ethyl isobutyrate A fruit-like additive used to flavor candies and ice creams.

ethyl-methyl-phenyl-glycidate A strawberry-like additive used to flavor candies and ice creams.

ethyl nonanoate A Cognac-like additive used to flavor candies and ice creams.

ethyl propionate A rum-like additive used to flavor candies and baked goods.

ethyl sorbate A tropical fruit-like additive used to flavor candies, ice creams, and baked goods.

European bake A baker's term that refers to a rich, deep golden-brown crust.

European plum See *plum.*

European-style butter See *butter.*

eutectic (u-'tehk-tihk) A combination of fats that lowers the melting point of a product.

evaporated milk Canned *homogenized* milk made by heating whole milk until 60% of the water is evaporated. Although there is no sugar added, the milk has a caramel-like flavor owing to the caramelization of the *lactose* during the evaporation process. It is available in whole, skim, low-fat, and nonfat varieties, and may be used as a substitute for milk by adding an equal amount of water by volume. Evaporated milk will last indefinitely if unopened.

Eve's pudding The English version of *tarte Tatin*. The use of apples represents the apple given to Adam by Eve in the Garden of Eden.

executive chef The person responsible for managing all aspects of the kitchen, including food production, menu development, staff management, food and labor costs, and purchasing and inventory control.

extensibility The dough's ability to stretch and hold a shape. See also *gluten*.

extension work Another name for *bridge*.

extract A concentrated flavoring mixture of ethyl alcohol and natural oils that may be pure, or imitation, which is synthesized from chemicals. Extracts are sensitive to heat and light and should be stored in a cool, dark place.

extraction rate The percentage of flour extracted from wheat once the bran and germ have been removed. It is typically 72% for white flour.

extra-virgin olive oil See *olive oil*.

eyelet embroidery A type of cake decoration by which a piece of rolled *fondant* is cut with a *decorative cutter*. The cutouts are removed and the remaining fondant, which has the design of the cutout pieces, is placed over the cake. The design may then be enhanced with piping to add further depth and design. The cutout pieces may also be attached for additional decoration.

Ezekiel mix (ah-zee-kee-ehl) A mixture of flour and grains, used in bread baking, that usually contains wheat flour, spelt, barley, ground lentils, and millet. Its name derives from the formula found in the Bible (Ezekiel 4:9).

E
e

Ff

F
f

F The abbreviation for *Fahrenheit*.

Fabbri See *amarena cherry*.

Fahrenheit ('fehr-uhn-hite) The temperature scale that records the freezing of water at 32°F (0°C) and the boiling of water at 212°F (100°C). It was invented by the German physicist Gabriel Daniel Fahrenheit. See also *Important Temperatures Every Pastry Chef and Baker Should Know* and *Conversion Formulas and Equivalents* appendices.

fairy floss The Australian term for *cotton candy*.

faiscre grotha ('fay-scrah groh-thah) A creamy Irish cheese made from cow's milk and similar to cream cheese in texture and flavor.

falernum (fuh-ler-nuhm) A sweet syrup from the West Indies, made with lime, ginger, and almonds.

falling number test A test that measures the degree of *amylase* activity in flour.

faluche (fah-loosh-eh) A small, round Belgian bread that looks like a mini pizza. It is cut open, spread with butter and sugar, and reheated before serving.

fancy patent flour See *flour, patent*.

Fantasia nectarine See *nectarine*.

far Breton A flan from Brittany, France, made with rum-soaked prunes and served warm or cold.

farina (fuh-'ree-nuh) The Italian word for flour, referring to a granular meal made from hard wheat flour, potatoes, tubers, or other grains. It is rich in protein and commonly used in puddings, porridge, or as a thickener.

farine (fah-rihn) The French word for flour.

farinette (fah-rihn-eht) A sweet or savory pancake from the Auvergne region of France.

farinograph A tool used to test a bread's resistance to break-down or collapse when made with a specific flour.

farl (fahrl) Similar to a scone, a thin Scottish griddle cake made of oatmeal. The name derives from "fardel," which means "fourth part," because these are made round and cut into four parts.

farmers cheese Similar to cottage cheese, a mild, slightly tangy American cheese made from whole or partially skimmed cow's milk; it can be sliced or crumbled.

farro See *spelt*.

Fasnacht ('fahs-nahkt) A yeast-raised potato doughnut, served on Shrove Tuesday. It is deep-fried in pork fat, a reference to using up animal fat, which was forbidden during Lent. It is not confirmed whether its origin is Pennsylvania Dutch or German, but it is traditionally served at breakfast, with jam or molasses.

fat See *fats and oils*.

fat rascal A large scone filled with candied fruit, almonds, and spices. It is a regional specialty of Yorkshire, England, and is typically served warm with butter.

fats and oils An essential ingredient in the production of baked goods and confections. There are many types of fats, including *butter, margarine, shortening, lard,* and *oil*. The main functions of fat are to provide tenderness, moisture, and flavor to baked goods. They also assist in leavening, prevent staling, and creating flakiness in *laminated dough*. Scientifically, fats are *lipids* that are solid at room temperature and oils are lipids that are liquid at room temperature. They are categorized as either saturated or unsaturated. *Saturated fat* is derived from animal meat and dairy fats. *Unsaturated fat* is derived from plants. See also *monounsaturated fat, polyunsaturated fat,* and *hydrogenated fat*.

fat substitute A product meant to replace traditional fats (butter, shortening, oil) in food in order to reduce calories and fat content. Owing to the many functions fat performs in food, no single substitute can produce the same texture, flavor, or color of a product made with traditional fats. See also *Leanesse, Olestra,* and *Simplesse*.

fatty acid A building block of fat, consisting of a long chain of carbon atoms that have hydrogen attached to them. They may be saturated or unsaturated. See *saturated fat* and *unsaturated fat*.

Fauchon A world-renowned Parisian shop that specializes in luxury foods, including confectionery, cakes, and pastries. It was founded by Auguste Fauchon in 1886, at the Place de Madeleine.

FDA The acronym for the U.S. Food and Drug Administration. It is part of the U.S. Department of Health and Human Services, and is responsible for protecting the nation's health against unsafe foods and other products. The agency approves and regulates food additives and sets food-labeling standards.

feijoa (fay-yoh-ah) A South American fruit that resembles an elongated egg and has a thin, light green skin surrounding a highly aromatic cream-colored flesh with a jelly-like center. The flavor is a sweet combination of guava, pineapple, and mint. The fruit is cultivated in New Zealand and California. They are a popular item for fruit salad and dessert garnishes. New Zealand feijoas are available from spring to early summer and California feijoas are available from late fall to January. Also known as *pineapple guava*.

fendu A French bread that resembles a *bâtard*, or short baguette, with a crease down the center. Also known as *split bread*.

fennel ('fehn-uhl) A native Mediterranean plant whose seeds are used as a spice and whose bulbous root is used as a vegetable. The two types of fennel are common fennel or *Roman fennel* and *Florence fennel* or *finocchio*. The small, oval greenish-brown seeds come from common fennel; they are available whole or ground and used in many Italian breads and desserts. Florence fennel has the flavor of sweet anise.

fenugreek ('fehn-yoo-greek) A bittersweet herb native to Asia and southern Europe, whose seeds are used whole in spice blends and teas, and ground to produce an artificial maple flavor for candies and ice cream.

Feqqas (fehg-'ghahs) A variety of Moroccan cookies typically served with mint tea. Popular versions include peanut feqqas that are made from cream cheese dough, filled with butter and roasted peanuts, then rolled into a cylinder and chilled before being cut into rounds and baked. Almond-anise feqqas are made with pastry dough flavored with ground almonds, anise, golden raisins, sesame seeds, and orange flower water; the dough is baked in a flat cylinder and then sliced into individual pieces and baked again until dry and crunchy.

F
f

fermentation The process by which yeast breaks down sugars and converts it into alcohol and carbon dioxide. This is one of the most crucial stages in the creation of bread because it provides both leavening and flavor. It also refers to the period that the dough is allowed to rest after kneading, which affects the flavor, appearance, and texture of the finished product. Various factors control the rate of fermentation, including the temperature of dough, amount of salt, type and amount of sugar, *pH* of the dough, and type and amount of yeast.

feuilletage (fuh-yuh-tahz) The French word for "flaky," referring to *puff pastry* or the process of making it.

fiadone (phee-ah-'doh-nay) A Corsican cake made with eggs, sugar, lemon peel, brandy, and Broccio cheese, a soft, creamy ewe's milk cheese from Corsica.

fiber The parts of fruits, vegetables, legumes, and grains that the body is not able to digest. This roughage in a person's diet has been linked with lowering cholesterol levels and risks of certain cancers.

ficelle (fee-'sell) The French word for "string," referring to a French bread that resembles a very thin *baguette.*

fidget pie A Welsh pie of potatoes, apples, onions, and unsmoked bacon, baked with a top crust.

FIFO The acronym for "first in, first out," referring to an inventory system that rotates products, particularly perishables, so that they are used in order of their receipt. This reduces spoilage and waste, and helps control food cost.

fig A soft "fruit" of any of a variety of wild or cultivated trees grown in a Mediterranean climate. It is an ancient food whose use can be traced back to the early Greek and Roman Empires. There are hundreds of varieties that come in a wide range of colors and shapes, and may be purchased fresh, dried, canned, or candied. The most common varieties are *Brown Turkey, Mission, Kadota,*  *Calimyrna,* and *Symrna.* The Brown Turkey is also known as *Black Spanish;* they are large with mahogany-purple skin and a juicy red flesh. The Mission or Black Mission fig is named after the Spanish missionaries who brought them to California; they have a dark pink interior and are best for cooking or eating fresh. The large Kadota is used primarily for canning; it has a yellowish-green skin and purplish-white interior. Calimyrna from California and Smyrna from Turkey are large, sweet figs that are greenish in color and used mostly for drying. Unripe figs can be ripened at room temperature, and once ripe, may be stored in the refrigerator up to three days.

Fig Newton An American fig bar produced by Nabisco. It is a soft, cakelike square of pastry that surrounds a sweet fig filling, created in 1891 by the Kennedy Biscuit Works in Cambridgeport, Massachusetts, and believed to be named after the nearby town of Newton. Variations on the original are now available with strawberry, apple, and raspberry fillings. It also comes in low-fat and 100% whole-grain versions; Fig Newton Minis were also recently introduced. The cookie is the company's number-three bestseller, at more than a billion a year.

figuette A drink made from dried figs and juniper berries.

filbert See *hazelnut.*

filhós See *malassadas.*

F
f

filo See *phyllo.*

filigree work A cake-decorating technique made by piping *royal icing* on a sheet of parchment paper. Once the pieces have hardened, they are attached to the cake. The pieces may be one-dimensional or made multidimensional by attaching various pieces together. They are generally large and used as adornments for the tops of cakes and between tiers.

filter To strain solids from liquids, using a sieve or cheesecloth.

financier A delicate sponge-like cake made with egg whites, *beurre noisette,* and ground almonds. Individual financiers are traditionally rectangular but also found in oval and round shapes. Large financiers  are baked in molds, with almonds lining the pan so they adhere to the cake as it bakes. They may also be baked in thin sheets and layered, or cut in ovals to use as a base for small pastries and petit fours. They were created by pâtissier Lanse and called *financiers* because they were dry so that when financiers ate them on the floor or the Stock Exchange they would not get their fingers sticky.

fine olive oil See *olive oil.*

Finger banana See *banana.*

finish In pastry, refers to the completion of a dish by decorating it.

fino ('fee-noh) The Italian word for "fine." See also *olive oil* and *sherry.*

finocchio See *fennel.*

firm-ball See *Sugar Cooking Stages* appendix.

firni (firr-nee) A rice flour and milk pudding from Pakistan, often flavored with rose water and garnished with almonds or pistachios.

flake To break or separate small pieces of food, usually pastry, with a fork or other utensil.

flaky A term to describe the light, crisp texture of a product. It is often associated with *pie dough* and *puff pastry.*

flaky pastry A term used to describe a pastry with a flaky texture. See *flaky.*

flaky pie dough See *pie dough.*

flambé (flahm-'bay) The process of pouring liqueur over a sweet or savory item and setting it on fire. This is done for showmanship and to enhance the flavor of the food. Also known as *flaming* a product or a product that has been "*flambéed.*"

flambéed See *flambé.*

flambé trolley A small rolling table with one or two burners, used in restaurants for *flaming* dishes at a table. Classically known as a *guéridon.*

Flame grape See *grape.*

flaming See *flambé.*

flamusse (flahm-'oos) An apple pudding similar to *clafoutis,* a specialty of Nivernais and Burgundy, France.

flan (flahn) 1. The Spanish term for *crème caramel,* a baked custard with a soft caramel top. 2. An open-faced custard tart filled with fruit, cream, or a savory mixture. 3. The British term for a *tart.*

flan de naranja (flan day nah-'raan-jga) An orange-flavored Spanish custard, usually garnished with crystallized oranges.

F
f

flan de queso (flahn day 'kay-soh) A Peruvian custard made with cottage cheese, condensed milk, and eggs. It is traditionally served with stewed fruit.

flan ring A bottomless, straight-sided 1-inch (2.5 cm)-high metal ring with a rim, used to support the pastry for a flan or tart. The rim is rolled over to prevent a sharp edge.

flapjack 1. A British bar cookie made from rolled oats, butter, brown sugar, and light treacle. 2. An American slang term for a *pancake*.

flatbread 1. A form of bread that may or may not contain *leavening*. Usually very thin, flatbreads have textures that range from chewy to crisp. They are generally served with soups, salads, and cheeses, although some ethnic breads, such as *naan* and *pita bread*, and are used as an edible utensil to hold or scoop food.

flatbrod ('flaht-brahd) A Scandinavian, thin cracker-like bread made from rye flour.

flat icing A pourable simple icing made by adding liquid, such as citrus juice, water, milk, or maple syrup, to sifted *confectioners' sugar* and mixing until smooth. It is typically drizzled over baked goods such as cinnamon buns, danish, and coffee cakes to add a bit of sweetness and enhance their appearance.

Flavor Fall See *pluot.*

Flavor Gator See *pluot.*

flavoring agent See *extracts.*

Flavor King See *pluot.*

Flavorosa See *pluot.*

Flavor Queen See *pluot.*

flaxseed A small, nutritious seed with a mild nutty flavor. If ground and mixed with liquid, it forms a gelatinous mixture that is similar to egg whites. Although it may be substituted for eggs in baked goods, it does not have the same leavening ability. It is also used in the production of linseed oil.

Fleur-de-lis (flohr-duh-lee) The French word for "lily flower," referring to a piped decorative design that resembles a lily flower. It may be made from buttercream or royal icing, with a plain or star tip.

fleur de sel (flehr duh sell) See *salt.*

fleur de sel de Carmargue (flehr duh sell duh 'kahr-mahr-goo) See *salt.*

fleuron (fluh-rawng) A crescent-shaped piece of *puff pastry*, usually used as a garnish.

Fleximold See *flexipan.*

Flexipan A nonstick flexible *silicone mold* used for baking or freezing. They come in many shapes and sizes and are manufactured by the Demarle company, in France. Also known as fleximold.

floating island A dessert of poached *meringue* balls topped with caramel and served in a pool of *crème anglaise*. The French name for this dessert is *île flottant;* also known as *oeufs à la neige.*

floodwork See *run-out.*

floodwork monogramming A technique used in cake decoration whereby a letter or series of letters is traced onto parchment paper. Royal icing is then used to outline the traced letter(s) and allowed to dry. Once the royal icing outline has dried and formed a dam, thinned royal icing is flooded in using floodwork techniques. This dries until hard, and is then removed and used as needed to form a 2-dimensional piece.

Florence fennel See *fennel.*

florentine A confection of butter, honey, sugar, cream, almonds, and candied orange peel, cooked to the soft ball stage (240°F/155°C) and then dropped by mounds onto cookie sheets and baked until the mounds flatten out. The result is a chewy candylike cookie traditionally coated with a thin layer of wavy tempered chocolate on one side.

flour The finely ground and sifted meal of grains, vegetables, grasses, or nuts. A vital baking ingredient, its main functions are to provide structure, absorb liquids, and contribute color, flavor, and nutritional value. The most common flours are:

All-purpose Typically a blend of hard and soft wheat flours, it has a protein content of 9.5 to 11.5% and may be bleached or unbleached.

Artisan An unbleached flour milled from hard red winter wheat. It has a low protein content of around 11.5% but the high quality allows artisan breads to develop good gluten and undergo a long fermentation process, which develops flavor.

Atta flour A coarse-grained wheat flour found throughout Asia. It is used in traditional breads and pancakes.

Baker's A wheat flour containing a high degree of protein or gluten, between 12 and 26%. This high concentration of gluten is beneficial in the production of yeast breads requiring high gluten content. Also known as *strong flour.*

Barley See *barley.*

Besan See *flour, gram.*

Bleached Flour that has gone through a whitening process to remove the natural yellow pigment. This is accomplished through either aging the flour or adding bleaching agents such as *benzoyl peroxide* or *chlorine* gas.

Bread Flour used for products that require good-quality gluten formation. It contains between 11 and 13% protein content, and is milled from either hard red winter wheat or hard red spring. It may be purchased bleached or unbleached, and is typically used for breads, rolls, and sweet yeast dough products.

Buckwheat Made from buckwheat, it has a strong, distinct flavor and dark color and is often used in combination with wheat flour owing to its low gluten-forming abilities. It is most often used to make Russian *blini.*

Cake Enriched, bleached flour from soft winter wheat that has a protein content of 7 to 8%. Used primarily for cakes and biscuits.

Chickpea See *flour, gram.*

Clear A low-quality commercial flour. It is less refined and higher in protein than bread flour; it is milled from the outer layer of the wheat endosperm and is slightly darker in color. It has a 16% protein content and is often used in combination with low-gluten flours in bread production.

Corn A no-gluten flour milled from either white, yellow, or blue cornmeal.

Durum Flour ground from durum wheat, with a high protein content of between 12 and 15%. Its bright yellow color makes it popular for pasta products and semolina breads.

Enriched A white flour enriched with B vitamins, minerals, and iron to replace many of the nutrients lost during the milling process.

Graham Similar to whole wheat flour but with the bran finely ground. Typically used in soft breads and cookies.

F
f

Gram A pale yellow high-protein flour made from chickpeas that have been dried and ground. It is used extensively in Indian cooking. Also known as *besan* and *chickpea flour.*

Green White flour that has been aged either naturally or with the use of chemical additives. It yields bread that has poor volume, pale crust color, and a gummy crumb.

High gluten A flour with a protein level of about 14%. Its good gluten-developing properties make it a popular choice for yeast products that require strength and structure.

Instant A partially cooked, pregelatinized wheat flour that is low in protein and has malted barley added. It has been formulated to dissolve quickly in either hot or cold liquids, and is most often used to thicken gravies and sauces. Because of its low-protein content, it is also sometimes used in making pie crusts and other recipes that call for cake flour. The most well-known brand is Wondra.

Nut A flour-type product made by grinding nuts, such as almonds and hazelnuts, into an extremely fine powder. It is commonly used in cakes, doughs, and macaroons. Also known as *almond meal, hazelnut meal*, etc.

Oat Made from oat groats that have been ground into a powder. It does not contain any gluten.

Pastry Available bleached or unbleached, it is milled from soft winter wheat and has a protein content of 8 to 9%. It is a good choice for cookies and pastries.

Patent The highest-quality white flour available. It consists of the first streams of flour and does not contain any bran or germ, which renders it low in ash content and very white. There are different grades depending on which streams of flour are blended during the milling process, but the highest quality is called *fancy patent flour* or *extra short flour.*

Potato A gluten-free flour made from potatoes that have been cooked and dried. It is used as a thickener and a flour substitute in some baked goods for people who have wheat allergies.

Rice A finely ground, powdery flour made from white rice. It is popular in Asia as a thickener and also in place of flour to make cookies, cakes, and pastries. It is not recommended for bread baking as it does not contain any gluten.

Rye See *rye flour.*

Self-rising Available as a cake or all-purpose flour, it has baking powder and salt added to it.

Sorghum A high-protein flour made from finely ground sorghum. It is used in India to make *flatbread*. Also known as *jowar.*

Soy A high-protein flour made from finely ground soybeans. It is often mixed with other flours to make cakes and is used to make confections in Japan, where it is known as *kinako.*

Stone-ground Flour that has been ground between two slow-moving stones. Some bakers believe this milling process produces a better-tasting bread.

Straight Milled from the whole endosperm, this high-ash content, hard-wheat flour is made from a combination of all streams of flour created during the milling process. It has a protein content of around 11.5% and is a good choice for hearth breads.

Strong A flour with strong gluten-forming ability. Strong flours generally have a high protein content and form good-quality, elastic gluten. Common examples are *bread flour* and *high gluten flour* and they are typically used in bread production.

Unbleached A naturally aged flour that has not been bleached. This helps maintain the flavor, aroma, and crumb color of the bread.

Weak A flour with weak gluten-forming ability. This is desirable for making tender cakes and pastries. Common examples are *cake flour* and *pastry flour.*

Wheat A general term for white flour that has been milled from the endosperm. It does not contain the same nutrients as whole wheat flour and often has caramel coloring or molasses added to it to resemble whole wheat.

Wholemeal Flour that is made from the whole wheat grain and is available finely ground or coarse ground. It has a shorter shelf life than other flours and creates a dense, crumbly loaf with an earthy taste. Typically it is used in combination with other flours to yield a less dense product.

Whole wheat An unbleached, whole-grain flour that contains the bran, germ, and endosperm. It may be coarse or fine and milled from soft wheat with a low protein content (11%) or hard wheat with a high protein content (14%). Breads made from whole wheat flour have a darker color, stronger flavor, and denser texture.

Whole white wheat A relatively new type of wheat grown in North America. The bran of the white wheat is lighter in color and milder in flavor than whole wheat. It is milled from hard white winter wheat and has a golden color and slightly sweet taste. It is also comparable to whole wheat flour in dietary fiber.

flower, crystallized Flowers that have been preserved by *crystallization.* The most common crystallized flowers are violets and rose petals. Also known as *candied flowers.*

flower, edible Edible flowers that are typically used as a garnish or ingredient.

flower former A plastic form used in the production of icing flowers. Flowers are piped and dried on a form shaped like an inverted bell. This allows the flowers to dry with a natural curve. The forms can be found in many sizes depending on the desired size of the finished flower.

flower nail A flat 1-inch (2.5 cm) disc that sits on a pinlike stem, used in the production of icing flowers. Icing flowers are piped onto the round platform and removed with a small spatula or scissors. Also known as *rose nail.*

floyeres ('floh-yah-rays) An almond-stuffed pastry roll, popular in Greece.

fluffernutter sandwich An American sandwich made with white bread, preferably *Wonder bread,* peanut butter, and *Marshmallow Fluff,* a brand of marshmallow cream.

fluid ounce A liquid volume measure the equivalent of 1⁄16 of a pint; abbreviated as fl. oz. in recipes. It is used in the U.S. system of weights and measures.

flummery A British dessert of fruit, semolina pudding, jam, and fresh cream. The recipe dates back to the 17th century and was similar to porridge because at one time oatmeal was used as the thickening agent.

flute 1. To *crimp* the edge of a pie crust. 2. To carve a decorative design into a vegetable, usually a mushroom. 3. A stemmed Champagne glass, tall and with a narrow body.

F
f

flûte A long, thin loaf of French bread that is between a *baguette* and a *ficelle* in size.

fluted A decorative pattern that resembles a scalloped or ruffled edge. Many tart pans and molds have fluted edges to create a decorative effect on the product.

foam-type icing See *boiled icing.*

focaccia (foh-'kah-cha) A square or rectangular, rustic Italian bread. It should be 1 to 1¼ inches (2.5 to 3.1 cm) thick, with a substantial golden brown crust and a tender, large-holed crumb. It is generally baked in a flat sheet pan and its characteristic dimpled top can be sprinkled with coarse salt, olive oil, herbs, cheeses, and/or other items. The name is derived from the Latin word for "hearth," referring to how the breads were baked before the advent of ovens.

foguete (fo-gha-tay) Literally "rocket" in Portuguese, a deep-fried tube of pastry that is filled with pineapple, cashews, and raisins. It is flavored with rose water, dipped in sugar syrup, and dusted with confectioners' sugar before serving.

foil candy cup A small fluted foil cup used to hold candies and truffles. They are usually silver or gold, but can be found in other colors.

fold 1. To gently combine light, airy ingredients into heavier ingredients, with the intention of losing as little air as possible. 2. To create layers in *laminated dough* by "folding" the dough with a *letter fold* or *book fold.* 3. To release the gasses in a bread dough and strengthen it.

fondant (fohn-'dhont) See *poured fondant* and *rolled fondant.*

fondant funnel A conical tool with a hinged handle used to control the flow of liquid with one hand. It is used to pour fondant or glazes onto petit fours and pastries. It can also be used to fill truffle shells and dispense sauce onto plates. There are different tip sizes to adjust the rate of product flow and a stand is available to hold the funnel while being refilled. Also known as *sauce gun.*

fondant icing See *icing.*

fondant sugar Another name for 12X *confectioners' sugar.*

fond de pâtisserie (fohn deh pah-tiss-ehr-ree) A French term to refer to a sweet base or shell used for cakes or pastries. It can be a *pie dough, puff pastry, sponge, meringue,* or *cookie* base.

fondue A Swiss specialty that calls for cooking food in a central, tabletop pot; it may be sweet or savory. A popular sweet fondue is made with melted chocolate to which cream or liqueur may be added. The mixture is kept warm in a fondue pot and used for dipping pieces of cake, fruit, or pastries.

food additive A substance added to processed foods to help improve taste, color, and shelf life. The additives may be natural or synthetic, and are typically not consumed as food in and of themselves. They must be approved by the FDA and clearly identified on the label.

food coloring A food-safe dye used to color pastry products such as chocolate, fondant, and marzipan. They are available in a wide range of colors and may be purchased as a paste, powder, or liquid that is either water or oil based.

food cost percent The amount of money an establishment spends on food, whether it is sold, stolen, wasted, or given away. This is generally figured by adding up all receipts for products purchased through vendors or other sources of material goods. Gross profit is calculated by subtracting food cost from gross revenue, or the amount the establishment takes in during a given period. It is expressed as a percentage that is called *food cost percent* (FC%), a ratio of the amount of money used in order to generate a particular dollar amount. Generally food cost percent is ⅓ or less the total revenue received by an establishment. For instance, an establishment that makes $500,000 a year in total sales and has a 32% food cost means that $160,000 actual money is spent on food purchases. Traditionally bakeries, pastry shops, and pastry departments generate a FC% between 9 and 20 percent, although establishments that use an extensive quantity of imported items or prepackaged pastry items may realize a much higher FC%.

food lacquer A food-grade product used to add shine and protection to chocolate and sugar showpieces. It is available in both glossy and matte.

food mill A kitchen tool used for straining, pureeing, and separating food solids from pulp or liquids. The food mill is a hopper with a hand-crank mechanism that forces food through small holes in changeable disks at the bottom.

food processor A kitchen appliance with a motor base and drive shaft and bowl, with an S-shaped steel blade that fits over the shaft and provides cutting ability. A lid locks into place on top. By turning the machine on, it will chop, puree, mince, and even knead. Other attachments allow the machine to shred, slice, and perform other cutting chores. Foods may be fed through a shoot that is attached to the lid.

foo-foo ('foo-foo) A West African bread made from mashed boiled plantains.

fool A chilled British dessert of strained fruit puree that is sweetened and mixed with twice its volume of whipped cream. It dates back to the 15th century.

foot A large, flat spot on the bottom of a confection owing to excess chocolate that has accumulated at the base. It is common in dipped confections and is not desirable because it diminishes the product's appearance.

Forastero See *chocolate.*

Forelle pear (fuhr-'rehl-pehr) See *pear.*

form V The stable form of cocoa butter crystals obtained through proper *tempering.*

Formosa oolong tea A Taiwanese tea renowned for its exquisite bouquet. It is considered one of the world's best and most expensive. Its leaves turn a rich copper color when steeped. It has the delicate flavor of fresh peaches and a hint of spice with no astringency or bitterness. *Formosa* is the former name of Taiwan and also means "beautiful" in Dutch, which was what they called the island.

Formosa pouching tea An expensive Tawainese oolong tea with a light peachy flavor and pale yellow color.

fortified wine See *wine.*

fortune cookie A thin, crisp crescent-shaped cookie that contains a small paper that offers a "fortune" or words of wisdom. It is believed to have originated in California, in 1916, introduced by a noodle manufacturer named Davis Jung. It is believed he got the idea from the ancient Chinese practice of exchanging covert messages inside buns.

fouet The French word for whisk.

fougasse (foo-gahs) A bread shape made by slitting an oval piece of dough with long alternating cuts on either side, then pulling them open prior to baking. It is somewhat flat and thin. The name derives from the Latin *focus,* which means "fireplace," because it was originally cooked on a hot hearthstone. It is sometimes called *ladder bread* because the openings have a ladder-like appearance.

F
f

four fold See *book fold*.

fourrer (foor-'reh) A French term that refers to the insertion of a raw or cooked filling into a sweet or savory item such as pastry cream into an éclair.

fractionation A technique developed in the 1950s that enables flour to be produced with a much higher or lower protein content.

fragole al aceto ('frah-goh-leh ahl ah-'chet-toh) An Italian dessert of wild strawberries that have been marinated in *balsamic vinegar*.

fragole al vino ('frah-goh-leh ahl 'vee-noh) An Italian dessert of wild strawberries that have a mixture of sugar and wine poured over at tableside.

fraise (frehz) The French word for *strawberry*.

fraise des bois (frez day bwah) French for "strawberry of the woods," referring to a tiny, triangular wild strawberry with an intense flavor. They are native to France and grow in northern Scandinvia and Central Europe. Also known as *alpine strawberry*.

fraisier See *bagatelle*.

framboise (frahm-'bwahz) 1. The French word for raspberry. 2. A clear French raspberry liqueur distilled from the juice of raspberries.

francesina (fran-che-zee-nah) A thick, soft type of breadstick.

Frangelico (frahn-'jell-ih-koh) A golden-brown liqueur made from an extraction of hazelnuts. It is produced in Canale, Italy, and has 24% alcohol by volume (48 proof). Legend has it that the name comes from its inventor, a hermit called Fra Angelica, who was known for his unusual liqueur creations. Its distinctive packaging is a bottle shaped like a monk, with a white waist cord. It is a popular addition to coffee and espresso.

frangipane (fruhn-juh-'pahn) An almond cream used as a filling for pastries such as *pithivier* and *jalousie*, or baked as a cake and used as a base for *petit four glace* and other pastries. It is named after an Italian nobleman named Marquis Muzio Frangipani. While he was living in Paris, he invented a bitter almond-scented perfume that was used on gloves; this inspired the French pastry cooks to create this popular pastry item, also known as *frangipani*.

Frangipani (fruhn-juh-'pahn-ee) The Italian word for *frangipane*.

frappe A confectionery ingredient added to some products such as taffy and fudge in order to aerate them. It typically has a base of gelatin and sugars or albumen.

frappé (frah-'pay) 1. A sweet or savory slushy made from fruit juice or other liquid flavorings and sometimes sugar, served as a drink or dessert.

freddo The Italian word for "cold."

freestone A stonefruit variety whose pit can easily be removed from the flesh.

freeze 1. The freezing point of water, 32°F (0°C). 2. To place food items into a freezer where the temperature is 0°F (–18°C) or lower, which causes the water molecules to collect into a frozen suspension, for the purposes of preservation.

freeze-dried coffee See *coffee*.

freeze-drying A method of food preservation whereby food items are frozen and then through a pressure reduction process the water that is present in the food is heated slightly and converted to a gas which dissipates and results in a dried finished product.

freezer An insulated cabinet where the temperature is at 0°F (–18°C) or lower, for the purpose of freezing foods for an extended time or to retain consistency, as in ice cream.

freezer burn The destructive process that occurs to items stored in the freezer whereby surface dehydration makes the product unpalatable. The surface will have white or gray spots or streaks.

French apple pie An apple pie topped with *streusel*.

French bread Any of a range of sizes and shapes of crusty white bread, by law made from only flour, water, yeast, and salt. The *baguette* is the most well known.

French buttercream See *buttercream*.

French cruller See *cruller*.

French doughnut See *doughnut*.

French ice cream A rich variety of ice cream that is made with a high percentage of eggs and cream.

French knife An all-purpose kitchen knife used to chop, cut, slice, etc., ranging in length from 8 to 14 inches (20 to 35 cm), with a blade that is wide at the heel and tapered toward the tip. Also known as a *chef's knife*.

French meringue See *meringue*.

French parfait See *parfait*.

French press A coffee-brewing device with a narrow cylindrical jug, typically made of glass or clear plastic, equipped with a lid and a plunger and filter that fit tightly in the cylinder. Coffee is brewed by placing the ground coffee and water in the cylinder and allowing it to steep for several minutes; then the plunger is depressed and pushes the grinds to the bottom of the press. The device was popularized by the French, and its operation is simple and produces a stronger coffee than other devices. Because the coffee grounds are in direct contact with the brewing water, coffee brewed with the French press captures more of the coffee's flavor and essential oils, which become trapped in a traditional drip-brew machine's paper filter. French pressed coffee is usually stronger and thicker, and has more sediment than drip-brewed coffee. Because the used grounds remain in the drink after brewing, French pressed coffee should be served immediately so as not to become bitter from overextraction. A typical 8-cup French press is considered expired after 20 minutes. It can also be used to brew loose tea. Also known as a *press pot, coffee plunger*, or *cafetière*.

French toast Bread that is dipped into beaten eggs and pan-fried in butter until golden brown on both sides, then served with syrup, fruit, and butter. This popular breakfast was originally intended to use up stale or leftover bread. The origin of its name is unclear, but one story claims that it was created in 1724 in Albany, New York, by a man named Joseph French. See also *pain perdu*.

fresh yeast See *yeast*.

friand ('free-ohnd) A French term that refers to a small, sweet pastry.

friandise (free-ohn-deeze) A sweet delicacy of petit fours and confections that are served after dessert. Also known as *mignardise*.

friction factor In breadmaking, the amount of heat generated when mixing the dough. This depends on the type of mixer used, mixing time, and speed, but in general is between 24° and 28°F (−5° and −2°C). It is important in determining the desired dough temperature. See also *12 Steps of Baking* appendix.

fritelle (phree-'tehl) A Corsican specialty of yeast-leavened dough made from chestnut flour, eggs, olive oil, and fennel, fried to a golden brown and served warm with a sugar coating and jam filling.

fritter A small piece of raw or cooked food, such as fruit, that is dipped in batter and deep-fried. Fritters may also be made from *yeast dough* or *choux pastry*. They are typically served warm, dusted with confectioners' sugar. Also known as *beignets* in France.

fromage (froh-'mazh) The French word for *cheese*.

fromage blanc (fro-'mahz blahngk) A very soft, creamy French cheese often eaten as a dessert with fruit and sugar.

fromage glacé (fro-'mahz glah-'say) A cone-shaped flavored ice cream. It was popular in the 18th and early 19th centuries, and is believed to be the original *bombe*.

front of the house An industry term that refers to the area of the hotel or restaurant where staff are in direct contact with the guests, such as servers and bartenders.

frost To encase a cake with frosting.

frosting See *icing*.

froth The foam formed from tiny light bubbles made by frothing milk. This is done to make the *crema* for espresso.

frozen soufflé A still frozen dessert that consists of a custard-type base that has whipped cream or beaten egg whites folded into it. This mixture is poured into individual ramekins that have a collar of *parchment paper* or *acetate* extending at least 1 inch (25.4 mm) above the rim. The product is frozen until firm and the collar is removed just before service, which gives the impression of a risen soufflé. A wide variety of flavors can be used in the preparation, including lemon, cassis, strawberry, coffee, and many others.

frozen yogurt A healthy alternative to ice cream, with a consistency similar to soft-serve ice cream. See also *yogurt*.

fructose ('fruhk-tohs) A simple sugar that is a natural by-product of fruit and honey. It is present in molasses and honey, but can also be purchased as dry crystals. It is more water soluble than *glucose* and sweeter than *sucrose*. It can be used by diabetics and is available in granular and liquid forms. It should not be substituted for regular sugar because it loses some of its sweetening power when heated. Also known as *fruit sugar* and *levulose*.

fruit beer A beer or mild ale that is flavored with fruit, fruit concentrates, or fruit extracts. These have been made for centuries, particularly in Belgium.

fruit butter A sweet, smooth spread of stewed fruit, sugar, and spices.

fruitcake A dense cake packed with fruit, nuts, and spices, and often soaked in brandy or rum. If it is a dark fruitcake, it is made with molasses or brown sugar and dark fruits and nuts. If it is a light fruitcake, it is made with light corn syrup or granulated sugar and light fruit and nuts. They have extraordinary staying power and are traditionally made during holiday time.

fruit cocktail A mixture of diced fruits, typically served chilled. The original canned version contains grapes, pears, peaches, and cherries in a syrup.

fruit compote Lightly poached fruit that is cooked in a sweet syrup. The original shape of the fruit remains; it is usually served as an accompaniment to dessert.

fruit leather A sweet dried-fruit snack that is made by pureeing fruit with sugar or honey and drying it in thin strips, which are then rolled into cylinders. They are available in a variety of flavors.

F
f

fruit mince A thick, rich mixture of dried fruits, sugar, butter, and alcohol, used as a base in many desserts, such as *Banbury tarts* and pies or cobblers.

fruit mince tart See *fruit mince pie.*

fruit mince pie A sweet British pastry traditionally served during Christmastime. They are filled with a mixture of fruit and spices and usually 2 to 3 inches (5 cm to 7.5 cm) and were originally made in the shape of a cradle to symbolize the birth of Christ. If the pie has no top it is known as a *tart.*

fruit oil The essential oil derived from certain fruits, particularly citrus rinds, and used to flavor sauces, creams, fillings, and other pastry products.

fruit pie See *pie.*

fruit powder A natural coloring and flavoring ingredient made from finely ground dehydrated fruit.

fruit smack A liquid concentrate for a water-based beverage. It was the original *Kool-Aid;* owing to breakage problems, the product was produced in powder.

fruit soufflé A fruit-based *soufflé* made by cooking sugar to the *hard crack stage* and then adding fruit puree. The mixture is then cooked to the softball stage and cooled before the whipped egg whites are folded in.

fruit soup A warm or cold soup of fruit cooked with milk or cream and spices or other flavorings and then pureed. It is a specialty of Scandinavia.

fruit sugar See *fructose.*

Früli (fruhr-lee) A *fruit beer* made from 70% wheat beer and 30% fruit juice.

frutta di martorana ('froo-tah dee mahr-toh-'rah-nah) An Italian confection made by molding *marzipan* into various bite-size fruits.

fry To cook food in hot fat; use a frying pan for shallow frying; use a deep-fat fryer to completely submerge the food in fat.

fry bread A Native American *flatbread* made from flour, water, salt, and sometimes baking soda. It is shaped into thin rounds, deep-fried, and served warm.

frying pan A long-handled, round pan with slightly angled sides, used to fry foods in oil or butter. It comes in a variety of diameters and is also known as a *skillet.*

fu (foo) A spongy dough made from dried wheat gluten. It is a Japanese specialty.

fudge A semi-soft, creamy candy made with sugar, butter, and cream that is cooked to softball (240°F/115°C) and beaten until thick, then poured out onto a marble slab to cool and set before cutting. Although chocolate is the most popular fudge, it may be made with other flavorings and additions, such as nuts. Although the exact origin is unknown, there is a story that the first batch of fudge resulted from a bungled batch of caramels made in 1886, hence the name.

fudge-type icing A thick, rich icing made with ingredients such as chocolate and caramel. These store well but should be covered tightly to prevent crusting and drying.

fufu ('foo-foo) A West African carbohydrate made by drying and grinding yams into a powder or pounding them into a paste. In the Caribbean it may be boiled, fried, baked, or made into a meal. Nigeria imports an instant powder that can be found in African markets, and depending on the region, fufu takes the place of rice, biscuits, and/or mashed potatoes.

Fuji apple See *apple.*

fungal amylase An *amylase* obtained from fungal sources. It is dried and added to flour as a powder in order to correct enzymatic deficiencies. It may be substituted with *malted barley.*

F
f

funnel cake A Pennsylvania Dutch specialty made by swirling batter into hot fat through a funnel. The batter spirals are deep-fried until crisp, then doused with confectioners' sugar or maple syrup and served warm.

furmint grape See *grape*.

futari (foo-tah-re) A Tanzanian dessert of pumpkin or other squash, sweet potatoes, lemon juice, cloves, cinnamon, and coconut milk, simmered until soft and slightly thick, then baked in a dish until set.

Fuyu persimmon See *persimmon*.

fuzzy melon See *muskmelon, winter melon*.

F
f

Gg

g The abbreviation for *gram*.

Gala apple See *apple*.

galactose (gah-'lack-tohs) A type of sugar found in dairy products and beets. It is less sweet than glucose and not soluble in water. It is considered a nutritive sweetener because it provides food energy.

G
g

galaktobúreko (gah-lahk-toh-'boo-rehk-oh) A crisp Greek dessert that consists of baked phyllo filled with vanilla custard.

galangal ('guh-lang-guhl) See *Thai ginger*.

galapong (ga-lah-pong) A batter or dough of ground glutinous rice and water, used in the Philippines to make pastries and breads.

galette (gah-'leht) A flat pastry of varying size, made of sweet flaky pastry dough, yeast dough, or unleavened dough, and filled with fruit, nuts, jam, or meat and cheese, depending on the region of France where it is made. The pastry dates back to Neolithic times and was made from a honey-flavored cereal paste that was baked on hot stones. The most well-known galette is the  *galette de rois*, which resembles a *pithivier* and has a filling of *almond cream*. It is also popular as a form of *Twelfth Night cake* or *Epiphany cake*, served on January 6 and baked with a trinket inside that gives the finder a wish of good luck or the title "King for the day."

galette de rois See *galette*.

Galia melon See *muskmelon*.

Galliano (gal-'lyah-noh) A slightly sweet Italian liqueur blended from herbs, berries, and spices. It is a brilliant orange-yellow and is used to flavor pastries and confections.

gallon A U.S. unit of liquid volume measurement that is equivalent to 128 fluid ounces, or 3 L (840 ml).

gamma crystals See *cocoa butter*.

ganache (gahn-'ahsh) A filling or coating used in cakes, tarts, pastries, and confections, made from scalded heavy cream, and sometimes butter, combined with chopped *couverture* and stirred until velvety smooth. Created in Paris around the 1850s, it may be flavored with liqueurs, pastes, extracts, or infusions. The consistency of the ganache is determined by the proportion of ingredients used and may be adjusted from thin to firm depending on use.

gandaria A small mango-like tropical fruit from Thailand. It has yellowish-orange skin and a sweet yellow flesh. Both the pulp and the skin are edible. Available March to May.

garambullo The fruit of a cactus that grows in Mexico, resembling small reddish berries. It is used fresh in making preserves or dried and eaten raw as a snack.

garam masala ('gah-rahm mah-'sah-lah) The principal spice blend used in Indian cuisine. Although it may contain any combination of spices, *cardamom, coriander,* and *mace* are popular choices.

garde manger (gahrd mahn-zhay) The cold station in the classic *brigade* system. This station focuses on cold salads, pâtés, and cold buffet items. In many kitchens, the garde manger and pastry cooks assist each other during plate up because they are the first and last courses to be served.

garibaldi An Italian raisin-butter cookie.

garland Another name for *drapery.*

garlic An edible bulb in the onion family, made up of small papery-covered sections called *cloves.* There are several varieties that differ in size and flavor, including an American white-skinned with a strong flavor, a Mexican or Italian purplish-pink skinned with a milder flavor, and *elephant garlic,* which is the largest and mildest variety. Although garlic is traditionally used in savory dishes, it is often used as a topping on flatbreads such as *focaccia* and more recently in sweet creations such as *garlic ice cream.*

garnish ('gahr-nish) An edible decoration on a dessert or pastry to enhance and complement its flavor, texture, and visual appeal. Popular pastry garnishes include *chocolate-dipped strawberries,* sprigs of mint, *chocolate cigarettes,* small sugar decorations, and *tuiles.*

garniture ('gahr-nig-teur) The French word for *garnish.*

garland ('gahr-lahnd) A term used in cake decorating that refers to a decorative swag of icing that is piped on the side of a cake. The finished product resembles garland that is hung on a Christmas tree.

garlic ice cream A garlic flavored ice cream that became popular in the 1990s. It is made from a vanilla custard base that is infused with fresh garlic. Don't knock it 'til you try it.

Gascon pastis A savory French pastry from Gascony, in southern France. The *puff pastry dough* is spread over an entire work surface; it is then heavily brushed with goose fat and cut into rounds. Half of the rounds are spread with finely sliced apples that have been *macerated* in *Armagnac;* they are then topped with the plain pastry rounds and baked, then sprinkled with more Armagnac and served warm.

gastronome ('gas-truh-nohm) A person with a refined palate and appreciation of gourmet food and dining. Also known as an *epicure* or *gourmand.*

gastronomy ('gas-trohn-uh-mee) The art and science of gourmet food, drink, and dining. The term derives from the Greek *gastros,* meaning "stomach," and *nomos,* meaning "laws." It was first used in France in the early 1800s and made official by the Académie Francaise in 1835, when they placed it in their dictionary.

gâteau ('ga-toh) The French word for cake, referring to pastry items based on *choux pastry, puff pastry, short dough, génoise,* or *meringue.* It is traditionally multilayered and filled with fresh cream, *pastry cream,* or *buttercream.* It is differentiated from a *cake* or *torte,* in that each portion is identically garnished.

gâteau de sirop ('gah-toh duh 'she-roph) A Louisiana spice cake made with cane syrup and frosted with a brown sugar and butter mixture, then decorated with pecan halves. Also known as *Cajun syrup cake.*

gâteau l'opera See *opera torte.*

gâteau Saint-Honoré (ga-toh sahnt-ohn-oh-ray)
A classic French gâteau named after the patron
saint of bakers and pastry cooks. It is also said
that the name comes from the pastry cook
Chiboust, who invented the cream used in the
filling, because in 1846 he lived in the Rue
Saint-Honoré in Paris. It consists of a pâte brisée
or puff pastry base with concentric circles of
choux pastry piped on top of the dough. After it
is baked to a golden brown it is filled with
Chiboust cream and finished with small, baked
choux puffs that are filled with Chiboust cream,
glazed with caramel, and attached to the outer rim with additional caramel.

gâteau Saint-Honoré tip A specialty pastry tip that is designed specifically for
decorating gâteau Saint-Honoré. It has a V-shaped notch that produces the characteristic wave-like design on top of the gâteau.

gau (gah-oo) A Chinese steamed rice cake made with sticky rice, coconut, flour,
and brown sugar, and garnished with sesame seeds and red dates. It is often
served during the lunar New Year celebration.

gaufre ('goh-freh) The French word for *waffle.*

gaufre de Bruxelles ('goh-freh duh 'brew-sehl) A *Belgian waffle* lightened by
the addition of whipped egg whites. It is garnished with sugar, whipped cream, or
chocolate.

gaufrette (goh-freht) A thin, crisp fan-shaped wafer served with ice cream.

Gaya melon See *muskmelon.*

gelateria (jeh-lah-toh-'ree-ah) An Italian shop where *gelato* is served.

gelatin ('jeh-lah-tihn) A colorless, tasteless product extracted from the bones
and connective tissues of animals. It acts as a binder, and ranges from soft to firm
depending on the ratios used. It is available in powdered or leaf/sheet form and
may be substituted for each other in equal weights. The dry form is sprinkled over
water to soften the granules and then heated to a clear liquid before use. The
leaf/sheet form is *bloomed,* or submerged in water, until soft and the excess water
is wrung out before use. It may be melted in a double boiler to a clear liquid
and added to the product, or added to the warm liquid to melt. Gelatin melts at
86°F (30°C) and sets at 68°F (20°C). It is used in the preparation of many molded
desserts. Note that some acidic fruits impede the setting power and must be
heated to 175°F (80°C) before use.

gelatinization A reaction that occurs during the baking process in which the
starches absorb moisture and swell. They reach their bursting point between
180° and 212°F (82° and 100°C) and set in a solid mass that gives the bread its
structure.

gelato (jeh-'lah-toh) An Italian style of ice cream made with milk instead of cream
and churned in a machine that produces less air so that it is denser than American
ice cream.

gem pan A small pan used to make miniature *muffins.*

génoise ('zhehn-whaz) A French sponge cake made with whole eggs and sugar
that are warmed and whipped to the ribbon stage before being folded in sifted
flour and melted butter; the incorporation of air is what gives volume to the cake.
It is different from other sponge cakes in that the eggs are not whipped separately.
Used as a base for many classic cakes, it is named for the Italian city of Genoa,
from where it was adopted in the 15th century.

G
g

geranyl isovolerate A food additive with an apple-pear flavor, used in beverages, candy, baked goods, and ice cream.

germ See *wheat kernel.*

German buttercream See *buttercream.*

German chocolate cake An American cake made up of layers of rich chocolate sponge cake and frosted with a cooked coconut-pecan icing. The cake first appeared in a food column in a 1957 Dallas newspaper, and got its name from the *Baker's German sweet chocolate,* used to create the cake. The chocolate was created in 1852 for the Baker's Chocolate Company by an Englishman named Sam German.

Gewürtztraminer (guh-'vurts-trah-mee-ner) A specialty of the Alsatian region of France, this crisp, spicy white wine may be dry or sweet. The late harvest varieties make excellent dessert wines.

ghee A cross between *clarified butter* and *beurre noisette,* produced by slowly melting the butter to separate the milk solids and then simmering it until the moisture evaporates and the milk solids brown. The result is a nutty caramel-like flavor that is popular because of its high *smoke point.* Although it originated in India with butter made from *buffalo milk,* it is readily available in other countries such as Scandinavia, the Netherlands, and Australia and may be made from any unsalted butter.

Ghiradelli chocolate Chocolate made by a U.S. company that has been manufacturing premium products since 1852.

ghoraiybah (go-ray-bah) A traditional Middle Eastern cookie that resembles a buttery, shortbread flavored with toasted cardamom and almonds.

gialetti (jee-ah-leh-tee) A cornmeal biscuit from the Romagna district of Italy.

gianduja (zhahn-doo-yah) 1. A smooth and creamy Swiss mixture of dark, or more commonly, milk chocolate and roasted hazelnut paste. 2. Confections made with chocolate and *hazelnuts.*

giant poha berry A large *cape gooseberry* grown in the United States and New Zealand. It is about 1 inch (25.4mm) in size with a waxy orange skin. The interior yields a sweet-tart flavor that is used for making jams and glazes.

gild To brush an egg wash over a pastry surface in order to produce a shiny finish after baking. 2. To apply *gold dust* or *gold leaf* to a confection.

gilka koutalioú (geel-kah coo-tah-lee-oh-oo) A Greek dessert of fruits preserved in syrup.

ginger The swollen root, or rhizome, of a Chinese leafy plant, now grown in India, Africa, and the Caribbean, used for seasoning and, when crystallized, as a confection. It has a sweet, peppery flavor and spicy aroma. It is sometimes referred to as a "hand" because its flat, spreading branches resemble a thick hand with knobby fingers. The name derives from the Sanskrit word *sringavera,* meaning "root shaped like a horn." There are two major types of ginger: mature and immature. Mature ginger is peeled before use and is more pungent than immature ginger, or spring ginger, which shows green sprouts and is available only in the spring. If the skin is dull and wrinkled rather than smooth and shiny, it indicates that the ginger is past its prime. The fresh root sections may be refrigerated for up to a week or frozen for a longer period of time. When dried and ground, ginger is widely used in pastry making as a flavoring agent.

ginger ale A sweet carbonated beverage flavored with ginger, first introduced in 1866 by James Vernor, in Detroit, Michigan. Vernors Ginger Ale is considered one of America's oldest soft drinks.

gingerbread A sweet, ginger-flavored cake, cookie, or bread. This age-old treat was introduced to Europe when the first crusaders returned from the holy wars with Middle Eastern spices that included ginger. The varieties of gingerbread range from region to region and may be light, dark, sweet, or spicy, but thin cookies are typically cut into shapes. An English village tradition encourages unmarried women to eat gingerbread "husbands" at local fairs in order to gain husbands. By the 17th century, gingerbread making was so important that it was recognized as an exclusive profession and a Guild of Master Bakers was formed. Making gingerbread houses became popular during the 19th century, when the story of Hansel and Gretel, who discovered a house made of bread, cake, and candies, became popular. As European immigrants settled in America, they brought with them their family recipes and customs, and Americans have been making gingerbread ever since. It is particularly popular during holiday time.

ginger root See *ginger*.

gingersnap A thin, crisp cookie flavored with ginger and molasses.

ginkgo nut ('ging-koh) The seed or nut of the ginko, or maidenhair, tree, which is native to ancient China. The fruit is about the size of a nectarine and has a sweet, light yellow-green flesh that is covered with a thin yellow skin and a smooth, hard shell. The hard outer shell must be cracked open to reveal the meat inside, and the nut must be soaked in warm water to remove the skin. The brownish-tan nut can be found in Asian markets during the fall and winter months, and is available fresh, canned in brine, or dried. The Chinese believe that the ginkgo nut will bring good fortune and dye the shells red for weddings. In Japan the nuts are popular grilled or used in egg custard and cookies.

Girl Scout cookies The cookies sold annually as a fundraiser for Girl Scouts of America. The sale dates back to 1917, when Girl Scouts supervised by their mothers would bake cookies to sell in their neighborhoods to raise money for their local chapters. Today, the licensed commercial bakers produce eight varieties, including three mandatory ones that are thin mint, peanut butter sandwich, and shortbread. All Girl Scout cookies are *kosher*.

glace (glahs) The French word for "glazed" or "frozen." It also means to frost or cover a cake or pastry with frosting.

glacé (glah-'say) The French word for *ice cream*.

glacé fruit Fruit that has been dipped in sugar syrup and used as a garnish or dipped in chocolate as a petit four. The syrup has been cooked to the *cracked stage* so that it has a hard, shiny exterior. The fruit should be stored in an airtight container. Also known as *candied fruit*.

glacier See *brigade*.

glayva ('gli-vah) A Scottish liqueur of herbs, honey, and Scotch whisky.

glaze 1. A thin icing that gives shine to a baked good and helps prevent it from drying out. The most common glazes are *apricot glaze* for fruit tarts and other pastries and baked goods, *chocolate glaze* for cakes and petit fours, and *confectioners' sugar* glaze for donuts and baked goods such as *danish*. Sometimes the glaze contains gelatin to thicken and stabilize it. 2. To apply a glaze on a baked good.

glazironanniye sirki (glah-zih-roh-nahn-nyah 'sehr-kee) A Russian candy with a cream cheese or farmers cheese base mixed with cream, sugar, egg yolk, lemon zest, and lemon juice; it is drained overnight in cheesecloth, shaped into bite-size balls, and dipped in chocolate.

gliaden (gly-ah-dehn) See *gluten*.

glister pudding A British steamed pudding flavored with marmalade and ginger.

Globe grape See *grape*.

glop See *gorp*.

glucose ('glue-kose) A natural sugar found in fruits, vegetables, maple syrup, and honey. It consists of simple and complex sugar properties that have half the sweetening power of granulated sugar. Glucose resists *crystallization* and is therefore used in to make *pulled sugar* and *blown sugar* work and a variety of candies and pastry items such as frostings, baked goods, and soft drinks. The most common type of glucose is called *dextrose* and it can often be substituted with *light corn syrup*.

glucose corn syrup Another name for *corn syrup*.

glucose crystal See *corn syrup*.

glucose-fructose The Canadian term for *high fructose corn syrup*. It contains equal parts *fructose* and *glucose* and is similar to *invert sugar* in composition and properties.

glutathione (gloo-tah-thee-'oh-neh) A protein that weakens gluten, found in milk and improperly used *active dry yeast,* as well as *wheat germ* that has not been heat-treated.

gluten ('glue-tihn) The primary protein in wheat that provides structure and flavor. It is composed of two partial proteins called *glutenin* and *gliadin,* which link together when hydrated and form gluten. Flours contain different amounts of gluten and must be chosen carefully to achieve desired gluten development. Typically, the higher the protein, the more gluten the flour contains. The main components of gluten serve different purposes: glutenin provides elasticity to the dough, while gliadin offers extensibility and volume to the dough. See also *gluten development*.

gluten development The formation of a strong, cohesive network of fibers that can stretch into a thin film without tearing and still retain elasticity. The many factors that affect the gluten's ability to develop include the type of flour, type and amount of liquid used for hydration, mixing time and dough temperature, salt and any other additions to the dough such as conditioners, fats, or other products.

glutenin ('glue-tin-ehn) See *gluten*.

glutinous rice flour Flour made from glutinous white polished rice, used extensively in Asian pastries such as sweet dumplings and buns.

glycerine See *glycerol*.

glycerol The commercial name for *glycerine,* a sugar alcohol obtained from three fatty acids that produce *triglyceride*. It is odorless, colorless, and syrupy, and is used in the commercial production of candies and confections.

glycyrrhizin (glee-seer-rhee-'tseen) A food additive derived from licorice root, used to sweeten low-fat dessert products.

glykys, glykys vrastos See *Greek coffee*.

goat's milk Milk derived from goats, most commonly used to produce *chèvre*.

gold dust See *gold powder*.

Golden Delicious apple See *apple*.

golden raisin See *raisin*.

golden syrup See *treacle*.

gold kiwifruit See *kiwifruit*.

gold leaf A micro-thin sheet of 22-karat edible gold. It is sold in small square sheets separated by tissue papers. It is very expensive and difficult to work with, but makes a spectacular adornment to confections and desserts. Using tweezers or a dry artist's brush is recommended for transferring the leaf onto the product. Also know as *vark* or *varak.*

Goldmine nectarine See *nectarine.*

Gold pineapple See *pineapple.*

gold powder A decorating powder that is made from 22- to 24-carat edible gold. It is used to decorate desserts and show pieces. The powder may be used as is or mixed with a small amount of *pure grain alcohol* to produce a gold paint. As the alcohol dissipates, the gold remains in a dry state.

gold spray An aerosol spray that contains 22-karat gold flecks, used to decorate desserts and pastries.

Goldwasser The German word for "gold water," referring to a pale yellow liqueur flavored with herbs and spices. Tiny flecks of 22- karat gold are suspended in liqueur. Danziger Goldwasser is the most common brand, and it is used in pastry and dessert preparations.

goma (goh-mah) The Japanese word for *sesame seeds.*

goober A U.S. Southern slang term for a peanut. The name derives from the African word *nguba.*

GooGoo Cluster A candy bar that is a mixture of caramel, marshmallow, and roasted peanuts, dipped in milk chocolate. A Southern favorite, it was the first combination candy bar ever created, produced by the Standard Candy Company in 1912, and believed to have gotten its name because it is a baby's first words. It is one of the longest-running sponsors of the Grand Ole Opry, and every Saturday night the Opry announcer leads the audience in the cheer "Gotta get a GooGoo!"

goop See *gorp.*

gooseberry See *berry.*

gorp A trail mix of nuts, raisins, seeds, dried fruits, and oats. Many hikers and outdoorsmen use this mixture as an energy snack. It is also known as *glop* and *goop.*

gougére (goo-zhair) A savory pastry of *pâte à choux* flavored with Gruyère, comté, or *Emmental* cheese, piped into a ring and baked. This is often served at wine tastings either warm or cold.

gourmand (goor-'mahnd) See *gastronome.*

gourmet (goor-'may) A connoisseur of fine food and drink.

graham cracker A cracker made with whole wheat, traditionally sweetened with honey or molasses. It was invented by Reverend Sylvester Graham in 1829, as part of the vegetarian diet he proposed to his followers. It was known as a health food, but soon became a snack for children and an indispensable ingredient in many desserts, such as *s'mores,* as well as the major ingredient for pies with a *graham cracker crust.*

graham cracker crust A pie crust made by mixing graham cracker crumbs and just enough melted butter for it to hold its shape. It is a popular crust for *Key lime pies* and *cheesecake.*

graham flour See *flour.*

grain The edible seed of grasses such as wheat, corn, rice, barley, and rye.

gram A standard metric weight measure that is the equivalent of .035 ounces.

28.35 grams = 1 ounce
1000 grams = 1 kilogram

gram flour See *flour.*

granadilla The Brazilian word for *passion fruit.*

grande The size of an *espresso*-milk beverage, usually a 16-ounce (480 ml) portion and normally made with a double shot of espresso.

Grand Marnier A Cognac-based amber-colored liqueur infused with Haitian bitter oranges, spices, and vanilla, and aged in oak vats for six to eight months. It was created by Alexandre Marnier-Lapostolle in 1880 and is still highly regarded. It is used extensively in the pastry kitchen to flavor *buttercreams,* ice creams, sauces, and *truffles.* A less expensive substitute is *Cointreau.*

granité ('grah-neh-tay) A frozen ice dessert made of fruit juice and syrup. Its name refers to granite rock because the rough texture of the ice crystals resembles the coarse grain of granite. The mixture may be intermittently stirred during freezing for larger ice crystals or put directly into the freezer for smaller ones. It is typically served as a dessert or *intermezzo.*

Granny Smith apple See *apple.*

granola A mixture of rolled oats, dried fruits, nuts, honey, and other ingredients, used primarily as a breakfast cereal. It has a cereal consistency stemming from the stirring during the baking process to break up clumps. It is popular with hikers because it is a high-energy food and is often served with yogurt or as a topping for pastries or desserts. A convenient bar form is also available in a crunchy or chewy texture.

granose See *Kellogg, John Harvey.*

granulated sugar See *sugar.*

grape The edible berry of small shrubs or climbing vines that grows in clusters in temperate climates throughout the world. California is the largest producer of American grapes for both wine and table. Grapes are one of the oldest cultivated fruits, and there are thousands of varieties, but in general they have smooth skin and may be seeded or unseeded. Wine grape varieties are highly acidic and too tart to eat fresh. Table grapes are low in acid, popular to eat fresh or to make jams, jellies, and juice. Grapes are categorized as white, green, red, or black and the most common varieties are:

> **Cabernet Sauvignon** A small black wine grape that may also be eaten fresh. Available early fall.
>
> **Catwaba** An oval, medium, seeded grape with an intense sweet flavor. It is used primarily in the commercial production of white wines, jams, and jellies. Available September to November.
>
> **Champagne** A petite, sweet table grape with a color that ranges from reddish-brown to purplish-black. They make attractive garnishes. Available June to September.
>
> **Common Black Seedless** A very juicy, sweet table grape with mild acidity. Color ranges from purple to purplish-black. Available August to January.
>
> **Common Green Seedless** A tangy, sweet table grape with low acidity and a pale green skin. Available May to December.
>
> **Common Red Seedless** A medium table grape with a sweet-tart flavor and juicy, crunchy texture. Available May to December.
>
> **Concord** A large, oblong, seeded grape with a sweet flavor and thick, blue-purple to black skin. It is used primarily in the commercial production of juice, jams, and jellies. Available August to September.
>
> **Delaware** A sweet American hybrid whose small, round berries have a light red skin. They are sweet and are used for both wine and table grapes. Available May to September.

Emperor A firm, crisp European table grape with a thick, reddish-purple skin and sweet flesh.

Flame Seedless A medium table grape with a crisp, sweet flavor and pale to dark red skin. Available May to December.

Furmint A highly prized white wine grape used to make the famed, sweet Tokay wines.

Globe Large, oval red grape that usually has seeds. It has a sweet-tart flavor and crisp, juicy texture. Available August to January.

Magnolia A muscadine grape variety; see below.

Muscadine (muhs-kuh-dine) An American grape found primarily in the Southeast. It has a thick dark purple skin and a strong, musky flavor. It is known as one of the first grapes used to make wine in America. The *Scuppernong* variety is popular in the South. Available March to October.

Muscat (muhs-kat) A name that refers to a large variety of grapes that range in color from light yellow to almost black. They have a sweet, rich, musky flavor and are grown all over the world in temperate climates. They are popular as table grapes and are also used to make sweet wines that pairs well with desserts. Available March to May.

Muscato A medium, seedless, oval grape that is either green or red skinned. The green variety is a cross between Thompson seedless and the Muscat variety and are sweeter than common green grapes. The red variety is a cross between the Italia, Tokay, and Muscat grape varieties and is sweeter than the common red grapes. Available June to October.

Niagara A large, American hybrid with a light green skin. It is used for wine and as a table grape and for commercial juice production. Available May to December.

Perlette A seedless, European grape with a thin, tender, pale yellow skin and juicy, slightly sweet flavor. Available March to October.

Ribier A large, juicy, European dessert grape with a purplish-black skin and nonacidic flavor. Available March to October.

Thomson Seedless The most common green grape variety for commercial production in the United States. It is the leading table grape and also used to make golden raisins. It is small to medium and has a pale golden-green skin and crisp, juicy flesh. Available May to December.

Tokay A large, firm, European table grape that grows in clusters of bright red berries. Available August to December. Also known as Flame Tokay.

Zante A small, bright purple European grape cultivated primarily to make currants. California is the largest producer of the seedless, sweet zante and they may also be eaten out of hand or used as a garnish or ingredient in pastries and cakes. Available March to October.

grapefruit A tropical citrus fruit available in several varieties, cultivated in Florida, California, Arizona, and Texas. The name derives from the observation that it grows on the tree in clusters, like grapes. They may be seeded or seedless, and are classified as white, pink, or ruby red. The white have a pale yellow flesh and are typically smaller and more tart than the pink. The pink are higher in vitamin A and have a mildly sweet pink flesh. The large ruby reds have a sweet, bright ruby flesh. All are available year-round, but Arizona and California grapefruits are best from January through August, while Florida and Texas grapefruits are available October through June. See also *cocktail grapefruit, melogold, oro blanco,* and *pomelo.*

G
g

grapefruit knife A small knife with a slightly curved blade that has a double-sided serrated edge, used to detach individual sections from the fruit.

grape pie See *jelly pie.*

grape sugar Another name for *dextrose.*

grappa ('graph-pah) Italian for "grape stalk," referring to an aromatic Italian alcohol made by distilling the skins, stems, and seeds of grapes leftover from wine making. It has been commercially produced since the 18th century, and the flavor depends on the type and quality of grape residue used as well as the style of distillation. It is popular in Italy as an after-dinner drink and is sometimes added to espresso, which is known as *caffè corretto.*

grasshopper pie A Southern pie from the 1950s that consists of a filling of *crème de menthe,* gelatin, and whipped cream in a graham cracker or cookie crust. Its name refers to the grasshopper green color of the pie that is a result of the green crème de menthe.

grate To reduce large particles of food to smaller particles or shreds by rubbing it against a serrated surface known as a *grater.*

grater A kitchen tool used to reduce hard food products to small pieces or shreds by moving the food over sharp holes or slots. There are graters for different purposes, including specialized graters for ginger and nutmeg. The most common is the *box grater,* which has four perforated sides, each with different size holes; it is open on the top and bottom, and has a handle on the top for gripping during use. See also *Mouli grater.*

Gravenstein apple See *apple.*

grease 1. The rendered fat from animal products such as bacon, chicken, or beef. 2. To apply fat to a surface in order to prevent foods from sticking to the surface and allowing for easy removal after cooking.

Greek coffee A very rich, strong coffee made in a *brik,* or brass coffee pot with a wooden handle. The coffee may be made in a variety of ways: *sketos,* or strong and bitter without sugar; *metrios,* or medium with one teaspoon of sugar; *glykys* or *vari glykos,* sweetened with honey; or *glykys vrastos,* sweet but boiled more than once so it loses most of its froth. Once the mixture boils, it is left to steep for a minute to allow the grounds to settle to the bottom and then is served immediately. If it is served cold it is known as Greek frappe.

Greek frappe See *Greek coffee.*

green flour See *flour.*

Green Fuerte avocado See *avocado.*

Greengage plum See *plum.*

green mango See *mango.*

green papaya See *papaya.*

green peppercorns See *peppercorns.*

green tea See *tea.*

grenadine ('grehn-uh-deen) A red syrup made from the juice of pomegranates that may or may not contain alcohol. Its name comes from the French *grenade,* which means "pomegranate." It is often used in pastry for both its flavor and the reddish-pink hue it imparts.

griddle A flat, solid surface used to cook foods with little or no fat. Griddles are typically made of iron or another heavy metal that is a good conductor of heat.

griddle cake A batter-type bread cooked directly on a *griddle.* The most popular griddle cakes are *pancakes;* however, *English muffins* also fall into this category.

grill 1. A metal grate placed over a heat source, usually a flame, to cook food on. 2. An eating establishment that has a casual atmosphere and broad food selection. Also spelled *grille*. 3. A dry-heat cooking method.

grind To reduce a food item to small particles, by grinding, crushing, or milling. The finished texture may be fine, medium, or coarsely ground.

grinder A tool used to grind food, either manually or electrically operated. Small, specialty grinders are used to grind beans for freshly ground coffee and espresso.

griottine (grih-yoh-teen) A French cherry that has been partially cooked and bottled in brandy with sugar. Both the griottine and its liquid are used in desserts, including *cherries jubilee*. Also known as *guinette*.

grissini Thin crisp Italian breadsticks. They originated in Turin in the Piedmont district of Italy.

grits A side dish of cornmeal mush made from coarsely ground corn. The name derives from the Old English *grytta,* which means "coarse meal." This Southern U.S. favorite can be made with either yellow or white cornmeal and from meal made from the whole kernel or from hulled kernels (*hominy*). The cornmeal is boiled in water or milk until it reaches a soft semi-solid state with a gritty texture, and typically is served at breakfast but has also become popular at other meals as well. Also known as *hominy grits.* See also *hominy.*

Grittibaenz ('grit-ih-bynzh) A German holiday bread formed in the shape of St. Nicholas. It is made for children and first appeared in the early 1800s.

groats The kernels of a grain such as oats or barley, from which the husks have been removed.

gros sel The French word for an unrefined crystalline salt.

ground cherry Another name for *cape gooseberry;* see *berry.*

groundnut Another name for *peanut.*

gruel ('groo-uhl) A thin, warm cereal made by cooking oatmeal with water or milk.

grunt A colonial American steamed cobbler made of fruit covered with a biscuit-like dough and sprinkled with sugar. Also known as a *slump.*

guar gum A thickener obtained from the beans of a plant that grows in India and Pakistan. It is also added to frozen foods such as pasteurized egg whites and ice cream to prevent freezer damage and to reduce the growth of ice crystals.

guava A tropical fruit with a thin edible skin that encloses a flesh with edible seeds, native to South America. There are several varieties, including a large green apple-size guava that is crisp but not very sweet; and two golf-ball-size guavas that are green skinned when unripe and golden yellow when ripe. One has a cream-colored sweet, juicy flesh while the other has a salmon pink flesh and perfume-like aroma. The fruit is high in pectin and often is used for jams, jellies, and preserves. *Guava juice* is also popular as a drink.

guava juice See *guava.*

guava paste A Latin confection of guava pulp, sugar, pectin, and citric acid that is cooked until very thick and molded into individually wrapped bars. It is typically sliced and eaten as a snack, or served with ice cream or yogurt.

gubana The Italian word for "snail," referring to a rich fruit and nut-filled sweet bread that is rolled into a spiral to resemble a snail. It is made with equal amounts of dough and filling, and is traditionally served at Easter. The rich filling consists of raisins, walnuts, hazelnuts, pine nuts, almonds, and five different wines and liqueurs. It is a specialty of Friuli, in northeastern Italy.

guéridon See *flambé trolley.*

G
g

Guittard A family-owned and -operated chocolate company based in San Francisco that has been producing chocolate products since 1868.

Gugelhopf See *Kugelhopf.*

guinette 1. A small red cherry grown in France; see *cherry.* 2. Another name for *griottine.*

guitar A tool used to cut confections. It has taught metal strings attached to a bar that is hinged to a flat, heavy metal, square base. There are interchangeable wire bars in order to achieve cuts of different widths.

gulab jamun ('goo-lahb jah-'moon) A north Indian confection of sweet sticky balls of dark milk fudge that have been boiled in milk until very thick, then deep-fried and steeped in rose water syrup spiced with cinnamon or cardamom.

gum arabic The purified and dried sap of the North African acacia tree, used as a thickener and to stabilize emulsions. It is used in fillings and icings because it maintains a flavorless, nongummy *mouthfeel.*

gumdrop A small, sweet, brightly colored candy made of gelatin and fruit flavor. Gumdrops are shaped like a fat thimble and coated in granulated sugar, which gives them a nice texture contrast to the smooth, "gummy" filling. They are often used for decorating cakes and cupcakes, and are a popular adornment for gingerbread houses during Christmastime.

gum paste An edible product that is used for cake decoration. It is made from confectioners' sugar, gum tragacanth, glucose, and water, which is kneaded to a soft dough-like consistency. It can be rolled very thin, and once dried, is both delicate and durable. The paste may also be colored before use or brushed with color once dried.

gum paste tool Any of several small, hand-held tools used to create decorative gum paste products, particularly flowers. They are typically made of heavy plastic but may also be available in metal.

gum tragacanth An ingredient in *gum paste* that is thicker than gum arabic. It is obtained from the Middle Eastern Astragalus shrub and is very expensive. It is also the binding agent in gum paste.

gunpowder tea A fine green tea from the Zhejiang province of China. It gets its unique name from the shape of the finished tea. The very dark green tea leaves are rolled into little pellets that look like gunpowder and "explode" into long leaves when steeped in hot water. It has a smoky flavor and slight aftertaste. Also known as *bead tea* or *pearl tea.*

guo kua ('goo-oh kwah) A Chinese breakfast bread that is a specialty of Sichuan. It may be sweet if made with raw brown sugarcane or savory if made with Sichuan peppercorns and scallions.

gur See *sugar, jaggery.*

Hh

Hachiya persimmon See *persimmon*.

half-and-half A combination of cream and milk in equal proportions. It contains between 10 and 18% butterfat, and may be purchased as a pint or a quart.

hálfmánar ('hahlf-mah-nahr) An Icelandic cookie of two half-moon-shaped butter cookies sandwiched together with fruit preserves or a prune spread. They are a traditional Christmas treat.

hallah (hahl-lah) See *challah*.

halo-halo ('hah-low 'hah-low) A *milk shake* made with jackfruit, coconut, and sweet red beans, popular in the Philippines.

halophilic (hahl-oh-phil-ihk) A term to describe an organism that needs a salty environment in order to thrive.

halva ('hahl-vah) See *halvah*.

halvah ('hahl-vah) A Middle Eastern confection made from ground sesame seeds, honey, and other ingredients such as pistachios or almonds, dried fruit, and semolina. It is also flavored with cinnamon, cardamom, or rosewater depending on the region. The name derives from the Arabic *halwa*, meaning "sweetmeat." After the ingredients are blended, they are heated and poured into long bars, which are sliced after cooling. Also known as *helva* in Turkey and *halva* in Greece.

Haman's hats ('hay-mehns) See *hamantaschen*.

hamantaschen ('hah-mahn-tah-shuhn)
A triangular, filled cookie whose shape is meant to represent the hat worn by the villain Haman in the Jewish story of Purim. The cookies are made with a *short dough* that is rolled out, cut into rounds, and filled with a poppy seed, prune, apricot, or nut mixture. It is then folded to resemble a three-cornered hat and baked.

hamburger bun A pre-split round, soft *yeast roll* that measures 3½ to 4 inches (8.7 to 10 cm) in circumference. It may be made from a variety of flours and topped with sesame seeds, poppy seeds, or chopped onions before baking. It is common to grill the top and bottom pieces before placing the hamburger between the roll.

hami See *muskmelon*.

hand-formed cookie A cookie dough that is shaped by hand into a log, individual balls, and other shapes before baking. Also known as *molded cookie*.

hard-ball stage See *Sugar Cooking Stages* appendix.

hard cider The fermented juice of apples or another fruit, with a slightly cloudy appearance and an alcohol content of around 5%. It may ferment naturally or in oak barrels with the addition of *yeast*.

hard-crack stage See *Sugar Cooking Stages* appendix.

hard pretzel See *pretzel*.

hard red spring wheat See *wheat*.

hard red winter wheat See *wheat*.

hard roll See *kaiser roll*.

hard sauce A nonliquid English dessert sauce made by creaming butter and sugar and then flavoring it with rum, brandy, or vanilla. It is traditionally served with *plum pudding*.

hardtack A hard, dry biscuit made from flour, salt, and water. It has a long shelf life and was given to sailors in the 1800s as nourishment during long voyages. The name derives from the British seamen's slang for food, "tack." Also known as *sea biscuit*.

hard water See *water*.

hard wheat See *wheat*.

hard white winter wheat See *wheat*.

hartshorn salt See *ammonium bicarbonate*.

hasty pudding A colonial American dish of cornmeal mush sweetened with molasses, maple syrup, or honey, served for breakfast or as a dessert. Also known as *Indian pudding*.

haupia (hoh-'pee-ah) A Hawaiian coconut pudding that is sometimes also used as a filling for a cake.

haystack A shortened reference to *coconut haystack*.

hazelnut The nut of the wild hazel tree, native to the Mediterranean region but now grown all over Europe and the northwestern United States. Turkey and Italy are the largest producers of this small, round golden nut that is wrapped in a papery brown skin and encased in a hard dark brown shell. The skin is slightly bitter and is typically removed by toasting the nuts and rubbing the skins off by hand with a towel. The toasting also brings out the rich, buttery flavor of the nut. The nuts are widely used in the pastry shop in whole, chopped, ground, or paste form. Their high oil content causes them to turn rancid in a short time, so they are best kept refrigerated in an airtight container or frozen. Also known as *filbert* and *cobnut*.

hazelnut meal See *flour, nut flour*.

hazelnut oil The rich, nutty oil pressed from hazelnuts. It is highly perishable and should be stored in a cool place. Although it is expensive, its concentrated form requires that only a small amount be used.

hazelnut paste A concentrated paste made by pressing roasted hazelnuts. The caramel-colored paste has a rich, nutty flavor and is used in pastry items as a flavoring agent.

hearth bread A bread that is baked directly on the hearth or hot deck of an oven. This is typically done with *artisan breads*.

heat lamp A key tool in the production of *pulled sugar* and *blown sugar*. It consists of a large infrared bulb that is generally 250 watts and 125 volts, attached to either a flexible gooseneck lamp or a *sugar warming case*. The top of the bulb is opaque and drives the light and its heat to the work surface below.

The lamp is elevated to leave enough room to work with the sugar, but may be moved up or down to adjust the intensity of the heat so that the sugar remains pliable. Also known as a *warming lamp* and *sugar lamp.*

heavy cream See *cream.*

heavy whipping cream See *cream.*

hedgehog Individual European cakes with an oval base and layered with chocolate-rum *buttercream* and studded with *pine nuts.* The whimsical cake is glazed with chocolate, and "eyes" are piped onto the front so it resembles a small animal. Known as *igel* in Austria.

Hefeteig ('hehf-uh-tlg) A basic *yeast dough* used to make cakes in Germany and Austria.

helva (hehl-vah) See *halvah.*

herb The edible leaf, stem, or flower of an herbaceous annual or perennial plant known for its flavor enhancement ability. Herbs are available fresh or dried, and are used in pastry primarily as garnishes, flavorings, or infusions.

herbal tea A tea made by steeping herbs in hot water. Some herb teas are believed to soothe and heal ailments.

herbsaint (ehrb-sahnt) An anise-flavored liqueur made primarily in New Orleans.

heraldic device A tart or cake decorated in the manner of a soldier's shield, using various jellies and fruits to designate the coat of arms. These desserts were originally served to soldiers before going into battle, as a symbol of good luck, or afterwards, to celebrate victory.

herman starter A sweet sourdough starter for producing yeast dough products. It is unclear why the starter is referred to as such, but it has become a Midwestern colloquialism.

hermit A chewy, spiced molasses cookie with nuts. The name comes from the belief that it tastes better after it is kept for several days.

heterofermentative lactobacilli Naturally occurring bacteria in sourdough cultures that produce both *acetic acid* and *lactic acid.*

hibiscus tea An aromatic, slightly tart tea with a striking magenta color, made by steeping the dark red leaves of the hibiscus flower in hot water. Its origin dates back to ancient Egypt, and it still served in the Nile Valley. The tea is believed to have powerful health benefits, such as lowering blood pressure and cooling the body in the heat. It is also revered in Egyptian culture, where people toast with a glass of hibiscus tea at every wedding.

hickory nut The nuts of over ten species of hickory trees, with the Shagbark being the fastest growing and most abundant in the eastern and central U.S. states. The most popular varieties are Eliot, Dover, and Papershell. Although they will produce nuts for over 300 years, it takes 100 pounds (47 kg) of seeds to make 1 pound (454 g) of nuts. The hard, bark-like shell contains a rich nutty meat and ripens between September and October. Since most of the nuts fall from their shells by December, the nuts are more readily available then because hand-hulling is minimal. See also *pecan.*

high-altitude baking Baking at higher altitudes requires that recipes be adjusted because the lower atmospheric pressure at these altitudes causes water to boil at a lower temperature. The following chart offers general guidelines, based on the number of feet above sea level. It is recommended that all high-altitude baking recipes be tested first for maximum quality.

H
h

INGREDIENT	ALTITUDE	ADJUSTMENT	NOTES
Eggs	2,500 feet 5,000 feet 7,000 and above	Increase by 3% Increase by 6% Increase by 12%	Will provide more structure and increase shelf life.
Leavening agent	2,500 feet 5,000 feet 7,000 and above	Reduce by 20% Reduce by 40% Reduce by 60%	Gas bubbles rise and pop more easily and may cause cake to fall because it may rise faster than it can set.
Flour	2,500 feet 5,000 feet 7,000 and above	Increase by 2% Increase by 4% Increase by 8%	Increased protein structure from gluten may help set the batter faster and prevent it from falling.
Sugar	2,500 feet 5,000 feet 7,000 and above	Reduce by 2% Reduce by 4% Reduce by 6%	Allows eggs to coagulate faster and helps prevent moisture loss.
Oven	2,500 feet to 7,500 feet	Increase temperature by 25°F	Will set cake structure faster and retain moisture.
Storage	Everything will dry more quickly in thin air so remove product from pans quickly and wrap air tight.		

high-conversion glucose corn syrup See *corn syrup.*

high fructose corn syrup See *corn syrup.*

high gluten flour See *flour.*

high-ratio cake A cake made with an *emulsified shortening*, enabling additional liquid to be added to the batter during the two-stage method of mixing. This produces an extremely tender and moist cake. Although butter or shortening may be substituted for emulsified shortening, the cake will be less tender. In addition, cake flour and an adequate amount of liquid are essential or the cake will be dry. See *high-ratio mixing method.*

high-ratio mixing method A two-stage mixing method used for batters when the weight of the sugar exceeds the weight of the flour. This method came about in the 1930s, when *emulsified shortening* and *chlorinated cake flour* were created. Previously, the low-gluten cake flour could not absorb as much liquid, which is necessary for a moist cake, but the chlorinated flour enabled it to absorb greater amounts of liquid. In addition, the new shortening dispersed the air and fat pockets better, producing a more tender cake. See also *two-stage mixing method* and *high-ratio cake*.

high-ratio shortening See *shortening*.

high tea A time of day, usually 4 to 6 PM, as well as the meal that is served then, consisting of brewed tea and a substantial selection of savory and sweet baked items. This British tradition originated in the 19th century as a supper for the working class. The "high" refers to how the meal was eaten, either sitting atop a stool or standing at a counter. High tea is often confused with the afternoon tea that is associated with a social gathering for women. See *afternoon tea*.

hiki-cha (hee-kee-'chah) A highly concentrated green tea powder from Japan. It can be used to color or flavor pastry items such as syrups, meringues, and mousses. Also known as *maccha*.

Hippenmasse ('hip-ehn-mahs) A stencil cookie similar to a *tuile* that is made with flour, sugar, butter, and almond paste spread over a stencil, baked, and formed while still warm. They are popular as garnishes and decorative cookies.

hoe cake A regional name for a cornmeal flatbread, of cornmeal, water, and salt. The name came about because field workers often cooked it on a hoe, over an open flame. See also *cornmeal flatbread*.

hogmanay See *black bun*.

hojuela de naranja (who-'whel-yahs day nah-'rahn-hah) A sweet orange puff from Colombia, made from pastry dough flavored with orange juice. The puffs are rolled out and cut into shapes before being deep-fried, and dusted with confectioners' sugar before serving.

hokey-pokey 1. A popular ice cream in New Zealand that has a crunchy toffee candy bar mixed in. 2. British slang for ice cream sold by street vendors.

holey-poke See *Baptist cake*.

hominy Hulled corn kernels, cooked and served as a side dish. American colonists learned from the Algonquian Indians how to make the tough corn grains edible by soaking the kernels in wood-based lye to remove the hulls. They would grind and boil the corn to make a cereal; today, the process is done mechanically. The word hominy refers to yellow or white corn without the hull and germ; it is served whole (available in cans) or ground as meal, the latter popularly called *grits* in the South. The name derives from the Algonquain word "rokahominy." See also *samp*.

hominy grits See *grits*.

homofermentative lactobacilli The naturally occurring bacteria in sourdough cultures that produce *lactic acid*.

homogenize (huh-'majh-uh-nize) To produce a uniform blended milk whereby the fat does not separate during storage. The process forces whole milk through very fine holes by spinning it at high speeds in order to break down the fat globules.

honey A pure, natural sweetener made from the nectar collected by bees from wild and cultivated flowers. There are over 300 types of honey available in the United States, and the extensive variety of floral sources creates an assortment of colors and flavors ranging from light and mild to dark and pungent. Honey has ancient origins and was the first sweetener known to humans. The Greeks and Romans referred to honey as "the nectar of the gods." When substituting honey for sugar in a recipe, use the following guidelines: Replace 1 cup (240 ml) of sugar with 1 cup (240 ml) of honey (note: honey is sweeter than sugar so adjust by taste) and reduce the amount of liquid by ¼ cup (60 ml). When baking with honey, add ½ teaspoon (2.5 ml) baking soda for each cup (240 ml) of honey

H
h

used and lower the temperature by 25 degrees. Honey batter becomes crisp and browns faster than sugar batter and will result in a firmer, heavier texture.

The most common varieties of honey are:

Acacia One of the few honeys that does not crystallize with age; this pale, clear honey can be found in Asia, Europe, and Canada. It has a delicate scent and is made from acacia blossoms.

Alfalfa Light and mild flavored, and produced extensively in Canada and the United States from purple alfalfa blossoms.

Avocado Dark with a rich, buttery taste; made from California avocado blossoms.

Blueberry Light amber, with a full, well-rounded flavor; produced in New England and in Michigan from the tiny white flowers of wild blueberries.

Buckwheat Dark and full-bodied; produced in the Midwest and eastern Canada from buckwheat flowers.

Clover The largest honey production in the United States. It is mild and varies in color from opaque to amber owing to the different colors of clover flowers.

Eucalyptus A California honey that varies in color and flavor owing to the different flowers in this group of plants, but tends to be on the stronger side.

Hymetus A dark brown, rich honey from Mount Hymettus in Greece, with a distinctive thyme flavor.

Lavender A delicate honey from the lavender flowers cultivated in the South of France.

Manuka A dark, thick, rich creamed honey flavored by the flowers of the New Zealand tea tree.

Orange Blossom A light citrus color and flavor; produced in citrus-growing areas of Florida, southern California, and parts of Texas.

Sage Light colored with a mild flavor and dense texture; produced in California and often blended with other honeys.

Tupelo A heavy-bodied, amber honey with a greenish hue and a mild, distinctive taste; produced in northwest Florida and has a high fructose content.

Wildflower A honey of many undefined wildflower sources.

honeybun A spiral breakfast roll made from a *yeast dough,* glazed with honey.

honey date A type of *date* grown in China, used in pastries and confections.

honeydew See *muskmelon.*

hoop A tall ring used in making large cakes, to extend their height.

Hoosier cake A coarse gingerbread cake from the U.S. Midwest, developed during the 19th century.

horchata (hor-'chah-tah) A popular Spanish and Mexican milky drink of water-steeped nuts, grains, or *chufa.* The mixture is sweetened with sugar and spices, usually cinnamon, and is served cold or at room temperature.

horehound A leafy, aromatic plant that is a member of the mint family. The juice is extracted and used to make *horehound candy*, throat medicine, and cordials.

horehound candy A bittersweet candy made from the extract of *horehound.*

horned melon See *kiwano melon.*

horno Another name for an *adobe oven;* see *oven.*

hors d'oeuvre (or 'derv) A small portion of warm or cold savory food, typically served during the cocktail hour preceding dinner.

hoska ('hos-kah) A braided holiday bread from Slovakia, flavored with almonds, raisins, and citron.

Hosui See *Asian pear*.

hotcake Another name for a *pancake*.

hot chocolate A rich, warm beverage of dark chocolate and hot milk or water, typically served in a mug and topped with whipped cream.

hot cocoa A warm beverage made with cocoa powder and hot milk or water, typically served in a mug and may be topped with mini-marshmallows or whipped cream. It is also commonly referred to simply as *cocoa*.

hot cross bun A small, spiced yeast bun studded with raisins and marked with a glazed cross on top, to symbolize Christ. It is a traditional Easter bread, historically served on Good Friday.

hotel pan A rectangular stainless steel pan with a lip. It rests in a well on a steam table to keep food warm during service. The pans come in standard sizes, such as full or half, and the depth of the pan is referred to as follows: 2 inches (5 cm) deep is a 200 pan; 4 inches (10 cm) deep is a 400 pan, etc.

hot fudge A thick chocolate sauce made with chocolate, butter, sugar, and cream, traditionally served warm over an *ice cream sundae*.

hot toddy See *toddy*.

huckleberry See *berry*.

huevo ('whey-voh) The Spanish word for egg.

huevo quimbo ('whey-voh 'keem-boh) A sweet egg cookie made by whipping egg yolks to the ribbon stage and baking them until set, then cutting them into shapes when cool and soaking them in a sweet rum syrup. They are named after the extinct Colombian tribe of Quimbaya Indians.

huff-juff See *Baptist cake*.

Huguenot torte ('hue-gah-not tort) A nut-filled baked apple, garnished with whipped cream and additional nuts. A popular dessert in Charleston, South Carolina.

huile The French word for oil.

hull 1. To remove the stem and calyx from a strawberry. 2. To remove the husk from a grain. 3. The outer coating of a fruit, seed, or nut.

humble pie An English pie once made from umbles, which are the less desirable innards of deer or other animals. Since it was considered inferior food, it was often served to servants and eaten by lower-class people. The term has become synonymous with the phrase "eat humble pie," which means to swallow your pride.

humbug See *berlingot*.

humectant A hygroscopic ingredient, such as *invert sugar*, added to a product to keep it moist and improve its shelf life.

hummingbird cake A moist, heavy cake made with bananas, pineapples, and nuts, usually pecans. It is layered and frosted with *cream cheese icing* and garnished with nuts.

hung bau (huhng-bow) The Chinese word for "red buns," referring to a steamed red pastry filled with red bean paste and traditionally given away to celebrate the birth of a baby girl.

hushva nan (hush-vanen) A thick, soft, lightly yeasted bread from Iran. It is made from whole wheat flour and has a bumpy, pebbled appearance. The breads are first cooked in a skillet on the stove and then transferred to the broiler. The finished bread has a glossy top and crusty bottom. Also known as *pebbled Persian bread*.

husk The protective outer coating of a grain.

hustler See *Baptist cake*.

Hutzelbrot ('hoot-serl-broat) The German name for a bread made with fruit.

hydration The percentage of liquid ingredients in a bread dough in relation to the weight of the flour in the dough.

hydrogenated fat Fats such as *all-purpose shortening, margarine,* and *high-ratio shortening* that have been hydrogenated by exposing them to hydrogen gas, pressure, and high heat. This saturates carbon atoms with hydrogen and coverts an *unsaturated fat* to a *saturated fat*. The product is typically only partially hydrated so that the fat remains soft, plastic, and easy to work with. See also *fats and oils*.

hydrogenated oil An oil that has been chemically manipulated from a liquid state to a solid state at room temperature. The hydrogenation process forces pressurized hydrogen gas through unsaturated fat, such as liquid vegetable oil, and creates trans fatty acids. Although this makes the product more spreadable and increases its shelf life, it is now a saturated fat, which is unhealthy.

hydromel An ancient beverage made from fermented honey and water. It was popular with the ancient Greeks and Romans and throughout the Middle Ages. Its name is from the Greek *hydro*, meaning "water" and the Latin *mel*, meaning "honey."

hydrometer An instrument used to determine the specific gravity of a liquid. See *saccharometer* and *refractometer*.

hygroscopic Refers to sugars that attract and absorb moisture from the air. A highly hygroscopic sugar such as *fructose* is desirable for moist, soft cookies and creamy icings, but is not recommended for sugar work because the result will easily become tacky.

hyssop ('hihs-up) An aromatic herb that belongs to the mint family. It dates back to Biblical times and is most often used for its oil to make *Chartreuse*. It is best used fresh, since drying diminishes its rich flavor; but if not available, substitute dried mint, thyme, savory, and/or rosemary.

Ii

Iago (ee-'ah-go) A small, round sponge cake filled with coffee *buttercream* and coated in *coffee fondant*. It is named after a character in the play *Othello* by Shakespeare and is typically served as petit fours or with afternoon tea.

ibarra (ee-'bahr-ah) See *Mexican chocolate*.

ibrik ('ibb-reek) A small brass pot with a long wooden handle, for making Greek and Turkish coffee.

ice bath A combination of ice and water, used to cool down food quickly. It is commonly used in the bakeshop to prevent eggs from overcooking in *crème anglaise* and control the color of *caramel*.

icebox cake A home-style cake or pie, typically consisting of alternating layers of thin chocolate cookies and pudding, chilled overnight, then topped with whipped cream.

icebox cookie See *cookie*.

ice cream A frozen dessert made from cream and/or milk. The origins of this American favorite can be traced back to the 4th century B.C., when the Roman emperor Nero combined fruit toppings with ice from the mountains. In the 13th century, Marco Polo learned about the Chinese method of creating ice and milk mixtures, and upon his return to Europe recipes appeared for ices and sherbets. The recipes found their way to America via immigrants, and it became a favorite of Thomas Jefferson, George Washington, and Dolly Madison. The U.S. standards require ice cream to contain a minimum of 10% milk fat and 20% total milk solids. There is a maximum of 100% overrun allowed. See also *overrun*.

ice cream cone A crisp, cornet-shaped wafer cookie used as a container to hold a single serving of ice cream. Although the origin of the cone has been greatly debated, it is thought to have been invented at the 1904 World's Fair in St. Louis, when an ice cream vendor ran out of paper cups and asked a nearby waffle booth to make some thin waffles he could roll up to hold the ice cream.

ice cream machine/maker An electrical or mechanical appliance used in the production of ice cream. Either machine operates on the same basic idea: the ice cream base is poured into a metal container that has a paddle (*dasher*) and then is placed into another, larger canister that holds the freezing agent. The mechanical ice cream maker is known as a hand crank and uses a wooden bucket filled with ice and rock salt to freeze the ice cream slowly as the paddle is turned. It generally produces 1 gallon (3 L, 840 ml) in 15 to 20  minutes. Although it is fun to use, it is not appropriate for the professional kitchen. Commercial ice cream makers vary in size, style, and price, but are meant to produce larger batches more efficiently.

ice cream scoop A tool to remove ice cream from its container. Scoops come in different shapes, sizes, and styles. Typically there is a number on either the handle or the metal band on the inside of the scoop that represents the number of scoops of ice cream per gallon or quart, depending on the brand of scoop.

ice cream soda A sweet beverage of ice cream and flavored syrup, topped with whipped cream and a *maraschino cherry*.

ice cream sundae See *sundae*.

ice kacang (i kah-'chang) A cold Chinese dessert of boiled red beans, corn kernels, and multicolored jelly cubes. The mixture is covered with crushed ice and shaped into a cone, then topped with colored syrup and condensed milk before serving.

ice milk A less creamy version of ice cream. It has a milk fat content of less than 10% and tends to be less expensive than ice cream because of the reduced fat content. In 1994 the Food and Drug Administration allowed it to be labeled "low-fat ice cream" so the term is rarely used nowadays.

iced soufflé A frozen dessert of a *pâte à bombe* mixture with meringue, whipped cream, and flavorings folded in, then put into a ramekin that has a paper or acetate collar extended over the top of the container. After the ramekin is filled and frozen, the paper is removed and the finished product resembles a hot soufflé just out of the oven.

ice-point method See *thermometer*.

ice wine A very sweet wine made from very ripe, frozen grapes. Known as *Eiswein* in Germany.

icing A sweet, creamy mixture used to cover, coat, or decorate baked goods, cakes, pastries, and petit fours. There are seven categories of icing: *buttercream, fondant, royal icing, fudge-type icing, flat icing, glazes,* and *boiled icing (foam-type icing)*. The type of icing used depends on the desired, texture, appearance, and flavor of the product being iced. Icing serves many functions, including enhancing the flavor, appearance, and texture of the product as well as prolonging shelf life by forming a protective coating to help prevent the item from drying out. Also known as *frosting*.

icing comb See *cake comb*.

icing sugar See *sugar*.

igel ('ee-gehl) See *hedgehog*.

île flottant (eel flow-'tahn) See *floating island*.

imitation vanilla A vanilla-flavored substitute for the higher-priced pure vanilla. It is made entirely of artificial flavorings and has a harsher quality and bitter after-taste. It is also necessary to use larger amounts in order to achieve the desired vanilla flavor.

immersion blender A slender hand-held blender that can be placed in a container to blend or puree the product in place. They are made with various speeds and in different sizes; their main advantage is their mobility.

impératrice, a l' (ahn-pair-ah-trees ahl) A French term that refers to desserts with cooked rice as their base. In pastry, it is most commonly used to describe a dessert made with rice, *Bavarian cream*, and candied fruits.

Imperial gallon The British term for a larger gallon than the American equivalent; it equals 1.2 U.S. gallons, or 160 fluid ounces, or 4.75 L.

Imperial system A system of measurement associated with the former British Empire; it uses pounds and ounces for weight measurements and pints, quarts, and fluid ounces for volume measurements. This is the measurement system employed by most commercial restaurants in the United States.

impossible pie A simple dessert that combines a package of biscuit mix with eggs, milk, coconut, sugar, and butter. When baked in a pie pan, the biscuit mix settles on the bottom of the custard and creates the "crust" of the pie.

imprinter A tool used for molding starch. It makes impressions in the starch and is typically made from plastic shapes that are attached to a wooden stick or board.

imu A Hawaiian outdoor oven made by digging a round pit with sloping sides. Kindling wood is then placed on the bottom of the pit along with stones, which retain heat. The food is sandwiched between grass or leaves, such as ti or banana leaves, and a mat or cloth covers the food to protect it from the dirt that is packed on top. The food is cooked by steaming and, depending on the food, may take several hours. Also known as a *lua*.

inch An American measurement of length that is equivalent to 25.4 millimeters.

Indian date See *tamarind*.

Indianerkrapfen (een-dee-'ahn-uhr-krap-fehn) A small, round Austrian cake of hollowed-out sponge layer that is filled with whipped cream and completely coated in a shiny chocolate glaze.

Indian nut See *pine nut*.

Indian pudding See *hasty pudding*.

Indian red peach See *peach*.

Indian saffron See *turmeric*.

indirect dough Bread dough that is produced with a *pre-ferment*, made with commercial yeast, wild yeast, or a starter. Also known as *sponge*.

induction burner/cooking A contemporary cooking technology that uses magnetic energy for heat conduction. The induction cooking surface is a flat, smooth ceramic cooktop with a magnified element underneath. When a special induction pot/pan is placed on the cooktop, its coils react with the heat source and quickly heat the contents of the pan. Once the pan is removed, the cooking surface remains cool. This makes it both safe and energy efficient to use.

infuse To steep an item in hot liquid in order to extract a pronounced flavor. Flavored teas, herbs, and fruits are infused.

infusion See *infuse*.

injera (in-'jehr-rah) An Ethiopian spongy, pita-like bread made from *teff*, a North African grain with a nutty flavor and high protein content. It is used as an edible plate on which stews are served; it soaks up spicy sauces. Also spelled *aenjera*.

instant active dry yeast See *yeast*.

instant cocoa A cocoa mix of cocoa, sugar, and dried milk solids that makes hot cocoa when added to hot water.

instant coffee A finely ground powdered coffee extract made by preparing and drying brewed coffee. The ground powder is combined with hot water to make a cup of coffee. See also *coffee*.

instant flour See *flour*.

instant oats See *oats*.

instant-read thermometer See *thermometer*.

intermezzo (ihn-teh-'meht-soh) A refreshing dish, usually sorbet, served in between courses to cleanse the palate.

invertase An enzyme used to soften and improve the shelf life of confectionery centers by inverting *sucrose*.

invert sugar See *sugar*.

instant dry yeast See *yeast*.

instant flour See *flour*.

iodized salt See *salt*.

IQF The acronym for individually quick frozen, referring to fruits or other foods that have been separated and blast-frozen. The food may be substituted for fresh once thawed, and the benefits are lower costs and year-round availability.

Irish breakfast tea A combination of black teas from Sri Lanka and India, typically served with the morning meal, but this robust beverage may be enjoyed any time of day or evening.

Irish coffee A coffee drink of hot coffee, Irish whisky, and sugar. It is topped with a generous dollop of whipped cream.

Irish oats See *oats*.

Irish soda bread An Irish quickbread that uses baking soda as the *leavening agent*. Although some bakers add nuts or fruit, the bread is traditionally made with flour, baking soda, salt, and buttermilk. The bread may be either brown or white, and became popularized in the 1840s when bicarbonate of soda was introduced to Ireland. It is believed that the loaf's round form with a cross sliced into it before baking is to ward off evil.

Irish whisky See *whisky*.

ironware See *cast iron*.

irradiation A preservation method that uses ionizing radiation to sterilize fruits and reduce ripening time.

ischl (eeshl) An Austrian cookie made from a cinnamon-spiced almond or hazelnut dough sandwiched with jam after baking. The center of the top cookie is cut out so that the jam shows through, and the cookie is dusted with confectioners' sugar before serving.

isinglass ('i-zuhn-glas) A gelling agent used before the invention of modern gelatin. It was produced from the air bladders of fish such as sturgeon and used to make jellies and European desserts.

isomalt ('i-soh-mahlt) A sweetener made by chemically altering *sucrose*. It is popular with pastry chefs because it does not brown easily, crystallize, or pick up moisture; it is used for sugar garnishes and showpiece work.

Italian bread An Italian version of the French *baguette*, with a softer texture and plumper shape.

Italian buttercream See *buttercream*.

Italian meringue See *meringue*.

Italian pine nut See *pine nut*.

izarra (ih-'zahr-ruh) An Armagnac-based liqueur flavored with herbs, available in yellow or the stronger and more full-flavored green.

Jj

jackfruit The oval fruit of a small evergreen tree that is native to India but is now prevalent all over Southeast Asia. The prickly greenish-yellow rind surrounds a rich yellow flesh with light brown seeds. It has a very strong odor; it is generally cut into sections and eaten fresh or boiled in coconut milk and eaten as a vegetable. The

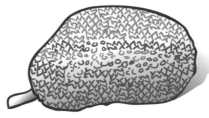

chewy flesh is a cross between a pineapple and a melon, but with a milder taste and less juicy texture. It is considered the largest fruit in the world. The seeds may be boiled in saltwater and eaten as a snack, while the wood of the tree is used extensively in wood carving. Jackfruit is also available canned.

Jacob's bâton (jhah-cob's bah-'than) A small, stick-shaped *éclair* filled with pastry cream and iced with *fondant*.

jaconde ('zha-kohnde) A light, thin sponge cake made with ground almonds, confectioner's sugar, egg whites, and flour, used for decorative linings for cake and charlotte molds. The design is incorporated by stenciling a colored tuile paste onto a silpat and then covering it with the jaconde batter before baking. Once baked the design is set on the outer layer of the cake. Also known as *ribbon sponge*.

jaggery See *sugar*.

jalebis ('gel-ei-bees) A sweet treat made in markets throughout the Middle East and in India. It consists of a thin batter poured into hot oil and fried until crisp, then soaked in a rosewater syrup.

jallab (gall-aab) A sweet, chilled Middle Eastern drink made from dates, grapes, and rosewater and garnished with pine nuts.

jalousie ('zhah-loh-zee) A French pastry of long rectangular strips of *puff pastry* filled with *frangipane* (although jam or poached fruit is also common), and topped with lattice-cut puff pastry, then baked and finished with either apricot glaze or a dusting of confectioners' sugar. The name is French for "venetian blind," as the filling is visible through the pastry.

jam A sweet fruit spread made from pureed fruit. It must contain a minimum of 45% fruit, combined with sugar and cooked to 220°F (104°C). Some fruits contain a natural gelling agent called *pectin* and during the cooking process, the acid and pectin in the fruit react and cause the mixture to set upon cooling. When the fruit is low in pectin granulated or liquid pectin may be added to achieve the proper set. The technique of fruit preservation can be traced back to the ancient Greeks who used honey in the preservation of fruit, such as quince. The Crusaders introduced fruit preservation to Europe where they improved the flavor and texture with cane sugar. Jam is used as a spread for breads, scones, and biscuits;

as a topping for waffles and pancakes; and as a filling for Danish, cakes, and doughnuts. See also *jelly, preserves,* and *marmalade.*

Jamaica pepper See *allspice.*

Jamaican rum See *rum.*

jameed See *labanah mackbouseh.*

janhagel ('yahn-hay-ghal) A Dutch almond cookie flavored with allspice and cinnamon, and topped with almonds.

Japanese pear See *pear.*

Japanese plum See *plum.*

Japanese rice wine See *sake.*

japonaise (zhah-poh-nays) A French baked meringue made with ground almonds or hazelnuts.

jar wonton A Chinese pastry of *wonton wrappers* filled with nuts, dates, lemon zest, and orange juice, then rolled into tubes, the ends twisted, and deep-fried. They are dusted with confectioner's sugar before serving.

jasmine ('jazz-mihn) A sweet-scented flower used to flavor teas and pastries.

jell To congeal a food substance into a firm state, often by using *pectin* or *gelatin.*

jellies Small European confections made from concentrated fruit juice and sugar, cooked to 220°F (104°C), cooled, and combined with gelatin to form a very firm, slightly chewy layer. It is then cut into desired shapes, usually squares, and coated with sugar. These are often served as part of a *mignardise* selection.

Jell-O A flavored and sweetened gelatin mix in powder form. It is dissolved in hot water, cold water is added, and it is allowed to gel. This popular American dessert dates back to 1845, when an inventor named Peter Cooper obtained the first patent for a gelatin dessert. Although he packaged the gelatin in neat little boxes with directions for use, it did not become popular until Pearle B. Wait, a carpenter and cough medicine manufacturer, created a fruit-flavored version in 1897. Pearle's wife, May Davis Wait, named it, and the original flavors were strawberry, raspberry, orange, and lemon. Today, over 300 million boxes of Jell-O are sold annually.

jelly A sweet fruit spread made from clear fruit juice and sugar. Generally fruits high in *pectin* are made into jellies. In England, *jelly* refers to sweet or savory gelatin-based food. See also *jam* and *preserves.*

jelly bag A canvas or cheesecloth bag used to strain fruit, so as to obtain the clear juice for making jelly.

jelly bean A very small, egg-shaped candy made with sugar, corn syrup, and food starch. It has a thin, hard exterior and a chewy fruit-flavored center. Jelly beans come in a wide variety of flavors and colors ranging from black licorice to hot pink cotton candy. It is believed they derive from the Middle Eastern confection known as *Turkish delight.* They became associated with Easter in the 1930s, and have been an American tradition ever since. Jelly Belly is the most well-known brand.

jelly cake A small sponge cake coated in jelly and rolled in *desiccated coconut,* eaten as is or sometimes split and filled with cream.

jelly melon See *kiwano melon.*

jelly pie A Southern pie with a filling of cooked *Concord grapes,* sugar, and lemon juice thickened with cornstarch and poured into a blind-baked pie crust (see *blind bake*), then topped with whipped cream. Also known as *grape pie.*

jelly roll A thin sheet of sponge cake spread with a thin layer of jam and rolled up into a cylinder. The cake is served cut into thin slices. Also known as *Swiss roll;* see also *English Swiss roll.*

jésuite (jeh-'sweet) A small, triangle of *puff pastry* that is filled with *marzipan* paste and covered with *royal icing.* Its triangular shape resembles the hats worn by Jesuits.

J. H. Male peach See *peach.*

Jiffy Pop See *popcorn.*

jilk A stabilizer sometimes used to help aerate *génoise.*

jimmies Tiny elongated pieces of chocolate, white, or multicolored candies, used to decorate cakes, cupcakes, and candies. They date to the early 19th century; known also as *sprinkles* in America, *vermicelli* in France, hundreds-and-thousands in England, and *nonpareils* in France.

Johannisberg Riesling See *Riesling.*

johnnycake A cornmeal flatbread made by early settlers in New England The name is believed to derive from the Shawnee Indian *jonakin.* Early versions were made simply with cornmeal, salt, and water; modern-day johnnycakes often include eggs, oil, and baking powder. Also known as *Shawnee cake* and *journey cake.* See also *cornmeal flatbread.*

jointoyer (jwahn-toy-'yay) A French term that refers to filling in any uneven surfaces of layered cakes and pastries. This is typically done with whipped cream or *buttercream* to ensure a smooth and uniform surface on the top and sides of the cake.

Jonagold apple See *apple.*

Jonathan apple See *apple.*

jordan almond A small confection of an almond encased in a hard sugar coating. These come in a wide range of colors and are popular wedding favors because they symbolize married life as being both bitter (almond) and sweet (sugar).

journey cake Another name for johnnycake, believed to be called such because it was easily prepared and carried by travelers. See also *johnnycake.*

jowar (joo-'wahr) See *flour, sorghum.*

juggery ('jooh-gehr-dhi) A tapioca dessert from India, made with *treacle,* coconut, and cream.

jugo ('hoo-goh) A Latin American drink made from fresh fruit pulp and ice, and sometimes sugar.

juicer A hand tool or electric machine that extracts the juice from fruits. The hand tool is a shallow flat-bottomed bowl for juicing citrus fruits; the fruit is cut in half and placed on a pointed cone in the center of the bowl. When the fruit half is pressed onto the cone and turned, the juice collects at the bottom. Electric juicers extract the juice from a variety of fruits and vegetables, separating pulp and residue using the same concept as the manually operated one.

jujube (joo-'joo-bee) 1. A small fruit-flavored candy with a hard gelatinous center. Originally the center contained cough medication; the name derives from the Chinese date *Ziziphus jujube,* the juice of which was used in the candy. 2. Another name for *Chinese red date,* used in Asian desserts.

julekaka (jhoo-'leh-kah-kah) A Norwegian Christmas bread made from a sweetened yeast-raised dough flavored with cardamom, citron, and raisins.

julienne (joo-lee-'ehn) To cut food into matchstick pieces, which generally measure ⅛ inch (3 mm) thick and vary in length.

jumbal 1. An English biscuit made with a honey-sweetened dough that is rolled into long, thin pieces, baked, and then covered with lemon icing and flavored with caraway. It dates to the 17th century. 2. A colonial American ring-shaped sugar cookie often flavored with sour cream and scented with rosewater. These crisp, delicate cookies date back to the 18th century and were also made in coconut and walnut flavors.

juniper berry See *berry*.

junket A British dessert of milk, sugar, and flavorings that are jelled with *rennet*. It has a custard-like texture and is traditionally served with *clotted cream*. The dessert dates back to medieval times.

juwar ('juh-wahr) The Hindi word for sorghum flour; see *flour*.

Kk

kaak ('kaa-k) A Lebanese yeast-raised pastry made from several pieces of sweet dough rolled into ropes and formed into rings, and topped with sesame seeds. After baking it is glazed with milk and sugar and dried.

kaaki ('kah-kee) A pretzel-like street food in Tunisia.

kab el ghzal (cab il gahl) A crescent-shaped Moroccan pastry filled with ground almonds, orange flower water, cinnamon, and sugar, and rolled in confectioners' sugar. Traditionally served with mint tea. The name means "gazelle's horn" and refers to the pastry's shape.

kadaif 1. Shredded *phyllo dough.* 2. A Middle Eastern confection of shredded phyllo dough filled with nuts and spices. It is coated with butter to keep it moist, and after baking is soaked in sugar syrup. Also spelled *kataïfi.*

kadayif See *kadaif.*

kadhi (kah-dee) An Indian dumpling made with chickpea flour and simmered in spices, vegetables, and yogurt.

kadin göbegi (kah-din gur-'beh-gee) The Turkish term for "lady's navel," referring to a sweet fritter made from a dough similar to *choux paste.* The walnut-size balls are piped onto a sheet pan and indented in the middle with a finger dipped in almond extract, then deep-fried and soaked in a lemon-sugar syrup.

Kadota fig See *fig.*

Kaffee ('kah-fay) The German word for *coffee.*

Kaffeekuchen ('kahf-fee-'koo-kuhn) The German word for *coffee cake.*

kaffir lime A pear-shaped citrus fruit with a bumpy, wrinkled bright yellow skin and a flowery, citrus aroma and flavor. The lime trees are grown in Hawaii and Southeast Asia. The dark green, shiny leaves are used as a flavoring agent.

kafir corn A sorghum grain introduced to the United States in 1876. It is a cereal grass with white, red, or black-hulled clusters of grain. It was popular because of its drought and heat resistance, and is used primarily as cattle and poultry feed. Named for the Kafir tribe in Natal, Africa where it is used for meal and syrup.

Kahúla A dark, coffee-flavored liqueur with the rich, sweet flavor of Mexican coffee. It has 20% alcohol content and is a popular flavoring agent for pastries and desserts. It is also used in cocktails.

kaimak (kl-'mahk) A thick, shiny sour cream served with bread, in Uzbekistan.

kaiser roll A large round, puffy roll with a crisp crust and soft, chewy center. Also known as *Vienna roll* and *hard roll.*

Kajü ('kah-jhoo) A Brazilian liqueur made from *cashew apples.* The name derives from the Brazilian *caju,* which means "cashew."

kaju burfi An Indian sweet made from ground cashews, sugar, ground cardamom, and *ghee.* It is often garnished with *silver varak.*

K
k

ka'kat ('kaa-kat) A ring-shaped Middle Eastern street bread that may be large or small, sweet or savory, and dense and chewy to soft and light, depending on the region.

kaltschale (kaylt-'shah-leh) Russian term for "cold cup," referring to a cold fruit dessert. It consists of fruit soaked in a mixture of white wine, sugar, and citrus juices and then pureed. The puree is served over fresh fruit.

kamut (kah-'moot) A high-protein wheat with distinctively large kernels and a pleasant nutty flavor. An ancient relative of modern *durum wheat*, its kernels are almost three times the size of normal wheat kernels. Today it is most often used in the production of commercial pasta and crackers.

kanom mo kaeng (kah-nom moe kah-hang) A sweet Thai custard. It is made by cooking, over a double boiler, coconut cream, brown sugar, eggs, and salt until thick, then baking until firm and briefly broiling to brown the top. It is then topped with sautéed shallots and cut into squares. *Kanom* is Thai for "dessert," *mo* means "pot" and refers to the cooking dish, and *kaeng* means "soup" or "curry," referring to the consistency of the dessert.

kanten Another name for *agar-agar*.

karakot (kah-raw-kott) A fruit and almond confection from Uzbek. It is made by cooking stewed fruit with sugar, finely ground almonds, egg yolks, and vanilla until thick; when it has cooled, whipped egg whites are folded in and the mixture is baked in a rectangular shallow pan on low heat until dry. It is traditionally cut into slices and served with lemon tea.

karidópita (kah-ree-doe-pee-tah) A Greek walnut cake that is soaked in brandy syrup after baking.

Karo A brand of *corn syrup*, available in light and dark versions.

kasha ('kah-sha) The Russian word for both the *buckwheat groat* that has been hulled, roasted, and crushed, and the *porridges* made with it. It has a distinctive nutty flavor and is one of the oldest meals in Eastern European cuisine.

kashata na nazi (kah-shaw-tah nah nah-zee) A Ugandan candy made by cooking sugar, coconut, salt, and cinnamon until firm and then cutting it into squares. It is served as a snack or during tea time.

kashi ('kah-shee) See *okashi*.

Kasnudeln ('kass-nood-lehn) A German noodle dish made with poppy seeds and fruit. It may also include savory fillings such as meat and cheese.

kataïfi See *kadaif*.

katakuri (kah-tah-koo-ree) A starch used as a thickener in Japan. It is made by drying and grinding the roots of the dogtooth violet.

kater A mixture of sugar, water, fresh lemon juice, and orange blossom water, used in many Middle Eastern confections, such as *nammura*.

katira (kah-'tee-rah) A Malaysian beverage of condensed milk, rosewater, and biji selaseh (the seeds of a type of basil that swell when in liquid), drunk during Ramadan.

ka'u orange See *citrus*.

kaymak (ghay-mak) A thick, dense cream similar to *clotted cream*, with a butterfat content of 60%. It made by slowly boiling buffalo or goat's milk over low heat for two or more hours. The cream is then skimmed off the top and fermented for a minimum of one day, which produces a slightly sour flavor. It is used extensively in desserts, baked goods, and as a spread for bread in the Middle East, particularly Turkey.

keemun ('key-moon) A black tea from China's Anwhei and Kiansi provinces, with a strong aroma and rich, nonastringent flavor.

keemun hao ya (key-moon ha-o eea) A black tea grown in the famous tea-growing region of China's Hao Ya mountain range. It has a slightly sweet aroma and delicate flavor that make it popular in blended teas, such as *Irish breakfast tea* and *English breakfast tea.*

kefir ('kah-feer) A frothy Middle Eastern drink originally made from fermented camel's milk but now produced from cow's milk. It is from the Caucasus region (between the Caspian and Black seas), and has the consistency of thin yogurt.

Kellogg, John Harvey A food pioneer and early advocate for vegetarianism, he was a medical doctor who used nutrition and exercise as a primary cure for ailments. He ran a sanitarium in Battle Creek, Michigan, where he developed a breakfast cereal called *granose*, which consisted of flaked wheat and toasted corn flakes. In 1884, he and his brother Will received a patent for a machine that perfected a method for flaking, and his brother William K. Kellogg founded the Battle Creek Toasted Corn Flake Company, which produced the *cornflake* breakfast cereal for the public.

Kelsey plum See *plum.*

Kentucky coffee tree During colonial times, the seeds of this native American tree were roasted and ground and used as a substitute for coffee.

Kerman pistachio A top-quality variety of pistachio created in 1950 from experimental plantings of pistachio seedlings in California. The variety was named in honor of Kerman, a city in California noted for the manufacture and export of fine carpets where the seeds were collected.

ketone An organic compound that contributes flavor and aroma to bread.

Key lime The fruit of the Key lime tree, native to Malaysia. The Spanish brought the tree to the Florida Keys in the 1500s, but when a hurricane wiped out the plantations in 1926, they were replanted with Persian limes, which are easier to pick and transport. Most Key limes are now imported from Mexico and Central America. The Key lime is smaller than the Persian lime and is juicier and more acidic. The thin, smooth, bitter yellow-green skin surrounds a pale yellow-green flesh. It has a distinct aroma and is most well known for its use in *Key lime pie.* The juice may be fresh squeezed or purchased fresh or frozen in concentrate form. Also known as *West Indies lime* and *Mexican lime.*

Key lime pie An American pie made with a *graham cracker crust* and a filling of *Key lime* juice and *sweetened condensed milk.* It is a Florida dessert staple and dates to the 1850s, when there was no refrigeration in the Florida Keys, and to 1856, when sweetened condensed milk was invented. The acid from the lime juice reacts with the sweetened milk and causes the filling to thicken without baking. There is much debate over whether the pie is topped with meringue or whipped cream, but either way, the true color of Key lime pie is a pale yellow. (The green that is commonly seen is the result of food coloring.)

kg The abbreviation for *kilogram.*

khachapuri (khah-chah-poor-ee) A small yeast-dough pastry filled with cheese, commonly sold by street vendors in the Republic of Georgia.

khamaliá (kah-mah-lee-'ah) A Greek marzipan-type delicacy made with grated white almonds, superfine sugar, lightly beaten egg whites, and flower essence. It is formed into various shapes and heavily dusted with confectioners' sugar after baking. It is traditionally served at weddings and other special occasions.

khamir (kha-meer) A natural yeast starter used in India to leaven *naan* and other soft breads.

K
k

khanom (khaa-nom) A variety of Thai liquid desserts and puddings.

khobaz (kho-bahz) A small, round or oval yeast-risen Middle Eastern bread, with a soft texture. It forms a pocket while baking that is used to hold foods.

Khoob (coob) A large melon from Iran that has pineapple-like flavor and orange skin and flesh.

Khourabia (koorab-'bee-ah) A crescent-shaped Armenian shortbread filled with walnuts, cinnamon, and sugar.

ki See *ti*.

kilogram A metric measurement of weight that is the equivalent of 2.2 pounds or 1000 grams.

kimochdun (kee-'mok-doon) A Pakistani skillet bread from the Hunzu Valley. It is often made for marking the end of Ramadan. There are several variations and methods of preparation, but are typically baked in a heavy skillet that is covered with hot coals. The bread is cut into wedges and served warm.

kinafa (kin-a-fah) An Arab dessert of long strips of buttered phyllo dough layered with either nuts, sugar, and spices or cream cheese and fruit. Once baked, it is soaked in a lemon and rosewater syrup.

kinako (kee-nah-koh) The Japanese word for soy flour. It may be found in health food stores under this name and it is very popular in Japan for the production of confections. See also *flour*.

King coconut A coconut from Sri Lanka, known for its very sweet juice.

King orange A large Florida orange with a loose, rough skin that encases a juicy, sweet-tart flesh. Available December to April.

kinome (kih-noh-meh) A Japanese herb with a flavor very similar to *mint*.

Kipferln ('kip-fairln) A Viennese crescent-shaped butter cookie made with ground almonds and rolled in confectioners' sugar. It is traditionally served during the Christmas holidays. Also known as *Viennese horn*.

kiping A brightly colored, leaf-shaped rice wafer from the Philippines. It is made from a thin paste of rice flour and water poured onto banana leaves and steamed. The wafers are peeled off before hardening and dried. The wafers are then deep-fried and coated with a thin layer of coconut jam or dipped in sweet syrup. They are most popular during the Lucban town festival, where they are stitched together with thread and made into decorative items.

kir (keer) An apéritif of white wine and *cassis liqueur*.

kir royale An apéritif that consists of *Champagne* and *cassis liqueur*.

Kirsch (keersh) See *Kirschwasser*.

Kirschtorte See *Zuger Kirschtorte*.

Kirschwasser ('keersh-vah-ser) A distilled cherry brandy whose name derives from the German *Kirsch* (cherry) and *Wasser* (water). It originated in the Black Forest region of Germany and is used as a flavoring in desserts and pastries, including *Black Forest torte* and *cherries jubilee*. Also known as *Kirsch*.

kishik ('kisk-kah) A Middle Eastern starch and thickener made from a ground mixture of sun-dried *bulgur* and *yogurt*.

kishk (keehk) The Arabic word for *yogurt* fermented with dried and ground *cracked wheat*.

kissel ('kee-suhl) A Russian custard-like dessert made by cooking a puree of red berries with sugar and thickening it with cornstarch or potato flour. It may be served warm or cold, and is typically topped with whipped cream.

K
k

Kit-Kat An American candy bar introduced in London in 1935 and called *Rowntree's Chocolate Crisp.* The name was changed in 1937, and is believed to have been a reference to the famous 1920s KitKat Club in South East London. Since the building had very low ceilings, it could accommodate paintings that were wide but not very high. In the art world, this size painting was known as a "kat" and the edge had to be snapped off to fit into a room with a low ceiling, just as the crisp wafer covered in milk chocolate "snaps" when eaten.

kiwai A small, fine-skinned variety of kiwi grown in Europe. The skin is edible.

kiwano melon An oval tropical fruit with a bright orange-yellow skin that is studded with small horns. The jelly-like flesh is pale yellow with a greenish hue, and tastes like a cross between banana, lime, and cucumber. It comes from New Zealand and ranges from 3 to 5 inches (7.5 to 12.5 cm) in size. It is also known as *horned melon, jelly melon,* and *cucumber melon.*

kiwifruit A small egg-shaped fruit with a thin, fuzzy brown skin and emerald green flesh, with small edible black seeds. It has a sweet-tart flavor that tastes like a cross between a pineapple, melon, and strawberry. Previously known as Chinese gooseberry, the name was changed by New Zealand growers. They are cultivated in California and New Zealand, which have opposite seasons, so they are available year-round. They are a good source of vitamin C and are used in pastries and desserts, particularly *pavlova,* because of their unique color and flavor. There is also a *gold kiwifruit* and *baby kiwifruit* variety. The gold kiwifruit has a smoother skin and a golden yellow flesh with a milder, more honey-like flavor; they are not available domestically but are in season from June to November. Baby kiwifruit are fuzzless and only about 1 inch (2.5 cm) long, with a firm green flesh; they are typically eaten whole and unpeeled and are available September to October.

K
k

klepon (kleh-'pon) An Indonesian confection that is a boiled dumpling made from sticky rice flour, rolled in grated coconut. See *rice, sticky.*

kloben An apricot-glazed European yeast cake filled with dried and candied fruits.

klosse (kloz-zeh) An Austrian *potato dumpling* made with eggs, flour, cornstarch, pureed cooked potatoes, bread crumbs, ginger, cinnamon, and cloves. The mixture is formed into balls and poached in a syrup of sweet wine and spices. Before serving, they are coated with buttery bread crumbs and drizzled with *crème anglaise* or *treacle sauce.*

klouskis ('klows-kihs) A Polish version of *klosse* made with flour, eggs, and spices. The dumplings are yeast-risen and proofed several times before being poached in sweet wine syrup.

kluay budt chee (kloo-i boot che) A Thai dessert of bananas cooked in coconut milk and sugar, topped with chopped *mung beans* and served warm or cold.

knäckebröd (kneh-keh-brud) A Swedish crispbread made from rye flour and meal.

Knauzenwecken (keh-'nout-zen-vek-ken) A German bread made with wheat flour, yeast, malt, vinegar, and salt. A specialty of Biberach.

knead To mix dough into a smooth, pliable mass. Kneading helps develop the *gluten* in the dough, and can be accomplished either by hand or in an electric mixer with a *dough hook.*

knife See *cake slicer, French knife, pairing knife, serrated knife,* and *slicing knife.*

Knödel (keh-'no-dehl) A German dumpling made from either flour or potato and leavened with yeast or egg whites. It is served as a dessert with sauce or on top of a stewed *fruit compote.*

Knusper (keh-'noo-spehr) An Austrian dessert that is a large cinnamon-flavored *shortcake* topped with crushed lump sugar and chopped almonds. It is traditionally cut into squares or rectangles and eaten with coffee or tea. Its name derives from the German *knusprig,* which means "crunchy."

koch (ko-khuh) A Slovakian rice pudding flavored with cinnamon.

Koche ('keuch-reh) A light, sweet or savory German pudding that may be baked or steamed.

koeckbotteram ('kook-bah-ter-am) A brioche-like bread of Dunkirk, England, made with flour, yeast, butter, milk, and raisins and formed into a loaf.

koeksister (ko-'ehk-sis-tehr) A South African pastry that originated in Malaysia, consisting of soft dough pieces cut into small triangles and twisted around a finger to resemble a snail's shell. The twists are deep-fried, drizzled with cinnamon-lemon sugar syrup, and rolled in sugar.

koji A steamed Japanese rice dish that has had koji-kin, or koji mold spores, cultivated on it. This mold creates enzymes that break the rice starches into sugars that can be fermented by the yeast cells, which then give off carbon dioxide and alcohol. It is used primarily in the production of *sake.*

kokei cha (koh-kay-ee cha) A fragrant Japanese tea.

kola nut The edible seed of a tropical tree native to Africa. It contains *caffeine* and is used to reduce hunger and fatigue. Although initially bitter in taste, the nuts turn sweet and are most well known for their use in *cola* soft drinks.

kolache (koh-'lah-chee) A sweet flaky pastry made from a yeast risen-dough filled with poppy seeds, cream cheese, jam, nuts, or fruit. Originating in Czechoslovakia, kolaches or "pockets" are believed to have been created when a mother (mimka) and her daughter (Lebuse) were baking the family bread in the 1700s, the little girl took her portion of dough, shaped it into a disc, and placed a plum slice in the center of the disc and folded it over to form a pocket. Also known in Poland as *kolacky.*

kolacky See *kolache.*

Komijne Kaas See *leyden.*

kompot ('kohm-poht) A Jewish dish that is a combination of fruit, sugar, fruit juice, and wine or liqueur. It may be baked or served as is.

Kona An Arabica coffee bean grown on the Big Island of Hawaii. It produces a premium, rich-flavored coffee with medium body and acidic flavor.

Konditorei (kon-dee-'toe-rey) The German word for a pastry or confectionery shop.

Kool-Aid An artificially flavored soft drink mix created by Edward Perkins of Hastings, Nebraska, in 1927. It was originally called Kool-Ade, but government regulations required fruit juice be used in any product labeled "ade," so the name was changed in 1931. The recipe was sold to General Foods in 1953. The original flavors were cherry, strawberry, raspberry, grape, orange, lemon-lime, and root beer. See also *fruit smack.*

Korean melon See *muskmelon.*

kosher Food prepared by the strict dietary laws followed by the Jewish people. The laws entail the separation of milk and meat products, avoidance of any pork products, and restrictions on certain types of fish, poultry, and meat products. The pastry chef must be aware that people who keep the kosher laws will not eat a dessert made with milk products after having eaten a meat meal. Many bakery items are made *pareve,* or without milk or meat products (no dairy produces such as cheese or butter). In a commercial kitchen, for items to be deemed *kasher* (pure), the Hebrew root for *kosher,* all food preparation must be overseen by a certified Rabbi.

kosher salt See *salt.*

kouing-aman (kween-ah-mahn) A rich flaky pastry from Breton, France, whose name means "bread and butter." The large, flat cake was created by Yves René Scordia in 1860, when he experimented by adding sugar to a yeasted *laminated dough.* The large amount of sugar in the dough creates an intense *caramelization* during baking and results in a crisp, sugary top.

kourabiede (koo-rah-bee-yay-deh) A rich Greek butter cookie. They are rolled in confectioners' sugar while warm and then again before serving. Often they have ground nuts mixed into the dough. The cookies come in different shapes and sizes, and are traditionally served at holidays and special occasions; at Christmastime, a whole clove is inserted in the centers of the cookies to symbolize the spices brought by the Magi.

krakelinge ('krah-keh-leen-geh) A cinnamon-flavored cookie with a figure-eight shape. They are brushed with egg whites, sugar, and ground almonds. Originally from Denmark, they are popular in South Africa.

kransekage ('krahn-sah-kah-geh) The Danish word for "wreath cake," referring to its shape, and made primarily from *marzipan.* It resembles a tower of stacked concentric marzipan circles that become progressively smaller as they reach the top. *Royal icing* is randomly piped on as decoration, and it is traditionally served at weddings and special occasions.

Krapfen ('krap-fan) A deep-fried Austrian pastry similar to a doughnut; see *Bismarck.*

krentewegge (kran-ta-wah-ghe) A long, flat Danish raisin roll, made with a yeast dough and traditionally given to new mothers as a gift.

krepik pisang (kreh-'peek pee-'song) A Malaysian dessert or snack of sliced plantains that are dipped in sugar syrup and deep-fried.

kringle ('kreen-gleh) 1. The Norwegian name for a Christmas butter cookie with lemon flavor. 2. A flat, wide Danish pastry made from flaky dough and filled with fruit or nuts. Also called *Racine Danish kringle.*

kringler ('kreeng-ler) 1. A Danish sugar pretzel. 2. A Swedish breakfast pastry made from yeast dough that is baked and drizzled with almond glaze.

Krispy Kreme A doughnut chain started by Vernon Rudolph in 1937 in Winston-Salem, North Carolina. Although they have a wide selection, they are well known for their original warm glazed doughnut.

krokant (kroh-kahnt) A rich, chewy nut brittle made from cooked sugar, butter, vanilla, and nuts, usually almonds. It is used as a decoration for cakes or as a petit four that may or may not be dipped in chocolate; broken into small pieces, it is an ingredient in cakes and pastries. Also spelled *croquant.*

krumkake ('kroom-kah-kah) A cardamom-flavored Norwegian Christmas cookie. It measures 5 inches (12.5 cm) around and is wafer-thin, from a thin batter poured onto a decorated *krumkake iron* and rolled into a loose cone shape while still warm. In Germany they are commonly filled with sweet stuffings such as raspberry compote or whipped cream.

krumkake iron A flat, two-piece hinged iron griddle with an intricate scroll design that imprints the *krumkake* as they are cooked. They are available in manual and electric models.

K
k

Kuchen ('koo-kehn) The German word for "cake," referring generally to a *coffee cake* made with sweet yeast dough that is either topped with sugar, spices, and nuts or filled with fruit or cheese.

kueh The Malaysian word for cakes or pastries.

kueh baulu ('koo-eh 'bow-loo) A small Malaysian cupcake made from flour, sugar, eggs, and vanilla, baked in a small mold that resembles a tiny *Bundt pan* with no center hole.

kueh denderam ('koo-eh 'dehn-deh-rahm) A deep-fried rice flour cake from Malaysia. These are made with rice flour, cane sugar, and coconut milk, which is kneaded into a dough and rolled out to a ¼-inch (1 cm) thickness, then cut into a large four-leaf clover shape with a hole in the center. After frying, they look and taste similar to *gingerbread.*

kueh sepit ('koo-eh 'seh-peet) A delicate wafer cookie from Malaysia. They are made with a thin batter of coconut milk, flour, eggs, sugar, and ground fennel seeds, cooked between two iron plates that are engraved with designs and words, and then rolled into cylinders while still warm. The name means "love letters" and refers to the decorative inscriptions embossed on the wafers.

kue lopes ('koo-eh 'loh-pehs) An Indonesian confection made with steamed sticky rice that is wrapped in a triangular palm leaf and boiled. It is topped with freshly grated coconut and served warm with palm sugar.

kue talam ('koo-eh tah-'lahm) An Indonesian steamed layer cake made with one layer of pink steamed ground rice mixed with brown sugar and one layer of green steamed ground rice mixed with coconut milk.

kugel ('koo-gehl) A Jewish baked noodle pudding. It may be savory or sweet and served warm or cold. Sweet versions are typically made with nuts, raisins, spices, and sour cream.

Kugelhopf ('koo-guhl-hopf) A sweet yeast-risen cakelike bread filled with raisins, nuts, and dried fruits. It is considered a type of *coffee cake* and is generally dusted with confectioners' sugar, and served for breakfast or afternoon tea. Although it is uncertain whether it originated in Austria or Poland, it is considered a specialty of Alsace, France, and is traditionally baked in a *Kugelhopf mold.* Also known as *Gugelhopf.*

Kugelhopf mold A round, deep aluminum mold with angled fluted sides and a narrow center tube. It is used specifically to bake *Kugelhopf* and the most common size holds just over 1 quart (946 ml).

kukicha (koo-kee-cha) A Japanese green tea blend made from roasted stems, stalks, and twigs. It has a unique creamy, nutty flavor and is popular in macro-biotic diets because it is a powerful *antioxidant.*

kulcha ('kool-cha) A *tandoor* baked bread from India, typically made from *maida flour.*

kulfi ('kull-fee) A rich Indian ice cream made by boiling water buffalo milk until thickened. Sugar and flavorings such as dried fruits, cardamom, saffron, or nuts, are added, and it is boiled again before being poured into molds and frozen. Since there is no overrun, the product is solid and dense.

kulich ('koo-lihch) A tall, cylindrical Russian Easter cake that made from a yeast-leavened dough packed with raisins, spices, and candied orange peel. The cake is dusted with confectioners' sugar and traditionally served with *pashka* and brightly colored eggs.

kulolo (koo-loh-loh) A Hawaiian pudding of brown sugar, coconut milk, honey, and *taro*, baked in an *imu* and served at a *luau*. Also known as *taro pudding*.

kumiss ('koo-mihs) A milk drink from Mongolia with a slight alcohol content. It is made from fermented mare's milk and a liquid starter culture, and is named after the paddle used to churn the fermenting milk. Commercially produced kumiss is more likely made from cow's milk.

Kümmel ('kihm-uhl) A sweet, colorless liqueur believed to have been developed in Holland during the 16th century. It is produced in Germany and Russia today and is flavored with caraway seeds, cumin, and fennel.

kumquat ('kuhm-kwaht) A small citrus fruit the size of a large olive, with golden orange rind and orange flesh. The rind is sweet, while the flesh is tart. The fruit is eaten whole, and may also be purchased candied, pickled, or in marmalades. Although kumquat trees are native to China, where its name means "golden orange,"  it is cultivated in Japan and the United States. Kumquats are an excellent source of vitamin A, potassium, and calcium.

K
k

kvass (keh-'vahs) A Russian drink made from fermented rye or barley. It has a low alcohol content; the bittersweet flavor is often masked with the addition of fruit or mint.

kyauk kyaw (keh-yoo-'ahk keh-'yow) A clear, fudgelike candy from Myanmar, made by cooking softened *agar-agar* in coconut milk and sugar and flavoring it with rosewater. The mixture is poured into a square mold and allowed to set, then cut into squares, rectangles, or diamonds and eaten as a snack.

kyogashi (kyoh-'gah-she) A variety of Japanese sweets made for weddings and special occasions. The type and color of the confections are determined by the season.

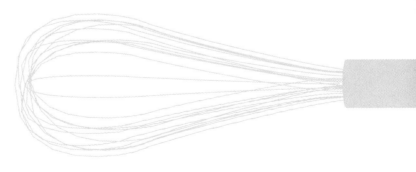

Ll

L The abbreviation for *Liter*.

laban ('lah-buhm) The Arabic term for cultured milk or yogurt.

labanah mackbouseh (lah-bah-nah mahch-boo-sak) A sun-dried ball of drained yogurt, eaten as a snack in Middle Eastern countries. Also known as *jameed*.

lacqua ('lac-kah) A fruit spread made with pureed cooked prunes and lemon juice and zest, used in Jewish cuisine.

la cuite (lah 'kweet) A Southern candy made by cooking thick, dark sugar syrup until just before it turns bitter. It is also used to top breads and as a flavoring in baked goods.

Lactaid The brand name of a packaged milk that is lactose free. It may be purchased as whole or reduced-fat milk, and it contains *lactase*, which breaks down lactose into *glucose* and *galactose*. It is also sweeter than regular milk.

lactase See *lactose intolerant*.

lactic acid ('lak-tik) A bitter acid produced when *lactose* (milk sugar) is fermented, which is a process that occurs naturally when milk sours. It can be found in cheese, yogurt, buttermilk, and sour cream. It is also important in bread baking because along with *acetic acid* it is the acid in a *sourdough culture* that is responsible for the sour taste of sourdough breads.

Lactobacillus A genus of bacteria that is primarily responsible for creating the acidity in *sourdough starters*.

lactose ('lak-tohs) A sugar that occurs naturally in milk. It is the least sweet of all natural sugars and is also called *milk sugar*; it is used in commercial candy making.

lactose-free milk See *milk*.

lactose intolerant A condition in some humans whereby they do not have high enough levels of the enzyme *lactase*, which breaks down *lactose* into *glucose* and *galactose*. Therefore, the undigested lactose produces acid and gas, which cause intestinal discomfort. See also *Lactaid*.

ladder bread See *fougasse*.

Lady apple A small, sweet-tart apple; see *apple*.

Lady Baltimore cake A moist three-layered white cake filled with raisins, nuts, and sometimes figs or other dried fruits. It is covered with fluffy white icing, usually a *boiled icing*. It is mentioned in the novel *Lady Baltimore*, by Owen Wister, 1906.

ladyfinger A delicate individual sponge cake that resembles a large, fat finger. This classic cakelike cookie is an accompaniment to ice cream, mousses, puddings, and other desserts. Ladyfingers are also known as *biscuit de savoie* and are used in the preparation of *charlottes, trifles*, and *tiramisu*. In France,

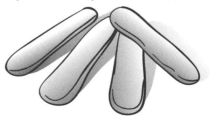

the ladyfinger is called *biscuit à la cuiller,* which means "spoon cookies," because they were originally formed with a spoon.

lagrima See *Port, white.*

lahvosh See *lavash.*

lait (lay) The French word for *milk.*

lait perfume A cold Algerian drink made from mint steeped in hot milk.

lakka A liqueur from Finland, made from the *Arctic cloudberry.*

Lambert cherry See *cherry.*

Lambeth method A highly decorative and ornate style of cake decorating created by Joseph A. Lambeth in the late 19th century to early 20th century.

lame (lom) A razor blade with a handle, used for scoring breads before baking.

laminated dough A pastry dough made by the *lamination* process. Also known as *rolled-in dough.*

lamination A technique of dough preparation that layers fat and dough in a long process of rolling and folding to create alternating layers. This method, along with a high baking temperature (which creates steam and leavens the product), causes the flaky layers characteristic of pastries made by this method. *Croissants, danish,* and *puff pastry* are examples of laminated doughs. See also *fold* and *turn.*

Lamington An Australian pastry or small chocolate-glazed butter cake that is rolled in shredded coconut. It was named in honor of Lord Lamington, governor of Queensland from 1895 to 1901. This cake is served for morning or afternoon tea, either plain or split in half and filled with cream and jam.

lampone (lahm-po-nay) The Italian word for *raspberry;* see *berry.*

Lancashire cake ('lank-ah-shur) A fruit-filled bun made from a yeast-risen dough, sprinkled with lump or raw sugar before baking. It was first produced in Lancashire, England, and is believed to be a variation on *Eccles cake* and *Banbury cake,* which are made with puff pastry.

Lancashire cheese A creamy white cow's milk cheese with a soft and crumbly texture. This farmhouse cheese, made in Lancashire, England, has a full flavor and excellent melting qualities, but does not travel well.

landaise (lahn-'days) A type of brioche from Andernos-les-Bains, in the Gironde region of southern France.

Lane cake A Southern white or yellow cake layered with rich custard, coconut, nuts, and dried fruits and iced with fluffy white frosting. It is believed to have originated in Clayton, Alabama, where its creator, Emma Rylander Lane, won a prize for it at the state fair.

Langra mango A sweet mango grown in India, with pink to red skin and juicy orange flesh.

Langsamenkneter (long-sahm-'ahn-kah-nay-tehr) A German rye bread mixer that slowly and gently mixes *rye doughs.*

langsat ('lung-saat) A sweet, slightly acidic fruit native to Southeast Asia. It is the size of a large grape and is yellowish brown when ripe.

langue-de-chat ('lawng-de-sha) Literally "cat's tongue" in French, a long, thin, delicate cookie often served with sorbet, iced desserts, and sweet wines. They can be sandwiched together with ganache, jam, or buttercream to make a richer cookies.

langue-de-chat pan A flat, rectangular tinned steel pan for making *langues-de-chat.* It has ten 3-inch-long (7.5 cm) shallow indentations per sheet. The pan can also be used to form *ladyfingers* and *éclairs.* See *cat's tongue mold.*

L
I

Laos ginger See *Thai ginger.*

Lapsang souchong tea ('lap-sang 'soo-shawng) A black tea from China's Fukian province, with a distinctive smoky aroma. See also *tea.*

lard Rendered pork fat, favored for its ability to produce a tender, flaky pie crust. It is a flavorful fat for frying as well, and has a high *smoke point,* but it is a *saturated fat* high in *cholesterol* and lacks nutritional value. When substituting lard for butter in baking, reduce the amount by 20 to 25%. All lard should be tightly wrapped to avoid absorbing other flavors while stored in the refrigerator.

lardy cake A small English cake made from a sweet, rich dough filled with dried fruit, lard, and sugar. It is similar to a *Chelsea bun;* many bakers now replace lard with butter.

Laroda plum See *plum.*

lassi ('lah-see) A chilled yogurt drink from India. It can be made salted or sweet and include fruit, fruit juices, spices, and herbs.

La Stupenda (lah stew-'pen-dah) An Australian dessert created to honor opera singer Dame Joan Sutherland (La Stupenda) for her last performance at the Sydney Opera House. It was created by Serge Dansereau, executive chef of the Regent Hotel in Sydney. It is made with *japonaise biscuits,* raspberry and mango *coulis,* a garnish of *chocolate curls, sable biscuits,* and a *passion fruit* filling, and served in a pool of *crème anglaise.*

late harvest An American wine term referring to wines made from grapes picked at the end of the harvest (usually late fall), preferably those with *Botrytis cinerea,* a fungus that shrivels the grape, thereby increasing its sugar content. Late-harvest wines are very sweet and usually have a high alcohol content. The most popular grapes used for these dessert wines are *Riesling, Gewürztraminer,* and *Sauvignon Blanc.*

latik A Filipino snack or dessert topping made by heating coconut milk until the oil separates and produces a brown, curdlike product.

latke ('lat-ke) A pancake usually made from grated potatoes, eggs, onions, *matzo meal* and onions, traditionally served during Hanukkah; the oil used to cook latkes represents the lamp oil that continued to burn for eight days when the Maccabees rededicated the holy Temple.

latte ('lah-tay) The Italian word for *milk.* See also *caffè latte.*

lattice ('lah-tis) A design for the top crust of a pie or tart, made by overlapping or weaving thin strips of dough to produce a criss-cross open pattern. It is a popular top for *linzertorte* and *fruit pies.*

lattice dough cutter A tool for forming a lattice design in rolled-out pastry dough. It consists of a round, thin, two-piece stencil that, when pressed into the dough, cuts out the lattice design without having to weave individual pieces.

lattice dough roller A small tool that cuts a uniform lattice pattern when rolled over pastry dough. It has a metal roller disc and a short wooden handle; the roller has 17 notched blades that cut the pattern.

laurel leaf See *bay leaf.*

lavash ('lah-vash) A very thin, crisp *flatbread* eaten throughout the Middle East and now around the world. It dates back 3000 years and is a form of the earliest known bread. Also known as *Armenian cracker bread* and also spelled *lavosh, lahvosh, lavoche.*

lavender An evergreen shrub in the mint family, native to the Mediterranean. It has aromatic purple flowers and sage-green leaves, in the mint family. The flowers and leaves are used both fresh and dried, as a flavoring in cooking, confections, and to make herbal tea.

L
l

lavender gem A citrus fruit that is a cross between a white grapefruit and a tangelo. It has pale pink skin and a sweet flavor. Also called *wekiwas*.

lavoche See *lavash*.

lavosh See *lavash*.

lawtonberry See *berry*.

laxtonberry See *berry*.

layer cake A cake with two or more layers joined with cream or filling.

Lazarroni di Saronno See *amaretti*.

lazy-daisy cake An American cake made with a single layer of yellow cake, topped with coconut, butter, and brown sugar and browned under a *salamander*.

lb. The abbreviation for the *pound* measure.

leaf gelatin Another name for *sheet gelatin;* see *gelatin*.

lean dough A bread dough made with flour, water, salt, and yeast and little to no fat and sugar, which gives it a characteristic crisp crust. *French bread* is a common example of a lean dough.

Leanesse A fat substitute made from oat flour, produced by ConAgra. The process of heating and cooling yield a gel that resembles the texture of *fat*.

lear oil The Canadian term for *rapeseed oil,* which is best known in America as *canola oil*.

leaven To make a dough or batter rise through the addition of a *leavening agent* such as *ammonium bicarbonate, baking powder, baking soda, beaten eggs,* or *yeast*.

leavening agent/leavener A substance that raises or lightens a dough or batter by incorporating air, steam, or gas. For baking, leavening agents include *yeast* (organic), *baking powder* or *baking soda* (chemical), or *steam* (physical/mechanical).

Lebkuchen ('layb-koo-kuhn) A gingerbread cakelike cookie baked in a decorative mold and dipped in chocolate or topped with a hard confectioners' sugar glaze. It is a specialty of Nuremberg, Germany.

leblebi (lehb-lehb-ee) Roasted chickpeas eaten as a snack in India.

lebneh (lebbkneeh) A Lebanese cream cheese made with *laban* (yogurt).

leche ('lay-chay) The Spanish word for *milk*.

leche flan ('lay-chay flahn) A Filipino *crème caramel* made with evaporated milk and lime zest.

leche frita ('lay-chay 'free-ta) A Spanish dessert of fried custard squares flavored with lemon zest and cinnamon sugar.

lecithin ('less-a-thin) An *emulsifier* found in egg yolks and vegetables, used in chocolate and confectionery making to preserve and moisturize the food. It also acts as a *stabilizer* by preventing the fat from separating out of the mixture.

leckerli (leh-'chur-i) Either of two Swiss cookies: *Baseler leckerli* is a sweet mixture of honey, flour, spices, nuts, and candied peel, which is baked and covered with fondant. *Zurich leckerli* is a mixture of almonds, sugar, and egg whites that is dried and then cooked quickly to brown the top; the dough is pressed into wooden molds, which imprint designs on the surface of the cookies. Also spelled *leckerlie*.

Le Concorde (luh 'kohn-khord) A French pastry of three layers of *chocolate meringue* that is filled and iced with *chocolate mousse,* and garnished with small sticks of chocolate meringue.

lees (leez) The sediment that settles in the bottom of the wine barrel as a result of fermentation.

lefse ('leff-suh) Norwegian *flatbread.*

lefse rolling pin A 16.5-inch (41.2 cm) rolling pin with a ribbed face, used to score the surface of *lefse.*

legume ('lay-goom) Any of a group of plants that have roots with nodules that contain nitrogen-fixing bacteria, most of which are important food sources. The most common include soybeans, lentils, peanuts, beans, and peas, all of which have seed pods that split lengthwise when ripe.

Leicester cheese ('less-ter) An English whole-milk cow's cheese similar to *Cheddar cheese,* but with a higher moisture content. It is orangey-red in color and has a tangy, rich flavor.

Leipziger Lerchen ('lip-zhig-her lehr-hkehm) See *Leipzig skylark.*

Leipzig skylark ('lip-zhig ski-lark) A German shortcrust pastry tartlet created when the hunting of skylarks was banned. The pastry slightly resembles a bird's belly, and the two strips of thin dough that form a cross on the top symbolize the nets that were used to trap the birds. Also known as *Leipziger Lerchen.*

lekach ('lay-kakh) A honey and spice cake served on the Jewish holiday Rosh Hashanah.

lekvar ('lehk-vahr) A thick, intensely flavored pureed fruit spread used to fill pastries and cookies. This Hungarian favorite is traditionally made with prunes or dried apricots cooked with sugar.

lemon The fruit of the lemon tree, a cultivated hybrid of lime and citrus trees. The lemon was developed in Southeast Asia, but is now grown in other tropical and temperate climates, particularly Florida and California. The fruit ranges in size from a large egg to a small grapefruit, and contains 30 to 45% juice depending on variety. The bright yellow rind may be thick or thin, and surrounds an acidic pulp whose juice contains about 5% citric acid. The most common varieties are *Eureka lemon* and *Lisbon lemon,* and they are available year-round. The juice and rinds are used extensively in the production of pastries and desserts. See also *Meyer lemon.*

lemonade A cold drink made by combining water, sugar, and lemon juice.

lemon aspen A yellow fruit the size of a grape, native to the Australian rainforest. It has a strong lemon flavor, with hints of honey and eucalyptus, and is often used as a flavoring in cakes, desserts, and stewed fruits.

lemon balm A lemon-scented herb in the mint family, native to Europe. It is often used to infuse a lemon flavor in herbal teas and pastry products.

lemon bar A *bar cookie* that consists of a short dough base filled with *lemon curd.* After baking it is dusted with confectioners' sugar and cut into squares.

lemon chess pie See *chess pie.*

lemon curd A creamy, thick custard made from lemon juice, butter, sugar, and egg yolks. It is served with *scones* for *afternoon tea* and is also used as a filling for cakes and tarts.

lemongrass A lemon-flavored grass that is an important ingredient in Thai and Vietnamese cooking. It is used as an herb and may be purchased dried or fresh. See also *citral.*

lemon meringue pie An American pie made with a prebaked *flaky pastry* shell that is filled with *lemon curd* and topped with a thick layer of *meringue,* then lightly browned.

lemon possit An English dessert made from sweetened cream that has been reduced by boiling and infused with lemon. It is a sweet yet tart dessert with a velvety smooth texture.

lemon verbena (vehr-'bee-nuh) A lemon-scented herb native to South America. The long slender leaves may be purchased dried or fresh, and are often used to infuse a sweet lemon flavor in herbal teas, sorbets, and other pastries and desserts. See also *citral.*

leopard skin loaf A loaf of bread that has been brushed with liquid yeast and rice flour before baking. This yields a crisp, leopard-looking skin and adds a slight yeasty flavor.

lepet ('leh-peht) An Indonesian confection made by boiling sticky rice and black beans, and wrapping the mixture in a coconut palm leaf, then tying it with seaweed.

Le Régent (luh ray-j'hahnt) A rich chocolate gâteau made by layering chocolate cake with chocolate whipped cream and covering it with chocolate icing and chocolate sprinkles. The cake was created in Paris in the late 19th century.

letter fold A fold used in producing *laminated dough,* whereby the dough is folded in thirds like a letter. The rectangular sheet of dough has butter smeared over two-thirds of the surface and then the unbuttered third of the dough is folded into the center and the remaining third folded on top. Also known as *three-fold* and *simple fold.*

levain (luh-vahn) The French word for "leaven," referring to a *sourdough starter* cultured by wild yeast.

level 1. To make a cake the same height all around. This is accomplished by shaving off areas that are higher than others. 2. To cut off the domed area of a cake that may be present after baking, thereby making it level.

leve seco See *Port, white.*

levulose A simple sugar found in honey and fruits. It is also known as *fructose* or *fruit sugar.*

leyden ('li-din) A semi-soft Dutch cheese made from partially skimmed cow's milk and buttermilk. It is flavored with caraway or cumin seeds and is also known as *Komijne Kaas.*

lichee See *lychee.*

licorice A black confection made from the root of a leguminous plant native to southeastern Europe and the Middle East. The root contains the substance *glycyrrhizin,* which is 40 times sweeter than sugar. Also known as *sweet root* and *liquorice.*

Liégeois café (lee-'ayjh-eh-wah ka-feh) An iced coffee drink made by filling a wine or Champagne glass ⅓ full with hot coffee and a small scoop of coffee ice cream, then topping it with whipped cream and garnishing with toasted almond slices. It was created in Liége, Belgium, and is served with petit fours. The coffee ice cream may be substituted with other flavors, such as vanilla, chocolate, or strawberry.

Liège waffle See *waffle.*

lier A thickening agent of egg yolks or cream, used in *crème anglaise* and other sauces.

Life Saver A small, hard candy with a center hole. It was created in 1912 by Clarance Crane, father of poet Hart Crane, and became a summertime treat because it would not melt in the heat. Life Savers originally came in one flavor, Pep-O-Mint, and were the first candy in America to be wrapped in tinfoil to keep them fresh. Approximately 548 million rolls of Life Savers are produced annually.

light brown sugar See *sugar, brown.*

light corn syrup See *corn syrup.*

light cream See *cream.*

light sour cream See *sour cream*.

lightning cake An orange-flavored butter cake with nuts. It is named lightning cake because it rises very quickly, owing to the baking powder.

light treacle See *treacle*.

light whipping cream See *cream*.

lilikoi (lil-lah-koy) The Hawaiian word for *passion fruit*.

Lillet (luh-lay) A French apéritif made from wine, brandy, fruits, and herbs. It was developed in the French village of Podensac, and has been made since the late 1800s. Lillet Blanc is made from white wine and Lillet Rouge is made from red wine. Both are served over ice, with a twist of orange.

lime A small, oval citrus fruit that ranges in color from light to medium green and sometimes has a yellowish hue, depending on the variety. The *Persian lime* is the most common and is available year-round, particularly May through August. The porous skin encases a juicy, pale green pulp and is an excellent source of vitamin C. British sailors during the 19th century were fed limes as a way of preventing scurvy and this is believed to be the basis for the nickname "limey." See also *kaffir lime* and *Key lime*.

limeade A cold drink made by combining water, sugar, and lime juice.

limequat The small, oval fruit of a citrus tree that is a cross between a lime and a kumquat. The sweet-tasting skin is greenish yellow, while the tart lime-flavored pulp is high in vitamin C. It may be eaten whole or used for its juice or rind to flavor drinks and pastries. Although it was developed in China, the tree is now grown in Israel, Britain, Spain, California, and Florida, but can be found in the United States only in small quantities during the fall and winter.

limoncello A sweet, bright yellow lemon liqueur produced in the south of Italy. It is made from lemon rinds, sugar, alcohol, and water.

limone The Italian word for *lemon*.

limestone A dehumidifying agent used to protect sugar pieces, *tuile*, and other pastry products that would otherwise deteriorate when exposed to moist air. The limestone is placed on the bottom of an airtight container and covered with a piece of parchment paper to prevent its coming into contact with the food. It is very important to keep the limestone away from water, or it will cause a reaction that produces hot steam.

limpa bread ('lihm-puh) A moist Swedish bread flavored with anise, fennel, cumin, and orange peel.

lingonberry See *berry*.

linzer leaf A leaf-shaped cookie made from linzer dough that is sold in many *Konditorei* as an accompaniment to coffee. They are typically made at Christmas time and coated in a fine European chocolate. See also *linzertorte*.

linzertorte ('lihn-zuhr-tort) A Viennese pastry with a nutty, spicy pastry and raspberry or apricot filling. The specialty originated in Linz, Austria, and is made with a dough of ground hazelnuts and/or almonds. The top is decorated with a *lattice* pattern of dough and brushed with apricot glaze or dusted with confectioners' sugar.

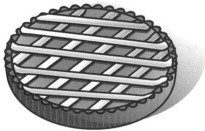

lipid See *fats and oils*.

liquefier An ingredient that helps loosen or liquefy a dough or batter; for example, water, milk, or oil.

liqueur (li-'kyoor) A sweet alcoholic beverage often flavored with herbs, spices, flowers, fruits, seeds, or plant stems and bark. The base is typically whisky, rum, brandy, or another spirit and ranges in alcohol content from 20 to 60%. Propietary liqueurs are made by specific producers with secret recipes; generic liqueurs are made by various producers with general recipes. *Cream liqueurs* are sweet, syrupy mixtures flavored with cream. The word *liqueur* is derived from the Latin *liquifacere,* which means "to dissolve" and refers to how the flavor is dissolved to make the liqueur. This may be done in one of four ways: *percolation,* whereby the alcohol is dripped through the flavorings to extract their taste; *distillation,* whereby the alcohol and flavorings are mixed before being distilled; *maceration,* whereby the alcohol base is steeped with their flavorings; and *infusion,* whereby the flavorings are steeped in hot water before being mixed with the alcohol base. Liqueurs are used extensively in pastry and dessert production as flavoring agents. They are also served as after-dinner drinks and then sometimes referred to as *cordials.*

liquor ('lih-kuhr) A distilled alcoholic drink made from the fermented mash of grains or other plants. The word is derived from the Latin *liquere,* which means "to be fluid."

liquore (lee-koh-reh) The Italian word for *liquor.*

liquorice See *licorice.*

Lisbon lemon See *lemon.*

lite Another spelling of the word *light,* which is now an accepted food-label term. Being called "lite" requires that the product to be ⅓ fewer calories than the regular product, or less than 50% of fat per serving.

Liter A metric measurement of volume that is equivalent to 33.8 fluid ounces. Liters are divided into milliliters (ml), centiliters (cl), and deciliters (dl):

> 10 milliliters = 1 centiliter
>
> 10 centiliters = 1 deciliter or 100 centiliters = 1 Liter
>
> 10 deciliters = 1 Liter

loaf sugar See *sugar.*

lo cha A *lychee*-flavored oolong tea from Taiwan.

locust bean See *carob.*

loganberry See *berry.*

lokma (loke-mah) A Turkish pastry of deep-fried yeast-risen dough balls that are dipped in a syrup of honey, lemon, and rosewater. They are sprinkled with cinnamon sugar and served warm. Also called *loukoumades* in Greece.

lollipop A hard sugar candy attached to the end of a small, thin wooden or paper stick, created in the early 19th century and made in different shapes, sizes, colors, and flavors.

longan See *dragon's eye.*

long-grain rice See *rice.*

long john See *Bismarck.*

longyan dou fu ('lahng-yahn doo-'oh foo) A chilled almond-milk gelatin dessert from Singapore, garnished with a *longan* poached in sweet syrup.

Lorna Doone A shortbread cookie introduced in 1912 but now produced by Nabisco. It is believed that the name came from the novel by R. D. Blackmore. The book and its Scottish main character were named *Lorna Doone.*

L
l

loska ('lohs-kah) A Slovak sweet poppy-seed bread served on Christmas eve.

loquat The oval or pear-shaped fruit of the loquat tree, distantly related to the apple and pear. Although it is native to China, loquat trees are now also cultivated in Turkey, Portugal, Israel, Brazil, Japan, and Hawaii. The fruit has a smooth yellow to orange skin and a sweet juicy pulp. The flesh ranges in color from cream to orange, and is high in sugar, acid, and pectin. It may be eaten fresh or used for making jam, jelly, pies, tarts, or wine.

Lord Baltimore cake A three-layered yellow cake filled with chopped pecans or almonds, candied cherries, and crushed macaroons, and covered with a fluffy white *boiled icing*. It is believed to have been created to use up the egg yolks left over from making *Lady Baltimore cake*.

lotus 1. A tree that is a member of the buckthorn family. Its large fruit is used to make breads and fermented drinks. 2. An Asian water plant whose leaves, roots, and seeds have culinary uses: the seeds may be candied or eaten raw as a snack; the leaves are used to wrap sweet or savory mixtures.

loukoumades (loo-koo-mah-thes) See *lokma*.

low-conversion glucose corn syrup See *corn syrup*.

low-fat milk See *milk*.

low-methoxyl pectin A chemically modified pectin that requires calcium, but not a high sugar content, to gel a liquid.

lua See *imu*.

luau ('loo-ow) 1. A traditional Hawaiian feast. 2. Hawaiian for taro leaves.

Lucullus A dessert with a *savarin* base that is soaked in a sweet liqueur syrup and placed in a wafer-thin sweet pastry base; the middle of the savarin is filled with a raspberry soufflé and then baked. It is served with a raspberry sauce that is flavored with the same liqueur as used to soak the savarin. It was named after the famed Roman general Lucius Licinius (110–56 B.C.).

lumpia A transparent pastry sheet from the Philippines, made from wheat flour, eggs, and cornstarch and used to wrap spring rolls of the same name.

luo bo gao (loo-'oh boh 'gow) A sweet dessert from Singapore, made with fried slices of grated white turnip.

Luster Dust The brand name of a *pearl dust*.

lychee A small, round fruit native to China. The translucent white flesh is encased in a bumpy, bright red skin that is easily removed. The flesh is sweet and has a single brown seed.

Mm

m The abbreviation for *meter.*

maamoul ('maah-mool) A small Middle Eastern cake formed with a *qalib.* It is flavored with orange flour water and filled with nuts.

macadamia nut (mak-uh-'day-mee-uh) A small, round, rich, buttery nut of a large tree native to Australia and Indonesia. They have a hard coating in a green husk that splits as the nut grows. Even with the husk split, the nutmeat is difficult to extract from the shell and requires pressured force to release it. They are up to 80% fat and 4% sugar and should be stored in the refrigerator to prevent spoilage. The tree and nut are named after John Macadam, who worked with botanist Ferdinand von Mueller to develop the cultivar. They pair well with tropical fruit and desserts. In the late 1800s, the trees were planted on the Big Island in Hawaii, which now produces 90% of the world's production.

macaroon (mah-kah-'roon) A small confection made from egg whites, sugar, and ground almonds or almond paste. It has a crisp exterior and a soft, chewy interior. It may be flavored with other ingredients such as citrus, coffee, chocolate, or coconut; other ground nuts may be substituted for the almonds. In France, macaroons are sandwiched together with a thin layer of *ganache* or raspberry or  apricot jam. Their origin dates back to 14th century Venice and its name is derived from the Venetian word "macarone" which means "fine paste." It is said that they are made in the shape of a monk's navel because the first recipe was made in the Cormery monastery; in the 18th century, they were made by the Carmelite nuns to pay for housing when they needed protection during the French Revolution. According to some historians, the nuns were following the principle of "almonds are for good girls who do not eat meat." During this time, two nuns living in the town of Nancy specialized in making and selling macaroons, and they became known as the "Macaroon Sisters." In 1952, the street where they operated was named after them and macaroons are still made there today.

maccha See *biki-cha.*

macchiato (mah-kee-'yah-toh) An espresso drink made with a dollop of steamed milk foam. Also known as *caffè macchiato.*

mace (mays) The bright red membrane that covers the nutmeg seed, ground and used as a pastry spice for fruit fillings and Middle Eastern confections. The membrane is removed and dried to a yellow-orange color. It is most commonly sold ground, but is also sometimes available whole, when it is known as *blade mace.* The flavor is similar to nutmeg but not as intense.

macédoine (mas-eh-dwahn) A mixture of small diced fruit or vegetables. The fruit is typically soaked in fruit syrup or sugar syrup flavored with liqueur and served cold.

M
m

macerate/maceration ('mas-eh-ryat) To soak a product, usually fruit, in a flavored liquid, usually alcohol, to soften and infuse it with flavor.

Macoun apple (muh-'koon) See *apple*.

maculan ('mah-coo-lahn) An Italian dessert wine that tastes like a mixture of orange, apricot, honey, and walnuts. It is slightly sweet and pairs well with nut cakes and fruit tarts.

Madeira (mah-'deer-uh) A fortified wine named after the Portuguese island where it is made. There are four distinct types, named after the white grape they are made from. They range in flavor from dry to sweet, and in color from pale yellow to deep ruby.

> **Sercial** The driest, with a tangy bite.
>
> **Verdelho** A medium-dry that is more full-bodied than Sercial.
>
> **Bual** A medium-rich type.
>
> **Malmsey or Malvasia** The richest, sweetest type.

These quality wines are not to be confused with the low-quality cooking Madeira made from the Tinta Negra Mole red grape. The finest Madeiras undergo a lengthy heating process and may be aged in oak caskets from three to 20 years. Their natural acidity makes them refreshing on their own or paired with food. The drier ones are generally served cool as an apéritif and pair well with salads or soups, while the sweeter versions are served room temperature and excellent with chocolate or cream-based desserts.

Madeira cake A rich sponge cake flavored with lemon peel and served with *afternoon tea*. Its origin dates back to 19th-century England, and is so named because it was popular to eat a slice of this cake with a glass of Madeira.

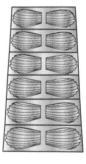

madeleine ('mahd-ehl-lihn) A small, light sponge cake baked in a madeleine pan, which gives it its distinct elongated scallop shell shape. It is traditionally served with tea or coffee, and may be made in a variety of flavors including lemon, orange, coffee, or chocolate. Madeleines have a crisp exterior and moist interior, and were originally flavored with orange flower water. Although their origin is debated, it is believed they are named after King Stanislaw Lesczeynski's cook, Madeline, who created them in 1755. See also *madeleine pan*.

madeleine pan A pan used in the production of madeleines. It has small, shallow, scalloped shaped indentions and may be made of metal or silicone (*Flexipan*).

magdalena (mahg-duh-'lay-nuh) A Spanish version of the French *madeleine* that is made with olive oil instead of butter. It also differs in shape and may be oblong, or round with a domed or flat top.

Magenbrot ('mah-gehn-braht) The German word for "stomach bread," referring to a spiced cookie that is supposed to be good for digestion.

Magnolia grape See *grape*.

magnum ('mahg-nuhm) A 1.5-Liter (50 oz.) wine bottle, equivalent to two bottles of wine. A double magnum is a 3-Liter (100 oz.) wine bottle that is equivalent to four bottles of wine.

mahleb (ma-hha-lub) An aromatic Middle Eastern spice made from ground black cherry pits. It has a nutty, sweet-tart flavor and is commonly added to breads, cakes, and cookies in Greece, Syria, Armenia, and Turkey.

Maibowle ('mi-bov-leh) See *May wine*.

maida flour (mai-daa) A flour used in India to make *flatbreads* and other baked goods.

maid of honor A small English tartlet made with *short dough* or *puff pastry* and filled with almonds, curd cheese, and lemon or orange flavoring. It originated in the 16th century in the town of Surrey, and was named after Anne Boleyn, who was the maid of honor to King Henry VIII's sister. He said they were as sweet as she was; shortly thereafter, she became his second wife.

Mai landerli (mi 'lahnt-ayr-li) A traditional lemon-flavored German Christmas cookie.

Maillard browning The browning or caramelization of baked goods due to the *Maillard reaction.*

Maillard reaction (may-yahrd) The caramelization in baked goods that occurs between 212° and 350°F (100° and 175°C), as a result of a reaction between reducing sugars and amino acids or proteins. It causes the sugar-protein bonds to brown at a lower temperature and creates different shades of color ranging from yellow-gold to rich brown. The effect of caramelization is apparent in both the look of the finished product and the flavor. It is an integral part of crust formation in bread baking and is affected by the oven temperature, fermentation time, and enzyme activity. Named after its discoverer, the chemist Dr. Louis-Camille Maillard.

maison (may-'zohn) The French word for "house," referring to a menu item that is a specialty of the restaurant or house.

mai tai (my tie) A strong alcoholic cocktail that consists of light rum, Triple Sec, orange or almond syrup, grenadine, and lime juice. It is garnished with a skewer of fresh pineapple and maraschino cherries. In the Polynesian islands it is traditionally served with an orchid floating on top. The name derives from the Tahitian word *maita'i*, which means "good." The story goes that when the drink's creator, Victor Bergeron, the original owner of Trader Vic's restaurant, served it to a couple of Tahitian friends, they exclaimed that the flavor was *maita'i roa*, which means "out of this world."

Maiwein See *May wine.*

makowiec (mah-koh-ve-eck) A poppyseed cake of Polish origin, made by filling a rolled out piece of *yeast dough* with a mixture of poppy seeds, almonds, honey, sugar, and citrus peel; the dough is then rolled into a cylinder and baked. It is traditionally served during the Christmas and Easter holidays.

Makrut lime A pear-shaped member of the citrus family that is cultivated in Hawaii and Southeast Asia. The bright yellow to green skin has a bumpy texture and the juice is acidic. The leaves are also used and may be purchased dried or fresh.

malai (ma-laa-ee) An Asian term that refers to a food similar to *clotted cream.* Buffalo milk produces the highest fat content, and the cream is used in a variety of desserts.

malakoff (mah-lah-koff) The name given to a variety of cakes that include nuts. The most popular consists of two layers of *japonaise* filled and covered with a strong coffee mousse. The torte is then topped with confectioners' sugar and the sides are covered in toasted almonds.

malassadas (mah-lass-sah-dahs) A Portuguese doughnut, made by frying *yeast dough* and then rolling it in cinnamon sugar. They are traditionally stretched into a rectangular shape, but are also popular as balls. In 1952, Leonard's Bakery began producing malasadas in Hawaii, and they have become a popular treat there ever since. Also known as *filhós* in Portugal.

Malay apple See *water apple.*

maldon See *sea salt.*

malic acid ('mal-ihk) A naturally occuring acid found in some fermented fruits. It is used as an acidulant (see *acidulated water*) and as a *flavoring agent* in some processed food products. During the wine-making process, the malic acid from the grapes is converted to *lactic acid* and produces malolactic fermentation. This reduces the wine's tartness and enhances flavor.

Malmsey See *Madeira*.

malsouqua (mahl-so-'ooh-goo-ah) Delicate, paper-thin sheets of pastry made with semolina flour. The name means "to adhere" in Arabic, and it is used in Tunisian dishes, particularly *brik*. The Moroccan version is called *warka*, which means "a leaf" and the Algerian version is called *dioul*.

malt A fine powder derived from barley and used for brewing beer, distilling liquor, and as a nutrient additive to food. The germinated grain is kiln-dried and ground. The malting process creates *amylase*, which converts the starch in the grain to a sugar called *maltose*. The resulting malt, also known as malted grain or *malted flour,* can be used for fermentation. Malt is also important in bread baking because it coverts the flour starch to sugar, which provides food for the yeast and adds a sweet, nutty flavor. Some flours already contain *malted barley flour*, or it may be purchased separately and added to the dough.

malted barley flour A flour made from barley that has been soaked, sprouted, dried, and ground. It is high in *amylase* enzymes and is typically added to the flour during the milling process.

malt extract A nutritious extract derived from malt that is added to bread to aid in fermentation and provide moistness in baked goods. It also adds color to the crust because it caramelizes at a low temperature (see *Maillard reaction*). There are two main types of malt extract: *diastic malt* and *nondiastic malt*. Diastic malt contains an enzyme called *diastase*, which converts starch to sugar; however, it should not be used in products with a long fermentation process because too much of the starch will be broken down. Nondiastic malt is processed at a higher temperature, which kills the diastase but the maltose and flavor component remain intact. The product may be purchased in dried or powdered form and may be substituted with honey at a 2:1 ratio. Also known as *malt syrup*.

maltose Another name for *malt sugar*.

malt sugar See *sugar*.

malt syrup See *malt extract*.

Malvasia See *Madeira*.

mamey sapote The large fruit of a tree native to the West Indies but now cultivated in Mexico, South and Central America, and South Florida. It has a thick, rough, fuzzy brown skin that encases a creamy-sweet reddish-pink flesh that tastes like a cross between pumpkin and almond. It is primarily eaten raw and used to make smoothies, ice cream, and shakes.

Mandarine Napoléon ('mahn-duh-rihn nuh-'pohl-lee-uhn) An aromatic brandy-based liqueur made with tangerines. It is produced in Belgium and tastes like candied oranges.

mandarin orange ('manh-duh-rihn) Any variety of orange that is distinguished by a loose, easily peeled skin. They vary in size, shape, and flavor and are grouped into three varieties:

Satsuma Small Japanese orange that is the most popular because it is virtually seedless. The majority of canned mandarins are produced from this variety.

Tangerine The most common variety found in the United States, it is named for the Moroccan city of Tangier and has a thick skin and sweet flavor.

M
m

Hybrid A group that includes *tangelo, tangor, clementine,* and *Dancy orange.*

All varieties originated in China, but today the majority of the commercial crop is grown in Florida and California. They are available from November to June and can be stored in the refrigerator for up to two weeks.

mandelbrot ('mahn-duhl-broht) A crisp almond bread similar to *biscotti,* in that it is twice baked. The name derives from the German word *Mandel,* which means "almond" and *Brot,* which means "bread." It is a Jewish specialty of German origin. The formed dough is baked, then sliced and baked again until dry and crisp.

mandelspan A lacy, almond wafer cookie from Sweden. It is made by combining almond paste, sugar, and eggs into a batter that is thinly spread onto wafer paper and baked on a semi-circular metal form. Once cooled, they are lightly dusted with confectioners' sugar and arranged to look like a crown.

M&M's Known throughout the world as the candy that "melts in your mouth, not in your hands," these milk chocolate candies have a colored sugar coating. Legend has it that while on a trip to Spain during the Spanish Civil War, Forrest Mars, Sr., encountered soldiers who were eating pellets of chocolate encased in a hard sugary coating, which prevented them from melting. Inspired by this idea, he and R. Bruce Murrie created what was then known as "Smarties" in England. When they wanted to market them in the United States, they needed a different name because there was already a product called Smarties. So they took the last initial of both their names and created M&M'S Plain Chocolate Candies. They were first sold domestically in 1940. In 1954, brown M&M'S Peanut Chocolate Candies was introduced, and in 1960 red and green colors were added. In 1976 orange was added and red was taken off the market owing to the controversy over red food dye. Once it was shown that the red dye used did not contain amaranth (FD&C Red #2), the red candies reappeared in 1987.

Almond M&M's were introduced in 1988. In 1995, the Mars Company had a global vote for the new color and blue was the winner. They held another public vote and purple was chosen. In 1996, M&M's Minis were made available, and in 1998, Crispy M&M's hit the market. Today M&M's can be found in a variety of colors and are marketed all over the world.

M
m

mandoline ('mahn-duh-lihn) A stainless steel, hand-operated kitchen tool used to julienne and slice firm fruits and vegetables. It has sharp adjustable blades to set how thick or thin the slices will be and foldable legs for easy storage.

manger (mahn-zhay) The French verb for "to eat."

mangiare (mahn-'jah-ray) The Italian verb for "to eat."

mangkok kueh ('mahng-kahk koo-'eh) A spongy, individual steamed rice cake from Malaysia, served with sugarcane and grated coconut, and eaten for breakfast or as a snack.

mango ('mang-goh) The fruit of the mango tree, native to India but cultivated in subtropical climates all over the world. There are dozens of varieties that vary in shape, size, color, and flavor. The two basic types are unripe, also known as green mangoes, and ripe, which are golden yellow to red in color. Green mangoes have a sharp, sour flavor and are used predominately in Asian cooking to make chutneys, savory salads, and dips. Ripe mangoes are prized for their sweet, juicy flavor and are used extensively in pastry to make ice cream, sorbet, fillings, sauces, and fresh fruit salads. Mangoes contain a large stone in the center, so the flesh has to be cut off around it. The fruit contains an enzyme that inhibits gelatin from setting, but this may be neutralized by bringing the pulp to a boil before use. Mangoes can be purchased canned, dried, and pureed. Fresh mangoes from Peru, Mexico, Ecuador, and Brazil are available year-round. The most common varieties are:

Atalufo A small, canary yellow variety from Mexico with a flattened oval shape. The yellow flesh is buttery with a distinctive sweet and spicy taste. Available February to May.

Keitt A large, oval variety from Mexico with a green skin that is blushed with red. It has a smooth texture and rich, fruity flavor. Available June to August.

Kent A large, oval variety from Mexico, Ecuador, and Peru with a greenish skin that is blushed with dark red and small yellow spots. It has a juicy, tender texture and vibrant mango flavor. Available January to March and May to August.

Haden A medium-large oval to round variety from Mexico, Ecuador, and Peru. It ranges in color from green to yellow with red highlights. The orange flesh is firm and fruity. Available October to December and March to May.

Tommy/Atkins A medium to large oval or oblong variety from Mexico, Brazil, Ecuador, and Peru. It has a golden-greenish skin blushed with dark pink. The deep yellow flesh is mildly sweet and has a firm, fiborous texture. Available year-round.

mangosteen The fruit of the mangosteen tree, native to Southeast Asia. The hard, dark brown skin is thick and tough, but cracks easily and reveals a tart, juicy segmented flesh with exquisite flavor. Mangosteens are typically eaten raw, but also produce unique creams and sorbets.

Manhattan A cocktail created in 1874 by a bartender at the Manhattan Club in New York City. It consists of blended whisky and sweet Vermouth. A dry Manhattan uses dry Vermouth, and a Perfect Manhattan uses equal parts dry and sweet Vermouth.

manioc ('man-ee-ok) Another name for *yuca*.

manjar (mahn-hahr) A Brazilian coconut and prune pudding.

manjar blanco ('mahn-harh 'blahnk-koh) A South American milk pudding made by slow-cooking milk, cinnamon, and sugar until very thick. It is eaten as is or used as a pastry filling or bread topping.

mannitol ('mahn-ih-tahl) A sweetener used to thicken, stabilize, and flavor processed food.

mantou (mahn-'too) A type of Chinese steamed bun made from milled wheat flour, water, and leavening agents. It is eaten as a bread staple and may be filled or unfilled. A popular dessert version is made by deep-frying the buns and serving them with sweetened condensed milk.

manufacturing cream See *cream*.

Manzanilla See *sherry*.

Manzano See *banana*.

maple cream A thick, sweet, creamy maple spread made by heating the syrup, cooling it over an ice bath, and then whipping it until thickened.

maple syrup The sap of the native sugar maple tree, extracted and boiled to a thick, syrupy consistency. Native Americans discovered this process and passed it on to the colonists. It takes approximately 40 gallons (151 L) of sap to make 1 gallon (3L 840 ml) of pure maple syrup. The syrup is produced primarily in Vermont, and the quality and quantity produced depends on the weather because the saps flows after the first thaw. Maple syrup is graded by color; the darker the color, the stronger the flavor. The grades are as follows:

Grade AA Light amber color and mild flavor.

Grade A Medium amber color and more intense mild flavor.

Grade B Dark amber color and strong flavor.

Grade C Very dark with a molasses flavor, used primarily for commercial purposes.

There are many products that blend maple syrup and corn syrup, use artificial flavorings, and use maple-flavored substitutes, but none compares to the rich maple flavor of pure syrup. It is used as a topping for pancakes and also to flavor candies, ice cream, and dessert sauces.

Marado See *papaya.*

maraschino cherry ('mahr-uh-shee-noh) See *cherry.*

maraschino liqueur A clear Italian liqueur typically made from the *Royal Ann cherry.* It has a slightly bitter cherry flavor and is a popular flavoring in fruit compotes and many Italian desserts. It may be substituted with *Kirschwasser.*

Marathon Bar 1. An American candy bar consisting of a twisted braid of caramel surrounded by chocolate, produced by Mars Inc. and marketed as "the world's longest candy bar." It was a full 8 inches in length, as shown by an 8-inch ruler printed on the back wrapper. It was introduced in 1973, but because of lackluster sales was discontinued in 1981. However, some will always remember its tagline, "Lasts a Good, Long Time." 2. Prior to 1990, Snickers was called Marathon Bar in Great Britain.

marbelize To give a product the appearance of marble by streaking two contrasting colors together. It is often used with chocolate, sugar, *marzipan,* and *rolled fondant.*

marble slab A sheet of marble used for chocolate and sugar work because the surface retains a cool temperature.

marc (mahr) The French version of *grappa.*

margarine ('mahr-juh-rihn) An imitation butter invented by a French chemist in the mid-1800s. *Vegetable oil margarine,* known as margarine, is made from partially hydrogenated corn or soybean oil; *oleomargarine,* known as *oleo,* is made from beef and veal fat, with vegetable and other oils added. The latter is similar to butter in that it contains at least 80% fat, but the remainder is made up of liquids, flavoring, coloring, and other additives. Margarine has the same number of calories and may be purchased salted or unsalted. It contains no cholesterol and has low levels of saturated fat, but some products have high amounts of trans fatty acids. Low-fat and fat-free margarines contain a higher percentage of water and rely on starches and gums to provide a butter-like consistency, which do not work as well in baking. Specific oleomargarines have been created for the baking industry that have a high melting point and/or cream well. Vegetable margarines are commonly used for products that must be vegan or pareve.

marigold A yellow or orange flower whose edible petals are used as garnish.

marinade ('meh-rihn-ade) The flavored liquid in which a food item is *marinated.*

marinate, marinated ('meh-rihn-ate) To soak a food item in a liquid for the purpose of infusing the flavor of the marinade into it.

maritozzi (mahr-ee-'to-tsee) A fat Italian sweet bun from Rome, filled with raisins and flavored with citrus zest. During medieval times, it was eaten as a Lenten sweet bread and is still enjoyed today for breakfast or as an afternoon snack with white wine.

M
m

marjolaine ('mahr-zho-lahn) A rectangular French gâteau created by Ferdinand Point, consisting of alternating layers of *japonaise,* chocolate *buttercream,* and *praline cream.*

marjoram ('mahr-juhr-uhm) An aromatic herb that is a member of the mint family and has a sweet, delicate flavor of oregano and sage. There are several varieties cultivated for culinary use, including French, knotted, winter, pot, and sweet marjoram.

Marlborough pie A custard-like pie from Massachusetts, often served as a Thanksgiving dessert. It consists of a pie shell filled with applesauce, eggs, cream, sherry, and nutmeg.

marmalade ('mahr-muh-layd) A citrus preserve that contains pieces of rind. The most common is made from Seville oranges, but limes, lemons, and grapefruits may also be used. The name derives from the Portuguese *marmalade,* which means "quince jam" because quince was the first fruit used to make this product. It is popular as a spread for sweet breads or to make dessert sauces, fillings, and glazes.

Marmite ('mahr-mite) A British spread of brown concentrated paste made from yeast extract, with a salty, slightly sweet taste. This British favorite was created in 1902.

marquise (mahr-'key) Most often a chocolate cake made in a rectangular mold lined with sponge cake and filled with a rich mousse and finished with a chocolate glaze. The term may also refer to a variety of other delicate desserts.

marron ('ma-rohn) The French word for *chestnut.*

marron glacé ('mah-rohn ' glah-say) Whole chestnuts that have been peeled and steeped in a concentrated sweet vanilla syrup. Once the sugar penetrates the chestnuts, they are glazed with a final coat of sugar syrup to give them a glossy finish. They are a French delicacy and are eaten as is or used as a garnish on cakes and pastries.

Marsala (mahr-'sah-lah) A fortified wine from Sicily, named after the ancient port city of Marsala. It was created by Englishman John Woodhouse in the 1770s and is primarily made from Grillo and Catarratto Bianco grapes. It comes in three colors: oro (golden), ambra (amber), and rubino (ruby). Each type is fortified to 17 to 18% alcohol and may be secco (dry), semisecco (semisweet), or dolce (sweet). Fine Marsala is aged one year, Superiore is aged two years, Superiore Riserva is aged five years, and Vergine Stravecchio is aged ten years.

marshmallow A soft, fluffy confection originally made from the sweetened extract of the marsh mallow plant. Today, it is commercially produced from a mixture of gelatin, corn syrup, sugar, gum Arabic, and flavorings.

Marshmallow Fluff A thick, fluffy marshmallow cream used to make fudge, candies, and fillings. It was created in the 1920s by Fred L. Mower and H. Allen Durkee, and is used to make the renowned *Fluffernutter* sandwich.

martini (mahr-'tee-nee) A cocktail traditionally made with gin and dry Vermouth. There are many variations on the original, ranging from peach to chocolate and made with different liqueurs and flavorings.

Martinshörnchen ('mahr-tin-shoorn-ken) A crescent-shaped pastry of Erfurt, Germany, that consists of yeast dough or flaky pastry filled with jam or fruit preserves. It is made in honor of Martin Luther, a Protestant reformer, and served on St. Martin's day.

maryann pan A baking pan with a convex bottom to give the baked product a hollowed-out center that is then typically filled with fruit or cream.

marzipan ('mahr-zih-pan) A thick, pliable mixture of almond paste, sugar, glucose, and sometimes egg whites. It may be colored. It is used extensively in creating edible figurines such as animals and flowers, and also rolled into thin sheets and used to cover cakes and pastries. Confectioners' sugar, rather than flour, is used to work with marzipan. If the dough is overworked, the almond oil will rise to the surface and make the dough sticky; this may be corrected by kneading in a bit of water and confectioners' sugar. Owing to its high sugar content, marzipan dries out quickly and should be kept covered. If it becomes too dry, it may be reconstituted with a bit of water, but this will reduce shelf life. It is best stored in an airtight container in a cool place. Also known as *pâte d'amande* and *almond paste*.

marzipan tool Any of several small, hand-held tools used to create decorative *marzipan* products, such as flowers and figurines. They are typically made of heavy plastic but may also be available in metal.

masa ('mah-sah) The Spanish word for "dough," referring to a cornmeal dough made from *masa harina*. Masa is used in Mexican and Latin American cooking to make tortillas and tamales. It is also used as a thickening agent.

masa harina ('mah-sah ah-'ree-nah) Cornmeal made from ground dried hominy, or hulled corn kernels. The corn is boiled in limewater, also known as calcium oxide, and then soaked overnight to release the hulls. It is then dried and ground to a fine powder.

masala (mah-'sah-lah) A variety of Indian spice mixtures. See *garam masala*.

mascarpone (mahs-kahr-'pohn) A soft, smooth, rich, triple-cream cheese from the Lombardy region of Italy. It is most well known for its use in *tiramisu,* but also makes a creamy cheesecake and pairs well with fruit, particularly figs.

mash 1. To crush a product to a smooth consistency. 2. The mixture of crushed grain or malt and hot water, steeped for the production of whisky and beer.

mastic The resin of the mastic tree, native to the Mediterranean region. It has a sweet, licorice flavor and is used throughout Greece, Turkey, and the Middle East to flavor desserts, bread, gum, and liqueurs.

masticha ('mas-tee-ka) A Greek liqueur made with mastic. It is typically served as an *aperitif* and is similar to *ouzo*.

mata kucing tea ('mah-tah 'koo-king 'tee) A Malaysian fruit tea made with fresh ginger, brown sugar, pandanus leaves, and the dried pulp of the mata kucing *longan* fruit.

matzo ('mat-suh) A thin unleavened bread eaten by Jewish people during Passover. It is made from flour and water that is processed quickly to prevent any fermentation. According to the Torah, when the Israelites were fleeing Egypt, they had no time to wait for the bread to rise, so they baked it immediately and the result was matzo.

matzo brei ('mat-suh bri) A version of French toast made with matzo, typically served with jam, honey, or cinnamon sugar.

matzo meal The fine or medium-fine flour made from grinding matzo, often used as a flour substitute in Passover cooking.

Mayapple The small yellow fruit of a herbaceous plant in the barberry family, native to the eastern United States. Only the ripe fruit is used, largely to make preserves, as it may be poisonous when green.

mayhaw A small red fruit of a tree that grows wild in the swamps of southwestern Georgia and along the Gulf coast. It has a floral, sweet-tart flavor and is used for making jelly.

May wine A German wine drink made with white wine and woodruff, an herb. It is traditionally served in springtime on the May Day holiday. Also known as *Maiwein* and *Maibowle*.

M
m

mazarek or mazurek (mah-zoo-rek) A Polish pastry with a soft, shortbread-like texture, topped with almonds or walnuts and decorated with fruit, jam, or colorful icing. Traditionally made for Easter.

mazurka (mah-'zhoor-kah) A small Russian confection similar to meringue, made with whipped eggs, honey, lemon juice and zest, and finely ground nuts such as almonds or walnuts. It is dusted with freshly grated nutmeg and served cold with whipped cream, traditionally at Easter.

Mazzard cherry See *cherry.*

McCallum A Scottish dessert of vanilla ice cream served with raspberry sauce. It originated in Glasgow during the 20th century, and is named after Mr. McCallum, who requested the white-and-red combination because it represented the colors of the Glasgow football (known as soccer in America) team.

McIntosh apple ('mak-ihn-tahsh) See *apple.*

mead (meed) A sweet alcoholic beverage made by fermenting honey, water, and yeast, that dates back to medieval times. If flavored with herbs and/or spices, it is called *metheglin*, and if it contains fruit, it is called *melomel. Mulled mead* is warm spiced mead traditionally served during the winter holidays.

meal 1. The coarsely ground seeds of any edible grain. 2. A fine powder made from nuts that can be substituted for or used in combination with flour in the production of cakes and other pastry products.

mealy Something with a dry or crumbly texture. A term often used for pie dough when the fat is worked into the dough until it resembles cornmeal.

mealy pie dough See *pie dough.*

measuring cup 1. Any one of a set of metal or plastic nested containers used to measure dry and wet ingredients by volume. They come in increments of ¼ cup (55 g/60 ml), ½ cup (115 g/120 ml), ⅓ cup (155 g/150 ml), ¾ cup (170 g/180 ml), 1 cup (225 g/240 ml), and 2 cups (450 g/480 ml). The ingredient should be leveled off at the top for an accurate measurement. 2. Any one of a set of metal, glass, or plastic containers used to measure liquid ingredients. They come in increments of ¼ cup (60 ml) to 4 quarts (3 L 840 ml). The measurement should be read at eye level for accuracy.

measuring spoon Any of a set of handled half-scoop spoons used to measure small amounts of dry and liquid ingredients. They come in increments of ¼ teaspoon (1.25 ml), ½ teaspoon (2.5 ml), ¾ teaspoon (3.5 ml), and 1 tablespoon (5 ml).

Mediterranean pine nut See *pine nut.*

medium-grain rice See *rice.*

medivnychky (metty-fah-'neech-kee) A Ukrainian honey cookie flavored with dried fruit or nuts.

medovik (meh-'do-veek) A Russian honey cake flavored with dried fruits, nuts, or spices.

mei kwei lu (moo-ee kwah-ee lou) A fragrant Chinese wine made from rose petals.

Meilleur Ouvrier de France See *MOF.*

meini (may-ee-nee) An Italian sweet bun that is a delicate cross between a scone and a corn muffin. It is a specialty of Lombardy, traditionally eaten on April 24 to celebrate the liberation of the countryside during the Middle Ages.

mélangeur (may-'lahn-goo-her) A refiner used in products such as *marzipan* and *gianduja* to reduce the particle size.

Melba peach See *peach.*

Melba sauce A sweetened raspberry puree created by Auguste Escoffier in honor of the Australian opera singer Dame Nellie Melba, who was rumored to be his mistress. It is most well known as the topping for *peach Melba.*

Melba toast A dry, crisp, thinly sliced toast created by Auguste Escoffier in honor of Australian opera singer Dame Nellie Melba. It is rumored that he created it to ease her upset stomach during an illness.

melogold grapefruit A large white grapefruit variety with a thick, green-tinged yellow skin. It can be up to 6 inches (15 cm) in diameter and weigh several pounds. It has very few seeds and is sweet and juicy with low acidity. Available October to April.

melomel See *mead.*

melon Any of a large variety of sweet fruits that belong to the gourd family. They are categorized as either *muskmelon* or *watermelon,* with each having its own varieties.

melon baller A small hand tool with a half-sphere scoop at the end of the handle to shape fruit, usually melon, into uniform balls. Some models have different size scoops on either end.

melting moment A rich, buttery cookie typically shaped into a ball, rolled in coconut flakes, and topped with a candied cherry or piece of angelica. These British cookies are popular for their melt-in-the-mouth quality and are often served with afternoon tea.

merengada (may-rayn-'gah-dah) A Latin American drink similar to a *milkshake,* consisting of milk, sugar, fresh fruit pulp, and ice. If it is made with water and milk, it is called *batido;* if it is made with no water or milk, it is called *jugo.*

meringue A light and delicate mixture of egg whites and sugar that has been whipped to the desired consistency. The name is believed to refer to the Swiss town of Meringuen. There are three types:

> **Common or French** Egg whites and sugar whipped to desired peak.

> **Swiss** Egg whites and sugar warmed over a double boiler to 120°F (49°C) and then whipped to desired peak.

> **Italian** A mixture of sugar and water cooked to 240°F (115°C) and poured over egg whites that are then whipped immediately, so the whites do not cook. This is the most stable of the three meringues.

Meringues are an essential component of pastry making, used to leaven cakes and soufflés, lighten mousses, and provide a base for creams. They may also be used as a topping for pies and desserts, which are then browned in an oven or with a *blowtorch.* In addition, they can be colored and piped in different shapes that are then dried in a low oven and used as cookies. It is best to use room-temperature whites, as they will whip faster and provide more volume. To guard against salmonella, use pasteurized whites if the meringue will not be baked. It is important that there is no water or yolk residue when making meringues, or they will not whip sufficiently. As a rule of thumb, there should be at least one ounce of sugar per egg white or the meringue will not be stable. Once the meringue is whipped to the desired consistency, it should be used immediately or it will begin to deflate.

meringue disc A baked circle of meringue used as a base or layer in many cakes and gateaus. It is piped into rounds of varying sizes and baked in a slow oven 250°F (122°C) oven for 2 to 3 hours until completely dry.

meringue powder A substitute for fresh egg whites when making meringues and icings. It consists of dried egg whites, sugar, and vegetable gum, ground into a fine white powder.

M
m

Metaxa (muh-'tahk-suh) A sweet, amber-colored Greek liqueur invented by Spyros Metaxa in 1888. It is produced from Savatiano, Sultanina, and Black Corinth grapes that have been twice distilled and then blended with aged Muscat wine. It is then flavored with a secret botanical mix before being aged in handmade limousine oak casks. It is most commonly available as 3 star, 5 star, and 7 star. Each star represents the number of years it has been aged, while the Private Reserve is aged a minimum of 20 years.

Meteor cherry See *cherry.*

meter A metric measurement of length, equivalent to 39.37 inches.

> 10 millimeters = 1 centimeter
>
> 10 centimeters = 1 decimeter or 100 centimeters = 1 meter
>
> 10 decimeters = 1 meter

metheglin See *mead.*

méthode champenoise ('meh-tohd 'shahm-peh-nwahz) See *Champagne.*

metric system A system of weights and measurements developed in France and used throughout the world. It differs from the American system in that it is based on decimals. Weight is based on the *gram,* volume is based on the *Liter,* and length is based on the *meter.*

methylated spirit See *denatured alcohol.*

metrios See *Greek coffee.*

Mexican chocolate A variety of sweet chocolate flavored with cinnamon and a hint of almond. It is grainier than other chocolates and has visible sugar crystals. The most well known brand is Ibarra. As a substitute for Mexican chocolate, use 1 ounce semi-sweet chocolate, ½ teaspoon ground cinnamon, and 1 drop of almond extract.

Mexican lime See *Key lime.*

Mexican wedding cookie A rich, buttery cookie loaded with almonds or pecans, rolled in confectioners' sugar immediately after baking and then again when cool. Also known as *Russian tea cake* and *polvorone.*

Meyer lemon A cross between an orange and a lemon, with a thin, smooth lemony skin. They are named after Frank Meyer, who first imported this Chinese fruit to the United States in 1908. They are prized for their sweeter, less acidic flavor, and are available from October to May.

m'hanncha (ehm-'hahn-chah) The Moroccan word for "the snake," referring to a confection of ground almonds, cinnamon, confectioners' sugar, and orange flower water or rosewater, mixed into a thick paste and then rolled into a cylinder. The cylinder is then rolled in buttered *phyllo dough* and shaped like a coiled snake. After baking, it is topped with cinnamon sugar and cut into slices. The slices are served for special occasions.

miche (meesh) A flavorful, naturally fermented, dense, chewy country bread created by the renowned French baker Lionel Poilâne.

microplane A hand-held tool used to finely grate zest, chocolate, whole spices, and other pastry ingredients. The surgical-grade stainless steel grater comes in a variety of sizes and coarseness, and is typically attached to a handle for ease of use. It was designed as a woodworking tool for shaving wood, but has become popular among pastry professionals.

M
m

midori (mih-door-ee) A bright green liqueur from Japan, flavored with honeydew melon.

miglia foglia ('mee-glee-ah 'fo-glee-ah) The Italian name for *mille-feuille.*

mignardise See *petit four.*

mijiu ('mee-joo) A Chinese sweet rice wine served as dessert.

mikong ('mee-kong) A Chinese honey cake lightly flavored with ginger.

milk A natural combination of water, proteins, minerals, lactose, vitamins, milk solids, and milk fat produced by domesticated cows. It is classified by the amount of *milk fat* it contains, which ranges from 3.25% for whole milk to 0% for fat-free or skim milk. Although water or a lower-fat milk may be substituted for whole milk, the reduced fat content may affect the flavor, color, and/or texture of the end product. Milk is an important ingredient in the bakeshop, serving many functions, including achieving improved crust color and softness, obtaining a longer shelf life, developing a fine, even crumb, and adding flavor and richness. When using milk in yeast doughs, heat it to 180°F (82°C) because it will denature the whey proteins that interfere with gluten development.

Milfoil See *yarrow.*

milk chocolate See *chocolate.*

milk crumb A mixture of chocolate liquor, sugar, and milk solids sometimes added to milk chocolate during the manufacturing process to produce a caramel-like flavor.

milk dough A bread dough that is primarily hydrated with fresh milk. These are typically enriched white breads made with natural dough conditioners, fat, sugar, and milk. This combination causes the crust to caramelize quickly and gives the bread a soft, airy texture. Common examples are hamburger and hot dog buns.

milk fat See *milk.*

milk powder See *dry milk.*

milk shake An American dessert drink of ice cream, milk, and/or a flavored syrup or fruit. It is typically served topped with whipped cream and a maraschino cherry.

milk solid The protein found in *milk.*

milk sugar Another term for *lactose.*

milk toast Toast that has been buttered, sprinkled with cinnamon, and moistened with hot milk.

Milky Way An American candy bar that consists of a chocolate-malt flavored nougat covered with caramel and enrobed in milk chocolate. It was created in 1920 by Frank C. Mars, and was the first filled candy bar. Its taste was inspired by the chocolate malted *milk shake* that was popular at the time. The European version does not contain any caramel.

mille-feuille (meel-'fwee) French for "thousand layers" or "thousand leaves," referring to a rectangular pastry of three strips of puff pastry layered with cream, jam, or another filling. It is topped with confectioners' sugar or white fondant with spider web lines of chocolate. Also known as a *Napoleon* or *miglia foglia.*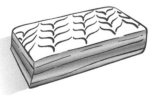

millet ('mihl-leht) Any of a variety of cereal grains that have been cultivated for thousands of years, such as *common millet, pearl millet, teff,* and *sorghum.* It is an important food source for the poor regions of Asia and Africa, where the plants

M
m

thrive in hot, arid climates. The grains are high in protein and generally cooked in water to make porridge or ground and used as a flour to make breads and cakes.

milliliter A metric measurement of volume, equivalent to .034 ounces. See also *Liter.*

millimeter See *meter.*

mimosa (mih-'moh-sah) 1. A popular brunch cocktail of equal parts orange juice and Champagne. 2. The small yellow flower from the acacia tree, generally used in the production of liqueurs and fritter batters for their flavor and color.

mince To finely chop.

mincemeat A rich, spicy, preserved fruit mixture, usually consisting of dried fruit, candied fruit, apples, and beef suet and steeped in spices and brandy, rum, or Madeira. Originally mincemeat contained meat, hence the name, but modern versions no longer use beef. The mixture is used as a pie filling, or as a filling for cakes, cookies, and pastries.

Minneola See *tangelo.*

mint A large perennial herb group that has over 30 species and 600 varieties. Many are prized for their oil and aromatic leaves, and are used extensively as a flavoring agent and garnish. See also *peppermint* and *spearmint.*

mique (meek) A French cornmeal dumpling, either savory of sweet. They originated during the Middle Ages, and are made by shaping cornmeal, yeast, eggs, and butter into a small flat discs and then poaching or frying it. It is often served with jam and sugar for dessert.

Mirabellan Geist ('meer-ah-bell-an guyst) A famous German *eau-de-vie* made from the *Mirabelle plum.*

mirabelle plum ('mihr-uh-behl) A very small, round European plum with a thin golden-yellow skin and a firm, sweet, juicy flesh. It is used in jams and tarts. Known in Great Britain as *cherry plum.*

mirliton 1. A puff pastry tartlet filled with almond cream and garnished with three almond halves that are arranged to form a star. 2. A crisp petit four flavored with orange flower water.

mise en place (meez ahn plahs) French for "everything in its place," referring to having all items properly prepared and set up for production.

Mission fig See *fig.*

mixer An electrical tool with metal whisks that is used to combine and beat ingredients to make breads and pastries. Mixers vary in size, shape, and model design, and come with different size stainless steel bowls. The machines come with a variety of attachments; see *mixer attachment.*

> **Floor mixer** Larger and heavier than tabletop mixers, it is generally bolted to the floor to prevent it from shaking during mixing.
>
> **Oblique mixer** Similar to the spiral mixer, but has a rotating arm that is paddle-shaped and placed on an angle.
>
> **Planetary mixer** A floor or tabletop mixer with a fixed bowl and removable attachments such as a dough hook, paddle, and whip that hang vertically in the bowl.
>
> **Spiral mixer** A fixed mixer with a spiral arm that turns simultaneously with a rotating bowl.
>
> **Tabletop mixer** Small, portable mixer with the most common bowl sizes of 5 quart (5 L) and 20 quart (20 L).

mixer attachment Interchangable parts for standard mixers, including a *dough hook, paddle,* and *whip.* The *dough hook* is a J-shaped metal attachment used to mix and knead bread dough. The *paddle* is a flat, round metal frame with six evenly spaced parallel bars, used to cream ingredients and mix heavier batters, such as pound cakes. The *whip* is a batch of thin or thick metal wires looped around a flat metal base, designed to whip air into ingredients; the width and flexibility of the whip vary, based on the designed lightness of the product, such as with eggs and cream, or the thickness, such as with heavy batters and icings. Other attachments and accessories include a *sweet dough arm,* which is an open loop made in an irregular winding shape, used to mix doughs such as cookie and short doughs, which should be blended without incorporating air. The *pastry knife* is similar to a sweet dough arm, but has a smooth edge and a bottom loop that ends in a slightly curved point, designed for mixing pie doughs and other items when the fat should remain in small pieces and not be creamed. A *mounted bowl scraper* is a wide, heavy plastic scraper that fits tightly against the sides of the mixer bowl from top to bottom, used to scrape down the sides of the bowl; it saves time from having to stop the machine to scrape down the sides. A *bowl truck* is a heavy metal ring on wheels that sits under the bowl and allows the mixing bowl to be pulled rather than lifted.

mixing methods The techniques used to mix doughs and batters, influencing their ultimate texture and appearance. The following briefly describes the most common mixing methods in the bakeshop:

Angel food Egg whites and sugar are whipped to soft peaks and then sifted dry ingredients are gently folded in. Used for angel food cake.

Biscuit Dry ingredients are sifted, fat is cut into the dry ingredients, liquid is slowly added, and it is mixed just until combined. Used for biscuits, scones, and pie dough. For flaky pie dough, the fat is cut into pieces the size of hazelnuts. For mealy pie dough, the fat is cut in until it resembles coarse cornmeal.

Chiffon Egg yolks, oil, and part of the sugar are combined; dry ingredients are sifted and added to the yolk-oil mixture; egg whites are combined with the remaining sugar and whipped to soft peaks; and then whites are gently folded into the mixture. Used for chiffon cake.

Creaming The fat and sugar are creamed until light and fluffy and then the eggs are added slowly. The remaining liquids (if any) are combined and added alternately with the sifted dry ingredients. Used for cakes, cookies, and sometimes muffins and quickbreads.

Direct dough Another name for *straight dough method.*

Egg-foam Another term for *sponge method for cakes and cookies.*

Indirect dough Another name for *sponge method for yeast doughs.*

Modified straight A variation on the *straight dough method;* the fat, sugar, salt, milk solids, and flavorings are blended together first and then the eggs are added slowly; the liquid is added next and only then the flour and yeast. Used for rich, sweet doughs to ensure even distribution of fat and sugar.

Muffin The wet and sifted dry ingredients are mixed separately and then the wet mixture is added to the dry, just until combined. Used for muffins and other quickbreads.

One-bowl Another name for *one-stage method.*

One-stage All the ingredients are added in one step. Also known as *one-bowl method.*

M
m

Sponge method for cakes and cookies Whole eggs or yolks are warmed with some of the sugar and whipped to *ribbon stage;* the sifted dry ingredients are gently folded in and then the whipped whites, which may have sugar whipped with them or sometimes melted butter, are folded in last. Used for sponge cake, gênoise, and ladyfingers. Also known as *egg-foam method.*

Sponge method for yeast doughs A preferment or sponge made with liquid, flour, and yeast and fermented before being added to the dough. Also known as *indirect dough method.*

Straight dough All ingredients are added at once and combined until the dough is smooth. Used for some yeast breads. Also known as *direct dough method.*

Two-stage The fat is cut into the sifted dry ingredients and liquids are added in two stages; the eggs and the sugar are added in the second stage and the batter is whipped for aeration. Used for *high-ratio cakes.*

ml The abbreviation for *milliliter.*

mm The abbreviation for millimeter. See *meter.*

mocha ('moh-kah) A combination of coffee and chocolate flavors, used in pastries.

mochi (moh-chee) A sweet Japanese short-grained rice with a high starch content and glutinous texture, used to make rice cakes and confections.

mochiko (moh-chee-koh) A rice flour made from *mochi.*

modeling chocolate A pliable chocolate used for covering cakes or making decorative garnishes. The addition of corn syrup to the chocolate creates a firm, flexible dough-like product similar to *marzipan.* The chocolate may be dark, white, or milk chocolate. Also known as *plastic chocolate.*

modeling tool Any of a set of hand tools used to shape and sculpt *marzipan* figures and flowers. They are made of plastic and have different shapes on both ends, that include round, pointed, flat, and blunt bottoms.

modified straight dough method See *mixing methods.*

MOF The acronym for Meilleur Ouvrier de France (Best of France), which is the highest honor a pastry chef can receive in France.

moh sein buong (moh zeh-ihn boo-'ong) A Burmese steamed sponge cake made with rice flour and palm sugar. It is steamed in a tall mold and has light and dark layers, and is garnished with grated coconut, toasted sesame seeds, and salt. It is served on banana leaves for breakfast or as a snack.

moisten To add a small amount of a liquid to ingredients to make them damp but not wet.

moistener An ingredient such as water, milk, oil, eggs, cream, or syrup that helps produce a moist product.

mojito (moh-'hee-toh) A Cuban cocktail of mint, rum, sugar, lime juice, and club soda.

molasses (muh-'las-sihz) The brownish-black thick syrup that remains when sugar is refined from sugarcane. The type and quality of molasses depends on the maturity of the sugarcane, the amount of sugar extracted, and the method of extraction. There are three grades:

Light Derived from the first boiling of the sugar syrup, which results in a syrup that is light in color and flavor.

Dark Derived from the second boiling, which results in a thicker texture, darker color, and less sweet version of the light.

M
m

Blackstrap Derived from the third boiling, which results in a darker, thicker, and more bitter syrup.

Molasses is available as sulphured or unsulphured, depending on whether or not sulphur was used in the refining. Molasses is used in breads and cakes to add flavor and improve shelf life. Molasses made from sugar beets, rather than sugarcane, is generally used as animal feed and in alcohol manufacturing.

mold 1. A container used to form or shape a product. 2. To form or shape a product by hand. 3. A fungus that grows on products such as bread, fruit, and cheese. Mold is desirable on cheese such as *Roquefort* and *Stilton,* but is an indication of spoilage on other foods.

molded chocolate A chocolate confection that has been molded in a decorative form (see *chocolate mold*). They may be solid or have a soft center.

molded cookie See *cookie.*

molinet (mo-lee-'neht) A wooden tool used by the Aztecs and Europeans to froth *xocotal.* Today, they are still an important part of Mexican cuisine, and the bottoms have ornamental carvings.

monkey bread A type of bread formed by arranging small balls of yeast dough in a pan so that they stick together as they rise and bake. They are typically brushed with melted butter and may be sweet or savory.

monosaccharide A simple sugar with one sugar unit or *saccharide.* The most common examples of a monosaccharide are *glucose* and *fructose.*

monounsaturated fat See *unsaturated fat.*

monstera (mon-steh-ruh) A tropical fruit that resembles a large pine cone, with a thick green scaly skin and firm, creamy flesh; it tastes like a combination of banana, pineapple, and mango. The tree is cultivated in California and Florida, and the fruit should be ripened at room temperature until the scales fall off.

Mont Blanc (mawhn blahn) French for "white mountain," referring to a rich dessert made with a sweet, *short pastry dough* topped with *crème chantilly* and thin strands of *chestnut puree.* The cream is piped to resemble a small mountain peak, as the dessert is named after the high mountain on the border between France and Italy. Known in Italy as *monte bianco.*

monte bianco See *Mont Blanc.*

Montmorency (mahnt-mo-'rayns) A French term that refers to any cake or dessert, such as ice creams, bombes, mousses, and tarts, in which the predominant flavor is of the Montmorency cherry. The cherries may be fresh, candied, or soaked in brandy. See *cherry.*

Montmorency cherry (mont-muh-'rehn-see) See *cherry.*

Montmorency gâteau A French cake of *génoise* topped with brandy-soaked cherries and *Italian meringue,* and garnished with candied cherries.

Montpensier (mahnt-pahn-see-'her) A French name given to a variety of sweet and savory dishes created in honor of the Duchesse de Montpensier. Cakes cooked in a pan lined with the ingredient that gives it its predominant flavor are termed à la Montpensier.

moon cake A round, moon-shaped Chinese cake filled with sweet black bean or lotus paste or a mixture of pickled melon and nuts. According to legend, these decorative cakes were created to conceal news of a revolt against Mongolian rulers. They are traditionally served with green tea during the Moon Festival, which is the 15th day of the 8th lunar month, when the moon is at its fullest and brightest.

Moon Pie A cakelike cookie of marshmallow cream sandwiched between two round graham crackers and dipped in chocolate. Created by the Chattanooga

M
m

Bakery in 1917. Its origin is not certain, but it is believed that one of the employees, Mr. Mitchell, visited a coal mine and asked the miners what kind of snack they would like for their lunch pail. One of the miners replied, "Something big and filling" and Mr. Mitchell asked, "How big?" At the time the moon was rising, so the miner pointed to the moon and said, "As big as the moon." Also known as *Scooter Pie* in New England.

Moravian Christmas cookie (moh-'ray-vee-uhn) A cookie made with ginger, molasses, and spices, from the Moravia region of the Czech Republic.

Morello cherry (mohr-'rehl-oh) See *cherry*.

mortar and pestle A two-part tool used to grind and pulverize herbs, spices, and other ingredients. The *mortar* is a bowl-shaped container and the *pestle* resembles a small baseball bat. The rounded end of the pestle is ground into the ingredients in the mortar until the desired consistency is reached.

Mouli grater ('moo-lee) A hand-held rotary grater used for small quantities of hard foods, such as chocolate and nuts.

mountain cranberry See *cowberry*.

mounted bowl scraper See *mixer attachments*.

mousse The French word for "froth" or "foam," referring to a velvety smooth dessert. It may be made from chocolate or fruit purees and lightened with whipped egg whites and/or whipped cream. It may also include gelatin for a firmer texture. It is a dessert and also used as a filling for cakes and pastries.

mouthfeel A term used to describe the consistency and texture of food in your mouth such as creamy ice cream.

muddle To mash ingredients together, usually relating to the preparation of cocktails.

Muesli ('myoos-lee) The German word for "mixture," referring to a breakfast cereal of raw rolled oats, wheat flakes, dried fruits, nuts, seeds, or other ingredients. It may be eaten dry or with milk or juice. It was created as a health food in the 19th century by Swiss nutritionist Dr. Bircher-Benner.

muffin 1. A small sweet or savory quickbread baked in a muffin pan, and made with various ingredients and flours. Muffins are most commonly eaten for breakfast or afternoon tea. 2. English term for a yeast-risen cake that is eaten as a snack or for breakfast; see *English muffin*.

muffin method See *mixing methods*.

muffin pan A metal or *Fleximold* baking form with small, medium, or large round indentions to hold muffin batter and to shape them during baking. The pans range in capacity from 6-cup to 4 dozen and come in full or half sheetpan size.

mulberry See *berry*.

mull To heat wine, ale, or cider and flavor it with sugar, spices, herbs, and/or fruit.

mulled mead See *mead*.

mulled wine An aromatic alcoholic drink of red wine, sugar, spices, and citrus fruit. It is served very warm and sometimes fortified with brandy or another spirit.

mung bean A small, oval bean that is eaten either whole, usually as bean sprouts or dried and made into flour. Whole mung beans are typically made from dried beans that have been cooked until they are tender and slightly sweet. The beans are green with the skin and light yellow without. They are used extensively in Chinese, Indian, and Japanese cooking to make sweet soups, dessert snacks, and ice cream. The flour is also used for breads and noodles.

Muscadine grape ('muhs-kuh-dine) See *grape*.

Muscat grape ('muhs-kat) See *grape*.

Muscatel wine ('muhs-kuh-tehl) A rich, sweet dessert wine made from the Muscat grape.

muscato See *grape*.

muscavado sugar See *sugar, Barbados*.

muskmelon A melon that contains seeds in a semi-hollow fibrous center and has either a smooth or netted skin. The most common varieties are:

Bitter An elongated, round, bumpy-skinned fruit with brown seeds. It is native to China, where it is used as a vegetable. When first picked it has a yellow-green skin and mildly sour flavor, but forms a bitter flavor as it ripens. Also known as *balsam pear*.

Canary An oblong melon with a smooth, bright yellow skin and firm, juicy, cream-colored flesh. It has a mild, sweet flavor. Available May through September.

Cantaloupe A round, netted melon with a golden yellow skin and bright orange flesh. It has a sweet, juicy flavor and tender texture. Available May through September.

Casaba A large, round to oval melon that is pointed at one end. It has a golden yellow skin and pale green flesh that has a mildly sweet flavor with a hint of cucumber. Available May through September.

Charentais A small, spherical melon with a greenish-tan skin that has long green streaks. The deep orange flesh is juicy with a sweet taste and floral aroma. Available May through September.

Crenshaw A large, oblong melon with a wrinkled, ridged dark green skin that turns yellow when ripe. The bright, salmon-colored flesh is tender and sweet with a hint of spice. Available May through September.

Galia A medium, sphere-shaped melon with a netted, dull green skin and pale green flesh. It has a firm, dense texture and sweet flavor. Available May through September.

Gaya A very small, roundish melon with a white flesh and smooth, white skin that is splotched with yellowish-green streaks. Available May through July.

Hami A large, oblong melon with an orange flesh and yellow skin that is streaked with green. It has a sweet, juicy flavor and crunchy texture. Available May through July.

Honeydew A sweet, smooth-skinned melon that has a round to oval shape. The three varieties are green, gold, and orange and the skin changes color from pale green to creamy yellow as it ripens, except for the gold variety, which has a light gold skin. The flesh is light green, except for the orange variety, which is orange. Available May through July.

Korean A small melon with a ridged, bright yellow skin and white flesh. It is very sweet and has a crisp texture. Available May through September.

Pepino A medium, oval melon with a point at one end. It has a pale yellow-green skin that has long, purple-red streaks and blotches. The smooth, tender flesh ranges in color from yellow to coral and has a sweet, mild cantaloupe-like flavor. Available November through April.

Persian A medium, round to oval melon with a netted, grayish-green skin and a pinkish-orange flesh. It is sweet with a firm, buttery texture. Available May through September.

M
m

Santa Claus A round or oval melon with a pale or dark green skin and light green flesh. It has a crunchy texture and mildly sweet flavor. Also known as *Christmas melon*. Available May through September.

Sharlyn An oblong, medium melon with a netted, tannish-yellow skin and tender, pale green flesh. It is sweet with a hint of spice. Available May through September.

Spanish A large, oval, sweet, juicy melon with a ribbed green skin and pale green flesh. Available July through October.

Sprite A small, oval, very sweet, crisp melon with a creamy yellow skin and white flesh. Available May through June.

Winter melon A muskmelon variety that resembles a large honeydew. The frosted green skin encases a porous white flesh that tastes like zucchini. Although it is a fruit, it is used mostly as a vegetable in Asian cooking. Available year-round in Asian markets. Also known as *fuzzy melon*.

must The fresh juice of grapes or other fruit that has been pressed, before the fermentation process occurs. It may include seeds, pulp, or skins.

M
m

Nn

naan bread A soft-textured round or teardrop-shaped flatbread from India. It resembles a thick pita and has a golden bottom crust and a rippled surface that is typically brushed with *ghee* or butter. It is cooked in a *tandoor oven* and served warm. It may be stuffed with a variety of fillings or used to scoop other foods.

nammura A Lebanese dessert made by baking semolina, yogurt, sugar, *kater*, baking powder, and *tahini*, topped with coconut and almonds. When golden brown, it is cut into squares and soaked with lemon syrup.

nanas goreng (nah-nass go-rang) An Indonesian pineapple fitter, made by dipping thinly sliced fresh pineapple into a batter of rice flour, eggs, baking soda, salt, sugar, and water. They are served warm as a snack with coffee or tea.

nanaimo bar (nah-'nehm bahr) A three-layered Canadian pastry that consists of a cookie crumb layer topped with custard or buttercream and then topped with dark chocolate. The graham cracker crumb layer may include chocolate, coconut, butter, sugar, or walnuts; the middle layer may be flavored with vanilla, mint, mocha, or other. It is cut and served in individual squares. The dessert was created in the 1930s and named after the city of Nanaimo, in British Colombia.

nangka goring ('nahng-kah 'gohr-ingh) Indonesian fried *jackfruit*, eaten as a sweet snack.

Nanterre See *brioche*.

Nantes cake (nahnt kayk) A small, round French cake flavored with citrus and baked in a mold lined with sliced almonds. Once baked, the cake is brushed with apricot glaze and iced with *fondant*.

Napoleon See *mille-feuille*.

Napoleon cherry Another name for *Royal Ann cherry;* see *cherry*.

Napolitain (nah-po-lee-'tay) A large cylindrical cake made with rings of almond pastry layered with jam and elaborately decorated with *marzipan* and candied fruits. Traditionally used as a buffet centerpiece, it is believed to have been created by Carême, who favored such dramatic showpieces.

nappage (nah-pah-zha) An apricot glaze commonly brushed on desserts and pastries to provide shine. It also helps protect fruit toppings from the air, so they will have a longer shelf life. The glaze may be made fresh or purchased in bulk from specialty vendors. The word derives from the French *nappé*, which means "to cover."

nappé (nah-pay) French for "to cover," used in the pastry kitchen to mean "to coat the back of a spoon." This term is used in the production of sauces, particularly *crème anglaise*, to determine its thickness.

naranjilla (nah-rahn-'hee-lah) A small South American fruit that tastes like a cross between citrus and pineapple. It has an orange skin that encases a yellowish-green segmented flesh dotted with tiny, flat seeds.

nashi The Japanese word for "pear," referring to a fruit with the texture and taste of a pear but the shape of an apple. The skin is yellowish green and the flesh is cream colored, sweet, and juicy.

nasturtium (nah-'ster-shuhm) An edible flower used as a garnish.

natilla (nah-'tee-yah) A soft Spanish custard made from ewe's milk and flavored with spices.

navel orange See *orange*.

navette A small boat-shaped butter cake flavored with orange flower water. The name derives from the Latin *navis*, which means "boat." It is believed to have originated in ancient Egypt, where the cake represented the boat that carried Isis, the goddess of fertility.

Neapolitan ice cream A layered ice cream dessert with three different flavors—vanilla, chocolate, and strawberry. The layers are stacked on top of or beside each other, and molded into a rectangle so that slicing reveals the layers. It was devised by a pastry chef named Tortoni in the 19th century.

NECCO The acronym for New England Candy Company, best known for their NECCO Wafers, hard little pastel-colored candy discs. The company has been in operation since 1847 and is headquartered in Revere, Massachusetts, and also makes Thin Mints and Haviland.

Nectacotum pluot See *pluot*.

Nectar peach See *peach*.

nectarine A peachlike fruit, but typically smaller and sweeter, with a smooth bright skin. It is a stone fruit, and its name derives from the Greek *necter*, which means "drink of the Gods." The thin, bright yellow skin is streaked with red and the flesh is creamy white or golden yellow. They are available from late spring to late summer but peak in July and August. Although there are many varieties, the most common are all *freestone*:

> **Gold Mine** A large white variety originally from New Zealand. Its skin is blushed with red.
>
> **Fantasia** A slightly oval medium to large variety with a generous covering of red blush. It originated in California and has firm, smooth yellow flesh.
>
> **Silver Lode** A juicy white nectarine from California. It has a yellow-red skin with red dots and a smooth, white flesh.

neenish A small, sweet tart with a *short dough* filled with gelatin-set lemon cream and topped with pink or white icing on one side and chocolate on the other. It is believed to have been created by Ruby Neenish of Australia in 1913.

neige (nehz) The French word for "snow," referring to egg whites that have been whipped to stiff peaks. They are used in desserts such as *floating islands;* see *oeufs à la neige*.

nelusko A *petit four* that consists of a pitted cherry soaked in *Kirsch* and then dipped in *fondant*. Once set, the bottom of the confection is typically dipped in chocolate to provide a flat base.

Nesselrode ('nehs-uhl-rohd) One of several sweet or savory dishes named in honor of a 19th-century Russian diplomat, Count Nesselrode. The most well known is *Nesselrode pudding*, a mixture of custard cream, chestnut puree, candied fruit, currants, golden raisins, and whipped cream, created by Nesselrode's head chef, M. Mouy.

Nesselrode pudding See *Nesselrode*.

N
n

Nestlé Crunch Bar The first chocolate bar to combine milk chocolate and crunchy crisps, created in 1938. Today it is Nestlé's third-largest-selling confectionery, available in about 40 countries worldwide. The candy is also made in the following varieties: Nestlé White Crunch, Nestlé Crunch Pieces, Nestlé Buncha Crunch, Nestlé Crunch with Caramel, and Nestlé Crunch Assorted Minis.

Nestlé, Henri Founder of the Nestlé Company, this German pharmacist was first known for inventing a food for babies who were unable to breastfeed. He changed his name from Heinrich to Henri when he moved to Vevey, Switzerland, and started the company in 1866. Although Nestlé is one of the largest food and beverage companies in the world, it is well known for its chocolates and confectionaries. In 1875, a friend and neighbor of Nestle, Daniel Peter, figured out how to combine milk and cocoa powder to make milk chocolate. He formed a company called Peter, Cailler, and Kohler, and relied on Nestlé for milk and marketing expertise. In 1929, Nestlé acquired the company and it soon became one of the world's leading makers of chocolate.

Nestlé Toll House cookie See *Toll House Cookie.*

Neufchâtel ('noo-shuh-tell) A soft, unripened French cheese similar to *cream cheese* and *mascarpone*. It has a high fat content (35–45%) and creamy, mild flavor. It has been made in the small town of Neufchâtel, France, since the Middle Ages and is used extensively for desserts.

new century See *Asian pear, shinseiki.*

Newton Pippin apple See *apple.*

New York style cheesecake See *cheesecake.*

Niagara grape See *grape.*

nib See *cocoa nib.*

nieulle (nee-eh-'ool) A small, French cake from Flanders that resembles a waffle. It is made by combining eggs, flour, sugar, milk, and butter into a batter and baking it in a waffle iron.

niflette (nee-'fleht) A French cake that consists of *puff pastry* filled with *frangipane*. It is made on All Saints Day in the town of Brie.

nigella A tiny black seed with a distinct peppery flavor, commonly used for breads, particularly *naan*, and savory items in India and the Middle East. Also known as *black onion seed.*

nijisseiki See *Asian pear.*

nipa palm fruit The fruit of a palm tree that grows along rivers in Southeast Asia. The young shoots and the pulp of the immature seeds are edible and have a slightly sweet flavor. They are often boiled in sugar syrup or mixed with other fruits before eating.

nitter kibbeh ('niht-tehr 'kihb-eh) An Ethiopian clarified butter flavored with aromatic spices.

nixtamal The Latin American word for *hominy.*

noble rot See *Botrytis cinerea.*

Nocello An Italian liqueur flavored with walnuts.

Nockerln An Austrian dessert that is a type of sweet dumpling. This specialty of Salzburg is made with a soufflé-type mixture set afloat a vanilla-flavored milk and then baked. The result is light and rich and is served using a crisp cookie as a spoon.

nog A slang term for *eggnog.*

N
n

noisette (nwah-'zeht) The French word for *hazelnut*.

noix (nwa) The French word for nut, especially *walnut*.

nondairy creamer A milk or cream substitute made from sweeteners, emulsifiers, and coconut, palm, or hydrogenated oil. A common ingredient found in most nondairy creamers is *sodium casienate*, which is a milk protein that does not contain *lactose* so therefore is not considered a dairy product. The first powdered nondairy creamer was introduced in 1961 by *Nestlé* under the name Coffee-Mate. Today these creamers may be found in liquid, powder, and frozen form. Also known as *coffee whitener*.

nondiastic malt Malt in which the natural *amylase* enzymes have been neutralized.

nonfat sour cream See *sour cream*.

nonnette (non-'neht) The French word for "nun," referring to a small spice cake iced with white fondant to resemble nuns' robes. These were originally made by nuns in convents and have been a specialty of Reims, France, since the Middle Ages.

nonpareil (non-puh-rehl) 1. A tiny sugar pellet for decorating cakes and other baked good, available in many colors. 2. A small flat chocolate candy covered with tiny white sugar pellets.

nonreactive cookware Cookware that is lined or made with a nonreactive material, such as stainless steel, ceramic, or glass, that does not have a negative reaction on the flavor or color of the food being cooking in it.

nopale (noh-'pah-lay) The oval leaves of the *nopal*, or prickly pear cactus. They are pale to medium green in color and have a light slightly tart flavor. They are used in Mexican cooking and may be purchased fresh or canned.

Northern Spy apple See *apple*.

Northwest Greening apple See *apple*.

no-time dough A yeast-raised bread dough that does not undergo bulk fermentation. Although this dough saves time, it compromises the flavor and texture of the bread.

nougat ('noo-guht) A sweet made with a cooked mixture of sugar, honey, and nuts, eaten as candy or used as an ingredient. Depending on the country, the ingredients, texture, and production method vary; the most well known is French white almond nougat, called *Nougat de Montélimar*, which is lightened with whipped egg whites. Nougat is susceptible to humidity, so is typically pressed between sheets of rice paper for storage.

nougatine ('new-gah-teen) A French confection made by combining sliced almonds and a cooked sugar syrup. The thick mixture is rolled out onto oiled marble while still warm and cut into decorative shapes or molded into baskets or other edible containers. The result is hard and crisp when cooled and may also be crushed and used as a flavoring in buttercreams, ice creams, and pastries.

nouvelle cuisine ('noo-vehl 'kwee-zeen) The French term for "new cuisine," referring to a style of cooking that started in the early 1970s as a departure from rich classic cooking. It was based on using natural flavors and serving smaller portions.

noyau (no-yeh) The French word for "stone," referring to liqueurs produced by infusing the flavor of a fruit's stone (pit), such as apricots or cherries. These may be consumed straight or used to flavor sorbets or cocktails.

Noyau de Poissy ('no-yeh duh pwahs) A French liqueur made from the pits of cherries.

nozzle A small metal or plastic funnel fitted into a *piping bag* to create designs, especially on pastries. It was invented by a French pâtissier named Trottier in the 19th century.

N
n

nulle ('noo-leh) A simple custard of egg yolks and cream baked in a mold and sprinkled with spiced sugar. It was created by an Italian chef named Nullio in the 17th century.

nuo mi ci (noo-oh 'mee see) A Singaporean confection of small green balls of glutinous rice filled with a paste of peanuts, sesame seeds, sugar, and butter and then rolled in grated coconut.

nuo mi fen (noo-oh mee fan) A Chinese rice flour.

nut A hard-shelled seed or dry fruit with an edible kernel surrounded by a papery skin. Note that many items called "nuts" in the bakeshop are actually seeds, legumes, or kernels. True nuts are high in fat, but considered healthy because they are also a good source of protein, vitamins, minerals, and fiber. They should be stored in an airtight container in a cool, dry place to prevent rancidity. See *almond, black walnut, Brazil nut, butternut, candlenut, cashew, chufa, hazelnut, hickory nut, macadamia, nutmeg, peanut, pecan, pine nut, pistachio,* and *walnut.*

Nutella A sweet hazelnut spread, produced by the Italian company Ferrero. It makes an excellent flavoring for pastries and confections.

nut flour See *flour.*

nut meat The inner, edible kernel of a *nut.*

nutmeg The seed of a tropical evergreen tree, grated and used as a spice. The exposed seed is surrounded by a lacy membrane that is also ground to make another spice, mace. The nutmeg is oval and about 1 inch (2.5 cm) in length. It is used throughout the world and may be purchased whole or ground; however, freshly ground has a far superior flavor. This versatile spice is used extensively in baking and pastry to add a spicy, slightly sweet flavor to custards, sauces, creams, and dessert drinks.

nutmeg grater A small hand-held tool used to grate whole *nutmeg.*

nut flour See *flour.*

nut mill A tool to pulverize nuts without releasing their oils. It is typically made of cast iron and attaches to a tabletop.

nutmeg grater

Nutrasweet The brand name of an artificial sweetener, *aspartame.*

N
n

Oo

oat bran See *oats*.

oat flour See *flour*.

oat groats See *oats*.

oatmeal See *oats*.

oatmeal cookie See *cookie, drop*.

oats A nutritious cereal grass that is processed into the following forms:

> **Instant oats** Cut groats that have been precooked and dried. This softens the oat pieces and so instant is not recommended for baking because once liquid is added, the mixture will turn gooey. Instant oats are sweetened and flavored, and sold in packages as a breakfast cereal.

> **Irish oats** See *steel-cut oats*.

> **Oat bran** The outer casing of the oat groat, prized for its high dietary fiber content and cholesterol-lowering qualities. It does not contain any gluten.

> **Oat flour** See *flour*.

> **Oat groats** Oat kernels that have been cleaned, toasted, hulled, and then cleaned again. The process leaves the nutritional value intact.

> **Oatmeal** A thick porridge made with hulled, sliced, and cooked oats.

> **Pinhead oats** Hulled oat groats that have been broken down and cleaned only once.

> **Quick oats** Oat groats that have been cut, steamed, and rolled to reduce cooking time.

> **Rolled oats** Large oat flakes produced when oat groats are cut, steamed, and flattened with rollers.

> **Scotch oats** See *steel-cut oats*.

> **Steel-cut oats** Oat groats that have been cut into two or three pieces, which takes them longer to cook; they are not precooked or rolled. Steel-cut oats are used for making oatmeal. Also known as *Irish oats* and *Scotch oats*.

oblaten (o-'blah-ten) A thin edible wafer used to line pans for making confections such as *nougat*. It is also used during Communion in Christian churches. The name derives from the Latin oblate, which means "flattened." Rice paper may be used as a substitute.

oblique mixer See *mixer*.

Obsttorte ('ahbs-tor-tah) A German fruit torte that consists of a sponge cake filled with pastry cream and fresh and/or candied fruits, covered with almond meringue and garnished with toasted almonds.

oeuf (uhf) The French word for *egg*.

oeuf à la neige The French name for "snow egg"; see *floating island*.

offset spatula A metal pastry blade that is bent at the handle, used to spread a thin layer of cake batter across a sheet pan without interference from your hand or the handle. It has a rectangular blade with a rounded tip and varies in length from 3 to 10 inches (7.5 to 25 cm). It may also be used for other pastry tasks.

ohagi ('oh-ha-gee) Sweet "rice eggs" from Japan, made by mashing cooked sweetened short-grain rice into a paste and forming it into egg shapes. Another paste of bean paste, sugar, and salt is cooked until thick and then wrapped around the rice eggs; the eggs are then rolled in ground toasted sesame seeds. They are named after the flower Hagi, which means "bush clover" and are traditionally served as a sweet snack during the autumn, when the flower blooms.

oil A liquid form of fat that is 100% fat. It is most commonly made from a vegetable source, such as soybeans, and is often labeled "salad oil." The most well known baking oils are cottonseed, corn, peanut, and canola. They may vary slightly in color and flavor, but can be used interchangeably in most recipes. Unlike *plastic fats*, oils cannot trap water or air and therefore do not aid in leavening. They do, however, produce a moist, tender crumb in quickbreads. Oils can be extracted either by *solvent extraction* or *cold pressing*. Solvent extraction grinds the source ingredient and immerses it in a solvent that is later extracted during boiling. In cold pressing, despite its name, the source ingredient is heated before the oil is pressed out. *Refined oils*, which are what are most commonly found in supermarkets, are treated to make them lighter and increase both the *smoke point* and *shelf life*. *Unrefined oils*, such as nut oils, are not treated and should be stored in the refrigerator to avoid rancidity.

oilstone A knife-sharpening tool made of very hard carborundum. The rectangular blocks are fine grained, and one side is coarser than the other. An oilstone must be lubricated with oil or water before use. Also known as *whetstone*.

okashi (oh-kah-shee) The Japanese term for sweets, pastries, or confections. Also known as *kashi*.

oke See *okolehao*.

okolehao (oh-koh-leh-hah-oh) A Hawaiian liquor made with aged whisky, tropical flavors, and the ti root. The islanders believe that ti not only wards off evil spirits but also brings goodness and strength. The liquor may be clear or golden colored and is 80 proof. It may be substituted with rum. Also known as *oke*.

olallie berry (ahluh-lee) See *berry*.

old dough 1. See *pâte fermentée*. 2. An overfermented dough.

oleo See *margarine*.

oleomargarine See *margarine*.

Olestra A fat substitute that contains no calories. It was created by Procter & Gamble, but is still awaiting approval by the FDA.

oliebollen (o-lee-'bo-lehn) A rich, fried Dutch doughnut filled with a spiced fruit mixture, usually apples, and rolled in sugar. These are served during Christmastime.

olio (oh-lyoh) The Italian word for *oil*.

olive oil An oil produced by pressing tree-ripened olives. It is used in cooking and baking because it is cholesterol free and high in monounsaturated fat, but its low *smoke point* makes it undesirable for frying. Olive oils are graded according to their levels of acidity, with the best olive oils being *cold-pressed*. Lower-grade olive oils are produced from the second or third hot pressing, which produces higher levels of acidity and less flavor. Olive oils are labeled in descending order of quality as follows:

Extra-virgin The finest and most expensive because it is produced from the first pressing and contains only 1% acid. It has the smoothest and most fruity flavor; the color ranges from golden yellow to pale green.

Virgin A first-pressing oil with a slightly higher acidity level, between 1 and 3%.

Fine or Fino A blend of extra-virgin and virgin olive oils.

Olive oil or Pure A combination of refined extra-virgin and virgin oils.

Oliver biscuit See *Bath biscuit*.

Oloroso See *sherry*.

omelette surprise An oval-shaped, frozen dessert that consists of a sponge base that is soaked with flavored syrup, topped with ice cream and fruit, then covered in meringue, which is browned with a blowtorch or in the oven.

onde-onde ('on-deh-'on-deh) A sweet rice-flour ball from Indonesia, made with a paste of sweet rice flour, salt, and coconut formed into a small ball. Brown sugar is pinched into the center of the ball and it is rolled in sweet rice flour and poached, then rolled in shredded coconut. It is eaten as a sweet snack or after a meal.

one-bowl method Another name for *one-stage method*; see *mixing methods*.

one-stage method A *mixing method* whereby all the ingredients are combined in one step; also known as *one-bowl method*.

oolong tea See *tea*.

opera torte A French torte of very thin alternating layers of almond *jaconde* brushed with coffee syrup, chocolate *ganache*, and rich coffee *buttercream*. It is topped with a chocolate glaze and served with the sides cut off to expose the magnificent layers. It is believed to have been created in honor of the Paris opera. Also known as *gâteau l'opera*.

orange A citrus fruit originally from Southeast Asia, now cultivated in temperate climates all over the world. The four distinct groups of oranges include the *navel orange*, the common orange (both of these are also known as *sweet orange*), the *bitter orange* or *sour orange*, and the *blood orange*.

Bergamot A small acidic, pear-shape orange prized for its peel because it yields an essential oil used in perfumes and candies. The peel is also used to flavor *Earl Grey tea*.

Bitter A tangy orange high in pectin. It is most popular for making marmalade, and the most well known varieties are the Bergamot and Seville. Available December to May.

Blood Named for the deep red color of its flesh, it is prized for its distinctive rich flavor. Used to make sorbets and sauces. Available December to May.

Cara Cara A sweet, juicy variety that has a bright orange skin and dark, salmon-colored flesh. Available December to April.

Common A very sweet, juicy orange used predominately for its juice. The most widely grown is the Valencia variety.

Dancy Similar in size, color, and flavor to the *clementine*, but with seeds. See also *mandarin orange* and *clementine*.

Mandarin See *mandarin orange*.

Navel Known for its crisp, rich flavor and ease of peeling and separating, these varieties are the most popular eating oranges worldwide, with thick, bright orange skin and sweet, juicy flesh. Available October to May.

Seville An aromatic orange with a thick, yellowish-orange skin and tart, acidic flavor. Used to make orange liqueurs such as *Grand Marnier;* also, its peel is used in making candy. Available January to February.

Valencia A sweet, juicy orange variety grown in Florida and California. It has a thin-orange skin and contains very few seeds. It is often used for its quality juice and is in season from June to September.

orangeat (o-rahn-jhey-'ah) A disc-shaped petit four made with *almond paste* mixed with candied orange pieces, covered with *fondant,* and garnished with candied orange peel.

orange flower water A highly aromatic liquid distilled from *bitter orange* blossoms. It has been used for centuries in Iran, Africa, and Turkey in cakes, confections, and desserts, including *Turkish delight,* sorbets, and ice creams.

orange liqueur See *Cointreau, Curaçao, Grand Marnier,* and *Triple Sec.*

orange pekoe tea See *tea.*

oregano (oh-'rehg-oh-'noh) An herb that comes from a bushy perennial mint plant. It is used is used as a seasoning for many applications, particularly ones that call for an Italian flavor. Also known as *wild marjoram.*

oreillettes (or-ray-'leht) A French fritter that is a rectangular strip of yeast dough slit down the center and twisted into a knot, fried, and rolled in cinnamon sugar. These are served warm at festivals.

Oreo A chocolate sandwich cookie made by Nabisco. The original version is two round chocolate wafer cookies sandwiched together with a sweet white cream filling. It was introduced by the Nabisco Biscuit Company in 1912, and it is estimated that over 345 billion have been consumed since then. The origin of the name is unknown, but some believe that it is from the French *or,* meaning "gold," which was the main color on early Oreo packages. Another theory is that it was named for the Greek oreo, meaning "mountain," because early test batches were hill-shaped. There is also much debate over the best way to eat an Oreo cookie, including dipping it in milk, twisting it open and eating the cream center first, or eating it as is. Today, there are at least nine varieties of Oreos: Double Stuff, Oreo Minis, Chocolate Cream filled, Reduced Fat, Vanilla Oreos, Fudge Covered, Fudge Mint Covered, White Chocolate Covered, and Baked.

organic Refers to food that has been cultivated or processed without the use of insecticides, chemicals, fertilizers, additives, or artificial colors or flavors. In 1990 Congress passed the Federal Organic Foods Production Act, which called for national organic food guidelines including certified growers and standards for organic food production.

orgeat syrup (ohr-zhay) A sweet syrup made from almonds, sugar, and orange flower water. It has a predominant almond flavor and is used as a flavoring agent in cocktails and confections. The name derives from the French *orge,* which means "barley," because the syrup was originally made with a barley-almond blend.

organic acid A naturally occurring acid that is produced in doughs, particularly doughs with preferments, that provides aroma and flavor to the bread.

oro blanco ('ohr-ro 'blahn-koh) The Spanish term for "white gold," referring to a *pomelo* hybrid that was developed in the 1950s. It is the size of a grapefruit and has a thick, bright yellow skin and sweet, juicy flesh. They are available from November to March.

O
o

osmotolerant See *yeast, SAF*.

ostia ('os-tee-ah) An Italian edible wafer paper, made from wheat starch and used to line molds and baking pans for making pastries, desserts, and confections such as *torrone* and *panforte*. Rice paper may be used as a substitute.

Othello A sweet confection of two small sponge cakes sandwiched together with chocolate pastry cream and brushed with apricot glaze, then covered in chocolate fondant. It was created by an English pastry chef in honor of the Shakespearian character Othello.

ounce A volume unit of measurement equivalent to 2 U.S. tablespoons or ⅛ cup, and the metric equivalent of 28.35 grams or 30 ml.

ouzo ('oo-zoh) A strong, sweet, anise-flavored liqueur from Greece. It is typically served as an *aperitif* straight or with the addition of water, which turns it milky white.

oven A self-contained piece of equipment used to bake, roast, and heat foods. There are many types of ovens, and they may be gas, electric, or wood-fired.

> **Adobe** A beehive-shape oven found in the pueblo villages of the U.S. Southwest. It is approximately 4 feet (1 m 20 cm) tall and 4 feet (1 m 20 cm) in diameter at the base. The bread is baked on the floor of the oven. Also known as *horno*.

> **Combi** Known as a combination oven, it holds half- or full-size sheet pans on wire shelving, and allows the operator to bake with convection heat with or with out the addition of steam heat. This dry/moist heat feature offers great flexibility in making breads where some steam is required, as well as the convenience of convection baking without steam. The oven may also be used on a steam-only setting. The oven is self-cleaning and generally bakes up to 30% faster than the standard convection oven.

> **Convection** A large oven designed to hold full-sheet pans on multiple wire racks. The oven is heated either by a gas-fired or an electric element. The back of the oven holds a fan that circulates the heated air in the oven to provide even heating and cooking. Convection ovens may also be outfitted with the ability to pump water into the oven to provide limited steam for bread baking. It is generally recommended that oven temperatures be lowered 25 degrees when operating a convection oven, so as not to overbake the products. Convection ovens are popular in many commercial kitchens and bakeshops.

> **Deck** A large oven with a stone hearth floor for baking directly on the hearth, providing consistent heat for crisping breads and pizzas. These ovens are well insulated and are capable even when fully loaded and steam is applied to their chamber. Deck ovens may be gas fired, heated by an electric element, or even wood fired. Deck ovens take their design from wood stone hearth ovens that were used centuries ago and are still highly sought by bakers.

> **Rack** A large convection oven that can hold up to four baker's racks designed for each particular model. They are typically equipped with steam injection and, although expensive, can produce a large quantity of evenly baked products at one time.

> **Rotating** A large, bulky oven with long shelves that revolve like a Ferris wheel. Since the product is in constant motion, there are no hot spots. However, many bakers are replacing them with smaller rack ovens.

> **Tandoor** ('tahn-door) A traditional Indian oven used to bake flatbreads or cook other products. It is typically barrel-shaped and made of brick

and clay. The walls are heated by a wood or coal fire made at the base of the oven. Flatbreads are baked by slapping the dough against the very hot walls, which produces a golden brown bottom and a puffy, light top. Chicken and other meats are generally skewered and placed in the oven to cook, and referred to as tandoori chicken or tandoori beef, etc. Also known as *tandoori oven.*

oven brush A long (12 to 14 inches /30 to 35 cm), wide (2 to 3 inches /5 to 7.5 cm) brush attached to a long handle, used to reach the back of the oven. It is used to sweep out the oven after baking, to remove seeds, crumbs, or flour so they do not burn onto the oven's surface during the next bake.

oven spring The rapid initial rise of a yeast dough when it is placed in a hot oven. The heat causes the carbon dioxide gas to expand until the dough reaches a temperature of 140°F (60°C). See also *12 Steps of Baking* appendix.

oven thermometer See *thermometer.*

overrun The increase in volume of ice cream as a result of incorporating air during the freezing process. Overrun is expressed as a percentage; for example, if the base doubles in volume, it has 100% overrun. In general, the higher the percentage of overrun, the lower the quality of ice cream. The amount of overrun is determined by the amount of fat in the base, the type of machine used, the amount of base used, and the length of time it is churned.

overpiping A cake decorating technique whereby, after an initial design is piped onto a cake or confection, the decorator goes back over the design and pipes a second design with a small tube so that depth is created. For quality depth of design, the technique is accomplished in *royal icing*, allowing each piped layer to dry completely before applying a second layer. The technique creates an ornate design and demonstrates a mastery of skills. Overpiping was introduced by Joseph Lambeth in the later part of the 19th century and is commonly known as the *Lambeth method.*

ovos moles d'aveiro ('oh-vohs mohl-ehs dee-ah-'vehr-oh) A rich Portuguese egg custard eaten as is or used as a filling for cakes, tarts, and confections or as a sauce for puddings. It is from the town of Aveiro.

O
o

oxidation The chemical reaction that occurs when a product is exposed to oxygen. In dough making, mixing incorporates oxygen and helps strengthen the gluten bonds, but when done in excess, may result in artificial maturing and breakdown of the dough. Also, oxidation occurs after milling flour to strengthen the flour proteins, either naturally by allowing the flour to age a few weeks or artificially by treating it with a chemical additive.

oz. The abbreviation for *ounce.*

Pp

pachade (pah-'shahd) A dessert from the Auvergene region of France that consists of a crêpe batter mixed with fruit, usually plums or prunes, and baked in a deep dish.

paddle See *mixer attachments.*

pain (pan) The French word for *bread.* Commonly used as a prefix for a bread-related product, such as *pain au levain* (*sourdough bread*).

pain à l'ancienne (pahn auhl-ahn-'see-uhn) The French term for "ancient bread," referring to a lean, rustic bread with a distinct natural sweetness and nutlike character. It is made with a unique, delayed-fermentation method. This method uses ice water to release flavors from the flour by delaying the activation of yeast until after the *amylase* enzymes have begun breaking down the starch into sugar. This creates a reserve of sugar in the fermented dough that adds flavor and caramelizes the crust during baking.

pain au chocolate (pahn oh sha-coe-'laht) A chocolate-filled *croissant.* It is made by rolling a rich, dark chocolate bar in a small, rectangular square of croissant dough. It is eaten by French children as an after-school snack, or for breakfast.

pain au levain (pahn o luh'va) A rustic French bread made with a levain starter and traditionally shaped into a *boule.* It is characterized by its crisp crust, delicate flavor, and open cell structure.

pain de campagne (pahn duh cuhm-'puhn-yuh) The French term for "country bread," referring to a rustic bread made with a dough similar to *baguette* dough but also with whole grains, such as whole wheat, white rye, or cornmeal. The grain gives the bread more character and flavor, and contributes to the brownish-gold country-style crust.

pain d'epeautre (pahn deh-peh-o-'trah) A simple Swiss breakfast bread made from *spelt* and sometimes flavored with honey.

pain d'épice (pahn deh-'pees) The French term for "spice bread," referring to a rich, breadlike cake made with honey, candied orange, and spices such as cinnamon, ginger, nutmeg, and anise.

pain de mie (pahn duh mee) The French term for "bread of the crumb," referring to white breads, including *Pullman loaf* and breads made from milk dough, such as sandwich bread and hamburger or hot dog buns.

pain perdu ('pahn pehr-do) The French term for "lost bread" that refers to a hard bread that is softened in a mixture of milk and eggs and fried, thereby making it useable for consumption. See also *French toast.*

pairing knife See *paring knife.*

pakora ('pah-koor-ah) An Indian deep-fried fritter made with *besan* and filled with sweet or savory items, eaten as a snack.

palacsinta (pah-lah-'shihn-tuh) A Hungarian dessert of stacked paper-thin sweet pancakes layered with jam. The six or seven pancakes are sliced into wedges and served with coffee.

palet (pa-lay) A crisp petit four flavored with anise, rum, vanilla, and brown sugar. Some varieties include candied citrus peel or ground almonds. *Palets de dames* are made with currants.

palets de dame See *palet.*

palette knife See *spatula, flexible.*

palmier (pahl-'me-yay) The French word for "palm leaves," referring to crisp, buttery strips of puff pastry that have been rolled up to resemble a palm leaf. It is topped with sugar, which caramelizes as it is baked. They are served with coffee or tea, or as an accompaniment to ice cream or dessert. In America, they are sometimes referred to as *elephant ears.*

palm kernel oil A pale yellow oil extracted from the kernel or nut of a palm tree. It is very high in saturated fat and milder in flavor than *palm oil.*

palm oil A reddish-brown oil extracted from the kernel or nut of an African palm tree. It is very high in saturated fat and is used in Brazilian and West African cooking.

palm sugar See *sugar.*

palm vinegar See *vinegar.*

Palo Cortado (pah-loh kohr-'tah-toh) See *sherry.*

pamplemousse ('pahm-pluh-moose) The French word for *grapefruit.*

pan (pahn) The Spanish word for *bread,* commonly used as a prefix for bread-related products, such as *pan de Aranada.*

panada Another name for *panade.*

panade (pah-'nahd) A paste of varying consistency, used as a base for *soufflés* and *choux pastries.* Also known as *panada.*

panadería (pan-uh-deh-'ree-ah) The Spanish word for *bakery.*

panary action The rising of bread dough by yeast action. *Panare* is Latin for "bread" and refers to fermentation or aeration.

pan bagna (pahn 'bahn-yuh) A large bread roll that is split and brushed with olive oil, then stuffed with any of several fillings.

pancake 1. A thin, flat cake made by cooking a batter on a griddle over high heat, served as a breakfast item with butter and maple syrup. 2. A cooked batter product with hundreds of varieties around the world that vary in thickness and ingredients, and may be served as breakfast, an appetizer, entree, or dessert. See also *blini, palacsinta,* and *Swedish pancake.*

pancake syrup A syrup served with American pancakes. Maple syrup is the most common, but it may also be fruit based.

pandanus leaf The green, strap-shaped leaf of the pandanus tree. It has a vanilla-like flavor and is used to flavor and color Southeast Asian desserts, pastries, beverages, and confections.

Pan de Aranada (pahn day 'ah-rah-'nah-dah) A flat, moist bread from Aranada de Duero in the Castilian province of Burgos, Spain.

P
p

pan di spagna (pahn dee 'spahn-yuh) The Italian term for "Spanish bread," referring to a light spongecake similar to *génoise.*

pan di Toni See *panettone.*

pandoro (pahn-'doh-roh) The Italian word for "golden bread," referring to a sweet yeasted bread from Verona, Italy. The bread gets its distinct star shape from being baked in a *pandoro mold;* it is dusted with confectioners' sugar and served at Christmas.

pandoro mold A deep, star-shaped mold for making *pandoro* bread.

pandoro mold

pandowdy A deep-dish dessert from New England that is a mixture of fruit, usually apples, butter, brown sugar or molasses, and spices, topped with a biscuitlike dough and baked. The name derives from a technique used to make the dessert, called "dowdying," which entails breaking the crust halfway through the baking so that it can absorb the fruit juices and result in a crisp crust. Pandowdy is served warm with whipped cream, ice cream, or hard sauce.

pane ('pah-neh) The Italian word for *bread,* commonly used as a prefix for bread-related products, such as *pane del marinaio.*

pané del marinaio ('pah-nay dehl mah-ree-ni-'o) The Italian term for "sailor's bread," referring to a dome-shaped sweet bread full of raisins, pine nuts, and candied orange. It is spiced with fennel seeds and flavored with *Marsala.* Its name derives from its popularity in Genoa, a seaport town on the Italian Riviera.

pané di ramerino ('pah-nay dee rah-may-'ree-no) A lightly sweetened Italian egg bread filled with raisins and flavored with rosemary. It resembles a *hot cross bun* and was traditionally eaten in Tuscany on Holy Thursday, but can now be found throughout the year.

paneer (pah-nayr) A fresh, unaged *farmers cheese* made from whole buffalo or cow's milk. It does not melt when heated and does not contain *rennet* so it is vegetarian. It is traditionally pressed into a firm cube that is chopped or sliced for cooking. It is widely used in Indian and Middle Eastern cuisine as a source of protein. Also spelled *panir.*

panela (pah-'nehl-ah) See *sugar.*

pane Siciliano ('pah-neh sihs-il-lee 'ah-noh) The Italian term for "Sicilian bread," referring to a rustic, enriched bread made with semolina flour, which adds a slightly sweet, nutty flavor and pale-yellow hue. It is S-shaped and topped with sesame seeds.

panetteria (pah-nah-teh-'ree-ah) The Italian word for *bakery.*

panettone (pahn-ah-'toh-nay) A traditional Italian festive bread baked in a tall cylindrical mold. It is a sweet and rich, yeasted bread packed with dried fruits and sometimes almonds. It is believed to have been created in Milan during the 15th century, and its name is said to derive from *pan di Toni,* the baker believed to have created it. Folklore says that a wealthy young Italian wished to marry the baker's daughter, but her lower-class status prevented this from happening, so the wealthy Italian gave the baker the ingredients to create a special bread that became so popular the baker prospered enough for them to marry.

panforte (pahn-'fohr-tay) The Italian term for "strong bread," referring to a strongly spiced flat, rich cake from Siena, made with honey, spices, nuts, and dried

P
p

fruits. It is served in thin slices during Christmastime, and dates back to medieval times. Also known as *Siena cake*.

panini (pah-'neen-nee) A small Italian bread roll stuffed with savory items such as prosciutto and cheese. Depending on the region, they may be soft or crisp and round to star-shaped.

panino (pah-nee-no) Italian for roll or sandwich.

panir (pah-'neer) See *paneer*.

panko ('pang-koh) Coarse Japanese bread crumbs that lend a crunchy, crisp, airy texture to fried foods.

panmarino (pah-mah-'ree-no) The Italian name for a potato-rosemary bread. Using mashed potatoes in the dough yields a tender product because potato starch softens the dough.

panna ('pah-nah) The Italian word for *cream*.

panna cotta ('pah-nah 'koh-tah) The Italian term for "cooked cream," referring to a light, refreshing eggless custard often molded and served with fresh fruit or sauce. It is made by simmering cream, milk, sugar, and a flavoring such as vanilla, and setting it with gelatin.

pannekoeken (pahn-neck-coe-ken) A sweet or savory Dutch pancake. The sweet version is made with apples and served with a light brown syrup made from sugar beets.

pannequet (pan-neh'kuh) A French sweet or savory pancake. The sweet version is typically filled with a pastry cream flavored with candied fruits, liqueur, or praline and either flamed or browned under a broiler.

panocha See *sugar*.

panola (pah-'noh-lah) A sweet Mexican pudding made from dried corn and spices.

pan tramvai (pahn trahm-'vah-ee) A sweet bread from Milan that is basically half bread and half raisins.

pa-pao-fan (pah-'poh-fahn) The Chinese term for "eight treasures," referring to a rice pudding elaborately decorated with eight different nuts and/or dried or candied fruits. It is typically served at special occasions with an almond-flavored syrup.

P
p

papaw (pa-paw) The fruit of a native North American tree, a member of the cherimoya family. It ranges in size from 2 to 6 inches long (5 to 15 cm) and resembles a fat, dark brown banana. It has an aromatic, pale yellow flesh that tastes like a cross between a sweet banana and a pear. It has a unique custard-like texture and is not widely available.

papaya (puh-'pie-yuh) A tropical fruit with a mildly sweet, tender flesh and exotic, slightly musky aroma. The leafy trees are cultivated in warm temperate climates around the world, including Hawaii, Florida, Mexico, Central and South America, India, Africa, Southeast Asia, and the Philippines. The mostly large, oval fruits are eaten fresh, sprinkled with lime, or used in salads and 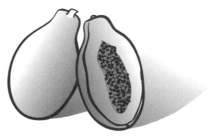 as a garnish, or pureed as a flavoring ingredient in sorbets, ice creams, and pastry creams. With the exception of the green papaya, they make an excellent fruit display owing to their striking contrast of bright orange flesh and dark seeds. The most common varieties are:

Green With deep green skin and firm, crunchy, creamy white flesh; used as a vegetable in Asian cuisine.

Maradol A common Caribbean variety. Similar to *Solo,* but larger with an oblong shape and salmon-colored flesh.

Solo A pear-shaped American variety approximately 6 inches (15 cm) long and 1 to 2 pounds (455 to 910 g). It has a thin, golden yellow skin and rich golden yellow-orange flesh, with a smooth, juicy texture and sweet-tart flavor. The large, center cavity is packed with small, shiny, grayish-black seeds that are edible but usually discarded.

Strawberry A smaller version of the *Maradol* but pear-shaped.

papelón (pah-peh-'yohn) Hardened raw sugarcane pulp. A Venezuelan drink called *papelón con limón* is made with water and lime, sweetened with papelón.

papelón con limón (pah-peh-'yohn kohn 'lee-mohn) See *papelón.*

paper cone A small, disposable piping bag made from parchment paper. These are typically filled with chocolate and used to decorate and write on cakes.

papillon ('pah-pee-yohn) The French word for "butterfly," referring to a pastry made by stacking thin strips of puff pastry and twisting the slices in the middle so that they resemble a bow tie or butterfly. The pieces are heavily dusted with sugar and baked until lightly caramelized. Small papillons are also sometimes referred to as *pig's ears.*

papillote ('pah-pee-yoht) See *en papillote.*

pappadam ('pah-pah-duhm) A crisp, wafer-like Indian *flatbread* made with lentil flour. It is usually sold dried at the market, and then roasted, grilled, or fried at home.

para (pah-'rah) See *Brazil nut.*

paratha (pah-'rah-tah) An Indian *flatbread* made with whole wheat flour and sometimes flavored with herbs and spices, and baked on a griddle. There are many variations depending on the region, whether round, square, or rectangular and stuffed with fruit or vegetables, or simply brushed with *ghee.*

parchment paper A nonstick paper used to line baking pans and make *paper cones.* The paper is available in light, medium, and heavy grades and comes in rolls, full- and half-sheet pan rectangles, and circles or pre-cut triangles.

pareve ('pahr-uh-vuh) A Jewish term to describe a food that has been made without dairy or animal ingredients. To be considered pareve, breads and cakes must be made with vegetable oils, and not butter or other animal fats or dairy products. Kosher dietary laws require dairy and animal products to be eaten separately, but pareve products may be eaten with either simultaneously.

parfait (pahr-'fay) 1. An American dessert of ice cream layered with a flavored syrup and sometimes fruit, and topped with whipped cream, nuts, and a maraschino cherry. It is traditionally served in a *parfait glass,* which is a tall, narrow, footed glass with a fluted top. 2. The French word for "perfect," referring to a still-frozen dessert made by folding whipped cream into a flavored *pâte à bombe* mixture. It has a light, airy texture and is typically molded to enhance its appearance.

parfait glass See *parfait,* no. 1.

paring knife A small, short-bladed knife used for slicing and peeling fruits and vegetables. Also spelled *pairing knife.*

P
P

Paris-Brest ('pah-ree brehst) A French pastry that consists of *pâte à choux* piped into a ring, topped with sliced almonds, and baked; once cooled, it is sliced in half horizontally and filled with a praline-flavored cream. The pastry was created in 1891 in honor of the bicycle race from Paris to Brest, France. The shape is meant to resemble a bicycle tire. Other variations omit the almonds and may be filled with whipped cream or *crème diplomat.*

Parisien (pah-rhee-zhee-'uhn) French cake that is lemon-flavored *spongecake* filled with *frangipane* and candied fruits, then covered in *Italian meringue* and lightly browned. It dates back to the 18th century.

Parker House roll A soft yeast roll with a center seam that splits open easily. The roll is formed by flattening the center of a round piece of enriched white-flour dough and folding it over to make a crease. The roll is named after the Parker House Hotel in Boston, where it was created.

parkin A British version of gingerbread, made with oatmeal and golden syrup. It is formed as a loaf or cookie, and is served on Guy Fawkes Day (November 5), in honor of the 17th-century man who fought to have Roman Catholic priests recognized in the Protestant Parliament.

Parmesan cheese A hard, sharp-flavored aged Italian cheese made from skim or part skim cow's milk. The cheese is often grated onto food to enhance its flavor; the authentic version is called *Parmigiano-Reggiano.*

Parmigiano-Reggiano cheese (pahr-meh-zhon-oh rehj-ee-'ah-noh) See *Parmesan cheese.*

partially hydrogenated fat A fat that has been partially hydrogenated to render it soft and plastic.

paskha ('pahs-kuh) A sweet Russian molded cheese that is a mixture of *pot cheese,* candied or dried fruit, and almonds. It is shaped as a four-sided pyramid with the letters *XB* on top, which stands for "Christ has risen," and is traditionally served at Easter with *kulich.*

passion fruit The fruit of a lush tropical vine with large, colorful flowers. The fruit is round to oval, with a hard purplish-brown skin that wrinkles when ripe and soft, jelly-like pulp with edible seeds. The fruit is native to Brazil, where it is known as *granadilla,* but today is cultivated in Hawaii (where it is known as *lilikoi*), New Zealand, Australia, California, and Florida and is available year-round. The flavor is intensely sweet-tart and tastes like a combination of honey, lime, banana,

and guava. The fruit is cracked open and the pulp scooped out and eaten straight, but more commonly the strained pulp is used to flavor drinks, ice cream, yogurt, and many other foods. The name was given by early European missionaries, who saw symbols of Christ's crucifixion, such as a crown of thorns, in its flowers and named the fruit after the Passion of the Christ. Although harder to find, there is also the *vanilla passion fruit,* also known as *banana passion fruit.* It is shaped like a small, straight banana with pointed ends. The soft skin wrinkles and turns from green to pale yellow as it ripens. The flesh has a greenish-orange hue, with a hint of vanilla and banana, and the edible seeds are larger and darker than the more common variety. Available March to June.

passion fruit liqueur A liqueur made from *passion fruit.* It is slightly acidic, with an intense flavor and aroma.

P
p

pasta frolla ('pahs-tah 'froh-lah) The Italian term for "tender dough," referring to a rich, sweet pastry dough that is used for many Italian desserts and pastries, such as *crostata, pastiera,* and fruit tarts.

pastel de nata ('pas-tell da nya-tah) A Portuguese pastry that is a flaky pastry shell filled with sweet custard cream.

pasteurization (pas-chuh-rize-'a-shun) The process by which the bacteria in milk are killed by heating it to a high temperature (161°F/72°C) for a minimum of 15 seconds. The process was developed by Louis Pasteur in the mid-1800s.

pasticceria (pah-stee-tcheh-'ree-ah) The Italian word for pastry shop.

pastiera (pahs-tee-'ehr-rah) A Neapolitan lattice-topped pie with a *pasta frolla* crust filled with cooked wheat grain, ricotta cheese, butter, milk, eggs, sugar, candied orange peel, walnuts, cinnamon, and orange flower water, then dusted with confectioners' sugar. Served at Easter.

pastillage ('past-tee-ahz) A very white, pliable pastry dough used to make pastry decorations such as ribbons, bows, and large-scale three-dimensional pieces. The dough is a combination of confectioners' sugar, cornstarch, gelatin, and sometimes *gum arabic*; it is kneaded until it is soft and smooth, and rolled to the desired thickness and cut and formed. It is very strong and dries rock hard. Although the dough is easy to roll and cut, it dries out quickly. Food coloring may be worked into the dough prior to rolling, or the finished piece may be *airbrushed* or painted with rehydrated cocoa powder or edible food coloring.

pastille (pas-'teel) A small, round, hard, flat, or drop-shape French confection. It is made from a mixture of cooked sugar syrup and *gum arabic,* flavored with mint, citrus oils, or licorice. It may be colored and is sometimes covered in chocolate. The name is believed to be after its creator, a confectioner named Jean Pastilla.

pastilles de leche (pahs-'stehl-laze day 'lay-chay) A chewy, fudge-like holiday confection from the Philippines. It is made by cooking milk, sugar, and lemon zest until very thick and then spreading it out in a ½-inch (1.2 cm) layer on a sugared surface. The candies are then cut into individual 2-inch (5 cm) pieces and rolled in sugar, then wrapped in brightly colored tissue paper that is cut in designs such as stars, leaves, and flowers.

pastis (pas-'tees) 1. A strong, licorice-flavored liqueur popular in the south of France. The name derives from the French *pastis,* which means "confused" or "mixed" because the drink has a cloudy appearance when mixed with water, which is how it is always drunk. 2. A pastry made in southwestern France, whose ingredients and preparation vary from region to region. See *Gascon pastis, landaise,* and *pastis bourrit.*

pastis bourrit (pas-tees boo-'rhee) A raised-dough *pastis* from Béarn, southern France. It is flavored with vanilla and rum or anisette and typically served with caramel custard at weddings, or sliced, toasted, and eaten as a snack or accompaniment with sweet or savory dishes.

pastry 1. A variety of sweet baked goods, such as *danish* and *éclairs.* 2. A variety of unleavened pastry doughs, such *pâte sucrée* and *pâte brisée,* that typically consist of flour, liquid, and fat.

pastry bag A hand-held, cone-shaped bag with a small opening at the bottom and a wide opening on top, used to pipe creams, light doughs, and such onto surfaces. A variety of pastry tips can be inserted into the bottom of the bag for different effects; the wide top enables the bag to be filled with the ingredient and twised, so that the pressure forces the product through the tip to form the decorative shapes. Pastry bags are available in different sizes and may be made from canvas, nylon, or disposable plastic. The canvas bags have a tendency to absorb the odors of the ingredients but can be refreshed by gentle cleaning in boiled lemon water. Also known as *piping bag.*

pastry blender A hand-held tool used to cut fat into a pastry dough. It consists of a metal or wooden handle with five or six U-shaped, sturdy steel wires attached. The pastry blender is often used in place of hand mixing to keep the fat from being warmed while it is worked into the dough.

pastry blender

pastry brush A hand-held tool used to brush a coating ingredient onto a pastry or other item before or after baking, most commonly used for egg wash on pastries, glazes on fruit, and melted butter on baked goods. The bristles are attached to a wooden or plastic handle, and range from hard to soft depending on whether they are nylon, silicone, plastic, or natural fibers. Nylon bristles may melt if they are not heat-resistant; they are also hard and may scratch or tear dough, so softer bristles are generally recommended for delicate brushing. The brushes come in a range of lengths and widths.

pastry chef The person responsible for the production of all pastry products and desserts, as well as for managing the pastry kitchen and its staff.

pastry cloth A large, lightweight canvas or plastic-coated cotton cloth used to roll out pastry dough without its sticking to the surface. The canvas version should be dusted with flour and the excess flour shaken off before storing it. Some plastic cloths have different sizes of circles drawn on them to act as a guide for rolling doughs to particular sizes.

pastry comb See *cake comb.*

pastry cream A creamy, rich, cooked custard that may be flavored with vanilla, chocolate, coffee, fruit purees, or liqueurs. It is used as a filling for pastries such as *éclairs* and *Napoleons,* and as a base for creams such as *crème diplomat.* Also known as *crème pâtissière.*

pastry cutter A sharp-edged cutter in a variety of sizes and shapes, used to cut out cookie doughs and make interesting garnishes for cakes and desserts. Possible shapes include circles, ovals, squares, stars, hearts, and flower petals.

pastry dough Any form of dough that is used to make baked pastry shells or pies. It generally consists of flour, fat, salt, and perhaps sugar and eggs. The dough may be made flaky or short, and is generally rolled before being used to line a pie or tart pan. See also *pâte brisée, pâte sablé, pâte sucrée,* and *pie dough.*

pastry flour See *flour.*

pastry scraper See *bowl scraper.*

pastry tip A metal or plastic attachment for a pastry bag, used to pipe batters, doughs, fillings, creams, icings, and ganaches into decorative shapes. There is a wide variety of tips available, and they may be purchased as sets or individually. Metal tips should be washed and dried immediately after use to prevent rusting and carefully stored to prevent their bending. Plastic tips are available in light and heavy gauge.

pastry wheel A hand-held tool used to cut small strips of dough into various shapes, sizes, and designs. It consists of a small, straight- or flute-edged wheel attached to a short wooden handle. The fluted variety will give the dough sides a wavy pattern; some brands of wheels have a combination of straight and fluted edges.

pâte (paht) The French word for *dough* or *batter.*

pâte à bombe (paht ah bohm) A base for making *mousses, bombes,* French *parfaits,* and iced *soufflés.* It is a mixture of sugar and water cooked to the *softball stage* and poured over egg yolks while whipping to the ribbon stage; it may then be flavored with fruit purees, chocolate, vanilla, or coffee. The name is sometimes used interchangeably with the word *bombe.*

pâte à choux (paht ah shoo) A French pastry dough used for making many pastry products and desserts, including *éclairs, cream puffs, gâteau Saint-Honoré,* and *croquembouche.* It is made by boiling milk or water with salt, sugar, and butter, adding the flour all at once, and stirring with a wooden spoon until it is thick and slightly dried. The mixture is then paddled until it cools to a temperature of 140°F (60°C), so that the eggs can be added one by one until they are fully incorporated. The finished dough is soft, shiny, slightly sticky, and able to hold a very soft peak. It is piped into the desired shapes and sizes, and baked at a high temperature in order to create the steam that leavens the pastry and creates its distinct soft, tender, hollow interior and crisp, golden-brown exterior. Choux pastries may be made in advance and frozen. Also known as *choux paste* and *éclair paste.*

pâte à glacer (paht ah glah-say) A commercially made chocolate glaze imported from France and available from specialty vendors. It comes in white or dark chocolate, and gives a shiny, glossy appearance with a smooth texture and chocolate flavor. Also known as *chocolate glaze.*

pâte brisée (paht bree-zay) The French term for "broken dough," referring to a flaky pastry dough made by the *biscuit method.* The term "broken" is a reference to the broken pieces of fat that are cut into the dough; the size of the fat and length of mixing time determine the dough's flakiness. The dough's mixing method and lower percentage of fat and sugar make it sturdier and easier to handle than *pâte sucrée,* so it is generally used for larger tarts. It is also a good choice for savory tarts because it is not sweet. The dough may be wrapped and stored in the refrigerator for up to five days or frozen for several months.

pâte d'amande (paht duhmahnde) See *marzipan.*

pâte fermentée ('paht fuhr-mehn-'tay) A *pre-ferment* that is taken from a piece of white flour dough, reserved after mixing and added into the next batch of dough. This reserved dough enhances the flavor of the bread and is the only yeasted pre-ferment that contains salt. Also known as *old dough.*

pâte feuilletée ('paht fuh-yuh-'tay) The French term for *puff pastry.*

patent flour See *flour.*

pâte sablée ('paht sah-'blay) The French term for "sand dough," referring to a sweet, rich, crumbly short dough made by the *creaming method.* The dough is softer and more delicate than *pâte brisée* and is recommended for small tarts, petit fours, and cookies. The dough may be wrapped and stored in the refrigerator for up to five days or frozen for several months.

pâte sucrée ('paht sue-'kray) The French term for "sugar dough," referring to a sweet, rich, crisp short dough made by the *creaming method.* The dough is softer and more delicate than *pâte brisée* and is recommended for small tarts, individual pastries, petit fours, and cookies. The dough may be wrapped and stored in the refrigerator for up to five days or frozen for several months.

pâtisserie (pah-'tis-uh-ree) A French word that refers to the art of pastry making, a shop where pastries are made and sold, and a general category of sweet baked products, such as cakes and pastries.

pâtissier ('pah-tees-syah) The French word for pastry cook. See *brigade*.

patranque (pa-trahn-'kuh) A French dish consisting of stale bread that is soaked in a cheese-flavored milk until soft and then fried in butter on both sides. A specialty of the Auvergne, this dish traditionally uses a soft, unripened cheese.

patty cake A small, round, individual butter cake that is baked in a *patty pan*. It is cut in half and filled with jam, then iced with fondant or buttercream.

patty pan A metal baking tray for baking *patty cakes*. There are 12 to 16 individual holes, with slightly curved indentions that measure ¾ inch (2 cm) deep.

pavé (pah-vay) The French word for "paving stone," referring to a square or rectangular sponge cake layered with buttercream. It can also be a thick block of gingerbread or a square sweet or savory molded mousse.

Pavlova (pav-'loh-vah) An Australian dessert of a large, round meringue disc spread with *crème chantilly* and topped with assorted fruits. The meringue has a light, crisp exterior and soft, delicate interior. The dessert was created in 1935 by chef Herberst Sachse; folklore has it that it was named in honor of the Russian prima ballerina Anna Pavlova, supposedly because when the owner of the hotel where Sachse worked saw the dessert, he remarked that the marshmallow center was as soft as the ballerina's personality, the whiteness was as white as her skin, and the sides resembled her tutu.

peach A *stonefruit* that is native to China but now cultivated in Europe, Africa, South America, Australia, and the United States. The peach was originally known as the *Persian apple* because Persia was the first to introduce it to Europe, and subsequently to the Americas. In the United States, Georgia, California, and Virginia are the largest producers of the commercial crop, while in Europe peaches are primarily cultivated in the Mediterranean region. Peaches are classified as either *clingstone* or *freestone* and there are hundreds of varieties that vary in size, shape, and color. The most common varieties are:

> **Babcock** A small, semi-freestone peach from California. It has a slightly fuzzy, pale pink skin blushed with red and a very white flesh with a red center. Available May to August.
>
> **Dixi-red** A semi-clingstone, medium peach from Georgia. It has a bright red skin and juicy, yellow flesh. Available early May to September.
>
> **Elberta** A large, semi-oval, freestone peach from Georgia. It has a deep golden skin that is blushed with red and a firm, juicy yellow flesh. Available June to September.
>
> **Indian Red** A freestone or clingstone peach with a soft, fuzzy deep red skin and sweet, juicy, white flesh blushed with red. Available August to September.
>
> **J. H. Male** A large freestone peach from Connecticut. It has a slightly fuzzy, yellow skin that is blushed with red and a smooth, juicy flesh. Available mid-June to October.
>
> **Melba** A large freestone peach from Texas. It has a pale yellow skin and honey-like, sweet white flesh. Available June to October.
>
> **Nectar** A large freestone peach from California. It has a pinkish-red skin and soft, juicy white flesh that is blushed with red. Available May to August.

P
p

Redhaven A medium freestone peach from Michigan. It has a yellow skin streaked with a bright red and sweet, juicy flesh. Available early May to September.

Rio Oso Gem A freestone peach from California. It has a bright red skin and smooth, buttery yellow flesh. Available mid-June to October.

Saturn A small, circular freestone peach with a flat top. It has a pale yellow flesh blushed with red and a smooth, firm, sweet, juicy white flesh. Available June to August.

White-fleshed Peaches that are usually freestone, with a tender, smooth, red skin and sweet, juicy, creamy white flesh. Available May to October.

Yellow-fleshed Peaches that are usually freestone, with a fuzzy, red blushed yellow skin and sweet, juicy, golden-yellow flesh. Available May to October.

peach Melba A French dessert of two poached peach halves served over vanilla ice cream and topped with Melba sauce and sometimes sliced toasted almonds. It was created by August Escoffier in honor of Dame Nellie Melba, an Australian opera singer rumored to be his mistress. Also known as *pêche melba*.

peanut The oily, nutlike seed of a legume plant, whose fertilized flowers bend down into the soil and develop into pods. The light tan seed has a thin, papery dark brown skin; the netted shell is tan as well, with an hourglass shape that holds two seeds. Peanuts are grown extensively in the U.S. South, with much of the crop used to make peanut butter and peanut oil. The two most well known varieties are the *Virginia peanut* and the *Spanish peanut*. The Virginia is larger and more oval than the smaller, rounder Spanish. They are available shelled and unshelled, and are high in fat and protein. Upon harvesting, most peanuts are dry-roasted and sometimes salted; however, *boiled peanuts* (which are peanuts that have been cooked in salted water) are a snack in the South. The peanut is also known as *groundnut* and *goober*.

peanut butter A smooth, creamy peanut paste invented in 1890 and marketed as a health food. Peanut butter gained national popularity after its introduction at the St. Louis World's Fair, 1904. Many commercial peanut butters contain ground roasted peanuts, salt, oil (often times hydrogenated), and some sugar. Natural peanut butter contains only ground peanuts and salt. Peanut butter may be purchased as either smooth or chunky, with the latter having bits of chopped peanuts. Peanut butter is used extensively in the bake shop to flavor creams and cookies.

peanut butter cookie A soft, chewy, peanut butter flavored cookie that typically has a criss-cross pattern on top, which are made with the tines of a fork before baking.

peanut oil The oil obtained by pressing peanuts. It is light in color and has a distinctive peanut smell and slight peanut flavor. Peanut oil is used extensively for frying, as it has a high *smoke point* of 450°F (232°C).

pear A tender, juicy fruit native to western Asia and now cultivated in temperate climates around the world, particularly France, California, Oregon, and Washington. There are thousands of varieties, and they vary in shape, size, color, and flavor. The most common varieties are:

    Anjou, Red Anjou A large pear with a stocky neck and sweet, juicy flesh. The skin is either greenish cream or red. Good fresh or cooked. Available September to July.

Asian See *Asian pear.*

Bartlett, Red Bartlett A bell-shaped aromatic, sweet, juicy pear with a smooth texture. The skin turns from green to yellow as it ripens; the red variety has the same flavor and texture. Good fresh or cooked. Available June to March.

Bosc A large, narrow pear with an elongated neck. It has a pebbled, russet skin and firm, crisp, grainy texture. Good fresh or cooked, but should not be refrigerated. Available June to March.

Comice A medium, squat pear with a rounded shape and short neck. It has a greenish-yellow skin that is sometimes tinged with red and a buttery, sweet flavor, and juicy, tender texture. Excellent dessert pear. Available September to March.

Forelle A very small pear, only 2½ inches (6.2 cm) long, the skin turns from green to bright yellow as it ripens and is speckled with red. It is mildly sweet with a crisp texture. Available September to March.

Seckel A petite, slightly rounded pear with a yellow-green skin that is heavily blushed with a reddish-brown. It has a sweet, slightly spicy flavor and crisp, juicy texture. Good fresh or poached and pairs well with cheese. They do not keep well. Available September to February.

Winternelis Medium pear with a rough-textured greenish-brown skin. It has a spicy flavor and mildly gritty texture. It has a long shelf life and is available September to March.

pear belle Hélène See *belle Hélène.*

pearl dust A colored, edible dusting powder used to give a pearlescent sheen to *gum paste* flowers, rolled *fondant,* and *pastillage.* The dust may be mixed with a clear alcohol, such as gin, to make it liquid enough to be painted on a surface. Also known as *Luster Dust.*

pearl millet See *millet.*

pearl sugar See *sugar.*

pearl tapioca See *tapioca.*

pearl tea See *gunpowder tea.*

peasant bread A category of rustic breads characterized by their coarse crust. These breads were originally made by European peasants who lived on small farms.

pebbled Persian bread See *bushva nan.*

pecan The nut of a variety of hickory tree, native to North America, grown mainly in the U.S. southern states. It has a thin, hard, tannish-brown shell that is about 1 inch (2.5 cm) long and encases a rich, buttery, golden-brown nutmeat. Pecans are used in the production of pies, fillings, and confections. The peak season is September through December. Their high fat content makes them susceptible to rancidity and so they should be stored airtight in a cool, dry place or in the freezer. They are available in the shell, shelled, whole, or in pieces.

pecan pie An American pie that is a pie crust that is filled with a mixture of eggs, brown sugar, corn syrup, butter, and pecans. This sweet, rich pie is a Thanksgiving and Christmastime dessert, often served with vanilla ice cream or whipped cream.

pèche melba (pesh 'mehl-ba) The French name for *peach melba.*

pectin ('peck-tihn) A natural gelling agent present in some fruits. Different fruits contain different amounts of pectin: apples, blueberries, lemons, limes, plums, and cranberries are high in pectin, while apricots, blackberries, and raspberries are medium in pectin, and cherries, strawberries, pineapple, peaches, nectarines,

P
p

figs, and grapes are very low in pectin. In the presence of acid and high amounts of sugar, pectin produces a clear gel with a glossy sheen. It is also available as a powder or liquid, and is used to thicken or gel fruit products such as jams, jellies, marmalades, bakery fillings, glazes, and fruit confections.

Pedro Ximénez (peh-droh 'hee-mehn-ez) See *sherry*.

peel 1. A flat, long-handled metal or wooden shovel used to load or unload bread or other products from the oven. Also known as *baker's peel*. 2. The rind or skin of a fruit or vegetable. 3. To remove the rind or skin from a fruit or vegetable, typically with a peeler or small knife.

Peeps An Easter confection of sugar-coated chick- or bunny-shaped marshmallow. These candies are very sweet and come in a different colors, including yellow, pink, green, and purple.

baker's peel

pekoe souchong tea ('pee-koh 'soo-chohng) See *tea, grading*.

pekoe tea ('pee-koh) A grade of tea in which the leaves medium size and slightly coarse. See also *tea*.

pentosan gum A polysaccharide found in plants that has a higher proportion of rye flour (8%) than any other flour. Pentosans are important in the production of rye breads because they increase the water absorption of the dough and also limit the gluten's ability to develop. Their fragility can cause them to break easily and result in a sticky dough, so the flour should be mixed in gently.

penuche (peh-'noo-chee) A creamy brown-sugar fudge from Mexico.

Pepino melon See *muskmelon*.

pepita (puh-'pee-tah) The delicate, dark-green edible seed of the pumpkin, used in Mexican cooking and eaten as a snack food. They are available raw, salted, or roasted and may be hulled or unhulled.

pepper Commonly used as a shortened reference to peppercorns, which typically refers to black pepper. See *peppercorn*.

peppercorn The berry of the pepper plant, native to Indonesia. The berries grow in grapelike clusters, and were once so prized that they were regarded as currency in some societies. Their distinct, spicy-hot flavor is used to season savory foods, but some pastry chefs use them, particularly pink and white peppercorns, to obtain a sweet-hot/spicy flavor contrast in ice creams, sauces, creams, and desserts. The most common varieties of peppercorns are:

> **Black** A peppercorn picked when green and slightly under ripe, then dried until hard and black. It is the most pungent of the peppercorns and has a strong, slightly hot flavor and aroma. They are available whole, cracked, and coarsely or finely ground, but freshly ground peppercorns yield the freshest, fullest flavor; ground peppercorns quickly lose their flavor.

> **Green** Harvested before they are ripe, these are difficult to obtain fresh and are usually sold packed in brine or freeze-dried. They are peppery but more mildly flavored and fruitier than black peppercorns.

> **Pink** See *pink peppercorn*.

> **White** A smoother, more mildly flavored peppercorn obtained by fully ripening the berries and removing the red skins before they are dried. They blend into foods better and do not leave the flakes that black peppercorns do. They are available whole and ground, but freshly ground peppercorns yield the freshest, fullest flavor.

P
p

pepper mill A hand-held kitchen tool that grinds peppercorns.

peppermint A pungent, peppery member of the mint family, with bright green leaves and square stems tinged with purple. It has a high menthol (mint oil) content, which gives it its distinct fresh flavor; it is often used as a flavoring in confections, ice creams, tea, and chewing gum.

peppermint Schnapps A distilled spirit with a distinct peppermint flavor. It is one of the most well known of the Schnapps varieties. See also *Schnapps*.

pera ('pay-rah) The Italian word for pear.

percolation (pehr-koh-'lay-shun) A method that is used to extract liquid from a product, such as coffee. The liquid is heated in the bottom of a container and then pumped to the top through a tube where it douses the product and the liquid drips down to the bottom. This process is repeated until the desired flavor is achieved.

percolator (pehr-koh-'lay-tohr) An electric coffee pot that works by pumping boiled water over the perforated container that holds the coffee grinds.

perforated sheet pan A sheet pan with tiny holes throughout the surface, which promote formation of a crisp crust and even bottom baking of breads and rolls in a rotating oven. It also helps evenly distribute steam around the baking item. These pans are not recommended for use in a deck oven because the bottom of the baking goods may become too dark.

perilla See *shiso*.

Perlette grape See *grape*.

permanent emulsion See *emulsion*.

Pernod ('pehr-noh) A licorice-flavored French liqueur.

Persian apple See *peach*.

Persian lime See *lime*.

Persian melon See *muskmelon*.

Persian walnut Another name for *English walnut*; see *walnut*.

persicot (pehr-see-'koh) A homemade French liqueur used to flavor pastries and confections, made by steeping peach stones, almonds, and spices in a sweetened alcohol.

persimmon (puhr-'sihm-muhn) The fruit of any of a group of trees in the ebony family. Most common are the large orange oriental persimmons, which are eaten out of hand; but there is also a native U.S. persimmon that is smaller and darker, harvested in the fall and whose cooked puree is used in pudding and fudge. The most common varieties of the commercially grown oriental persimmon are:

> **Cinnamon** A lesser known but attractive Hachiya variety, shaped like a tomato, with golden yellow-orange skin and golden-yellow flesh dotted with cinnamon specks. It is very sweet and low in astringency, and can be eaten firm or slightly softened. Available October to December.

> **Fuyu** Smaller than the Hachiya, this tomato-shaped variety has a reddish-orange skin and flesh. It is sweet and tangy, and can be eaten firm or slightly softened. Available October to December.

> **Hachiya** The most common available in the United States, it is heart-shaped with a bright orange skin and sweet, tangy, jelly-like pulp. When unripe, these are highly astringent so they must be eaten ripe. When ripe, they feel like an overfilled water balloon.

> **Sharon** A sweet, round Fuyu variety grown in Israel. Available December to February.

P
P

persipan A paste made from ground peach or apricot kernels, sugar, and *glucose.* It is kneaded until it forms a dough, and may be used as a substitute for *marzipan* and *almond paste.*

pestiños al anis (pess-'tee-nyos al 'ah-ness) A Spanish fried pastry flavored with anise. These are made with a pastry dough that has been mixed with lemon-anise infused oil and white wine. The dough is cut into small rectangles and fried, then dipped in honey syrup and dusted with confectioners' sugar.

pestle See *mortar and pestle.*

pet-de-nonne (peht-duh-non) The French term for "nun's farts," referring to a fritter made with small balls of *choux paste* that are fried until golden brown, then sprinkled with sugar. They are served warm with fruit sauce or filled with cream or jam and served cold.

Peter Heering A ruby-red Danish liqueur with a mildly sweet black cherry flavor. It was created in the 1830s by Peter Heering. Also known as *Cherry Heering.*

petit-beurre (puh-'tee-burr) A French butter cookie that is topped with coarse sugar; traditionally oblong in shape with fluted edges.

petit déjeuner (pah-'teet 'day-zhoo-nay) Name for the first meal of the day in France, typically a cup of tea, coffee, *café au lait,* or hot chocolate and *croissants* or bread, served with honey and jam.

petit four ('peh-tee fohr) The French term for "small oven," referring to a small, bite-size confection. According to Câreme, the name dates back to the 18th century and is named for the small ovens that were used to bake these products; Also, the items were baked *à petit four,* meaning they were baked at a low temperature after the large cakes had been taken out of the oven and the temperature had dropped. In America, many people mistakenly associate the term with only a square, bite-size confection with a *frangipane* base and layered with raspberry or apricot jam, topped with *marzipan* and glazed with *fondant.* Traditionally the fondant is white, but it may be colored as well. Although many people refer to all small sweets served after a meal or with coffee or tea as petit fours, they are actually categorized as follows:

> **Petit Four Glacé** The term *glacé* is French for "iced" or "glazed" and refers to the largest and most diverse group of petit fours. They are made from cakes layered with jam, *ganache,* pastry cream, or buttercream and glazed with a thin coating of chocolate, caramel, or fondant. They may be cut into rounds, squares, diamonds, and rectangles, and are garnished with a decorative piping of chocolate or icing or topped with candied fruits, flowers, or nuts. Other popular products that fall into this category are *éclairs* and sugar-coated fruits.
>
> **Petit Four Sec** The term *sec* is French for "dry" and refers to small cookies or biscuits such as *madeleines* and *financiers,* baked meringues, *palmiers,* and other plain items that are ready to eat after baking.
>
> **Petit Four Demi-Sec** The term *demi-sec* is French for "half dry" and refers to petit fours that combine a petit four sec with a cream, jam, or ganache filling, such as *macaroons.*
>
> **Petit Four Varitété** The term *varitété* is French for "variety" and refers to all other petit fours that do not fall into the above categories, such as savory petit fours.

Petit fours that are traditionally served after a meal or a dessert course are referred to as *mignardise.* They are also popular with afternoon tea or coffee.

petit four cup A small paper cup with a fluted edge, for holding a petit four. They come in different colors and may be made of thin paper or foil. They enhance the appearance of the petit four and also make it easier to pick up and package.

petit four cutter A small metal cutter used to cut out individual petit fours. They are typically sold in sets and are available in different shapes, including hearts, hexagons, fluted circles, and teardrops. They range in size from 1 to 2 inches (2.5 to 5 cm) high and 1 to 1½ inches (2.5 to 3.7 cm) in diameter.

petit four demi-sec See *petit four.*

petit four glacé See *petit four.*

petit four mold A miniature shallow metal or plastic form for making petit fours. They come in a variety of shapes, including circles, squares, ovals, diamonds, and triangles, and may have a fluted or straight edge; they range in size from 1¼ to 1½ inches (3.1 to 3.7 cm) in diameter and are usually ½ inch (1.2 cm) deep. They are often sold in sets of assorted shapes.

petit four sec ('peh-tee fohr sehk) See *petit four.*

petit four varitété ('peh-tee fohr vehr-uh-'tay) See *petit four.*

petit pain ('peh-tee pahn) The French term for "small bread," quite similar to the American bread roll.

petit Suisse ('peh-tee swees) A rich, creamy French cheese that contains between 60 and 75% milkfat, which gives it a soft, cream cheese–like consistency. It has a mild, sweet-tangy flavor and pairs well with bread and fruit. It is typically formed into small cylinders or flat squares.

petticoat tail See *shortbread.*

Pfeffernüsse (pfehf-fehr-noorz-zuh) The German word for "peppernuts," referring to a small, round, spicy Christmas cookie flavored with black pepper, cinnamon, cloves, ginger, cardamom, and nutmeg. During the holidays they are rolled in confectioners' sugar or glazed with a white icing. They are very hard and contain no fat, so they keep for a long time.

pH A measurement of the acidity and alkalinity of a product, on a scale of which 7 is neutral, below 7 is acidic, and above 7 is alkaline. The pH of an ingredient plays an important role in baked goods. It can affect the color, flavor, gluten strength, and crumb texture; the addition of an acid such as cream of tartar and fast-acting baking powder tends to decreases the pH of batters and doughs, while the addition of an alkali such as baking soda increases the pH. The increase of pH in cookies weakens the gluten and yields a more tender cookie that spreads more and crisps more quickly; it also results in a coarser, drier crumb and increases browning. Recipes that call for naturally acidic products, such as honey (3.5 to 4.5 pH) and cocoa powder (5 to 6 pH), use baking soda to neutralize the acidity and assist in leavening. Cream of tartar and other acids prevent the crystallization and browning of sugar owing to a lower pH. A small amount of baking soda added to chocolate brownies and gingerbread increases the pH and yields a darker, richer-looking product. See also *water pH.*

Philadelphia Cream Cheese A major brand of *cream cheese,* named for the city of Philadelphia, where it was introduced in 1880.

phyllo dough ('fee-loh) The Greek word for "leaf," referring to a paper-thin sheet of dough made from flour and water, and sold in a stack of sheets or leaves. Phyllo is used extensively in the pastry shop to make desserts such as *baklava* and crisp garnishes or edible containers or wraps for desserts. The dough dries out very quickly, so it is important to keep it covered with a damp cloth when working with it. It is available fresh in some Greek and Middle Eastern markets, or more commonly frozen in supermarkets, and should be thawed in the refrigerator

P
p

overnight before use. It can be stored airtight in the refrigerator for a few days, but once used should not be refrozen or it will become brittle. Also spelled *filo*.

physalis ('fih-zal-his) Another name for *cape gooseberry*.

picanchâgne (pee-kahn-shahn-'yeh) A pastry that consists of a rich, sweet dough filled with sliced pears and shaped into a large ring and brushed with apricot glaze. It is a specialty of Bourbonnais, France, and its name derives from a French children's game called Piques Comme en Chane, which means "to bristle like an oak tree" and refers to handstands that children do during the game. The small cooked pears in the pastry stick up like the legs of the children doing handstands.

pickling The act of preserving food, such as cucumbers and watermelon rind, in a vinegar mixture or *brine*.

pie A savory or sweet dish baked with a bottom, and sometimes a top, crust. The origin of the pie is believed to date back to the ancient Egyptians, from whom the early Romans probably learned the dish. These first pies were made in containers of grass reeds, which held the fillings. The first known pie recipe is a rye-crusted goat cheese and honey pie that was published by Romans in the 14th century. The first pies made in England predominately had meat fillings; their thick crusts were referred to as coffyn. Pie came to America with the first English settlers, and the colonists cooked their pies in long, narrow pans they similarly called coffins. As in Roman times, early American pie crusts often were not eaten; they simply held the filling during baking. It was during the American Revolution that the term *crust* replaced coffin. As ingredients such as butter and shortening became more readily available, the improved flavor and texture of the bottom crust became an edible addition to the pie.

In America, pies have evolved into a traditional dessert and are associated with American culture, as in the phrase "as American as apple pie." They are traditionally baked in a shallow pie pan and consist of a bottom crust filled with a sweet or savory filling; they may or may not have a top crust as well. The crust is typically made from pie dough, but crusts are also made from crushed cookie crumbs, such as graham crackers or chocolate or vanilla wafers. The crust may be *blind-baked* and filled with a pre-cooked filling, or baked together with the filling and/or top crust. Pie fillings include fruit mixtues, custard, and chiffon. In general, fruit pies are made by lining a pie pan with raw dough that is then filled with fruit and topped with raw dough that may be whole or cut into a lattice design; custard pies are made by lining a pie pan with raw dough, filling it with custard mixture, and baking until set; it usually does not have a top crust. Chiffon pies are made by filling a prebaked pie shell with a flavored mixture that has been lightened with whipped egg whites or whipped cream. Starch or gelatin sets the filling so it does not require additional baking. If the pie does not have a top crust, it is often garnished with fresh fruit, whipped cream, or meringue. See also *pie dough, banana cream pie, Boston cream pie, coconut cream pie, Key lime pie,* and *lemon meringue pie.*

pièce montée (pee-ehs mohn-'tay) The French term for "mounted piece," referring to a lavish, ornamental pastry created to decorate tables at a banquet or party. These were popular with nobility during the Middle Ages, often made in animal shapes. They reached their height of popularity in the 18th and 19th centuries, and mainly depicted historical or allegorical subjects. They can be constructed using *pulled sugar* or *blown sugar, nougat, chocolate, crystallized fruit, petit fours, dragées,* and *marzipan.* Although they are less popular and more modest in size today, they are still made for special occasions.

pièce montée à l'espagnole (pee-'ehs mohn-'tay al-ehs-pahn-'yol) The Spanish version of a *pièce montée* with separate trays of confectionries arranged in layers on top of each other and separated by pillars that stand on the outer edges of the tray beneath.

pie crust See *pie.*

pie dough A *pastry dough* made by the biscuit method (see *mixing methods*). It is used to line a pie pan for a bottom crust and may also be used to put a top crust or lattice top on the pie. It is made with a low-gluten flour, salt, cold water or milk (which will make it richer but brown more quickly), shortening or butter, and sometimes sugar. The choice of fat depends on cost and type of dough desired. Shortening produces a flaky product and is easy to work with, but lacks flavor. Butter is more expensive and more difficult to work with since it melts faster, but provides a rich, buttery flavor. Many chefs use a combination of the two to gain the benefits of both. If butter replaces all the shortening in the recipe, it should be increased by ¼ and the water decreased slightly, as butter contains moisture.

The two types of pie dough are mealy and flaky. *Mealy pie dough* is produced by cutting in the fat until it resembles coarse cornmeal. The benefits of this type are that the crust is tender because less gluten is developed and the crust is less likely to absorb moisture from the filling and become soggy. For these reasons some chefs prefer to use it as a bottom crust. *Flaky pie dough* is produced by cutting in the fat until it resembles hazelnut pieces. In order to ensure a flaky, tender pie crust, it is important to use only the amount of cold liquid necessary to bring the dough together and to not overmix the dough.

pie filling See *pie.*

pie pan/pie tin A metal, glass, or disposable aluminum pan used to bake pies. It has slanted sides and comes in sizes that range from 8 to 10 inches (20 to 25 cm) in diameter and 1 to 2 inches (2.5 to 5 cm) deep.

pie plant See *rhubarb.*

pie weight A small, ceramic or metal pellet or bead used in a batch of others to weight down pie dough in order to *blind-bake* the crust, preventing it from blistering as it cooks.

pignoli (peeg-no-lee) The Italian term for pine nuts. See *pine nut.*

pig's ear See *papillon.*

pikelet (pihk-eh-'leht) A thin English pancake or griddle cake flavored with cinnamon. It measures no more than 4 inches (10 cm) in diameter and is served with raspberry jam and fresh cream.

piki ('pee-kee) A crisp, gray-blue *flatbread* made by the Hopi Indians of Arizona. The batter is made from blue cornmeal, water, and ash; the ash usually comes from the chamisa bush and along with the blue cornmeal, gives the bread its unique color and nutrients. It is baked on a hot *piki stone,* which varies in size and shape but is typically a long rectangle of granite 2 inches (5 cm) thick.

piki stone See *piki.*

pillar A cylindrical piece of plastic that is used to separate the layers in a wedding cake, thus creating a tiered appearance. They range in size from 4 to 8 inches (10 cm to 20 cm) and are also referred to as a column. See also *wedding cake.*

piloncillo ('pee-yohn-'chill-yoh) See *sugar.*

piña colada ('pee-yuh koh-'lah-dah) The Spanish term for "strained pineapple," referring to a chilled tropical drink made with rum, coconut cream, and pineapple juice.

pinch See *dash.*

pineapple A juicy, sweet-tart tropical fruit that is indigenous to Central and South America but commercially grown in Hawaii. The name derives from its appearance, since it resembles a pine cone; *apple* was added to indicate that it is

P
p

a fruit. The fruit is available year-round, with peak season March to July. The most common varieties are:

Baby Hawaiian A small Gold pineapple 5 to 8 inches (12.5 to 20 cm) high. It has a sweet, crunchy texture with an edible core and brown exterior.

Cayenne A large, commercial variety from Hawaii. It is longer and more cylindrical than other varieties and has a golden yellow skin and flesh with long, sword-like green leaves sprouting from the top.

Gold or Common A very large variety ranging from 17 to 22 inches (42.5 to 55 cm) long, with an intensely sweet bright yellow flesh and golden exterior.

Red Spanish A large, squat, commercial variety grown mainly in Florida and Puerto Rico. It has reddish golden-brown skin and several pointed leaves on top.

South African Baby A very sweet, aromatic pineapple 5 to 7 inches (12.5 to 17.5 cm) high. It has a golden flesh with an edible core and golden exterior.

Sugar Loaf A large Mexican variety seldom available in the United States owing to its poor shipping ability. It has intensely flavored golden flesh and an exterior that is still green when ripe.

pineapple guava See *feijoa*.

pineapple sage See *sage*.

pine nut The edible seed of pine trees that grow in Italy, China, North Africa, Mexico, and the southwestern United States. The nuts are high in fat and expensive owing to the labor-intensive process of harvesting them. The two main varieties are the *Italian pine nut* or *Mediterranean pine nut* and the *Chinese pine nut*. Both have a thin shell that encases an ivory-colored nutmeat approximately ½ inch (1.2 cm) long. The more expensive Italian and Mediterranean pine nut is shaped like a tiny torpedo and has a light, delicate flavor. The Chinese pine nut is shaped like a squat triangle and has a pungent pine flavor and aroma. All pine nuts are highly susceptible to rancidity and should be stored in an airtight container in the refrigerator or freezer. They are a popular ingredient in desserts, pastries, and confections, and are often toasted to enhance their flavor and aroma. Also known as *Indian nut, piñon nut,* and *pignoli*.

pineapple upside down cake See *upside down cake*.

pinhead oats See *oats*.

pink lady A rose-colored cocktail that consists of gin, grenadine, lemon or lime juice, egg whites, and cream.

Pink Lady apple See *apple*.

pink peppercorn The dried berry of the baies rose plant, cultivated in Madagascar and imported via France. Although these expensive berries are not true peppercorns, they resemble them in size and shape, though they have a distinct rose-colored hue and strong, slightly sweet flavor.

piñon nut (pihn-'yohn) The Spanish word for *pine nut*.

Pinot Noir ('pee-noh nwahr) A red grape used to produce a broad spectrum of wines, such as Champagne, lesser Burgundies, and sparkling wines.

pint 1. A U.S. measurement of liquid volume, equivalent to 16 fluid ounces or 480 ml. 2. British slang for a beer.

pipe To push a product such as choux paste, buttercream, chocolate, or another smooth mixture out of a pastry bag or paper cone onto a pastry surface in order to create a particular shape or decorative effect. This technique is used extensively in the pastry shop.

P
p

piped cookie See *cookie.*

Pippin apple See *apple, Newton Pippin.*

piping bag See *pastry bag.*

piping chocolate A fluid chocolate used to decorate cakes and pastries. It is typically put into a paper cone and piped onto a pastry using a fine point. The chocolate may be purchased ready-made from specialty vendors or made by adding a small amount of *inverted sugar* to melted chocolate. *Tempered chocolate* may be used as a substitute.

piping gel A smooth, jelly-like, translucent, ready-made mixture of sugar, corn syrup, and *gum arabic.* It may be tinted with food coloring and used to decorate cakes and pastries, via a *pastry bag* and *pastry tip* or *paper cone.*

pip Another term for a small seed, usually found in fruits such as grapes, apples, and oranges.

piquant (pee-'kahn) The French word for "pungent," used to describe a flavor that may be spicy, tart, or strong.

pirouette (pir-oh-'eht) A thin rolled wafer cookie shaped like a hollow cigarette. The ends are often dipped in chocolate. It makes a great accompaniment to ice creams and sorbets because its crisp texture contrasts well with a creamy dessert.

pirozhki (peh-'rawsh-kee) A small Russian turnover filled with a sweet, usually fruit, or savory mixture. They may be baked or fried, and shaped like a rectangle, triangle, or crescent.

pisang goring (pee-sung goh-'rehng) A warm snack from Indonesia, made by dipping thinly sliced bananas into a batter of rice flour, sugar, salt, eggs, water, and baking soda and then deep-frying them.

pisco ('pee-skoh) A strong, pale yellow South American brandy that is primarily produced in Peru and Chile. It is typically made from a Muscat wine and has a spicy, exotic flavor with a hint of orange blossom.

pistachio (pih-'stash-ee-oh) A distinctly green nut produced by a tree in the cashew family, native to Asia. Pistachios are cultivated in California, Turkey, Italy, and Iran. The nut has a hard tan shell that is sometimes dyed red or green with vegetable dyes. The nuts may be shelled or unshelled, salted or unsalted, and eaten raw or roasted. They are used in confections, ice creams, and as garnishes. If buying the nuts unshelled, choose ones that are partially open; otherwise the nutmeat has not properly matured. To enhance the green color of the nut, briefly blanch the nuts in boiled, salted water. Toasting will bring out their delicate nut-like flavor and aroma.

pistole A packaging term for *couverture* that refers to small, round discs of chocolate. Some pastry chefs prefer purchasing chocolate this way because it reduces the amount of chopping; the uniform size and shape assist in even melting as well.

pit 1. The stone or seed of fruits such as apricots, plums, peaches, and cherries. 2. To remove the stone or seed of a fruit.

pita, pita bread ('pee-tah) A round Middle Eastern *flatbread* that has a horizontal opening about one-third of the way down the bread. This creates a deep pocket that is typically stuffed. Pita may be grilled or baked and sliced into wedges for dipping. It may be made from white or wheat flour, or a combination of both. Also known as *pocket bread.*

pitaya (pee-'tay-ah) A Latin American fruit that is a member of the cactus family. It is shaped like a large egg and has a prickly skin that ranges in color from pink to yellow. The juicy flesh has small, edible seeds and is pink or ivory depending on the variety. It is not widely available outside Latin America, but may be found in cans or jars in Latin American markets.

P
p

pith The spongy, white layer in citrus fruits that lies between the rind and the flesh. It is often attached to the rind when it is zested, but should be removed because it will impart a bitter flavor.

pithivier ('pee-tee-vyay) A French dessert that consists of two large round circles of puff pastry that are filled with *frangipane,* the edges are scalloped, and the egg-washed top is scored into a sunburst design. This is a specialty of the town of Pithiviers, in the Órleans region of France. It is traditionally served as a *Twelfth Night cake* in that region.

pitter A small, hand-held tool used to extract the pits of cherries and olives.

pitti (pitt-ee) A sweet, chewy *flatbread* from the Hunzu Valley of Pakistan. It is made from a combination of wheat berry sprouts and apricots, and served with goat cheese and apricot preserves.

pixbae (pee-'bah) The small fruit of the peach palm, native to Latin America and the Caribbean. It resembles a persimmon, with a hard, shiny red skin. It must be boiled before eating, and tastes like a cross between a chestnut and a sweet potato. It is typically ground into meal and fermented to make alcoholic beverages, or mashed and used to flavor pastries.

pizelle (pih-'zehl) A large, round, crisp cookie with an ornate design imprinted on the surface from the iron on which it is baked. While still warm, the cookie may be formed into a shape that can then be filled with cream or mousse. Its crispy texture makes a nice contrast to creamy desserts such as ice cream, custard, and sorbet. See also *pizelle iron.*

pizelle iron A two-piece form for cooking *pizelles.* It consists of two 5-inch (12.5 cm) round, engraved cast iron plates hinged together. These irons are available in manual and electric models. The manual has a long handle attached to each plate and makes one cookie at a time; the electric, which is larger, makes one or two large pizelles or four mini-pizelles.

plantain See *banana.*

plastic chocolate Another name for *modeling chocolate.*

plastic fat See *shortening, high-ratio plastic.*

plättar ('plah-tahr) A small, Swedish pancake served with *lingonberries.*

plett pan (pleht) A cast iron griddle with shallow sides, used to make *Swedish pancakes.* It is approximately 3 inches (7.5 cm) in diameter.

plisson (plee-'zoh) A thick, sweet dessert cream made by heating milk and sugar very gently, without boiling, and repeating the process until it thickens. It is a specialty of Poitou, France.

plombière (plom-bee-'ayr) A French dessert of a custard-based ice cream mixed with whipped cream and candied fruit that has been steeped in *Kirsch* and frozen in a square mold. The name derives from the French *plomb,* which means "lead," because originally the dessert was made in a lead mold.

Plugra ('ploo-grah) A European-style butter made with added cultured cream. The high butterfat content and creamy texture make excellent *laminated doughs* and pastries.

plum A stonefruit of a variety of trees in the genus *Prunus,* a member of the rose family. There are both clingstone and freestone varieties, and the three main categories are Japanese, European, and American. *Japanese plums* originated in China and are typically larger with a softer, juicy flesh and skin of many shades of yellow, red, and purple. *European plums* originated in southwestern Asia, but have been cultivated in Europe for over 2,000 years; they are typically blue or purple, with a firm flesh and round or oval shape. *American plums* were developed from wild plum trees in North America; they are not as commercially produced as the European or Japanese plums. The most common plum varieties are:

Beach A wild, dark purple plum found in sandy areas along the Atlantic coast. It is tart and bitter, so the fruit is used mostly in jams and jellies.

Beauty A Japanese variety developed in California. It is heart-shaped with a bright red skin and dark yellow-red flesh. Available March to August.

Casselman A large, cone-shaped Japanese variety developed in California. It has purplish skin speckled with yellow and firm, yellow flesh. Available June to August.

Damson A small European variety that originated in Syria. It has a blue-purple skin and juicy, golden flesh that is slightly acidic. It is popular for jams and preserves. Available May to August.

Greengage A round, medium European variety named for Sir William Gage, who brought it to England. It originated in Italy and was brought to France in the 16th century, where it is known as *reineclaude*. It has a yellow-green skin with a blush of red and green flesh that is good fresh or cooked. Available March to August.

Kelsey A large, heart-shaped Japanese variety with yellow-green skin and firm, sweet flesh. Available May to August.

Laroda An oval Japanese variety developed in California. It has a dark, reddish-purple skin and firm, fragrant, amber flesh. Not recommended for cooking. Available May to August.

Mirabelle A petite, round European variety from Syria. It has a very thin yellow skin and juicy, sweet, firm red flesh. Available May to August.

Queen Ann A large, heart-shaped Japanese variety developed in California. It has dark purple skin and sweet amber flesh that is good fresh or cooked. Available May to August.

Santa Rosa A Japanese variety developed by Santa Rosa resident Luther Burbank. It is large with a deep purplish-red skin and a firm, juicy yellow flesh that is slightly tart. Available March to September.

Shiro A medium Japanese variety developed in California. It has a yellow skin and very flavorful yellow flesh that is good fresh or cooked. Available March to July.

Wickson A large, heart-shaped Japanese variety developed in California. It has yellow-green skin and flavorful yellow flesh. Not recommended for cooking. Available May to August.

plum cake A British cake flavored with rum, currants, and candied orange peel.

plumcot The hybrid fruit created by crossing a plum (50%) and an apricot (50%), developed by horticulturist Luther Burbank. It has a tart golden yellow skin and sweet bright yellow flesh. Available May to July. See also *aprium* and *pluot*.

plump To soak dried fruit such as raisins in a liquid to soften and rehydrate them so that they are "plump" and juicy.

plum pudding An English steamed pudding, originally made with plums but later including suet, dried fruit, nuts, spices, and usually dark *treacle*. It is flamed with brandy and served warm during Christmastime with a *hard sauce*. Also known as *Christmas pudding*.

P
p

plunger A small, hand-held tool used to cut decorative pieces for decorating cakes. It consists of a small cutter attached to a spring-loaded tube. When the top is pushed down onto the rolled fondant, marzipan, or gum paste, the tool cuts out the design and holds it in the plunger. The cutter is then placed on a cell pad, so that when the plunger is pressed again, it releases the cutout design. Plungers are available in flower designs and also bells, birds, and abstract shapes.

pluot (plu-oht) The fruit of a hybrid, produced by crossing an apricot (75%) and a plum (25%). The fruit resembles a plum in taste and appearance, but has a more intense, sweet flavor. Available May to September. The most common varieties are:

> **Dapple Dandy** The most widely available variety, it is large with a reddish purple skin dotted with yellow specks. The very sweet flesh ranges from golden yellow to bright red.
>
> **Emerald Baut** The sweetest variety with a green-yellow skin and yellow flesh.
>
> **Flavor Fall** A late-season variety with a deep purple skin and sweet yellow flesh.
>
> **Flavor Gator** A variety with very sweet yellow flesh that has a marbled red and yellow-green skin.
>
> **Flavor King** A medium sweet variety with low acidity and a yellow speckled red skin and red-blushed yellow flesh.
>
> **Flavorosa** A medium variety with a deep purple skin and pinkish-red flesh. Typically the first variety available during the season.
>
> **Flavor Queen** A very sweet variety with complex flavor and with a pale yellow-green skin and golden yellow flesh.
>
> **Nectacotum** A variety with very sweet, nectarine-like flavor, pale yellow specked red skin, and red-yellow flesh.
>
> **Sweet Treats** An intensely sweet variety with a pale yellow-green skin and red flesh.

poach To cook food by gently simmering it in a liquid just below the boiling point. Fruit is often poached in a sugar syrup with ingredients such as red or white wine and/or spices in order to infuse those flavors into the fruit.

pocket bread Another name for *pita*.

poe (po) A chilled custard dessert from Tahiti. It is a mixture of pureed tropical fruits such as pineapple, mango, or papaya and brown sugar, vanilla bean, and arrowroot-thickened fruit juice. It is baked in a buttered dish until set and served with coconut cream.

poha ('poh-hah) The Hawaiian name for *cape gooseberry;* see *berry.*

poirat (pwah-'rah) A pie filled with sweetened pears that have been soaked in honey, baked with a top crust, and served hot with fresh cream poured through the open holes in the crust. It is a traditional pastry of Berry, France.

poire (pwahr) The French word for *pear.*

poire Hélène (pwahr heh-'leen) See *belle Hélène.*

Poire William (pwahr 'weel-yahm) A clear, pear-flavored *eau-de-vie* made in France and Switzerland. It is distilled with a pear-infused brandy; the premiere brands have a whole pear in the bottle, which is accomplished by placing the bottle over the budding fruit and allowing it to grow inside. Poire William is used to flavor creams, sauces, and confectionery fillings.

polka A gâteau that consists of a ring of *choux pastry* on a base of *short dough.* After baking, the choux is filled with pastry cream and heavily dusted with confectioners' sugar. A red-hot iron in the shape of a criss-cross pattern is pressed into the sugar and caramelizes the pattern onto the top. The design is said to resemble the steps of the polka dance.

polka bread A round, flat French bread with deep criss-cross grooves on top, which allows it to be divided without being cut. It is from the Loire Valley. The criss-cross pattern is said to resemble the steps of the polka dance.

polonaise (poh-loh-'nays) A brioche that is soaked in *Kirsch* or rum and filled with a mixture of pastry cream and candied fruit. The pastry is covered in meringue and garnished with sliced almonds, then browned in the oven.

polvorone (pohl-voh-'rohn-aa) The Spanish name for *Mexican Wedding cookie.*

polydextrose A food additive primarily used as a *bulking agent, humectant,* and tenderizer in baked goods, confections, candies, and frozen dairy products.

polysaccharide The term for "many sugars," referring to large molecules that are made up of many sugar molecules linked together. They are distinguished by the type and amount of sugar molecules and how they are linked together.

polysorbate A food additive primarily used as an *emulsifier* in baked goods, chocolate products, frozen desserts, icing mixes, and shortenings. It is also sometimes used as a dough conditioner and dispersing agent in gelatins.

polyunsaturated fat Also known as polyunsaturated fatty acids. See *unsaturated fat.*

pomace ('puh-muss) The residue that remains after the fruit for a wine or juice has been pressed. It consists of skins, pulp, seeds, and pits and is processed to make pomace brandy, *marc,* and *grappa.*

pomegranate ('pom-uh-gran-uht) A many-celled large red berry, the fruit of a tropical Asian tree. Cultivated in Asia, the Mediterranean, the Middle East, and California, this labor-intensive fruit is about the size of a medium orange, with a thin, leathery skin that ranges in color from pink to deep red and encases a seed-packed interior. The tiny, edible seeds are individually surrounded by a translucent, bright red, jelly-like flesh that has a juicy, sweet-tart flavor. Pomegranates are excellent fresh or as a unique garnish for sweet or savory items. The juice may also be extracted to flavor sorbets, creams, and sauces. The ripe fruit should be heavy for its size and show no sign of deterioration. It may be stored in a cool, dry place for one to two weeks or in the refrigerator for up to a month. The seeds and juice should be stored in an airtight container in the refrigerator for one week or frozen up to three months. They are rich in potassium and vitamin C. Available August to December, but most commonly found in September and October.

pomelo ('pom-eh-loh) A very large citrus fruit that is native to Malaysia and believed to be related to the grapefruit. The fruit varies in size, shape, color, and flavor, but may weigh up to 25 pounds (11 kg). The soft, thick rinds may be yellow, yellowish-brown, lime green, or pink. The juicy flesh ranges in color from light yellow to deep pink and may be tangy-tart to spicy-sweet. It is a popular ingredient in many Asian dishes and is also known as a *Chinese grapefruit.* Also spelled *pommelo* and *pummelo.*

pomme (pom) The French word for *apple.*

pommelo (pom-'eh-loh) See *pomelo*.

pompe An assortment of sweet or savory French pastries that vary from region to region. *Pompe aux pommes* is a pastry from the Auvergne region; it is a buttery, flaky pastry spiced with cinnamon and filled with jam, fruit mixtures, usually plums, and sometimes cream cheese. In Provence, *pompe à l'huile* is a flat Christmas cake served with mulled wine; it is made from a leavened dough that contains olive oil and is flavored with orange flower water, lemon zest, and sometimes saffron, then garnished with sugared almonds.

pompe à l'huile See *pompe*.

pompe aux pommes See *pompe*.

pompelmo (pohm-'pehl-moh) The Italian word for *grapefruit*.

pone (pohn) The Native American word for "baked."

Pont l'Eveque (pon lay-'vehk) An uncooked, ripened cheese made from whole or partially skimmed cow's milk. It has a fat content of 50%; it is square with a golden yellow-orange rind and a soft, creamy pale interior that has a sweet-tart flavor. The cheese dates back to the 13th century and pairs well with fruit, nuts, and dessert wines.

pönnukörkur (poor-new-koor-kuhr) A large, thin pancake from Iceland, served with whipped cream and jelly.

pontefract cake A small, round, flat British cake flavored with anise.

pont-neuf (puh'nt-nuhf) A small French pastry with a sweet-dough tartlet base that is filled with *frangipane* and crushed macaroons. Thin strips of dough are placed in a cross pattern on top, the pastry is baked, then it is glazed with apricot jam while still warm and dusted with confectioners' sugar before serving. It is named after the Parisian bridge.

pony A liquid measurement used for preparing drinks; it is equal to 1 fluid ounce, or 30 grams.

poolish ('poo-leash) A loose *pre-ferment* made of equal amounts flour and water and a small amount of yeast (.08 to 1%). It is of Polish origin and is used to increase the extensibility of bread dough and add a sweet, nutty, mildly acidic flavor and aroma. It also improves loaf volume.

poor knight's pudding A British dessert of bread soaked in milk and beaten eggs, then fried in butter. The pieces are spread with fruit or jam and sandwiched together.

popcorn A snack of dried corn that is heated either in oil or by dry heat until the moisture in the hull of the kernel "pops" open from the pressure created by the heat. It is a low-calorie snack believed to date back over 6,000 years, and must be made with a variety of corn that pops. Pre-packaged microwave popcorn was developed in the 1940s and is available buttered and/or salted or natural. Theatre popcorn is popped in a popcorn machine and is available with or without a melted butter topping. Raw corn kernels may also be purchased and popped in a skillet with oil. *Jiffy Pop* is a brand of popcorn that combines unpopped popcorn kernels with an aluminum pan and folded aluminum foil lid; as the pan is heated, the popping corn causes the foil to unfold and puff up. It was created in 1958 by Fred Mennen of Indiana, and is currently manufactured by Con Agra Foods.

popover A puffy, muffin-size *quickbread* with a crisp brown crust and moist, tender, somewhat hollow interior. It is made with a batter of eggs, milk, butter, and flour, and sometimes flavorings such as cheese, herbs, and/or spices. It is baked at high heat, and the high proportion of liquid creates steam that leavens the bread.

P
p

popover pan A heavy baking pan used for making *popovers* and *Yorkshire pudding*. It is similar to a *muffin pan*, but has deeper, tapered indentions that are spaced farther apart.

poppy seed The small, dried dark bluish-black seed of the poppy plant, used extensively in cakes, fillings, pastries, and as a topping for bread. It takes about 900,000 seeds to produce 1 pound (455 g). The seeds may be purchased whole or ground, and are also available in white and brown varieties. They have a high oil content and are susceptible to rancidity, so they should be stored in an airtight container in a cool, dry place. Also known as "mohn" in Hebrew where it is used extensively as a filling in cakes and pastries such as hamentaschen.

porridge ('por-ihj) A thick dish made of cereal or grain, usually oatmeal that is cooked in water or milk. It is usually served warm for breakfast with sugar and cream or milk.

Port A sweet, fortified wine from Portugal. The finest ports still come from the Douro region, where production is strictly regulated to ensure quality. These wines are referred to as *porto*. Port is made by adding grape alcohol to red wine while it is fermenting; this stops the fermentation process and results in a sweet wine that has about 10% residual sugar and 20% alcohol. The two main categories of Port are those that are aged predominately in wood or a tank and those that are aged in the bottle. The wood-aged Ports are ready to drink after they have been bottled and shipped, and should be consumed within two years after bottling. Unlike bottle-aged Ports, they do not need to be decanted. The major styles of Port are as follows:

Colheita A tawny Port from a single harvest. It is aged a minimum of seven years and is ready to drink after bottling.

Crusted A full-bodied, moderately priced Port that is a blend of two to three wines from different years. It is generally aged in the bottle for three to four years and gets its name because a heavy crust or sediment forms and must be decanted before drinking.

Late-bottled vintage Made from a single vintage and aged in wood for four to six years. These are ready to drink after bottling and are considered high-quality ruby Ports, but do not have the complex flavor or richness of vintage.

Ruby The least complex of the reds, it is a blend of young wines from different years that have been in barrels for two to three years. It has a fruity, straightforward flavor and is generally the least expensive.

Single quinta vintage A vintage that is produced from a single high-quality wine estate. These are generally wood-aged for two years and then bottle-aged for ten or more years. They are slightly less expensive than vintage and have a less intense richness.

Tawny Made from a blend of grapes from several years, they are either young or aged. Young tawnies are less than three years old and have a basic flavor and lighter color. Aged tawnies are usually designated on the label as 10, 20, 30, or 40 years. The long barrel-aging gives them a deep red or tawny color and nutty, sweet flavor with a hint of vanilla. They have a soft, silky texture and are made with the highest quality wines.

Vintage character High-quality ruby Ports that are blended from several vintages and wood-aged. They are fairly inexpensive and ready to drink when bottled. They have a light, fruity flavor and are usually sold under proprietary names, such as Fonseca Bin 27.

Vintage Regarded as the best and most expensive of all Ports, they are made from grapes from a single vintage and bottled within two years. They may be aged up to 50 years and have an intense, rich flavor. The long-bottle aging requires the ports to be decanted before drinking.

White Made from a variety of white grapes, these represent only a small portion of all production. The basic varieties are aged briefly in tanks, but there are some finer brands that are aged briefly in wood. They have a slightly nutty flavor and range in sweetness from light and dry (*leve seco*) to very sweet (*lagrima*). They are typically drunk chilled straight up or mixed with soda water and served with a twist of lime.

porto A label given to true Ports, produced and bottled in the Portuguese city of Oporto. See *Port.*

Port-Salut (por-'suh-loo) A mild, smooth, semi-soft French cheese with an orange rind and pale yellow interior. It dates back to the 19th century, when it was made by Trappist monks at the Port-du-Salut monastery in Brittany. It has a savory flavor that pairs well with fruit.

posset ('pos-iht) A hot drink of milk, wine, or ale and sugar and spices. Some versions add eggs to make it even richer. It dates back to medieval times.

Postum The proprietary name for a caffeine-free, powdered coffee substitute made from cereal grain.

pot A round, deep cooking container with one or two handles and a lid. Pots are available in various sizes, from 1 pint (480 ml) to 2 gallons (8.5 L).

potato starch A non-gluten-forming starch derived from potatoes. It has twice the thickening power of flour, and in baked goods provides tenderness and added moisture. It has no cereal flavor and swells and gels at a lower temperature. Since it contains no protein, some chefs replace a portion of the flour in cake batters so the cake will bake at a lower internal temperature and retain moisture. See also *starch.*

pot cheese A soft, fresh cheese similar to *cottage cheese* but drier because the majority of liquid has been pressed out.

potica ('paht-ee-kah) A Czech pastry of paper-thin pastry dough filled with a rich mixture of nuts, milk, and honey, then rolled up like a strudel and served in slices to highlight the spiral filling.

pound A U.S. measurement of weight, equivalent to 16 ounces or 454 grams. In professional recipes, the pound is also expressed with the # symbol.

potato flour See *flour.*

pot de crème (poh duh krehm) French for "pot of cream," referring to a rich, creamy custard typically baked and served in small ramekins. Vanilla is the classic flavoring, but coffee and chocolate are popular variations.

pound A standard measurement used in the United States that is the equivalent to 16 ounces by weight or 453.6 grams metric. 2. To beat or punch dough or other food with excessive force in an effort to tenderize or alter the texture in some manner.

pound cake A fine-textured loaf cake that got its name because it was originally made with 1 pound (455 g) each of butter, sugar, eggs, and flour. Many variations have evolved over the years, and now include baking powder or baking soda as *leaveners* and flavorings such as spices, nuts, dried fruit, and extracts.

poured fondant A shiny, pourable sugar icing used to coat *petit four glacé,* pastries, cakes, confections, or as a filling. The natural color is white, but it may be colored or flavored. Although it can be made by hand, it is labor-intensive, so it is typically purchased ready-made from specialty vendors. The *fondant* should be heated to approximately 100°F (38°C) before use, but if overheated it will be matte rather than shiny. Water may be added to adjust the consistency.

P
p

poured sugar The result of pouring prepared sugar syrup onto a lightly oiled surface or mold, to use for decorating pastries and desserts. The mixture may be colored and made into different shapes and sizes; it is used as a decorative base or component or background of a sugar showpiece or as a support for unstable decorations. Also known as *castor sugar*.

powdered gelatin See *gelatin*.

powdered milk See *dry milk*.

powdered sugar See *sugar*.

praline ('pray-leen) 1. A brittle, sweet confection made in the U.S. South. A mixture of caramelized almonds and/or hazelnuts nuts is poured into small, round, flat patties on a lightly oiled marble surface and cooled. The candies can be eaten as is or crushed and used as a garnish or in fillings for cakes and pastries and confections. In Louisiana, pralines are made with brown sugar and pecans. The name derives from the French *praliner,* which means "to brown in sugar."

praliné (prah-lee-'nay) A confectionery term that refers to a bite-size, chocolate-coated confection.

praline paste ('pray-leen) A thick, smooth paste made by grinding caramelized almonds or hazelnuts to release their natural oils. It is used as a flavoring agent in creams, confectionery fillings, and other pastry products.

pratie bread A fried *quickbread* from northern Ireland, made with mashed potatoes. It was devised as a way to use up leftover mashed potatoes and is typically served for breakfast, like pancakes.

pre-ferment A mixture of flour, water, yeast, and sometimes salt that is mixed together and allowed to ferment before being incorporated into the final dough. A pre-ferment gives the fullest range of flavor to the wheat flour and adds to the extensibility of the dough. It reduces production time and produces breads with more complex flavor and increased moisture retention and loaf volume. Unlike *sourdough* cultures, which can be perpetuated for years, pre-ferments have a limited life expectancy and typically last no more than 48 hours before they start to loose leavening power. The three main types of pre-ferments are *biga, pâte fermentée,* and *poolish*.

preserve 1. A cooked fruit mixture that is sweetened with sugar and set with pectin. Chunks of the fruit are visible in the product and add to its flavor and texture. It is a popular spread for toast. 2. To prepare food so as to extend its shelf life; methods include *canning, smoking, freeze-drying, pickling,* and *dehydrating*.

preserved lemon A lemon that has been cured in a mixture of lemon juice and salt. This specialty product is used extensively in Moroccan cooking and makes an interesting ingredient for flavoring pastries, desserts, and confections.

pressed cookie See *cookie*.

press pot Another name for *French press*.

pretzel ('preht-zuhl) A snack food made from wheat flour and yeast, and dipped in lye solution before baking; it may or may not be topped with coarse salt. Pretzels can be either hard and crisp or soft and chewy. *Soft pretzels* are shaped like an interlocking, twisted, loose knot meant to resemble hands folded in prayer. They are often sold hot by street vendors and spread with mustard. *Hard pretzels* also come in the traditional knot shape, but are also available in nuggets and thin or thick sticks. The first American commercial pretzel factory was established in Litilz, Pennsylvania, in 1861. In Germany, the pretzel is a preeminent symbol of baking that dates back hundred of years; pretzels were given as gifts to children who finished their prayers, and to this day, wooden or iron pretzels still hang above some baker's doors.

P
p

prezzo fisso ('preht-zoh 'fee-soh) The Italian term for "fixed price," referring to a complete restaurant meal for a preset price.

prick To make tiny holes in an unbaked product, such as pie or tart dough, in order to prevent it from blistering while baking.

prickly pear The pear-shaped fruit of a cactus. Its prickly skin ranges in color from green to reddish purple and encases a soft, porous flesh studded with black seeds and color that ranges from pale yellow-green to deep pink. It has a melon-like aroma and a somewhat bland, sweet flavor. Prickly pear puree is available from specialty vendors, and the deep magenta color and unique flavor makes an interesting sorbet. It is also a popular ingredient in Mexican, Latin, and Mediterranean cooking. Also known as *cactus pear*.

princess cake A dome-shaped Swedish cake that consists of *sponge cake* layered with whipped cream and custard, and covered in colored *marzipan*. It is typically decorated with *marzipan* flowers and leaves. This cake is known as *prinsesstårta* in Sweden, where it is traditionally served at celebratory occasions.

prinsesstårta (prayn-ses-'stuhr-tah) See *princess cake*.

prix fixe (pree fihks) The French term for "fixed price," referring to a complete restaurant meal for a preset price.

profiterole (proh-'fih-ter-ohl) A small cream puff filled with a sweet or savory filling. The classic version is made by filling the *choux puffs* with *crème chantilly*, ice cream, or *pastry cream* and arranging them in a small pyramid topped with chocolate sauce. In the production of *croquembouche* and *gâteau Saint-Honoré*, the profiteroles are filled with flavored pastry cream or *crème diplomat* and dipped in caramel.

progrès (proh-grehs) A cake composed of crunchy baked meringue discs sandwiched together with praline, coffee, or chocolate *buttercream* and garnished with confectioners' sugar and roasted almonds. The meringue layers are made with a mixture of whipped egg whites, sugar, and ground almonds or hazelnuts.

proof 1. See *12 Steps of Baking* appendix. 2. A term used to describe the amount of alcohol in spirits and liqueurs.

proof box An atmosphere-controlled piece of baker's equipment used to proof bread and other yeast-risen products. Industrial *proofers* come in a variety of shapes that range from under-the-counter machines on rollers to walk-in ones with room for several racks. Many of these models can be set to a specific temperature and humidity setting, as well as be electronically turned on and off. An inexpensive alternative is to place the yeast product in a closed cabinet with an electric or gas burner under a bain-marie of water. Once heated, the water will create the warm moisture that is necessary to proof the bread. Although this is an effective alternative to a proof box, it is difficult to control the temperature and humidity level, so the product should be watched carefully to prevent overproofing.

P
p

proofer Another name for a *proof box*.

Prosecco (proh-'sehk-koh) A popular Italian *spumante* wine that is made from the grape of the same name. The white grape grows in the eastern part of the Veneto region and produces a sparkling wine that has a crisp flavor. Although they are primarily dry, a sweet variety is also available. It is traditionally blended with the juice of fresh white peaches to make the refreshing beverage *bellini,* but may also be enjoyed on its own.

protease A class of enzymes that digest gluten proteins. They are important in bread baking because an excess of them will result in a slack, sticky dough.

protein A large molecule made up of amino acids. Protein is obtained from animal and vegetable sources and plays an important role in baking and pastry making; the proteins in eggs coagulate when heated, which enables them to thicken custards, sauces, and fillings. The proteins in wheat flour affect the amount of water absorbed in the dough; the gluten-forming proteins, glutenin and gliadin, make up about 80% of the proteins in the endosperm. In addition, when baked goods cool, the protein molecules bond and solidify, which sets the structure of the product.

prove Another word for *proof.* See *12 Steps of Baking* appendix.

prover Another name for *proof box.*

prune The dried fruit of the red or purple plum. Originating in Rome, prunes have been a traditional snack and pastry ingredient in Europe for centuries. They are harvested in the fall to obtain maximum sweetness and plumpness, and are traditionally dried in the sun, but modern dehydrating technology has largely replaced this technique. Prunes come in different sizes, including small, medium, large, and jumbo. They have a bluish-black skin that should be soft and malleable to the touch. 2. A variety of Italian plum.

pruneau ('prew-noh) The French word for *prune.*

prunelle ('proo-nehl) A sweet, brandy-based liqueur that is pale green and flavored with wild plums.

prune puree A smooth paste made from finely ground prunes. It can be used as a fat substitute in baked goods to reduce the calories by 30% and render it cholesterol free. Despite its nutritional benefits, prune puree adds sugar and moistness to the product, which can interfere with structure development and may also give a distinct pruny flavor. See also *lekvar.*

pudding A variety of desserts that may be served warm or cold. Custard-based or baked puddings include *bread pudding, tapioca pudding,* and *rice pudding.* They are generally creamy and are flavored with ingredients such as chocolate, vanilla, fruits, nuts, or spices. Steamed puddings such as *plum pudding* are steamed in a *pudding mold* and have a firm, cake-like texture.

pudding mold A deep, cylindrical mold with fluted or grooved sides and a fluted top and center tube, used to steam puddings. The mold sometimes has a lid that can be clamped on. It may be made of aluminum, steel, or glazed earthenware; molds range in size from 2-cup (480 ml) to 2-quart (1 L 920 ml) capacity.

pudgy pie A campfire treat of two slices of white bread that have been buttered and filled with a variety of fillings such as a fruit mixture, peanut butter, or cheese, then put in a hinged iron and cooked over a fire. The bread slices are pinched together by the iron, enclosing the filling until bread is toasted on both sides. Gladys Flynn introduced the pudgy pie to the co-author of this book.

pudim molotoff (poo-deem 'mo-loh-toph) A rich egg-custard from Portugal, thickened with cornstarch and baked in a mold lined with butter and sugar. Once

P
p

cooled, it is turned out and garnished with toasted almonds and served with a sweet fruit sauce.

pueblo bread An adobe-baked bread made by Native Americans of the Southwest. The bread is round and tender while warm but becomes crisp as it cools and then is more akin to a cracker than bread.

Puerto Rican cherry See *acerola.*

puff pastry A rich, buttery, flaky French *pastry dough* used extensively in the production of pastries and baked goods such as *Napoleons, palmiers,* and *cream horns.* It is believed to date back to ancient Greece, but historians debate whether it was invented by Claude Lorrain, a 17th-century landscape painter who served as a pastry cook's apprentice, or by Feuillet, the chief pastry cook of the house of Condé. As a *laminated dough,* its preparation is labor-intensive and takes a skilled pastry cook to produce a light, flaky result.

To make puff pastry, a *détrempe* is rolled out and covered with a sheet of butter; margarine, shortening, goose fat, lard, or oil may be used in place of the butter but flavor will be sacrificed. The quantity of rolled-in fat may range from 50 to 100% of the weight of the flour. The dough is then folded, turned, rerolled, and folded again repeatedly, with a minimum of 30 minutes rest time, in the refrigerator, between each fold. The dough may be folded a maximum of eight times; the number of turns and folds determines the number of layers, which can be over 1,000. When the dough is baked at high temperature, the fat melts and creates steam, which leavens the dough to between six and eight times its original thickness. Since it is not a sweet dough, it is often used for savory items as well. Also known as *pâte feuilletée.* See also *Blitz puff pastry, reverse puff pastry,* and *demi-feuilletage.*

puff pastry dough See *puff pastry.*

pugliese (poo-'lyeh-she) A round, rustic Italian bread with a crunchy crust and soft, tender crumb, and with a big-hole structure and nutty flavor. The bread is from Apulia. It is a very wet dough traditionally made with durum flour, but if not available, may be substituted with only one-third the amount of semolina flour and the rest with either unbleached high-gluten flour or bread flour.

puit d'amour (pwee dah-more) A small hollowed-out shell of baked *puff pastry* that is filled with jam or vanilla *pastry cream.* It is dusted with confectioners' sugar. It is believed to be named after the 1843 opera of the same name.

pulled sugar A decorative sugar technique made by pouring a prepared sugar syrup onto a lightly oiled marble surface and moving it around and folding it over with a spatula until it is cool enough to be handled by hand. In order to get the best shine, it should be pulled as cold as possible. The cooled sugar mass is pulled out into long strands, twisted, brought back together, folded, and the process is repeated until it has a smooth, shiny appearance. It is important not to overpull the sugar or it will appear dull and crack. When the pulling is complete, the sugar is put under a heat lamp to keep warm while various objects such as flowers or ribbons are shaped. The pulled sugar pieces and unused sugar blocks are highly susceptible to moisture and should be stored in an airtight container in a cool, dry place. The unused sugar blocks may be reserved and re-used at a later time. See also *blown sugar.*

pullman loaf A long, narrow, rectangular loaf of bread. It was named after the inventor of the railroad Pullman car, George Mortimer Pullman, because the finished loaf resembles the long, narrow car. It gets its shape by being baked in a *pullman loaf pan,* which has a lid that slides over the top, forcing the dough to conform to the shape of the pan. The finished bread has a soft, even, golden-brown crust and tender white crumb. It is typically used for sandwiches, *canapés,* and *melba toast.*

P
p

pullman loaf pan See *pullman loaf.*

pulque ('pool-keh) A thick, milky white, slightly alcoholic Mexican drink that is made from the fermented juice of the agave plant. The drink dates back to the Aztecs, and is often flavored with chiles, nuts, fruits, spices, or herbs.

pullman loaf pan

Pulco A French citrus product with a strong lemon-lime flavor, used to flavor sauces, creams, and fillings.

pulse 1. A setting on a food processor or blender that rough chops the ingredients in stop-and-start action. 2. The dried seeds of legumes, including peas, beans, and lentils.

pulverize To reduce to a powder or dust by grinding, crushing, or pounding.

pummelo (puh-'mehl-oh) See *pomelo.*

pumpernickel ('puhm-puhr-nihk-uhl) A term that refers to both the coarsely ground flour made from the rye berry and the bread made from it. In the United States, pumpernickel bread is typically darkened with an artificial caramel color.

pumpernickel flour See *rye flour.*

pumpkin A large, round member of the gourd family with thick orange skin and a mildly sweet orange flesh. Although it is often referred to as a vegetable, it is actually a fruit. Pumpkins were a staple food of Native Americans, who introduced it to the colonists. The colonists used the flesh to make beer and soup, and toasted the seeds, also known as *pepitas,* to eat as a snack. *Pumpkin pie* was served at the first settler's Thanksgiving feast and this tradition remains today. Fresh pumpkins are available in the fall and winter, but canned puree is available year-round. In addition to pie, pumpkin puree is used to flavor *ice creams, mousses, custards, quickbreads,* and *cookies.*

pumpkin pie A traditional Thanksgiving pie with a bottom crust and a creamy filling of pureed pumpkin, sugar, eggs, cream or evaporated milk, and spices such as cinnamon, nutmeg, cloves, and ginger. It is often topped with whipped cream.

pumpkin seed See *pepita.*

pumpkin seed oil A pungent, viscous, army-green oil made from roasted pumpkin seeds. Owing to its strong flavor, it should be used sparingly or in combination with milder oils.

punch 1. A beverage that is a mixture of liquor, wine, fruit juices, and carbonated products. It may be drunk cold or warm and is typically served in a large glass decorative bowl called a *punch bowl.* 2. See "fold/punch," *12 Steps of Baking* appendix.

punch bowl A wide bowl made of glass, silver, silver plate, or other metal that holds several gallons of liquid. Used for serving punch; most commonly set up so that guests may serve themselves.

Punschtorte ('poon-shtor-tuh) The Austrian name for "punch cake," referring to a cake made by soaking the sponge layers in a punch-like rum syrup, filling it with apricot jam, and coating it in pink *fondant.*

punt The indentation in the bottom of a Champagne or wine bottle that allows for a strong handhold when pouring. It also catches the sediment and reinforces the bottle strength.

P
p

puree ('pyuh-ray) 1. To grind or mash a food until completely smooth. This may be accomplished with a blender, food processor, or sieve. 2. A fruit or vegetable that has been mashed to a fine, smooth consistency. Fruit purees are used extensively in the pastry shop to make sauces, sorbets, and as a flavoring agent in fillings, creams, and chocolates.

pure olive oil See *olive oil.*

pure vanilla See *vanilla.*

puri ('poor-ee) A deep-fried Indian *flatbread* made with *atta flour,* whole wheat flour, *ghee,* and sometimes spices such as cumin, turmeric, or black pepper. It is a popular street food and also served as an accompaniment to curries and chutneys.

putu ayu ('poo-too 'ah-yoo) An Indonesian confection that resembles a tiny Bundt cake. It is made from ground rice cake and dyed with the juice of *pandanus leaf.* The bottom is green and the top is a creamy white.

putu piring ('poo-too pehr-'reyng) A sweet steamed rice cake from Malaysia. These are made from coarse-grained rice and filled with chopped *palm sugar* before being steamed in a funnel-shaped mold. They are served hot with grated coconut.

pyramide cheese ('pih-rah-meed) A small French goat cheese covered with an edible, dark-gray vegetable ash. It is shaped like a pyramid and, depending on the aging process, has a texture that ranges from soft to crumbly and a flavor that ranges from mild to pungent. It pairs well with bread and fruit.

pyrolisis (pie-roh-'lihs-ihs) A process in bread baking that occurs when no steam is injected into the oven during the baking process. The dry atmosphere prohibits the starches from gelatinizing and results in a bread with a matte, dull crust.

P
p

Qq

qahweh bel habahan (kah-va behl hah-bah-hahn) A thick Egyptian coffee that is sweetened and flavored with cardamom. *Qahweh* is the Arabic word for coffee.

qalib (koo-lib) A wooden mold used in the Middle East, with small, deep engravings that make decorative impressions on bread and pastry dough.

qater (kah-tar) A Middle Eastern pastry syrup made with honey and sugar, used to soak pastries such as *maamoul* and *awwam*.

qt. The abbreviation for *quart*.

Quady A California winery that specializes in the production of dessert wines. They have been in operation since 1975. A few of their award-winning dessert wines include:

> **Electra** A light, delicate dessert wine with a crisp, floral flavor and hints of peach and melon. It is made from Orange Muscat grape juice and has an alcohol content of only 4%. It pairs well with strawberries, nectarines, peaches, or melons.

> **Elysium** Named for the Greek term for heaven, it is made from the Black Muscat grape. It has a rose-like aroma and litchi-like flavor. It pairs well with blue cheese, vanilla, dark chocolate, ice cream, and desserts containing red fruits such as strawberries and raspberries.

> **Essencia** Made from 100% Orange Muscat grapes, it has an aroma reminiscent of orange blossom and apricot, and a lingering refreshing aftertaste. The wine is lightly fortified to about 15% alcohol and aged for three months in French oak casks. It pairs well with chocolate and desserts containing almonds, peaches, apples, or apricots. It is also excellent for dipping biscotti, or as a flavoring agent in syrups, sauces, and beverages.

quaking pudding A British dessert of bread crumbs, cream, eggs, sugar, and spices that resembles a cross between a light sponge and a custard. It dates from the 17th century and its name refers to the fact that it wobbles or "quakes" when set.

Qualitaschäumwein ('kwooahl-it-ahs-shoim-vine) See *Sekt*.

quark (kwark) A soft, unripened cow's milk cheese from Austria, where it is known as *Topfen,* which means "pot cheese." The texture is somewhere between yogurt and cottage cheese.

quart A U.S. measurement of volume that is the equivalent of 32 fluid ounces or 946 ml. It is abbreviated in recipes as qt.

Quart de Chaume (qwahrt du shOm) A sweet white wine from Anjou, France.

quarter To slice a food item into four even parts.

quatre-quarts (kw'aht-reh kwahrt) A French rectangular sponge cake. It is rich in flavor, the equivalent of a *pound cake*. The name means "four of one quarter" because each of the four main ingredients (butter, sugar, flour, and eggs) is added in equal amounts.

Q
q

Queen Ann plum *See plum.*

queen of puddings A British dessert that consists of a baked custard flavored with lemon-vanilla and thickened with bread crumbs. Once set, it is spread with jam and topped with browned meringue.

queen of Sheba An airy French chocolate cake that is made with a mixture of flour and ground almonds and lightened with whipped egg whites. After baking, the center sinks slightly as it cools and it is served cold with crème anglaise in the center. Also known by its French name, *Reine de Saba.*

Queensland arrowroot See *canna.*

Queijadas (qwah-he-'hah-dahs) A small fresh cheesecake from Portugal, flavored with coconut, almonds, and cinnamon.

quenelle (kweh-'nehl) A small oval French dumpling, usually savory but sometimes a sweet item. It is shaped with two spoons. Its unique shape makes it useful as a garnish.

Queso ('kay-soh) The Spanish word for cheese. Some of the most popular Spanish cheeses are:

> **Añejo** (ahn-'yea-ho) An aged Mexican white cheese made from skimmed cow's or goat's milk. It has a dry, crumbly texture and slightly salty flavor.
>
> **Blanco** ('blahnk-koh) A white Mexican cheese similar to farmers cheese, with a mild, slightly salty taste. Also known as queso fresco.
>
> **De Cabra** ('kah-brah) A strong goat cheese from Chile, made from raw milk.
>
> **De Crema** ('crehm-mah) A rich cream cheese from Costa Rica.
>
> **De Mano** ('mahn-oh) A cow's milk curd cheese from Venezuela.
>
> **Del Pais** (pie-'eeze) A mild semi-soft Puerto Rican cheese made with cow's milk.
>
> **De Puna** ('poo-nah) A Puerto Rican cottage cheese made from skimmed cow's milk.
>
> **Requeson** (reh-'kway-sohn) A fresh, mild, curd-like cheese similar to ricotta. It is used in fillings and desserts.

queso de tuna ('kay-soh day 'too-nah) A sweet paste made from fermented *prickly pear* juice. It is used in the production of Mexican confections and desserts.

Quetsch (ketch) An Alsatian *eau-de-vie* made from a plum of the same name. The plum is also used to make tarts, compotes, and jams.

Quetzalcoatl Believed to have been a Toltec king who was also a mythological god, an important figure in the history of chocolate. His purpose was to bring cocoa seeds to humans and teach them how to cultivate cacao. When he left the capital, owing to political uprisings, Aztec astrologers predicted he would return in 1519; when Cortes arrived in 1519, Montezuma believed he was Quetzalcoatl and showered him with gifts, including a cacao plantation and *xocolatl.*

quiche (keesh) A French savory custard tart. It originated in Lothringen, Germany, which the French later renamed Lorraine. The word *quiche* derives from the German *kuchen,* which means "cake." The bottom crust was originally made from bread dough, but today it is made with a *short pastry dough* or *puff pastry.* The original quiche Lorraine is an open tart filled with eggs, cream, and smoked bacon; today, it also contains cheese. There are many ingredients that may be used to make quiche filling, including, vegetables, meats, and seafood.

quickbread A category of breads, muffins, scones, and biscuits that are quick to make because the batter or dough uses chemical leavening rather than yeast.

quicklime See *limestone.*

quick oats See *oats.*

quillet (qee-'leh) A small round *sponge cake* layered and decorated with butter-cream flavored with *orgeat syrup* and vanilla. It is named for the pastry cook who created it.

Quinalt strawberry (qee-n'ahlt strawberry) An everbearing strawberry variety that is large and sweet.

quince The fruit of the quince tree, a member of the rose family. The fruit resembles and tastes like a cross between an apple and a pear; its thin yellow skin encases a hard, bitter, tart cream-colored flesh. The tree has grown in the Mediterranean region for over 4,000 years. The ancient Romans referred to it as "golden  apple," and the flower was used to scent honey and perfume. It was also given as a symbol of love.

Owing to the fruit's high pectin content, it is used to make jams and preserves, but Europeans also cook quince for use in tarts, custards, and pies. It is available fresh or as a paste, and pairs well with aged cheeses.

quindin (qeen-d'ayn) A Brazilian custard-like dessert of coconut milk, sugar, and eggs.

quinine ('kwi-nine) An alkaloid derived from the bark of the cinchona tree, which is native to the mountainous regions of South and Central America. It has a bitter flavor and is primarily used to flavor *tonic water* and other beverages.

quinine water See *tonic water.*

quinoa (keen-wa) A cereal grain with a light, fluffy texture and mild nutty flavor. It resembles tiny clear balls and was revered by the Incas as "the mother of all grains." It is a staple of Peruvian cuisine, prized for its nutritional value because it is high in protein and contains all eight essential amino acids. It is also gluten-free and may be ground for use as flour or thickener in soups.

Q
q

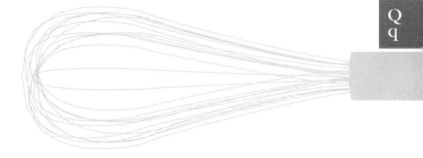

Rr

rabadi A rich dessert sauce from India, made by reducing milk until it is maple colored and has a honey-like consistency. It may be sweetened and topped with nuts and eaten as a pudding, or thinned with water or milk and served as a drink.

rabote (rah-'bot) A ball-shaped French pastry that consists of an apple or pear enclosed in *puff pastry* and baked, then served warm or cold.

Racine Danish kringle See *kringle*.

rack oven See *oven*.

radiation heat An indirect method of heating. It may be done through the transfer of heat to the surface of a product via appliances such as toasters, broilers, heat lamps, and conventional ovens; or with a microwave, which transfers the heat to the interior of a product. Dark-colored and dull surfaces radiate more heat than light-colored or shiny surfaces.

rahat loukoum (rah-hat loo-koom) See *Turkish delight*.

raisin ('ray-zihn) A grape that has been dried, either by the sun or by hot air. California produces about half of the world's raisin supply. Raisins added to baked goods will retard staling because the high sugar content enables them to retain moisture. Soaking raisins prior to adding them to recipes is beneficial because it adds flavor and rehydrates them. In addition, raisins to be added to a frozen product such as ice cream should be first soaked in alcohol to prevent them from freezing rock-hard. The type of raisin depends on the grape used; varieties are as follows:

> **Dark** A sweet, brownish-black raisin produced from the Thomson Seedless grape. It is the most common variety and is sun-dried, which gives it its dark color and shriveled appearance.
>
> **Golden** Moist, plump raisin made from the Thompson Seedless grape treated with sulfur dioxide to prevent it from turning dark. It has a pale, golden-yellow color and is air-dried, which produces a plumper, moister raisin. It is sweet and is used in desserts and breads for both its color and its flavor. Thompson golden seedless raisins are known as *Sultanas* in Britain.

raita (rah-'ee-tah) A yogurt dip from India, served with street foods such as *puri* and *chapatti*.

raki ('rah-kee) A Turkish brandy distilled from grapes, grains, or plums and flavored with anise.

rakott palascinta (rah-'koht pah-la-'skeen-tah) A Hungarian dessert of three layers of crepes, filled with alternating layers of (1) grated chocolate, chopped walnuts, and vanilla; (2) apricot jam and brandy; and (3) curd cheese, vanilla sugar, eggs, and lemon zest. The last crepe is put on the top, covered with meringue, and baked. The dessert is served warm.

rambutan ('rahm-boo-than) A small tropical fruit related to the lychee, native to Malaysia. It grows all over Southeast Asia, and is recognized by its thick, reddish-orange leathery rind covered with bristly strands that look like hair. The firm, juicy, grape-like edible pulp is translucent white and contains a single pit. The flesh has a sweet, slightly acidic flavor. Available October to May.

ramekin ('rahm-uh-kihn) An individual, straight-sided baking dish, made of either porcelain or earthenware. It is used to bake custards, warm desserts such as cobblers or soufflés, or chilled desserts. It is available in 2-, 4-, and 5-ounce (55, 115, 140g) sizes.

rancid The deteriorated condition of a food item caused by the decomposition of fats that results from a breakdown of fatty acids. A food turns rancid as a result of oxidation, light, heat, metal exposure, or enzymes.

Ranier cherry See *cherry*.

Rapadura See *sugar*.

rapeseed oil Another name for *canola oil*.

råröda (rah-'roor-dah) A Scandinavian spread made with gently crushed and lightly sweetened raw *lingonberries*. It makes a nice accompaniment to bread, crepes, waffles and desserts.

ras el hanout ('ray-sehl-hahn-o-oot) The Moroccan term for "head of shop," referring to a shop owner's mix of spices, which may include cinnamon, ginger, anise, nutmeg, peppercorns, cardamom, lavender, rose petals, or anything else that makes it their unique spice blend.

rasgulla A Bengalese dessert that consists of a mixture of sweetened *chenna* cheese and *semolina*, formed into small balls, boiled, and soaked in light sugar syrup. Considered by some to be the national dessert of India.

ras malai An Indian dessert of delicate cheese balls simmered in syrup until they resemble dumplings. Once cooled, they are topped with toasted pistachios and almonds, and served with a thick cream sauce.

raspberry See *berry*.

raspberry liqueur See *Chambord* and *framboise*.

ratafia 1. A *liqueur* made from an infusion of apricot or peach kernels and bitter almonds. The name is believed to be from the Latin *rata fiat,* which means "let the deal be done," because it was used as a toast when a treaty or settlement was ratified. 2. A type of almond-flavored *macaroon*.

ratafia essence A flavoring agent made from bitter almonds, used to flavor pastries, confections, and desserts.

raw milk Unpasteurized milk. It is believed to have a higher nutritional value than pasteurized milk because the natural vitamins and enzymes have not been destroyed by the heat of pasteurization. It can be found in health food stores, but may contain harmful bacteria.

raw sugar See *sugar*.

R
r

RDA The acronym for Recommended Dietary Allowance, referring to the U.S. government's recommendations of how much protein, vitamins, and minerals people should consume to maintain healthy living.

reblochon cheese ('reh-bluh-shohn) An uncooked French cow's milk cheese with a delicate flavor and creamy, soft texture. It pairs well with fruit.

reconstitute (rhee-'kohn-stih-toot) To rehydrate a dried product, usually through the addition of milk or water.

red banana See *banana*.

red bean paste A sweet paste that is made from *azuki* beans that have been cooked.

red currant See *currant*.

red date See *jujube*.

Red Delicious apple See *apple*.

Red Electra See *Quady*.

Redhaven peach See *peach*.

red rice vinegar See *vinegar*.

red shiso See *shiso*.

Red Spanish pineapple See *pineapple*.

reduce To cook a liquid until the evaporation reduces the volume and thickens the product.

reduced-fat milk See *milk*.

red velvet cake An American cake of rich chocolate cake layers that have been dyed bright red with food coloring; the layers are sandwiched with sweet cream cheese frosting. It is particularly popular in the South.

red wine vinegar See *vinegar*.

refined oils See *oil*.

refiner A machine that uses rollers to reduce the particle size of mixtures such as *gianduja* and *marzipan*.

refractometer A tool used to measure *Brix*. It is more expensive than a *hydrometer,* but faster and easier to use.

refrigerator cookie See *cookie*.

Rehrüken ('reh-ruhr-kehn) The Austrian word for "deer," referring to a delicate chocolate-almond cake baked in a mold that resembles a saddle of venison. It is covered in chocolate glaze and garnished with toasted almonds that are meant to look like the fat on a real roast of venison.

Reims biscuit (rayms biscuit) A small, light crunchy French biscuit, created in the 18th century as a way to use the remaining heat of an oven after baking bread. The original biscuit was white and heavily dusted with confectioners' sugar, but was later colored pink and flavored with vanilla. They pair well with Champagne.

Reineclaude plum ('rehn-eh-clod-eh plum) See *plum, greengage*.

Reine de Saba ('rehn-eh deh zah-bah) See *queen of Sheba*.

Reinette ('reh-neh) A variety of French apple that has a dull green skin and slightly dry, sharp flavor.

religieuse (rehl-li-zhoos) The French word for "nun," referring to a pastry of two *pâte à choux* puffs, one larger and one smaller, that are filled with a flavored *pastry cream* and glazed with *fondant* of the same flavor. The smaller choux is attached to the top of the larger choux and decorated with *buttercream* of the same flavor. The pastry was created in 1856 by a French pâtissier named Frascati. The original version was made with chocolate buttercream and white fondant, in an effort to create a pastry that resembled a nun in her habit.

rennet ('rehn-net) A coagulating enzyme obtained from the stomach lining of a young animal, usually a calf. It contains an enzyme called *rennin,* which causes the milk to curdle. It is used to make *cheese* and *junket,* and is available in tablet or powdered form. A form of vegetable rennet is also available to make kosher and vegetarian cheeses, which comes from plant enzymes that have similar coagulating effects.

rennin See *rennet.*

rest See *12 Steps of Baking* appendix.

retard To slow down the yeast fermentation in a bread dough by placing the product in a *retarder* or refrigerator. This gives the baker flexibility in the production schedule and also the ability to change the flavor and aroma of the bread. For example, fermenting *levain* in a retarder overnight increases the acidity of the bread, affecting the taste.

retarder A piece of bread equipment that resembles an upright refrigerator and is used to *retard* doughs. It is often available with a humidity control feature as well as a retarder/proofer combination. This electronic device allows the baker to control the temperature and time.

retsina (reht-'see-nah) A Greek wine flavored with pine tree resin, which gives it a distinctive turpentine flavor. It has been made for over 3,000 years, and is available in either white or rosé; it should be served very cold.

revani (rey-vah-ne) A Greek semolina cake that is soaked in sugar syrup flavored with orange flower water, almond extract, and lemon zest.

reverse puff pastry A technique for making *puff pastry dough,* whereby the butter encloses the dough rather than the dough enclosing the butter. Although it is more difficult to prepare, it can be made and baked without a final rest; also, it shrinks less than classic puff pastry.

reverse shell See *shell.*

rheology A variety of tests performed on a sample of flour in order to measure its strength and baking ability.

Rhode Island greening apple See *apple.*

rhubarb ('roo-bahrb) The edible stems of a leafy vegetable in the buckwheat family. The leaves are toxic, owing to their high level of oxalic acid, so only the pinkish-red stalks are used. When cooked, rhubarb turns soft and stringy but its tart flavor is often paired with strawberries and ginger in pie fillings. Available early winter to early summer. Also known as *pie plant.*

rhubarb relish A condiment made of cooked rhubarb, onions, brown sugar, salt, pepper, cinnamon, and cloves. It makes an excellent spread for breads.

ribbon A culinary term referring to the thickness of a batter after it has been cooked or whipped. When the spoon or whip is lifted up and moved from side to

R
r

side, the batter falls in "ribbons." Also, when a product is whipped to a ribbon-like consistency, it is said to have reached the *ribbon stage*.

ribbon sponge See *jaconde*.

ribbon stage See *ribbon*.

Ribier grape See *grape*.

rice The edible seed of a cereal grass, a major food staple for over half of the world's population. There are many varieties, classified as short-grain, medium-grain, or long-grain. *Short-grain rice* has fat, white, roundish grains that have a high starch content. It is preferred in Asia because, when cooked, the grains stick together, making it easy to handle with chopsticks. *Medium-grain rice* is shorter and plumper, but not as starchy. It produces a fluffy product, but has a tendency to become sticky when cool. *Long-grain rice* is four times as long as it is wide and produces a fluffy product whose grains separate easily. White rice is the most commonly used long-grain rice.

> **Arborio** An Italian rice that is shorter and fatter than regular short-grain rice. Its high starch content renders a creamy texture and it is traditionally used to make risotto.
>
> **Basmati** An aromatic, nutty, long-grain rice from India.
>
> **Brown** Made from the entire grain, with only the inedible outer husk removed. It has a chewy texture and nutty flavor. It is more nutritious than white rice, but the high fiber content shortens its shelf life.
>
> **Carolina** A popular American long-grained rice that was first planted in North Carolina in the late 17th century. It is now cultivated in Texas, California, Louisiana, and Arkansas.
>
> **Converted/Parboiled** More commonly known by the brand name Uncle Ben's, the grain is treated with a pressurized steam that takes the vitamins and minerals out of the bran and concentrates them in the kernel. This process also gelatinizes the starches, which yield a fluffy, separated cooked product.
>
> **Flaked** Short-grain rice that has been flattened, parboiled, and sometimes tinted green. It is used in Asia to make puddings and other sweets.
>
> **Glutinous** A short-grain rice that has a high starch content.
>
> **Instant/Minute/Quick** Rice that has been fully or partially cooked before being dehydrated and packaged.
>
> **Jasmine** A fragrant long-grained rice from Thailand.
>
> **Mochi** A sweet, short-grained, glutinous rice from Japan.
>
> **Sticky** A short-grained rice from Asia that is sticky when cooked. It is used extensively in Southeast Asian pastries, desserts, and confections. In Thailand, a popular dessert called sticky rice with mango is made by cooking the rice in coconut milk and serving it with sliced fresh mango.
>
> **White** Long- or medium-grained rice that is whitened by removing the husk, bran, and germ of the kernel. This process strips it of its nutritional value but increases its shelf life. It also gelatinizes the starch in the grain, which produces a fluffy, separated rice when cooked. It is often enriched with iron, calcium, and vitamins to compensate for the loss of nutrients during the whitening process.
>
> **Wild** Mistakenly referred to as a rice, this nutty-flavored, chewy textured product is the long-grain seed of a marsh grass.

rice bran The outer layer of the rice kernel, which is high in soluble fiber and believed to lower cholesterol.

rice flour See *flour.*

Rice Krispies A breakfast cereal produced by the Kellog Company since 1928. The flakes are made of rice grain that is cooked, dried, and toasted. When the cereal is mixed with milk, the thin walls collapse and the famous "Snap, Crackle and Pop" can be heard.

Rice Krispie treats An American snack of Rice Krispies, melted butter or margarine, melted marshmallows, and vanilla, shaped into a bar cookie and baked. They were invented in the 1930s by a Kellogg's employee named Mildred Day, as a way to raise money for the Campfire Girls organization.

rice paper A thin, edible, translucent paper made from finely ground rice flour or the pith of the Chinese rice-paper plant and water. It is available in different sizes and shapes, including round, square, and rectangular. The flavorless sheets are used as separators for stacked tiers of wedding cakes, as baking liners, as wrappers that may be deep-fried, and for decorative purposes because they can be painted or printed on with edible dyes.

rice pudding A creamy, custard-like dessert made by slow-cooking rice in milk or another liquid and flavoring it with spices, vanilla, chocolate, nuts, fruit, or sugar. Virtually every country has some version of this popular dessert.

ricer A kitchen tool that reduces food to rice-like particles. The food is placed in a metal hopper and is pushed through a grated die with a plunger. It is often used to make mashed potatoes and other items where creaminess is desired.

rice starch A widely used starch in the commercial food industry, due to its ability to vary gelatinization temperatures, produce desireable texture, and stabilize. It can replace fat or give sheen to a sauce. The starch is extracted from white rice that has been steeped in a caustic soda solution to separate the rice starch from the protein. See also *starch.*

rice syrup A healthy sweetener made from rice starch. It has a brownish-tan color and distinct flavor.

rice wine A sweet, low-alcohol Asian wine made from fermented rice. The most well known is Japanese sake.

rice wine vinegar See *vinegar.*

ricotta (rih-'kaht-tuh) The Italian word for "recooked," referring to a rich, fresh, white Italian cheese that has a slightly grainy texture and moist, slightly sweet flavor. It was originally made by recooking the *whey* that is drained off while making other cheeses such as *provolone* and *mozzarella.* Today, it is made with a combination of whey and whole or skim cow's milk. In other countries it may also be made from sheep or water buffalo milk, which gives it a richer flavor. It is used as an ingredient in many classic Italian desserts such as *cassata,* and *cannolis.* It may also be used in *cheesecakes* or sweetened and served with fruit for dessert.

R
r

Riesling ('reez-ling) A white wine made from the Reisling grape, native to Germany. It ranges from dry to very sweet and is characterized by a floral aroma and spicy, fruity taste. It is considered by many wine experts to be the most noble white grape variety in the world. In the United States, Rieslings are sometimes referred to as *Johannisberg Riesling,* after the German city of Johannisberg, which is famous for its Riesling, and are primarily produced in California. The very sweet German Rieslings can contain up to 30% residual sugar and are referred to as *Trockenbeerenauslese.* They make excellent dessert wines and pair well with fruit and nuts.

Ricó Jancsi A chocolate pastry from Hungary that consists of two layers of rich chocolate cake filled with a whipped orange-flavored chocolate *ganache* and covered in chocolate ganache. It is named after a famed 19th-century gypsy violinist who was said to have broken many hearts.

rigodin (ree-go-'dayn) A pudding from Burgundy, France. It is made by combining milk-soaked brioche pieces with chopped walnuts, hazelnuts, and cinnamon. After baking it is traditionally served warm with fruit compote.

rijsttafel ('rah-jahst-fuhl) The Indonesian word for "rice table" that refers to a lavish feast with multiple dishes and courses.

rind The outer skin of citrus fruits. See also *zest*.

rioler (re-yoh-lee) A French culinary term that refers to arranging straight or fluted strips of dough on top of a pastry item to form a crisscross pattern or lattice design.

Rio Oso Gem peach See *peach*.

rissole (rih-sohl) A sweet or savory pastry that resembles a turnover. It may be filled with cooked fruit, cream, or jam and either baked or fried. There are many regional variations around the world; it is a popular snack in Australia, Brazil, and Indonesia.

riz à la Conde A ring-shaped chilled rice pudding set with gelatin and filled with poached apricots, served with Kirsch-flavored fruit sauce. It is one of many dishes that are named in honor of the famed French general, Conde.

riz à l'imperatrice (ree ah lahn-pehr-ah-trees) French for "as the empress likes it," referring to a rich rice pudding made with whipped cream, candied fruit, and vanilla custard.

rizcous (reez-koos) A California product made from broken brown rice grains, which is no longer available in the United States.

Robusta coffee bean See *coffee*.

rocher (roh-shay) A French confection made by baking slivered almonds in a sugar mixture until crystallized. Once cooled, they are broken into small, irregular pieces and thinly coated with dark chocolate. The name derives from the French word for "rock" because the finished product resembles small rocks.

rock and rye An American liqueur based on rye whisky flavored with citrus and bottled with a chunk of rock candy in it.

rock bun A spicy, cookie-like British cake packed with coarsely chopped dried fruit and baked in a small mound, which gives it a rock-like appearance.

rock candy A sweet, hard candy that is made by slowly evaporating a concentrated sugar syrup until it crystallizes into chunks. It is typically formed around small wooden sticks and dipped into cocktails, coffee, or tea to sweeten the beverage.

rock salt See *salt*.

rock sugar See *sugar*.

rocky road A bumpy looking candy that consists of miniature marshmallows, nuts, and chocolate pieces. It is also a popular flavor combination for ice cream.

rodgrod ('rahd-grod) A Norwegian pudding made by cooking crushed berries and fruit with starch until thick. Once set, it is served chilled with whipped cream.

rolled cookie See *cookie*.

rolled fondant A wedding cake icing with a pliable, doughlike consistency, made from confectioners' sugar, corn syrup, glycerine, and gelatin. It is rolled out with confectioners' sugar and draped over a cake to create a smooth surface. It is also used to make swags, bows, flowers, and other decorative items; although it is white, it may be tinted. Although it can be made by hand, it is labor-intensive, so it is usually purchased from specialty vendors in bulk. Fondant must be stored in a cool, dry area or it will dry out and crack; if this happens, it may be reconstituted with a little water.

rolled-in dough See *laminated dough*.

rolled oats See *oats*.

rolling pin A long wood, plastic, brass, glass, marble, or porcelain tool used to roll out dough. Rolling pins are available in different sizes, and wood is the most popular. Some pins contain a hollow tube, meant to be filled with ice water in order to keep the dough cool during rolling. There are several types of rolling pins, including:

> **American** A sturdy, heavyweight pin with a handle on each side.
>
> **Basketweave** A plastic pin with a decorative pattern. It is typically rolled over *fondant* or *marzipan* to produce a basketweave effect. Different varieties produce deeper and more defined patterns than others.
>
> **French** A thinner version of the American pin, with no handles.
>
> **Marzipan** A decorative pin used to create a checkered design or a pattern of fine parallel lines.
>
> **Pizza** A one-handled pin that requires only one hand to roll the dough so the other is free to turn the dough as it is rolled out.
>
> **Springerle** A German rolling pin with an etched design that imprints the dough as it is being rolled.
>
> **Tapered** A pin with tapered ends, popular for rolling out circles of dough since the dough can be rotated easily during rolling.
>
> **Tarla** A hardwood pin covered with a thin sheet of copper, and with short knobbed handles. It maintains coolness when rolling out dough with a high butter content and warm products such as *nougatine*.
>
> **Tutové** A heavy-duty French rolling pin made of hardwood or plastic, used to distribute butter evenly between layers of dough.

roll out To flatten a piece of dough with a *rolling pin* until it is a smooth, even layer, extensively for pie and tart doughs.

roly-poly A British steamed pudding made by filling a suet pastry crust with jam and dried fruits, and then rolling it into a cylinder with a moist cloth.

Roman fennel See *fennel*.

Rome Beauty apple See *apple*.

rooibos ('roy-boss) The South African word for "red bush," referring to a shrubby legume used to make a popular tisane called *African Red tea*.

root beer A soft drink made with root beer extract, carbonated water, and other flavored syrups. It was created by a Philadelphia pharmacist named Charles Hires, in the mid-1800s, and the original version was alcoholic and made by fermenting a blend of sugar, yeast, sassafras root, cherry tree bark, licorice root, and spices.

root starch See *starch*.

Roquefort cheese ('rohk-furt) A pungent French ewe's milk blue cheese with a rich, crumbly texture and tangy, slightly salty flavor. It is characterized by its creamy white color streaked with veins of blue mold. European law dictates that only cheeses aged in the Cambalou caves of Roquefort may be called such. Considered to be the king of cheeses, it is used in savory breads and pairs well with dessert wines.

R
r

Rosalind A sweet confection of two light *sponge cakes* sandwiched together with raspberry jam and coated with a pink cherry-flavored *fondant*. Named in honor of the Shakespearian character Rosalind in the play *As You Like It*.

rosé (roh-'zay) 1. A highly regarded style of Champagne made with a blend of Chardonnay and Pinot Noir grapes. Depending on the percentages of each grape used, the color can range from light pink to coppery salmon, and the body from light and delicate to full and rich. The flavor profile ranges from dry to sweet, with a variety of overtones including fruit, honey, vanilla, and flowers. See also *Champagne*. 2. A pink-hued, nonsparkling wine that ranges from dry to sweet.

rose hip The reddish-orange berry-like fruit of the wild, rugosa, or dog rose. It is used to make jam, syrup, and tea. Rose hips are high in vitamin C; they may be dried and ground into a powder. They are sold in health food stores.

rosemary An aromatic herb native to the Mediterranean but now cultivated throughout Europe and the United States. It is a member of the mint family; it has needle-like evergreen leaves that have a pungent piney flavor. Rosemary is a popular flavoring for breads and pairs well with lemon. It is available fresh, dried, or ground and should be used sparingly owing to its strong taste.

rose nail A small, flat metal disc attached to a thin, screwlike handle, used to make *buttercream roses*. See also *flower nail*.

rosette (roh-'sette) 1. A decorative swirl piped on a cake with a *star tip*. Whipped cream, *buttercream,* or *ganache* may be used. It can also be created with a firm *cookie dough*, which will retain its shape after baking. 2. See *rosette iron*.

rosette iron An L-shaped iron rod with interchangeable metal plates, used to make small, deep-fried cookies from Sweden. The iron comes in various shapes, including hearts, butterflies, snowflakes, stars, and flowers. The iron is dipped into a thin, sweet batter and then dipped into hot oil and the dough fried until golden brown. The rosette cookies are then drained on paper towels and sprinkled with sugar. The cookies are known as *sockerstruvor* in Swedish.

rosewater A highly perfumed distilled liquid made from rose petals. It is used as a flavoring agent in Middle Eastern confections.

rosé wine A light-bodied and slightly sweet rose-colored wine, also known as *blush wine* in the United States.

rotating oven See *oven*.

Rothschild The name given to dishes created in honor of the Rothschilds, a famous banking family. One of the most well known is *Rothschild soufflé,* created by Antoine Carême.

Rothschild soufflé A soufflé containing candied fruits soaked in *Goldwasser;* created by Antoine Carême in honor of the famous Rothschild banking family.

roti ('roh-tee) A round, flat unleavened bread from India. It is usually made with whole wheat flour and baked on an iron griddle called a *tava*. Depending on the region, there are many variations of roti, each with its own name. In Sri Lanka, roti are made with white flour and coconuts, and eaten as a snack with coffee, tea, or fresh juice. In Rajasthani, they are called *batia roti* and filled with salt, cumin, pepper, and fresh coriander, and spread with *ghee* before baking. In northwestern India, they are called *besan roti* and made with chickpea flour; they are thin, have a pale-yellow color, and are flavored with onion and cumin seeds. There is also a *roti jala,* which is made from a thin batter and resembles a lacy, layered pancake. In Thailand (maida paratha), Malaysia (*roti canai*), and Singapore (*roti prata*), the bread is typically drizzled with condensed milk and eaten as a warm snack. Roti are also popular in the West Indies, where there are many variations as well.

roti canai See *roti.*

roti jala See *roti.*

roti prata See *roti.*

roughage See *fiber.*

roulade (roo-'lahd) The French word for "roll," referring to a sweet or savory item that has been stuffed and rolled. In pastry, it is typically a thin *sponge cake* that is filled with jam or cream and rolled into a cylinder. It is similar to a *Swiss roll* but richer and smaller in circumference.

roxédes (rok-'say-dees) An unbaked Greek *marzipan*-type delicacy made with grated white almonds, coarse sugar, lightly beaten egg whites, and flower essence. It is formed in various shapes and served at weddings and other special occasions.

Rowntree's Chocolate Crisp See *Kit-Kat.*

Royal Anne cherry See *cherry.*

royal icing A smooth, glossy white icing made from sifted confectioners' sugar, egg whites, and a few drops of lemon juice. *Glycerin* is sometimes added to prevent the icing from becoming too hard. It is used as a decorating medium on cakes, particularly wedding cakes, and may be tinted with food coloring.

royal shortbread See *shortbread.*

rubber spatula A hand tool used for scraping batter or other mixtures from a bowl, or for mixing or folding ingredients. Spatulas come in different shapes and sizes, but all are flexible pieces of rubber attached to a short handle. It is recommended to use heat-resistant ones as they do not melt or absorb odors.

Ruby Port See *Port.*

rugalach ('ruhg-uh-luh) A rich, crescent-shaped, bite-size Jewish pastry made with a *cream cheese dough* and filled with jam, nuts, fruits, poppy seeds, cinnamon, chocolate, or raisins.

ruisleipa (roo-ee-slee-pah) A lightly yeasted Finnish rye *flatbread.* They may be eaten fresh and soft and dry and crisp. Traditionally they are made in large batches only a few times a year. A hole is cut out of each center so they can be hung high on poles or cords to dry.

R
r

rum A distilled spirit made from fermented sugarcane juice. The majority of rum is produced in the Caribbean. Depending on type, it is aged from one to 10 years and ranges in proof from 60 to 151. There are several varieties, including light, dark, spiced, or flavored. *Jamaican rum* refers to any dark rum from that region. *Demerara rum* is the strongest and darkest rum, made from sugarcane that grows along the Demerra River in Guyana. Rum is used as a flavoring in many desserts and confections.

rum butter A traditional hard sauce consisting of a mixture of unsalted butter, sugar, and rum, served with *Christmas pudding* in Britain.

Rumtopf (rhoom-tahpf) The German word for "rum pot," referring to a German dessert made by mixing various fruits, sugar, and rum and aging it in a stoneware or glazed pottery pot with a lid. It is stored in a cool, dry place for several months until the fruit is fully ripe and still firm, then served with whipped cream, ice cream, or custard.

run-out A decorative garnish made from *royal icing.* The design is placed under a sheet of parchment paper and outlined with a thick layer of royal icing. Once hardened, a thin royal icing is flooded in. The result is a smooth, slightly raised design that is used as a two-dimensional garnish on wedding cakes and other confections. This technique can also be used with chocolate. Also known as *floodwork.*

rusk (ruhsk) A thick or thin slice of yeast bread that has been rebaked until dry, crisp, and golden brown. It may be plain, sweetened, or flavored with nuts, dried fruits, or spices. A European snack, the plain version is known as *Zwieback* in Germany.

Russian tea cake See *Mexican wedding cookie.*

rye bread A dense, strong-flavored bread made from a *rye dough* that contains a high percentage of rye flour. The bread may be light or dark, and is often made with a sour starter.

rye dough Used in the production of *rye bread,* it consists of clear flour, rye flour or rye sour dough starter, yeast, and salt. Many rye doughs contain molasses for flavor and color and are garnished with caraway seeds.

rye flour A low-gluten flour milled from the grain of hardy rye cereal grass. Although it contains a similar amount of protein as wheat flour, it is low in *glutenin* and high in *pentosan gums,* which interfere with its gluten-forming ability. The high gum content helps provide structure, but also causes it to absorb large amounts of water, which can make the dough gummy and sticky. Wheat flour is usually added to compensate for the gluten deficiency. There are various types of rye flour, which include:

Dark Produced from the outer layer of the endosperm.

Medium Produced from whole rye grain with the bran removed.

Light or White Produced from the center of the rye endosperm.

Pumpernickel A coarse grade of rye meal that is ground from the whole kernel.

R
r

Ss

sabayon ('sah-bah-yohn) See *zabaglione.*

sablé (sah-blay) The French word for "sand," referring to a cookie that consists of butter, flour, sugar, and sometimes egg yolks, and with a light, crumbly texture. These are made in different sizes and shapes but are typically round with a fluted edge. They can be flavored with citrus zest or nuts and may be dipped in chocolate or sandwiched together with jam. They are also popular as a base for fruit tarts and other desserts.

sablé biscuit Another name for *sablé.*

Sabra liqueur ('sah-bruh) An Israeli liqueur flavored with chocolate and orange.

saccharide See *monosaccharide* and *disaccharide.*

saccharin ('sak-uh-rihn) An artificial sweetener. It is 300 times sweeter than sugar and lower in calories. It was discovered in 1879 by scientists at John Hopkins University and is the sweetener used in Sweet'N Low. Although it is used primarily as a sweetener in commercially processed foods and beverages, its composition does not lend itself well to baking because it does not provide the same volume, tenderness, and browning capabilities of sugar. When used in large amounts or heated, it is also said to have a bitter aftertaste.

saccharometer See *thermometer.*

saccharomyces cerevisiae (sahk-kah-'ro-mee-sees she-reh'vee-see-ah) The strain of yeast most commonly used in bread baking because of its rapid gas production.

saccharomyces exiguous (sahk-kah-'ro-mee-sees ek-'see-goo-oos) A strain of wild yeast that thrives in acidic environments and is thereby important for making sourdough bread.

Sachertorte ('sha-kuhr-tohrt) A Viennese torte created in 1832 by Franz Sacher, the pastry chef to Prince Metternich. It consists of a rich chocolate cake that is either coated or filled with apricot jam. The torte is covered completely in a rich chocolate glaze and the word "Sacher" is written on top with tempered chocolate. It is served with a whipped cream. In the 1960s, a great rivalry developed between the Hotel Sacher and Demel's pastry shop in Vienna, when both claimed to possess the original recipe passed down from Franz Sacher's descendants. The six-year court battle resulted in favor of the Hotel Sacher, but Demels continues to serve his version (torte is covered not filled with jam and then glazed) and calls it "Ur Sacher," meaning "Original Sacher."

sacristain (sah-kree-'stay) A small French pastry made by twisting a thin strip of puff pastry and dusting it with sugar and chopped almonds. It is served as a tea biscuit.

SAF See *yeast.*

safflower oil A colorless, flavorless, cholesterol-free oil pressed from safflower seeds. It is a good choice for deep-frying because it has a high *smoke point;* it is also popular for salad dressings because it does not solidify when chilled. It can be substituted with other vegetable oils such as canola, sunflower, or corn.

saffron ('saf-rohn) The thread-like stigmas of a small purple crocus plant. It is the most expensive spice in the world. The bright yellowish-orange threads are harvested from plants that produce only three stigmas each, which must be hand-picked and dried. It takes over 75,000 flowers to produce 1 pound (455 g) of saffron, or approximately 14,000 stigmas for 1 ounce (30 g) of saffron. Saffron has been used since ancient times to flavor and color food and beverages, and has a pungent taste and aromatic fragrance. It is recommended to buy the fresh threads, as ground saffron looses its flavor and aroma quickly and may also be adulterated with yellow or orange food coloring.

safra The Arabic term for "yellow," referring to a semolina-date cake that is soaked in honey syrup and served as a snack with tea or coffee.

Saga blue cheese A *double-cream cheese* from Denmark. It has a rich, mild flavor and fine blue veins; its soft white rind is edible.

sage (sayj) An aromatic herb native to the Mediterranean region and a member of the mint family. The name derives from the Latin *salvus,* meaning "safe" because it is believed to have healing powers. The oval, grayish-green leaves have a pungent, slightly bitter flavor with a hint of mint. There is also a popular variety called *pineapple sage,* which has an intensely sweet pineapple aroma.

sago ('say-goh) A starch extracted from the pith of the sago palm. It is available as a flour, meal, or in pearl form, similar to *tapioca.* It is used as a thickener for puddings and fillings, particularly in the South Pacific and Asia.

Saint André cheese (san ohn-'dray) A very rich *triple-cream cheese* with a mild, mellow flavor.

Saint-Honoré See *gâteau Saint-Honoré.*

Saint John's bread See *carob.*

sakamai See *sake.*

sake ('sah-kee, 'sah-kay) A Japanese alcoholic beverage made from steamed fermented rice that is filtered, heated, and aged. Specific rice varieties are used, such as *sakamai* and *yamada nishiki,* and each type yields specific flavor profiles. It generally has an alcohol content of 12 to 17% and is used for drinking, cooking, and flavoring sauces, marinades, and desserts.

salamander ('sal-uh-man-duhr) 1. A gas-fired broiler whose heat source is on top, used to quickly brown or caramelize foods such as *meringue* or sugar. 2. A hand-held iron disk attached to a long metal shaft with a wooden or metal handle; the disc is held over an open flame until it is very hot and then placed on top of an item to be caramelized or browned.

salambô (sah-lahm-'bo) A small, round French pastry of *choux pastry* filled with a Kirsch-flavored *pastry cream,* dipped in green *fondant,* and dusted with chocolate sprinkles. It was created in the late 19th century in honor of a character in an opera.

Sally Lunn A rich, sweet, yeast-risen British bun, split open and served warm during tea time, spread with butter or *clotted cream.* The origin of the bun is debated, but they are said to be named after the creator, a woman from Bath who produced them in her bakery during the 18th century. Another version is that the small, round brioche-like bread is named after a similar Alsatian bun called *solilmeme.* Lastly, some believe the name derives from the French *sol et lune,* which means "sun and moon" and refers to the round shape of the bun.

salmonella (sahl-muh-'nehl-uh) A food-borne illness caused by a strain of *Salmonella* bacteria that is present in contaminated water, poultry, and fresh eggs.

It is imperative to practice safe food handling to prevent the illness. In pastry, it is particularly important when working with fresh eggs in the production of ice cream and other pastry products.

salt A seasoning derived from seawater or rock layers of salt laid down eons ago by oceans. It is a crucial ingredient in cooking and baking, providing many functions, which include enhancing the flavors of food and baked goods, intensifying and setting colors in cooked green vegetables, retarding yeast development, strengthening gluten structure, aiding in crust coloring, preserving flavor and color of flour, browning, and preventing spoilage owing to its ability to draw moisture out of food. It is commercially produced by solar evaporation, rock salt mining, or solution mining. Solar evaporation produces solar salt, which is coarser than other varieties and is made by using the heat of the sun to evaporate the water from the ocean or inland salt lakes. Rock salt mining involves bringing the salt to the surface from salt domes or underground salt mines, and crushing it to the desired coarseness. Solution mining forces water through a pipe into an underground salt mine and pumps the brine to the surface, where it is purified and dehydrated into granular form. The United States is the world's largest producer of salt; the most common types are as follows:

Celtic A natural, hand-harvested sea salt made through solar evaporation. It has a mild, sweet-salty flavor and is named after the ancient Celtic tradition once used to harvest the salt from the Atlantic marshes of Brittany, France.

Citric Salt extracted from acidic fruits such as limes and lemons. Also known as *sour salt*.

Curing A mixture of 94% salt and 6% sodium nitrate, which is often colored pink. It is used primarily for curing charcuterie items.

Fleur de Sel A highly regarded sea salt obtained from the very top of the ocean surface off the Brittany coast of France.

Fleur de Sel de Carmargue The most esteemed of all sea salts, hand-panned from the seawater that is pumped across the Carmargue marshes, in southern France.

Iodized Table salt that has had iodine added to it.

Korean yellow A salt with a moist, medium-coarse grain that is gray in color, with a slightly bitter aftertaste.

Kosher A pure mined additive-free coarse-grained salt. It dissolves readily and has a crisp, clean taste. It is used for its flaked rather than granulated form, which allows for a more even distribution over food. It is also used by people who observe strict Jewish dietary guidelines (see *kosher*). Also known as *coarse salt*.

Marsh A moist salt with medium-coarse grain that has a fresh, mild salty flavor. The algae residue from the marsh turns it a pale grayish-green color.

Pickling A fine-grained salt used primarily to make brine for pickles.

Popcorn Designed specifically for popcorn, this mildly salty, fine-grained salt has an anti-caking additive that allows it to cling to the fat on the popcorn.

Rock Chunky crystals of unrefined salt, used primarily to retard ice from melting when manually churning ice cream.

Saltpeter Made of 100% sodium nitrate, it is used to cure food.

Salt substitute A salt product that contains little to no sodium.

Sea A type of salt obtained by sun-drying ocean water until some or all of the water is evaporated and the mineral-rich salt crystals remain. It may be refined or unrefined, and is available in whole crystals or ground. The color and flavor depend on the refinement process and where it is harvested.

Table A fine-grained all-purpose salt most commonly used in cooking and baking. It has additives to prevent it from clumping and a pleasant salty taste.

salt dough A bread dough with a very high salt content. The salt renders the dough inedible, but it is used to create decorative pieces for buffets and show-pieces. The finished pieces may be frozen and used over and over. Also known as *dead dough*.

salt rising bread An 18th-century method of making bread that relied on a fermented mixture of milk or water, flour, cornmeal, and salt for leavening. This method was largely abandoned with the production of commercial yeast, but the bread had a tangy flavor and smooth texture.

saltwater taffy See *taffy.*

Salzburger Nockerl ('salts-buhr-guhr nah-kuhrl) A dessert from Salzburg, Austria, that is a sweet *soufflé* flavored with anise and lemon, and baked in three mounds in an oblong dish. It is served warm, dusted with confectioners' sugar.

Sambuca (sam-'boo-kuh) A strong, colorless, anise-flavored liqueur from Italy. Its name derives from the Italian *sambucas nigra,* which refers to the elderberry shrub, whose leaves and berries originally flavored the drink. It is 42% alcohol (84 proof); it is served *flambéed,* with a few coffee beans floating on top, which is said to bring good luck. (The flame heats the beans and infuses the drink with coffee flavor.)

sambusik (sam-boo-sihk) A crescent-shaped pastry from the Middle East filled with walnuts and sugar, then soaked in honey syrup flavored with lemon or rosewater.

samp Broken or coarsely ground *hominy.*

sanding sugar See *sugar.*

sandkage (sahnd-kah-geh) The Danish word for "sand cake," referring to a tender, moist loaf cake made with butter, sugar, eggs, potato flour, and sometimes brandy, then dusted with confectioners' sugar. Known in Sweden as *sandkaka.*

sandkaka 1. See *sandkage.* 2. The Norweigan term for "sandy" that refers to a rich, crumbly or "sandy" cookies made from finely chopped almonds and baked in small tin cups with fluted edges.

sangría (san-'gree-uh) A Spanish summer drink mixture of red wine, fruit, fruit juices, soda water, and sometimes liqueurs such as brandy or Cognac, served cold over ice. The name derives from the Spanish *sangre,* meaning "blood" and refers to its blood-red color. There is also a *sangría blanco,* made with white wine. In southern Spain, *zurra* is made with peaches or nectarines.

sangrita (sahn-'gree-tah) A spicy Spanish-Mexican drink of citrus juice, mashed tomatoes, and chiles, drunk chilled, accompanied by *tequila.*

sansho ('sahn-show) See *Szechwan peppercorn.*

sans sel French for "without salt."

Santa Claus melon See *muskmelon.*

Santa Rosa plum See *plum.*

sanwin makin ('sahn-wihn 'mahk-ihn) A Burmese semolina cake made with coconut milk, ghee, sesame seeds, raisins, and cardamom. After baking it is slightly broiled to brown the top and served in slices or diamond-shaped pieces.

sapodilla (sap-oh-'dee-yuh) The fruit of an evergreen tree native to Mexico and Central America. It has a rough, potato-brown skin and a sweet, soft, juicy flesh that ranges in color from yellow to pinkish brown. It may be eaten fresh or used to make compotes and other pastry products.

S
s

sapote (sah-'poh-tay) See *mamey sapote* and *white sapote*.

Sarah Bernhardt A French petit four of an almond macaroon topped with a kiss-shaped piping of chocolate ganache, enrobed in dark chocolate and sometimes garnished with gold leaf. It is named in honor of the famous French actress, who is believed to have been Escoffier's mistress.

sarsi A sarsaparilla-based beverage that is popular in the Phillipines and other Southeast Asian countries.

sarsaparilla (sas-puh-'rihl-uh) A carbonated drink popular in the 1800s, originally made from the roots of the sarsaparilla vine, native to Mexico and Central America. Today it is often combined with wintergreen oil and other flavorings to mask the natural bitterness of the root and flavor *root beer* and other beverages.

sassafras ('sas-uh-fras) A tree native to eastern North America, a member of the laurel family. Its leaves are dried and used to make tea and *filé powder,* and the root bark is used to flavor *root beer.*

satin stitch A royal icing decoration that resembles linen embroidery. It is generally piped over *floodwork monogramming* so that the edge is raised and has a "stitched" appearance. The recommended tip is #00, since it produces the smallest thread of icing.

satsuma orange (sat-'soo-mah) See *mandarin orange.*

saturated fat A fatty acid composed of a carbon atom that is saturated with hydrogen atoms. The more saturated fatty acids a fat contains, the more solid it is. Animal fats such as butter, *tropical oils* such as coconut oil, and *hydrogenated vegetable oil* and *cocoa butter* are all naturally high in saturated fatty acids. Dietary guidelines recommend that the intake of these types of fats be limited because they are believed to raise blood cholesterol levels and increase the risk of heart disease.

saturated solution A syrup that contains the maximum amount of sugar that it can hold at a given temperature.

Saturn peach See *peach.*

Sauerteig (zow-ehr-tig) The German word for sourdough bread, generally referring to rye-based breads.

sauce 1. A thick or thin flavored liquid used to complement the food with which it is being served. 2. To apply the sauce as a decorative component as well as a flavor enhancer to food about to be served; the common phrase is "sauce the plate."

sauce anglaise See *crème anglaise.*

sauce gun See *fondant funnel.*

saucepan A round, deep cooking container with a long handle and a tight-fitting lid, used to stew or boil food. Saucepans come in different sizes and may be stainless steel, aluminum, or copper.

sauce whisk See *whisk.*

sauté (saw-'tay) To cook a food item quickly, over direct heat and in a small amount of oil or fat, generally in a *sauté pan.*

sauté pan A straight-handled cooking pan used to *sauté* food. It is wide with straight or slightly curved sides, and comes in different sizes. It may be made from stainless steel, enameled cast iron, copper, or aluminum; some pans have a nonstick coating on the surface.

Sauternes (saw-'turn) An opulent, sweet, dessert wine produced in the Sauternes region of France. It is typically made from Sémillon grapes and sometimes Sauvignon that have been infected with the fungus *Botrytis cinerea,* which creates a high sugar

S
s

concentration. This luscious wine is well balanced with sweetness and acidity and is reminiscent of apricots and honey. The labor-intensive production of these wines renders them expensive; the most highly regarded Sauternes is Château d'Yquem. The term *Sauternes* is often used to refer to all sweet wines from Bordeaux, and also as a generic term for inexpensive dry to semisweet white wines.

savillum (sah-'veel-loom) A pudding made with wheat flour, curd cheese, honey, and eggs, baked in an oil earthenware mold with a lid, then brushed with melted honey and covered with poppy seeds.

savarin ('sahv-uh-rihn) A ring-shaped yeast-risen pastry similar to a *baba,* but made without raisins. It is baked in a *savarin mold* and steeped in sugar syrup flavored with rum or Kirsch. It is then coated with apricot glaze and the center filled with pastry cream, crème chantilly, and fresh fruit. It was created in the 19th century by Auguste Julien, one of the three famous French pastry cooks, in honor of Brilliat-Savarin, who taught him the secret of making the syrup to soak the cake.

savarin mold ('sahv-uh-rihn) A shallow ring mold with an open whole in the center. They range in diameter from 2¾ to 3½ inches (7 to 8.7cm) and are designed for baking *savarin,* although they may be used for other pastries and desserts as well.

savoie (sah-'vwah) The French name for *savoy sponge;* see *biscuit de savoie.*

savory ('say-vuh-ree) 1. A strong, aromatic herb in the mint family that tastes like a cross between thyme and mint. Summer savory is milder than winter savory; savory is available fresh or dried. 2. A culinary term that refers to food that is not sweet.

savory nut See *Brazil nut.*

savoy sponge See *biscuit de savoie.*

Sazerac ('saz-uh-rak) A cocktail of whisky, sugar syrup, and a dash of *Pernod* and *bitters.* Its name is from the Sazerac Coffee House in New Orleans, where it was created.

scald To bring a liquid to just below the boiling point. This technique is used extensively in regard to scalding milk or cream for custards. Since the temperature is just below boiling it prevents the sugars from caramelizing.

scale 1. To accurately measure ingredients or portion out dough into specific weights. 2. A device for accurately weighing ingredients. There are several types, including:

Balance A heavy metal scale that uses a durable plastic scale bowl on one side and counterbalance weights on the other. The brass or cast iron counterweights come in metric or U.S. customary sizes and range from 1 to 8 pounds (455 g to 3 kg). The center of the scale contains a metal bar with ¼ ounce (8 g) increments up to 1 pound (455 g). The product to be measured is placed in the bowl and the weights are adjusted until the scale is balanced on both sides. Used for measuring large amounts. Also known as *baker's scale* and *balance beam scale.*

Digital A scale that uses an electronic system to display weights. Available in a variety of styles and weighing capabilities, the product may be scaled and then the weight zeroed out so another product can be weighed on top of it. Many types allow the user to switch from metric to U.S. weights and vice versa. They are typically more expensive than the other scales but popular for their greater efficiency.

Portion Another name for spring scale; see below.

Spring A spring-loaded scale that uses a dial and needle to display the weight of a food item put on the flat metal top tray. They are available in ounces, pounds, or grams and are used when portioning out products such as bread dough.

spring scale

Schaumtorten ('showm-tohr-tehn) An Austrian dessert of meringue layers sandwiched with fruit and topped with *Schlag*.

schiacciata (skee-ah-kee-'ahta-uh) A rich, eggy, brioche-like Tuscan bread, similar to a coffee cake. It is usually made during the grape harvest so that Sangiovese grapes can used in the filling, but raisins are sometimes substituted.

Schlag (shlahg) The German word for "*whipped cream*," served with pastries, desserts, and coffee drinks.

Schnapps (shnaps) The German word for "mouthful," referring to strong, colorless spirits distilled from grains or potatoes. They are available in a variety of flavors including peppermint, apple, and peach.

Schokokuss (shoh-kok-kuhs) A German chocolate–coated cookie that is sandwiched together with buttercream.

Schwarzwälder Kirschtorte See *Black Forest torte.*

scone (skohn) A small, individual Scottish quickbread with a crispy, golden crust and soft, delicate interior. Scones were originally made from oats and baked on a griddle, but today they are flour based and baked in an oven. Usually triangular, but may also be round, square, or diamond shape. They may be sweet or savory, and are most commonly eaten as a breakfast item or served with *afternoon tea* with *clotted cream* and jam. The name is believed to be a reference to the Stone (Scone) of Destiny, where Scottish kings were crowned.

Scooter Pie See *Moon Pie.*

score See *12 Steps of Baking* appendix.

Scotch See *whisky.*

Scotch oats See *oats.*

scraper See *bowl scraper.*

Scottish shortbread See *shortbread.*

Scuppernong grape ('skuhp-uhr-nawng) A sweet variety of *muscadine grape,* popular in the South for making wine and jelly.

sea biscuit See *hardtack.*

seafoam See *divinity.*

sea salt See *salt.*

season 1. To add ingredients such as salt, pepper, herbs, and/or spices to enhance the flavor of food. 2. To prepare a cast iron pan for use by coating the bottom with a thin layer of vegetable oil and heating it to 300°F (149°C) for about 1 hour. This removes any residual particles embedded in the pan and keeps food from sticking.

S
s

seasoning The ingredients used to enhance the flavor of food. The most common are salt, pepper, herbs, and spices.

sec (sehk) The French word for "dry," used to describe the flavor of wines and Champagnes and the texture of petit fours.

Seckel pear See *pear*.

seed 1. To remove the seeds from fruits or vegetables. 2. The block or pieces of chocolate used to temper chocolate. See *tempering, seeding method*.

seeding method See *tempering, seeding method*.

seffa A Moroccan rice pudding–like dessert made by cooking couscous, butter, cinnamon, sugar, and orange flower water.

seitan ('say-tan) A protein-rich food made from wheat gluten. It has a firm, chewy texture and somewhat neutral flavor, that easily picks up the flavors of the food it is cooked with. It is used extensively in vegetarian dishes and can be found in Asian markets and natural food stores. Also known as *wheat gluten*.

seize A condition that occurs when chocolate comes into contact with water; it "seizes up" and becomes a hard, lumpy mass. Once this occurs, the chocolate is no longer useable for tempering, but may be re-melted with a small amount of cocoa butter or vegetable oil and used in recipes requiring chocolate, though smooth quality may be compromised.

Sekt (zehkt) A German word that is the shortened version of *Qualitaschäumwein*, which means "quality sparkling wine." It is the top category for sparkling wine in Germany, whose wines are characterized by a fruity sweetness.

sel (sehl) The French word for *salt*.

self-rising flour See *flour*.

seltzer water ('selt-suhr) An effervescent water made by charging it with carbon dioxide. It may be used plain as a mixer in cocktails or flavored and/or sweetened and used in beverages such as soda pop. Also known as *soda water* and *club soda*.

semifreddo ('she-mee-fray-doh) The Italian term for "half cold," referring to a creamy, *still frozen* dessert that may be molded and flavored with fruit puree, coffee, chocolate, or citrus.

Sémillon grape ('she-mee-yohn) A white grape variety grown primarily in the Bordeaux region of France and in California. It is used in the production of dessert wines such as *Sauternes* because of its susceptibility to *Botrytis cinerea*.

semisweet chocolate See *chocolate*.

semolina (she-muh-'lee-nuh) Coarsely ground durum wheat used in Italian puddings and pasta, Middle Eastern desserts, and breads.

serabi (she-'rah-bee) A small Indonesian pancake made with wheat flour, ground rice, egg, and coconut milk, simmered in a small earthenware pot with a lid. It is either a natural creamy white or colored green with the juice of the *pandanus leaf*. It is served warm with palm sugar or a sweetened syrup.

Sercial See *Madeira*.

serikaya dengan agar-agar (sehr-ee-'kah-yah 'dayng-ahn) A Malaysian jelly-like candy made from coconut milk, cinnamon, cardamom, water, and salt, and thickened with *agar-agar*. The thick mixture is strained and poured into rectangular or square molds, and cooled before serving.

serrated knife A long-bladed knife with a scalloped or serrated edge. It is recommended for slicing cakes and breads.

sesame ball A Chinese dessert made by boiling a thin batter of glutinous rice powder and water in a sugar syrup and then adding more glutinous rice powder to form a dough. The soft dough is kneaded and formed into small balls, which are filled with red bean paste, rolled in sesame seeds, and deep-fried.

sesame oil An aromatic oil pressed from sesame seeds. It may be light or dark, and ranges in flavor from mildly nutty to pungent. The dark variety is roasted sesame oil and is used extensively in Indian and Asian cooking. The light variety is offered as a healthier alternative.

sesame seed ('sehs-uh-mee) The tiny flat seed of a tropical annual plant. It has been used as a seasoning since 3000 B.C. They were brought to America by African slaves, who called them *benne seed*. They have a slightly sweet, nutty flavor and come in shades of ivory, brown, red, or black. They are used extensively in Middle Eastern, Asian, and Indian cooking, and as an ingredient in or topping for breads, confections, cookies, and cakes. Owing to their high fat content, they are susceptible to rancidity and should be stored in an airtight container in a cool, dry place.

sesame seed paste A creamy paste made from finely ground roasted sesame seeds. It is popular as a flavoring agent in Middle Eastern cuisine and is used in *tahini* and *halvah*.

set A term used with gelatin-based desserts to describe that the mixture has firmed up, or "set."

seven-minute frosting A fluffy, meringue-like frosting made from sugar, egg whites, cream of tartar, and vanilla. The mixture is whipped over a double boiler for approximately 7 minutes until it forms stiff peaks.

Seville orange See *orange.*

sfogliatelle (sfo-glee-ah-'te-lay) A scallop-shaped pastry from Naples made with a flaky pastry dough filled with a creamy mixture of ricotta cheese, semolina, and flavorings such as cinnamon, vanilla, candied fruit, or chocolate.

sharbat A sweet, chilled drink from India. It is flavored with fruit juice or flower petals and may be thin or thick enough to eat with a spoon.

Sharlyn melon See *muskmelon.*

Sharon fruit See *persimmon.*

sharpening steel A long, pointed thin round rod attached to a handle, used to sharpen knives. It is made of very hard, high-carbon steel and is available in different lengths.

shawnee cake See *johnnycake.*

sheet cake A cake made in a full- or half-size sheet pan. It may be thin and rolled for desserts such as *jelly rolls* or layered to make large, rectangular celebration cakes.

sheet cookie See *cookie.*

sheeter A fairly large piece of kitchen equipment used to evenly roll out dough. The dough is placed on a piece of stretched canvas and rolled through metal cylinders. The width of the space between the rollers may be adjusted manually to determine the thickness of the dough. There are tabletop and floor models available. It is also used to roll *marzipan, rolled fondant, gum paste,* and *modeling chocolate.*

sheet gelatin Another name for *leaf gelatin;* see *gelatin.*

shelf life The length of time a product can be stored or "sit on a shelf" before it begins to stale, spoil, or lose its quality.

shell The backbone of a cake decoration, made by piping icing through a fluted pastry tip onto a cake to form a round shell with a tapered end. Used mainly

S
s

to decorate borders and sides of cakes, the shell is also the basis for many other decorative designs, including *fleur-de-lis* and *reverse shells*.

sherbet ('sher-biht) 1. A frozen dessert of fruit juice or puree, sugar, water, milk or cream, and/or egg whites or gelatin. It is richer than sorbet but lighter than ice cream. Sometimes liqueur or wine is used to flavor the product. U.S. regulations require that sherbet contain a minimum of 1% and a maximum of 2% butterfat. 2. In England, a fizzy, fruit-flavored powder eaten as a sweet.

sherry A fortified wine originally made in Jerez, in Andalusia, southern Spain, but now produced other places as well. The flavors range from dry to sweet and fall into two categories: *Fino* and *Oloroso*. *Fino sherries* are light, dry, and crisp, while *Oloroso sherries* are more full-bodied, nutty, darker, and sometimes sweet. Within these two broad categories are seven styles that vary in color, flavor, and quality depending on where it is produced. The major grape used is a white variety called Palomino and the sweet dessert sherries use a minor white grape variety called Pedro Ximénez. The styles of sherry are as follows:

> **Manzanilla** A highly regarded fino-type sherry produced in the small seaside town of Sanlúcar de Barrameda. It has a delicate, slightly crisp flavor with a salty tang and aroma. It should be served cold and pairs well with seafood.

> **Amontillado** An aged fino-type sherry that is deeper in color with a rich, nutty flavor and medium-dry finish.

> **Cream** A very sweet oloroso-type sherry that has a broad spectrum of flavor, body, price, and quality.

> **Fino** The most refined, complex fino-type sherry. It is pale in color and low in alcohol with a dry tang and spring-like flavor. It should be drank young and chilled.

> **Oloroso** An aromatic, long-aged sherry that has an intense nutty flavor and darker color. It is typically sweet and has a richer, more full-bodied taste.

> **Palo Cortado** A rare type of dry amontillado with the full-body of a dry oloroso.

> **Pedro Ximénez** An oloroso-type sherry that is made from the grape of the same name. It is very dark, sweet, and dense. It is often used to sweeten other sherries or served as a dessert wine or topping for vanilla ice cream.

shinseiki See *Asian pear*.

Shirley Temple A nonalcoholic drink named after the 1930s child star, a mixture of ginger ale and grenadine syrup, garnished with a maraschino cherry.

Shiro plum See *plum*.

shiso ('shee-soh) An aromatic leaf of the perilla plant, which is a member of the mint family. It comes in red leaf and green leaf varieties, and tastes like a combination of mint, basil, and cilantro. It is used in Asian cooking, and the leaves and flowers are also used to make tea. Its jagged edges make it an interesting garnish as well. Also known as *perilla*.

shochu ('show-shoo) A clear, distilled spirit from Japan. It is typically mixed with oolong tea and fruit juices such as orange, peach, and grapefruit.

sholeh zard (shul-'lehh-zarrd) An Iranian rice pudding flavored with almonds, pistachios, cinnamon, and saffron.

shoofly pie A molasses pie topped with a crumb mixture of flour, butter, and brown sugar, of Pennsylvania Dutch origin. Its name is believed to be a reference to shooing away the flies that are attracted to the sweet pie.

shortbread A rich butter cookie with a tender, crumbly texture. It may be flavored with nuts, candied fruit, citrus zest, or spices, or dipped in chocolate (which is known as *royal shortbread*). Although today there are many variations in terms of shape, size, and flavor, shortbread originated in Scotland and was made in a large round shape, cut into wedges. This round shape comes from the ancient Yule cake called *bannock*, which was a symbol of the sun. The classic way of making Scottish shortbread is to press the dough into a *shortbread mold* and bake it to a pale straw color. Once removed from the oven, it is cut into wedges, which were known as "petticoat tails" because they resembled the petticoats worn by the women in the 12th century. Shortbread was traditionally served at tea during Christmas and Hogmanay (Scottish New Year's Eve), but is now made year-round.

shortbread mold A shallow, round, wooden or earthenware mold that imparts a decorative design on the dough when pressed into it.

shortcake A sweet, crumbly biscuit used to make the American dessert of the same name. The biscuit is sliced open and filled with and topped with sliced fresh fruit and sweetened whipped cream. *Strawberry shortcake* is the most well known; sometimes angel food cake or sponge cake is used instead of the biscuit.

short dough A cookie or pastry dough with a high ratio of fat to flour, that produces a finished product with a rich, tender, and crumbly texture. The fat is creamed into the flour, which "shortens" the gluten strands. Typical short doughs are *pâte sablée* and *pâte sucrée*.

shortening A bland, white fat made from either partially hydrogenated soybean oil or vegetable or animal fat. It is 100% fat and contains no water. The three main types of shortening used in the bake shop are:

> **All-purpose** Contains no added emulsifiers and is aerated by the manufacturer with 10% air or nitrogen, which plays an important role in leavening the product. It should be used in products made by the *creaming method* or *biscuit method* and is also appropriate for frying. Its low cost, pliability, and ability to work over a wide temperature range makes it less expensive and easier to work with than butter, but it lacks the rich flavor. Many chefs use a combination of butter and shortening to get the best of both worlds.

> **High-ratio Plastic or Emulsified** Similar to all-purpose in appearance, but has emulsifiers added to it. This type is best used in icings, cakes, and other products that have a high amount of liquid or air. It is not appropriate for frying.

> **High-ratio Liquid** A liquid shortening that contains a much higher level of emulsifiers than high-ratio plastic shortening and is also less hydrogenated. It is primarily used in cakes because it is effective at incorporating air into the batter, thus producing a lighter, more tender cake. It also provides the most volume, moistness, and longest shelf life of all the fats and oils. If substituting liquid shortening for plastic shortening, reduce the liquid shortening by 20%.

Short pastry dough See *short dough.*

short-grain rice See *rice.*

Shrewsbury A small English shortbread cookie named for the town in which it was created. They are typically sandwiched together with jam and dusted with confectioners' sugar. The top cookie usually has a hole cut out to expose the jam underneath.

shrub A cold beverage made from fruit juice, sugar, and vinegar that was originally spiked with brandy or rum in Colonial America. Today, they are typically nonalcoholic and made with sweetened fruit juice and vinegar, served over ice with or without soda water.

S
s

Sichuan pepper See *Szechwan peppercorn.*

Siena cake See *panforte.*

sieve (sihv) 1. To sift a product into finer particles with a sieve. 2. A type of strainer; see *tamis.*

sift To pass dry ingredients through a *sifter* to aerate them, remove or break up lumps, or combine evenly.

sifter A cylinder with a rotating blade and a mesh bottom that stirs and *sifts* food. It may be made of heavy plastic or metal, and either hand-cranked or battery operated.

silica gel A dehumidifying agent that changes color according to the amount of moisture it has absorbed. When dry, the crystals are blue. Once it has absorbed the maximum amount of water, the crystals turn pink. The silica gels may be dried in a 300°F (149°C) oven for a few minutes to return them to their original color and be reused.

silicone mold 1. See *Flexipan* 2. A decorative mold made from silicone, used for chocolate and sugar showpieces.

Silpat ('sihl-paht) A professional non-stick baking sheet made of food-grade silicone and fiberglass. It is effective at temperatures between −40° to 480°F (−40° to 248°C) and can be used for anything from baking sheetcakes to rolling out nougat. It is available in full and half sheetpan sizes.

silver leaf An ultra-thin edible sheet of pure silver, used for applying silver decoration to confections and desserts. The leaves are sold in small square sheets separated by tissue paper; they are very expensive and difficult to work with, and it is recommended to use tweezers or a dry artist's brush to transfer the leaf onto the product. Also know as *vark* or *varak.*

Silver Lode nectarine See *nectarine.*

silver powder An edible powder made from finely ground pure silver, used to decorate desserts and show pieces. The powder may be used as is or mixed with a small amount of clear alcohol to produce a silver paint. As the alcohol dissipates, the silver will remain.

silver varak See *varak.*

simmer To gently cook food in a liquid at just below boiling point. The low heat should produce tiny bubbles on the surface, not a rolling boil.

simnel cake An English spice cake packed with dried fruits and candied orange peel, and garnished with *marzipan* eggs. The cake batter is poured halfway into the pan and then a layer of marzipan or almond paste is placed in the center before the remaining batter is poured over the top and baked.

simple fold See *letter fold.*

simple syrup A pastry syrup with equal parts sugar and water, briefly boiled and then cooled. It may be used as is or flavored with extracts, juices, or liqueurs, and used to moisten cakes, sweeten or poach fruit, thin *fondant,* glaze baked goods, and as a base for *sorbets* and *granitas.*

Simplesse (sihm-'plehs) A whey protein product used as a fat substitute in low-calorie foods.

singapour A rich génoise sponge that has been sliced in half and filled with syrup-soaked fresh fruit. The cake is garnished with candied fruit and served in slices with whipped cream.

single-malt whisky See *whisky.*

siroper (see-ro-'pehr) A French term that refers to soaking a pastry item in syrup.

sketos See *Greek coffee.*

skewer ('skew-uhr) A very thin, pointed piece of wood used to support the weight of tiers of cakes or to impale fruit, which may then be grilled or used as a garnish.

skillet See *frying pan.*

skim To remove food particles or the top layer from the surface of a liquid, using a spoon or a *skimmer.*

skimmer A hand-held flat, fine-mesh metal strainer with handle, used to skim the top layer off a liquid.

skim milk See *milk.*

slicing knife A long, thin, narrow-bladed knife recommended for slicing cakes.

slump See *grunt.*

slurry A thin mixture of flour or cornstarch and water, added to thicken a mixture; once added, the mixture should be boiled to cook out the starchy flavor.

smen (smehn) A seasoned, preserved butter used in the Middle East and North Africa. It has a distinct, slightly fermented flavor and will keep for years unrefrigerated.

smocking A cake-decorating technique used in combination with *drapery* and *swag designs* to imitate the fullness of fabric in a woman's garment. First, a sheet of *rolled fondant* is gathered to achieve a pleated pattern. Then a #0 or #00 tip is used to pipe an embroidery pattern over the rolled fondant. This technique is an elegant decorative effect on wedding cakes.

smoke point The point at which a heated fat begins to smoke and impart undesirable flavors to the foods. The higher the smoke point, the more suited a fat is for frying and sautéing. Fats with a high smoke point include peanut, corn, and safflower oils as well as high-ratio plastic shortening.

smoothing A technique whereby *rolled fondant* is smoothed out so that there are no lines or wrinkles present when it is placed over a cake. *Cake smoothers* are used to achieve this technique. It is quite important to have the surface of a cake smooth so that it will display the applied decorations without any detractions.

smoothie A thick, smooth chilled drink of fresh or frozen fruit, yogurt, juice, and milk.

s'more A sweet, gooey dessert of toasted marshmallows and a thin piece of chocolate sandwiched between two graham crackers. Most commonly associated with camping and campfires. The name comes from their being so good that everyone wants "some more."

Smyrna fig See *fig.*

snickerdoodle (snihk-uhr-doo-dl) A rich, sweet, buttery American sugar cookie that originated in New England in the 19th century. They are traditionally sprinkled with cinnamon sugar and have a distinct crinkly top. They may be soft or crunchy, and are sometimes made with nuts, dried fruits, or spices.

snifter A small glass with a large bowl, for drinking fine brandy. Its short stem and rounded bottom allow the glass to be cradled by the drinker's hand, warming the brandy and bringing out its aroma.

snow 1. A 16th-century dessert of stiffly beaten egg whites, cream, sugar, and flavorings, originally served over other desserts to give the impression of snow. Today, it is typically served chilled and set with gelatin. 2. A treated confectioners' sugar that is resistant to moisture.

snow cone A cold snack of colored, flavored syrup poured over crushed ice and served in a paper cone.

soaker A mixture of whole or cracked grains or seeds with an equal amount of water, soaked until the grains are soft and palatable and used for whole-grain

S
s

breads; the soaker deprives the dough of moisture and inhibits gluten development. A soaker can be made by either the hot or cold method. The hot method requires the liquid to be brought to a boil before incorporating the grains; the mixture is then cooked for an additional 5 minutes over low heat and set aside to cool before adding it to the dough. This method pregelatinizes the starch of the soaker's grain, which may improve crust color and shorten the baking time of some whole-grain breads. However, some chefs feel that there is a loss of flavor and quality compared to the cold method. The cold method is typically done the day before; the grains and liquid are put in a container and allowed to soak overnight. Soakers are added to the dough after it has started to develop. Breads made with a soaker tend to have a light, whole-grain texture, and their high moisture retention prolongs shelf life.

sockerstruvor See *rosette iron.*

soda bread See *Irish soda bread.*

soda water See *seltzer water.*

soft-ball stage See *Sugar Cooking Stages* appendix.

soft-crack stage See *Sugar Cooking Stages* appendix.

soft flour See *flour.*

soft peak The consistency of a whipped product such as eggs or cream. When beaters are lifted up, the product should form soft peaks.

soft pretzel See *pretzel.*

soft red winter wheat See *wheat.*

soft water See *water.*

soft wheat See *wheat.*

soft white wheat See *wheat.*

solilmeme (zol-eel-may-muh) An Alsatian sweet bread similar to *brioche.*

Solo papaya See *papaya.*

sommelier ('saw-muh-lyay) A knowledgeable wine professional, trained in all facets of wine service.

soomsoom mah assal (soom-soom 'maa 'aah-ssal) A Middle Eastern confection made by reducing honey and lemon juice to a thick consistency. A mixture of toasted sesame seeds, almonds, pistachios, and shredded coconut is added to the syrup and it is cooled in a square or rectangular dish. Once cooled, it is cut into squares and served as a snack or dessert.

sopaipilla (soh-pah-'pee-yah) A crisp, puffy, deep-fried flour tortilla, drizzled with a sugar or honey syrup flavored with cinnamon. Thought to have originated in New Mexico over 200 years ago, there is also a South American version made from pastry dough that is cut into thin strips, deep-fried, and dusted with confectioners' sugar.

sorbet ('sohr-bay) The French word for *sherbet,* referring to a churn-frozen dessert of fruit puree or juice, sugar, and water. It is a refreshing low-fat dessert or a palette cleanser in between courses.

sorbetto (sohr-'beht-toh) The Italian word for *sorbet.*

sorbitol ('sor-bih-tawl) An artificial sweetener also used as a thickener and stabilizer in gum and candy. It is found naturally in some fruits, such as plums.

sorghum ('sor-ghum) A cereal grass related to millet and cultivated for its nutritious grain. It is an important cereal grain in Third World countries, where it is used to make porridge, flour, and bread. In Asia, it is an important ingredient in the production of alcoholic beverages. In the United States, it is primarily used as animal feed and for *sorghum molasses.*

sorghum flour See *flour.*

sorghum molasses A rich, sweet, dark syrup produced from sorghum stalks. It is used to flavor and sweeten baked goods and desserts. Also known as *sorghum syrup.*

sorghum syrup See *sorghum molasses.*

sotas lace A cake-decorating design with a series of overlapping, squiggly lines randomly piped to form an abstract, contemporary lace appearance.

soufflé (sue-'flay) A French dessert made with whipped egg whites folded into a base of sugar, flour or cornstarch, scalded milk, and egg yolks. The mixture may be flavored with vanilla, chocolate, liqueurs, fruit purees, and/or spices and is baked in a *soufflé dish* or *ramekin* that has been buttered and sugared to help the soufflé rise evenly and create a delicate crust on the sides. The high heat of the oven causes the air trapped in the whipped egg whites to rise; it  is served directly from the oven because it begins to fall as it cools. A well-made soufflé will double its size over the top of the baking dish and have a creamy, airy interior and light, delicate crust. It is dusted with confectioners' sugar and served with a complementary sauce, such as *crème anglaise.* The name derives from the French *souffler,* which means "to inflate." See also *fruit soufflé* and *frozen soufflé.*

soufflé dish A round, deep, straight-sided porcelain or earthenware dish used for baked or frozen soufflés, custards, and mousses. They are typically white with a smooth interior and fluted exterior; they range in size from 4 to 8 inches (10 to 20 cm) in diameter and 2 to 4 inches (5 to 10 cm) high.

sour 1. A term used to describe a sharp, tart taste. 2. A cocktail made by mixing liquor such as whisky or amaretto with lemon juice and a little sugar.

sour cream A thick, creamy, white dairy product that is 18 to 20% fat. The tangy or sour taste comes from the lactic acid bacteria with which it is fermented. Its consistency is a result of added ingredients such as gelatin, rennin, and vegetable enzymes. Light and nonfat sour cream are higher in moisture but less rich in flavor than regular sour cream. *Light sour cream* is made with half-and-half instead of cream and contains about 40% less fat. *Nonfat sour cream* is thickened with stabilizers. Sour cream is often used as an acidic ingredient in baking, particularly *cheesecake.* Although it is commercially produced, it may be made by adding vinegar to pasteurized cream and letting it set until it curdles.

sourdough bread A bread loaf with a distinct tangy, sour flavor, achieved through the use of a *starter.* The wild yeast and bacteria in the starter is specific to each area, and therefore breads made in different places have different flavor profiles and qualities. The characteristic sour flavor is produced not from the wild yeast but from the *Lactobacillus* and *Acetobacillus* bacteria. When the bacteria feed off the sugars in the dough, they create lactic and acetic acids, which are what produces the sour flavor.

sourdough culture/starter A mixture of microorganisms that contain wild yeasts and bacteria, used to initiate a bread dough. There are many ways to make and maintain a starter, but in general it is a mixture of flour, water, and wild or commercial yeast. The mixture ferments and is regularly refreshed with more flour and water, which provides the nutrients and sugar it needs to stay alive. This ongoing process allows the starter to continually develop flavor; some starters may be centuries old. Starters affect the structure, leavening, and flavor of the bread. Also known as *barm* and *wild yeast starter.*

S
s

sour orange See *orange*.

sour salt See *salt, citric*.

soursop The fruit of a tropical tree native to the Caribbean. It has an avocado-like skin and a white, pink, or yellow-orange custard-like flesh that has a delicate, slightly tart flavor. The fruit is used mainly for sherbets, ices, and a Jamaican drink. Frozen soursop pulp and bottled drinks are also available in Latin American markets.

sous chef See *brigade*.

sous vide (soo veed) The French term for "under vacuum," referring to a method of cooking food that maintains the integrity of the ingredients. This usually entails slow cooking the vacuum-packed food at a low temperature in order to maintain its original texture, appearance, and nutrients. This process was developed by Georges Pralus in the mid-1970s for the Restaurant Troisgros in Roanne, France, and is used today by many professional chefs. It may be purchased pre-packaged or done in-house.

South African baby pineapple See *pineapple*.

Southern Comfort A strong, sweet liqueur made from a secret blend of whisky, peaches, oranges, vanilla, sugar, and cinnamon. It was created in 1874 by W. M. Heron, a bartender at McCauley's Saloon in the French Quarter of New Orleans, as a way to improve the flavor of the rough-tasting barrel whisky used at the saloon. It is 100 proof and is now produced in St. Louis, Missouri.

soybean oil A pale-yellow oil extracted from soybeans. It is high in unsaturated fats (23% monounsaturated and 58% polyunsaturated) but low in saturated fats (15%) and therefore considered a healthful oil. It is used primarily in the manufacture of margarine and shortening, and is also a good choice for frying because of its high *smoke point*.

soy flour See *flour*.

soy ice cream A nondairy alternative to ice cream, made with *soy milk* instead of cream and flavored with fruit or chocolate. Since it does not contain any butterfat, partially hydrogenated soybean or palm oil is added to resemble the creamy texture of ice cream. It is a good choice for health-conscious menus.

soy margarine A health-conscious margarine made from *soybean oil*, which does not contain any saturated fat.

soy milk A high-protein, nondairy alternative to cow's milk, made by pressing ground, cooked soybeans. It is popular with people who have milk allergies, are lactose-intolerant, and/or follow a vegan diet. It is available plain or flavored.

soy nut A high-protein snack made by roasting whole, water-soaked dried *soybeans*. They resemble small peanuts and have a nutty flavor and crunchy texture.

soy sour cream A lactose-free product made by treating *soy milk* with a souring agent. It is thick and creamy like regular *sour cream* and may be substituted in equal quantities for it.

soy yogurt See *yogurt*.

Spanische Windtorte An Austrian confection of a *meringue* shell filled with fresh berries and whipped cream. The sides are decorated with a piped shell or rosette design and garnished with crystallized violets, while the top is finished with a decorated meringue disc.

Spanish melon See *muskmelon*.

Spanish peanut See *peanut*.

sparkling wine An effervescent wine, such as *Champagne, Asti Spumante,* or *Prosecco,* that is made fizzy by the infusion of carbon dioxide. This may be done by one of four ways: *méthode champenoise, transfer method, charmant* or *tank method,* or *carbonation;* see *Champagne* for detailed information.

Spätlese ('shpayt-lay-zuh) The German term for "late harvest," referring to a rich, sweet wine whose grapes are picked after the regular harvest. This allows the fruit to fully ripen and increase its sugar content. Owing to the grapes' high acid content, the wine is not as sweet as other German sweet wines, such as *Auslese* and *Trokenbeerenauslese.*

spatula A rubber, plastic, stainless steel, silicone, or wooden tool, used for spreading mixtures. They are available in a wide variety of shapes and sizes, with the most popular being:

>**Flexible** Used for icing cakes and spreading batters, chocolate, and creams, this spatula has a round-tipped, flat metal blade attached to a wooden or plastic handle. The blades range in size from 3 to 14 inches (7.5 to 35 cm) in length and 1 to 2 inches (2.5 to5 cm) in width. Also known as *icing spatula* and *palette knife.*

>**Icing** Another name for *flexible spatula.*

>**Offset** Identical to a flexible spatula (see above) except the blade is bent at a 90° angle from the handle to allow the product to be spread very thin without the spatula's hitting the edge of the baking pan.

>**Palette knife** Another name for *flexible spatula.*

>**Rubber** A spatula with a flat or slightly curved top that enables the product to be completely scraped from the bowl. Some are available in heat-resistant materials, which can be used with very hot products without worrying about the rubber's melting or absorbing flavors of the food.

>**Triangular** Resembling a putty knife, this has a wide triangular blade that tapers down to the handle. It is used primarily for tabling chocolate, cooling poured sugar, and forming chocolate ruffles and cigarettes.

>**Turning** A short, wide-bladed offset spatula that may or may not have slits in the blade. These are typically used for turning products over and/or moving them from one place to another.

spearmint A vigorous variety of mint native to southern Europe but grown widely. Its green leaves have sawtooth edges and are most commonly used to make spearmint oil and extract to flavor mint sauces, jellies, and gum.

speculaas A thin, crunchy Belgian cookie with rock candy and various spices. They are baked in ornately carved molds that come in various shapes and sizes, although the shape of St. Nicholas is the most popular.

spekkoek ('spehk-o-ehk) An Indonesian butter cake of Dutch origin, with 12 thin alternating layers of vanilla cake and vanilla cake spiced with cinnamon, cloves, and nutmeg, which gives the sliced cake a striped appearance. It is typically served after *rijsttafel* or with coffee or tea.

spelt A cereal grain native to southern Europe that is milled into whole-grain and white flours. It has a mild nutty flavor, and with the exception of celiac disease, can be tolerated by people with wheat allergies. Although it is high in protein, it contains less gluten and has lower water-absorption ability than wheat, and so it is easily overworked. Otherwise, it has good bread-making qualities, but will

S
s

produce a loaf with stronger flavor and less volume if not used in combination with other flours. Known as *Dinkel* in Germany and *farro* in Italy.

spice An aromatic and/or pungent seasoning used in cooking and baking to flavor food. Spices are obtained from the roots, fruits, buds, stems, or barks of many plants and trees. They are available dried, in whole or ground form.

spiral mixer See *mixer*.

spirit lamp See *alcohol burner*.

spirits A general term for distilled alcoholic beverages.

Splenda See *artificial sweetener*.

split bread See *fendu*.

sponge A *pre-ferment* mixture that is generally loose textured and consists of flour, water, and yeast. It ferments anywhere from 30 minutes to several hours before it is added to a yeast dough. This pre-ferment kick-starts the fermentation process and adds flavor to the finished product.

sponge cake A light, airy cake characterized by its high proportion of eggs to flour. Sponge cakes are typically leavened solely by the air whipped into the eggs, but sometimes *chemical leaveners* are added as a safety measure. Usually whole eggs or yolks are combined with sugar and whipped separately from the egg whites, which are whipped with some sugar and then folded into the heavier mixture. Sometimes only whites are used; a small amount of sifted flour is then folded in. Sometimes butter, milk, and/or flavorings such as citrus zest, cocoa powder, or ground nuts are added. Sponge cakes are baked at a high temperature to quickly set the cake; the high amount of egg protein and small amount of flour make them springy and flexible.

sponge method See *mixing methods*.

spoom A frothy sorbet made by combining a light sugar syrup with a liquid such as fruit juice, Champagne, or liqueur and freezing it half way; then uncooked meringue is added, which gives it its light, airy texture. The name derives from the Italian *spuma*, which means "foam."

spoon bread A pudding-like Southern U.S. bread made from cornmeal and baked in a casserole dish. Its name implies that it is soft enough to eat with a spoon.

Springerle ('shpring-uhr-luh) A German Christmas cookie that originated in the 15th century in Swabia, southwest Germany. It is flavored with anise and distinguished by the embossed design on its surface, done by either pressing the dough into a *Springerle mold* or with a *Springerle rolling pin*. The dough is firm and contains no fat, so these hold the detailed impressions very well. In addition, the imprinted dough is left to dry overnight so it keeps the decorative design after baking.

Springerle mold An elaborately carved wooden cookie mold used to impress decorative designs on *Springerele*.

Springerle rolling pin See *rolling pin*.

springform pan A round, straight-sided baking pan with a removable bottom. These pans are available in sizes that range from 2 to 4 inches (5 to 10 cm) in depth and 4 to 12 inches (10 to 30 cm) in diameter. They are typically used to bake cakes such as cheesecakes, which might otherwise be difficult to remove from the mold after baking.

spring ginger See *ginger.*

spring wheat See *wheat.*

sprinkles Another name for *jimmies.*

Sprite melon See *muskmelon.*

spritz (sprihts) A buttery almond cookie from Sweden that is piped out in a variety of designs or molded in a cookie press.

spritzer ('spriht-suhr) A chilled beverage made in a tall glass with wine and soda water.

spuma ('spoo-mah) The Italian word for *spoom.*

Spumante (spoo-'mahn-tay) The Italian word for "foaming," referring to a sparkling wine made from a variety of red, or more commonly, white grapes. See *Asti Spumante* and *Prosecco.*

spumone, spumoni (spoo-'mohn-ee) A molded frozen dessert from Naples, consisting of two layers of flavored ice cream sandwiched with sweetened whipped cream, toasted nuts, candied fruit, and rum or brandy. It is served in slices to expose the attractive layers.

spun sugar A decorative dessert garnish that resembles fine threads or strands of *angel hair,* by which it is also known. It is made by cooking sugar, water, and sometimes cream of tartar or glucose to the *hard crack stage.* The pan is then immediately dipped in an *ice bath* to prevent the sugar from cooking further. The threads are made by dipping a fork, whisk (with the bottom cut off so the thin metal pieces are separate), or a sugar tool that has nail-like spikes attached to a handle into the sugar and quickly waving it back and forth over rows of spaced wooden rods or onto parchment paper. It is then gathered into a nest by hand as the sugar is threaded off of the tool. Spun sugar is highly susceptible to humidity and should be worked with and stored in a cool, dry place. It will keep better in an airtight container with *dessicant* and last longer if it is made with *isomalt* rather than regular sugar.

squash blossom The edible flower of a summer or winter squash. These range in color from yellow to orange and have a mild, squash flavor. They may be used fresh, sautéed, or stuffed with sweet or savory items and baked, or batter-dipped and fried. They are perishable and in season only from late spring to early fall.

stabilizer A thickening or gelling agent added to foods to help prevent their deterioration and maintain emulsification. The most common stabilizers are *gelatin, guar gum, gum arabic, gum tragacanth,* and *xanthan gum.*

stage See *stagiaire.*

stagiaire (stah-zhee-her) The French word for "trainee," referring to a kitchen apprentice who works either for free or a nominal wage in exchange for learning the trade. The length of time involved varies and is referred to as a "stage" (*stahzhe*).

star anise An aromatic spice native to China that resembles a small, dark brown star and has a tiny seed in each of its eight segments. It has a slightly more bitter licorice flavor than *anise seed,* and is popular in teas, liqueurs, syrup infusions, and as an ingredient in *Chinese five-spice powder.*

starch Any of several powders made from potatoes, corn, sago, rice, wheat, arrowroot, or tapioca, used to thicken mixtures. Different starches possess unique properties; they are either high in *amylose,* such as cornstarch, or high in *amylopectin,* such as waxy maize. Root starches, such as tapioca, potato, and arrowroot, fall somewhere between the two. The major differences between the two types of starches are as follows:

AMYLOSE STARCHES	AMYLOPECTIN STARCHES
Cloudy when cool	Fairly clear when cool
Forms a firm gel when cool	Thickens, does not gel
Gel tightens and weeps over time	Does not weep over time
Not freezer stable	Does not weep when thawed
Much thicker cold than hot	Same thickness whether hot or cold
Tends to mask flavors	Less likely to mask flavors

*Adapted from *How Baking Works* by Paula Figoni

See also *arrowroot, cornstarch, flour, potato starch, rice starch, tapioca,* and *waxy maize.*

starch attack Refers to the breakdown of dough structure during baking, used in reference to rye bread. It is caused by *amylase* activity that weakens the crumb, and it may be prevented by using a *sourdough starter* because the starter reduces the amylase activity.

starch gelatinization The swelling and gelatinization process that occurs with starch in the presence of heat and moisture; it sets the loaf structure.

starch retrogradiation The staling process that begins after baking, when the starch in a baked good slowly begins to lose moisture.

starch wheat See *emmer wheat.*

star fruit See *carambola.*

starter A general term for a *sourdough culture.*

star tip A pastry tip with V-shaped cut-outs that produces star-shaped designs of the product being piped such as buttercream and *spritz* cookies.

Stayman Winesap apple See *apple.*

steam 1. A technique that cooks food on a rack or in a steaming basket over simmering water in a covered pan; this method best retains the food's shape, texture, flavor, and nutrients. It is a popular method for cooking vegetables and rice. 2. To inject moisture into an oven during the early stages of bread baking. This improves the volume by preventing the crust from forming too quickly. It also adds color and shine to the crust. 3. The water vapor that is formed when moisture-containing ingredients such as water, milk, and eggs are heated. The moisture plays an important role in obtaining volume and leavening of baked goods because when water expands, steam occupies over 1,500 times more space than liquid.

steamed bread A moist, tender batter bread that is cooked by steam method. The most popular version is *Boston brown bread.*

steamed bun See *mantou.*

steamed pudding A sweet or savory pudding steamed in a decorative mold. The finished product is imprinted with the design and usually served with a sauce. If a pudding mold is not available, pudding can be steamed in any heatproof container.

S
S

steamer A serving of foamed or steamed milk flavored with an Italian-style syrup and no espresso.

steel-cut oats See *oats*.

steep To soak dry ingredients in a liquid until the flavor is infused. Tea, coffee, herbs, and spices are commonly steeped in hot water, oil, or syrups.

stencil paste See *tuile*.

sticky bun An American breakfast item or afternoon snack made with a yeast-risen sweet dough that is smeared with a nut filling or cinnamon sugar. The dough is rolled into a cylinder and sliced into individual rounds. The rounds are put in a pan that has a bottom layer of a sticky mixture of pecans, butter, brown sugar, and honey or corn syrup. The buns are baked and then turned over to reveal a rich, sweet, caramelized, nutty topping. Many people joke that the name is from the fact that they "stick to your buns."

sticky rice See *rice*.

still-frozen A frozen product that is not machine churned. The air is incorporated through the use of whipped eggs and/or whipped cream, as with *mousse* and *French parfait,* or it may be stirred or frozen as is, as with *granité*.

Stilton cheese ('stihl-ton) A rich, creamy blue cheese with a slight crumbly texture. It contains 55% fat and pairs well with Port, grapes, and nuts. It is considered one of the best cheeses in the world, and is named for the English village where it was first produced.

stinger A cocktail that consists of equal parts Cognac or brandy and white *crème de menthe*.

stirred custard See *custard*.

Stollen ('stoh-luhn) A German Christmas bread that is a rich yeast dough packed with dried fruits and sometimes nuts. It is heavily dusted with confectioners' sugar. The bread was created in 1445 in Dresden; and the loaf symbolizes the blanket of the baby Jesus, while the colored fruits represent the gifts of the Magi. Although the original Dresden Stollen is the most well known, there are several varieties that soak the fruit in brandy or Schnapps before adding it to the dough and/or adding a thick band of *marzipan* or *almond paste* to the center before baking.

stonefruit See *drupe fruit*.

stone-ground flour See *flour*.

Stracchino (straht-chee-noh) A creamy, fresh cow's milk cheese from the Lombardy region of Italy. It contains about 50% milk fat and has a mild flavor similar to cream cheese but slightly more acidic.

straight dough See *mixing methods*.

straight flour See *flour*.

strain To separate a liquid from solids by passing the liquid through a *strainer* or *cheesecloth*.

strainer A mesh-bottomed bowl or disc with a handle attached to the rim. They come in various shapes and sizes. See *china cap* and *chinois*.

strap pan A commercial baking pan that consists of three or four loaf pans attached to each other by a metal strap.

Strassburger cookie A European butter cookie flavored with vanilla and cardamom. It is piped in a variety of designs, usually with a star tip, and may be sandwiched together with jam before being dipped in chocolate.

S
S

Strawberries Romanoff A dessert of strawberries soaked in orange liqueur or orange juice and topped with *crème chantilly*. Named in honor of the Russian royal family.

strawberry See *berry*.

Strawberry papaya See *papaya*.

strawberry shortcake See *shortcake*.

straw sugar A decorative sugar made by pouring sugar syrup on an oiled marble and allowing it to cool until firm. It is pulled into a long cord and folded in half lengthwise, bringing the ends together to form two strands that sit side by side. The process is repeated until there are eight strands. The long outside edges are brought together to form a hollow tube and the ends closed so that the air is trapped inside. The total folding process is repeated until the sugar starts to splinter on the outer walls and as much air as possible has been incorporated. The sugar may then be twisted into the desired shapes and will give the appearance of a tree branch. It may also be broken when cold and offers an interesting texture and appearance to showpieces and decorative garnishes. Traditionally it is not colored, but is cooked to a brown/yellow tone and used in its natural form.

Strega ('stray-guh) The Italian word for "witch," referring to a golden liqueur made from a secret combination of over 70 herbs, flowers, and spices. Its brilliant yellow comes from the use of the saffron flower, and its rich, slightly sweet flavor is used to flavor many Italian pastries, desserts, and confections.

Streusel ('stroo-zuhl) The German word for "sprinkle," referring to a crumbly topping of flour, sugar, butter, and sometimes spices. It is sprinkled on muffins, cakes, pies, coffeecakes, and other pastries before baking.

stroopwafel (stroop-'vahv-ehl) A Dutch cookie that is two crisp wafers spiced with cinnamon and nutmeg, and sandwiched together with molasses or caramel. The top of the cookie has a crosshatch pattern imprinted on it.

strong flour See *flour*.

strudel ('shtroo-duhl) The German word for "whirlpool," referring to a flaky pastry made by stretching a piece of strudel dough until it reaches paper-thin consistency and transparent appearance. It is then filled with a sweet or savory mixture and rolled up into a long rectangle. The pastry is baked and typically served warm. This famous Viennese pastry was inspired by the Turkish *baklava*, but originally created by Hungarians. There is an old wives' tale that a man will not marry a woman if he cannot read his newspaper through the stretched strudel dough.

stud To insert a flavored or decorative item into a food. For example, bread may be "studded" with raisins.

sübye ('soo-ehb-yah) A thickener used in Turkey, made from ground rice and milk.

succès A French cake that is two round layers of crisp almond *meringue* filled and iced with praline *buttercream*. The sides are covered with toasted sliced almonds and the top is heavily dusted with confectioners' sugar. It is also the name of the meringue mixture used to make the cake and various other petit fours and pastries.

sucralose An artificial sweetener. It is about 500 times sweeter than regular sugar, used in Australia and Canada under the name Splendar, but not yet approved by the FDA in the United States.

sucre neige ('sue-crah nehzh) The French word for "sugar snow," referring to the brand name of a treated confectioners' sugar product that is resistant to moisture.

sucrose ('soo-krohs) A disaccharide that is one molecule *glucose* and one molecule *fructose*. This dry, crystalline water-soluble sugar is what we most commonly know as regular sugar. It is commercially produced by removing and purifying the natural sucrose from sugarcane or sugar beets. It is also naturally present in maple and palm tree sap, and in many ripened fruits. It is less sweet than fructose but sweeter than glucose.

sugar A sweet crystallized substance that is mostly *sucrose,* used in baking and confectionery making. One of the most important ingredients in baking and pastry, sugar has many important functions, including sweetening and tenderizing products, retaining moisture and improving shelf life, aiding in caramelization and coloring of products, providing food for yeast, stabilizing whipped egg foams, promoting spread in cookies, reducing iciness in frozen desserts, assisting in leavening, and providing bulk and substance to sugar-based confections. Although granulated sugar is the most commonly used sugar product, there are other sugars, such as:

> **Barbados** A dark brown sugar that is very moist. It is used in the production of gingerbread fruit cakes and is made by combining cane or beet sugar with a large quantity of molasses. Also known as muscavado sugar.

> **Brown** Refined granulated sugar that is mixed with molasses. The color and flavor of the molasses determines if it is light or dark brown sugar.

> **Castor sugar** A British sugar that is similar to American superfine sugar. It is a granulated sugar that is more finely ground than regular sugar but coarser than confectioners' sugar. Its name is from the tall, cylindrical container with a perforated lid that is used to store the sugar, which is known as a castor in England. Also spelled caster sugar.

> **Coconut** Another name for palm sugar; see below.

> **Confectioners'** 1. Granulated sugar that has been ground into a powder. It contains 3% cornstarch, which absorbs moisture and prevents lumping. Also known as powdered sugar. There are varying degrees of fineness, which include:

>> **6X** A coarse powdered sugar that is most common to the nonprofessional. It is a good choice for dusting desserts and pastries because it is less likely to lump up or liquefy.

>> **10X** A finely ground sugar best used for items that need the sugar to melt quickly.

>> **12X** The finest ground powdered sugar available. It is best for icings and fondant. Also known as fondant sugar.

> **Crystal** The coarsest type of decorating sugar. It is formed into pellets that are five times larger than the grains of granulated sugar.

> **Cube** Damp granulated sugar that is pressed into molds, dried, and cut into desired cubes.

> **Decorating** Available in a variety of colors and textures, this sugar has larger grains than regular granulated sugar and is typically used to decorate cakes, cookies, and confections.

> **Demerara** Native to the Demerara region of Guyana, this raw cane sugar is light brown with coarse crystals that dissolve slowly. It is typically used as a topping for baked goods to add a sweet, crunchy texture to the product.

> **Glazing** A super-fine powdered sugar, typically 12X, that sometimes has stabilizers added to help retain moisture so that the glazed product will keep its glossy appearance longer.

S
s

Granulated The most common form of sugar used, this highly refined white sugar is made from either sugarcane or sugar beets. It is over 99% pure sucrose and is also referred to as regular sugar.

Icing The Canadian and British terms for *confectioners' sugar,* equivalent to American 12X.

Invert Sucrose sugar that has been inverted, or broken down into two components, *fructose* and *glucose.* The inversion process helps prevent *crystallization* and produces a smooth product. It is commonly used in the production of candies and confections. Natural products with invert sugar components include honey, molasses, maple syrup, and corn syrup.

Jaggery An unrefined, coarse brown sugar that is made by boiling sugarcane juice until it reduces to a thick crystallized syrup. It is the sugar used in India, where it is a honey-butter texture or cake-like solid form. Also known as *gur* and *palm sugar.*

Loaf Used in the creation of sugar sculptures, it is produced in a method that is similar to cube sugar.

Malt A *disaccharide that* consists of two glucose molecules, most commonly found in *glucose corn syrup* and *malt syrup.* It is formed when starch is broken down by enzymes and produces carbon dioxide. It also occurs when starch is converted into sugar during alcohol fermentation. It is one-third as sweet as sucrose and is also known as *maltose.* The name is also used to label the granulated malt extract used in baking. It is important in yeast-raised products because it ferments slowly, thus providing food for the yeast through the final proof. This ensures adequate carbon dioxide and results in properly leavened bread.

Palm The Thai version of *jaggery,* used in Thailand for sweets. Also known as *coconut sugar.*

Panela Made in Columbia, this unbleached and unrefined sugar is sold as bricks or round cakes. It has a golden-brown color and is popular as a beverage in South America. The drink may be made with milk and cheese, and served warm or with water and citrus and served cold.

Panocha An unrefined sugar from the Philippines.

Papelón Raw hardened sugarcane pulp. A popular Venezuelan drink called "papelón con limón" is made with water and lime and sweetened with papelón.

Piloncillo A cone-shaped variation of *panela,* made in Mexico.

Rapadura The juice of pure sugarcane that has been formed into bricks and dried. It is used as a substitute for refined sugar because of its high nutritional value. It has a mild caramel-like flavor, which makes it popular for baking. It is sold as organic whole sugar or organic powdered sugar and is 100% vegan.

Rock A decorative sugar produced when *royal icing* is added to a sugar syrup that has been cooked to 285°F (141°C). This causes the sugar to turn opaque and bubble up in the pan. As the heated air expands, the albumen in the egg white of the royal icing sets and the liquid evaporates. The remaining sugar crystallizes and forms a porous, rocklike appearance to the sugar. Once set, it is rock hard and may be colored as desired with an airbrush.

Sanding A type of decoratoring sugar whose granules are larger than granulated sugar but smaller than crystal sugar. Also known a *pearl sugar.*

Superfine A very small-grained sugar that melts and dissolves more quickly then regular granulated sugar. It is most commonly used in meringues, icings, and other products that benefit from its fine melting qualities. It may be substituted with granulated sugar in equal amounts.

Turbinado Similar in taste and color to light brown sugar, this granulated sugar is made by steaming unrefined raw sugar. It retains a small amount of molasses on both the surface and the crystal itself, which gives it its pale brown color and light molasses flavor. It is three times coarser than granulated sugar and is also known as raw sugar.

Wasanbon Toh A refined Japanese sugar made from a special variety of sugarcane. It is a fine, creamy white powder made by removing the molasses syrup. It has a delicate flavor that is important for Japanese sweets.

sugar apple See *sweetsop.*

sugarcane stalk A sweet snack or garnish made by boiling the stalk of the sugarcane to make it soft and edible.

sugar cookie A short dough cookie typically cut out into various designs and decorated with a variety of items such as royal icing, flat icing, jimmies, candy, or other products. They may be crisp or tender depending upon the baking time and are very popular during Christmastime.

sugarplum A small, sweet confection that consists of dried fruits enrobed in *fondant.*

sugar substitute See *artificial sweetener.*

sugar density refractometer See *thermometer.*

sugar flower Decorative flowers made from *gumpaste.*

sugar lamp See *heat lamp.*

Sugar Loaf See *pineapple.*

sugar syrup A syrup made by boiling sugar and water and allowing it to cool. The ratio of sugar to water varies according to the desired sweetness. The syrup may be flavored with spices, extracts, and/or liqueurs and is used primarily for moistening cakes, thinning *fondant* or other syrups, and *sorbet* and *granité* production.

sugar thermometer Another name for *candy thermometer;* see *thermometer, candy.*

sugar warming case A box-shaped piece of equipment for working with *pulled sugar* and *blown sugar.* It has a solid top and bottom with transparent sides and an open front. A heat lamp hangs from the top of the box and may be adjusted up or down depending on the amount of heat you want on the sugar. The box is large enough to work with the sugar by hand inside the box and has an elevated work surface that is removable for cleaning. The box helps prevent the sugar from being exposed to drafts, which will cool it and keeps the sugar free of debris.

sultana (suhl-'tan-uh) 1. A white seedless grape from Smyrna, Turkey, and named after the Turkish sultan. It has been used to make wine, but today is primarily cultivated for raisins and is known in the U.S. as Thompson Seedless. 2. British term for a golden raisin.

sumac ('soo-mak) An aromatic shrub native to the Middle East, with deep, purplish-red berries. The berries are dried and sold whole or ground to a powder that has a fruity, slightly astringent taste. It is used as a flavoring ingredient and also as a topping for breads and pastries.

summer pudding A British dessert of briefly cooked, sweetened fresh berries that are placed in a deep bread-lined dish or mold and topped with more sliced bread.

S
s

The dessert is weighted down overnight and the berry juices moisten the bread with their juices. After unmolding, the pudding is served chilled with whipped cream.

sundae An American ice cream dessert of one to three scoops of flavored ice cream, topped with a sauce such as chocolate, fruit, caramel, or butterscotch, and sometimes topped with sweetened whipped cream, nuts, and a maraschino cherry. It dates back to the 19th century, when serving an ice cream soda on Sunday was thought to be immoral because it was carbonated. The carbonation was removed and the name was changed with an alternate spelling so as not to be disrespectful of the day.

sunflower seed The seed of the sunflower plant, cultivated primarily for its oil. Russia is the largest producer of sunflower seeds, and uses them extensively also in confections and snack food. In the United States, California, Minnesota, and North Dakota are the largest producers of sunflower seeds. A single sunflower may measure more than 12 inches (30 cm) in diameter and contain over 2,000 seeds. The seeds are rich in iron and contain 24% protein and 47% fat. They are available dried or roasted, either in or out of the shell and plain or salted.

sunflower seed oil A pale, mild oil pressed from *sunflower seeds*. It is low in saturated fat and contains low cholesterol. It is not recommended for frying owing to its low *smoke point*.

sungkaya ('soong-kah-yah) A steamed coconut custard from Thailand.

superfine sugar See *sugar*.

sütlaç (soor-tlahk) A Turkish rice pudding flavored with vanilla or cinnamon and briefly placed under a broiler to brown the top before serving. It dates back to the Ottoman Empire, and may be served hot or cold.

swag design See *garland*.

sweat To cook foods, particularly vegetables, in a little amount of fat over low heat in a covered pot, so as to cook the foods in some of their own juices and soften them without browning.

Swedish pancake A small, moist, rich pancake served with *lingonberries* and butter. They are made in a *plett pan* and eaten as a dessert.

sweet chocolate See *chocolate, dark*.

sweet cider See *cider*.

sweetened condensed milk A thick, creamy sweet cow's milk product that has had 60% of the water evaporated and around 45% sugar added. It is popular for use in desserts such as puddings and pies, and as a sweetener for cocktails and beverages, particularly in Asia.

sweet potato The large, edible root of a vine in the morning glory family, native to tropical areas of the Americas and particularly popular in the South. There are two varieties, pale and dark. The dry-fleshed pale variety has a crumbly texture similar to a white potato and a light yellow skin and flesh. The moister orange-fleshed type has dark skin and sweet flavor that is often combined with brown sugar, honey, molasses, and marshmallows for use in pies and sweet desserts.

sweet red bean paste A mixture of pureed Chinese red beans, sugar, and shortening. It is dark red, thick, and sweet; it is used in steamed pastries and sweet dishes, and is available fresh or in cans.

sweetsop The small, oval fruit of a tropical New World tree that is cultivated in California and Florida. Its thick, yellow-green skin encases a sweet, segmented, custard-like flesh. It is available mid-summer to mid-winter and is also known as *sugar apple*.

Sweet Treats pluot See *pluot.*

Swiss buttercream See *buttercream.*

Swiss Chalet See *Specialty Vendors* appendix.

Swiss dots A simple cake-decorating technique whereby round dots are piped onto the sides and top of a cake to create a decorative pattern. The size of the dots can determined by the decorator; however, most designs are made with a #2, #3, or #4 decorating tip. This technique works with *royal icing* as well as *buttercream.*

Swiss meringue See *meringue.*

Swiss roll See *jelly roll.*

syllabub ('sihl-uh-buhb) An English dessert of whipped cream, white wine, sugar, brandy or sherry, and sometimes spices and lemon. It dates back to Elizabethan times. It may be eaten as is or used as a topping for cakes, fruit, or cookies.

syrniki (sihr-nee-kee) A rich, creamy Eastern European cake made from farmers cheese, flour or farina, sugar, eggs, milk or cream, and sometimes lemon or raisins; it is fried and topped with confectioners' sugar, jam, honey, or sour cream. The dish is popular in Russia, Poland, and the Ukraine, and is eaten for breakfast or as a dessert.

Szechwan peppercorn The tiny, reddish-brown berry of the prickly ash tree native to the Szechwan province of China. The berries have a distinct hot-spicy flavor and aroma; also known as *sansho* and *Sichuan peppercorn.*

S
s

T, Tbsp. Abbreviations for *tablespoon;* the letter is usually capitalized to avoid confusion with *teaspoon* (abbreviated as *tsp).*

table d'hôte ('tah-bluh doht) French for "the table of the host," referring to a complete meal of various courses for the price of the entrée.

tablespoon A U.S. measure of volume, equivalent to 3 teaspoons or .05 fluid ounces, and the metric equivalent of 15 ml.

tabliering method See *tempering.*

tabling See *tempering.*

taffy ('tah-fee) A soft, chewy, bite-size candy made with butter, sugar, and various flavorings. *Saltwater taffy* uses a small amount of saltwater in the mixture and was popularized as a boardwalk treat in Atlantic City, New Jersey, during the 1800s.

tahini (tah-'hee-nee) A thick, oily paste made from ground raw sesame seeds. It is most commonly used as a flavoring agent in Middle Eastern cooking and candy making.

taiyaki See *waffle.*

Taleggio cheese (tahl-eh-zee-oh) A rich, semi-soft cow's milk cheese produced in the Lombardy region of Italy. Its flavor and color are determined by how long it is aged and ranges from mild to pungent and pale to golden yellow. It pairs well with fruit and dessert wines.

talibur (tah-lee'buhr) A French dessert of an apple stuffed with almonds, dried fruits, and spices and then wrapped in *puff pastry.* It is baked and then glazed with apricot jam and *fondant* flavored with *Calvados.*

tall A 12-ounce (360 ml) portion of an espresso-milk beverage.

tallow ('taah-loh) Animal fat rendered from beef or mutton, used in the commercial production of shortening, cooking oils, and cake mixes. It can also be colored and sculpted for use as a decorative showpiece.

taloa (tah-loh-ah) A yeasted corn cake from the Basque region of France.

tamarillo (tam-uh-'rihl-oh) A small (2½ to 3-inch/6.2 to 7.5 cm) oval fruit native to South America. It is related to the tomato, and the two varieties are red and gold. The red variety has a sweet-tart flavor and a scarlet skin with a golden yellow-orange flesh packed with tiny black seeds. The gold variety is slightly sweeter and has a golden yellow skin and flesh with greenish-white seeds. Available April to September. Also known as a *tree tomato.*

tamarind ('tam-uh-rihnd) The seed pod of a tropical tree native to Asia and Africa, but widely cultivated in India. The pods are long and reddish-brown, and contain small seeds surrounded by a distinct sweet-sour pulp. The pulp is available fresh in the pod, dried, as a syrup, or as a paste. Tamarind is used extensively in Asian and Indian cooking, in curries, and also to flavor desserts and beverages. Also known as *Indian date*.

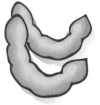

tamis ('tam-ee) The French word for "drum," referring to a metal or wooden drum-shaped sieve. It has a metal or nylon mesh that comes in various hole sizes, which determine the fineness of the product being sifted. Those made with nylon mesh are more durable and retain their shape better; however, the metal mesh is stronger and sharper, but susceptible to rust and discoloration from fruit purees.

tamper A tool used to pack freshly ground espresso beans, attached to the espresso machine under the water nozzle. It holds the grounds in place during brewing.

tandoor oven See *oven*.

tandori oven (than-'door-ee) Another name for *tandoor oven*.

tangelo (tan-'jell-oh) A mandarin orange hybrid that is a cross between a *tangerine* and a *pomelo*. There are many varieties that vary in size and flavor and range in color from light yellow to deep orange. The most common variety is *Minneola,* which is distinguished by its nipple-shaped end. They are available from November to March. A gourmet variety from Florida known as "Honey Bell" is distinguished by its intense sweetness and juiciness and is only available in January. See also *mandarin orange*.

tangerine (tan-juh-'reen) See *mandarin orange*.

tangor An oval, loose-skinned hybrid citrus that is a cross between a *tangerine* and an *orange,* most commonly the *Temple orange.* They are available from December to March. See also *mandarin orange*.

tank method See *Champagne*.

tannin ('tan-ihn) A substance derived from the seeds, stems, and skins of *grapes* and many other plants. It is important in the production of red wines because, if they are not properly aged, the tannin will produce an undesirable astringent, puckery taste. Tannins are an important natural ingredient in wine that helps prevent oxidation and is a major portion of sediment found at the bottom of the bottles of many well-aged red wines.

tant-pour-tant A French term that refers to a mixture of equal parts by weight superfine sugar and ground almonds. It is used in the production of cookies, batters, and petit fours.

tapioca (tap-ee-'oh-kah) A pure starch extracted from the root of the *cassava* plant, a tropical plant of the New World. It is used as a thickening agent, much like *cornstarch* or *arrowroot,* in pie fillings, fruit glazes, and desserts. It is available as a powder or flour, granules, flakes, or pellets, which are more commonly known as pearls. *Pearl tapioca* is used to make *tapioca pudding;* it should be soaked before use because during baking it becomes translucent and soft, rather than dissolving completely.

tapioca flour See *tapioca*.

tapioca pudding A pudding made from pearl tapioca with a custard-like consistency and a unique added texture of the softened tapioca pearls. Many people describe this dessert as "fish eyes and glue." See also *tapioca*.

T
t

taralli (tah-rah-lee) A small, round, unsweetened Italian semolina cookie that is sometimes flavored with fennel or pepper. It is first boiled and then baked.

tarla See *rolling pin*.

Taro A starch derived from the taro root, used mainly for ethnic savory cooking by people of West Africa, the Carribean, and the Polynesian Islands. It exhibits the same properties as most other starches. See *starch*.

taro pudding See *kulolo*.

tarragon ('tahr-uh-gon) An aromatic herb of the Artemisia genus, with pointed, narrow, dark green leaves and a distinct anise-like flavor. It is available fresh, powdered, or dried. There are two types of tarragon plant, but the French is preferred.

tart 1. A shallow pastry crust that is filled with a sweet or savory mixture before or after baking. The tart may be straight sided or fluted, and made free-form or in a *tart pan* or *flan ring;* flan rings and tart pans are available in different shapes and sizes. Small or individual tarts are called *tartlets*. In Britain, a tart is known as a flan. 2. A term used to describe a sharp, slightly sour taste.

tarta pasiega A Spanish cheesecake flavored with honey and orange flower water. It is served at Easter and dates back to medieval times.

Tartarian cherry See *cherry*.

tartaric acid (tahr-'tar-ik) A substance found in some fruits, but most commonly extracted from *grapes*. It is used in wine making to create a crisp flavor and mellow aging process. It is also used to make *cream of tartar* and to enhance the fruit flavor of sorbets and fruit desserts. It may also be used as a substitute for *acidulated water* or *citric acid*.

tarte aux fruits (tahrt oh fwee) The French term for "tart with fruit," referring to a pastry tart shell filled with a lightly sweetened custard cream and topped with fresh fruits. It is then glazed with apricot jam, which gives the fruit a nice sheen and helps prevent it from oxidizing. Some pastry chefs brush the bottom of the baked tart shell with tempered chocolate to prevent the cream from making the crust soggy.

tarte Tatin (tart tah-'tan) A French upside-down apple tart, made famous by the Tatin sisters, who lived in the Loire Valley. It is believed to have been created by accident at their hotel during the late 19th century, when one of the sisters left sliced apples cooking in butter and sugar too long. In an effort to save the dish, she placed a pastry crust over it and baked it in the oven. When the crust was browned, the tart was inverted to reveal a beautifully caramelized apple tart. It is traditionally served with *crème fraîche*.

tartine (tahr-teen) The French term for a slice of bread spread with butter, jam, or cheese.

tartlet See *tart*.

tart pan A metal baking pan for baking tarts, available in different shapes and sizes, and with straight or fluted sides. Some pans have removable bottoms.

tava A cast iron plate used to bake Indian *flatbreads,* such as *chapatti*.

Tawny Port See *Port*.

tayberry A large, cone-shaped Scottish berry that is a cross between a *blackberry* and a *raspberry*. It has a bright purple color and a blackberry taste.

Tayglach ('tay-glak) A Jewish confection of small pieces of honey-sweetened dough that are baked and then poached in a sweetened honey-ginger syrup. They are rolled in chopped nuts or shredded coconut before serving.

tea 1. A popular warm beverage made by steeping processed dried tea leaves in hot water until their aroma and flavor are infused. 2. The dried leaves used to make tea. 3. The evergreen plant in the Camellia family, from which tea is made.

T
t

The tea tree flourishes in warm climates that have a lot of rainfall. It is believed to date back to 2700 B.C., when Emperor Shen Nung, scholar and herbalist, was sipping hot water under a wild tea tree. As the leaves floated in his cup, the flavor was infused and tea was born.

Tea plays an important role in many cultures and influences art, social life, and economy. The British developed a meal around it, called *high tea.* The Japanese have an elaborate tea ceremony called *kaiseki.* And American history was made as a result of the Boston Tea Party, a rebellion against high taxes. It is also a major part of traditions in India, China, and the Middle East. The major tea-producing countries are India, China, Sri Lanka (Ceylon), Kenya, Tanzania, Japan, Turkey, and South America. To harvest tea, the leaves and buds are hand-plucked, then processed as follows:

1. **Withering** The leaves are thinly spread to evaporate the water and make them soft and pliable, either naturally or by forcing heated air over the racks.

2. **Rolling** After withering, the leaves are passed through a rolling machine, where they are twisted and rolled to release the juices that give tea its flavor.

3. **Roll-breaking** The twisted lumps produced from the rolling are broken up by coarse mesh sieves or roll-breakers. The fine leaves that fall through the sieve are fermented while the coarse leaves are re-rolled.

4. **Oxidation or fermentation** The leaves are spread on cement or tiled floors in a cool, damp room. The absorption of oxygen turns the leaves a bright copper color. This step is done only for black teas, not green teas.

5. **Drying or firing** The leaves are further oxidized and dried evenly with hot, dry air.

6. **Grading** After the drying process, large and small broken and unbroken leaves are mixed. They are sorted through sieves with different size mesh, which divides them into leaf and broken grades. Leaf grades are made up of the larger leaves that are left after the broken grades have been sifted out. They include *orange pekoe, pekoe,* and *pekoe souchong.* The broken grades are smaller and represent approximately 80% of the total crop. They make a darker, stronger tea and are primarily used for blending and teabags. These grades include broken orange pekoe, broken pekoe, and broken pekoe souchong, fannings, and fines.

There are over 3,000 varieties of tea. The three main types of tea are black, green, and oolong. The processing determines the quality and individual characteristics of the tea.

Black A tea processed with the most oxidation. It is typically very strong and contains more caffeine than the other varieties. In general these teas are named after the regions in which they are produced, with the most well known being Assam, Ceylon, and Darjeeling.

Green A tea known for its mild, slightly bitter flavor, which comes from leaves that are steamed and dried but not fermented. It has a light, slightly bitter flavor with leafy undertones. The light green color of the tea contributes to its name. It is popular for its health benefits as an *antioxidant.* The most common varieties are Tencha and Gunpowder.

Oolong A tea made from semi-fermented leaves. The flavor and color fall somewhere between black tea and green tea. The most well known is Formosa Oolong from Taiwan.

Instant Tea that has been dried and granulated. It dissolves quickly in cold and hot water and often has additives such as sugar and flavorings.

T
t

Herbal See *tisane*.

White A light, delicate tea made by steaming and drying the leaves.

tea ball See *tea infuser*.

tea cake 1. A light, buttery yeasted bun studded with dried fruits. After baking it is brushed with sugar syrup and then dusted with cinnamon sugar. It is served with jam and cream during tea time in Britain. 2. A variety of small cakes served with *afternoon tea*.

tea infuser A small container to infuse loose tea leaves in hot water, usually in a tea pot. The leaves are placed in a small basket-like cup with perforations and a hinged lid. Once infused, the container is pulled out via a small chain attached to the lid. Also called a *tea ball*.

teaspoon A U.S. measure of volume, equivalent to .17 fluid ounces, or the metric equivalent of 5 ml.

tea strainer A tiny handheld mesh strainer used to infuse tea in a cup. It is also used to remove impurities from sugar syrup when preparing it for decorative sugar work.

teff A tiny cereal grain native to Ethiopia, where it is the primary ingredient in the flatbread *injera* that serves as a dinner plate for stews and that is subsequently eaten. Teff is now cultivated in the United States. It has a mild, nutty flavor and is high in protein, fiber, carbohydrates, calcium, and iron. It contains no gluten and is available in natural food stores.

tekoua (ta-ko-wa′) A North African dessert made by rolling sesame paste and sugar into a small ball and then in confectioners' sugar.

teleme (tehl-uh-may) A creamy, semi-soft cheese with a distinct tangy flavor that is similar in texture to brie. Available primarily in northern California. It pairs well with fruit and nuts.

tempering The process by which chocolate is made workable. Chocolate is purchased in a tempered state, meaning it is hard, glossy, and has a brittle snap when broken, but in order to work with it, it must be melted and retempered to achieve the characteristics of its original form. This is accomplished with a process called tempering. It involves melting, cooling, and re-warming chocolate in order to bring the different cocoa butter crystals into alignment (see *cocoa butter*). The temperatures used vary according to the type and brand of chocolate, but the following is a guideline for working temperatures:

TYPE	MELT	COOL	REWARM
Dark chocolate	115° to 120°F	84° to 86°F	89° to 90°F
	(46° to 49°C)	(29° to 30°C)	(31° to 32°C)
Milk chocolate	110° to 115°F	82° to 84°F	86° to 88°F
	(43° to 46°C)	(26° to 29°F)	(30° to 31°C)
White chocolate	110° to 115°F	82° to 84°F	86° to 88°F
	(43° to 46°C)	(26° to 29°F)	(30° to 31°C)

There are four methods for tempering chocolate:

Tabliering or Tabling Melt chocolate to appropriate temperature. Pour ⅔ of the melted chocolate onto a marble slab. Cool the chocolate by repeatedly spreading it with a palette knife and scraping it together with a metal scraper until it begins to thicken. Keep the chocolate in constant motion to prevent any solidification. Scrape the cooled chocolate into the remaining ⅓ of the melted chocolate and stir until it is smooth. Check the temperature and warm slightly over a double boiler if it is too cool. Once it reaches its working temperature it is ready for use.

Seeding or Block Melt chocolate to appropriate temperature. Slowly add either a block or small pieces (seeds) of tempered chocolate into the mixture and stir continuously between each addition. The block or seed is considered the cooled chocolate, so once the chocolate reaches its working temperature it is ready for use.

Direct Warming Slowly melt chopped chocolate until it reaches the working temperature. If it goes above it must be re-tempered in order for the cocoa butter crystals to properly align.

Cold Water Cool the melted chocolate over a cold water bath just until the sides begin to set up and then stir until smooth and the chocolate is cooled to proper temperature. Return chocolate to warm water bath and stir until it reaches the proper working temperature.

Temple orange A hybrid of an *orange* and a *tangerine,* this medium, oval fruit has a dark orange flesh and a rough, thick dark orange rind. It has many seeds and a sweet-tart flavor. Available January through mid-March.

temporary emulsion See *emulsion.*

tencha tea A premium Japanese green tea most commonly used in Japanese tea ceremonies.

tenderizer An ingredient such as fat, oil, sugar, syrup, or leavening agent that interferes with structure formation and produces a moist, tender product. Excess use of a tenderizer may cause the product to crumble and fall apart.

Tennessee whisky See *whisky.*

tennis cake See *Battenberg.*

tequila (teh-'kee-luh) A pale-yellow Mexican liquor made by fermenting and distilling the sweet sap of the blue agave plant, a succulent of dry habitats. It is named for the town in which it is produced and is bottled, in the following categories:

Blanco (white) It is bottled shortly after distillation and has a fresh, smooth flavor with hints of pepper and herbs. Also known as Silver or Plata.

Oro (gold) or Joven Abacado (young) A Tequila Blanco that has flavoring and coloring added to resemble an aged tequila.

Resposado (rested) Aged for a minimum of two months in wood casks. This produces a mellow tequila with hints of vanilla and spices.

Anejo (old) Aged for a minimum of one year but less than three years. It has a smooth, complex flavor. Extra Anejo, also known as Maduro (mature), is aged for a minimum of three years and is considered the finest of tequilas.

terrine A sweet or savory food prepared in a mold, also called a terrine. The mold is oblong with straight sides and a flared edge to hold the cover. Sweet terrines do not use the cover and may be made from Bavarian creams, mousses, ice creams, or gelled fruit.

terrinée A dessert of slow-baked rice, milk, sugar, cinnamon, ginger, cloves, and sugar, from Normandy, France. The long baking time produces a sweet crust of moist, soft, spiced rice that is served warm or cold.

T
t

tête de nègre (teht duh 'nehg-ruh) Literally, "black head," a round French confection of two dome-shaped white *meringue* discs sandwiched together with chocolate *buttercream,* coated with the buttercream, and rolled in grated chocolate.

Thai coffee Coffee mixed with *sweetened condensed milk.*

Thai ginger A white-fleshed rhizome, or underground swollen stem, of a ginger plant native to Southeast Asia. It has a hot, peppery-ginger flavor and is used extensively in Thai cooking. Also known as *galangal* and Laos (the powdered form).

thala guli ('tah-lah 'goo-lee) A Sri Lankan candy made from ground raw sesame seeds, salt, and *palm sugar.*

Theobroma cacao A tropical evergreen tree native to Central and South America, cultivated for its cacao pods, which are the source of cocoa, chocolate, and cocoa butter. *Theobroma* means "food of the Gods."

theobromine See *xanthine.*

thermal death point The temperature at which yeast dies, 140°F (60°C).

thermometer A tool to measure the temperature of doughs, chocolate, sugar, and other items, such as refrigerators and freezers. Thermometers are necessary to ensure proper food safety and sanitation. The type of thermometer used depends on the product being made, but to ensure an accurate reading, they should all be properly calibrated. With the exception of the *Baumé thermometer* and *Brix hydrometer,* this can be done by either the *ice-point method* or the *boil-point method.* To use the ice-point method, place the thermometer in a container of ice water without its touching the container. If it does not read 32°F (0°C), either push the reset button or, if it does not have one, use a pair of needlenose pliers to turn the nut under the top of the thermometer until it reaches the correct reading. To use the boil-point method, place the thermometer in boiling water; if it does not read 212°F (100°C), adjust it using the same instructions as for the ice-point method. The following are the major kinds of thermometers used in the bake shop:

> **Baumé** Another name for Saccharometer; see below.
>
> **Brix hydrometer** Similar to the Saccharometer but expressed in decimals rather than degrees.
>
> **Candy** A glass thermometer suspended in a metal cage or rectangular metal sheet to protect the glass and prevent it from touching the bottom of the pan. It is used to read the temperature of sugar, candies, confections, jams, and jellies. It is typically marked in 2-degree increments, from 100° to 400°F (38° to 205°C). Some types are marked with the stages of cooked sugar (see *Sugar Cooking Stages* appendix). Also known as *sugar thermometer.*
>
> **Chocolate** Designed to read the temperature of chocolate during the tempering process. It is also good for warming fondant. It reads in 1-degree increments from 40° to 130°F (4° to 54°C). It is recommended to use the style that has a temperature dial on top of a silicone spoon, so that the temperature may be read while stirring. A mercury thermometer that is encased in glass and protected by a wire cage is available and many pastry chefs utilize this when boiling sugar, although because of the chance of breakage all other mercury thermometers are not recommended for bakeshop use.
>
> **Deep-frying** Designed to read the temperature of the hot fat used for deep-frying.

T
t

Digital Measures temperatures with a metal probe or sensing area and displays it on a digital readout. These range in size, shape, and ability to read both Fahrenheit and Celsius. Some can store data and be programmed to take and record temperatures at different times.

Instant-read Measures temperatures from 0° to 220°F (−18° to 104°C) through a metal probe that has a sensor on the end. The reading is displayed on the top of the round face with a needle that registers the numbered temperature markings. It is typically made with an adjustable calibration nut and comes in a thin plastic tube with a clip so it can be attached to a chef's jacket.

Oven Designed to read the internal temperature of an oven. It is typically set in a metal frame with a stand or hanging clip, and reads from 100° to 650°F (38° to 343°C). The temperatures are marked on a face dial with a needle that points to the temperature reading.

Refrigerator/freezer Designed to read the internal temperature of a refrigerator or freezer. It looks and works like an oven thermometer, but reads from −20° to 80°F (−29° to 26°C).

Saccharimeter Measures the sugar concentration in a liquid by measuring the angle of refracted light. It is typically used in the food processing industry and for the distillation of alcoholic drinks.

Saccharometer Designed to determine the concentration of sugar in a liquid, which affects the density of the solution. It is a small, thin glass tube marked with readings of 0° to 58°BE. To use this instrument, place enough of the solution in a container (there are small, thin metal containers for this use) so that the saccharometer can float. The reading is taken from the marking that sits directly on the surface of the solution. To get an accurate reading, the solution should be around 58°F (14°C). Also known as Baumé thermometer.

Sugar Density Refractometer Uses the *Brix scale* to measure sugar concentrations, using the same principles as the Saccharimeter.

thermoreversible A gel such as *gelatin* or *agar-agar* that, once set, may be rewarmed to a liquid state.

thimbleberry See *berry.*

thin To dilute or make a mixture thinner by adding liquid.

Thompson Seedless grape See *grape.*

thong muan ('tahng moo-ahn) The Thai term for "rolled gold," referring to a cigarette-shaped wafer flavored with *coconut milk* and *kaffir lime.*

thread stage See *Sugar Cooking Stages* appendix.

three-fold See *letter fold.*

Three Musketeers A milk chocolate candy bar filled with a light, creamy chocolate *nougat* center.

thyme (time) An aromatic herb, native to southern Europe, that is a member of the mint family. It has a strong, minty, lemon-like flavor and is available fresh or dried. There are several varieties, including garden thyme, lemon thyme, French thyme, and lime thyme.

ti A fast-growing, woody plant or shrub, an Asian and Pacific member of the lily family. It is known as *ki* in Hawaii, and its leaves were used by the Kahuna priests

T
t

in their religious ceremonial rituals, to ward off evil spirits and to call in good. Today, the leaves are used to wrap food for cooking and are boiled in water to make a relaxing drink. The boiled roots are used to make a strong liquor called *okolehao* and the large, sweet starchy roots are baked and eaten as a dessert.

Tía Maria ('tee-uh muh-'ree-uh) A Jamaican liqueur made from rum and Blue Mountain coffee. It is similar to Kahlúa, but drier and lighter.

tier (teer) A level of a multilevel celebration cake; the cake layers are either stacked on top of each other or separated by *pillars*.

tiger nut See *earth almond*.

tigeladas (tea-zha-lah-das) A thick, fluffy, pudding-like Portuguese dessert made with milk, eggs, sugar, and cinnamon baked in a clay dish.

timbale ('tihm-buhl) 1. A small, high-sided, drum-shape mold with a closed, tapered bottom. It is used to bake sweet and savory dishes. 2. A baked pastry shell filled with fruits, pastry cream, or ice cream.

tippaleivat (tip-pah-le-fhat) A Scandinavian dessert made with a yeast-raised batter that is piped into a cruller shape, fried, and then rolled in sugar.

tipsy (Parson's) cake A British sponge cake layered with sherry-flavored custard and topped with whipped cream. There are two stories as to how it got its name. The first was that a parishioner named Parson made the cake for the local priest and had added too much sherry; the other is that the cake is so laden with custard and sherry that it always tips to one side.

tiramisu The Italian word for "pick me up," referring to a dessert of *ladyfingers* soaked with espresso and Marsala-flavored *mascarpone* mousse. It is garnished with cocoa powder and/or chocolate shavings.

tisane (tih-'zahn) An herb tea, made by steeping herbs, spices, and/or flowers in hot water; believed by many to have a calming effect, especially when made with *camomile*.

toddy ('tod-ee) A warm cocktail made by steeping spices and alcohol, usually rum, whisky, or brandy, in hot water. It is believed by some to relieve the symptoms of a cold or flu. Also known as *hot toddy*.

toffee A buttery, crunchy confection made by cooking sugar, water, and butter until it caramelizes, about 300°F (149°C). The mixture is then poured onto an oiled marble slab, cooled, and broken into pieces. It may be dipped in chocolate and/or nuts, and eaten as a candy or used to garnish cakes. The caramel-like flavor pairs particularly well with apples.

Tokay grape See *grape*.

Tokay wine ('toh-kay) A sweet white wine produced in the Tokay region of Hungary, primarily with the Furmint grape. Tokay Aszú is considered to be a leading, well-balanced sweet wine. In Hungary, it is served with celebratory desserts such as apricot cake or crepes filled with a thick chocolate cream.

Toll House cookie A rich butter cookie with chocolate chips. This famous American cookie was created in the 1930s by Ruth Wakefield, who owned the Toll House Inn, on the outskirts of Whitman, Massachusetts. In 1939, she sold the recipe to the Nestlé Company, and the original recipe for Nestlé Toll House Cookies is still printed on the back of every bag of its semisweet chocolate morsels.

Tom and Jerry A warm cocktail made with eggs, hot milk or water, sugar, spices, and a liquor such as brandy or rum. It is named after the two central characters in the 19th-century novel *Life in London*.

tonic water ('tohn-ik) Water that has been charged with carbon dioxide and flavored with quinine, fruit extracts, and sugar, used as a mixer for cocktails. Also known as *quinine water*.

tonkinois (than-kee-nwah) 1. A two-layer French almond sponge cake filled and iced with praline *buttercream*. The sides are decorated with toasted almonds and the top is iced with orange *fondant* and sprinkled with grated coconut. 2. A square petit four of *nougatine* filled with praline-flavored *frangipane*. The top is iced with chocolate and sprinkled with toasted chopped pistachios.

Tootsie Pop A fruit-flavored lollipop created in 1931; it has a hard candy shell and *Tootsie Roll* center.

Tootsie Roll A small, chewy candy in the shape of a cylinder, with chocolaty flavor. It was created in 1896 by Leo Hirschfield, who wanted a chocolate candy that would not melt in the heat; he used his daughter's nickname.

Topfen See *quark*.

toque (tohk) The traditional white pleated chef's hat. It dates back to the 16th century, and the different heights of the hat originally indicated the cook's rank in the kitchen. The pleats are believed to represent how many different ways there are to cook an egg.

torrone (toh-'roh-nay) The Italian version of *nougat,* made from honey, sugar, egg whites, and toasted almonds.

torta ('tohr-tuh) 1. The Italian word for tart, cake, or pie. 2. The Spanish word for a loaf or cake. 3. The Portuguese word for cake or tart.

torta delizia (t'or-tah day-leet-see-ah) An Italian *sponge cake* filled with *pastry cream* or jam and covered in almond *macaroon* paste. It is briefly baked, then brushed with a sweet glaze. Owing to its sweetness, it is eaten in bite-size pieces.

torta di mandorle ('tor-tah dee mahn-'dor-lay) A pastry shell filled with *frangipane,* topped with whole almonds, and then baked until golden brown. It is made in a variety of shapes and sizes, and is heavily dusted with confectioners' sugar. A specialty of Venice.

torta diplomatica ('tor-tah dee-plo-mah-tee-kah) A rich, round Italian cake made by layering *puff pastry* with pastry cream and with *sponge cake* that has been brushed with rum syrup. The cake is iced in *pastry cream* and covered with broken pieces of puff pastry. It is dusted with confectioners' sugar before serving.

torta nicolotta A simple bread pudding from Venice, made with leftover bread, milk, sugar, and flavorings such as lemon zest, raisins, rum, and cinnamon.

torte (tohrt) A rich, single or multi-layered cake typically made by replacing all or some of the flour with ground nuts or bread crumbs. It may be filled with butter-cream, jam, or other flavorings. The most well-known tortes are *Sachertorte, Dobos torte,* and the tart-like *linzertorte.*

torteil (tohr-'tay) A variety of *Twelfth Night cake* that consists of brioche dough shaped like a crown and flavored with citrus, anise seed, rum, and dried fruit, then decorated with candied fruit to resemble the jewels on the crown.

tortillon (tohr-'teel) A *petit four sec* that is made by twisting *puff pastry* into a corkscrew shape and sprinkling it with ground almonds or candied fruit.

tortoni (tore-'toh-nee) An individual frozen Italian dessert of either sweetened whipped cream or ice cream and rum, chopped almonds, and crumbled macaroons. It is named after the owner of a popular 18th-century Parisian café.

toscatårta ('tohs-kah-'tahr-tah) A Swedish almond butter cake, served warm.

tôt-fait (toht-fay) 1. A lemon pound cake served at tea in slices or with poached fruit. 2. A soufflé-like dish made with sugar, flour, butter, milk, vanilla, and eggs in a shallow ramekin. It is eaten warm, directly from the oven before the dough collapses.

T
t

toughener An ingredient such as eggs, flour, cocoa powder, or starch that builds structure and holds the volume and shape of a baked item.

tourage (too-'rahj) The technique of rolling puff pastry dough, folding it, turning it 90°, and repeating until the desired number of folds are made to produce the flaky finished product.

tourier (too-rhee-'ayr) See *brigade.*

trans fatty acid A type of fat produced during the hydrogenation process. Trans fats can be found in processed foods such as margarine and cookies, and are believed to contribute to cholesterol problems. See also *hydrogenated oil.*

transfer method A way to make sparkling wine, whereby the secondary fermentation takes place in individual bottles and the wine is then transferred to large pressurized tanks, where the sediment is removed by filtration. See also *Champagne.*

transfer sheet A small, rectangular sheet of clear acetate used to transfer designs onto chocolate. The designs are printed on with colored cocoa butter, and are available in hundreds of designs or can be custom made with specific logos, patterns, or designs. The chocolate pieces can be cut and formed into shapes or broken into abstract pieces. The decorated chocolate work is popular as a garnish and to wrap around the sides of cakes and desserts. When working with transfer sheets, it is important to make sure the chocolate is properly tempered and completely cooled before gently peeling off the acetate.

treacle ('tree-kuhl) A sweet, syrupy by-product of sugar refining. There are two types, light and dark. Light treacle, also known as *golden syrup,* has a golden color and light caramelized flavor. Dark treacle, also known as *black treacle,* is similar to molasses in flavor and color. They are both used in baked goods to provide sweetness, color, moisture, and longer shelf life. They are also used to flavor and color, puddings, sauces, and confectionery, particularly in Britain.

treacle sauce See *treacle.*

tree tomato See *tamarillo.*

Tres Ricos A variety of Arabica coffee bean grown in Costa Rica. These beans are aromatic and produce a fresh, tangy flavor.

trifle ('tri-fuhl) A British pudding of pieces of sponge cake that have been soaked with sherry, Port, or another fortified wine, and topped with candied and/or fresh fruits, a sweet thin custard, whipped cream, and sometimes nuts or grated chocolate. Trifle was created as a way to use stale cake, and is still popular for that reason today. Although it may be served in any type of bowl or dish, trifle is usually presented in a straight-sided glass trifle dish with a pedestal base.

triglyceride A class of fats and oils that have three fatty acids linked by a molecule of glycerol.

trinitario See *cacao bean.*

trois frères (twa frehr) French for "three brothers," referring to a dessert that was created by the three Julien brothers, who were all celebrated Parisian pastry chefs. It consists of a mixture of rice flour, butter, eggs, sugar, and maraschino cherries that is baked in either a *savarin mold* or *trois frères mold.* When cooled it is turned out onto a lightly baked disc of sweet pastry dough. It is then glazed with apricot jam and decorated with candied angelica.

trois frères mold A decorative shallow tube pan with a fluted pattern on the bottom and lower part of the sides. The remaining side portion has a slightly larger plain band. The mold is approximately 8 inches (20 cm) in diameter and 2 inches (5 cm) high. It is used for baking cakes and molding cold desserts. See also *trois frères.*

T
t

triple cream cheese A soft, ripened cheese made by enriching the fresh cheese curds with cream to increase the fat content to a minimum of 75%. Its natural, mild sweetness and creamy texture make it good as a dessert cheese and it pairs well with fruit and nuts.

Triple Sec ('trih-pl sehk) A clear orange liqueur. Although the name is French for "thrice dry," it is actually sweet. It is produced in a range of qualities, with the generic Triple Sec label usually referring to a less expensive grade. The higher-quality Triple Secs include *Curaçao, Grand Marnier,* and *Cointreau.*

triticale A hybrid of wheat and rye grains that is higher in protein and lower in gluten than wheat. It has a sweet, nutty flavor and is available in flakes, flour, and whole berries. It was developed in 1876 by a Scottish botanist named A. Stephan Wilson.

Trokenbeerenauslese (trawk-uhn-bay-ruhn-ows-lay-zuh) A class of Germany's richest, sweetest, rarest, and most expensive wines.

truffle, chocolate A rich bite-size confection made with dark, white, or milk chocolate, cream and/or butter, and flavorings such as fruit purees, liqueurs, spices, and extracts. Truffles are traditionally ball shape and rolled in cocoa powder to resemble the fungus of the same name.

truffle screen A cooling rack for truffles. It is similar to a cooling rack but with more tightly woven wire mesh to give chocolate truffles a rough, spiked surface. After the truffles are dipped in tempered chocolate, they are rolled around the screen with a dipping fork; as the chocolate cools, the tiny spikes are solidified. The screen may also be used to ice cakes and petit fours with ganache or fondant, but the screen should be suspended as it does not have any feet to elevate it from the work surface.

truffle shell A commercial product that consists of a hollow chocolate truffle shell with a small, round opening on the top. The truffle shells sit in a plastic tray with a separate plastic top that fits perfectly over the shells. The opening at the top allows the truffles to be filled and sealed with tempered chocolate, with no chance of excess filling or chocolate spilling onto the outside of the shell. They are available in dark, milk, or white chocolate from specialty pastry vendors.

tsp. The abbreviation for *teaspoon.*

tuaca (too'ah-kah) A slightly sweet, golden-colored Italian liqueur flavored with vanilla, almond, coconut, and orange. It is used to flavor sauces, creams, confections, and desserts.

tube pan A round, deep-sided cake pan with a hollow tube center. The tube promotes even baking in the center of the cake, and produces a ring-shaped cake. The most common tube pans are *angel food cake pans, Bundt pans,* and *Kugelhopf molds.*

tuile The French word for "tile," referring to a light, thin, delicate stencil cookie. The name is a reference to their distinct curved tile appearance, made by placing the baked discs over a rolling pin while still warm. They may be flavored with extracts, cocoa powder, or spices and/or sprinkled with nuts before baking. Their crisp texture makes them an excellent accompaniment to ice creams, mousses, and sorbets.

tuile mold A tinned steel mold used to shape *tuile* cookies. It has six narrow half-cylinders that lie side by side. The warm cookies are placed in the mold, which allows them to form their distinct arched shape. The mold may also be used to shape chocolate and sugar.

tuile stencil A thin, rectangular sheet of strong plastic with a cut-out design, used to make *tuile* cookies. The batter is placed inside the cut-out design and spread thinly across the plastic onto a parchment- or Silpat-lined sheet pan. When the

T
t

plastic sheet is removed, the design remains on the Silpat. There is a wide variety of designs available from specialty pastry vendors or they may be custom made. Although a stencil may also be cut from a cake box or other thin material, the commercial stencils are sturdier and can be washed for repeated use.

tulipe ('too-leep) The French word for "tulip," referring to an edible container with a ruffled edge that resembles a tulip flower. It is most commonly made from *tuile* batter and formed over a cup or mold while still warm. It may be filled with mousse, berries, ice cream, or other pastry items.

tulumba tatlisi (too-loom-bah tah-tlee-see) A Turkish sweet made by deep-frying a piped batter and then dipping it in a sugar syrup.

tunneling The large, irregular holes that form inside a muffin because of overmixing.

turbinado sugar See *sugar*.

turfjes met bessensap (tour-fees met 'bessen-zahp) A Dutch bread pudding, served chilled with whipped cream and raspberry sauce.

Turkish coffee Very strong coffee, made by boiling ground coffee, sugar, and water three times in an *ibrik*. It is cooled slightly in between boilings and served in small cups immediately after the third boiling. Sometimes spices such as cardamom, nutmeg, or cinnamon are added to the water before boiling.

Turkish delight A Middle Eastern confection that is a chewy, gelatinous, rubbery mixture typically colored pink or green. It is called *rahat loukoum* in Turkish, which means "a rest for the throat." It is made from fruit juice, honey, sugar, glucose, and cornstarch or gelatin. Sometimes nuts such as pistachios, almonds, hazelnuts, or pine nuts are added for texture, and it is cut into small squares and coated with confectioners' sugar.

turmeric (ter-'muh-rihk) An Indian and Middle Eastern spice derived from the root of a tropical plant related to ginger. It has an intense golden yellow-orange color and strong, exotic flavor and aroma, and is most commonly used to flavor and color products such as mustard and curry powders; it gives an interesting twist to sweet items.

turn A step in the production of *laminated doughs*, whereby the folded dough is turned 90 degrees before rolling out again and adding another fold. The number of turns depends on how many times the dough is folded. See also *fold* and *laminated dough*.

turnover A flaky pastry that is filled with sweet or savory fillings. It is shaped as either a triangle or half-moon, and may or may not have crimped edges. It can be baked or fried, and served as an appetizer, dessert, or breakfast item.

turntable A thin, flat metal or plastic disc attached to a heavy pedestal base, used for cake decorating. The discs come in various sizes but the most common is 10 inches (25 cm). The disc is rotated by hand as the cake is iced or decorated, and the turning makes it easier to create a uniform appearance.

turrón The Spanish version of nougat, made during Christmastime. It is believed to be of Arabic origin, made in Spain as early as the 16th century. There is the original hard version from Alicante and the soft version from Jijona. Traditionally, they are made from pure orange blossom honey, sugar, almonds, and dried fruit. Other regions add hazelnuts, pistachios, coconut, chocolate, and liqueurs.

tutové See *rolling pin*.

tutti-frutti ('too-tee 'froo-tee) 1. The Italian word for "all fruits," referring to desserts such as ice cream, cakes, custards, and fillings that use a mixture of minced fresh, candied, or poached fruits. 2. An artificial fruit additive used to flavor candy and gum.

Twelfth Night cake A cake eaten on Epiphany, January 6. There are many variations, specific to each country and region. They vary in size and shape, and may be made from cake, brioche, or puff pastry and flavored with frangipane, candied fruit, spirits, orange flower water, or other combinations. One common characteristic of all cakes is that a bean or small token is placed inside before baking. The person who receives the slice of cake with the bean or token is crowned king or queen of the day. Also known as *Epiphany cake*.

twelve steps of baking See *12 Steps of Baking* appendix.

twentieth century See *Asian pear, Nijisseiki*.

Twinkie A packaged snack of golden sponge cake with a creamy filling, made by Hostess.

two-grain spelt See *emmer wheat*.

two-stage mixing method See *mixing methods*.

Tyler pie A Southern pie that consists of butter, eggs, brown sugar, cream, and eggs and is garnished with toasted, grated coconut. It was created in honor of President John Tyler.

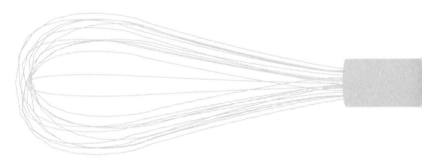

T
t

Uu

ube The Filipino word for purple yam. Although it is a vegetable, it is commonly cooked with sugar and eaten as a dessert or made into a jam. It is also used for the bright violet color and unique flavor it imparts to ice cream, sorbet, cakes, and other pastries. This is a true yam, not a sweet potato.

ubod (oo-bod) A Filipino vegetable that comes from the inner core of the coconut palm. It is used in savory items such as salads and egg rolls, but may be cooked with sugar for a sweet snack. It also absorbs the other flavoring agents that it is cooked with and is a good source of fiber. Also known as heart of palm.

udon (oo-dohn) A flat, spaghetti-like Japanese noodle made from either wheat or corn flour. It is available fresh or dried.

ugali (oo-'gah-lee) A thick cornmeal porridge from Kenya and Tanzania.

Ugandan coffee Most of Uganda's coffee is the *Robusta coffee bean*, but the *Arabica coffee bean* is similar to Kenyan coffees. The best coffee is produced on the western slopes of Mt. Elgon and is called *bugishu*. It has a heavy body and rich, rustic, fruity character.

ugli fruit ('uhg-lee) A hybrid of the *tangerine* and the *grapefruit*. It is referred to as "ugly" because it has a thick, wrinkled, baggy rind. The peel comes off easily, and contains a segmented flesh. It may weigh up to 2 pounds (910 g) and is available from January to May.

Ugni Blanc (ooyhn blahnk) A French white grape that is the predominant grape used to make *Cognac*.

ujeqe (oo-ye-quay) A whole wheat and cornmeal dumpling from South Africa.

uj-wee ('ujj-wee) A Middle Eastern confection of dates stuffed with almonds and rolled in sugar.

ulanda (oo-'lahn-dah) A cocktail of Pernod, gin, and Cointreau.

uld man's milk An alcoholic Scottish drink of whisky, milk, cream, sugar, nutmeg, and whipped egg whites.

ulekan ('oo-lee-kan) An Indonesian version of a mortar and pestle, made from granite or volcanic rock. It is used to grind spices.

ullage The space that develops at the top of a wine bottle when there is leakage or evaporation. This may cause oxidation and spoil the wine.

Ulmer Wasserweck ('ool-mehr 'vahz-zehr-vehk) A small German wheat roll made with water instead of milk.

Ulmer Zuckerbrot ('ool-mehr 'zoo-kehr-'broht) A German yeasted bun flavored with sugar, fennel seeds, and rose oil.

ultra pasteurization A process for prolonging the shelf life of milk and cream. The pasteurization is done at a higher temperature (280°F/138°C) than regular pasteurization. Ultrapasteurized cream is not recommended for use in the bake shop because will attain less volume when whipped.

ulu ('ooh-looh) The Hawaiian word for *breadfruit*.

umm Ali (umm-'aah-lee) The Arabic word for "mother of Ali," referring to an Egyptian bread pudding of milk, cream, pistachios, almonds, cinnamon, rosewater, and phyllo.

umami (u-mom-ee) The Japanese word for "tastiness," which is debated to be a fifth basic taste. It applies to the sensation of savoriness in high-protein foods.

umbrella pine A Japanese pine tree shaped like an open umbrella. It is one of several varieties that produce *pine nuts*.

ume (oo-meh) The Japanese word for a plum used to make a several products including *umeboshi* and *umeshu*. They are high in potassium and calcium and are believed to bring good health.

umeboshi (oo-meh-boh-she) A Japanese condiment of unripe plums pickled in brine and *red shiso* leaves. The leaves add flavor and turn the product pink. It has a salty-tart flavor; it is often served with the breakfast meal. It may also be pureed and used as a seasoning, which is called *bainiku*.

umeshu (oo-meh-shoo) A Japanese plum wine made from green ume plums and a white liquor called *shochu*. It has been consumed for over 1,000 years; it has an alcohol content of about 35% and a sweet-tart flavor.

unbleached flour See *flour*.

Unicum ('yoon-ee-kuhm) A Hungarian liqueur, made from a secret formula of over 40 herbs and spices that are blended and distilled, then aged in oak casks for six months. It is believed to have gotten its name in 1790, when the Habsburg monarch, Joseph II, tasted it and exclaimed to its creator, his court physician, Dr. Zwack, *"Das ist ein Unikum,"* meaning, "This is a specialty." It is still produced by the Zwack family, and may be drunk as an *apéritif* or as a *digestif*.

unleavened (uhn-'lehv-uhnd) A baked good that contains no leavening, typically used to describe *flatbreads*.

unmold To remove a baked or gelled mixture from its mold. This may be accomplished by briefly heating the mold to loosen the frozen or chilled dessert, or by running a thin blade around the inner circumference to release the item.

unrefined oil See *oil*.

unripened cheese A cheese made from acidified skim milk, which has milk fats added to it during the curd stage. It is eaten fresh and usually has a high moisture content.

unsalted butter See *butter*.

unsaturated fat A type of fat derived from plants. With the exception of partially hydrogenated vegetable shortenings, it tends to be liquid. It may be monounsaturated, meaning one double bond between carbon atoms, or polyunsaturated, meaning more than one double bond between carbon atoms. See also *saturated fat*.

unsweetened chocolate Another name for *baker's chocolate*; see *chocolate*.

unsweetened cocoa See *cocoa powder*.

upside down cake A cake that is made by covering the bottom of a pan with sugar, butter, and fruit; the batter is poured on top, and as the cake bakes, the sugar caramelizes so that when the cake is turned upside down, the glazed fruit is on top. The most well known is *pineapple upside down cake*.

uva A strong, aromatic black tea grown on the eastern slopes of the central mountains of Sri Lanka. It has a deep, rich, coppery color and smooth, full-flavored taste.

uva ursi A perennial herb that is infused to make a medicinal tea, used to treat urinary tract infections. It is the Latin word for "bear berry," which is also its common name because bears are fond of the plant's red sour berries.

U
u

vacherin ('vahs-ran) A cold French dessert of rings of baked *meringue* that are piped into the shape of a basket and filled with *crème chantilly* or ice cream and fruit. It may be left open and garnished with crystallized flowers or topped with a baked meringue lid. It is named after a cheese of the same shape and color.

vadai ('wah-dl) A warm, spicy street snack of southern India, particularly Kerala. It has a hole in the middle and is fried like a doughnut.

Valencia orange (vuh-'lehn-see-uh) See *orange*.

Valrhona A French chocolate company, known for its high-quality chocolate products.

vandyke To make a V-shaped cut or zigzag pattern around the circumference of a fruit or vegetable, for decorative purposes. It is commonly done for lemon crowns, tomato garnishes, watermelon baskets, and buffet displays.

Van Houten, Coenraad Johannes A Dutch chocolate maker who, in 1828, invented the press that extracts cocoa butter from cocoa solids, to produce cocoa powder.

vanilla, vanilla bean The seed pod of the orchid *Vanilla planifolia,* native to tropical regions. It has been used as a flavoring agent for hundreds of years, and was cultivated by the Aztecs for their cocoa-based drink *xocolatl.* Owing to its time-consuming and labor-intensive cultivation and collection, vanilla is an expensive ingredient. The vines must be pruned regularly and bent into loops for easy access by workers. The clusters of buds that form on the vine take many weeks to develop into flowers, which must be hand-pollinated during their short blooming period. Once pollinated, the flowers develop long, thin, green cylindrical seed pods that range in length from 8 to 12 inches (20 to 30 cm). After eight months, the pods are harvested. Since the green pods have no vanilla flavor or fragrance, they must be cured, a process that takes between three and six months and requires sundrying; they become hot, so when they are wrapped in blankets, they sweat and begin to ferment; this is repeated for several weeks until the pods turn dark brown. Lastly, they are dried in the sun for several months before being packed and shipped. The three most common types of vanilla beans are:

> **Bourbon-Madagascar** Named for the region in which they are grown, they make up approximately 75% of commercial bean production. They are the thinnest variety and have a rich, sweet flavor.

> **Mexican** The thickest variety, with a rich, smooth flavor. They are produced in the Veracruz region of Mexico.

> **Tahitian** Grown in Tahiti, these beans are sweeter, softer, wider, and more floral than the other varieties.

vanilla extract A concentrated flavoring essence, used in pastries, desserts, and confections. It is categorized as follows:

Imitation A vanilla-flavored product made entirely of artificial flavorings. It is significantly less expensive than pure vanilla extract, but has a harsher quality and bitter aftertaste. It is also necessary to use larger amounts to achieve the desired vanilla flavor.

Pure A flavoring agent made by aging chopped vanilla beans and alcohol. To be considered pure, there must be a minimum of 13.5 ounces (385 g) vanilla beans per gallon (3 L 840 ml) and 35% alcohol.

vanilla passion fruit See *passion fruit.*

vanilla powder A vanilla-flavored product made when the whole, dried vanilla bean is ground to a powder.

vanilla sauce The American word for *crème anglaise.*

vanilla sugar Flavored granulated sugar, made by infusing it with vanilla beans. The longer the beans are left in the sugar, the stronger the flavor. It is used to flavor cakes, pastries, fillings, and confections.

vanillin The aromatic, white, powdery crystals that form on the outside of the vanilla bean during the curing process. It is also made synthetically and used to flavor imitation vanilla extract.

varak (vah-ruhk) The Indian word for paper-thin sheets of *gold leaf* or *silver leaf.* They are packaged in small, square sheets that are separated by tissue paper. They are very expensive and somewhat difficult to work with, but make a stunning garnish on desserts and confections. Also known as *vark.*

varietal wine A wine produced from a particular variety of grape. To be named a grape varietal, the wine must contain a minimum of 75% of that grape. For example, Chardonnay, Pinot Noir, and Cabernet Sauvignon are varietals.

vari glykos See *Greek coffee.*

vark See *varak.*

vatrouchka A Russian cheesecake made with curd cheese and dried fruits, baked onto a *sable dough* base. It is topped with a lattice of sweet pastry dough and dusted with confectioners' sugar before serving.

vatrouchki A Russian turnover made with a rich *brioche dough* that is filled with curd cheese and sometimes fruit, and either fried or baked.

vegan ('vee-guhn) A person who does not eat anything derived from animals, including meat, butter, eggs, cheese, and milk. It is a challenge for the pastry chef to produce tasty vegan desserts, but it can be done by using fruits, vegetables, and *soy milk.*

Vegemite ('vej-uh-mite) A yeast extract produced by Kraft Foods. It is the Australian version of the British product *Marmite,* and was created in 1922 by Australian scientist Cyril Callister. The thick, salty brown paste is flavored with onions and celery, and is a breakfast spread on toast.

vegetable oil An edible oil derived from a plant. The most common vegetable oils are *canola oil, corn oil, peanut oil,* and *safflower oil.*

vegetable oil margarine See *margarine.*

vegetable peeler A hand-held metal tool used to peel the skin off vegetables and fruits. It is available in various shapes and sizes, but all have a blade that is slit in the middle to allow the skin to pass through. The blade usually swivels, so that the shape of the fruit or vegetable may be followed as it is peeled to minimize waste.

vegetable shortening A solid fat made from vegetable oils.

vegetarian A person who does not eat meat.

V
v

Veneziana A sweet Italian holiday bread very similar to *pannetone* but with no candied fruit or citron. It is a tradition of Venice, made for Christmas and New Year's Eve, and the top is dusted with confectioners' sugar and whole almonds.

verbena See *lemon verbena.*

Verdelho See *Madeira.*

Vergine Stravecchio (vehr-j'hee-nay strah-veh-'kee-o) See *Marsala.*

verjuice The acidic juice of unripened grapes. It was used extensively as a sour flavoring agent in medieval cooking, before citrus was commonly available. It is sometimes labeled *verjus* when marketed in wine bottles for cooking.

verjus See *verjuice.*

vermicelli 1. Another name for *jimmies.* 2. The Italian term for "little worms" that refers to very thin strands of pasta.

vermouth A fortified red or white wine that has been infused with aromatic spices, herbs, flavorings, and barks. It was created in Piedmont, Italy, in the 1700s; the name derives from the German *Wermut,* meaning "wormwood," because it was the primary flavoring agent before that substance was banned because of toxicity. Red vermouth is generally sweet while white vermouth is dry or semi-sweet. It is served as an apéritif and is also an essential ingredient in Manhattans and Martinis.

Vernors Ginger Ale See *ginger ale.*

vettalapam ('veht-tah-lah-pahm) A national custard dish of Sri Lanka that is made with coconut, coconut cream, and palm sugar.

Victoria sandwich cake An English cake consisting of two layers of buttery *sponge cake,* filled with either raspberry or strawberry jam and *buttercream* or sweetened whipped cream, named in honor of Queen Victoria. It is served at *afternoon tea.*

Victoria sponge cake A rich, buttery *sponge cake* used to make *trifle,* petit fours, and *Victoria sponge cake.*

vidiler (vee-dee-'layr) To decoratively pinch a pastry dough to give it a neat, even, stylish border.

Vienna roll See *kaiser roll.*

Viennese bread See *Danish pastry.*

Viennese coffee ('vee-uh-neeze) A strong, rich, sweetened coffee from Vienna, served warm in a tall glass and topped with whipped cream.

Viennese horn See *Kipferln.*

viennoiserie (vee-uhn-wah-zah-rhee) A French term that refers to baked goods other than breads, such as *danish* and *coffee cakes.*

vin (vahn) The French word for *wine.*

vinegar ('vihn-uh-ger) The sour liquid produced when bacterial activity converts a fermenting mixture such as cider, beer, or wine into *acetic acid.* The word derives from the French *vin aigre,* which means "sour wine." There is a wide variety of vinegars, including:

> **Apple Cider** Made from fermented apple cider. It is light amber colored and has a tangy taste.
>
> **Balsamic** An Italian vinegar made from the juice of Trebbiano grapes. It is aged in casks of different woods, which produce complex, pungent sweetness.
>
> **Black Rice** Made from glutinous sweet rice. It has a dark color and rich, mild flavor.

Cane Made from sugarcane, with a rich, slightly sweet flavor.

Cuka A colorless vinegar from Indonesia. It may be substituted with malt vinegar.

Distilled White Made from a grain-alcohol mixture. It is colorless and has an astringent taste.

Fruit Made from fruits such as blueberries and raspberries.

Herb Made by infusing herbs in vinegar.

Malt Made from malted barley. It has a mild taste and is popular in Britain.

Palm A mild white vinegar popular in the Philippines.

Red Rice A Chinese product that has a clear, pink color and sweetish-tart, salty flavor.

Red Wine Made from red wine.

Rice Made from fermented rice. It has a mild, slightly sweet flavor.

Sweet Rice A Chinese product that is flavored with star anise and has a brownish-black color.

Turkish Mildly sweet with a strong, sharp flavor. It may be substituted with a combination of balsamic and wine vinegars.

White Wine Made from white wine.

viniculture ('vihn-ih-kuhl-cher) The science of wine making. Also known as *enology*.

vino ('vee-noh) The Italian word for wine.

vintage Port See *Port*.

Virginia peanut See *peanut*.

viscoelasticity The ability of a product to stretch and change shape without tearing or breaking, such as *gluten*.

viscosity A measure of fluidity: low-viscosity fluids flow easily and high-viscosity fluids do not flow easily.

visitandine (vee-see-tan-'daan) A small boat-shaped cake made by lining a *barquette mold* with a sweet pastry base and filling it with ground almonds, egg whites, butter, and sugar. After baking, these are glazed with apricot and thinly brushed with a Kirsch-flavored *fondant*. They were originally made in French and Italian monasteries in the 16th century as a way to use up leftover egg whites.

vital wheat gluten Dried wheat *gluten* that contains approximately 75% protein. The wet gluten is dried in a way that retains its vital properties when reconstituted. It is purchased as a creamy tan powder and added to *yeast doughs* to improve flour quality, volume, dough elasticity and strength, and shelf-life.

vitamin C See *ascorbic acid*.

violet An edible flower used as a garnish.

viticulture ('viht-ih-kuhl-cher) The science of growing grapes.

vodka A clear, colorless distilled spirit made from potatoes and other grains such as barley and wheat. Its name derives from the Russian *zhiznennaia voda*, which means "water of life."

voiler To cover pastries and desserts with fine threads of sugar that have been cooked to the *hard-crack stage*.

volatile oil An oil that evaporates easily and provides strong, aromatic flavor. All spices contain volatile oils, and the quality of the spice depends on the amount of volatile oil it contains. Also known as *essential oil*.

V
v

vol-au-vent ('vawl-oh-vahn) The French term for "flying in the wind," referring to a light-as-air *puff pastry* container that resembles a small pot with a lid. It was invented by renowned pastry chef Carême, and although it is filled with a warm savory mixture, it may be filled with sweet mixtures as well.

Volkornbrot The German word for "full-grained bread," referring to a bread that is made either entirely or almost entirely with whole grains.

volume measurement See *Weight and Volume Equivalents for Most Common Ingredients* appendix.

vort limpa A sweet Swedish rye bread made during the Christmas holidays.

vouvray (voo-'vray) A white wine produced in the Loire Valley of France from 100% Chenin Blanc grapes. They are categorized by sweetness as follows: *sec* = dry; *demi-sec* = medium dry; *moelleux* = medium sweet; *doux* = very sweet. The great sweet Vouvrays are popular as a dessert wine.

VS; VSOP; VVSOP See *Cognac.*

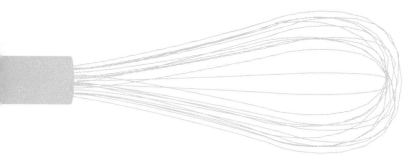

V
V

Ww

wafer A very thin, crisp biscuit or cookie. They vary in size and may be round, fan-shaped, or rolled into a cigarette. They may also be embossed with a design, such as those using a *pizelle iron* or *krumkake* iron.

wafer cookie See *cookie*.

waffle There are many variations of waffles around the world, with the most popular being:

> **American** A thin, crisp, batter cake that is baked on a waffle iron, which gives it its distinct grid appearance. It is an American breakfast item typically topped with butter and maple syrup. The batter may be leavened with baking powder or yeast and flavored in numerous ways.

> **Belgian** A thick, fluffy, and crisp waffle, a specialty of Brussels; it is both a breakfast item and a dessert, where it is topped with strawberries, whipped cream, and sometimes ice cream.

> **Liège** A small, sweet, and dense waffle named for the Belgian city. It is coated in caramelized sugar and eaten as is or topped with fruit, whipped cream, or chocolate.

> **Taiyaki** A Japanese batter cake that resembles a fish-shaped waffle. It is traditionally filled with a sweet bean paste.

waffle cone A crisp ice cream cone made by pouring a thin batter onto a *pizelle iron*. While warm, the wafer is wrapped around a cone and cooled. It is used as an edible container for ice cream, but may also be used to hold other desserts such as sorbets, mousses, and fruit mixtures.

waffle iron An appliance with two hinged metal plates that have a honeycomb design, for cooking waffles. It is available in electric or stovetop models and comes in different shapes and sizes, including round, square, and heart shaped.

wagashi (wah-'ga-shee) An assortment of small Japanese confections, made from glutinous rice, adzuki beans, fruit, sugar, rice powder, agar-agar, and red bean paste. They are crafted into artistic shapes and figures, such as flowers and fish, and are served with green tea during the Japanese tea ceremony.

wajik ('vah-jich) An Indonesian confection made with sticky rice boiled in palm sugar. They come in a variety of colors and shapes.

walnut The fruit of the walnut tree, native to Asia but now cultivated in Europe and North America. California, in particular, produces 90% of the most common commercial walnut, the *English walnut,* which is also known as *Persian walnut.* They are easy to shell and have a mild-nutty flavor. The nuts are available year-round and may be purchased whole, shelled, in halves, in pieces, or ground (walnut flour or meal). The other type of walnut is the *black walnut,* native to North America. It has a hard black shell that is difficult to remove and therefore the nutmeats are more expensive. The strong, rich nutmeat has a distinctive flavor that is slightly bitter and smoky. The high oil content of walnuts makes them susceptible to rancidity, so they should be stored in the refrigerator or freezer.

W
w

walnut oil An oil extracted from the nutmeats of the English walnut. It is expensive and perishable, so it should be refrigerated.

warka (war-kah) See *malsouqua*.

warming lamp See *heat lamp*.

wasabi (wah-'sah-bee) A pungent, fiery-hot green Japanese green condiment. It is made from horseradish, and is available fresh or dried. Although it has been traditionally served with sushi and sashimi, many pastry chefs use it as a flavoring agent to provide heat and color to ice creams, sauces, and desserts.

wasanbon toh (wah-'sahn-bon toe) See *sugar*.

wassail (wahs-'uhl) A warm Nordic punch of sweetened wine or ale, flavored with cinnamon, nutmeg, and ginger. The word derives from the Norweigan "ves heil," which is a toast that means "in good health."

water An essential ingredient that serves many functions, including hydrating flour so that gluten can form; converting to steam, which acts as a leavener and also prevents bread crust from forming too quickly; adjusting the temperature in batters and doughs; and gelatinizing starches during the baking process. See also *water hardness* and *water pH*.

water apple See *wax apple*.

water bath A container that sits in water, used for baking to provide even distribution of heat to the baking item and help prevent overcooking. A water bath is also used to keep foods warm and to melt chocolate. It may set up on the stovetop or in the oven. Also known as *bain-marie* in French.

water biscuit A crisp, bland cracker often served with wine and cheese.

water chestnut The edible tuber of a water plant, native to Southeast Asia. Although water chestnuts may be purchased canned, fresh ones are crunchier and sweeter. They are shaped like a chestnut and have a purplish-brown skin that must be removed before eating. They may be cooked in sugar syrup and eaten as a sweet snack.

water chestnut powder An Asian starch made from ground dried water chestnuts. It is used as a thickener and also as a flour.

water hardness The amount of minerals in water. *Hard water* is high in minerals and *soft water* is low in minerals. This is important because minerals affect *gluten* development. If the water is too hard, the dough may be too strong or elastic, while dough made from water that is too soft may be too slack, soft, or sticky. The water hardness may be adjusted with a water softening system or through the addition of a *dough conditioner*.

water ice A smooth frozen dessert of water, sugar, and fruit juice, puree, or an infusion of other flavors such as coffee or liqueur.

watermelon A category of melon native to Africa and characterized by a thick, smooth rind and crunchy, juicy flesh. There are many varieties that range in shape, size, color, and flavor, but the most common is the *Charleston Gray watermelon*, which has an elongated-oval shape and weighs between 15 and 35 pounds (7 K to 18 K). It has a two-tone green or grayish-green rind that is striped or marbled. The flesh color ranges from pink to red and contains scattered shiny black seeds. Other varieties may have a yellow or orange flesh and the seeds may be white, brown, or speckled. They may also be seedless, which actually have a few small beige seeds scattered throughout; the baby variety offers a mini alternative to the larger types.

Watermelon is a refreshing summer treat eaten cold and raw, and it is also popular as a decorative container for fruit salads on buffets, where the skin is often carved into intricate patterns for display. In other countries, watermelon seeds are roasted as a snack and the rind is pickled. Although they are available year-round, peak season is June to August.

water nozzle The part of the espresso machine that automatically dispenses water at about 210°F (99°C).

water pH A measure of the amount of acidity or alkalinity in water. The *pH* scale ranges from 0 to 14, with 7 being neutral. The ideal water pH for gluten development is 5 to 6. It may be adjusted by adding an acid such as cream of tartar or lemon juice, or an alkali such as baking soda.

wattle seed The seed of the Australian wattle tree. They are roasted and ground, and used to impart a nutty flavor to cakes and pastries or made into a form of coffee.

wax apple A tropical bell-shaped berry with a crunchy texture and juicy, sweet flavor, native to Malaysia and Indonesia. Also known as *water apple*.

waxed paper A thin opaque piece of paper that has been coated with a thin film of wax on both sides. It is used to line baking pans in order to prevent sticking. See also *parchment paper*.

waxy maize A cornstarch typically modified to increase its stability against excessive heat, acid, or freezing. It is generally clear, with a clean taste. See also *starch*.

wedding cake An elaborate cake made to celebrate a wedding. The history of the wedding cake dates back to ancient Rome, where barley bread was crumbled over the bride's head to symbolize fertility. In medieval England, guests brought sweet cakes as gifts and stacked them on a table; the bride and groom would kiss over the stack of cakes to bring them good luck and prosperity. As baking methods advanced and ingredients became more readily available, the wedding cake evolved. In the mid-1840s, Queen Victoria married Prince Albert, and their single-layer cake was over 7 feet (2.5 m) in circumference and intricately decorated with pure white icing. The whiteness of the icing represents the purity of the bride and also the affluence of the family, because refined sugar has been an expensive commodity. The tiered wedding cake as we know it today first appeared at the marriage of the Queen's daughter in 1859. A photograph of the cake in newspapers inspired other brides to imitate this style.

Today, the design and decoration of the wedding cake has become an art form and the possibilities are endless. The joint act of cutting the cake has come to symbolize the first task the bride and groom do together as they begin their new life as husband and wife. In America, it is a tradition for the top tier to be reserved and eaten on the couple's one-year anniversary. Although each country may have its own designs and traditions, the wedding cake is an integral part of the celebration.

Weinchaudeau (vine-kow-do) An Austrian version of *sabayon;* it should be used immediately because it is slightly more delicate and will not hold.

wekiwas See *lavender gem.*

West Indies cherry See *acerola.*

West Indian lime See *Key lime.*

wheat An ancient cereal grain. Wheat has been cultivated for at least 6,000 years, and there are over 30,000 varieties, distinguished by color and growing season. *Hard wheat* or *soft wheat* refers to the hardness or softness of the wheat kernel and also to the protein content. Hard wheat contains more protein and less starch, while soft wheat contains less protein and more starch. Winter and spring are the two growing seasons. *Winter wheat* is planted in the fall and harvested in early summer. It is grown in areas with milder winters, such as Kansas and Nebraska. *Spring wheat* is planted in the spring and harvested in late summer. It is grown in areas with harsher winters, such as Minnesota, Montana, and the Dakotas. The wheat color ranges from white to red and affects the color and flavor of the flour. All wheat varieties fall under one of these categories:

Durum A very hard, high-protein wheat used to make semolina flour for pasta. The average protein content is 15%.

Hard Red Spring Constitutes 20% of the U.S. crop and produces a high-protein flour with a protein content of 13 to 15%. Used primarily for bread flour and high-gluten flour.

Hard Red Winter Constitutes 40% of the U.S. crop with an average protein content of 11 to 12%. Used primarily for all-purpose flour.

Hard White Winter The newest class of wheat grown in the U.S. The red pigment is bred out and results in a bran that is lighter in color and milder in flavor than Hard Red Winter. Produces flour with a protein content of 11 to 12%. Popular for use in *artisan bread* making.

Soft White Constitutes 10% of the U.S. crop with a protein content of about 10%. It is favored for use in flatbreads, cakes, pastries, and crackers.

Soft Red Winter A low-protein wheat, approximately 10%, typically grown in warm southern climates and used for cake and pastry flour.

wheat berry A whole wheat kernel that may be hulled or unhulled. These are popular in Middle Eastern cooking, and the chewy, slightly sweet kernels go well with sweet spices.

wheat bran See *wheat kernel*.

wheat flour See *flour*.

wheat germ See *wheat kernel*.

wheat gluten See *seitan*.

wheat kernel The seed of the wheat plant, which is milled into flour. It comprises three parts:

Bran The protective outer covering of the wheat kernel. It contains a high amount of dietary fiber.

Endosperm The largest part of the kernel. It is approximately 70 to 75% starch and contains the two gluten-forming proteins, *glutenin* and *gliadin*.

Germ The embryo of the wheat plant. Although it constitutes only 3% of the kernel, it is packed with nutrients but prone to rancidity because of its high fat content.

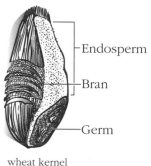

wheat kernel

whetstone See *oilstone*.

whey The liquid solid of coagulated milk that is produced during the cheese-making process.

whip 1. To beat heavy cream or egg whites in order to incorporate air and increase the volume to a firm or semi-firm consistency. 2. A cold dessert of fruit puree, whipped cream, and meringue. It is typically served in an edible bowl made from chocolate or *tuile*. 3. Another name for a *whisk*. 4. See *mixer attachments*.

whipped butter See *butter*.

whipped cream Cream that has been whipped to incorporate air and change the consistency from a liquid to a solid or semi-solid state. The cream must contain a minimum of 30% butterfat in order to whip properly; overwhipping will cause the cream to turn to butter. Whipped cream should be kept cold and used immediately, as heat will cause it to separate. This product is used extensively in pastry making as a garnish, filling, and ingredient in mousses and still-frozen desserts.

whipping cream See *cream.*

whisk

1. A hand-held kitchen tool used to mix ingredients and incorporate air. Whisks are made of rounded metal wires affixed to a handle. They come in different sizes, and the wires are stiff or flexible depending on their thickness. Different whisks are made for different jobs but they are most often used to whip egg whites and cream. The most common pastry whisks are:

> **Balloon Whisk** Recommended for whipping egg whites and cream because it has a large balloon-shaped end and light, flexible wires that maximize the incorporation of air. Also known as an egg whisk.

> **Sauce Whisk** Has stiffer metal wires and is recommended for whipping thicker products.

> **Batter Whisk** Recommended for mixing or beating batters to make them smooth with minimal incorporation of air; they have a rounded end but are flat and two-dimensional.

2. The act of whisking a product with a whip in order to mix ingredients and/or incorporate air.

whisky A distilled alcoholic beverage made from the fermented mash of a grain such as corn, barley, rye, or wheat. The type and quality of the whisky depends on the type of grain used, how it is distilled, and the aging process. Bourbon and rye fall under the whisky classification, while Scotch, Canadian, and Irish whisky are often referred to simply as their names. *Whisky* is the Gaelic word for "water of life."

white chocolate See *chocolate.*

white currant See *currant.*

white flour See *flour.*

white lady A cocktail of Cointreau, white crème de menthe, and lemon juice.

white peach See *peach.*

white pepper (corns) See *peppercorns.*

white poppy seeds See *poppy seeds.*

white Port See *Port.*

white rice See *rice.*

white sapote (sah-'poh-tay) A small, plum-shape tropical fruit native to Mexico and Central America, but now grown in Florida and California. It resembles a green-skinned apple with one pointed end. Its crisp, creamy, ivory flesh has a few inedible seeds and tastes like a combination of mango and banana with a hint of vanilla. Also known as *zapote blanco.*

white tea See *tea.*

white walnut See *butternut.*

white wine vinegar See *vinegar.*

white Zinfandel See *Zinfandel.*

wholemeal flour See *flour.*

whole wheat flour See *flour.*

whortleberry See *berry, bilberry.*

wiamanola ('why-amm-ann-ho-lah) A rich, buttery *macadamia nut* variety grown in Hawaii.

W
W

Wickson plum See *plum*.

wienerbrod ('vee-nehr-brod) See *danish pastry*.

wild majoram Another name for *oregano*.

wild rice See *rice*.

wild strawberry See *fraise des bois*.

wild yeast See *yeast*.

wild yeast starter See *sourdough culture/starter*.

wine An alcoholic beverage made from the fermented juice of grapes and sometimes other fruits. Wines are categorized as follows:

> **Fortified** A wine that has its alcohol content increased by the addition of a distilled spirit, usually brandy. They are generally categorized as dessert wine or liqueur, and have an alcohol content of 16 to 20%. See *Madeira, Marsala, Muscatel, Port, Setúbal, Sherry,* and *Vermouth*.

> **Sparkling** A wine with bubbles. See *cava, Champagne, sekt,* and *spumante*.

> **Still** Nonsparkling wine, which includes white wine, red wine, and rosé.

wine cream A thick, sweet wine custard made with thickened wine and sugar. It was created in Germany during the 18th century as a way to use leftover wine.

Winesap apple See *apple*.

wineberry See *berry*.

winnowing See *chocolate*.

wintergreen A native North American evergreen shrub that has small red berries and white, bell-shaped flowers. The highly aromatic leaves are prized for its oil, which is used to flavor candies and confections. Also known as checkerberry.

winter melon See *melon*.

winter wheat See *wheat*.

winternelis pear See *pear*.

wo bing A deep-fried lotus-paste pancake from China. A thin batter of flour, salt, water, and eggs is cooked in oil to form a very thin pancake. The center is filled with lotus paste, and the sides of the pancake are folded into the center and sealed with additional batter. The pancake is fried in hot oil, then cut into thin strips and served warm, topped with toasted sesame seeds.

wok (wahk) A round-bottomed metal cooking pan with sloping sides. It is used in Chinese cookery for stir-frying, steaming, braising, deep-frying, and poaching. Woks are available in various sizes and may be electric or come with a special ring trivet for use on a gas stove; or be flat-bottomed for use on an electric stove.

Wonder Bread A popular 1½-pound (680 g) American white loaf bread, It was created by the Taggart Baking Company of Indianapolis and named by Vice President Elmer Cline because he was inspired by the International Balloon Race at the Indianapolis Speedway. Upon seeing the sky filled with hundreds of colorful balloons, he felt a sense of wonder. Since that time, the colorful red, blue, and yellow balloons have been the cornerstone of Wonder Bread's logo and package. In 1925, the Continental Baking Company bought the Indianapolis bakery and Wonder Bread soon became a national brand. The Continental Baking Company altered the course of bread forever in the 1930s when it introduced "sliced" Wonder Bread. During the 1940s, several advances in its nutrition and baking were made, and in 1941, Wonder Bread was involved in a government-supported move to enrich white bread with vitamins and minerals to improve nutrition. At the same time, Wonder introduced a new way of baking that eliminated holes in

W
W

bread. In 1986, a new reduced-calorie Wonder Bread was launched and is one of the company's strong sellers today. In 1995, Interstate Brands Corporation acquired the Continental Baking Company, and continues to produce this soft, popular American white bread.

Wondra flour See *flour, instant.*

wonton wrapper A paper-thin square or round of dough, used to wrap sweet and savory items. Once filled, the wontons may be steamed or pan-fried.

woodruff A sweet scented leaf used in Germany and Austria to flavor *May wine,* jam, teas, and candies.

wood sugar See *xylitol.*

wormwood An aromatic, bitter herb whose leaves are used to flavor *absinthe* and its flowers are used to flavor *vermouth.* The name is from the fact that it was originally a medicine to treat intestinal worms. The oil extracted from the leaves may be toxic, and it is therefore banned for use in any products in the United States.

Wuchteln ('vook-tehlm) An Austrian dessert that is a rich, buttery yeast bun filled with plums or plum jam. After baking, it is usually served warm with *crème anglaise.*

W
w

Xx

X A label symbol used in the grading of confectioners' sugar that represents the degree of coarseness. The more X's, the finer the grade of sugar.

xanthan gum ('ksahn-thuhn) A food additive made from corn syrup. It is used as an emulsifier, stabilizer, and thickener in processed foods.

xanthia (ksahn-'thee-ah) A cocktail of cherry brandy, yellow Chartreuse, and gin.

xanthine (ksahn-'thee'nee) An alkaloid that, when *methylated,* can be found in the caffeine in coffee and the *theobromine* found in chocolate.

xathophyllus (ksah-tho-phee-lus) A pigment that aids in the yellow colorization of egg yolks. It is chemically related to *carotene* and is also found in onions and potatoes.

xérès ('zayr-rez) The French word for Sherry. The name derives from the Spanish city where sherry originated, Jerez de la Frontera, which was formerly known as Xeres.

xìn rén dòu fù (sheen 'rehn do 'foo) A Chinese almond bean curd that resembles tofu. It is made from jellied almond extract and condensed milk and is typically served in a fruit salad with syrup.

xithum ('ksee-thom) A type of beer produced from fermented barley in ancient Egypt.

xio vo (soy vah) A Vietnamese snack food of coconut rice and yellow mung beans.

XO A brandy term that means "extra old."

xocolatl ('zhock-ah-tehl) An ancient drink made by grinding cocoa beans into a paste and then adding cold water and chiles. The origin of the name is debated but is believed to be influenced by the ancient Aztecs and Mayan cultures, who referred to it as "bitter water." It was considered a royal drink and was so highly regarded that the ground paste was kept in golden containers and drunk from beakers made of pure gold. The Aztecs believed it had aphrodisiac powers, and Montezuma introduced it to the Spanish explorer Cortes in 1519. Cortes was also impressed with its stimulative properties and proclaimed that it "kept a soldier fresh for the whole day." He brought it back to to Spain, where sugar and other spices such as anise seed, cinnamon, and almonds were added, and the cold water was replaced with hot water, which dissolved the paste more effectively. Although the Spaniards were able to keep this cherished beverage a secret for over 100 years, it was eventually discovered by the rest of Europe, and led to the creation of chocolate houses, where it could be enjoyed by Europe's upper class. See also *chocolate.*

xoi (zhoy) A Vietnamese street food of sticky rice steamed in a banana-leaf wrapper. It may or may not also contain peanuts or mung beans.

xoi gat (zhoy 'gah) A bright orange carrot powder used to color rice in Vietnam.

xylem (ksee-lehm) The tissue in a tree trunk that transports food to the leaves. This is where maple sap flows and is tapped for *maple syrup* production.

xylitol ('ksee-lee-tol) A sugar alcohol used as a sugar substitute. It can be extracted from corn, birch bark, fruits, vegetables, and berries. It is popular in Finnish confections and also is an ingredient in chewing gum. Also known as *wood sugar* or *birch sugar.*

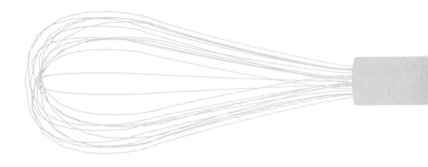

X
x

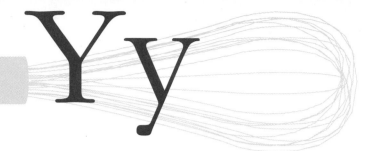

Yy

yak bap (yahk bahp) A Korean dessert of creamy rice sweetened with honey and flavored with dates, pine nuts, and chestnuts.

yakshik (yah-'shee) A Korean rice dessert made with *jujubes,* which are prized for their medicinal properties. *Yak* is Korean for "medicine."

yali (yah-ree) See *Asian pear.*

yam A root vegetable of the tropics, often confused with the sweet potato, but larger, with a starchy taste and higher moisture content. Its flesh ranges in color from creamy white to pink or purple and the skin may be off-white or light to dark brown. Depending on the variety, the texture may be moist and tender or dry and mealy. It is used extensively in the South Pacific, South America, and Africa. See also *fufu.*

yamada nishiki ('yah-mah-dah 'nee-shkey) See *sake.*

yarrow ('yah-roh) A widely naturalized European herb also cultivated in the United States. Its lacy green leaves have a pungent flavor and are dried and used to flavor tea. The flowers may be yellow, pink, or magenta and are used as a food coloring. Known as milfoil in Europe.

yeast A single-celled living organism that is a fungus. Although there are hundreds of yeast species, *Saccharomyces cerevisiae* is the strain most commonly used in baking because of its rapid gas production. Yeast will grow and multiply when the following conditions are met: moisture, dough temperature between 85° and 95°F (29° to 35°C), and sugar (either added to the dough or converted from the natural starch in the flour) for food. Yeast fermentation is retarded in temperatures below 60°F (16°C) and above 115°F (46°C), and it dies at 145°F (63°C). Yeast is a crucial ingredient in baking because, when yeast ferments, it breaks down the sugar and starches and converts them to alcohol and carbon dioxide, which leavens bread or other yeast-risen baked goods. Yeast fermentation is affected by several factors, including temperature of dough, amount of salt, amount and type of sugar, pH of the dough, and amount and type of yeast. It is important to not allow yeast to come into direct contact with salt because it can retard the effects of the yeast and slow or kill fermentation. Once a yeast package is opened, it will begin to absorb moisture from the air and lose its strength; therefore, it is important to keep yeast in an airtight container in the refrigerator or freezer. There are several types of yeast available.

> **Active Dry** Yeast that has been dehydrated and vacuum packed to extend shelf life. Once open, it can stay at room temperature for several months or longer if refrigerated or frozen. The process of drying the yeast kills the outside layer of each granule and yields 25% dead yeast cells per package. Once dead or damaged, the yeast releases a substance called *glutathione,* which adversely affects the quality of gluten in dough; therefore, this product is not popular with professional bakers. If used it should be dissolved in very warm water (110°F/43°C) that is four times its weight.

Brewer's Nonleavening yeast used specifically in beer making.

Compressed Fresh Although preferred by many bakers, it has a shelf life of only two to three weeks. It may be frozen, but will lose approximately 5% of its strength and should be thawed slowly and used immediately. It is typically sold in 1-pound rectangular blocks and should crumble easily. Also called fresh yeast. If not available, it may be substituted accordingly:

To convert fresh yeast to active dry yeast, multiply the weight of the fresh yeast by .4

To convert fresh yeast to instant dry yeast, multiply the weight of the fresh yeast by .33

Cream Used only in large commercial production facilities, the yeast and nutrient base are in liquid form, which makes it easier to blend into the dough.

Instant Active Dry Yeast that can be added directly to the dough and does not need to be hydrated first. It contains about 25% more living yeast cells than active dry yeast because it is processed more gently.

SAF An instant yeast called *osmotolerant*. It is used specifically for very sweet or very acidic doughs because it is able to tolerate the high amounts of sugar or acidity that typically slow down regular yeast strains. Regular yeast may be substituted, but it will take longer to activate. It is commonly known as SAF Gold because it is packaged in a gold wrapper.

Wild Yeast that live in the air as well as on seeds, grains, flour, and grape skins. This yeast plays a crucial role in the leavening of bread and the production of *starters*. The strain used to make sourdough bread is called *Saccharomyces exiguous*.

yeast bread Any bread that is leavened by yeast.

yeast dough Any dough that contains yeast as a leavening agent.

yeast extract A mixture of liquid yeast extract and vegetable extract. It is rich in vitamin B and is used as a seasoning and as a base for products such as *Marmite* and *Vegemite*.

yeast raised Any product leavened with yeast, such as bread or doughnuts.

yeast roll See *rolls*.

yeast starter See *starter*.

Yellow Baby A variety of baby watermelon. See *watermelon*.

Yellow Delicious apple See *apple*.

yellow peach See *peach*.

yergecheffe ('yehr-geh-chehf-eh) An Ethiopian Arabica coffee bean that produces a medium-bodied coffee with a sweet flavor and aroma.

yield The quantity or number of servings that a recipe makes.

ylang-ylang A Filipino flower prized for its perfumed aroma and bitter floral taste. The flower's oils are extracted and used to flavor confections, ice cream, and pastries.

yoe (yoh) 1. A Tibetan snack of toasted barley, soybeans, and corn millet. 2. A variety of corn millet known as white broom from the Gansu province of China.

yogurt A tangy, custard-like dairy product made by adding bacteria to milk and holding it at a warm temperature until it ferments and coagulates. According to folklore, it was accidentally created thousands of years ago by nomadic Balkan tribes in an effort to preserve milk.

Y y

Although the milk may be from any animal, cow's milk is the most prevalent. It may be purchased plain or flavored with fruit and/or sugar and artificial flavorings, and is available in whole milk, low-fat milk, and nonfat milk varieties. It is commonly eaten with fruit and/or nuts or granola as a breakfast item or snack and may also be used as a substitute for *sour cream* in baking. Frozen yogurt has a creamy consistency and is popular as an alternative to ice cream. Soy yogurt, which is made with soy milk, is available for people who do not eat dairy.

yogurt tatlisi (tah-'tlee-see) A Turkish yogurt cake that is soaked in sweet syrup and garnished with toasted pistachios.

yokan (yoh-kahn) A Japanese confection made with sweetened adzuki bean paste and gelled with *agar-agar*.

yolk See *egg*.

York Imperial apple See *apple*.

Yorkshire pudding ('york-shuhr) A savory British *popover*. It is named for the English region of Yorkshire, and is traditionally served with roast beef, made from the pan drippings; but it is also popular with other dishes that have gravy. It is made from a thin batter that is poured into muffin tins greased with beef drippings. The high heat of the oven produces the steam that leavens the popover and it bakes to a puffy, crisp golden brown.

youngberry See *berry*.

young dough An underfermented dough.

Yquem (kem) See *Sauternes*.

yuba ('yoo-bah) The skin produced from heating soybean milk. This film is skimmed from the top and dried in sheets or sticks. It is then rehydrated in water before being used to wrap foods or fried and eaten as a snack.

yuca ('yuhk-uh) The large root of a succulent plant of dry areas in the New World, now primarily imported from Africa. The root may be bitter (poisonous if not cooked) or sweet (used to make *tapioca*), and ranges in size from 6 to 12 inches (15 to 30 cm) in length and 2 to 3 inches (5 to 7.5 cm) in diameter. It has a tough brown skin and a crisp white flesh. It can be stored in the refrigerator for no more than four days. Also spelled yucca and known as *cassava* and *manioc*.

yucca Another spelling of yuca. See *yuca*.

yuè bìng (u-eh bing) A sweet Chinese moon cake filled with dried fruits and nuts.

yufka A Turkish bread dough similar to *phyllo* but thicker. It is rolled into a thin circle and used to wrap sweet and savory items.

Yule log See *bûche de Noël*.

yuzu (yoo-zoo) A sour citrus fruit from Japan, used almost exclusively for its aromatic juice and rind. It is the size of a small orange and has a green, pebbled skin that turns yellowish-orange as it ripens. The pale, yellowish-green flesh is heavily seeded and tastes like lime, lemon, grapefruit, and tangerine. It may be used as a garnish or to flavor various dishes.

Y
y

za'atar ('zah-ttarr) 1. The Arabic word for thyme, referring to another herb that tastes like a combination of thyme, marjoram, and oregano. 2. A spice blend made primarily of sumac, sesame seeds, and the za'atar herb. It is common as a topping on flatbreads.

zabaglione (zah-bahl-'yoh-nay) An Italian dessert made by whipping yolks, sugar, and Marsala over a double boiler until thick and creamy. It may be served as is or used as a sauce to top fruit or other desserts. Champagne or other dessert wines may also be used to flavor the mixture. The name is derived from the Neopolitan *zapillare,* which means "foam." It is known as *sabayon* in France.

zabaglione pot An unlined copper pot with a round bottom and long handle. It is designed so that the product, particularly *zabaglione,* can be easily whisked over simmering water.

zaletti (zah-'let-tee) An Italian cornmeal cookie flavored with lemon zest, vanilla, and golden raisins soaked in grappa or brandy. The cookie, a specialty of Venice, has a name derived from *gialetti,* which means "little yellow things."

Zante currant See *currant.*

Zante grape See *grape.*

zapatilla (zha-pah-'teel-yah) A somewhat flattened bread that is popular in Madrid, Spain. It is cut into large squares and filled with a variety of items such as cured ham, garlic, and tomato that is sprinkled with olive oil.

zapote, zapote blanco (zah-'poh-tay blahn-'koh) Another spelling of *sapote;* see *white sapote.*

zarda ('zahr-dah) A spicy, sweet Indian pudding flavored with saffron, nuts, and raisins.

zein (tsayn) A cream-colored protein powder used as a coating for processed baked foods.

zéphyr (zefer) The French word for "light wind," referring to sweet and savory dishes characterized by a light, frothy consistency. Both mousses and soufflés fall under this category.

zerde (zerr-dee) A sweet Iranian pudding flavored with cinnamon, rosewater, and saffron.

zero mist A dessert cocktail made with two parts crème de menthe and one part water.

zest The colored outer skin of the rind of a citrus fruit. It may be removed with a *zester,* knife or vegetable peeler; only the colored portion of the skin is desirable because the white pith under the skin is bitter. Zest is a popular ingredient in cooking and baking; the peel contains the fruit's aromatic and flavorful essential oils. It may also be candied and used as is or as an ingredient in custards, cakes, pastries, and other confections.

Z
z

zester A hand tool for harvesting the outer rind of citrus fruit. There are several varieties, including one that has five small holes that removes the zest in thin strips, one that removes the zest in one wide strip, and a miniature grater that removes the zest in flakes. It may also be purchased as a combination stripper/zester.

zhan mi fen (han me fan) A Chinese rice flour made from long-grained rice.

zhi ma jiang (shee ma 'gee-hang) A sesame seed paste from China.

zhoug (tsoos) A spicy dipping sauce for soft *flatbreads,* popular in the Yemini community of Israel. It is made with a mixture of fresh parsley and cilantro, chiles, garlic, cumin, and oil.

Zimtsterne ('tsimt-stehrn-eh) The German word for "cinnamon stars," referring to an almond Christmas cookie flavored with lemon or Kirsch and topped with a cinnamon-flavored meringue. Once baked, they are decorated with colored sugar crystals.

Zinfandel grape ('zihn-fuhn-dehl) A red grape that produces a light, slightly sweet white or a bold, fruity full-bodied red wine. Originally from Europe, this grape is now grown widely in California. The white wine is typically drunk as is or made into a *spritzer,* while the red pairs well with chocolate desserts. Although less common, there are also late-harvest zinfandels that are very sweet and served as a dessert wine.

Zitron ('ziht-trohn) A Swiss pastry of sweet tart dough filled with smooth, rich lemon curd and topped with a thin layer of yellow fondant. It is decorated with a chocolate Z on top.

zombie A dessert cocktail of pineapple, lime, and orange juice, apricot brandy, light and dark rum, and passion fruit syrup.

Zubrovka (zoo-'brahv-kah) Another name for *Zubrowka.*

Zubrowka (zoo-'brawv-kah) A yellowish vodka from Poland and Hungary, which contains a blade of bison grass in each bottle. Also called *Zubrovka.*

zuccotto (zoo-'koht-toh) A dome-shaped Italian dessert made by lining a mold with ladyfingers that have been soaked in liqueur and then filling it with sweetened whipped cream, candied fruit, chopped chocolate, and toasted hazelnuts. It is then topped with additional cake and chilled until set. The dessert is inverted and dusted with confectioners' sugar and cocoa powder. The name is believed to derive from the Italian *duomo,* which means "cathedral church," because these desserts are typically built with a similar dome-shaped ornamental top.

Zucker ('zook-kehr) The German word for *sugar.*

Zuger Kirschtorte ('zook-kehr Kirsch-tohrt) A Swiss torte made by sandwiching two almond or hazelnut meringue layers with Kirsch-flavored buttercream and genoise that has been brushed with a Kirsch syrup. The torte is iced with the Kirsch buttercream and the sides covered with toasted almonds or hazelnuts. The top is heavily dusted with confectioners' sugar and scored in a diamond pattern. It is named after the Swiss town of Zug, where it was created. Also known as *Kirschtorte.*

zuppa inglese ('zoo-pah een-'glay-zeh) Italian for "English soup," referring to a chilled dessert made by layering Kirsch-soaked sponge cake with pastry cream, candied fruit, whipped cream, and toasted almonds. The cake is topped with meringue and browned in the oven. It was invented in the 19th century by

Neapolitan pastry cooks who were inspired by the English puddings that were popular at the time.

Zurich leckerli See *leckerli.*

zurra ('zohr-ah) See *sangría.*

Zwetschgen im Strudelteig ('tsvehtsh-gehn-im-stroo-dehl-tihk) A deep-fried plum strudel from Germany.

Zwieback ('zwhy-bahk) The German word for "twice baked," referring to a cracker-like bread. It is made baking bread and then slicing it into pieces and baking it again until it is crisp and dry.

zymase (tsee-mah-she) A yeast enzyme that takes part in the breakdown of sugars during the fermentation process.

zymurgy ('zi-mahr-jee) The area of chemistry that deals with fermentation, particularly for brewing.

Z
z

Important Temperatures Every Pastry Chef and Baker Should Know

FAHRENHEIT	CELCIUS	IMPORTANCE
0°F	−18°C	Required freezer temperature
6° to 10°F	−14.5° to 12°C	Servable temperature for ice cream
32°F	0°C	Freezing point of water
40°F	4°C	Temperature of dormant yeast
41° to 135°F	5° to 57°C	Temperature danger zone
68°F	20°C	Temperature gelatin will begin to set
77° to 122°F	25° to 50°C	In bread baking, there is a rapid increase in yeast fermentation and enzyme activity; crust formation begins; starch swells; and increased gas production and expansion create oven spring
80°F	26°C	Ideal temperature for yeast multiplication
82° to 84°F	26° to 28°C	Temperature range for cooling milk and white chocolate for tempering
84° to 86°F	28° to 30°C	Temperature range for cooling dark chocolate for tempering
86°F	28°C	Gelatin dissolves
86° to 88°F	30° to 31°C	Temperature range for working with tempered milk and white chocolate
90°F	32°C	The ideal working temperature of tempered dark chocolate
100° to 105°F	38° to 40°C	Ideal temperature for working with coating chocolate and fondant

FAHRENHEIT	CELCIUS	IMPORTANCE
105° to 115°F	40° to 49°C	Temperature range for melting milk and white chocolate for tempering
115° to 120°F	46° to 49°C	Temperature range for melting dark chocolate for tempering
122° to 140°F	50° to 60°C	In bread baking, rye starch begins to gelatinize; bacteria die; enzymes in yeast are deactivated
135°F	57°C	The temperature danger zone ends at this degree, although many foods are still susceptible to bacterial growth
140°F	60°C	Yeast dies
140° to 158°F	60° to 70°C	In bread baking, wheat starch begins to gelatinize; expansion of loaf slows; coagulation of proteins begins; amylase enzymes reach maximum activity
158° to 176°F	70° to 80°C	In bread baking, the coagulation of gluten is complete and dough structure is formed; enzyme activity decreases. In rye breads, rye starch gelatinization ends
176° to 194°F	80° to 90°C	In bread baking, wheat starch gelatinization is complete and enzyme activity stops
180° to 200°F	82° to 94°C	Temperature range for drying products such as meringues and fruit slices
194° to 212°F	90° to 100°C	In bread baking, maximum internal loaf temperature is reached and caramelization of crust begins
212°F	100°C	Boiling point of water at sea level

FAHRENHEIT	CELCIUS	IMPORTANCE
212° to 350°F	100° to 175°C	Maillard reaction develops crust color and keytones and aldehydes form to contribute flavor and aroma of bread
220°F	104°C	The sheeting stage for jelly
220° to 234°F	104° to 112°C	Thread stage of sugar
240°F	115°C	Soft ball stage of sugar
245° to 248°F	118° to 120°C	Firm ball stage of sugar
250°F	122°C	Hard ball stage of sugar
270° to 290°F	132° to 143°C	Soft crack stage of sugar
300° to 310°F	149° to 154°C	Hard crack stage of sugar
300° to 325°F	149° to 163°C	Temperature range for baking custards and cheesecakes
300° to 400°F	149° to 205°C	In bread baking, caramelization further develops crust color and flavor
310° to 318°F	155° to159°C	The beginning stage for caramelization of sugar syrup
320° to 338°F	160° to 170°C	Caramel stage of sugar
325°F	163°C	Medium oven heat for baked goods such as macaroons
350° to 375°F	175° to190°C	Temperature range for baked goods such as cakes cookies, pies, muffins, and quickbreads
400° to 450°F	205° to 230°C	Temperature range for baked goods such as laminated doughs and pâte à choux
475° to 500°F	246° to 260°C	Temperature range for baked goods such as bread, pizza, and flatbreads

Weight and Volume Equivalents for Most Common Ingredients

PRODUCT	OUNCES IN 1 CUP	OUNCES/VOLUME
Active dry yeast		.13 oz. = 1 tsp.
All-purpose flour	4.25	
Almond paste	9.5	
Almonds, blanched sliced	4.5	
Almonds, natural sliced	3	
Almonds, natural whole	5	
Apricot glaze	12	
Apricot jam	12	
Apricots, dried	4.5	
Baker's dry milk powder	4.75	
Baking powder		.50 oz. (.45) = 1 T
Baking soda		.50 oz. (.57) = 1 T
Bran cereal	2.25	
Bran flakes	2	
Bread flour	4.75	
Butter	8	
Cake flour	4	
Cherries, dried	5	
Chocolate chips (mini)	6	
Chocolate chips (regular)	6	
Chocolate cookie crumbs	4	
Cocoa powder	3.75	
Coconut milk	8.5	
Coconut, cream of,	10	
Coconut, sweetened, flake	3	
Coconut, unsweetened	2.75	
Confectioners' sugar	4	

PRODUCT	OUNCES IN 1 CUP	OUNCES/VOLUME
Cornmeal, course	6	
Cornmeal, fine	5	
Cornstarch		1 oz. = 3 T
Cream of tartar		.33 oz. = 1 T
Dark/light brown sugar	8	
Dark/light corn syrup	12	
Diastic malt powder		.3 oz. = 1 T
Egg whites, frozen, pasteurized		1 white = 1.15 oz.
Egg yolks, frozen, sugared		1 yolk = .55 oz.
Eggs, fresh, large		1 egg (no shell) = 1.70 oz.
Espresso powder	4	.25 oz. = 1 T
Figs	6	
Fresh yeast		.66 oz. = 2 T, crumbled
Fruit puree	9	
Fruit, chopped, candied	5.5	
Gelatin		.25 oz. = 2¼ tsp.
Gold SAF yeast		.11 oz. = 1 tsp.
Graham cracker crumbs	4	
Granulated sugar	7	
Half-and-half	8.5	
Hazelnuts, whole, unblanched	4.75	
Heavy cream	8.5	
High-gluten flour	4.75	
Honey	12	
Instant active dry yeast		.11 oz. = 1 tsp.
Macadamia nuts	4.75	
Malt syrup	12	
Malted milk powder	4	

PRODUCT	OUNCES IN 1 CUP	OUNCES/VOLUME
Maple syrup	12	
Meringue powder		.25 oz. = 1 T
Milk	8.5	
Milk, evaporated	9	
Milk, sweetened condensed	11	
Molasses	11	
Peanut butter	8	
Peanuts	4.75	
Pecan halves	4	
Pecan pieces	3.75	
Pineapple, crushed	8	
Poppy seeds		.65 oz. = 1 T
Potato starch		.37 oz. = 1 T
Prunes	6	
Pumpernickel flour	4	
Pumpkin	8.57	
Raisins	6	
Raspberry preserves	12	
Rolled oats	3.5	
Rye flour	4	
Salt, granulated		.50 oz. = 1 T
Salt, kosher		.33 oz. = 1 T
Sour cream	8.5	
Spices, ground		.25oz. = 1 T
Superfine sugar	7.33	
Tapioca		.5 oz. (.43) = 1 T
Vanilla beans		4 beans = 1 oz.
Vanilla extract		.5 oz. = 1 T
Vegetable oil	8	

PRODUCT	OUNCES IN 1 CUP	OUNCES/VOLUME
Vegetable shortening	5.75	
Walnut pieces	4	
Wheat germ	4	
Whole wheat flour	4.5	

Sugar Cooking Stages

The following chart results were obtained by placing a teaspoon of cooked sugar syrup in ice water to judge the stage of crystallization.

STAGE	TEMPERATURE	IN ICE WATER
Thread	230° to 234°F (110° to 112°C)	Sugar syrup spins a soft 2-inch thread
Soft ball	234° to 240°F (112° to 116°C)	Sugar syrup forms a soft, pliable ball*
Firm ball	244° to 248°F (118° to 120°C)	Sugar syrup forms a firm but pliable ball
Hard ball	250° to 265°F (121° to 129°C)	Sugar syrup forms a hard, compact ball
Soft crack	270° to 290°F (132° to 143° C)	Sugar syrup separates into hard but not brittle threads
Hard crack	300° to 310°F (149° to 154°C)	Sugar syrup forms hard, brittle threads
Carmel	320° to 338°F (160° to 170°C)	Sugar syrup forms hard, brittle threads and the liquid turns brown

*At the soft ball stage the sugar may also be able to be blown through a wire formed into a loop and will form a bubble.

Conversion Formulas and Equivalents

1. Conversion formulas:

When it is necessary to convert Fahrenheit temperature to Centigrade, the following may be used:

$$\text{Fahrenheit} - 32 \times 5 \div 9$$

When it is necessary to convert Centigrade to Fahrenheit temperature, the following may be used:

$$\text{Centigrade} \times 9 \div 5$$

2. Volume Equivalents:

	QUANTITY	EQUIVALENT
a.	3 teaspoons	1 tablespoon
b.	2 tablespoons	1 fl. ounce
c.	16 tablespoons (8 fl. ounces)	1 cup
d.	2 cups (16 fl. ounces)	1 pint
e.	2 pints (32 fl. ounces)	1 quart
f.	4 quarts (128 fl. ounces)	1 gallon

3. Metric Conversions: Weight

1 ounce = 28.35 grams

1 pound = 454 grams

1 gram = 0.035 ounces

1 Kilogram = 2.2 pounds

a. To convert ounces to grams, multiply by 28.35

b. To convert grams to ounces, multiply by 0.03527

c. To convert kilograms to pounds, multiply by 2.2046

d. To convert pounds to kilograms, multiply by 0.4535924

4. Metric Conversions: Volume

1 ounce = 29.57 ml

1 cup = 2 dl, 2 cl, 7 ml (237 ml)

1 quart = 9 dl, 4 cl, 6 ml (946 ml)

1 milliliter = 0.034 fl. ounces

1 Liter = 33.8 fl. ounces

a. To convert quarts to Liters, multiply by 0.946

b. To convert Liters to quarts, multiply by 1.05625

c. To convert Liters to pints, multiply by 2.1125

320

d. To convert Liters to ounces, multiply by 33.8

e. To convert pints to Liters, multiply by 0.473

f. To convert quarts to milliliters, multiply by 946

g. To convert milliliters to pints, multiply by 0.0021125

h. To convert milliliters to ounces multiply by 0.0338

5. Metric Conversion: Length

1 inch = 25.4 mm

1 centimeter = 0.39 inches

1 meter = 39.4 inches

a. To convert inches to millimeters, multiply by 25.4

b. To convert inches to centimeters, multiply by 2.54

c. To convert millimeters to inches, multiply by 0.03937

d. To convert centimeters to inches, multiply by 0.3937

e. To convert meters to inches, multiply by 39.3701

Seasonal Fruit Availability

The following chart is a general guideline. Please see specific fruit for varietal availability.

FRUIT	WINTER Nov. 20 – March 5	SPRING March 6 – May 30	SUMMER June 1 – Sept. 1	FALL Sept. 2 – Nov. 19
Apples			X	X
Apricots			X	
Blueberries		X	X	
Cantaloupe		X	X	
Cherries		X	X	
Chestnuts	X			X
Citrus	X	X	X	X
Cranberries	X			X
Dates	X			X
Figs			X	X
Grapes			X	X
Mangos		X	X	
Papayas		X	X	
Peaches			X	
Pears	X	X		X
Pecans	X			X
Persimmons	X			X
Pineapples		X	X	
Plums			X	X
Pumpkins				X
Raspberries			X	
Rhubarb			X	
Strawberries		X	X	
Watermelon			X	

The 12 Steps of Baking

The art of bread baking relies on 12 fundamental steps. An understanding of the factors involved in each of these steps is critical for quality bread production.

Step 1: Scaling/Mise en Place

All ingredients are accurately measured. As with all aspects of baking and pastry, properly scaled ingredients are crucial for creating consistency in quality and controlling cost. As part of the mise en place, the baker should take stock of the ingredients, noting temperatures of ingredients, equipment, and the room so that these temperatures may be calculated into the final temperature of the dough. It is also important that all equipment, especially the scale, is working properly and that the weights of the ingredients are double-checked before proceeding to the mixing process. This step should conclude with all ingredients accurately measured and lined up in order of use, as well as all tools and equipment ready for the second step in the bread-making process.

Step 2: Mixing

Ingredients are combined into a smooth, uniform dough; the yeast and other ingredients are evenly distributed through the dough; and the gluten is developed. Before mixing the dough, determine the desired dough temperature. For lean doughs, the ideal temperature is typically 75° to 80°F (24° to 27°C), while enriched doughs are slightly higher. Use the following formula to calculate the temperature of the water needed to achieve the ideal dough temperature:

Flour temperature + room temperature + friction factor = X

X − desired dough temperature = water temperature.

The friction factor is the amount of heat generated when the dough is mixed. It depends on the type of mixer used, mixing time, and mixing speed; but in general it is between 24° and 28°F (−5° and −2°C). It is important in determining the desired dough temperature. Once the water temperature has been adjusted so that the desired dough temperature is achieved, the dough is ready to be mixed. The mixing method used affects the final outcome of the dough; the methods are as follows:

- **Straight dough method:** All ingredients are placed into a bowl and then mixed at one time. We refer to this method as "everybody in the pool." Bakers also refer to this as a "direct" method because it has not undergone any previous mixing of fermentation. This method is used for quantity production of white pan bread, rolls, and other bread products. Because this dough has no pre-ferment, many bakers feel that it lacks the quality flavor and texture that can be achieved with other mixing methods. It is commonly used in commercial bread products.

- **Modified straight dough:** A variation on the straight dough method, typically used for rich sweet doughs to ensure distribution of fat and sugar. In this method, the fat, sugar, salt, milk solids, and flavorings are blended and then the eggs added slowly. After the eggs are incorporated, the liquid is added and then the flour and yeast are added.
- **Sponge method:** This method uses a pre-fermented dough or sponge, which adds flavor, texture, and volume to the bread. This method is also known as the "indirect" dough method because of the addition of a previously fermented dough. It is primarily used in the production of artisan breads. The most common pre-ferments are biga, pâte fermentée, and poolish (see entries in Terminology for detailed descriptions). The pre-ferment is made in advance and added to the final dough during the mixing process.

The development of gluten during this stage is what gives the dough its elasticity and extensibility and affects the texture and volume of the final product. The mixing time and speed are determined by the type of mixer used, the amount of dough in the bowl, hydration (the % of water in the dough in relation to the % of flour in the dough), the type of flour used, and the presence of other ingredients. An overmixed dough will result in lack of color, flavor, and texture. An undermixed dough will result in poor volume and texture. In artisan bread baking, there is an additional step called autolyse, which may or may not be used in the initial mixing of the dough. This involves mixing a percentage of the flour and water first and allowing it to rest for approximately 20 minutes. It enables the flour to become completely hydrated and increases the volume and extensibility of the dough.

Step 3: Bulk or Primary Fermentation
The dough is allowed to ferment. Most bakers feel that the fermentation of the dough is the most important step in bread making because it affects the volume, texture, and flavor of the result. Fermentation is the process by which the yeast acts on the sugar and starches and produces carbon dioxide and alcohol. An overfermented or underfermented dough will result in a product with poor volume, color, texture, and flavor. The key to proper fermentation is controlling time and temperature. The amount of time that a dough ferments is determined by the type and quantity of yeast used and the percentage of sugar that is present in the dough. In general, lean yeast doughs have a longer fermentation time because there has been no fat or sugar added and the yeast must feed off of the natural sugar and starch in the flour. Also, the warmer the dough, the quicker it will ferment. Temperature can be controlled by retarding (cooling) the dough in a retarder or refrigerator. This slows the process of fermentation, which allows the bread to develop fuller flavor and increases the gluten elasticity so that it stretches further and holds more gas.

Step 4: Punching, Degassing, or Folding

The dough is equalized. The purpose of this step is to degas the dough, redistribute the yeast for continued growth, and equalize the temperature. This may be accomplished by gently punching the dough or by performing a series of folds. Some bakers believe that folding rather than punching the dough produces a higher quality bread; in addition to expelling the carbon dioxide and redistributing the yeast, it increases the dough strength. It is important to note that doughs made with a high percentage of pre-fermented flour are already strong, and too many folds may adversely affect their extensibility and result in poor volume. On the other hand, doughs made with weak flour and/or a high hydration benefit from folding. Punching rather than folding the dough works well with stiff doughs and doughs with a short bulk fermentation time.

Step 5: Dividing or Scaling

The dough is divided or scaled into the desired portion weights. This may be done by hand with a scale and a metal dough cutter or by a dough-dividing machine. Either way, it is important that the dough is cut cleanly and quickly so it does not oxidize and form an undesirable skin. When scaling the dough, it necessary to allow for weight loss during baking owing to evaporation of moisture. Although it will vary according to the moisture content of the dough, in general the weight loss is approximately 10 percent of the weight of the dough, which should be made up with extra dough to achieve the desired final weight. For example, if a 1-pound (500 g) loaf of bread is desired, an additional 1.5 ounces (50 g) of dough should be added to the scaled portion.

Step 6: Preshaping or Rounding

The portioned dough is loosely shaped into smooth, round balls. This organizes the dough into consistent pieces and makes the final shaping easier and more efficient. It also stretches the gluten on the outside of the dough and forms a skin that helps it retain the gases produced by the yeast.

Step 7: Benching or Bench Rest

The shaped dough rests. If the loaves were rounded on a workbench (hence the name), they are gently covered with plastic or a vinyl zipper-top bag if they are on a rack. Either way, the covering prevents the loaves from forming a crust on the surface. The benching or resting lasts approximately 10 to 20 minutes and relaxes the gluten, making the final shaping of the dough easier. It is important to note that the dough is still fermenting during this stage.

Step 8: Makeup and Panning

The dough is formed into its final shape and placed in the pan or mold that it will be baked in. Hearth breads that will be baked directly on the oven deck are placed in bannetons or between the folds of baker's linen.

There is a wide variety of shapes to choose from, and the final shaping is crucial to the appearance of the finished product. During shaping, all of the gas bubbles should be expelled or air bubbles will form on the surface of the dough during baking. The seam of the dough should also be on the bottom to avoid the bread's splitting open during baking. It is also important to consider the size of the mold so that the proper amount of dough is used. After the loaves are shaped and panned, they are covered and put in a warm spot or put in a temperature/humidity-controlled proof box to prevent the surface of the dough from drying out. Applying a liquid such as an egg wash, milk, or water will add color and shine to the finished loaf as well as act as a sort of glue for toppings such as nuts, seeds, or rolled oats or bran. This should be done before the next step, otherwise the dough is at risk of deflating.

Step 9: Proofing or Final Fermentation

The dough has one final fermentation. This is an important step that affects the texture, volume, appearance, and flavor of the final product. An overproofed dough will result in a coarse texture and loss of flavor. An underproofed dough will have poor volume and a dense texture. The dough should be placed in a temperature and humidity controlled environment to allow the bread to rise to the desired volume before baking. Most bakers agree that the optimum rise for this stage is 80 to 85 percent of the dough's overall volume. The dough should never be taken to 100 percent rise because the bread may collapse under the lack of structure and produce a final product of poor quality. The remainder of the rise will occur in the oven during Step 10 by a process called ovenspring.

Step 10: Baking

The dough is baked. Depending on the desired finish, the dough is often scored (slashed) with a lame or sharp knife prior to baking. This not only enhances the appearance of the bread but also allows the bread to expand without bursting. At this point the proofed breads are very fragile and should be carefully loaded into the ovens so they do not deflate. Lean yeast doughs are baked with steam injected into the oven for the first part of the baking period; this keeps the crust soft and prevents it from forming too quickly so that the bread can expand rapidly and evenly. It also contributes shine and color to the crust. The moisture from the steam gelatinizes the starches on the surface of the loaf and causes them to swell and become glossy, which results in a shiny crust. When the moisture of the steam reacts with the starches on the surface of the dough, it breaks down the starches into dextrins and other simple sugars. At the end of the baking process, when the steam is withdrawn, the sugar caramelizes and yields a rich-colored crust. It is important to make sure that the temperature of the oven and baking time are accurate in order to achieve a quality product. Many changes occur during the baking process and the most important ones are:

- **Ovenspring:** The initial, rapid expansion of loaf volume that is caused when the trapped gasses in the dough expand as a result of the high heat of the oven. The yeast remains active in this final fermentation process until it is killed at a temperature of about 145°F (63°C).
- **Coagulation of proteins and gelatinization of starches:** This contributes to the formation of the crumb and sets the structure of the product. This begins at approximately 140°F (60°C) and continues until the temperature reaches between 180° and 194°F (82° and 90°C).
- **Formation and browning of the crust:** This begins when the surface of the dough reaches 212°F (100°C) owing to a process known as Maillard reaction. It is a complex chemical change that significantly contributes to the rich color and flavor of the bread. It occurs in baked goods in the presence of heat, moisture, proteins, and sugars and continues until the surface temperature reaches 350°F (175°C). Further crust color and flavor develop with caramelization that occurs between temperatures of 300° and 400°F (149° and 204°C).

When the bread reaches a maximum internal temperature of 210°F (99°C) the bread should be properly baked. Other signs that mark the completion of the baking process are a golden brown crust and a hollow sound emitted when the baked loaf is thumped. The baking process is now complete and the bread is ready to be cooled and stored.

Step 11: Cooling

The loaves are cooled on racks that allow the air to circulate around them and prevent the crusts from becoming soggy. The cooling process enables the excess moisture to evaporate and enhances the flavor and aroma of the bread. The bread should be cooled at least two hours to allow the crumb structure to stabilize and develop full flavor.

Step 12: Storage

The bread is packaged for storage, if appropriate. If the bread is to be sold that day, it may be left on racks for the fresh bread to be purchased. If longer storage is required, it should be packaged in moisture-proof bags, which will increase its shelf life. The bread should be thoroughly cooled before storing in a cool, dry place, or moisture will collect inside the packaging and reduce the quality of the bread. Baked breads will stale most quickly at temperatures between 32° and 50°F (0° and 10°C) and therefore should never be placed in the refrigerator. In order to delay staling and maintain the quality of the bread, it may be wrapped tightly after cooling and stored in the freezer.

Classic and Contemporary Flavor Combinations

Berries

	BLACKBERRY	BLUEBERRY	CRANBERRY	RASPBERRY	STRAWBERRY
Allspice			X		
Almonds	X	X	X	X	X
Amaretto	X	X		X	X
Angelica					X
Apples	X	X	X	X	X
Apricots	X	X	X	X	X
Balsamic vinegar					X
Banana	X	X		X	X
Banana liqueur	X	X			X
Basil		X		X	X
Black pepper	X	X	X	X	X
Blackberries	X	X	X	X	X
Blueberries	X	X	X	X	X
Brandy	X	X	X	X	X
Brown sugar	X	X	X	X	X
Caramel					X
Cardamom		X			
Cashews		X			
Cassis	X	X	X	X	X
Champagne	X	X	X	X	X
Cheese	X	X	X	X	X
Chestnuts	X	X	X	X	X
Cinnamon	X	X	X	X	X
Cloves			X		
Coffee				X	X
Cranberries	X	X	X	X	X
Cream cheese	X	X	X	X	X

	BLACKBERRY	BLUEBERRY	CRANBERRY	RASPBERRY	STRAWBERRY
Crème fraîche	X	X	X	X	X
Currants	X	X	X	X	X
Dark chocolate	X	X	X	X	X
Dates	X	X			
Figs	X	X			
Ginger	X	X	X	X	X
Goat cheese	X	X	X	X	X
Grapefruit				X	X
Hazelnuts	X	X	X	X	X
Honey	X	X	X	X	X
Kahula				X	X
Kumquat	X	X	X	X	X
Lemon	X	X	X	X	X
Lemon verbena	X	X		X	X
Lemongrass	X	X		X	X
Lime	X	X	X	X	X
Madeira					X
Mangos	X	X	X	X	X
Marsala				X	X
Mascarpone	X	X	X	X	X
Melon	X	X	X	X	X
Midori	X	X	X	X	X
Milk chocolate		X		X	X
Mint	X	X	X	X	X
Nectarines	X	X	X	X	X
Nutmeg	X		X		X
Orange	X	X	X	X	X
Orange liqueur	X	X	X	X	X
Papaya	X	X		X	X
Passion fruit	X	X		X	X

	BLACKBERRY	BLUEBERRY	CRANBERRY	RASPBERRY	STRAWBERRY
Peaches	X	X	X	X	X
Pears	X	X	X	X	X
Pecans	X	X	X	X	X
Pineapple	X	X		X	X
Pine nuts	X	X	X	X	X
Pink peppercorns					X
Pistachios	X	X	X	X	X
Plums	X	X	X	X	X
Port	X				X
Pumpkin	X				
Raspberries	X	X	X	X	X
Raspberry liqueur	X	X	X	X	X
Red wine	X				
Rhubarb	X	X			X
Ricotta	X	X	X	X	X
Rosemary	X			X	X
Roses					X
Rum					X
Sauternes	X	X	X	X	X
Sesame seeds	X	X	X	X	X
Star anise	X	X	X	X	X
Strawberries	X	X	X	X	X
Sweet potato	X	X	X		
Szechwan peppercorns					X
Thyme	X	X		X	X
Vanilla	X	X	X	X	X
Violets					X
White chocolate	X	X	X	X	X

Nuts Part I

	ALMONDS	BLACK WALNUTS	BRAZIL NUTS	CASHEWS	CHESTNUTS	HAZELNUTS
Allspice	X					
Almonds	X					X
Amaretto	X					
Apples	X	X		X	X	X
Apricots	X	X				
Bananas	X	X	X	X		X
Blackberries	X					X
Blueberries	X					X
Caramel	X	X	X	X	X	X
Cheese	X	X				X
Cherries	X					X
Cinnamon	X	X	X			X
Cloves	X					
Coconut			X			
Coffee	X				X	X
Cranberries	X					
Cream cheese		X				X
Currants	X				X	
Curry	X					
Dark chocolate	X	X	X	X	X	X
Dates	X				X	
Figs	X				X	X
Goat cheese	X	X				X
Honey	X					
Lemon	X					X
Mangos	X			X		
Mascarpone	X					X
Milk chocolate	X		X	X	X	X
Mint	X					X

	ALMONDS	BLACK WALNUTS	BRAZIL NUTS	CASHEWS	CHESTNUTS	HAZELNUTS
Nectarines	X	X				X
Nutmeg	X					
Orange	X		X	X		X
Passion fruit				X		
Peaches	X	X				X
Peanuts				X		
Pears	X	X		X		
Pecans						X
Pineapple				X		
Plums	X	X				X
Port	X					X
Pumpkin	X	X				X
Raisins	X			X		
Raspberries	X					X
Red wine	X					X
Rhubarb	X					
Ricotta	X					X
Rosemary	X					
Roses	X					X
Rum	X	X				
Strawberries	X					X
Sweet potato	X	X				X
Thyme	X					
Vanilla	X	X		X	X	X
White chocolate	X	X		X		X

Nuts Part II

	MACADAMIA NUTS	PEANUTS	PECANS	PINE NUTS	PISTACHIOS	WALNUTS
Apples		X	X	X	X	X
Apricots			X	X	X	X
Balsamic vinegar				X		
Bananas	X	X	X		X	X
Basil				X		
Blackberries			X		X	X
Blueberries			X		X	X
Brown sugar			X			X
Caramel	X	X	X	X	X	X
Cheese			X	X	X	X
Cherries			X	X	X	X
Cinnamon			X	X		X
Coconut		X				
Coffee	X		X			X
Cranberries						X
Cream cheese			X	X	X	X
Currants						X
Dark chocolate	X	X	X	X	X	X
Dates	X			X	X	X
Figs				X	X	X
Ginger	X	X				
Goat cheese			X	X	X	X
Grapes						X
Honey			X	X		X
Lemon			X	X	X	X
Lemon verbena					X	
Lemongrass					X	
Mangos	X					

	MACADAMIA NUTS	PEANUTS	PECANS	PINE NUTS	PISTACHIOS	WALNUTS
Maple syrup			X			
Mascarpone			X			
Milk chocolate		X	X			
Mint	X				X	
Molasses			X			
Nectarines			X	X	X	X
Orange			X	X	X	X
Passion fruit	X					
Peaches			X	X	X	X
Pears			X	X	X	X
Pineapple	X					
Plums			X		X	X
Pumpkin			X			
Raisins		X	X	X		X
Raspberries						X
Red wine						X
Rhubarb						X
Ricotta			X	X		X
Rosemary				X		X
Roses	X					
Sweet potato			X			X
Vanilla	X	X	X	X	X	X
Violets	X					
White chocolate	X		X			X

Chocolate and Citrus

	DARK CHOCOLATE	MILK CHOCOLATE	WHITE CHOCOLATE	ORANGE	LEMON	LIME
Allspice	X	X	X	X		
Almonds	X	X	X	X	X	X
Amaretto	X	X	X	X	X	
Angelica	X	X	X	X	X	
Apples	X	X	X	X	X	X
Apricots	X	X	X	X	X	X
Bananas	X	X	X	X	X	X
Banana liqueur	X	X	X	X	X	X
Basil	X	X	X	X	X	
Black pepper			X	X	X	
Black walnut	X		X	X	X	
Blackberries	X	X	X	X	X	X
Blueberries	X	X	X	X	X	X
Brandy	X	X	X	X	X	
Brazil nuts	X	X	X	X	X	X
Brown sugar	X	X	X	X	X	X
Caramel	X	X	X	X	X	X
Cardamom	X		X	X	X	
Cashews	X	X	X	X	X	X
Cassis	X	X	X	X	X	
Champagne	X	X		X		
Cheese				X	X	
Cherries	X	X	X	X	X	X
Cherry liqueur	X	X	X	X		LIME
Chestnuts	X	X	X	X	X	X
Chinese five-spice	X	X	X	X	X	
Cinnamon	X	X	X	X	X	
Cloves				X		

	DARK CHOCOLATE	MILK CHOCOLATE	WHITE CHOCOLATE	ORANGE	LEMON	LIME
Coconut	X	X	X	X	X	X
Coffee	X	X	X	X	X	
Cranberries	X	X	X	X	X	X
Cream cheese	X	X	X	X	X	X
Crème fraîche	X	X	X	X	X	X
Currants	X	X	X	X	X	X
Curry	X		X	X	X	
Dark chocolate	X	X	X	X	X	X
Dates	X	X	X	X	X	X
Figs	X	X	X	X	X	X
Ginger	X	X	X	X	X	X
Goat cheese	X	X		X	X	
Grapes	X	X		X	X	
Grapefruit				X	X	
Green tea	X		X	X	X	
Hazelnuts	X	X	X	X	X	X
Honey	X	X	X	X	X	X
Kahula	X	X	X	X	X	
Kirsch	X	X	X	X	X	
Kumquat	X			X	X	X
Lemon	X		X	X	X	X
Lemon verbena			X	X	X	
Lemongrass			X	X	X	
Lime	X		X	X	X	X
Macadamia nuts	X	X	X	X	X	
Madeira			X		X	
Mangos	X	X	X	X	X	X
Maple syrup	X	X	X	X	X	
Marsala			X	X	X	

	DARK CHOCOLATE	MILK CHOCOLATE	WHITE CHOCOLATE	ORANGE	LEMON	LIME
Mascarpone	X	X	X	X	X	X
Melon			X	X	X	X
Midori			X	X	X	X
Milk chocolate	X	X	X	X		
Mint	X	X	X	X	X	X
Molasses	X					
Nectarines	X	X	X	X	X	X
Nutmeg	X		X	X	X	
Orange	X	X	X	X	X	X
Orange liqueur	X	X	X	X	X	X
Papaya	X	X	X	X	X	X
Passion fruit	X	X	X	X	X	X
Peaches	X	X	X	X	X	X
Peanuts	X	X	X			
Pears	X	X	X	X	X	X
Pecans	X	X	X	X	X	
Pineapple	X	X	X	X	X	X
Pine nuts	X	X	X	X	X	X
Pink peppercorns	X	X	X	X	X	
Pistachios	X	X	X	X	X	X
Plums	X	X	X	X	X	X
Port	X					
Pumpkin	X	X	X	X	X	
Raisins	X	X	X	X	X	
Raspberries	X	X	X	X	X	X
Raspberry liqueur	X	X	X	X	X	X
Red wine	X			X	X	
Rhubarb				X	X	

	DARK CHOCOLATE	MILK CHOCOLATE	WHITE CHOCOLATE	ORANGE	LEMON	LIME
Ricotta	X	X	X	X	X	X
Rosemary	X		X	X	X	
Roses	X		X		X	
Rum	X	X	X	X	X	X
Sambuca	X	X	X	X		
Sauternes	X					
Sesame seeds	X	X	X	X	X	X
Star anise	X	X	X	X	X	
Strawberries	X	X	X	X	X	X
Sweet potato	X	X	X	X	X	
Szechwan peppercorns	X	X	X	X	X	
Tamarind	X		X	X	X	X
Tequila				X		X
Thyme	X		X	X		
Vanilla	X	X	X	X	X	X
Violets			X	X	X	
Walnuts	X	X	X	X		
Whisky	X	X	X	X		X
White chocolate	X	X	X	X	X	X
White pepper	X		X	X		

Fruit

	APPLES	DATES	FIGS	MELONS	PEARS	PERSIMMONS
Allspice	X	X	X		X	
Almonds	X	X	X		X	
Amaretto	X					
Apples	X		X		X	X
Apricots	X				X	
Bananas		X				
Banana liqueur		X				
Basil	X				X	
Black pepper	X		X		X	X
Black walnuts	X				X	
Blackberries	X			X	X	
Blueberries	X			X	X	
Brandy	X	X			X	
Brown sugar	X				X	X
Caramel	X				X	
Cardamom	X	X			X	
Cassis					X	
Champagne				X	X	
Cheese	X	X			X	
Cherries					X	
Chestnuts	X	X			X	
Chinese five-spice	X				X	
Cinnamon	X	X	X		X	X
Cloves	X				X	
Coffee		X				
Cranberries	X				X	
Cream cheese	X	X	X		X	
Crème fraîche	X	X	X		X	
Currants	X				X	

	APPLES	DATES	FIGS	MELONS	PEARS	PERSIMMONS
Curry	X					
Dark chocolate	X	X				
Dates					X	
Figs	X	X	X		X	
Ginger	X		X		X	X
Goat cheese	X	X	X		X	
Hazelnuts	X		X		X	
Honey	X				X	
Kumquats			X			X
Lemon			X			
Lemon verbena				X		
Lemongrass				X		
Maple syrup	X				X	
Marsala					X	
Mascarpone	X	X	X		X	
Melon				X		
Midori				X		
Milk chocolate					X	
Mint	X			X	X	
Molasses	X				X	
Nutmeg	X				X	
Orange	X	X	X	X	X	
Orange liqueur	X	X	X		X	
Peanuts	X					
Pears	X		X		X	X
Pecans	X				X	
Pine nuts	X		X		X	
Pink peppercorns					X	
Pistachios	X		X		X	
Port			X		X	
Pumpkin	X				X	

	APPLES	DATES	FIGS	MELONS	PEARS	PERSIMMONS
Raisins	X				X	
Raspberries					X	
Red wine			X		X	
Rhubarb	X				X	
Ricotta	X		X		X	
Rosemary					X	
Rum	X	X	X		X	
Sauternes					X	
Sesame seeds					X	
Star anise	X				X	
Sweet potato	X				X	
Szechwan peppercorns					X	
Tamarind	X				X	
Thyme					X	
Vanilla	X	X	X		X	
Violets					X	
Walnuts	X	X	X		X	X
Whisky		X	X		X	
White chocolate					X	
White pepper					X	

Stone Fruits and Vegetables

	CHERRIES	PEACHES & NECTARINES	PLUMS	APRICOTS	PUMPKIN	CARROTS	SWEET POTATO
Allspice	X	X	X		X	X	X
Almonds	X	X	X	X			
Amaretto		X					
Apples					X		X
Apricots	X	X		X			
Balsamic vinegar		X					
Basil		X					
Black pepper	X		X	X			
Black walnuts					X		X
Blackberries		X					
Blueberries		X					
Brandy	X	X	X			X	
Brazil nuts		X					
Brown sugar	X	X			X	X	X
Caramel		X		X	X		X
Cardamom	X	X		X	X		X
Cassis		X		X			
Champagne		X		X			
Cheese	X	X		X	X		X
Cherries	X	X		X			
Cherry liqueur	X	X		X			
Chestnut	X		X		X		X
Chinese five-spice		X					
Cinnamon	X	X	X	X	X	X	X
Cloves			X		X		X
Cranberries					X		X
Cream cheese	X	X		X	X		X
Crème fraîche					X		X

	CHERRIES	PEACHES & NECTARINES	PLUMS	APRICOTS	PUMPKIN	CARROTS	SWEET POTATO
Currants						X	
Curry					X		X
Dark chocolate	X			X	X		X
Dates				X			
Figs		X		X			
Ginger	X	X	X	X	X	X	X
Goat cheese				X			
Green tea		X					
Hazelnuts		X	X	X			
Honey		X	X	X			
Maple syrup					X		X
Marsala			X	X			
Mascarpone	X			X			
Melon		X					
Milk chocolate	X						
Mint		X		X			
Molasses					X	X	X
Nectarines		X		X			
Nutmeg	X			X	X	X	X
Orange	X	X		X		X	
Orange liqueur	X	X					
Passion fruit		X					
Peaches		X		X			
Pears	X						
Pecans		X		X		X	
Pistachios		X					
Plums				X	X	X	X
Port	X		X				
Pumpkin					X		X

	CHERRIES	PEACHES & NECTARINES	PLUMS	APRICOTS	PUMPKIN	CARROTS	SWEET POTATO
Raisins					X	X	X
Red wine			X				
Ricotta	X						
Rosemary			X	X			
Sauternes				X			
Star anise			X			X	
Strawberries		X					
Sweet potato					X		X
Vanilla	X	X	X	X	X	X	X
Walnuts					X	X	X
Whisky					X	X	X
White chocolate	X	X	X		X		X

Tropical Fruit

	MANGO	COCONUT	PAPAYA	PASSION FRUIT	PINEAPPLE	BANANA
Allspice	X					X
Bananas	X	X	X	X	X	X
Banana liqueur	X	X	X	X	X	X
Basil					X	
Black pepper			X			
Black walnuts						X
Blackberries	X		X			
Blueberries	X					
Brandy						X
Brazil nuts		X				X
Brown sugar	X				X	X
Caramel	X				X	X
Cardamom						X
Cashews		X				X
Cheese	X					
Cherries						X
Chinese five-spice	X					
Cinnamon	X		X		X	X
Cloves	X				X	X
Coconut	X	X			X	X
Coffee						X
Cream cheese	X				X	
Dark chocolate	X	X		X	X	X
Ginger	X					X
Goat cheese	X					
Hazelnuts						X
Honey					X	X
Kahula						X

	MANGO	COCONUT	PAPAYA	PASSION FRUIT	PINEAPPLE	BANANA
Lemon verbena	X					
Lemongrass	X					
Lime	X	X	X			
Macadamia nuts	X	X			X	
Madeira						X
Mangos	X	X	X	X		X
Mascarpone	X					
Midori						X
Milk chocolate		X				
Mint	X				X	
Molasses						X
Nutmeg	X					
Orange	X		X	X	X	X
Orange liqueur	X					
Papayas	X	X	X			X
Passion fruit	X	X				
Peanuts						X
Pecans						X
Pineapple	X	X			X	
Pink peppercorns					X	
Rosemary					X	
Rum	X	X	X		X	
Sauternes	X					
Sesame seeds						X
Star anise					X	
Strawberries	X		X			X
Tamarind						X
Tequila						X

	MANGO	COCONUT	PAPAYA	PASSION FRUIT	PINEAPPLE	BANANA
Thyme	X				X	
Vanilla	X	X	X	X	X	X
Walnuts						X
Whisky						X

What Went Wrong and Why

Buttercream

WHAT WENT WRONG	WHY
The finished buttercream looks broken or curdled.	Insufficient quantity of butter added to the sugar/egg mixture. The butter has not been thoroughly beaten into the sugar/egg mixture. The butter was too cold when added to the sugar/egg mixture.
The finished buttercream is too soft and does not thicken up.	The sugar/egg mixture was not cool enough when the butter was added.
The finished buttercream has a grainy texture.	The buttercream was overbeaten. The sugar may not have dissolved completely during the heating process of sugar/egg mixture (Swiss buttercream).
The finished buttercream is too stiff to spread.	Buttercream is too cold. Soften at room temperature or temper over hot water or a heat source while continually beating.
The finished buttercream is lumpy.	Sugar crystals may be present, formed during the incorporation of the sugar into the eggs.

Cakes

WHAT WENT WRONG	WHY
The crust is too dark.	There was an excessive quantity of sugar added. The heat of the oven was too high.
The crust is soggy.	The cake was underbaked. The cake was cooled while still in the baking pan or without proper ventilation. The cake was wrapped in plastic wrap before it was completely cooled.
The crust burst or cracked on top.	There was an excessive quantity of flour added to the batter. A flour high in gluten was used in preparation of the batter. There was an insufficient quantity of liquid added to batter. The batter was not properly mixed. The temperature of the oven was too hot.

WHAT WENT WRONG	WHY
The crust is too light.	There is an insufficient quantity of sugar added to the batter. The temperature of the oven was too cool.
The flavor is poor in quality.	Inferior ingredients were used in the production of the cake. Incorrect storage of the cake. Improper sanitary conditions in the bake shop. The formula is unbalanced.
The texture is dense or heavy.	An insufficient quantity of leavening was used in the production of the batter. There was an excessive quantity of liquid used in the production of the batter. There was an excessive quantity of shortening used in the production of the batter. The temperature of the oven was too cool.
The texture is coarse or irregular.	There is an excessive quantity of leavening in the batter. There is an inadequate amount of egg product for the quantity of batter. The batter has not been mixed properly.
The texture is crumbly.	There is an excessive quantity of shortening or fat in the batter. There is an excessive quantity of leavening in the batter. There is an excessive quantity of sugar in the batter. The incorrect type of flour was utilized in the make-up of the batter. The batter was not mixed correctly.
The texture is tough.	An inadequate amount of sugar was used in the make-up of the batter. An inadequate amount of fat was used in the make-up of the batter. The flour had a high gluten content. There was an excessive amount of flour used for the quantity of batter. The batter was not mixed correctly.

WHAT WENT WRONG	WHY
The cake exhibits poor volume.	An excessive amount of liquid was used in the make-up of the batter. An inadequate amount of flour was used in the make-up of the batter. An inadequate amount of leavening was used in the make-up of the batter. The temperature of the oven was too hot.
The cake exhibits an uneven shape.	The oven that the cake was baked in had uneven heat distribution. The distribution of the batter in the cake pans was uneven. The batter was not mixed correctly. The cake pans were baked on uneven racks or oven decks. The cakes pans are warped or misshapen.
The egg foam cake collapses.	Too much air was incorporated into the egg foam during the make-up of the batter. Too little air was incorporated into the egg foam during the make-up of the batter.

Chocolate

WHAT WENT WRONG	WHY
During the melting process the chocolate becomes thick and grainy and hardens to an unusable mass.	The chocolate has seized, usually due to the addition of water. Even a single drop of water will cause the chocolate to seize up and become unusable.
Chocolate smells "hot" and does not harden when it cools down.	Chocolate was overheated. Improper tempering technique used.
After dipping ingredients or candy centers into melted chocolate, a grayish white streaky texture develops on the surface.	The streaks that have developed are known as bloom and are the result of the fat separating in the chocolate and rising to the surface. This occurs because the chocolate was not correctly tempered or the items to be dipped were too cold.
When folding whipped cream into melted chocolate, the chocolate solidifies and flecks of hard chocolate form in the cream.	The items were of two extreme temperatures (cream too cold, chocolate too warm). Allow chocolate to come to room temperature before combining. Add a small amount of chocolate to the cream and whisk in vigorously, then fold in the remaining chocolate quickly.

WHAT WENT WRONG	WHY
Finished ganache is curdled or separated.	The ganache has separated and must be tempered by heating a small amount of heavy cream and then beating small amounts of the separated ganache into the warm cream until the ganache "comes back together."
Finished ganache looks grainy and is extremely thick.	The fat in the chocolate has recrystallized. The ganache must be rewarmed and whisked to a smooth creamy state.

Cookies

WHAT WENT WRONG	WHY
The cookie is too brown.	The temperature of the oven was too high. There was an excessive amount of sugar used in the cookie dough. The cookies were overbaked.
The cookie is not brown enough.	The temperature of the oven was too low. There was in inadequate amount of sugar used in the cookie dough. The cookies were underbaked.
The cookie is too dry in texture.	There was an inadequate amount of shortening or fat incorporated into the cookie dough. There was an inadequate amount of liquid incorporated into the cookie dough. There was an excessive amount of flour incorporated into the cookie dough. The cookies were overbaked. The temperature of the oven was too low.
The cookie is too crumbly in texture.	There was an excessive amount of shortening or fat used in the cookie dough. There was an excessive amount of leavening used in the cookie dough. There was an excessive amount of sugar used in the cookie dough. There was an inadequate amount of eggs used in the cookie dough. The dough was improperly mixed.

WHAT WENT WRONG	WHY
The cookie is too hard in texture.	There was an excessive amount of flour used in the cookie dough. The gluten content of the flour was too high. The cookies were overbaked. The oven temperature was too low. There was an insufficient amount of liquid used in the make up of the cookie dough. There was an insufficient amount of shortening or fat used in the make up of the dough.
The cookie exhibits an undesirable sugary crust.	There is was an excessive amount of sugar used in the cookie dough. The cookie dough was improperly mixed.
The cookie exhibits too much spread during the baking process.	There was an insufficient amount of flour used in the cookie dough. There was an excessive amount of leavening used in the cookie dough. There was an excessive amount of sugar used in the make-up of the cookie dough. There was an excessive amount of liquid used in the make-up of the cookie dough. The oven temperature was too low. The baking pans were overgreased.
The cookie exhibits too little spread during the baking process.	There was an excessive amount of flour used in the cookie dough. The gluten content in the flour was too strong. There was an insufficient amount of sugar used in the cookie dough. There was an insufficient amount of leavening used in the dough. There was an insufficient amount of liquid used in the dough. The temperature of the oven was too low. The baking pans were undergreased.
The cookie sticks to the baking pan.	The baking pans were undergreased. There was an excessive amount of sugar used in the cookie dough.

WHAT WENT WRONG	WHY
The finished cookie is too tough.	There was an excessive amount of flour used in the make-up of the cookie dough. The gluten content of the flour was too strong. There was an in adequate amount of shortening or fat used in the cookie dough. The amount of sugar was incorrectly measured. The cookie dough was overmixed. The cookie dough was incorrectly mixed.

Custards

WHAT WENT WRONG	WHY
The custard is lumpy and curdled.	Eggs have been improperly tempered. Custard was overcooked. Custard was not strained correctly. Carryover cooking time allowed custard to continue to cook.
The custard developed a skin.	The custard was not properly covered. Overoxidation.
The custard breaks down and forms watery areas.	The alpha-amylase, which is an enzyme that is found in egg yolks, attacked the starch, causing the custard to thin out. Custard must come to a boil to kill the enzymes. After the addition of flavorings the custard may become "overstirred," causing the starch granules to break down. An excessive quantity of sugar or acid was used.
The custard is exhibiting small hard yellow clumps.	The egg yolks and sugar should be combined just before they are combined with the milk so that the sugar does not "cook" the yolks, which means the proteins in the yolks have dried out as a result of contact with the sugar.

Frozen Desserts

WHAT WENT WRONG	WHY
The ice cream base never freezes or takes a very long time to freeze.	There was insufficient salt used in the ice brine to freeze the ice cream. The equipment never reached freezing temperature. The ice cream base was not sufficiently chilled.
The finished frozen dessert is soft and slushy.	An excessive amount of sugar or alcohol was in the base.
The ice cream is soft and slushy.	The ice cream base was not spun long enough to allow proper freezing. The ice cream base was not sufficiently chilled. The custard was undercooked and therefore did not properly thicken.
The frozen dessert lacks flavor.	The flavoring ingredients have been added in insufficient quantities without taking into account the chilled temperature.

Pies and Tarts

WHAT WENT WRONG	WHY
The finished crust is crumbly.	There was insufficient water used in the dough. There was excessive shortening used in the dough. The gluten content in the flour was insufficient. The dough was incorrectly mixed.
The dough was too stiff.	There was insufficient water used in the dough. There was insufficient shortening used in the dough. The gluten content in the flour was too strong.
The finished crust is tough.	There was insufficient shortening used in the dough. The dough was overmanipulated during the make-up process. The gluten content in the flour was too strong. There was excessive water used in the dough. The dough was rolled too much. Scrap dough was overworked.

WHAT WENT WRONG	WHY
The finished crust is not flaky.	There was insufficient shortening used in the dough. The dough was overmixed or overmanipulated. The shortening that was cut into the flour was blended too much, resulting in a mealy texture. The dough was overrolled. The dough ingredients were too warm.
The finished pie exhibits a soggy or undercooked bottom.	The temperature of the oven was too low. The pie was placed in the oven so as not to receive sufficient bottom heat. The pie was underbaked. The filling was hot when placed in the shell. The filling did not contain enough starch and "watered out" during baking. The wrong dough was used: mealy dough used on the bottom will assist in preventing a soggy crust.
The finished crust has shrunk from the sides of the pie pan.	There was insufficient shortening used in the dough. There was excessive water used in the dough. The dough was overmanipulated during the make-up process. The gluten content in the flour was too strong. The dough was not given a rest period in the refrigerator in order for the gluten to relax. The dough was stretched when it was placed in the pie pan.
The filling in the pie boiled over during baking.	There was excessive filling in the pie pan. Not enough starch was present in the filling. Steam holes or vents were not cut into the top crust. The fruit in the pie was too acidic. There was excessive sugar in the filling. The top and bottom crusts were not sealed together on 2-crust pies.
The custard filling curdled during baking.	The pie was overbaked.

Sugar

WHAT WENT WRONG	WHY
In the preparation of a cooked sugar the syrup thickens and becomes grainy.	There were undissolved sugar crystals on the side of the pan or on the thermometer or spoon/whisk used to stir the syrup and this caused a chain reaction that resulted in the crystallization of the sugar syrup; these crystals must be washed down with a pastry brush dipped in water to prevent crystallization. The shaking or movement of the pan caused a chain reaction and crystallization of the sugar occurred; if a small amount of acid such as lemon juice or tartaric acid is added to the pan, it will help to prevent crystallization.
The sugar syrup did not display the correct characteristics associated with the temperature that it was cooked to—i.e., hard crack stage.	The syrup did not reach the correct temperature. A calibrated candy thermometer should be used to determine final temperature.

Quickbreads

WHAT WENT WRONG	WHY
The quickbread is compact and not fully risen.	There was insufficient leavening used in the batter. The temperature of the oven was too low. With batters that are made by the creaming method, the shortening and sugar were not sufficiently creamed.
Muffins did not peak above the edge of the muffin pan.	If paper liners were used, omit the liners and grease the muffin pan cups and bake muffins directly in pan.
The texture of muffins is not cakelike.	The muffin method was used, resulting in an inadequate amount of air being beaten into the batter; the creaming method may eliminate this problem.
The quickbread is tough and has undesirable eating qualities.	The protein in the flour was too strong for quickbreads. The bread was overbaked. The batter was overmixed, causing an excessive amount of gluten to form.

WHAT WENT WRONG	WHY
There is tunneling or holes on the interior of the quickbread, or it has a "knobby" shape on the top.	The batter was overmixed, causing an excessive amount of gluten to form. The leavening agents used in the batter were not sufficiently distributed.

Yeast Breads

WHAT WHEN WRONG	WHY
The finished bread exhibits poor volume.	Poor choice of flour. Oven was too hot, which allowed the bread to form a crust too quickly. Insufficient liquid was used in the mixing process. Yeast was not activated. The proportion of yeast was insufficient for the quantity of dough. The proportion of salt was too much for the quantity of dough. The dough has been under- or overmixed.
The finished bread exhibits split or burst crust.	The dough has been overmixed. The dough was not sufficiently fermented. Poor shaping; seam not on bottom. Lack of scoring. The oven was too hot, which allowed the steam from the dough to split the newly formed crust. There was an insufficient steam when the bread was first placed into the oven.
The finished bread exhibits too much volume.	The proportion of salt was insufficient for the quantity of dough. Too much yeast was used in the formula. The scaled weight of dough was too heavy. The finished product was overproofed.
The finished bread product exhibits poor shape.	The proportion of salt was insufficient for the quantity of dough. High gluten flour was not used. Incorrect shaping or makeup of dough. Fermentation or proofing was incorrectly performed. Too much steam was introduced into the oven during baking.

WHAT WHEN WRONG	WHY
The finished bread product is too dense or close grained.	The proportion of salt was too much for the quantity of dough. Insufficient liquid was used in the mixing process. The proportion of yeast was insufficient for the quantity of dough. The dough was not sufficiently fermented. The dough was not sufficiently proofed.
The finished bread product is too coarse or open.	Too much yeast was used in the formula. An excessive amount of liquid was used for the quantity of dough. The dough was mixed for an incorrect time period. The dough was not sufficiently fermented. The finished product was overproofed. The pan that the bread product was baked in was too large for the quantity of dough.
The finished bread product exhibits a streaked outer crumb.	The dough was improperly or insufficiently mixed. Incorrect shape or makeup of dough. Too much flour was used for dusting.
The finished bread product exhibits a gray crumb.	The fermentation time was too lengthy. The fermentation temperature was too hot.
The finished bread product exhibits a crust that is too dark.	There was too much sugar or milk added to the dough. The dough was not sufficiently fermented. The temperature of the oven was too hot. The baking time was too long. There was an insufficient steam injected at the onset of the baking process.
The finished bread product exhibits a crust that is too pale.	An insufficient amount of sugar or milk was added to the dough. The dough was overfermented. The dough was overproofed. The temperature of the oven was too low. The baking time was insufficient. There was too much steam injected at the onset of the baking process.

WHAT WHEN WRONG	WHY
The finished bread product exhibits an outer crust that is too thick.	There was an insufficient quantity of sugar or fat added to the dough. The fermentation was improperly performed. Bread was baked too long or at an incorrect temperature. There was insufficient steam injected at the onset of the baking process.
The finished bread product exhibits blisters on the crust.	Too much liquid was added for the quantity of dough. The fermentation was improperly performed. The finished bread was improperly shaped.
The bread exhibits flat taste or poor flavor.	There was an insufficient quantity of salt in dough. Ingredients are rancid, old, or not of top quality. The sanitation standards of the bake shop are substandard. The product was under- or overfermented.

Specialty Vendors

Albert Uster Imports, Inc.

Specializes in pastry and confectionery ingredients and equipment.

9211 Gaither Road
Gaithersburg, MD 20877
800-231-8154
www.auiswiss.com

American Chocolate Mould Company

Specializes in confectionery equipment and modeling work for chocolate molds. Also acts as a service organization to the confectionery industry.

1401 Church Street Unit #5
Bohemia, NY 11716
631-589-5080
www.americanchocolatemould.com

Chef Rubber

Specializes in silicone rubbers for making molds and specialty tools for mold making.

702-614-9350
www.chefrubber.com

Chocolate à la Carte

Specializes in chocolate with over 3,000 products. Will also custom design.

28455 Livingston Avenue
Valencia, CA 91355
800-818-CHOC (2462)
www.chocolates-ala-carte.com

CK Products

A wholesale distributor with over ten thousand products for the cake decorating, candy making, kitchen tools, and wedding accessories industries.

310 Racquet Drive
Fort Wayne, IN 46825
260-484-2517
www.ckproducts.com

International Sugar Art Collection

Specializes in tools, equipment, and educational resources for cake decorating and sugar art.

6060 McDonough Drive, Suite F
Norcross, GA 30093
800-662-8925 or 770-453-9449
www.nicholaslodge.com
www.internationalsugarart.com

JB Prince Company

A distributor of fine chefs' tools and equipment from around the world.

36 East 31st Street
New York, NY 10016-6821
800-473-0577
www.jbprince.com

Paris Gourmet

Specialty importer of fine French products and ingredients.

145 Grand Street
Carlstadt, NJ 07072
201-939-5656 ext. 1 or 800-727-8791 ext. 1
www.patisfrance.com

Swiss American Imports, LLC

Specialty importer of pastry ingredients and Swiss chocolate.

9455 NW 40th Street
Miami, FL 33178-2941
800-444-0676
www.swissamericanimports.com

The Chicago School of Mold Making

Specialty tools, equipment, and educational resources for mold making. Custom molds available.

CSMM, 1131 Lake Street
UPS Box 143
Oak Park, IL 60301
708-660-9707
www.chicagomoldsschool.com

The Chocolate Gallery

Specializes in novelty chocolate products.

5705 Calle Real
Goleta, CA 93117-2315
800-426-4796 or 805-967-4688
www.chocolate gallery.com

Tuile Time

Specializes in high-quality, durable design templates for tuile and other products. Custom designs also available.

984 SW 1st Avenue
Pompano Beach, FL 33060
954-907-7292
www.tuiletime.com

Wilton Industries

Specialty equipment and tools for cake decorating, candy making, and cookie production.

2240 W. 75th Street
Woodridge, IL 60517
800-794-5866 or 630-963-1818
www.wilton.com

Professional Development Resources

Organizations

Académie Culinaire de France

45, Rue Saint-Roch
75001 Paris, France
www.academieculinairedefrance.com

American Culinary Federation (ACF)

10 San Bartola Drive
St. Augustine, FL 32086
800-624-9458
www.acfchefs.org

American Dietetic Association (ADA)

120 South Riverside Plaza, Suite 2000
Chicago, IL 60606-6995
800-877-1600
www.eatright.org

American Institute of Baking (AIB)

P.O. Box 3999
Manhattan, KS 66505-3999
800-633-5137
www.aibonline.com

American Institute of Wine and Food (AIWF)

304 West Liberty Street, Suite 201
Louisville, KY 40202
800-274-2493
www.aiwf.org

American Society of Baking

533 1st Street East
Sonoma, CA 95476
707-935-0103
www.asbe.org

Bread Bakers Guild of America (BBGA)

3203 Maryland Avenue
North Versailles, PA 15137
412-823-2080
www.bbga.org

Chefs Collaborative

262 Beacon Street
Boston, MA 02116
617-236-5200
www.chefscollaborative.org

International Association of Cooking Professionals (IACP)

455 South Fourth Street, Suite 650
Louisville, KY 40202
502-581-9786
www.iacp.com

International Cake Exploration Societe (ICES)

www.ices.org

International Council on Hotel, Restaurant and Institutional Education (CHRIE)

2810 North Parham, Suite 230
Richmond, VA 23294
804- 346-4800
www.chrie.org

James Beard Foundation

167 West 12th Street
New York, NY 10011
800-36-BEARD
www.jamesbeard.org

Les Dames d'Escoffier International

P.O. Box 4961
Louisville, KY 40204
502-456-1851
www.ldei.org

National Restaurant Association

1200 17th Street N.W.
Washington, DC 20036
202-331-5900
www.restaurant.org

Personal Chefs Network

877-905-CHEF
www.personalchefsnetwork.com

Retail Baker's Association

14239 Park Central Drive
Laurel, MD 20707-5261
800-638-0924
www.rbanet.com

Round Table for Women in Food Service

3022 West Eastwood Street
Chicago, IL 60625
800-898-2849

Slow Food USA

434 Broadway, 6th Floor
New York, NY 10013
212-965-5640
www.slowfoodusa.org

Société Culinaire Philanthropique

305 East 47th Street, Suite 11B
New York, NY 10017
212-308-0628
www.societeculinaire.com

Continuing Education and Professional Development

American Institute of Baking (AIB)

1213 Baker's Way
Manhattan, KS 66502
913-537-4750
www.aibonline.org

Barry Callebaut Institutes

7 locations worldwide
www.barry-callebaut.com

Bellouet Conseil Ecole Gastronomique de Paris

304-306, rue Lecourbe
Paris 75015, France
(33) 1 40 60 16 20
www.bellouet.web.com

Center for Advancement of Foodservice Education (CAFE)

959 Melvin Road
Annapolis, MD 21403
410-268-5542
www.cafemeetingplace.com

Ecole Chocolat

2023 West 4th Avenue
Vancouver, BC, Canada
604-484-1872 from Canada or International
213-291-8309 from US or International
www.ecolechocolat.com

Ecole Lenotre

40, rue Pierre Curie- BP 6
Plaisir Cedex 787373, France
(33) (0) 1-30-81-46-34
www.lenotre.fr

International Cake Exploration Societe (ICES)

www.ices.org

King Arthur Baking Education Center

133 Route 5 South
Norwich, VT 05055
800-652-3334
www.kingarthurflour.com

La Varenne Ecole de Cuisine

Château du Fëy
89300 Villecien
Burgundy, France
800-537-6486
www.lavarenne.com

Retail Bakers of America

8201 Greensboro Drive, Suite 300
McLean, VA 22102
800-638-0924 or 703-610-9035
www.rbanet.com

The Chicago School of Mold Making

CSMM, 1131 Lake Street
UPS Box 143
Oak Park, IL 60301
708-660-9707
www.chicagomoldsschool.com

The Culinary Institute of America

433 Albany Post Road
Hyde Park, NY 12538-1499
1-800-CULINARY or 845-452-9430
www.ciachef.edu

The French Pastry School

226 West Jackson Boulevard
Chicago, IL 60606
312-726-2419
www.frenchpastryschool.com

The Notter School of Pastry Arts

8204 Crystal Clear Lane
Suite 1600
Orlando FL 32809
407-240-9057
www.notterschool.com

The San Francisco Baking Institute (SFBI)

390 Swift Avenue #13
South San Francisco, CA 94080
650-589-5784
www.sfbi.com

Valrhona Ecole du Grand Chocolat

F 26 600 TAIN L'HERMITAGE
(33) 4 75 07 90 90
Fax: (33) 4 75 08 05 17

Wilton Industries

240 W. 75th Street
Woodridge, IL 60517
800-794-5866 or 630-963-1818
www.wilton.com

References

Aharoni, I. (1999). *Eating al Fresco: The Best Street Food in the World*. New York: Harry N. Abrams.

Alford, J., & Duguid, N. (2003). *Home Baking*. New York: Artisan.

Alford, J., & Duguid, N. (Eds.). (1995). *Flat Breads & Flavors*. New York: William Morrow.

Almond, S. (2004). *Candy Freak*. New York: Algonquin Books of Chapel Hill.

Amendola, Joseph. (1978). *The Baker's Manual*. Rochelle Park, NJ: Hayden.

Amendola, Joseph., & Lundberg, Donald. (1992). *Understanding Baking*. New York: Van Nostrand Reinhold.

Baggett, Nancy. (2001). *All-American Cookie Book*. Boston: Houghton Mifflin.

Bailey, A. (1969). *The Cooking of the British Isles*. New York: Time-Life Books.

Beranbaum, R. (1998). *The Pie and Pastry Bible*. New York: Scribners.

Bilheux, R., & Escoffier, A. (2000). *French Professional Pastry Series: Doughs, Batters, and Meringues* (Vol. 1). New York: John Wiley and Sons.

Bilheux, R., & Escoffier, A. (2000). *French Professional Pastry Series: Creams, Confections, and Finished Desserts* (Vol. 2). New York: John Wiley and Sons.

Bilheux, R., & Escoffier, A. (2000). *French Professional Pastry Series: Petit Fours, Chocolate, Frozen Desserts, and Sugar Work* (Vol. 3). New York: John Wiley and Sons.

Bilheux, R., & Escoffier, A. (2000). *French Professional Pastry Series: Decorations, Borders and Letters, Marzipan, and Modern Desserts* (Vol. 4). New York: John Wiley and Sons.

Bilheux, R., & Escoffier, A. (2000). *French Professional Pastry Series: Decorative Breads* (Vol. 5). New York: John Wiley and Sons.

Bloom, C. (1995). *International Dictionary of Desserts, Pastries, and Confections*. New York: Hearst Books.

Boyle, T. (1997). *Grand Finales: The Art of the Plated Dessert*. Hoboken, NJ: John Wiley & Sons.

Brachman, W. (2003). *American Desserts*. New York: Clarkson Potter.

Brown, D. (1968). *American Cooking*. New York: Time-Life Books.

Brown, D. (1968). *The Cooking of Scandinavia*. New York: Time-Life Books.

Brown, D. (1970). *American Cooking: The Northwest*. New York: Time-Life Books.

Calvel, R. (2001). *The Taste of Bread* (R. Wirtz, Trans.). Gaithersburg, MD: Aspen Publishers.

Casas, P. (1983). *The Foods and Wines of Spain*. New York: Alfred A. Knopf.

Charsley, S. (1992). *Wedding Cakes and Cultural History*. New York: Routledge.

Child, J., & Beck, S. (1970). *Mastering the Art of French Cooking* (Vol. 2). New York: Alfred A. Knopf.

Child, J., Beck, S., & Bertholle, L. (1961). *Mastering the Art of French Cooking* (Vol. 1). New York: Alfred A. Knopf.

Claiborne, C., & Franey, P. (1970). *Classic French Cooking*. New York: Time-Life Books.

Clayton, B. (1987). *Bernard Clayton's New Complete Book of Breads*. New York: Simon and Schuster.

Corriher, Shirley O. (1997). *CookWise*. New York: William Morrow.

Culinary Institute of America. (2004). *Baking and Pastry: Mastering the Art and Craft*. Hoboken, NJ: John Wiley & Sons.

Danforth, R., Feierabend, P., & Shassman, G. (2000). *Culinaria: United States*. Cologne, Germany: Könemann Verlagsgesellschaft mbH.

David, E. (1999). *The History of Bread*. New York: Harry N. Abrams.

Davidson, Allen. (1999). *The Oxford Companion to Food*. Oxford, England: Oxford University Press.

Dominé, A. (1999). *Culinaria: France*. Cologne, Germany: Könemann Verlagsgesellschaft mbH.

Elizabeth, D. (1994). *English Bread and Yeast Cookery*. Newton, MA: Biscuit Books.

Escoffier, A. (1969). *Escoffier Cookbook*. New York: Crown.

Feibleman, P. (1969). *American Cooking: Creole and Acadian*. New York: Time-Life Books.

Feibleman, P. (1969). *The Cooking of Spain and Portugal*. New York: Time-Life Books.

Field, C. (1985). *The Italian Baker*. New York: HarperCollins.

Field, M., & Field, F. (1970). *A Quintet of Cuisines*. New York: Time-Life Books.

Figioni, P. (2004). *How Baking Works*. Hoboken, NJ: John Wiley & Sons.

Fisher, M. F. K. (1968). *The Cooking of Provincial France*. New York: Time-Life Books.

Friberg, Bo. (2002). *The Professional Pastry Chef*. New York: John Wiley & Sons.

Friberg, Bo. (2003). *The Advanced Professional Pastry Chef*. Hoboken, NJ: John Wiley & Sons.

Gergely, A. (1999). *Culinaria: Hungary*. Cologne, Germany: Könemann Verlagsgesellschaft mbH.

Gillespie, G. (1995). *1001 Cookie Recipes*. New York: Black Dog & Leventhal Publishers.

Gisslen, W. (2001). *Professional Baking*. Hoboken, NJ: John Wiley & Sons.

Glezer, M. (2000). *Artisan Baking Across America*. New York: Artisan.

Greweling, P. (2007). *Chocolates and Confections*. Hoboken, NJ: John Wiley & Sons.

Gundel, K. (1998). *Gundel's Hungarian Cookbook*. Budapest, Hungary: Kossuth Printing House.

Hahan, E. (1968). *The Cooking of China*. New York: Time-Life Books.

Hamelman, J. (2004). *Bread: A Baker's Book of Techniques and Recipes*. Hoboken, NJ: John Wiley & Sons.

Harris, M. (2001). *Marilyn Harris Cooking School Cookbook*. Gretna, LA: Pelican Publishing.

Hazelton, N. (1969). *Cooking of Germany*. New York: Time-Life Books.

Healy, B. (1994). *The French Cookie Book*. New York: William Morrow.

Heatter, M. (1982). *Maida Heatter's New Book of Great Desserts*. New York: Alfred A. Knopf.

Hensperger, B. (1999). *The Bread Bible*. San Francisco: Chronicle Books.

Herbst, R., & Tyler Herbst, S. (2003). *The New Wine Lover's Companion* (2nd ed.). Hauppauge, NY: Barron's Educational Series. (Original work published 1995)

Herbst, S. T. (2001). *Food Lover's Companion* (3rd ed.). Hauppauge, NY: Barron's Educational Series. (Original work published 1990)

Hill, T. (2004). *The Contemporary Encyclopedia of Herbs & Spices*. Hoboken, NJ: John Wiley and Sons.

Hutton, W. (2004). *Tropical Fruits*. Singapore: Periplus Additions (HK) Ltd.

Ingram, C., & Shapter, J. (1999). *The World Encyclopedia of Bread and Bread Making*. New York: Lorenz Books.

Juillet, C. (1998). *Classic Patisserie*. Woburn, MA: Reed Educational and Professional Publishing Ltd.

Karousos, G. (1994). *The Patissier's Art*. Hoboken, NJ: John Wiley and Sons.

Kendrick, R., & Atkinson, P. (1987). *Candy Making*. Los Angeles: HP Books.

King Arthur Flour Company, Inc. (2003). *The King Arthur Flour Baker's Companion*. Woodstock, VT: Countryman Press.

Labensky, S. (2005). *On Baking*. Upper Saddle River, NJ: Pearson Education.

Labensky, Steven. (2006). *Prentice Hall Dictionary of Culinary Arts*. Upper Saddle River, NJ: Pearson Prentice Hall. (Original work published 2001)

LaRousse. (1989). *Gastronomique* (Lesley Bernstein Translation Services, Trans.) (J. Harvey Lang, Ed.). New York: Crown Publishers.

Leader, D., & Blahnik, J. (1993). *Bread Alone*. New York: William Morrow.

Lenôtre, G. (1977). *Lenôtre's Desserts and Pastries*. Woodbury, NY: Barron's Educational Series.

Leonard, J. (1971). *American Cooking: The Great West*. New York: Time-Life Books.

Leonard, J. (1970). *American Cooking: New England*. New York: Time-Life Books.

Liddell, C., & Weir, R. (1995). *Frozen Desserts*. New York: St. Martin's Press.

MacLauchlan, A. (1999). *The Making of a Pastry Chef*. Hoboken, NJ: John Wiley & Sons.

MacNeil, K. (2001). *The Wine Bible*. New York: Workman.

Malgieri, N. (1990). *Great Italian Desserts*. New York: Little, Brown and Co.

Maree, A. (1994). *Patisserie*. Sydney, Australia: HarperCollins.

McGee, Harold. (1984). *On Food and Cooking: The Science and Lore of the Kitchen*. New York: Scribners.

Metzger, C. (2000). *Culinaria: Germany*. Cologne, Germany: Könemann Verlagsgesellschaft mbH.

Milona, M. (2004). *Culinaria: Greece*. Cologne, Germany: Könemann Verlagsgesellschaft mbH.

Morgan, L. (1997). *The Ethnic Market Food Guide*. New York: Berkeley Publishing Group.

Mowe, R. (1998). *Culinaria: SouthEast Asian Specialities*. Cologne, Germany: Könemann Verlagsgesellschaft mbH.

Nickles, H. (1969). *Middle Eastern Cooking*. New York: Time-Life Books.

Norman, J. (1995). *The Complete Book of Spices: A Practical Guide to Spices and Aromatic Seeds*. New York: Viking.

Notter, E., Notter S. (1992). *Das Ist Zucker That's Sugar*. Self-published.

Papashvily, H., & Papashvily, G. (1969). *Russian Cooking*. New York: Time-Life Books.

Parkinson, R. (1999). *Culinaria: Caribbean*. Cologne, Germany: Könemann Verlagsgesellschaft mbH.

Piras, C., & Medagliani, E. (2000). *Culinaria: Italy*. Cologne, Germany: Könemann Verlagsgesellschaft mbH.

Rau, S. (1969). *Cooking of India*. New York: Time-Life Books.

Reinhart, P. (2001). *The Bread Baker's Apprentice*. Berkeley, CA: Ten Speed Press.

Rice Lorenzetti, L. (2000). *The Birth of Coffee*. New York: Clarkson Potter.

Riely, E. (2003). *The Chef's Companion*. Hoboken, NJ: John Wiley & Sons.

Rolland, J. (2004). *The Cook's Essential Dictionary*. Toronto, Canada: Robert Rose.

Römer, J., & Ditter, M. (1995). *Culinaria: European Specialities*. Cologne, Germany: Könemann Verlagsgesellschaft mbH.

Root, W. (1968). *Cooking of Italy*. New York: Time-Life Books.

Rose, E. (1976). *The Complete International Jewish Cookbook*. New York: St. Martin's.

Sahni, J. (1980). *Classic Indian Cooking*. New York: William Morrow.

Scherber, A., & Dupree, T. (1996). *Amy's Bread*. New York: William Morrow.

Shenton, J., & Pellgerini, A. (1971). *American Cooking: The Melting Pot*. New York: Time-Life Books.

Silverton, N. (1996). *Breads From the La Brea Bakery*. New York: Random House.

Sokol, G. (2006). *About Professional Baking*. Clifton Park, NY: Thomson Delmar Learning.

Stechishin, S. (1984). *Traditional Ukrainian Cookery*. Winnipeg, Canada: Trident Press Ltd.

Steinberg, R. (1970). *Pacific and Southeast Asian Cooking*. New York: Time-Life Books.

Tannahill, R. (1988). *Food in History*. New York: Three Rivers Press.

Teubner, C. (1997). *The Chocolate Bible*. New York: Penguin.

Thomas, Cathy. (2006). *Mellissa's Great Book of Produce*. Hoboken, NJ: John Wiley & Sons.

Toussaint-Samat, M. (1992). *History of Food*. Cambridge, MA: Blackwell.

Trutter, M. (1998). *Culinaria: Spain*. Cologne, Germany: Könemann Verlagsgesellschaft mbH.

van der Post, L. (1970). *African Cooking*. New York: Time-Life Books.

Walter, E. (1971). *American Cooking: Southern Style*. New York: Time-Life Books.

Waugh, A. (1968). *Wines and Spirits*. New York: Time-Life Books.

Wechsberg, J. (1968). *The Cooking of Vienna's Empire*. New York: Time-Life Books.

Whatley, S. (1993). *Encyclopedia of Classic French Pastries*. Beverly Hills, CA: Royal House Publishing.

Wilson, J. (1971). *American Cooking: The Eastern Heartland*. New York: Time-Life Books.

Wolfe, L. (1970). *The Cooking of the Caribbean Islands*. New York: Time-Life Books.